Map pages s

G000147873

127
Grimsby

118   119
Skegness

Boston
104   105   Cromer
King's   106   107
Lynn

borough   Norwich
9   90   91   92   93
Thetford

Cambridge
5   76   77   78   79
rd   Ipswich

60   61   62   63
helmsford

ONDON
4   45   46   47

Maidstone
Sevenoaks   34   35   Dover
32   33   Folkestone

hton   Hastings
19   20   21

To help you navigate safely
and easily, see the AA's
France and Europe atlases...
theAA.com/shop

On the road or in your home call us in an emergency

Breakdown cover with the UK's
No.1 choice for breakdown recovery^

Home Emergency Response
Peace of mind at home too

Trust the AA to protect you against the cost of repairs in emergencies at home, as well as resolving breakdowns on the road. Both services are available 24/7, 365 days a year and you can even upgrade both – just ask for details from your 4th emergency service.

For **Breakdown** cover call us now on **0800 032 0687**

For **Home Emergency Response** call us now on **0800 975 6528**

 Your 4th Emergency Service

Atlas contents

Scale 1:250,000 or 3.95 miles to 1 inch

Map pages south	inside front cover
Route planner	II–VII
Mileage chart	VIII
Atlas Symbols	1
Road maps 1:250,000 scale	2–237

Western Isles 1:700,000 scale — 232–233
Orkney Islands 1:636,000 scale — 234
Shetland Islands 1:636,000 scale — 235
Channel Islands 1:150,000 scale — 236
Isle of Man 1:317,000 scale — 237

Restricted junctions	238–239
Index to place names	240–319

County, administrative area map — 240–241
Place name index — 242–319

Ireland	endpaper
Map pages north	inside back cover

12th edition June 2013

© AA Media Limited 2013

Cartography:

Now fully updated, the 1st edition of this atlas won the British Cartographic Society - Ordnance Survey Award for innovation in the design and presentation of spatial information. All cartography in this atlas edited, designed and produced by the Mapping Services Department of AA Publishing (A05052).

This atlas contains Ordnance Survey data © Crown copyright and database right 2013 and Royal Mail data © Royal Mail copyright and database right 2013.

Land & Property Services. This atlas is based upon Crown Copyright and is reproduced with the permission of Land and Property Services under delegated authority from the Controller of Her Majesty's Stationery Office, © Crown copyright and database rights 2013, Licence number 100,363. Permit No. 130004.

© Ordnance Survey Ireland/ Government of Ireland.
Copyright Permit No. MP000913

Publisher's notes:
Published by AA Publishing (a trading name of AA Media Limited, whose registered office is Fanum House, Basing View, Basingstoke, Hampshire RG21 4EA, UK. Registered number 06112600).

All rights reserved. No part of this publication may be reproduced, stored in a retrieval system, or transmitted in any form or by any means – electronic, mechanical, photocopying, recording or otherwise – unless the permission of the publisher has been given beforehand.

ISBN: 978 0 7495 7451 2 (flexibound)

A CIP catalogue record for this book is available from The British Library.

The publishers would welcome information to correct any errors or omissions and to keep this atlas up to date. Please write to the Atlas Editor, AA Publishing, The Automobile Association, Fanum House, Basing View, Basingstoke, Hampshire RG21 4EA, UK.
E-mail: roadatlasfeedback@theaa.com

Acknowledgements:
AA Publishing would like to thank the following for their assistance in producing this atlas:

RoadPilot® Information on fixed speed camera locations provided by and © 2013 RoadPilot® Driving Technology. Crematoria database provided by Cremation Society of Great Britain. Cadw, English Heritage, Forestry Commission, Historic Scotland, Johnsons, National Trust and National Trust for Scotland, RSPB, The Wildlife Trust, Scottish Natural Heritage, Natural England, The Countryside Council for Wales.

Printer:
Printed in China by Leo Paper Products.

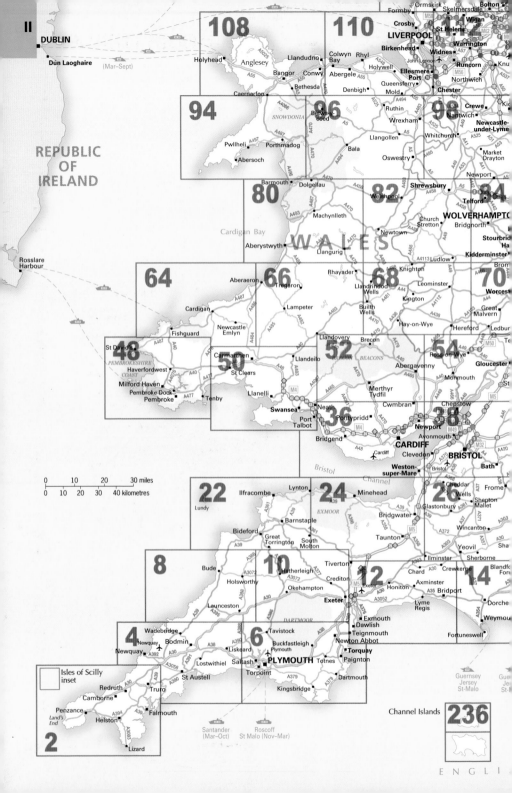

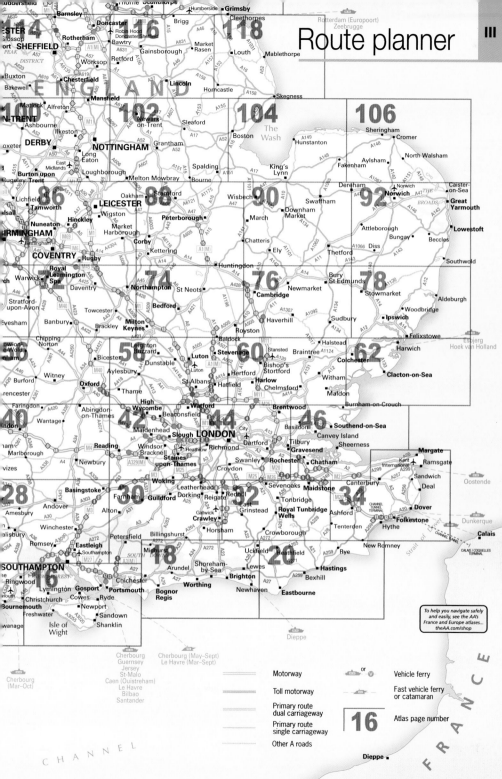

Motorway

Toll motorway

Primary route
dual carriageway

Primary route
single carriageway

Other A roads

Vehicle ferry

Fast vehicle ferry
or catamaran

16 Atlas page number

To help you navigate safely
and easily, see the AA's
France and Europe atlases...
theAA.com/shop

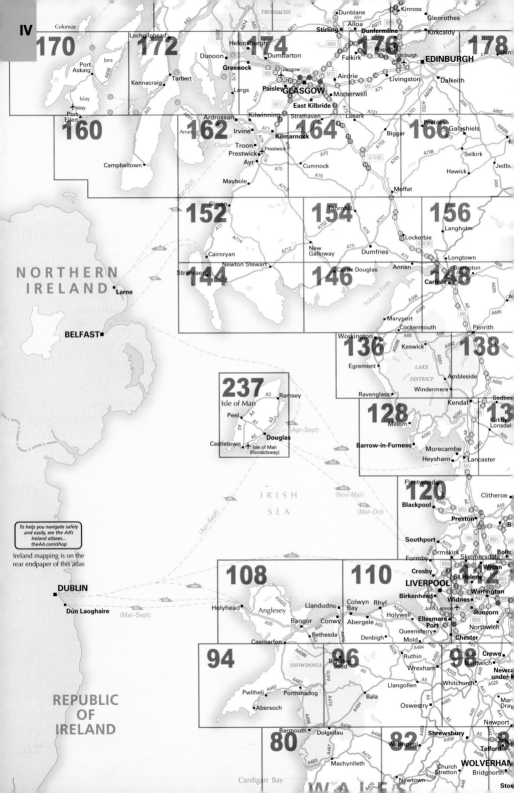

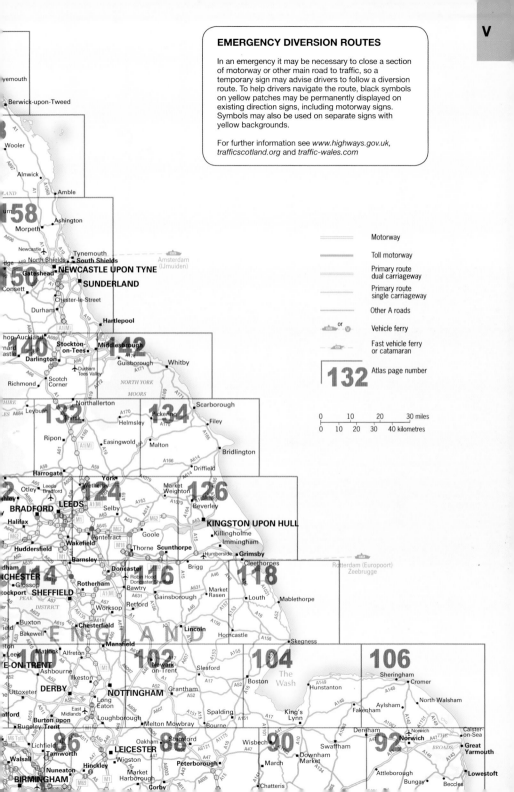

EMERGENCY DIVERSION ROUTES

In an emergency it may be necessary to close a section of motorway or other main road to traffic, so a temporary sign may advise drivers to follow a diversion route. To help drivers navigate the route, black symbols on yellow patches may be permanently displayed on existing direction signs, including motorway signs. Symbols may also be used on separate signs with yellow backgrounds.

For further information see *www.highways.gov.uk, trafficscotland.org* and *traffic-wales.com*

Motorway

Toll motorway

Primary route dual carriageway

Primary route single carriageway

Other A roads

Vehicle ferry

Fast vehicle ferry or catamaran

132 Atlas page number

0   10   20   30 miles
0 10 20 30   40 kilometres

FERRY INFORMATION

Hebrides and west coast Scotland

calmac.co.uk	0800 066 5000
skyeferry.co.uk	01599 522 236
western-ferries.co.uk	01369 704 452

Orkney and Shetland

northlinkferries.co.uk	0845 6000 449
pentlandferries.co.uk	0800 688 8998
orkneyferries.co.uk	01856 872 044
shetland.gov.uk/ferries	01595 743 970

Isle of Man

steam-packet.com	08722 992 992

Ireland

irishferries.com	08717 300 400
poferries.com	08716 642 020
stenaline.co.uk	08447 70 70 70

North Sea (Scandinavia and Benelux)

dfdsseaways.co.uk	08715 229 955
poferries.com	08716 642 020
stenaline.co.uk	08447 70 70 70

Isle of Wight

wightlink.co.uk	0871 376 1000
redfunnel.co.uk	0844 844 9988

Channel Islands

condorferries.co.uk	0845 609 1024

Channel hopping (France and Belgium)

brittany-ferries.co.uk	0871 244 0744
condorferries.co.uk	0845 609 1024
eurotunnel.com	08443 35 35 35
ldlines.co.uk	0844 576 8836
dfdsseaways.co.uk	08715 229 955
poferries.com	08716 642 020
transeuropaferries.com	01843 595 522
myferrylink.com	0844 2482 100

Northern Spain

brittany-ferries.co.uk	0871 244 0744
poferries.com	08716 642 020

Motorway

Primary route
dual carriageway

Primary route
single carriageway

Other A roads

Vehicle ferry

Fast vehicle ferry
or catamaran

192 Atlas page number

0	10	20	30 miles

| 0 | 10 | 20 | 30 | 40 kilometres |

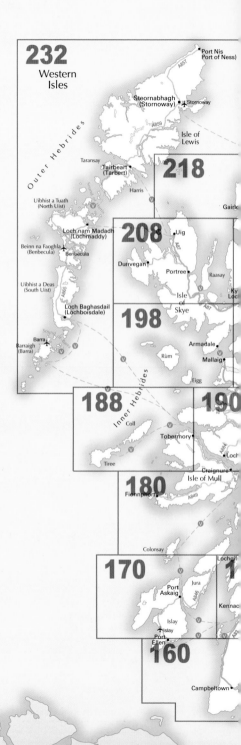

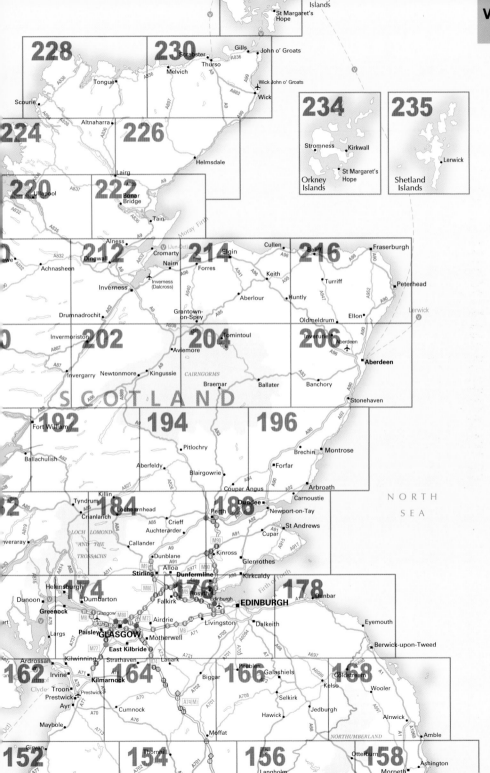

Mileage chart

The mileage chart shows distances in miles between two towns along AA-recommended routes. Using motorways and other main roads this is normally the fastest route, though not necessarily the shortest.

The journey times, shown in hours and minutes, are average off-peak driving times along AA-recommended routes. These times should be used as a guide only and do not allow for unforeseen traffic delays, rest breaks or fuel stops.

For example, the 378 miles (608 km) journey between Glasgow and Norwich should take approximately 7 hours 28 minutes.

journey times

The page contains a large triangular AA mileage chart giving distances in miles and journey times in hours and minutes between UK towns. The towns listed along the diagonal are: Aberdeen, Aberystwyth, Barnstaple, Birmingham, Brighton, Bristol, Cambridge, Cardiff, Carlisle, Carmarthen, Dorchester, Dover, Edinburgh, Exeter, Fort William, Glasgow, Gloucester, Guildford, Hereford, Holyhead, Hull, Inverness, Kendal, Leeds, Lincoln, Liverpool, Maidstone, Manchester, Middlesbrough, Newcastle, Northampton, Norwich, Nottingham, Oxford, Penzance, Perth, Peterborough, Plymouth, Portsmouth, Preston, Salisbury, Sheffield, Shrewsbury, Southampton, Stoke-on-Trent, Stranraer, Taunton, Wick, York, LONDON.

distances in miles (one mile equals 1.6093 km)

Atlas symbols

M4	Motorway with number	
Toll	Toll motorway with toll station	
3	Restricted motorway junctions	
S Fleet	Motorway service area	
Motorway and junction under construction		
A3	Primary route single/dual carriageway	
Primary route junction with and without number		
Restricted primary route junctions		
S	Primary route service area	
BATH	Primary route destination	
A1123	Other A road single/dual carriageway	
B2070	B road single/dual carriageway	

Minor road, more than 4 metres wide, less than 4 metres wide

Roundabout

Interchange/junction

Narrow primary/other A/B road with passing places (Scotland)

Road under construction/ approved

Road tunnel

Toll → Road toll, steep gradient (arrows point downhill)

5 Distance in miles between symbols

Railway line, in tunnel

Railway station and level crossing

Tourist railway

628 637 Height in metres, Lecht Summit mountain pass

30 Speed camera site (fixed location) with speed limit in mph

40 Section of road with two or more fixed speed cameras, with speed limit in mph

50 50 Average speed (SPECS™) camera system with speed limit in mph

V Fixed speed camera site with variable speed limit

or V Vehicle ferry

Fast vehicle ferry or catamaran

⊕ H F Airport, heliport, international freight terminal

H 24-hour Accident & Emergency hospital

C Crematorium

P•R Park and Ride (at least 6 days per week)

City, town, village or other built-up area

National boundary, administrative boundary

Scenic route	⊓	Aqueduct or viaduct	········	Forest drive	Horse racing, show jumping
Tourist Information Centre (all year/seasonal)	✿ ♣	Garden, arboretum	– – –	National trail	Air show venue, motor-racing circuit
Visitor or heritage centre	♣	Vineyard	☀	Viewpoint	Ski slope (natural, artificial)
Picnic site	♀	Country park	⊙	Hill-fort	National Trust property (England & Wales, Scotland)
Caravan site (AA inspected)	♥	Agricultural showground	Roman antiquity	Prehistoric monument, Roman antiquity	English Heritage site
Camping site (AA inspected)	☰	Theme park	✕ 1066	Battle site with year	Historic Scotland site
Caravan & camping site (AA inspected)		Farm or animal centre	⋘	Steam railway centre	Cadw (Welsh heritage) site
Abbey, cathedral or priory		Zoological or wildlife collection	⌒	Cave	Major shopping centre, other place of interest
Ruined abbey, cathedral or priory		Bird collection, aquarium	✕ ⊥	Windmill, monument	Attraction within urban area
Castle	RSPB	RSPB site	⚑	Golf course (AA listed)	World Heritage Site (UNESCO)
Historic house or building		National Nature Reserve (England, Scotland, Wales)		County cricket ground	National Park and National Scenic Areas
Museum or art gallery		Local nature reserve	∂	Rugby Union national stadium	Forest Park
Industrial interest		Wildlife Trust reserve	⚘	International athletics stadium	Heritage coast

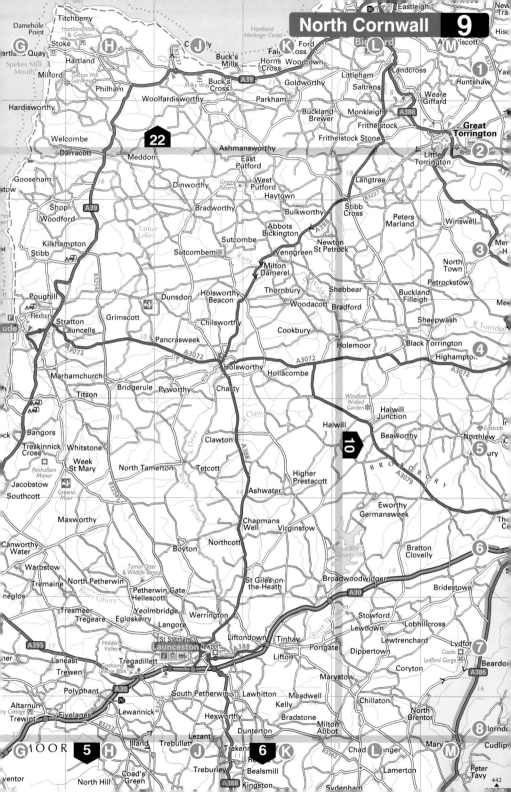

Ⓐ Ⓑ Ⓒ Ⓓ Ⓔ Ⓕ

1

2

North West
Point

*Lundy
Heritage Coast* LUNDY

3 ▲142
Marisco
Surf Point
Shutter Point

4

5 B A R N S T A P L E

O R

B I D E F O R D   B A Y **Westw**

*Shipload
Bay*

HARTLAND POINT

Titchberry Abbot

Damehole
Point *Hartland Abbey
& Gardens* Clovelly Ford

6 Stoke Fairy Cross

Hartland Quay Buck's
Mills Horns Woodtow
Cross

*Spekes Mill
Mouth* Hartland B3248 4
A39
Milford *Docton Mill
Gardens* Buck's Goldwort
Cross

Philham *Milky Way*

Woolfardisworthy Parkham

Hardisworthy Buck
Br

Welcombe
*South West
Coast Path* Darracott Ashmansworthy

7 Med **9** East
Putford

Gooseham Dinworthy *Gnome
Reserve* ★ West
Putford Haytown

Morwenstow Bradworthy Bulkwort

Higher Sharpnose Point Shop A39 Abbots
Bickington

*South West
Coast Path* Woodford Sutcombe Wenr

8 Lower Sharpnose Point *Tamar
Lakes* Milton
Damerel

Steeple Point Kilkhampton Setcom' ill *River* Thornbury

Ⓐ Ⓑ Ⓒ bb Ⓒ Ⓓ Ⓔ Ⓕ

0   1   2   3   4 miles
0 1 2 3 4 5 kilometres

Holsworthy

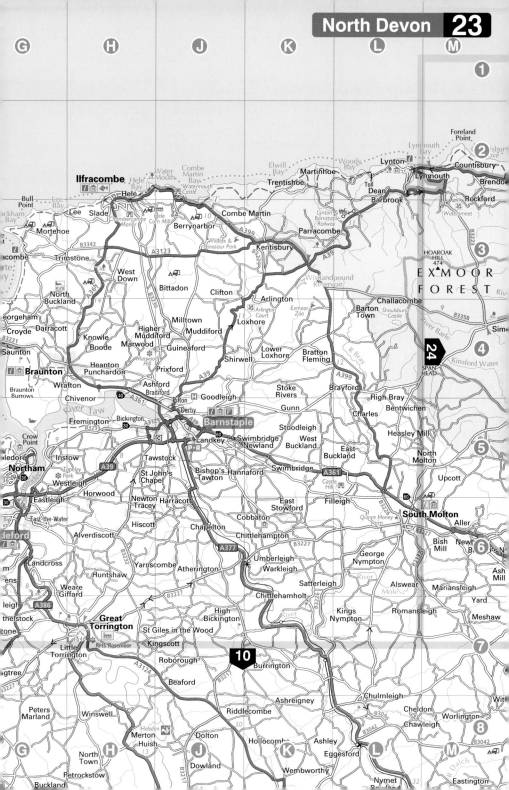

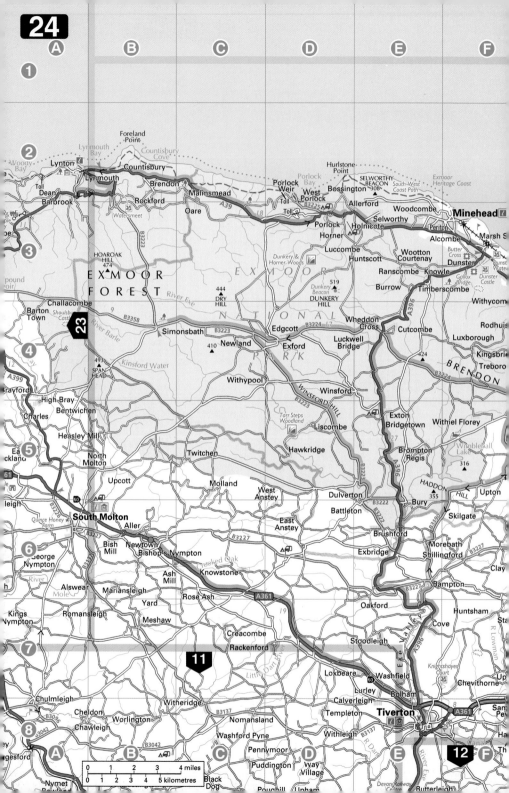

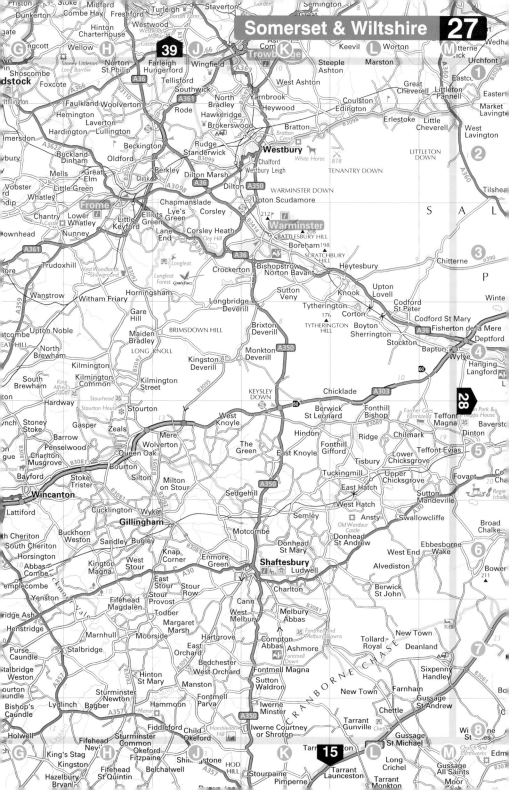

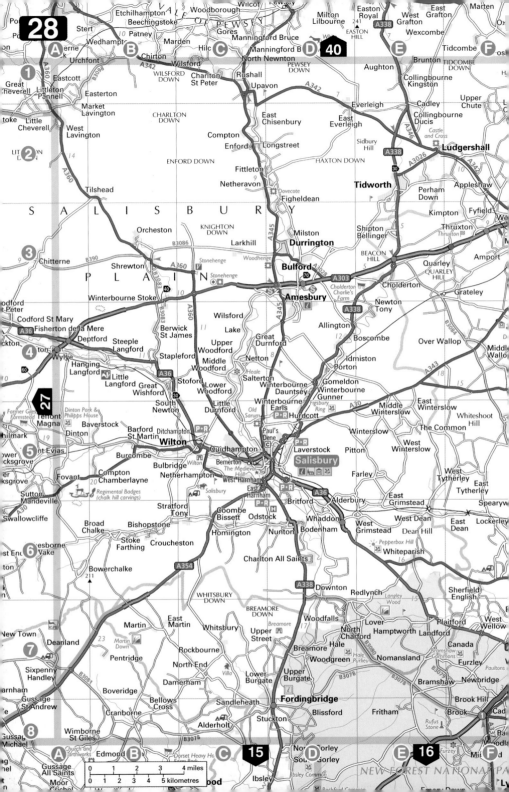

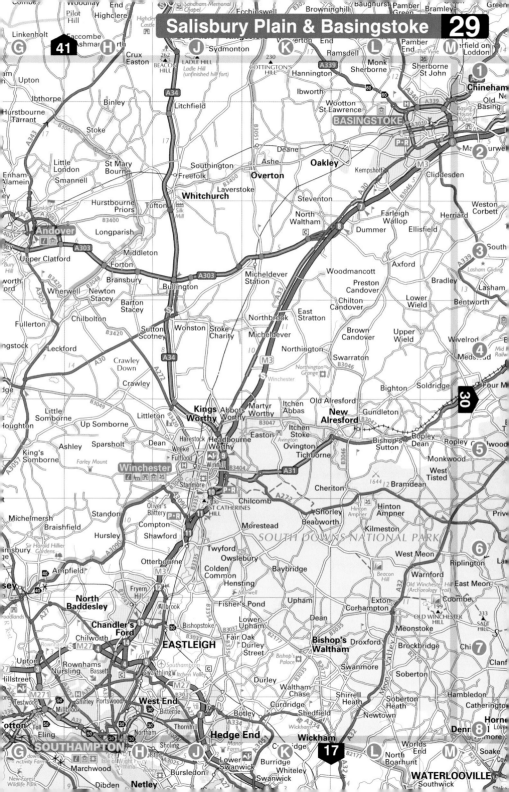

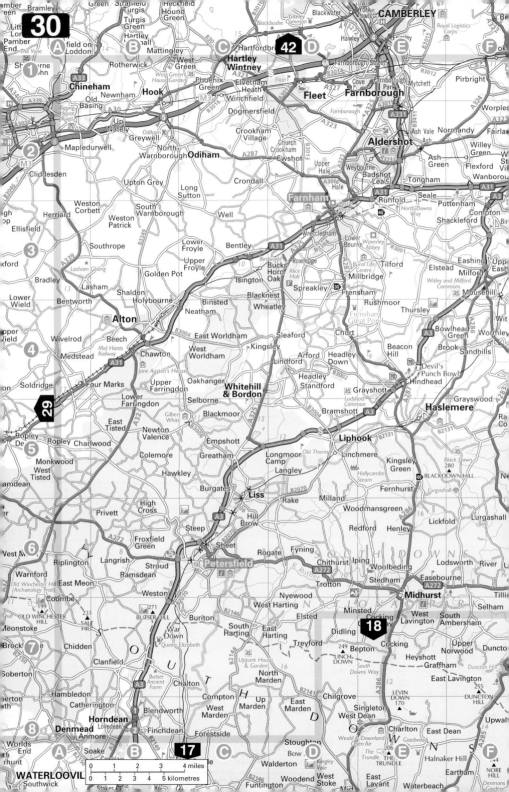

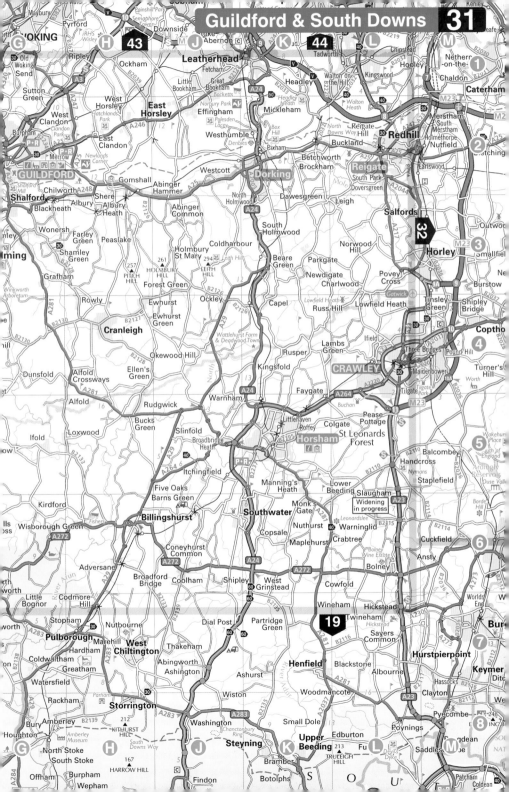

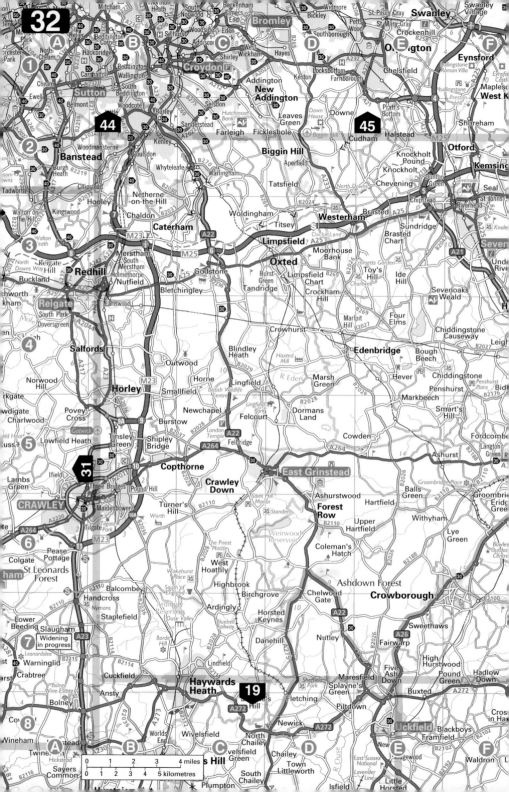

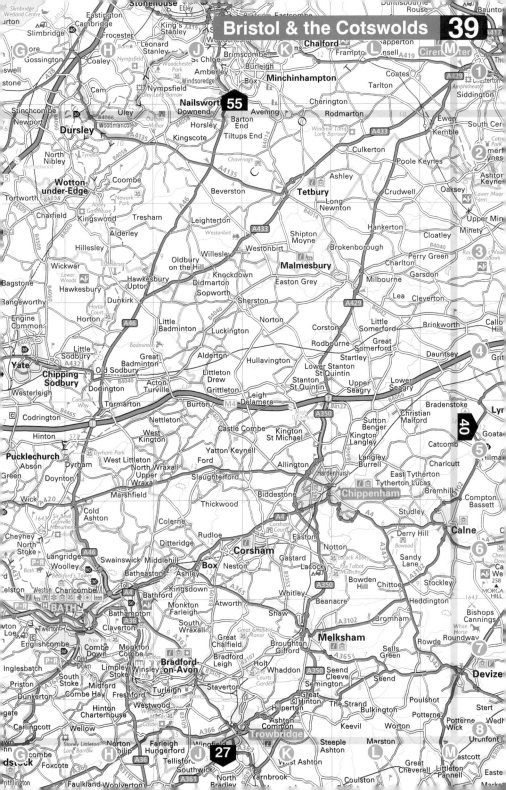

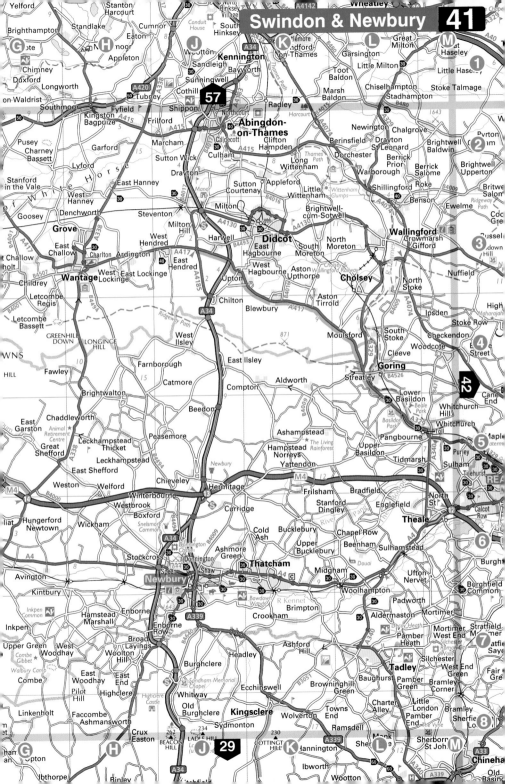

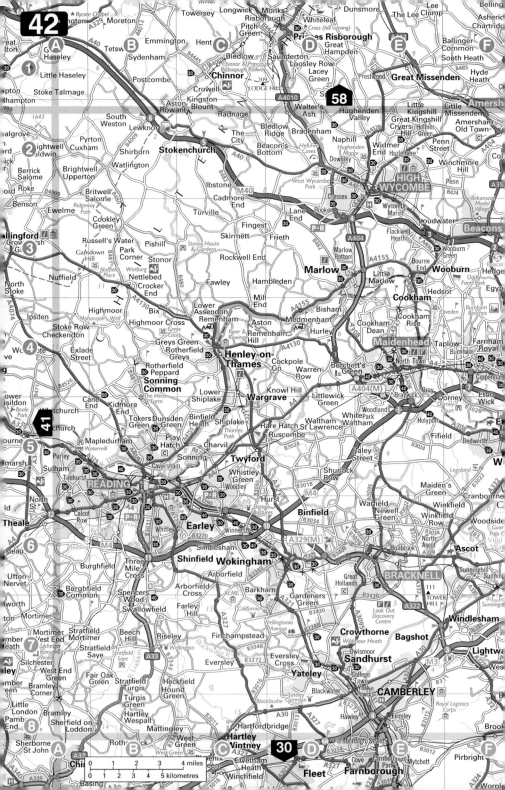

G H J K L M

1 2 3 4 5 6 7 8

62

Holliwell Point

Foulness Point

rouch

Courtsend

Churchend

LNESS LAND

Warden Point

Leysdown-on-Sea

A2500

EY

Isle of Harty

ne Swale

Shell Ness

Whitstable
Whitstable Bay

Tankerton

Seasalter

Oare

Dare

versham

Chapel Davington

Hill

Preston

North Street

eldwich

Hogben's Hill

A251

Badlesmere

Shottenden

Chilham

Dane Street

Goodnestone

Highstreet

Dargate

Hernhill

Staplestreet

Boughton St

South Street

Oversland

Selling

Old Wives Lees

Chartham

Shalmsford Street

Garlinge

Yorkletts

Denstroude

Dunkirk

Upper Harbledown

Blean

Rough Common

Harbledown

Thanington

Chartham Hatch

ackington Street End

Lower Hardres
Bishopsbourne

Druidstone Park

Tyler Hill

Hales Place

Sturry

Fordwich

Littlebourne

Canterbury

Howletts

Bridge

North Downs Way

Herne Bay
Hampton

B2205

Swalecliffe

Chestfield

South Street

Greenhill

Herne

Broomfield

Beltinge

Bishopstone

Reculver

Reculver Towers
& Raman Fort

Hoath

Upstreet

Hersden

Westbere

Stodmarsh

Broad Oak

Wildwood

A291

A299

A2050

A28

St Nicholas
at Wade

Boyden Gate

Sarre

Chislet

A253

West Stourmouth

Preston

Wickhambreaux

Ickham

Seaton

Bramling

Bekesbourne

Patrixbourne

Adisham

Ra

Aylesham

Nonington

Minnis Bay

Westgate on Sea

Birchington

Acol

Monkton

Durlock

Minster

East Stourmouth

Westmarsh

Elmstone

Hoaden

Durlock

Wingham

Staple

Goodnestone

Chillenden

Cop Street

Ash

Marshborough

Woodnesbor

Statenborou

Eastry

Betteshanger

35

MA

OF NE

RAF Manston

B2190

A299

Wes

A2

Richb
om

Stone Cross

Ha

34 35 6 6 7 8

G H J K L M

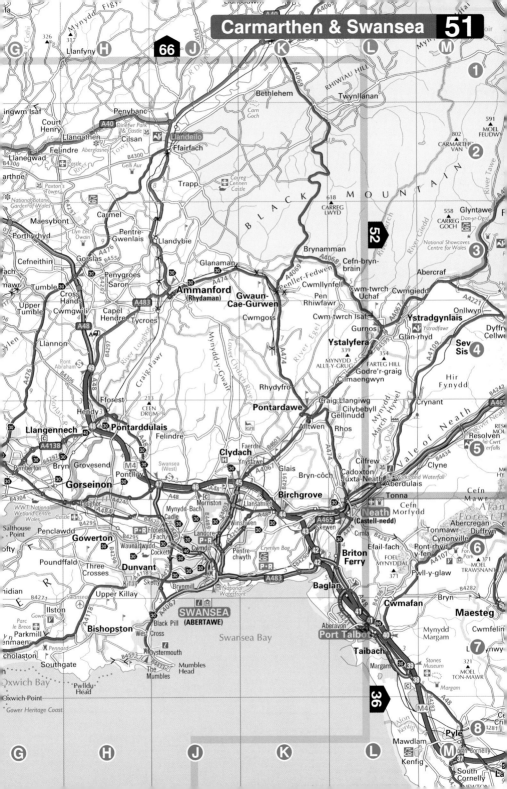

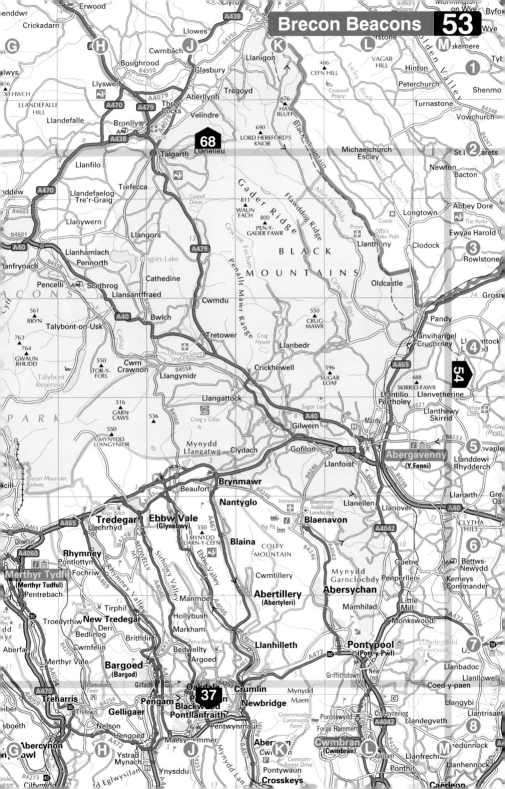

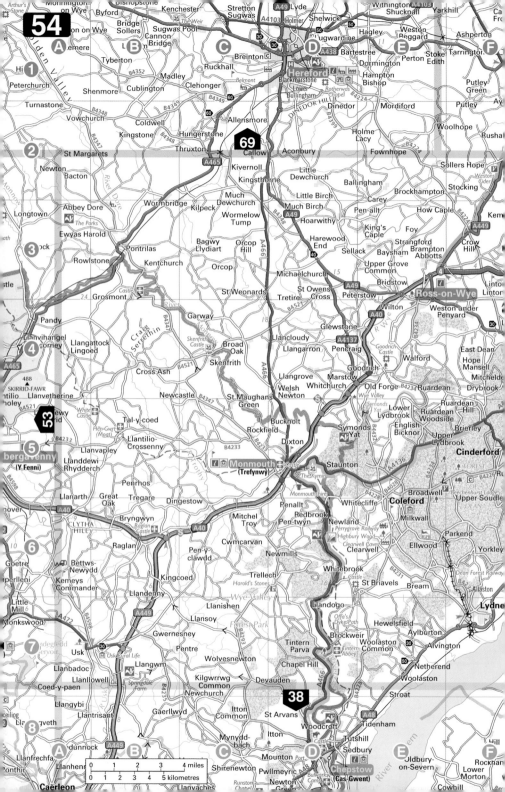

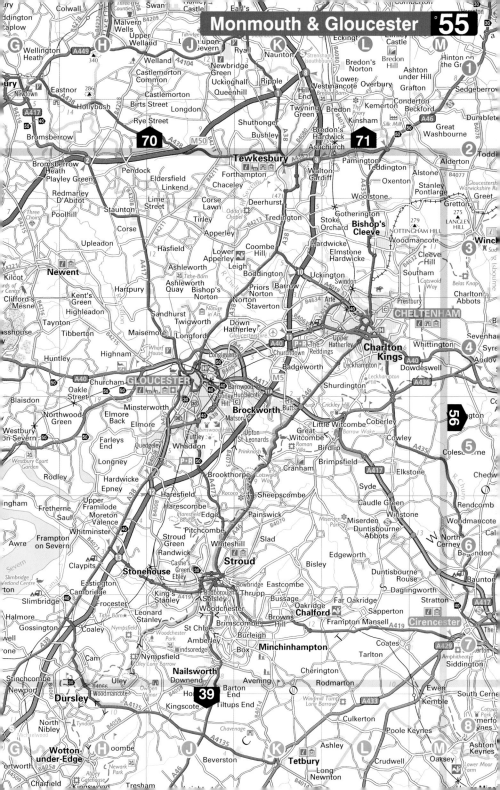

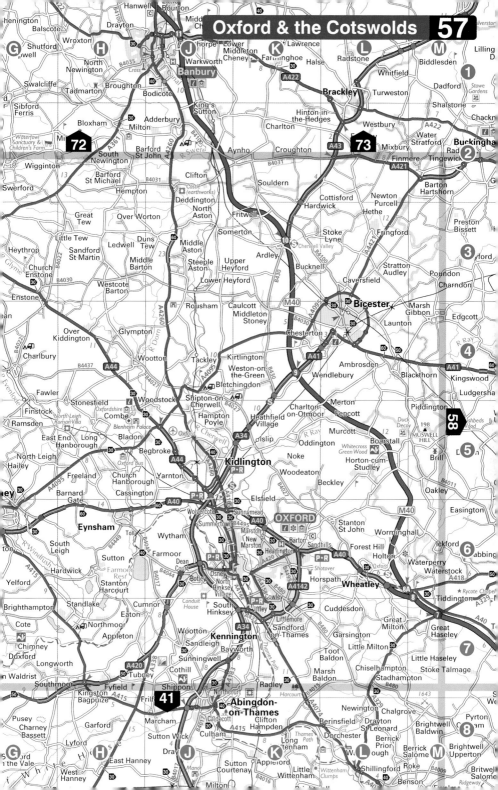

Oxford & the Cotswolds 57

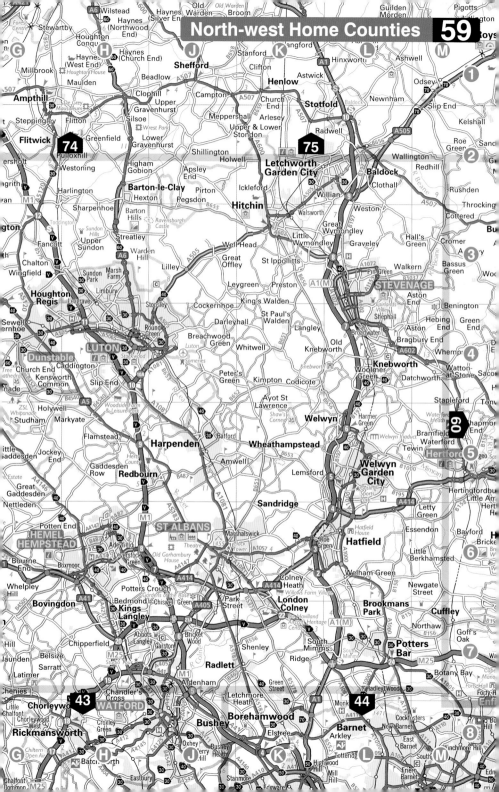

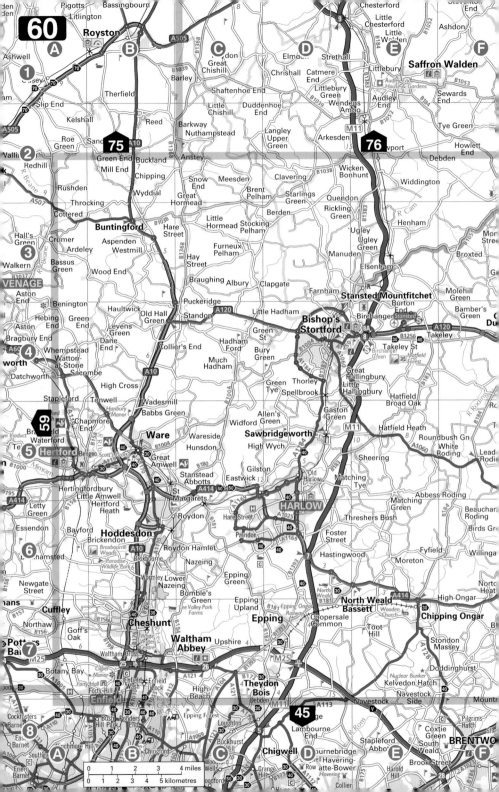

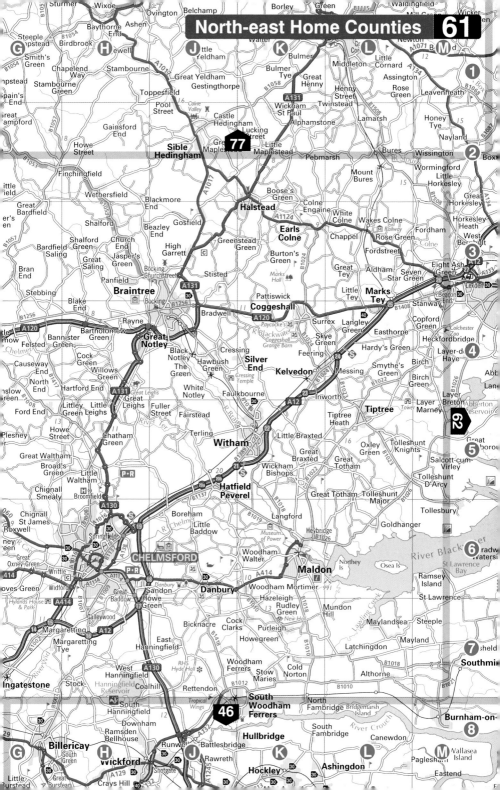

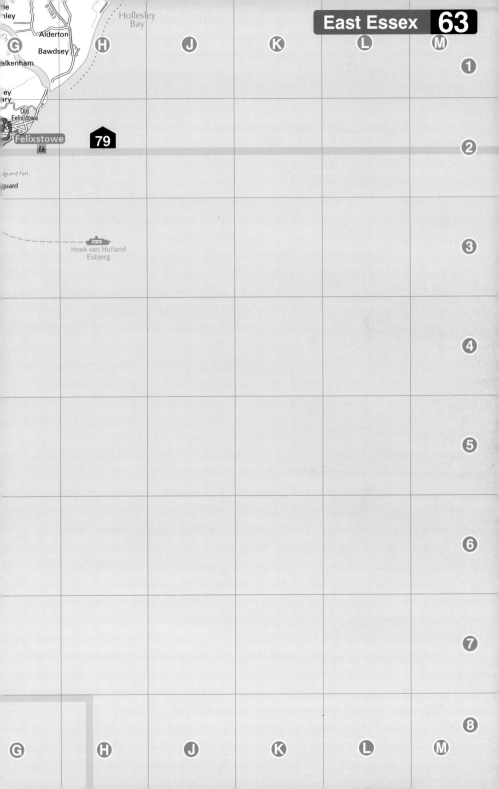

A   B   C   D   E   F

1

2

3

4

5

St Dogmaels Moylgrove
Heritage Coast

Moylegro

Rosslare Harbour

Pemb
Coa

6

STRUMBLE HEAD

Carregwastad Head

Dinas Head
Heritage Coast

DINAS
HEAD

Newport
Bay

Trwyn-y-bwa

Pen Brush

Nevern

Fel
Fa

Llanwnda

Fishguard
Bay

Bryn-
Henllan

Newport

Carreg
Coetan

Pwll Deri

Goodwick

Ocean Lab

A487

Dinas

Pentre
Ifan

Cros

Pembrokeshire
Coast Path

Trefasser

Lower Town

Mynydd
Melyn

311

Penlan-Uchaf

MYNYDD
CAREGOG

Manorowen

Fishguard
(Abergwaun)

PEMBROKESHIRE

St Nicholas

Llanychaer
Bridge

Ynys
Daullyn

Scleddau

Pontfaen

MYNYDD P

Carreg Sampson

Granston

Abercastle

A40

B4313

NATIONAL

Porthgain

Trefin

Mathry

Llangloffan

Jordanston

Trecwn

Foel
Eryr

536

FOEL
CWMCERWYN

Abereiddy

Llanrhian

A487

16

48

B4331

49

Puncheston

Rosebush

Berea

Croes-goch

Llangloffan
Fen

Letterston

Little
Newcastle

Castlebythe

26

Tufton

Maencloch

Treglemais

B4330

15

Henry's Moat
(Castell Hendre)

Llangolm

Caer
F...ell

River   Solva

Llandeloy

Whitchurch

Wolf's
Castle

Rinaston

Ambleston

New
Moat

Llany

Solva

A   B   C   D   E   F

Hayscastle
Cross

Treffgarne

Llys-y-fran
Res...

0	1	2	3		4 miles
0	1	2	3	4	5 kilometres

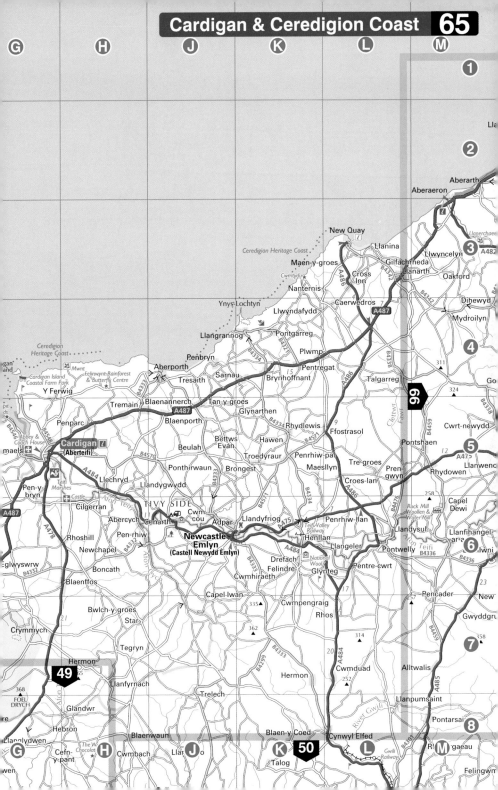

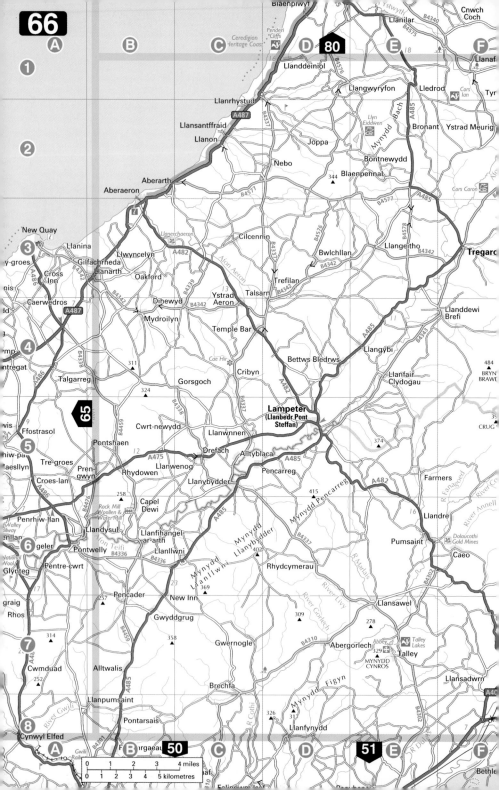

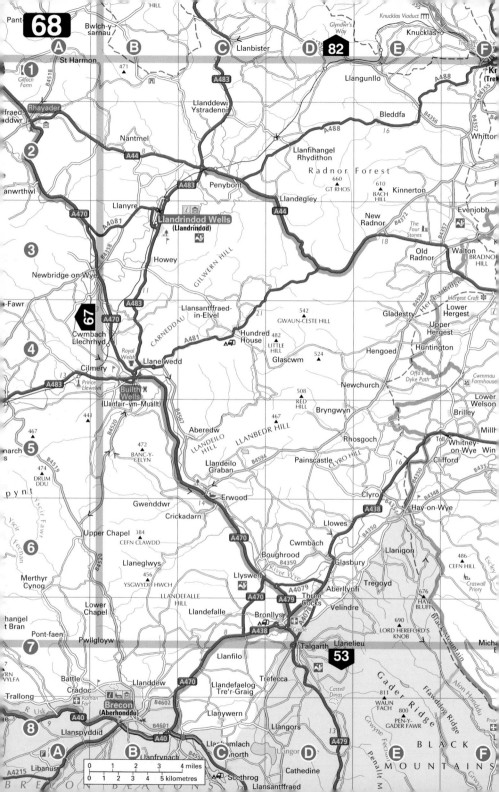

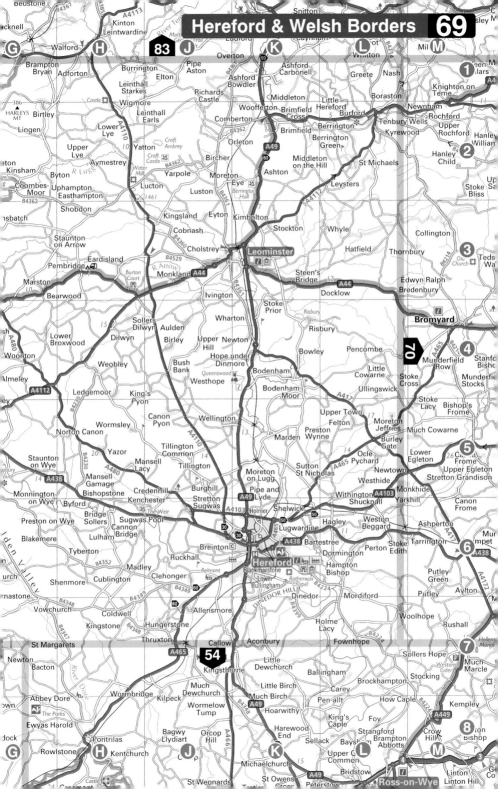

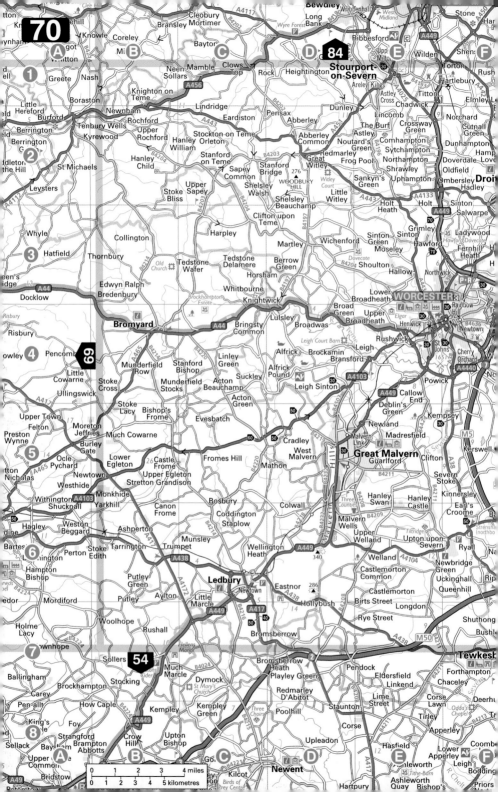

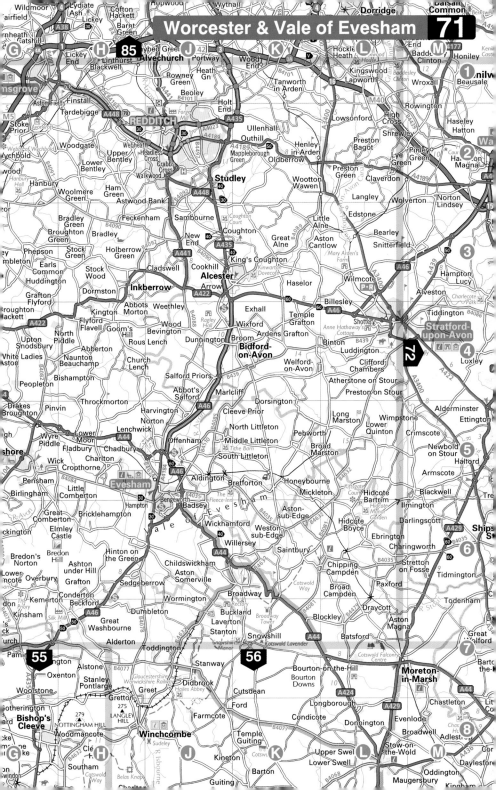

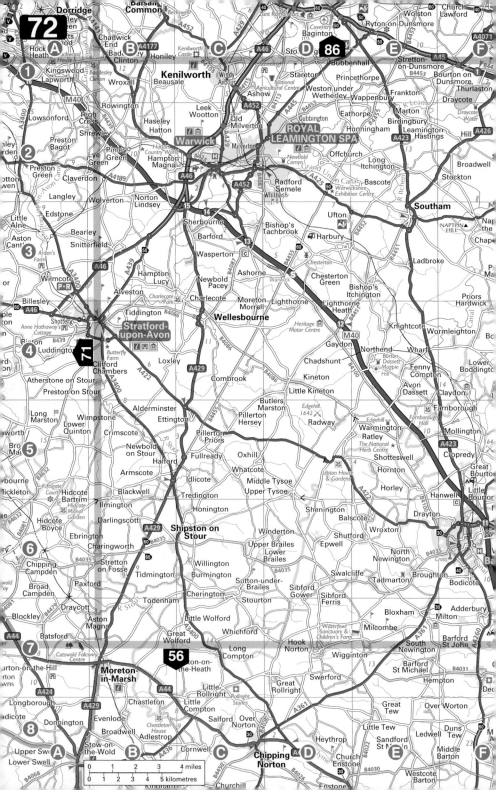

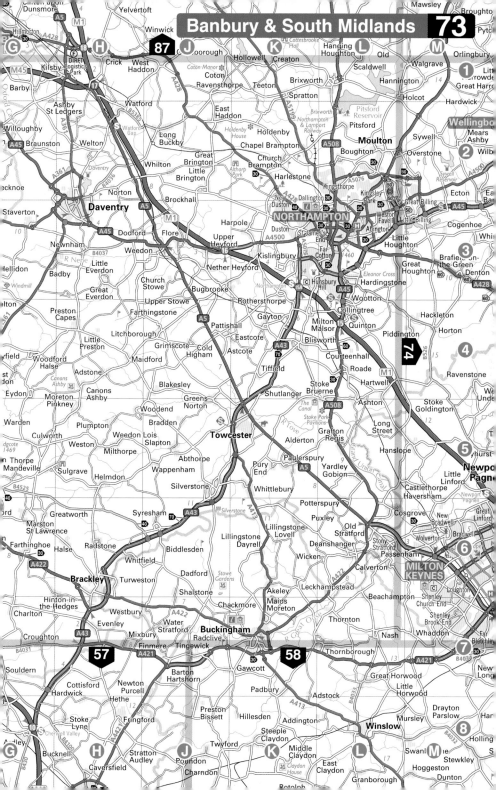

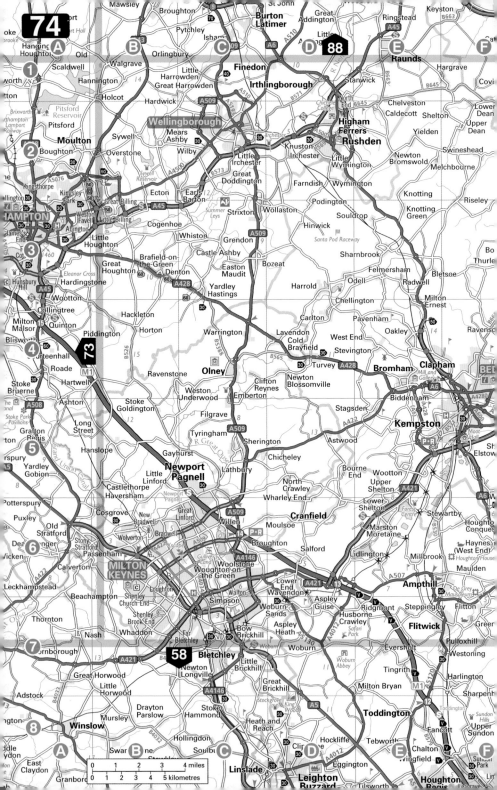

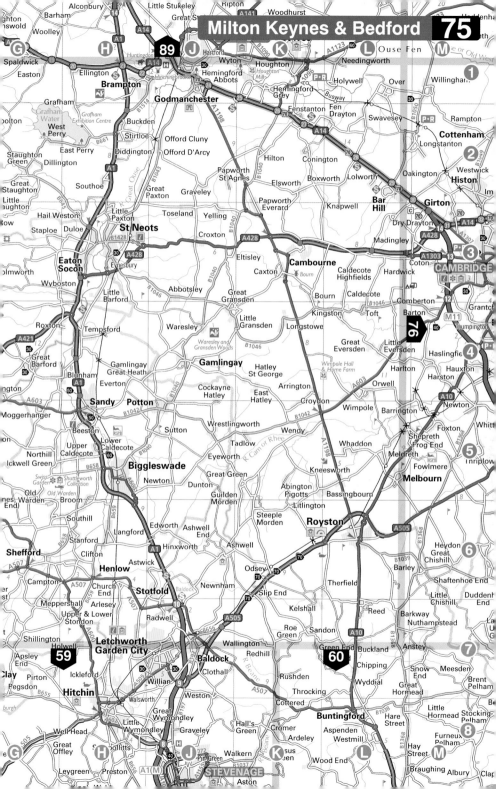

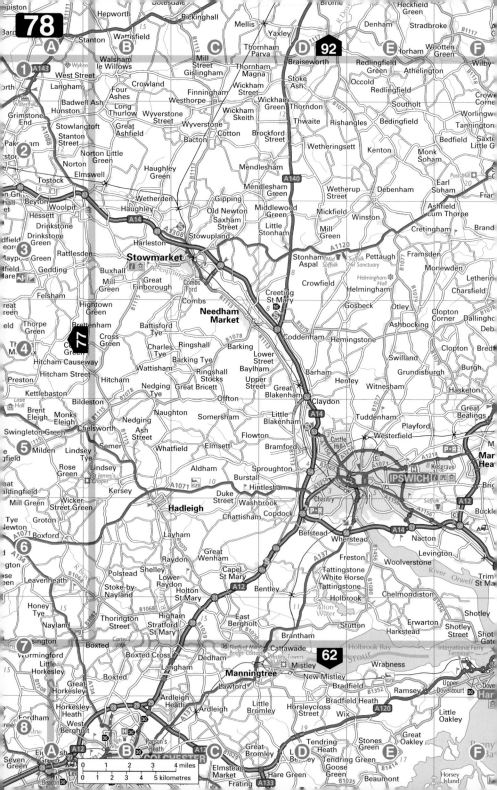

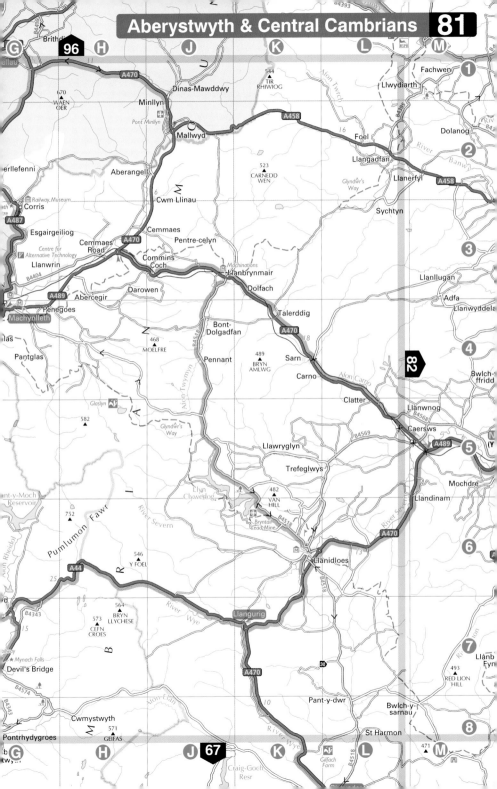

G 96 H J K L M

Brithdir

A470

670 WAEN OER

Dinas-Mawddwy

Minllyn

Pont Minllyn

Mallwyd

544 TIR RHIWIOG

Fachwen

Llwydiarth

A458

Foel

16

Dolanog

River

Llangadfan

River Banwy

Llanerfyl

A458

erllefenni

Aberangell

523 CARNEDD WEN

Glyndŵr's Way

Sychtyn

Railway Museum

Corris

Cwm Llinau

A487

Esgairgeiliog

Centre for Alternative Technology

Cemmaes

A470

Cemmaes Road

Pentre-celyn

Llanllugan

Adfa

Llanwyddela

Llanwrin

B4404

Commins Coch

Machinations

Llanbrynmair

Dolfach

Darowen

Abercegir

A489

Penegoes

Machynlleth

las

Pantglas

468 MOELFRE

Bont-Dolgadfan

Pennant

489 BRYN AMLWG

Talerddig

A470

18

Sarn

Carno

Afon Carno

Clatter

82

Bwlch-y-ffridd

4

Llanwnog

B4568

Caersws

A489

5

(Y

Mochdre

Llandinam

Glaslyn

582

Glyndŵr's Way

Llawryglyn

Trefeglwys

Llyn Clywedog

482 VAN HILL

B4518

River Severn

A470

6

nt-y-moch Reservoir

752

Pumlumon Fawr

A44

546 Y FOEL

Bryntail Lead Mine

Llanidloes

B4518

Afon Rheidol

25

B4343

564 BRYN LLYCHESE

573 CEFN CROES

River Severn

River Wye

Llangurig

Llanb Fyn

493 RED LION HILL

7

15

Mynach Falls

Devil's Bridge

B4574

A470

30

Pant-y-dwr

Bwlch-y-sarnau

8

Cwmystwyth

571 GEIFAS

River Wye

St Harmon

471

Pontrhydygroes

B4343

A470

10

Gilfach Farm

twy

G

H

J 67

K

L

M

Craig-Goch Resr

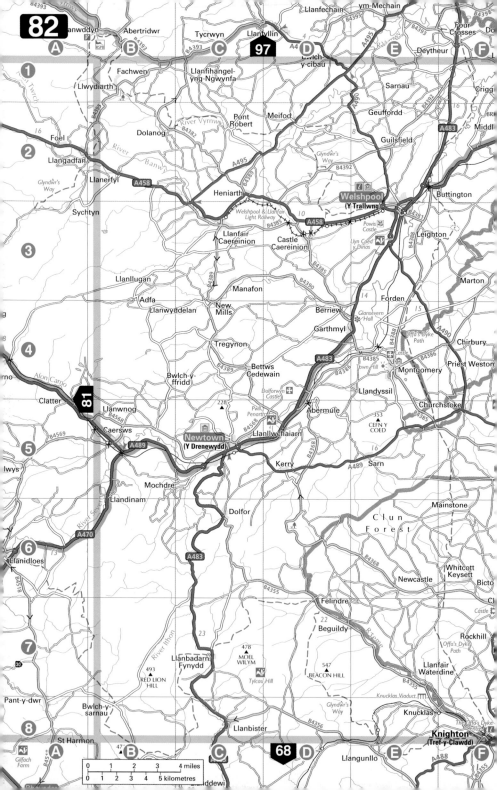

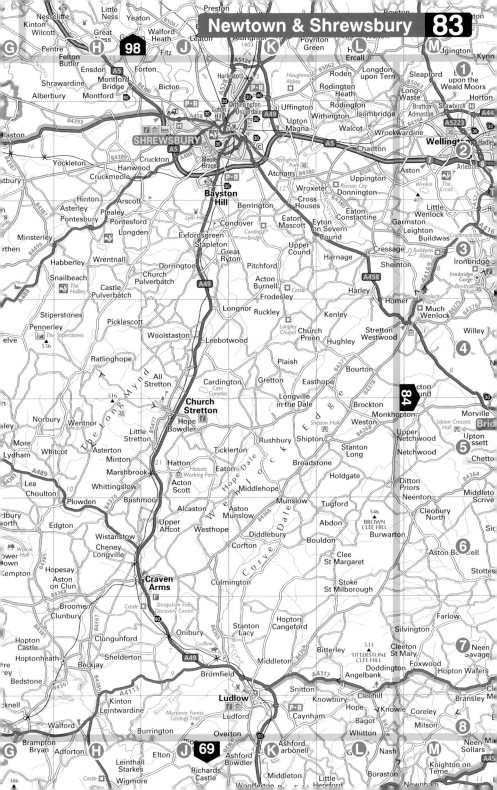

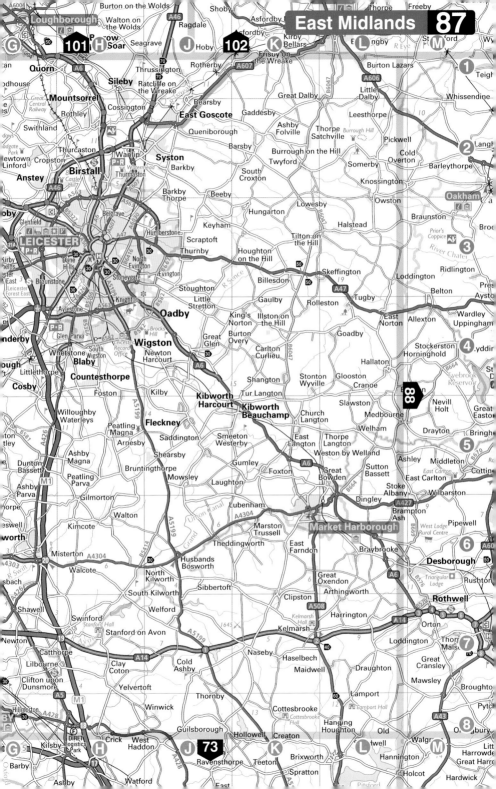

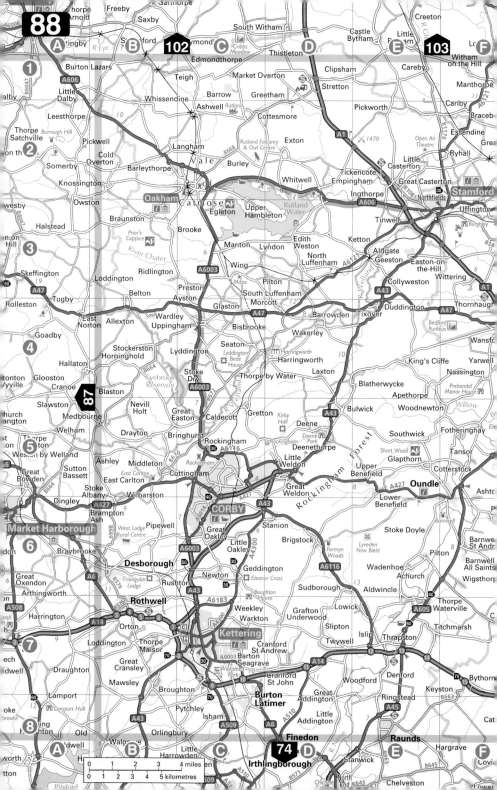

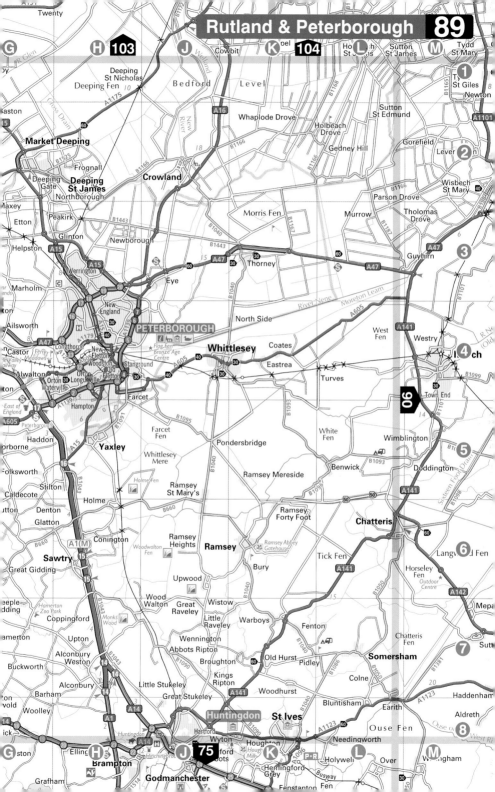

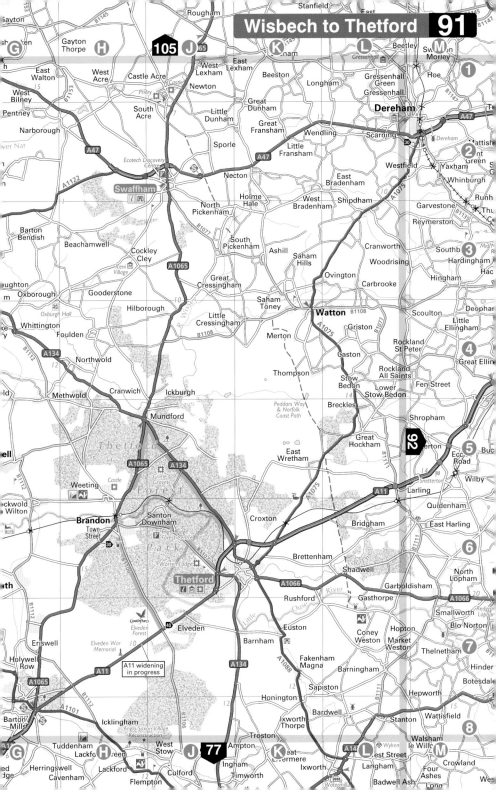

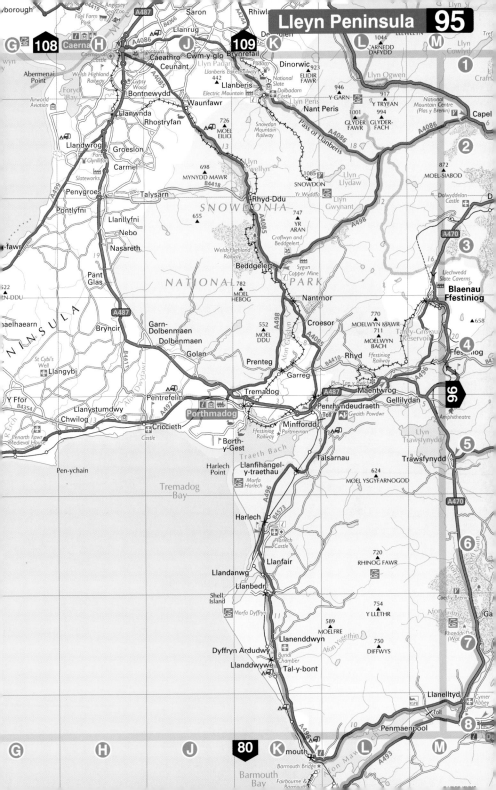

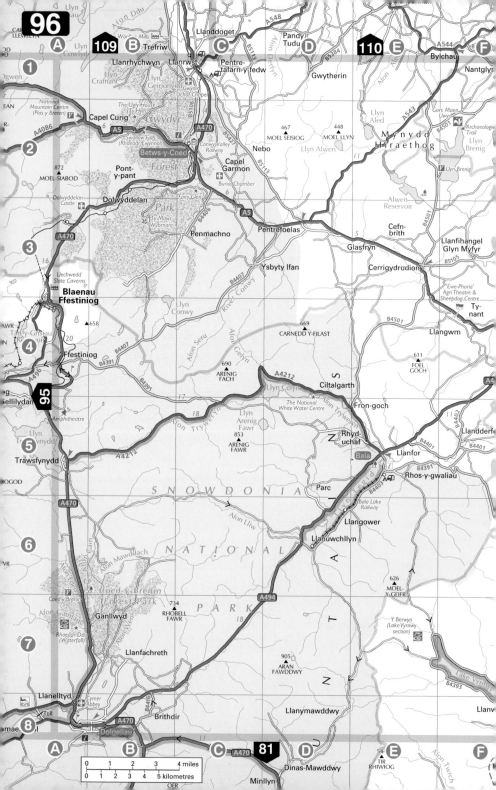

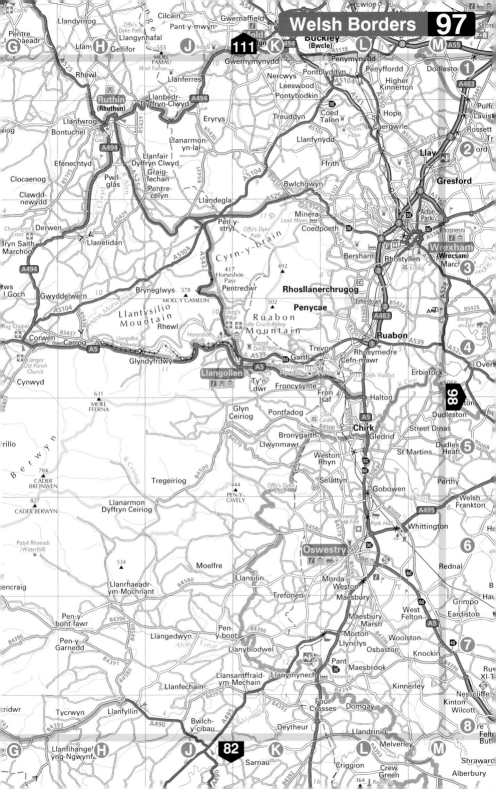

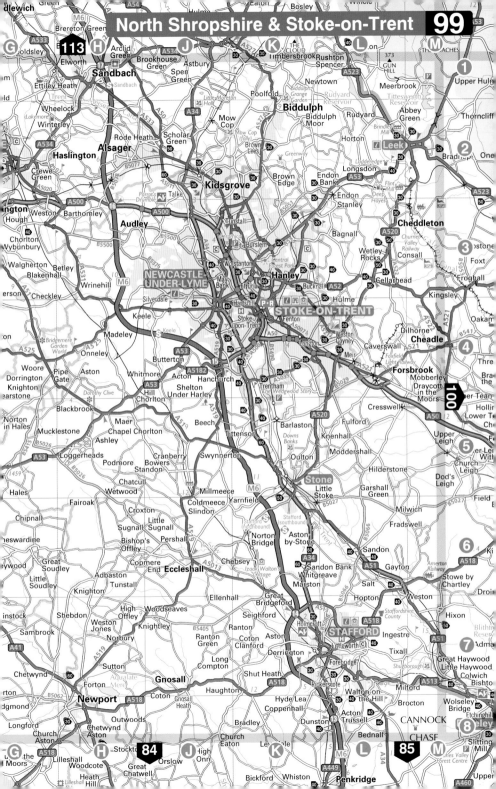

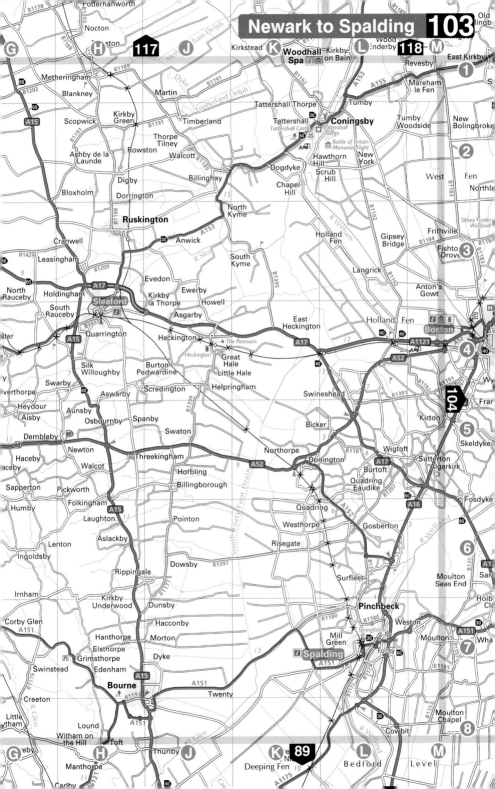

G H J K L M

① ② ③ ④ ⑤ ⑥ ⑦ ⑧

North Norfolk
Heritage Coast

Blakeney Point

Holkham Bay

Brancaster
Bay

Scolt Head
Island

Peddars Way &
Norfolk Coast Path

106

Old
Hunstanton
Holme next
the Sea
Holme
Dunes
Brancaster
Brancaster
Staithe
Burnham
Norton
Burnham
Overy
Staithe
Holkham
Wells-next-
the-sea
Mo
Stiffke
Co

Thornham
Titchwell
Brandonium
Roman Fort
Burnham
Deepdale
B1155
Holkham Hall
A149
Ringstead
Burnham Market
Burnham Overy
Warham St Mary
Warham
All Saints
Wighton
Bi

nton
eacham
Norfolk
Lavender
Summerfield
Peddars Way &
Norfolk
Coast Path
Burnham
Thorpe
North
Creake
Creake
Abbey
Wells & Walsingham
Light Railway
The Shrine of
Our Lady
Little
Walsingham
Great
Walsingham
Hindringham

Sedgeford
B1454
Docking
B1155
Stanhoe
South
Creake
North
Barsham
Houghton St Giles
Great
Snoring
Thursford

Snettisham
goldisthorpe
Fring
B1153
Bircham
Newton
B1155
Syderstone
West
Barsham
East
Barsham
Little
Snoring
A148
Croxton

ersingham
Shernborne
Great
Bircham
Bircham
Tofts
B1454
Wicken Green
Village
Sculthorpe
Fakenham
Kettlestone
owl
k

gham
Bog
Anmer
Houghton
Hall
West
Rudham
Tattersett
Dunton
Coxford
Shereford
Hempton
Stil

Sandringham
West Newton
New
Houghton
A148
East
Rudham
Tatterford
Little Ryburgh
Great
Ryburgh
A1067

Flitcham
Harpley
Helhoughton
West
Raynham
South
Raynham
East
Raynham
Colkirk
Toftrees
B146
Horningtoft
Gateley

Hillington
B1439
Congham
Roydon
A148
Little
Massingham
Great
Massingham
Weasenham
St Peter
Wellingham
Whissonsett
Brisley
North
Elmham

 sing
Castle
Grimston
B1153
B1145
Gayton
Gayton
Thorpe
Weasenham
All Saints
Rougham
Tittleshall
Stanfield
East
Bilney
Old
Beetley
Beetley

s Lynn
A149
Ashwicken
B1145
A1065
Litcham
Mileham
B1145
8

Fair Green
East
Winch
East
Walton
J 91 K West
xham
East
Lexham
L Bee M Gressenhall
Green

G H West
Bilney
A Acre
e Acre
Newton
Longham
Gressenhall

Middleton
Blackborough
End
Priory
Castle
South
Great
Dunham
Little
Dereham

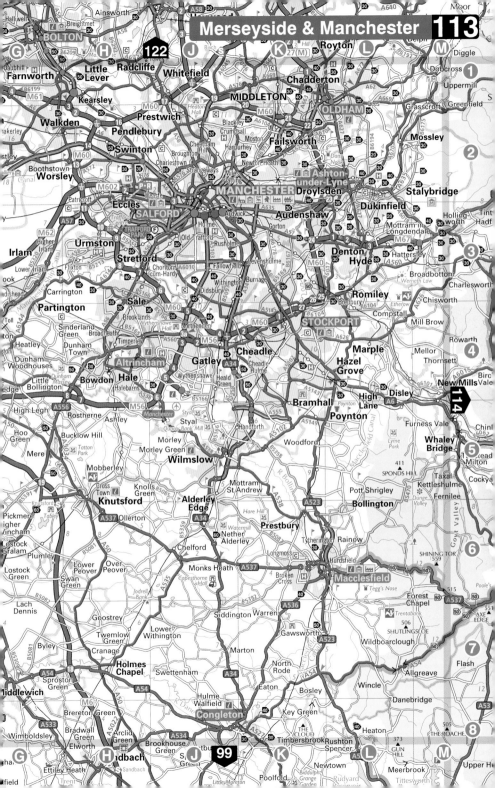

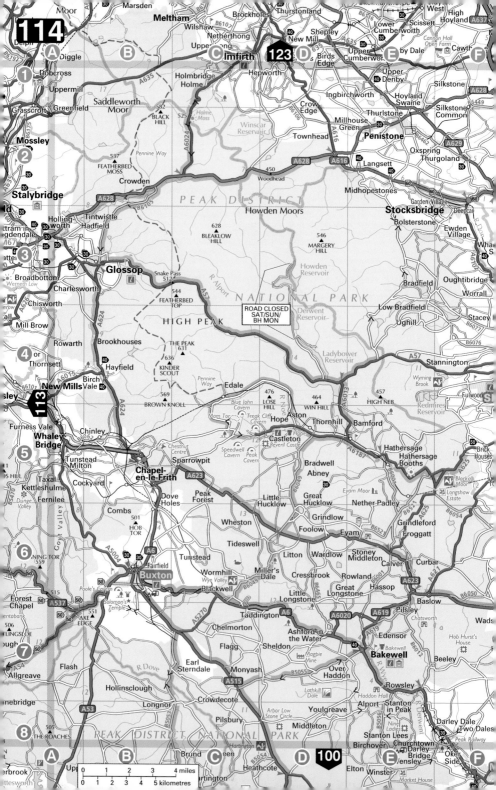

Peak District to Doncaster 115

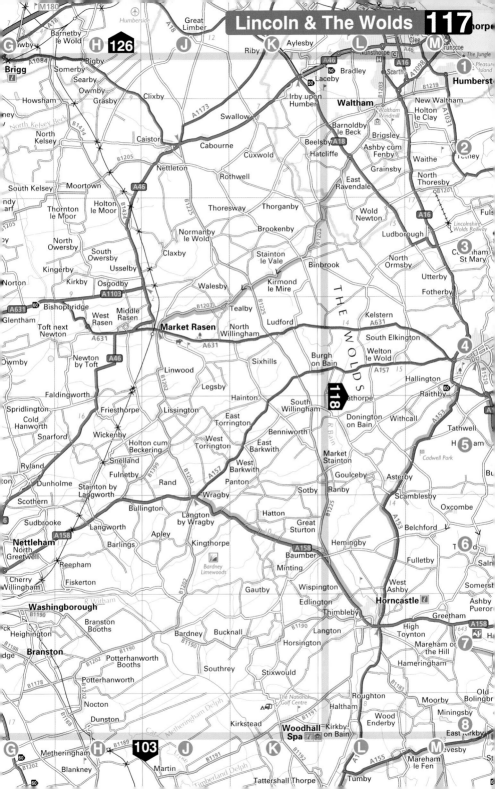

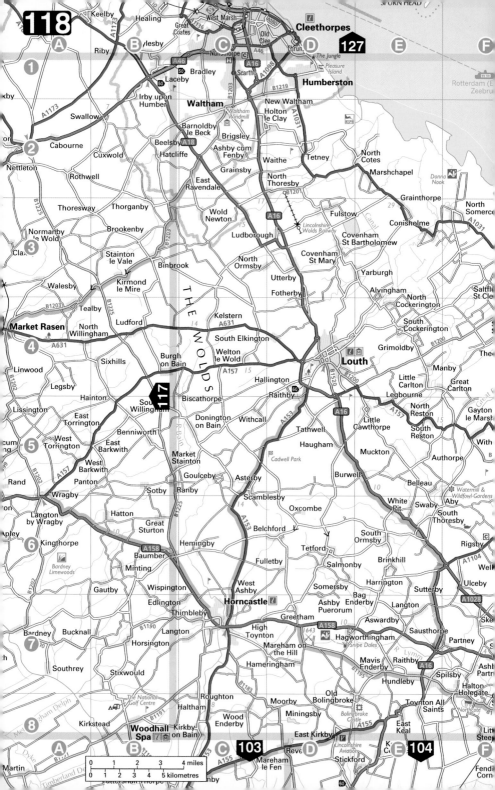

dlethorpe
len

Mablethorpe

Trusthorpe
Sutton on Sea
Sandilands

Markby

Huttoft
urlby

Anderby Creek

Anderby
thorpe Mumby
orth

Chapel Point

Hogsthorpe
hby

**Chapel
St Leonards**

Sloothby

Fantasy Island

Habertoft Addlethorpe
Ingoldmells

Ingoldmells
Point

Burgh le Marsh

A158

he Marsh

Skegness

104

Croft

St Peter
Wainfleet
Haven
Wainfleet

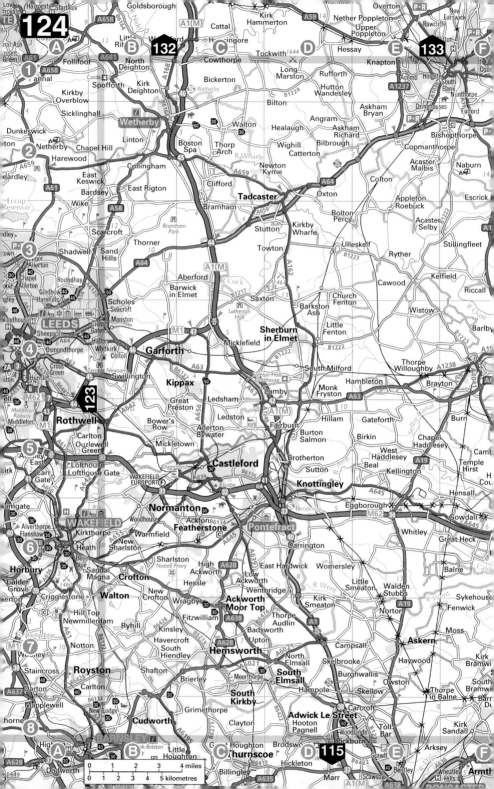

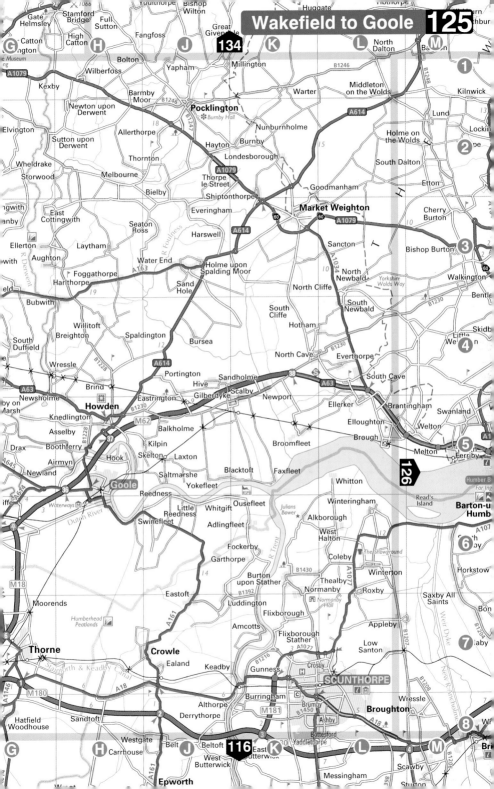

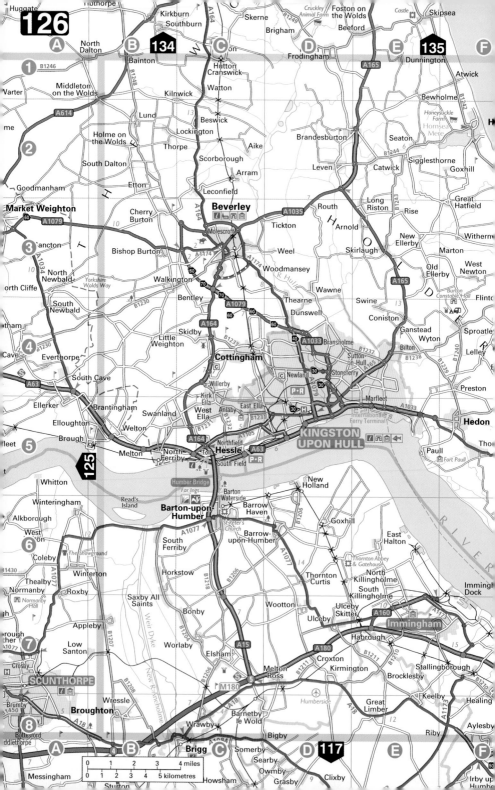

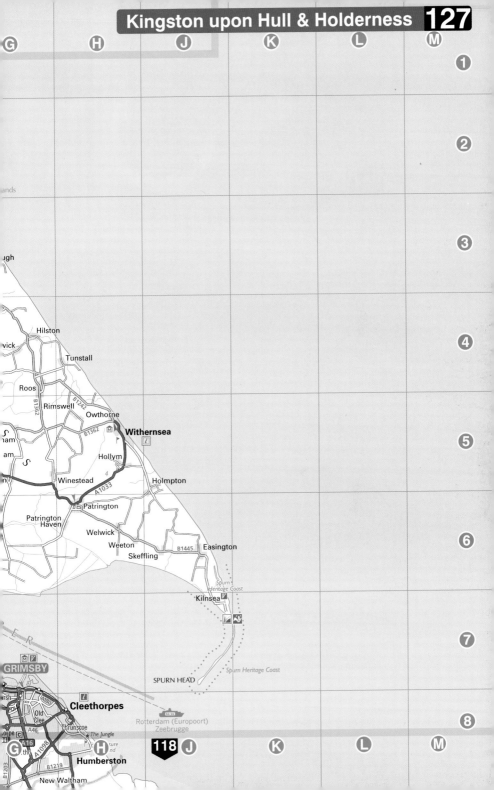

G   H   J   K   L   M

1
2
3
4
5
6
7
8

Hilston
vick
Tunstall
Roos
Rimswell
B1362
B1242
Owthorne
B1362
Withernsea
ham
am
Hollym
Winestead
A1033
Holmpton
Patrington
Patrington Haven
Welwick
Weeton
Skeffling
B1445
Easington
Spurn Heritage Coast
Kilnsea
Spurn Heritage Coast
SPURN HEAD

E R
GRIMSBY
Cleethorpes
Old Clee
A46
Thrunscoe
The Jungle
sure nd
A1098
J
B1203
B1219
Humberston
New Waltham

Green

Hallsenna Moor
Drigg
Holmrook
Muncaster
Mill
Ravenglass
and Eskdale
Railway

River Esk

ESKDALE

652
HARTER
FELL

Devoke
Water

Ravenglass
Roman
Bath
House
Muncaster

A595

Hall
Dunnerdale

Sea

136

137

Waberthwaite

573
WHITFELL

Ulpha

LAKE   DISTRICT

Hycemoor

Selker Bay

Bootle

NATIONAL

Swinside
Stone Circle

Broughton
Mills

PARK

Broughton

A595

Lady
Hall

Foxfield

600
BLACK
COMBE

Gutterby Spa

Whitbeck

The Green

Kirkb
B

Whicham

The Hill

A595

Silecroft

Soutergate

A595

Kirksanton

Millom

Haverigg

Ireleth

Haverigg
Point

Askam
in Furness

Linda
in Furne

Sandscale Haws

South Lakes
Animal Park

North Walney

Dalton-
in-Furness

Newton

Sandscale Haws

**BARROW-
IN-FURNESS**

Furness
Abbey

Bow
Bridge

Dendro

Vickerstown

Barrow
Island

30

A5087

**ISLE OF
WALNEY**

Sheep
Island

Piel
Ca

Piel

Hilpsford Point

South
Walney

Piel

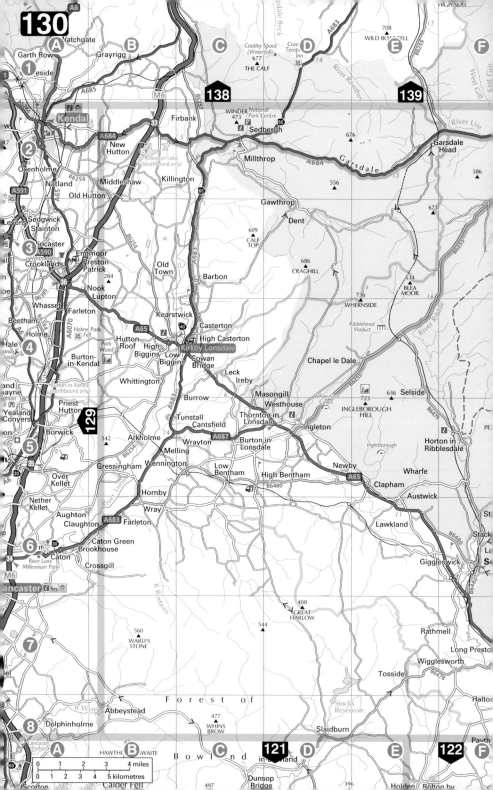

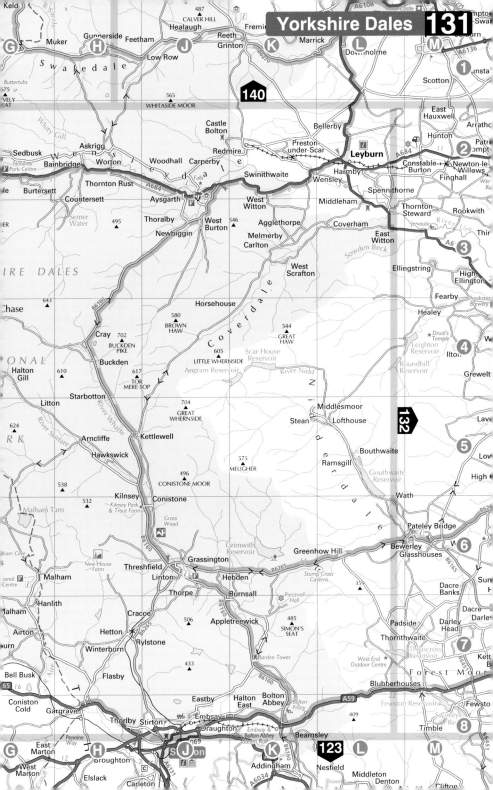

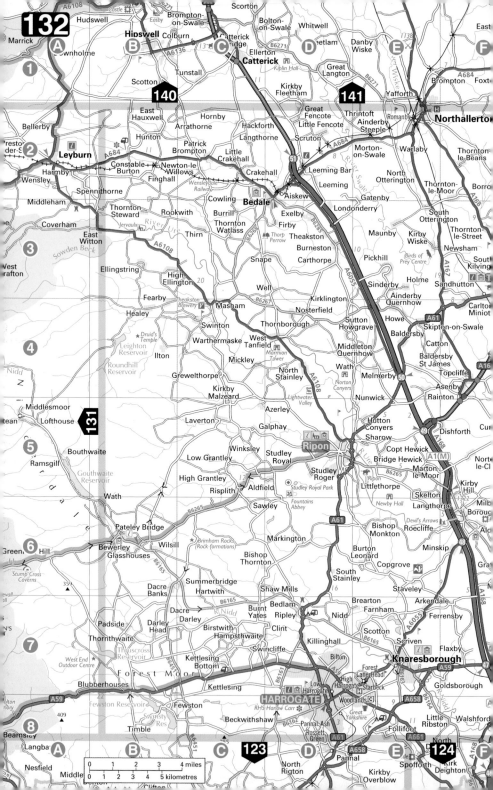

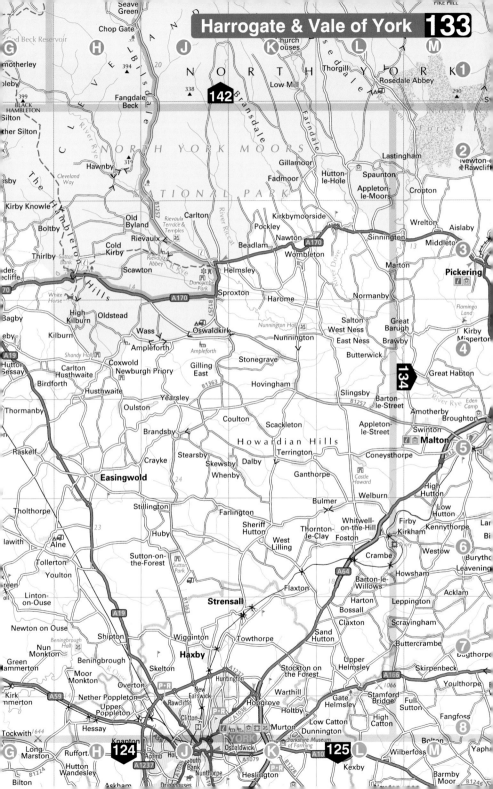

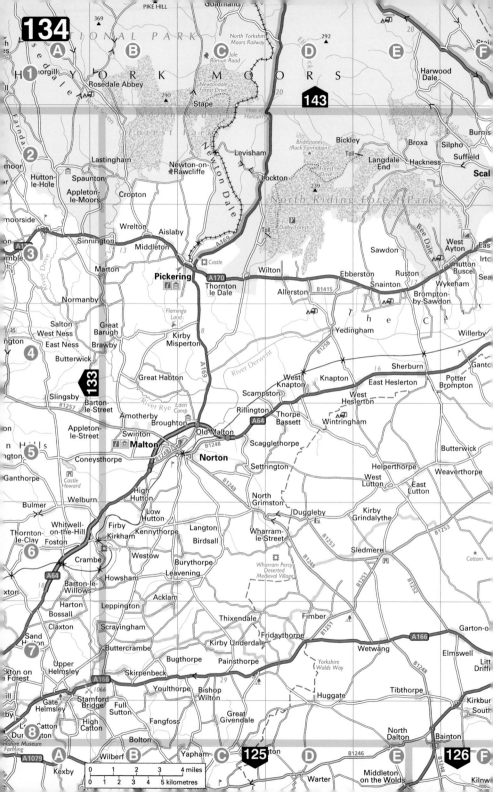

int

ay

rborough

fatherleigh
Deep-Sea-Trawler

s Mount

Osgodby
Cayton Bay

The Wyke

on

ebberston
Gristhorpe
Muston
R. Hertford

A1039

A1039

Filey Brigg

Filey

Filey Bay

Hunmanby

rdon

Reighton

Speeton

B1229

Flamborough Head
Heritage Coast

Thornwick Bay

Vold
ewton

Bempton Cliffs
RSPB

Buckton
Bempton

North Landing

Selwicks Bay

FLAMBOROUGH HEAD

Burton Fleming

Grindale

A165

B1229

B1259

Lighthouse

Flamborough

B1255

Bondville
Miniature Village

Sewerby

Rudston
Monolith

Boynton

Bridlington

BRIDLINGTON BAY

Bessingby
Hilderthorpe

Carnaby

A165

Kilham

Haisthorpe
Thornholme

Norman Manor House

Burton Agnes

arva
Harpham

S

A614

Lowthorpe

Fraisthorpe

Nafferton

Gransmoor

Great Kelk
Lissett

Barmston

Wansford

Gembling

B1242

Ulrome

Cruckley
Animal Farm

Foston on the Wolds

Castle

Skipsea

ne

Brigham

Beeford

North Frodingham

B1249

126

A165

Dunnington

Atwick

Bewholme

B12

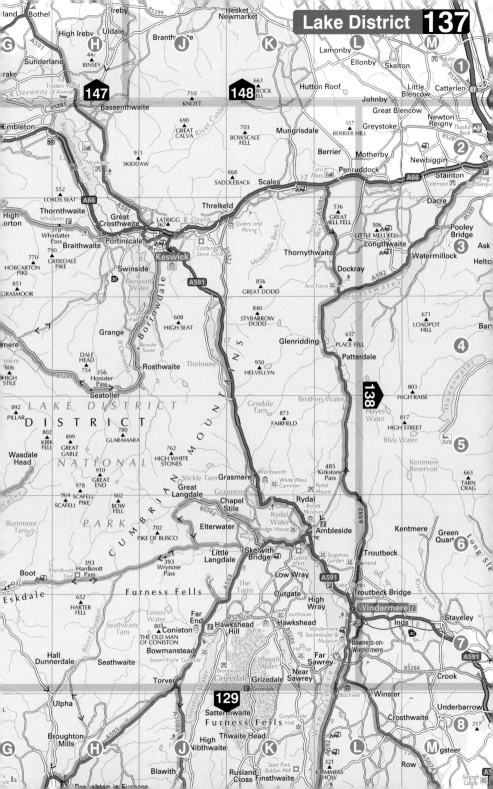

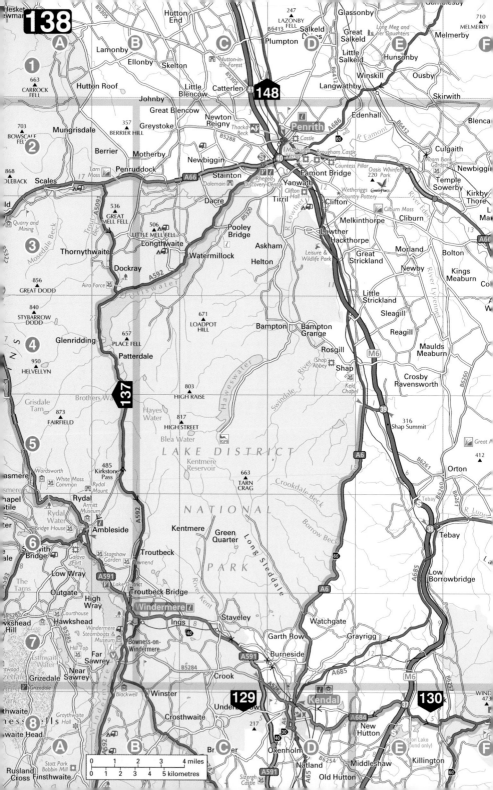

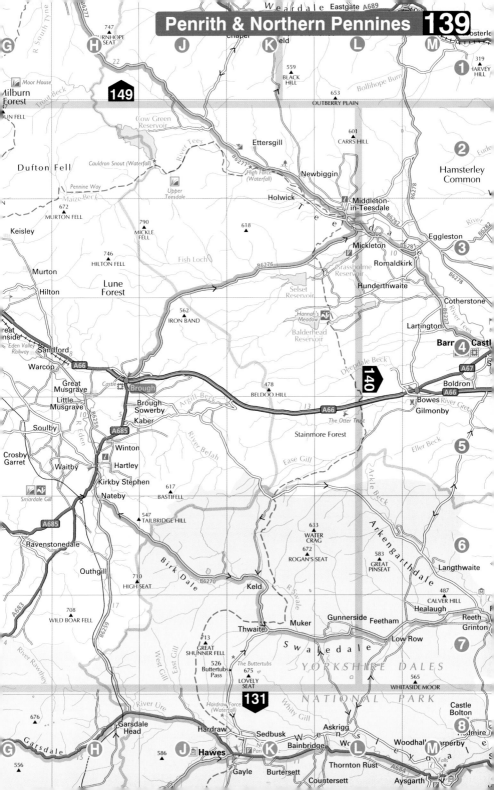

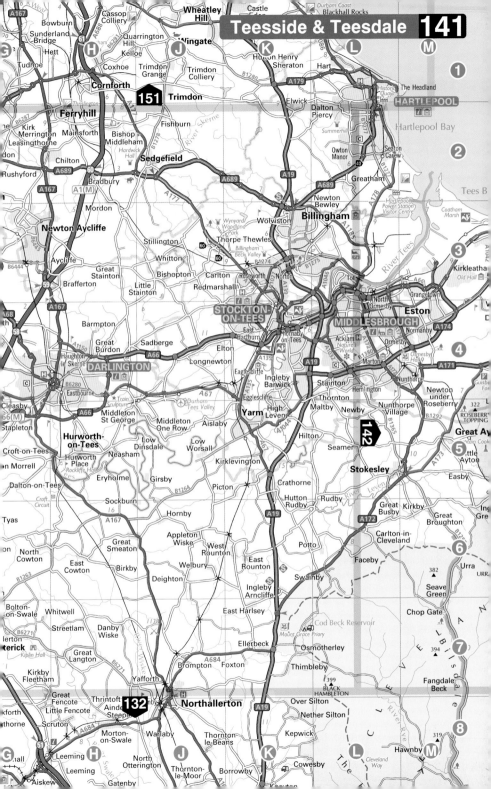

G H J K L M

1
2
3
4
5
6
7
8

thes
Heritage Centre

North Yorkshire and
Cleveland Heritage Coast

Runswick
Bay

Runswick

Ellerby

Goldsborough

Overdale
Wyke

Lythe

A174

Sandsend

Sandsend
Wyke

eby

West
Barnby

East
Barnby

Whitby

Saltwick
Bay

Dunsley

Abbey

gthorpe

Newholm

Ruswarp

Stainsacre

Briggswath

High Hawsker

Aislaby

Sneaton

A171

Sleights

Ugglebarnby

Iburndale

Ness Point or
North Cheek

Egton

Esk Dale

Grosmont

A169

Robin Hood's Bay

ge

Fylingthorpe

Robin
Hood's Bay

B1416

Old Peak or
South Cheek

A171

Ravenscar

Goathland

North Yorkshire
Moors Railway

292

Eller Beck

Staintondale

Shire Horse Centre

Hayburn
Wyke

Wheeldale
Roman Road

M O O R S

Newtondale
Forest Drive

20

Harwood
Dale

Cloughton
Wyke

Stape

Hole of
Horcum

Cloughton

134

Cromer Point

A165

Burniston

Levisham

Broxa

Silpho

Cleveland Way

Bickley

Bridestones
(Rock Formation)

Toll

Dalby
Forest
Drive

Langdale
End

Hackness

Suffield

Lock

239

Scalby

Scarborough

G H J K L M

North Riding Forest Park

Falsgrave

Hatherleigh
Deep Sea Trawler

Newton Dale

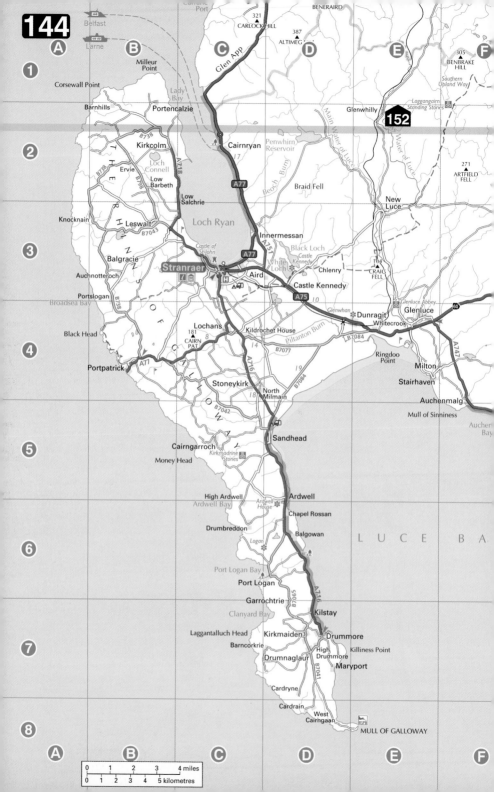

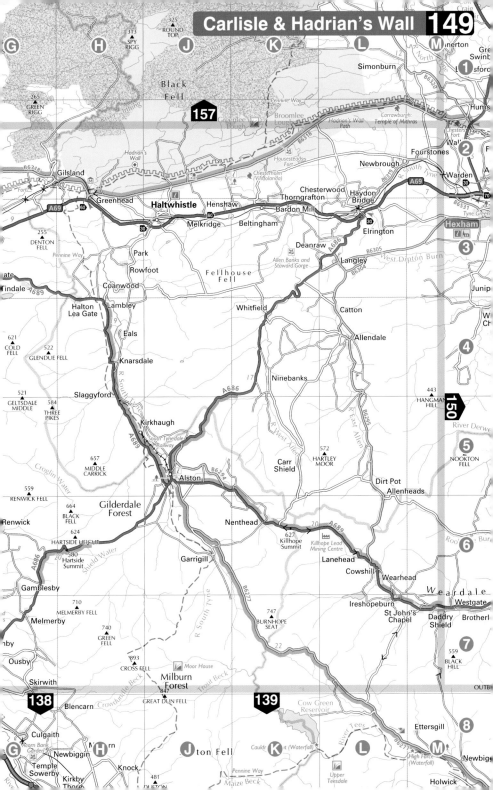

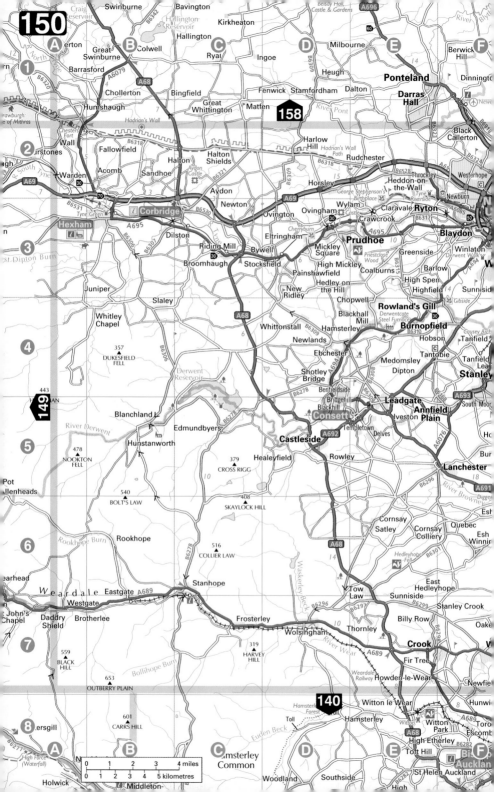

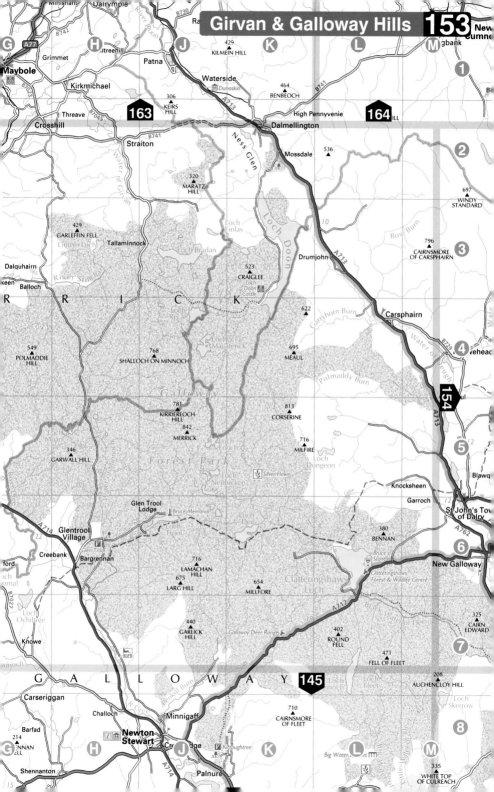

163

164

154

145

G A77 Maybole
Grimmet
Kirkmichael
Threave
B741
Crosshill
B7045
Straiton
Tallaminnock
Dalquhairn
Balloch
R R I C K
549 ▲ POLMADDIE HILL
346 ▲ GARWALL HILL
Glentrool Village
Creebank
Bargrennan
A714
G A L L O W A Y
Carseriggan
Challoch
Barfad
214 ▲ ANNAN ELL
Shennanton
Knowe

H Iltreehill
Patna
J
B730
River Doon
Waterside
Dunaskin
306 ▲ KEIRS HILL
320 ▲ MARATZ HILL
Ness Glen
429 ▲ GARLEFFIN FELL
Lintern Loch
Loch Bradan
Loch Finlas
Loch Doon
768 ▲ SHALLOCH ON MINNOCH
781 ▲ KIRRIEREOCH HILL
842 ▲ MERRICK
Galloway Forest Park
Glen Trool Lodge
Bruce Memorial
Loch Trool
716 ▲ LAMACHAN HILL
675 ▲ LARG HILL
440 ▲ GARLICK HILL
RSPB
Minnigaff
Newton Stewart
Crf dge
Palnure

429 ▲ KILMEIN HILL
K
464 ▲ BENBEOCH
High Pennyvenie
Dalmellington
536 ▲ Mossdale
523 ▲ CRAIGLEE
Loch Doon Castle
Loch Recar
Loch Macaterick
622 ▲
695 ▲ MEAUL
Drumjohn
A713
813 ▲ CORSERINE
716 ▲ MILFIRE
Loch Dungeon
Loch Enoch
Silver Flowe
Loch Neldricken
Loch Dee
654 ▲ MILLFORE
Galloway Deer Range
402 ▲ ROUND FELL
Clatteringshaws Loch
710 ▲ CAIRNSMORE OF FLEET
Kirroughtree
K

L
B741
A713
697 ▲ WINDY STANDARD
Bow Burn
796 ▲ CAIRNSMORE OF CARSPHAIRN
Garryhorn Burn
Carsphairn
Water of Deugh
B729
Polmaddy Burn
Knocksheen
Garroch
St John's Tov of Dalry
A762
380 ▲ BENNAN
Bruce's Stone
Clatteringshaws Forest & Wildlife Centre
New Galloway
471 ▲ FELL OF FLEET
208 ▲ AUCHENCLOY HILL
Loch Skerrow
L
Big Water et
335 ▲ WHITE TOP OF CULREACH
M

M gbank
1
2
697
3
4 veheac
5
Blawq
6
325 ▲ CAIRN EDWARD
7
8
New Cumn
B
Ill

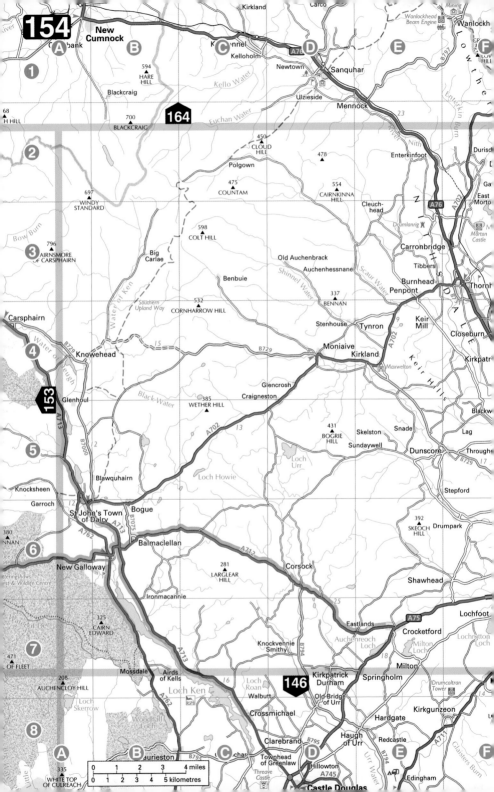

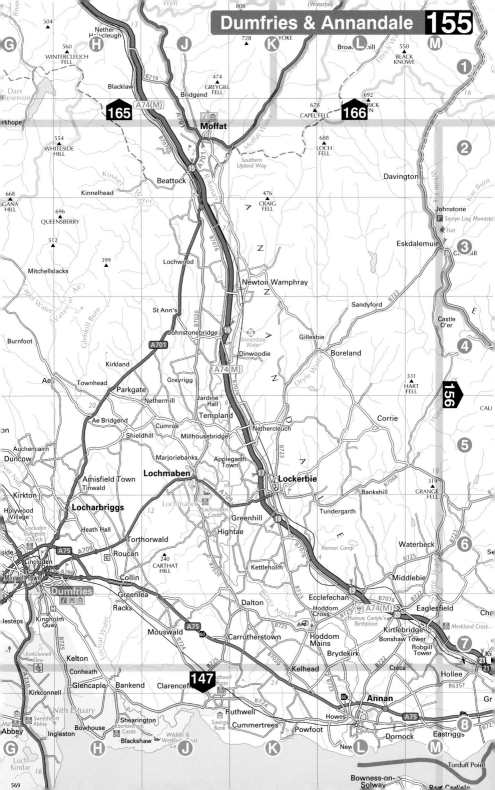

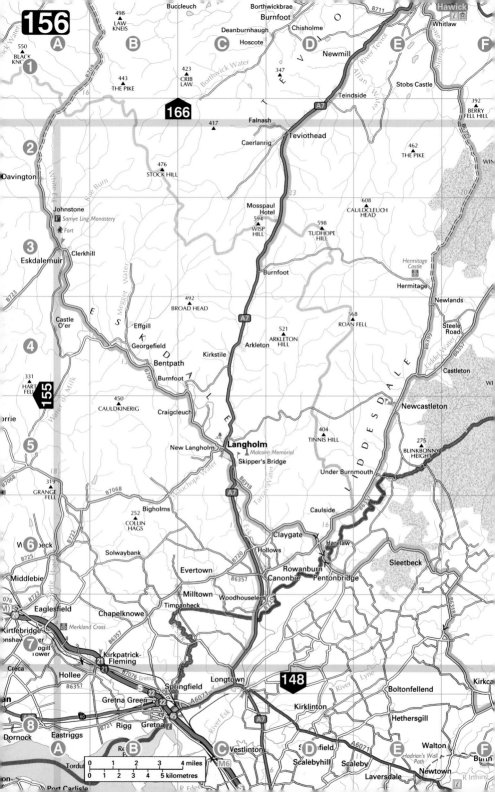

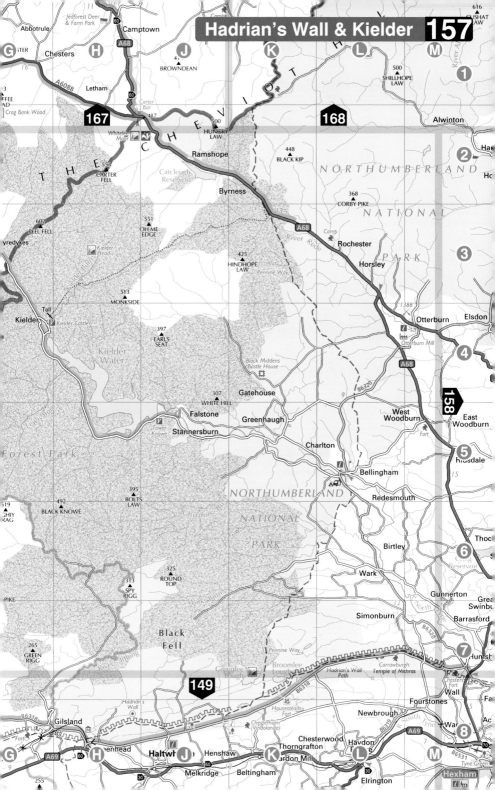

1

Abbotrule
Jedforest Deer & Farm Park
Camptown
A68
G ESTER
H Chesters
J BROWNDEAN
K
L
M
616 CUSHAT LAW
Letham
A6088
FFEE AD
Crag Bank Wood
60
Carter Bar
417
Whitelee Moss
167
C
551 CARTER FELL
THE
Catcleugh Reservoir
500 HUNGRY LAW
Ramshope
168
448 BLACK KIP
500 SHILLHOPE LAW
Alwinton
NORTHUMBERLAND
2
Ha
Ho

CHEVIOT HILLS
River A

E
Byrness
A68
River Rede
368 CORBY PIKE
NATIONAL
3

602 PEEL FELL
551 OH ME EDGE
Kielder Head
425 HINDHOPE LAW
Pennine Way
Camp
Rochester
Horsley
PARK

yredykes
513 MONKSIDE
1388
Otterburn
Otterburn Mill
A68
Elsdon
4

Kielder
Toll
Kielder Castle
397 EARLS SEAT
Kielder Water
307 WHITE HILL
Gatehouse
Black Middens Bastle House
B6320
9
West Woodburn
East Woodburn
158
5
riosdale
15

Falstone
Tower Knowe
Stannersburn
Greenhaugh
Charlton
Fort
Bellingham
A70
Redesmouth

Forest Park
395 BOLTS LAW
492 BLACK KNOWE
NORTHUMBERLAND
NATIONAL
Wark
Birtley
6
Thoc
Reservoir

519 GHY RAG
313 SPY RIGG
325 ROUND TOP
PARK
Gunnerton
Grea Swinbu
Barrasfor

PIKE
Black Fell
Simonburn
B6320
North Tyne

265 GREEN RIGG
Pennine Way
Broomlee Lough
Carrawburgh: Temple of Mithras
Hadrian's Wall Path
7
Humsh

Greenlee Lough
149
Hadrian's Wall
B6318
Housesteads Fort
Chesterholm Vindolanda
Fourstones
Wall
8
Ac

B6318
Gilsland
Fort
G
A69
60
reenhead
H
Haltwh
J Henshaw
Chesterwood
Thorngrafton
Wardon Mill
K
Havdon
L
War
Newbrough
A69
7
M
B6531
70
Melkridge
Beltingham
Elrington
Tyne Green
Hexham
255
30

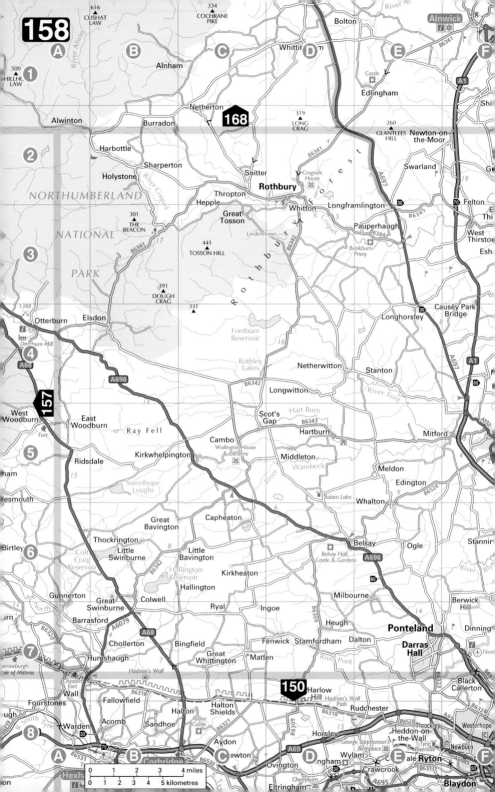

Seaton Point

G H J K L M

1

Alnmouth

Alnmouth
Bay

169

2

Warkworth

Amble Coquet Island

Hill

High
Hauxley

on

Broomhill

3

Druridge Bay

Druridge
Bay

North Northumberland
Heritage Coast

Widdrington

4

Widdrington
Station

A1068

Cresswell

m

Ellington

Lynemouth

A189

Beacon Point

Woodhorn

ington

A197

Hirst H

Newbiggin-by-the-Sea

Wansbeck
Riverside

B1334

5

al

Stakeford
Guide Post

30

dlington

B1331

A193 C

Cowpen

Blyth

A189

Newsham

A192

6

A1061

Seaton
Sluice

ington

A192

New
Hartley

A193

Seaton

B1326

A190

**Seaton
Delaval**

★ St.Mary's Lighthouse

C

Dudley

Vide
pen

B1322

Earsdon

A1148

Monkseaton

**Whitley
Bay** i

A1056

Killingworth

Shiremoor

A191

Cullercoats

7

Forest Hall

H

Tynemouth

A189

Rising
Sun

C

Tynemouth Priory
& Castle

151

Amsterdam
(IJmuiden)

South

Longbenton

**North
Shields**

A1058

Willington
Quay

**SOUTH
SHIELDS**

i

esmond

50

Wallsend

Heaton

40

Willington

C

Toll

Int. Ferry
Terminal

Westoe

A183

Marsden
Bay

8

Walker

Tyne Tunnel

ton

Jarrow

Souter Lighthouse

Byker

Hebburn

H

J

Marsden

A183

Souter Point

L

M

Felling

Monkton

C

West

Cleadon

G H J K L M

GIGHA
Ardminish
Achamore
G
V
H
Tayinloan
Rhunahaorine Point
Rhunahaorine
J
172
K
L
M

1
North Arr
Cara
Grogport
Barmollack
Pirnmill
Penrioch
Loch Tanna

354
CRUACH MHIC GOUGAIN
264
CNOC-AN SAMHLA
Cour

38

A83
CRUACH NAN GABHAR
Whitefarland
715
BEINN BHARRAIN
2
Glen Iorsa

Muasdale
Carradale
Imachar
Balliekine

Glenacardoch Point
Belloch
MacAlister Clan
Bridgend
Dippen
Carradale House
Carradale Point
162
A R R

Glenbarr
454
BEINN AN TUIRC
Torrisdale
Carradale Bay
Auchagallon Stone Circle
Machrie
Machrie Bay
3

319
Cleongart
408
BORD MOR
Saddell
Saddell Bay
Tormore
Machrie Moor Stone Circles
Balmichael

Bellochantuy Bay
N
Bellochantuy
Tangy Loch
396
SGREADAN HILL
Ugadale
Moss Farm Road Stone Circle
Torbeg
Balmichael
BEI

Glen Lussa
Peninver
Ardnacross Bay
Drumadoon Bay
Blackwaterfoot
Kilpatrick
4

Kilkenzie
A83
Kilmichael
B842
Brown Head
Kilpatrick Dun
Corriecravie
Slidder
La

achrihanish Bay
Campbeltown
Campbeltown
Campbeltown Loch
Island Davarr
Torr a' Chaisteal Fort
5

achrihanish
6
B843
Drumlemble
Kilkerran
Kildalloig
352
BEINN GHUILEAN
Achinhoan
Ru Stafnish

385
THE STATE
46
OC OY
Dalsmeran
10
K
Conie Glen
Glen Kerran
6

Stone Glen
Glen Breakevie
Cattadale
Polliwilline Bay
CE
Carskey
Southend
Macharioch
7
Dunaverty
Carskey Bay
Borgadalemore Point
Sanda Sound
Sheep Island
Sanda Island
8

G
H
J
K
L
M

Lochranza
V
Glen Catac
1

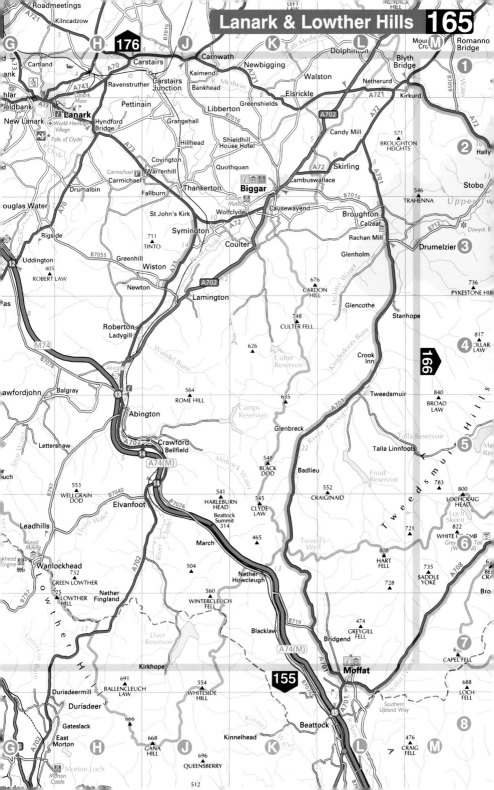

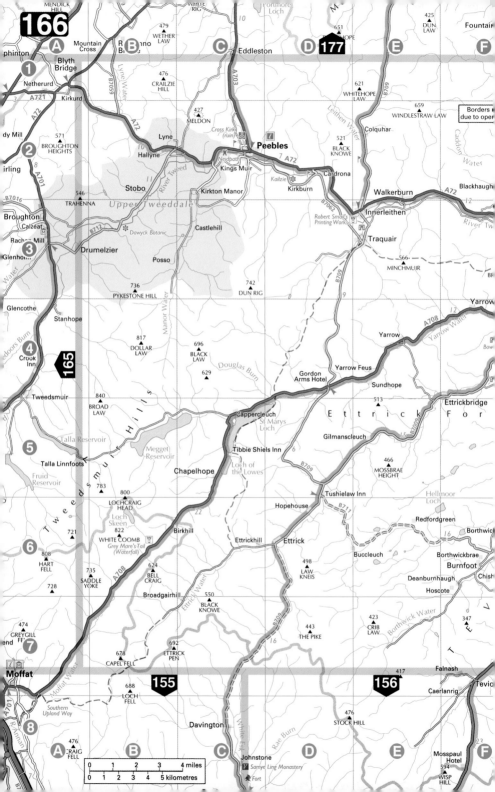

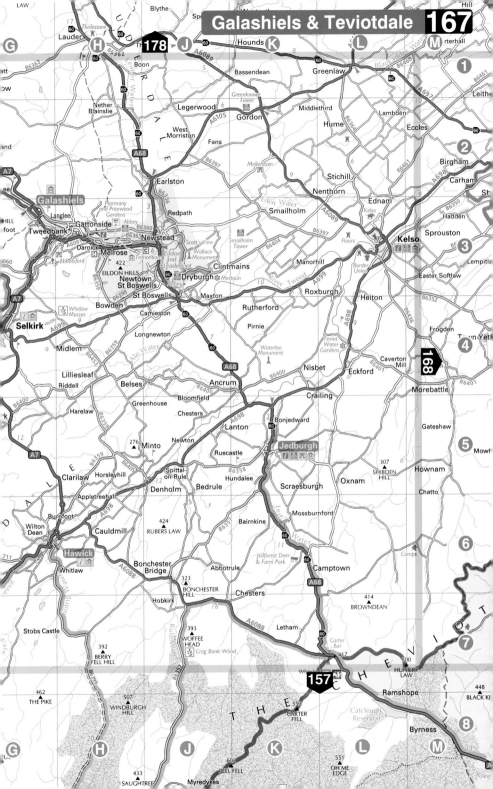

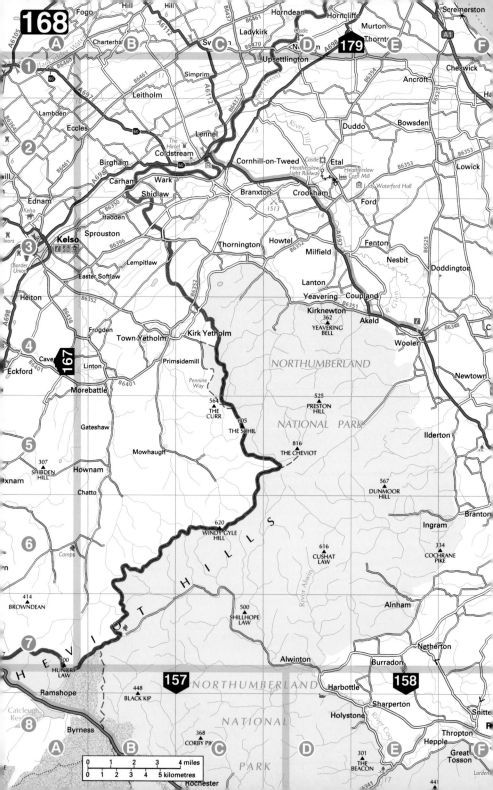

A   B   C   D   E   F

1

2

De

3

I S

Nave Island   Ardnave
Point

4
Ton Mhòr

Kilnave
Eilean Mòr   Sanaigmore

Rudha Lamanais   Loch
Gorr   Lecht Gruinart   Loch Gruinart   Gleann

Saligo Bay   B8018   B8017   Gruinart   Gleann
5   Loch
Gorm   Sunderland   B8018
Coul Point   Kilchoman   A847

Machir
Bay   Loch
Indaal
Bruichladdich   ISLAY

Kilchiaran Bay   Bowmore
6
15
231   Port
BEINN TART A'MHILL   Charlotte

Lossit Bay   RHINNS OF ISLAY   Nereabolls   Duich R

7   Rudha na
Faing   A847
Portnahaven   Port Wemyss   Laggan
Orsay   Bay
RHINNS
POINT

8   Rudha Mòr

A   B   C   D   E   F   165
MAOL BU

THE
Lower
Killevan

0   1   2   3   4 miles
0   1   2   3   4   5 kilometres

JURA

ORONSAY

Scalasaig
Machrins
G

Rudha Bàn

Eilean Ghurdmail

H

J

181

K

L

M

364

Corpach Bay

466
BEINN BHREAC

Glen Grundale

Lussa River

Ardlussa
Lussa Point
Lussagiven

Shian Bay

453
RAINBERG MÒR

Loch Righ Mòr

Rudh' ant-Sàilein

Loch Tarbert

Keills Cha

Rudha' a' Mhàil

Rudha Bholsa

363
SGARBH BREAC

506
SCRINADLE

398
BEINN TARSUINN

Dann Island

St Cormac's Chapel

Kilmory Knap Chapel

Kilmory Bay

Jura Forest

784
BEINN AN OIR

734

Point Knap

Bunnahabhain

316
GUIR-BHEINN

Loch a' Chnuic Bhric

Paps of Jura

J u r a

24

Knockrome
Ardfernal

560
GLASS BHEINN

Port Askaig
Kiells

Feolin Ferry

Keils

Small Isles

172

529
DUBHA BHEINN

Craighouse

Ballygrant

A846
8

Loch Finlaggan
Finlaggan

Loch Ballygrant

Loch Lossit

342
BRAT BHEINN

Rudha na Gaillich

Kilber Sculptu Stone

Kilberry Head
Keppoch Poir
Ti

chossan

266
BEINNE DUBH

Cabrach

Am Fraoch Eilean

Brosdale Island

Rudha na Tràille

Lo

Kilennan Burn

429
SGÒRR NAM FAOILEANN

471

McArthur's Head

Port Askaig - Kennacraig

490
BEINN BHEIGEIR

Rudha Liath
Ardtalla

Kinerara

454
BEINN URARAIDH
Loch Uraraidh

Claggain Bay

Tarbert

GIGHA

Kintour

Ardmore Point

Port Ellen Kennacraig

Rhunahaorine Point

346
BEINN SHOLUM

Kildalton Cross

Eilean a' Chuirn

Ardminish
Achamore

Port
en
G
A846

Ardbeg
Lagavulin

H

Rudha na Gainm

160

J

K

L

Tayinloan
M

Laphroaig
Texa

Cara

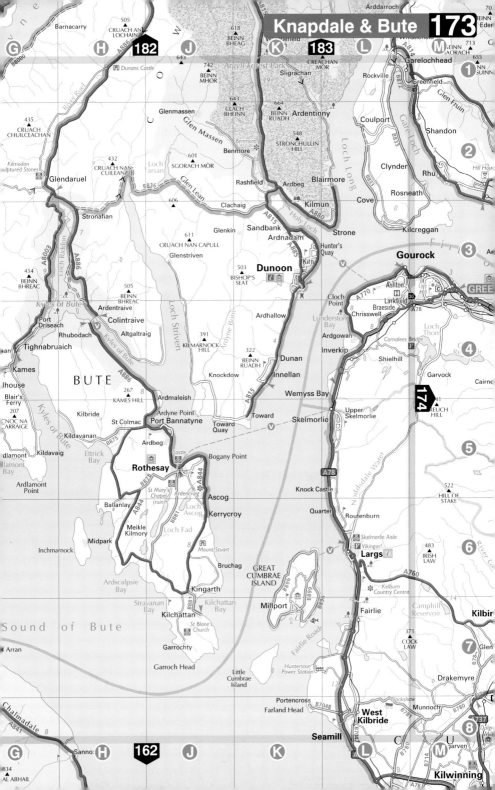

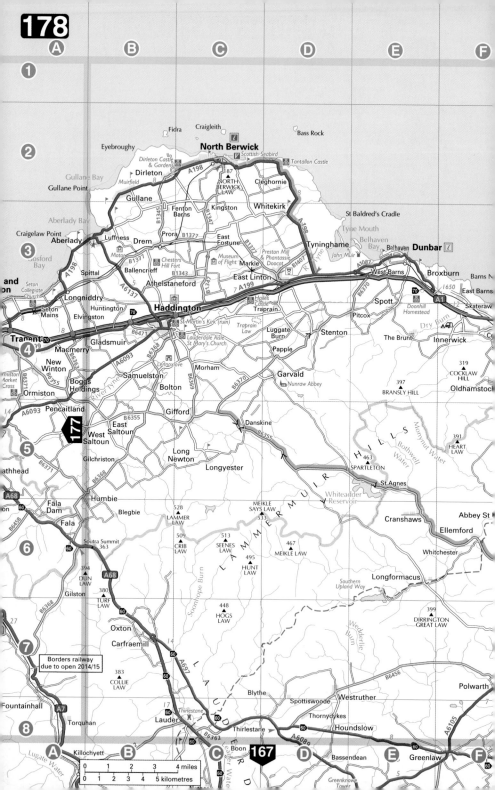

G   H   J   K   L   M

1
2
3
4

Pease Bay   Siccar Point   Fast Castle Head   ST ABB'S HEAD

A1107   196 BROWN RIG   Coldingham Loch

Pease Dean   St Abbs

Grantshouse   Coldingham   Coldingham Bay

Houndwood   Cairncross   Eyemouth

Heugh Head   262 HORSELEY HILL   Reston   Ayton   A1   Burnmouth

Auchencrow

Marygold   Lamberton

Lintlaw   Marshall Meadows Bay

Preston   North Northumberland Heritage Coast

Cumledge   Chirnside   1333

Edrom Church   Chirnsidebridge   Foulden   A6105

Manderston   Broadhaugh   Edington   Whiteadder Water   Foulden Tithe Barn   Castle   Berwick-upon-Tweed

Allanton   Hutton   Barracks

Blackadder   Paxton   Town Ramparts

Whitsome   Hilton   Tweedmouth   Spittal

Sinclair's Hill   Horndean   Horncliffe   Huds Head

Ladykirk   Murton   Scremerston

Swinton   Castle   Thornton   A1

Norham   A698   Cheswick

Leitholm   Simprim   Upsettlington   168   Ancroft   CAUSEWAY FLOODED AT HIGH TIDE

G   H   J   K   L   M

Haggerston

5
6
7
8

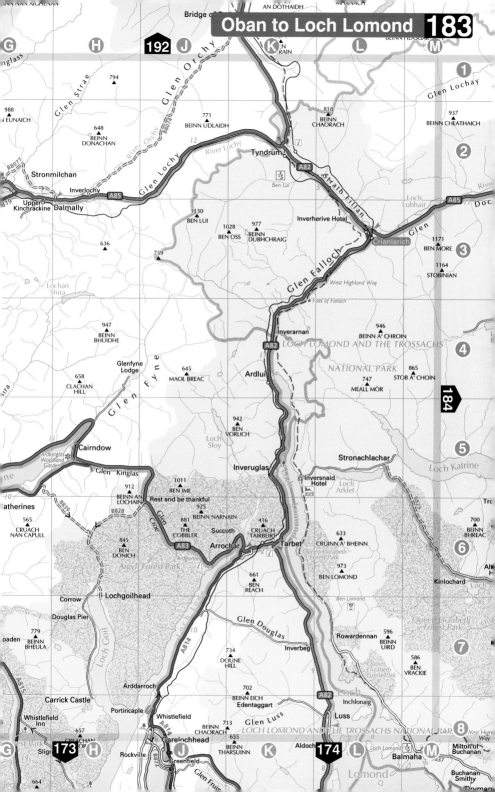

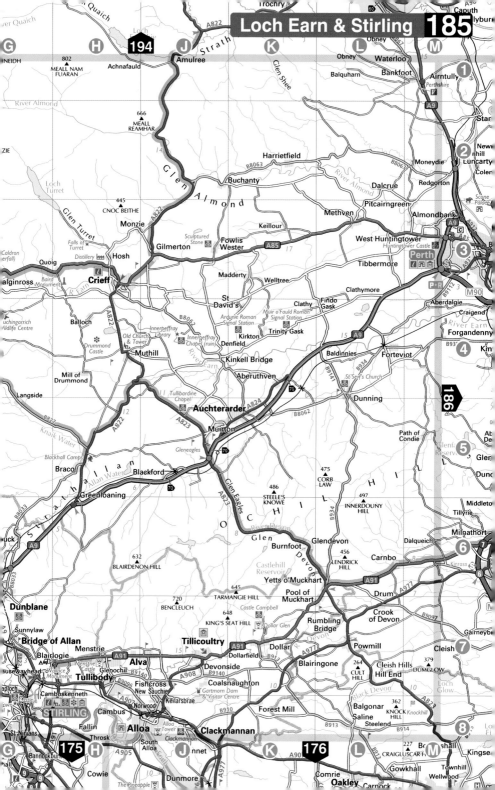

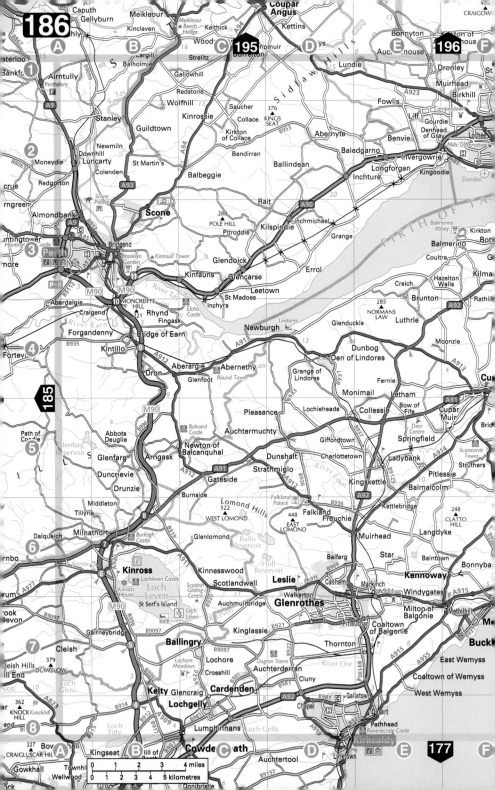

A B C D E F

① ② ③ ④ ⑤ ⑥ ⑦ ⑧

Grishipo
Clabhach
Hogh Bay Ballyhau
Totronald
Bagh a Chaisteil Coll Acha
(Castlebay) Arileod Uig
Feall
Bay RSPB
Calgary Point Crossapo
Bay Rudha
Gunna Fàsachd
Loch Bgathacha

Rudha Port Caoles Rudha Dubh
Bhiosd Clachan B8069
Mor Balephetrish Ruaig
Haugh Bay B8068 V
Bay Loch
Ballevullin Bhasapoll Gott
Cornoigmore Kenovay Bay
Kilkenneth Tiree
Moss B8065 Scarinish
Middleton Heylipoll
Barrapoll Crossapoll TIREE
Loch a B8065 Hynish Bay
Phuill B8067 Balemartine
Mannel
Rinn
Thorbhais Hynish
Balephuil
Bay

0 1 2 3 4 miles
0 1 2 3 4 5 kilometres

G   H   **198** J   K   L   M

1
2

Kildonnan
393

Eilean
nan Each
MUCK
Port Mor

Cail
tail

Sanna Point
Sanna Bay
Sanna Bay
Portuairk   Achnaha
Ardnamurchan
Point
Achosnich
B8007
342
BEINN
NA SEILG
Ormsaigmore
Kilchoan
Mingary

Kilmory   Ockle
Branault   3
ARDNAMU
Loch
Mudle
436
MEALL NAN CON
527
BEN
HIANT   4
Ardslignish

Ockle
Point

Ru
Dr

Rudha
Mòr
Eilean Mòr
Rudha
Sgor-innis
Bousd   Sorisdale
COLL

Bagh a Chasteil
(Castlebay)
Loch Baghasdail
(Lochboisdale)

Ardmore Point
Sorne
Point
Quinish Point
Glengorm Castle
Tobermory
Calve
Island
Drim   5

Coll - Oban

Caliach Point
Calgary
Calgary Bay
Treshnish Point   Ensay
342
CARN MÒR
ISLE
OF
MULL
Dervaig   B8073
Achnadrish House
292
'S AIRDE
BEINN
444
SPEINNE MÒR
Loch Frisa

A848

190
Auliston
Point
Oro

Sou   6

Rudh' a' Chaoil   Burg
Fanmore
CNOC AN DÀ CHINN   390
Glen Aros
Aros   Aros
Glenaros House   7

Fladda
Lunga
TRESHNISH
ISLES
Gometra
ULVA
Ballygown
Oskamull
Eas Fors (Waterfall)
B8073
333
BEINN
NAN CARN
Killiechronan
Gruline
Macquarie
Mausoleum
B8035

Bac Mòr or Dutchmans Cap
Bac Beag
Little Colonsay
Staffa
Fingal's Cave
Loch Tuath
Loch na Keal,
Isle of Mull
Eorsa
Loch na Keal
591
BEINN A' GH.   8

G   H   **180** J   K   L   M

Inch Kenneth
Inchkenneth hapel
(ruin)
Balnahard

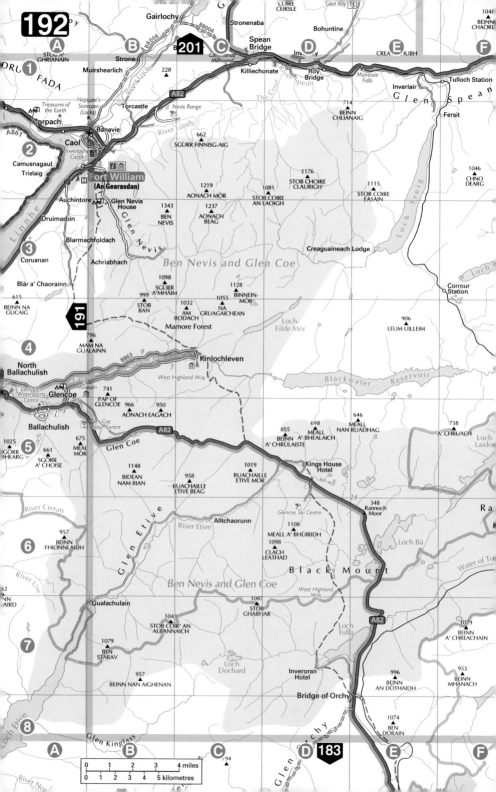

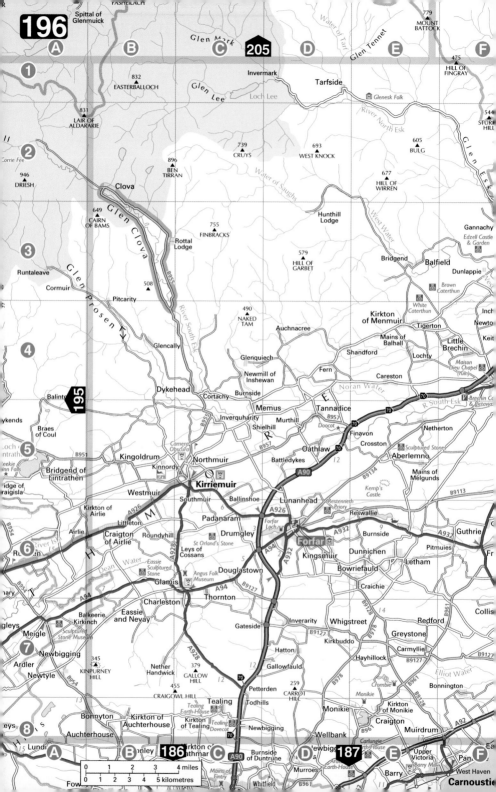

LEACHIE HILL
Goosecruives
465
GOYLE HILL
Bervie Water
206
J v Mill
Tar
Drumlithie
Temple of Fiddes
Crawton
Fowlsheugh
Trelong Bay
Glenbervie
414
FINELLA HILL
Auchenblae
Mondynes
Kinneff
Catterline
Todhead Point
70
B966
Fordoun
Pittarrow
Redmyre
Arbuthnott
B967
A92
Mains of Haulkerton
25
Laurencekirk
Inverbervie
Bervie Bay
B9120
B9120
50
Redford
Gourdon
B974
Dykelands
Benholm
70
A90
Marykirk
A937
13
Johnshaven
Craigo
Lochside
Bush
St Cyrus
Milton Ness
Logie
Morphie
Logie Pert
Hillside
A92
House of Dun
Dun
9 A935
Montrose Air Station
Montrose
Montrose Basin
Scurdie Ness
Barnhead
Maryton
Ferryden
A934
Craig
Usan
Westerton of Rossie
Boddin Point
Braehead
Lunan
Lunan Bay
Inverkeilor
13
Red Head
elton
uldcots
A92
Marywell
Auchmithie
Carlingheugh Bay
The Deil's Head
Arbroath

Talisker

Bay

BEINN
BHREAC
447

Gr.

Loch Eynort

Glen Eynort

434
AN CRUACHIN
Glenbrittle Hou

Bualintur

Loch Britt

Rudh' an Dùnain

CANNA

CARN A' GHAILL
210

A'Chill

Garrisdale Point

Canna
Harbour

Rudha
Shamhnan Ins

Sanday

Sound of Canna

MULLACH
MÒR
302

A Bhrideanach

ORVAL
570

RÙM

Oigh-sgeir

ASKIVAL
810

SGÙRR NAN
GILLEAN
763

The Small Isles

Rudha nam
Meirleach

Sou

Ru

Eilean
nan Each

0   1   2   3   4 miles
0 1 2 3 4   5 kilometres

ISLE OF SKYE

The Cuillin Hills

lin Hills

SOAY

SOUND

SOUND OF SLEAT

Sligachan
GLAMAIG
396
A87
Loch Ainort
Dunan
Luib
209
J
Balpay
K
27
Pabay
L
(Caol Loch A
Skye Bridge
M
Kyleakin
1

965
URR NAN GILLEAN
G
H
564
GLAS BHEIN
MHÒRN
Corry
Broadford Bay
Waterloo
Lower Breakish
Upper Breakish
Kyleakin
Lochalsh
Woodie
Garde

732
708 BEINN NA CAILLICH
BEINN DEORG MHÒR
Broadford
Harrapool
Skulamus
732
SGURR NA COINNICH
2
Kyleakin

927
BLAVEN
Loch Coruisk
Loch na Crèitheach
Torrin
14
BB083
605
BEN ASLAK
Otter Haven

894 GARS BHEINN
Kirkibost
Loch Slapin
300
BEINN NAN CARN
Heast
561
BEINN NA SEAMRAIG
Eilan

139
BEINN BHREAC
Mol-chlach
344 BEN MEABOST
Rudha Suisnish
Suisnish
Drumfearn
Sandaig Island
3

Elgol
Glasnakille
298 SGÒRACH BREAC
Duisdalemore
Isleornsay
Ornsay
Rudha Buidhe

Strathaird Point
Tokavaig
Ord River
17

Tarskavaig
Tarskavaig Bay
Achnacloich
Loch nam Uamph
Teangue
Knock
Knock Bay
Rudh' Ard Slisneach
Inverguse
4

Ferrindonald
Kilmore
Kilbeg
Airor
Sandaig
200
518 DRUIM NA CLUAIN-AIRIDHE
Glen Guseran
BE CA

Clan Donald
Ardvasar
Calligarry
Armadale
Sandaig
Sandaig Bay
Rudha Raonuill
Inverie Bay
erie
5

Aird of Sleat
Ard Thurinish
Inverie

Point of Sleat
Rudha Raonuill
Loch Ne
6

Courteachan
Mallaigvaig
547 CÀRN A' GHOBHAIR
Loch an Nostaire
437 SGÙRR BHUIDHE
Tarbet
Swordland

Mallaig (Malaig)
Glasnacardoch Bay
Beoraidbeg
Morar
Bracora
Bracorina

Bay of Laig
Cleadale
299 AN CRUACHAN
Laig
EIGG
Kildonnan
393 AN SGÙRR
Sandavore
Eilean Chathastail
Glenancross
Bunacaimb
Eilean Ighe
Back of Keppoch
Luinga Mhòr
Rudh' Arisaig
103 CRUACH DOIRE
Loch nan Ceall
Arisaig
Druimindarroch
Arisaig House
Loch nan Uamh
Glenfinnan
503 CÀRN A' MHÀDAIDH-RUAIDH
600 SIDHEAN MÒR
Prince Charlie's Cairn
Kinlochnanuagh
Lettermorar
Loch Mo
7

A830
BB088
10

190
K
Arisaig
Ardnish
Rudha Choalais
L
Polnish
Ardnish
Inverailort
Lochailort
8

G
H
J
190
K
L
M
Loch Ailort
861

G 603 CÀRN GLAC AN FICH

H

213

BEINN BHREAC

J Lodge

Tomatin

Tomatin Distillery Visitor Centre

Findhorn Viaduct

K

L

M CARN 471

1 ain ge

707 CÀRN NA SAOBHAIDH

Clune

Garbole

Strathdearn

406 Slochd Summit

A9

Bogroy

Carrbridge

Auchterblair

Duthil

A928

A9

10

Skye of Curr

617 CÀRN PHRIS MHÒIR

Dalnahaitnach

Drumuillie

Landmark Forest Adventure Park

A95

13

Nethy ridge

2

805 BEINN BHREAC MHÒR

750 CARN DUH' IC AN-DEÒIR

Kinveachy

B9153

7

Der Abe

Coignafearn

River Dulnain

Boat of Garten

RSPB

Loch Garten

Straanruie

River Findhorn

790 CÀRN COIRE NA H-EASGAINN

745 CNOC FRAING

712

Aviemore

Strathspey Railway

B970

3

824 GEAL-CHARN MÒR

Craigellachie

Glenmore Forest Park

809 MEALL A' BHUAC

813 ALPA MÒR

729 CAIRN DULNAN

Inverdruie

Rothiemurchus

Coylumbridge

Glenmore Lodge

River Spey

Glenmore

Reindeer Centre

M o u n t a i n s

878 CÀRN AN FHREICEADAIN

Loch Alvie

A9

Loch an Eilean

Glenmore Lodge

Loch Morlich

Rothiemurchus Lodge

4 Cairngorm Ski Area

Glen Mor

928 A CHAILLEACH

Raitts Burn

Highland Wildlife Park

Kincraig

B9152

B970

10

Feshiebridge

Lagganlia

204

C A I R N G O R M

5 han uidhe

Newtonmore

Baile Ur an t-Sleibh

Highland Folk

Kingussie

Pitmain

Ruthven

A9

Lynchat

Insh Marshes

RSPB

Farr

Ruthven Barracks

Drumguish

Insh

Inveruglass

Loch Insh

Auchlean

1108 SGÒR AN DUBH MOR

Loch Einich

1295 BRAERIACH

Lairig Ghru

1309 BEN MACDHUI

A86

Glentruim House

Phones

Ràlia

627 MEALL BUIDHE

Glen Feshie

River Feshie

1049 CÀRN BAN MOR

1293 CAIRN TOUL

6

Etteridge

593 GARBH-MHEALL MÒR

C A I R N G O R M S

1017 MULLACH CLACH A BHLAIR

1157 BEINN BHROTAIN

River Eidart

Glen Dee

A9

ore

Loch na Cuaich

768 MEALLACH MHÒR

857 CÀRN DEARG MÒR

Glenfeshie Forest

River Dee

7

N A T I O N A L P A R K

898 BAGHA-CLOICHE

Loch an t-Seilich

910 LEATHAD AN TOABHAIN

G R A M P I

River Feshie

941 CÀRN NA CAIM

Gaick Forest

999 CÀRN EALAR

1006 AN SGARSOCH

8

G

H an Dùin

194

J

K

L

M f Water

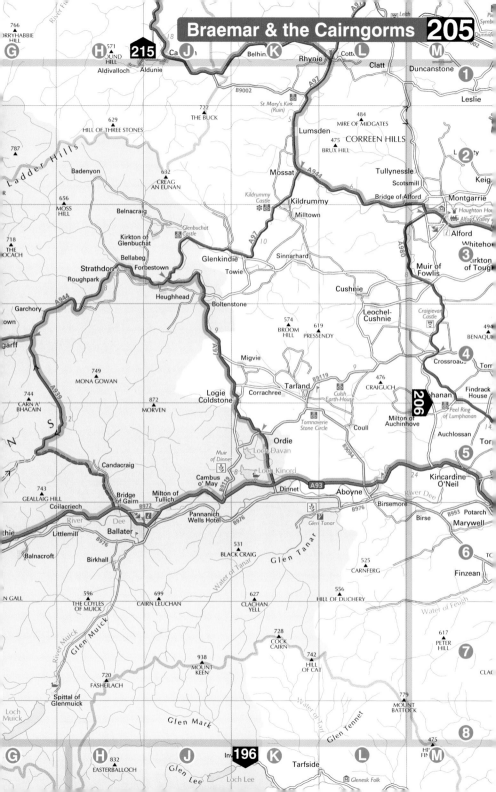

G H J K L M

766
ORRYHABBIE
HILL

571
HOUND
HILL
215

Ca...n
Belhin
Rhynie
Cott...
Clatt
Duncanstone
1
Aldivalloch Aldunie
Leslie

629
HILL OF THREE STONES
722
THE BUCK
B9002
St Mary's Kirk
(Ruin)
484
MIRE OF MIDGATES
Leslie

787
475
BRUX HILL
Lumsden
CORREEN HILLS
2
Keig...ty

Ladder Hills
Badenyon
632
CREAG
AN EUNAN
Mossat
A944
Tullynessle
Scotsmill
Montgarrie
Keig

656
MOSS
HILL
Belnacraig
Kildrummy
Castle
Kildrummy
Bridge of Alford
Haughton Ho...
Alford Valley

718
THE
OCACH
Kirkton of
Glenbuchat
Glenbuchat
Castle
Milltown
A97
Whitehou...
Alford
3

Strathdon
Bellabeg Forbestown
Glenkindie
Sinnarhard
Kirkton
of Toug...
Muir of
Fowlis

Garchory
Roughpark
Heughhead
Towie
Cushnie
Craigievar
Castle

A944
Boltenstone
574
BROOM
HILL
619
PRESSENDY
Leochel-
Cushnie
494
BENAQU...
4

744
CARN A'
BHACAIN
749
MONA GOWAN
A97
9
Migvie
476
CRAIGUCH
Crossroads
Torr
Findrack
House

N S
872
MORVEN
Logie
Coldstone
Corrachree
Tarland
Cush
Earth-House
Coull
...hanan
206
Milton of
Auchinhove
Peel Ring
of Lumphanan
14
Auchlossan
Tor

743
GEALLAIG HILL
Candacraig
Tomnaverie
Stone Circle
Ordie
Loch Davan
Loch Kinord
Kincardine
O'Neil
5

Coilacriech
Bridge
of Gairn
Milton of
Tullich
Cambus
o' May
Dinnet
A93
Aboyne
Birsemore
River Dee
Birse
B993
Potarch
Marywell

...chie
Littlemill
Ballater
Pannanich
Wells Hotel
B976
Glen Tanar
B976

Balnacroft
Birkhall
531
BLACK CRAIG
Glen Tanar
525
CARNFERG
Finzean
6

...N GALL
596
THE COYLES
OF MUICK
699
CAIRN LEUCHAN
627
CLACHAN
YELL
556
HILL OF DUCHERY
617
PETER
HILL
7

River Muick
Glen Muick
728
COCK
CAIRN
742
HILL OF CAT
Water of Feugh
CLAC...

720
FASHEILACH
938
MOUNT
KEEN
779
MOUNT
BATTOCK

Spittal of
Glenmuick
Glen Mark
Water of Tanar
Glen Tennet
475
HI...
FIN...
8

Loch
Muick

G H
832
EASTERBALLOCH
J
Glen Lee
196
Inv...
K
Tarfside
L
M
Glen Lee
Loch Lee
Glenesk Folk

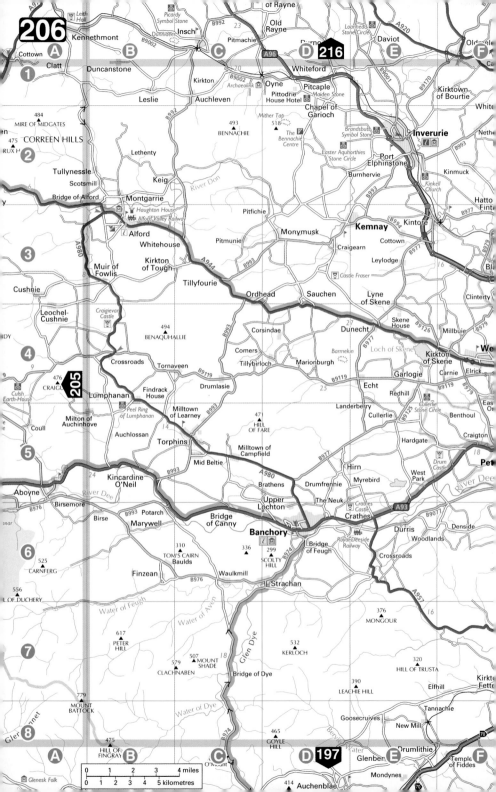

Ythsie
Ellon
Esslemont
A920
Pitmedden
A920 10
Kirkton of Logie Buchan
Collieston
G Logierieve **H**
Housieside
B9000
217
J
Forvie
Udny Station
A90
B9000
Newburgh
Pettymuk Cultercullen
Foveran
A975
Ilygreig

K **L** **M**

Delfrigs

Causeyend

Whitecairns
Belhelvie
B977
Balmedie
Balmedie

Potterton

B997
Blackdog

Dyce
Denmore
Middleton Park
V
Kirkwall
Lerwick
wood
40
Bankhead
A90
P·R
Bridge of Don
sburn 30
40 40 30
Northfield
Old Aberdeen
swells **H**
C B9119
RDEEN
Ruthrieston 40
Torry
Nigg Bay
Mannofield
Cults
Kincorth 40
side
Nigg
n of Banchory-Devenick A90
Altens Haven
lle
Charlestown
Cove Bay
usie
Marywell
Hillside
Auchlee 70
Findon
Portlethen
Cammachmore Bay
Downies
machmore
Newtonhill
Skateraw
Muchalls
Doonie Point
A90
70
Garron Point
Stonehaven Bay
Stonehaven
Dunnottar

G **H** **J** **K** **L** **M**
Crawton
Fowlsheugh
Trelong Bay

G H J K L M

Garloch

Eilean Horrisd

nan

1

South Erradale

Redpoint

Red
Point

2

Loch
Torridon

Lowe
Diaba

Loch
Diaba

Rudha
na Fearn

Fearnmore

Fearnbeg

3

Arrina Kenmore

Òb
Chuaig

Cuaig

Callakille

492
▲
AN GARBH-
MHEALL

Lonbain

493
▲
CROIC-
BHEINN

4

INNER SOUND

Applecross Bay

River Applecross

Applecross

Milton

626
▲
Pass of the
Cattle

5

Camusteel

774
▲
SGÙRR A'CHAO

Camusterrach

Bealach-
Na-Ba

Aird Dhubh

Culduie

6

Toscaig

River Toscaig

Caolas Mòr

Eilean
Meadhonach

Eilean
Mòr

CROWLIN ISLANDS

Loch Carr

Port-an-Eorna

7

Drumbuie

Badicaul

Kyle of Lochalsh

(Caol Loch Ailse)

Skye Bridge

Locha
Wood
Gard

8

Poldorais

Eilean Flodigarry

G H J K L M

Digg
CH

A Digg

Staffin
Bay

Staffin Island

brogaig

Stenscholl Staffin

218

Trotternish

Maligar

Marishader

Kilt Rock Waterfall

Ellishader

Valtos

611
▲
EINN
EDRA

Garros

Rudha nam Brathairean

Culnaknock

Lochan Bhràige

Lealt

Tote

A855

RONA

608
▲
CREAG A' LAIN

Eilean
Tigh

Old Man
of Storr

719
▲
THE
STORR

r Haulton

Loch
Leathan

SOUND OF RAASAY

Eilean
Fladday

Borve

A855

Loch
Fada

Manish
Point

Loch
Arnish

Torran

Arnish

muie

312
▲

Brochel

ngrasco

Torvaig

RAASAY

Portree
Seafield

444
▲
DUN CAAN

417
▲
BEINN NA
GRÈINE

Penifiler

412
▲
BEN
TIANAVAIG

hore

Rudha na' Leac

Glenvarragill

Camastianavaig

Oskaig

310
▲
BEINN NA LEAC

A87

ary

Tianavaig
Bay

Ollach

Clachan

Inverarish

Glen Varragill

The Braes

444
▲
BEN LEE

B883

Peinchorran

Eyre
Point

Suisnish
Point

SCALPAY

Sconser

67
▲
Longay

Pabay

27
▲

773
▲
GLAMAIG

Sligachan

564
▲
GLAS BHEIN
MHÒRN

396
▲
MULLACH
NA CARN

Dunan

Luib

A87

Loch Ainort

Caolas Scalpay

Broadford
Bay

G H J K L M

965
▲
GURR NAN GILLEAN

199

Corry

Waterloo

Lower
Breakish

A87

K kin

732

Lower

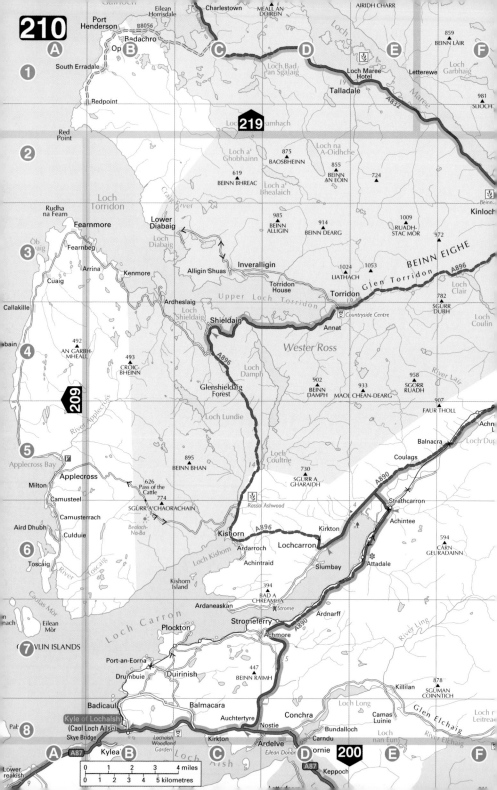

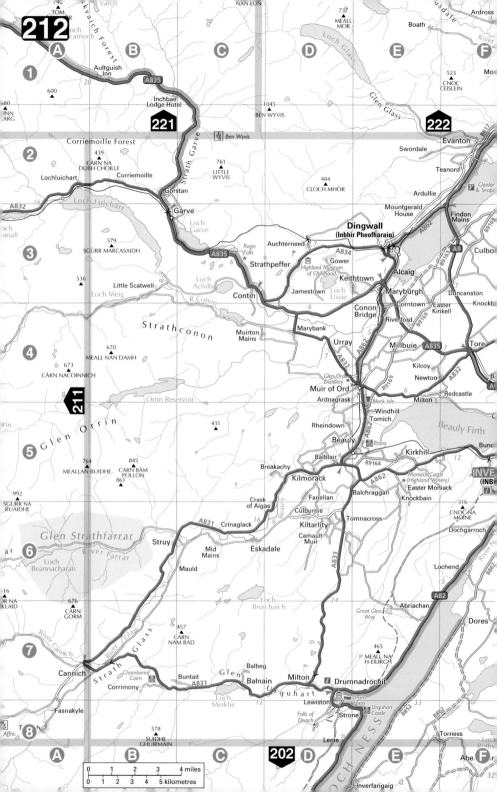

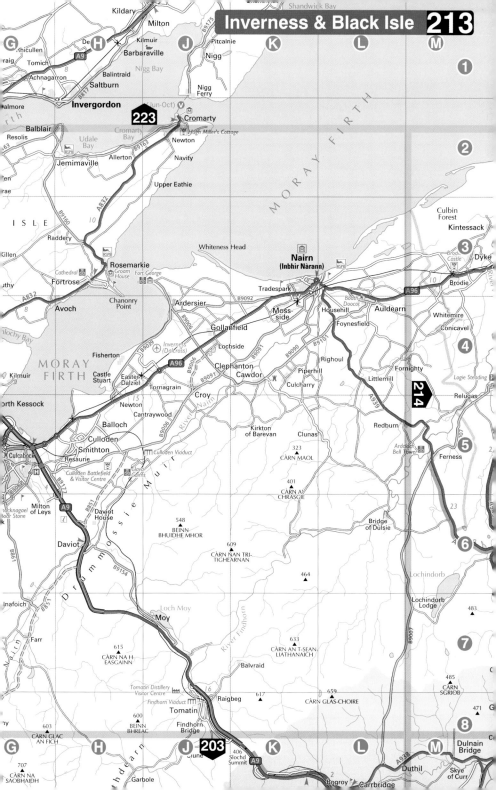

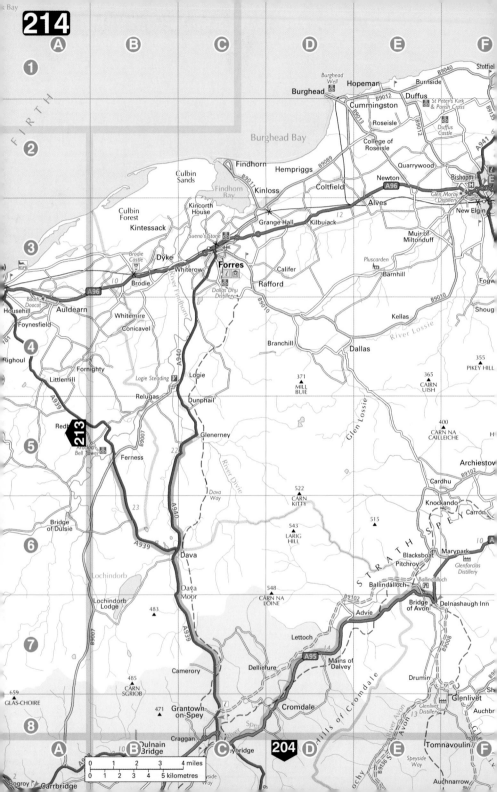

Mayor's Spring Tea

On Thursday 28th April the Mayor and Mayoress of Lewes, Cllr Stephen Catlin and Cllr Shirley-Ann Sains, will be hosting a traditional afternoon tea in the Town Hall Assembly Room from 3.00 – 4.30 pm.

This is the first time the Spring Tea has been able to happen for a couple of years due to Covid-19 restrictions. Spring flowers, gifts and lucky envelopes will adorn the tables and there will be music from Lewes Music Group to entertain the guests.

Older residents of the town are invited to book their space by calling the Town Hall on 01273471469, or emailing info@lewes-tc.gov.uk. Entry is free, but names must be added to the guestlist to attend.

G H J K L M

1

Isle Ristol
Polbain
Tanera Beg
Tanera Mòr
Badentarbat Bay
Steornabhagh (Stornoway)
Glas-leac Beag
Horse Island

2

Priest Island
Eilean Dubh

Greenstone Point
Rudha Beag
Cailleach Head
Scoraig

Mellon Udrigle
GRUINARD ISLAND
Stattic Point

3

Badluachrach
Gruinard Bay
A832
Badcau

Laide
Mellon Charles
Ormiscaig
Aultbea

Gruinard

4

Foura
Cove
347 CREAG-MHEAL BEAG

Rudha Reidh
296 AN CUAIDH
ISLE OF EWE
Loch Ewe
Loch Fada

B8057

Melvaig
Aultgrishin
293 CNOC BREAC
Inverasdale
Naast

681 BEINN A' CHAISGEIN BEAG

5

North Erradale
B8021
Inverewe Garden
13
Londubh
250 MEALL NA MEINE
Wester Ross

Poolewe

Big Sand
Strath
A832
Auchtercairn
Smithstown
Lonemore
Gairloch
Heritage C
Dubh Loch

6

Longa Island
Loch Gairloch
Eilean Horrisdale
Charlestown
421 MEALL AN DOIREIN
791 BEINN AIRIDH CHARR

Port Henderson
B8056
Badachro
Opinan
Loch

859 BEINN LÀIR

South Erradale
Loch Bad an Sgalaig
Loch Maree Hotel
Letterewe
Loch Garbhaig

7

Redpoint
Talladale
19
A832
981 SLIOCH

Red Point
Loch Ghaineamhach
Maree

8

Lower Diabaig
875 BAOSBHEINN
855 BEINN AN EOIN
724
1009 RUADH-STAC MÒR
Kinlocher

210

619 BEINN BHREAC
Loch a' Bhealaich

Rudha na Fearn
Fearnn
Loch Torridon
Craig River
Loch Diabaig
BEINN ALLIGIN
914 BEINN DEARG
972

Fearnbeg
Òb Chuaig

G H J K L M

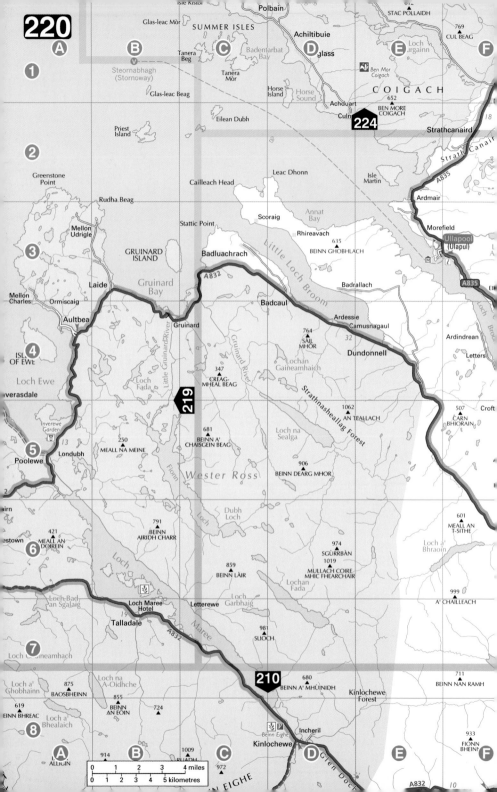

Strath
River Brora
Dalreavoch Lodge
Loch Horn
520 ▲ BEN HORN

G **H** **J** **K** **L** **M**

1

Dalchalm
Brora
378 ▲ CAGAR FEOSAIG
Golspie Burn
Doll
227
Backies
446 ▲ BEN LUNDIE
Carn Liath
A9
383 ▲ BEN BHRAGGIE
Rhives
Dunrobin Castle

2

Golspie
ambusavie Platform
Loch Fleet
minish
Skelbo
Skelbo Street
Fourpenny

3

Birichin
Embo
Embo Street
Pitgrudy
Evelix
A949
Royal Dornoch
ore A9
Camore
Dornoch
Historylinks
Cuthill

4

Tarbat Ness
Point
Innis Mhor
Brucefield
Wilkhaven
Dornoch Firth
Portmahomack
Morangie
Glenmorangie Distillery
Inver
Rockfield
B9165
Arboll
Tain
(Baile Dhubhthaich)
Toulvaddie

5

Lochslin
Loch Eye
Rhynie
Hill of Fearn
Newfield
B9165
Balmuchy
Hilton of Cadboll Chapel (ruin)
Fearn
Tullich
Hilton
Ichraggan
Arabella
Shandwick
Balintore
Kildary
Ankerville
Shandwick Bay
Milton
B9175
Kilmuir
Pitcalnie
Barbaraville
Nigg

6

ntraid
Nigg Bay
n
Nigg Ferry
(Jun-Oct)
7
Cromarty
Burghead
Cromarty Bay
Hugh Miller's Cottage
B9163
Newton
213
214
lerton
Navity
Findhorn
Hem
Culbin Sands
Upper Eathie
Findhorn Bay
B9011
8 ss
Culbin Forest
Kincorth House
Grange Ha

G **H** **J** **K** **L** **M**

MORAY FIRTH
Kintessack
Sueno's Stone
Whiteness Head

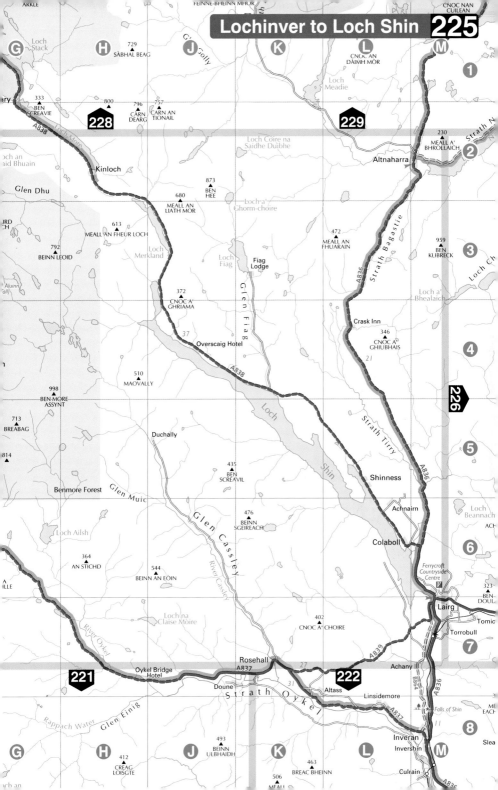

Altnabreac Station

CNOC NAN GALL

Loch an Thulachan

Loch Sand

Achavanich

Loch Stemster

Loch Rangag

STEMSTER HILL

Grey C of Car

Ros

Rumsdale Water

Strathmore

Dalnawillan Lodge

226 COIRE NA BEINN

Glutt Water

348 BEN ALISKY

230

Glutt Lodge

248 BEN-A-CHIELT

287

231

Upper Lybster

Swiney

Invershore

Lybster

Oc

M

NOCKFIN EIGHTS

264 CNOCAN CONACHREAG

Houstry

Land-hallow

Forse

Lybster Bay

Smerral

Latheron

317 CNOC LOCH MHADADH

Dunbeath Water

Latheronwheel

Janetstown

A9

Berriedale Water

Braemore

Laidhay Croft

Dunbeath

COIRE EARNA

484 MAIDEN PAP

Knockally

705 MORVEN

Ramscraigs

518 CNOC AN EIREANNAICH

626 SCARABEN

Borgue

Langwell Forest

20

Newport

554 CREAG SCALABSDALE

Langwell House

Berriedale

ge

401 CNOC NA MAOILE

416 EINN BHAIN

A897

A9

404 CREAG THORARAIDH

Ord of Caithness

n River Helmsdale

Torrish

Timespan

Navidale House Hotel

West Helmsdale

East Helmsdale

Helmsdale

591 BEINN NA MÈILICH

Gartymore

N

Glen Loth

Portgower

Lothmore

thbeg

G H J K L M

1

2

Whiten
Head

n Hoan

408
▲ BEN HUTIG
Strathan
Rabbit
Islands

Eilean
Nan Ròn

Ardmore
Point
Kirtomy Point
Neave Island
Farr Point
Armad.
Kirtomy
Swordly
3

Talmine
Skerray
Torrisdale Farr
Bay Bay
Farr

Melness
Midtown
Tongue
Bay
Achtoty
Torrisdale
Bettyhill

30
EN
BOLL
A838
Scullomie
Coldbackie
Borgie
Invernaver
Achina
Loch
Meadie

262
▲ DRUIM
NAN CLIAR
Kyle of Tongue
13
A836
Skelpick
228
N
BO
4

Tongue
310
▲ MEALL LEATHAD
NA CRAOIBHE
River Borgie
Strath Naver
Loch Mòr
na Caorach

230

h Hope
318
▲ CNOC
CRAGGIE
Loch
Craggie
12
Loch
nan
5

Kinloch
Kyle of Tongue
17
527
▲ BEINN
STUMANADH
213
▲ CNOC
MALPELLY
Loch Strathy

Loch na
Seilg
598
▲ MEALLAN
LIATH
763
▲ BEN
LOYAL
Loch
Loyal
B871
335
▲ MEALL BAD
NA CUAICHE

927
▲ BEN
HOPE
A836
6

Strath More
Loch an
Deerie
Loyal Lodge
345
▲ CNOC NAN
TRI-CHLAC

557
▲ CNOC NAN
CUILEAN
Loch
Syre
River Naver
404
▲ BEINN
MHADADH

656
▲ CNOC AN
DÀIMH-MÒR
Syre
259
▲ BEINN
ROSAIL
B871
16
7
BE

Loch
Meadie
294
▲ POLE
HILL
12
B873
Loch
Rimsdale
Loch
nan Clàr

h Coire na
he Duibhe
225
230
▲ MEALL A'
BHROLLAICH
Strath Naver
270
▲ BEADAIG
226
Loch
Truders
Loch
Badanloch
8

Altnaharra
Loch Naver
River Naver
Loch an
Altàn Fhearna

n a'
choire
G H J K L M

472
▲ MEALL AN
FHUARAIN
Bagastie
959
▲ BEN
ire Forest

434

A B C D E F

1
2
3
4
5
6
7
8

Brims Ness

St Mary's Chapel (ruin)

Crosskirk

16

Bridge of Forss

Skiall

Ardmore Point

Armadale Bay

Strathy Point

Strathy Bay

Melvich Bay

Sandside Bay

Upper Dounreay

Achreamie

Lythm

tomy Point

Brawl

Baligill

Portskerra

Isauld

Reay

Achvarasdal

Shebster

Cnoc Freiceadain Long Cairns

W

Point

Strathy Inn

Strathy

Melvich

Bighouse

A836

Forss Water

Armadale

A836

15

Kirtomy

River Strathy

Swordly

185
BEINN RUADH

242
BEINN RATHA

Broubster

Loch Meadie

228
BEINN NAM BO

229
BEINN RUADH

Loch na Seilge

Shurrery

Shurrery Lodge

elpick

229

Skelpick Burn

Loch Mòr na Caoraich

Upper Bighouse

A897

Dalhalvaig

290
BEIN NAM BAD MHOR

Loch Scye

Dorr

Loch nan Clach

Strath Halladale

Trantlemore

Trantelbeg

243
CNOC AN FHOARAIN BHÀIN

160
BRAIGH FÉITH HEMIGAL

DRU CHRAC

213
CNOC BAD AIRÈACH NA GAOITHE

Loch Tuim Ghlais

184
CREAG NA CRICHE

Loch Caluim

Loch Strathy

335
MEALL BAD NA CUAICHE

Dyke Water

Halladale River

203
CNOC PREAS A'MHADAIDH

200
CNOC BEUL NA FAIRE

345
CNOC NAM TRI-CHLACH

Loch Cròcach

217
CNOC A' BHREUN BHAID

280
SLETILL HILL

21

Altnabreac Station

Forsinard

RSPB

275
CNOC NAN GALL

Rumsdale Water

Strathmore Water

404
BEINN MHADADH

588
BEN GRIAM BEG

337
MEAL A' BHEALAICH

Dalnawillan Lodge

348
BEN ALISKY

16

590
BEN GRIAM MOR

Loch Druim à Chliabhain

A897

Glutt Water

Glutt Lodge

Loch an Ruathair

226

440

KNOCKFIN HEIGHTS

Loch nan-Clàr

Loch Badanlòch

Loch Arichlinie

432

317
CNOC LOCH MHADAIDH

Loch àn Fheàrna

B871

r Helmsc

KinBra le

A897

Kinbrace Burn

Ber

434

437
CNOC COIRE

484

0 1 2 3 4 miles
0 1 2 3 4 5 kilometres

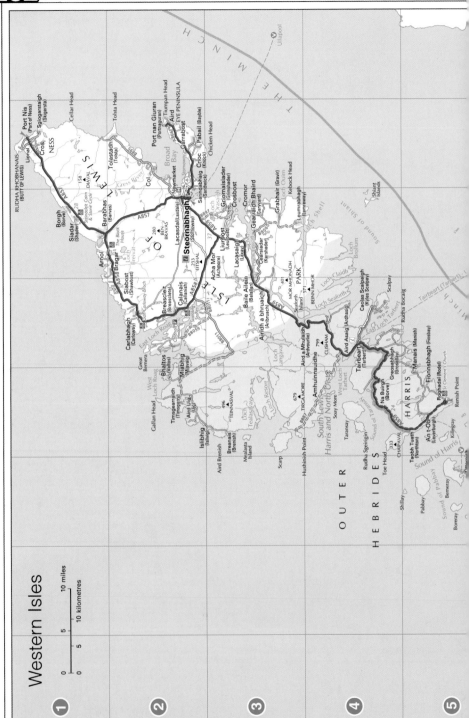

Western Isles

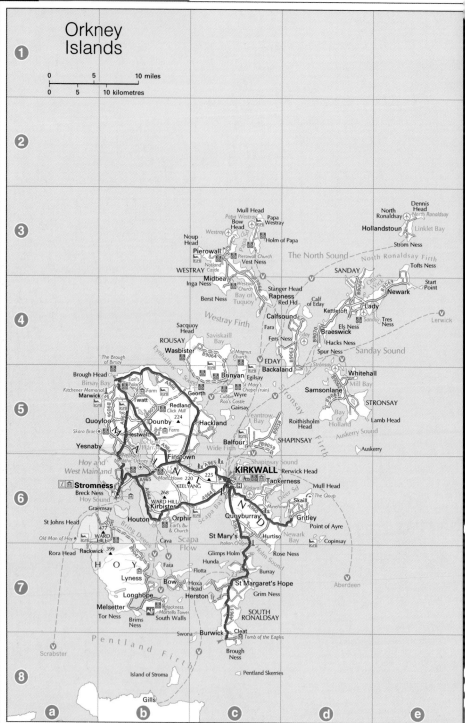

Orkney Islands

0 ___ 5 ___ 10 miles
0 _ 5 _ 10 kilometres

1

2

3

Mull Head
Papa Westray
Bow Head
Papa Westray
North Ronaldsay
Dennis Head
North Ronaldsay
Hollandstoun
Linklet Bay
Noup Head
Holm of Papa
Strom Ness
Pierowall
Vest Ness
Notland Castle
Pierowall Church
The North Sound
North Ronaldsay Firth
Westray
Papa Westray
WESTRAY
Midbea
Inga Ness
Westside Church
SANDAY
Tofts Ness
Berst Ness
Bay of Tuquoy
Stanger Head
Rapness Red Hd
Calf of Eday
Kettletoft
Newark
Start Point
Els Ness
Tres Ness
Lerwick

4

Sacquoy Head
ROUSAY
Saviskaill Bay
Wasbister
St Magnus Church
B9064
Fara
Fers Ness
Calfsound
EDAY
Backaland
Spur Ness
Braeswick
Hacks Ness
Sanday Sound
The Brough of Birsay
Eynhallow Sound
Brinyan
Egilsay
St Mary's Chapel (ruin)
Wyre
Whitehall
Mill Bay
Samsonlane
STRONSAY
Bay of Holland
Lamb Head
Auskerry Sound
Auskerry
Roithisholm Head
SHAPINSAY

5

Brough Head
Earl's Palace
Birsay Bay
Kitchener Memorial
Marwick
Earl's Farm
Twatt
Georth
Redland Click Mill
224
Dounby
Hackland
Cubbie Roo's Castle
Gairsay
Quoyloo
Skara Brae
Hestwall
Farm
Yesnaby
Harray
Veantrow Bay
Wide Firth
Balfour
B9059

6

Hoy and West Mainland
Loch of Stenness
Standing Stones of Stenness
Finstown
A965
Shapinsay Sound
KIRKWALL
Rerwick Head
Tankerness
Maes Howe
220
225
KEELYANG
Deer Sd
Mull Head
The Gloup
Stromness
Breck Ness
268
WARD HILL
Kirbister
Minehowe
Skaill
Hoy Sound
Graemsay
Houton
Orphir
Earl's Bu & Church
Scapa Bay
Quoyburray
A960
Point of Ayre
Gritley
St Johns Head
477
WARD HILL
Bring Deeps
Cava
St Mary's
Italian Chapel
Hurtiso
Newark Bay
Copinasy
Old Man of Hoy
Rackwick
399
Fara
Flotta
Glimps Holm
Hunda
Rose Ness
Scapa Flow
Aberdeen
Rora Head
H O Y
Burray
Lyness
Bow
Hoxa Head
St Margaret's Hope
Grim Ness

7

Longhope
Herston
Melsetter
Blackness
Martello Tower
South Walls
SOUTH RONALDSAY
Tor Ness
Brims Ness
Swona
Burwick
Cleat
Tomb of the Eagles
Scrabster
Pentland Firth
Brough Ness

8

Island of Stroma
Pentland Skerries
Gills

a   **b**   **c**   **d**   **e**

Shetland Islands

0 · · · 5 · · · 10 miles
0 · · · 5 · · · 10 kilometres

1

Muckle Flugga
The Noup
HERMA NESS
Herma Ness 171
Lamba Ness
LIBBERS HILL ▲
Burrafirth
Norwick
Loch of Cliff
Baltasound
Haroldswick
UNST 216
Harold's Wick
Keen of Hamar
Balta

2

Gloup Holm
Bluemull Sound
Sand Wick
Cullivoe
Uyeasound
98 ▲
Belmont
Ness of Ramnageo
Gutcher
Muness Castle
Ramna Stacks
Nev of Stuis
Sellafirth
Linga
Uyea
Point of Fethaland
Gruney
Whale Firth
Hascosay
Tressa Ness
Strandburgh Ness
Uyea
Brough Lodge
159
Wick of Gruting
Isbister
Horra
Mid Yell
Tresta
FETLAR
West Sandwick
188 ▲
Vatsetter
The Snap
453 RONASHILL
Collafirth
YELL
Colgrave Sound
Rams Ness
Heylor
Otterswick
Esha Ness
Ollaberry
Ulsta
Burravoe

3

The Faither
Ronas Voe
Hillswick
Copister
Tangwick
Toft
Shetland (North)
Bar Taing
Sullom Voe
Mossbank
St Magnus
Sullom
Lunna Ness
Out Skerries
Bay
Mavis Grind
Laxo
Lunna
Skaw Taing
Brae
Fora Ness
Brough
WHALSAY
Muckle Roe
Papa Little
Vidlin
Isbister
Papa Stour
Voe
Symbister
Vementry
Gonfirth
Neap
Brindister
Clousta
Brettabister
Sandness
Aith
South Nesting Bay
249 SANDNESS HILL
E Bridge of Walls
Twatt
Weisdale
Bixter
Moul of Eswick
Mu Ness
Staneydale Temple
Heglibister
Wats Ness
Walls
Tresta
Girlsta
Score Head
Gruting
Gardenhouse
Haggersta
Gunnista
Vaila
Whiteness
Veensgarth
Mail
BRESSAY
Culswick
Easter Skeld
FOULA
Westerwick
Hildasay
LERWICK
Isle of Noss
Skelda Ness
Scalloway
Clickimin Broch
Kirkabister
The Deeps
Trondra
Castle
Oxna
Hamnavoe
Quarff
Bard Ness
Shetland (South)
East Burra
Fladdabister
West Burra
Cunningsburgh
Kettla Ness
Helli Ness
Cliff Hills
293 ▲
South Havra
Hoswick
Stove
Mousa
Bigton
Sandwick
Mousa Broch
St Ninian's Isle
Levenwick
Scousburgh
Boddam
Croft House
283 ▲
Hillwell
Fitful Head
Toab
Sumburgh
Old Scatness
Lady's Holm
Jarlshof Prehistoric & Norse Settlement
Ness of Burgi
SUMBURGH HEAD
Sumburgh Roost
Kirkwall
Aberdeen

Inset:

Shetland Islands
Foula
Lerwick
To Aberdeen
Fair Isle
Orkney Islands
Stromness
Kirkwall
St Margaret's Hope
Scrabster
Gills
Wick
To Aberdeen

Fair Isle inset:

217 ▲
North Haven
FAIR ISLE
0 · · · 5 miles
0 · · · 5 kilometres

a b c d e

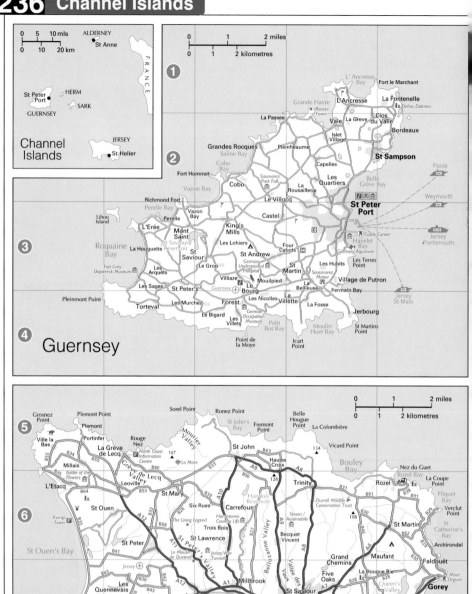

Channel Islands

ALDERNEY
● St Anne

FRANCE

St Peter Port ● HERM
GUERNSEY ◦ SARK

JERSEY
● St Helier

Guernsey

L' Ancresse Bay
Fort le Marchant
L'Ancresse
La Fontenelle
Grande Havre
Rousse Tower
Vale
La Grève
Clos du Valle
Bordeaux
La Passee
Islet Village
St Sampson
Grandes Rocques
Saline Bay
Pleinheaume
Capelles
Les Quartiers
Belle Grève Bay
St Peter Port
Fort Hommet
Cobo Bay
Cobo
Saumarez Park Folk
La Rousaillerie
Vazon Bay
Le Villocq
Castel
Richmond Fort
Perelle Bay
Vazon Bay
King's Mills
Four Cabots
Perelle
L'Erée
Mont Saint
Les Lohiers
St Andrew
Lihou Island
Roquaine Bay
La Houguette
St Saviour Reservoir
St Saviour
Le Gron
Villiaze
St Martin
Les Hubits
Castle Cornet
Guernsey Aquarium
Havelet Bay
Les Terres Point
Fort Grey Shipwreck Museum
Les Arquets
German Underground Hospital
Guernsey
Moulipied
Sausmarez Manor
Village de Putron
Les Sages
St Peter's
Le Bourg
La Bellieuse
Fermain Bay
Pleinmont Point
Les Murchez
Forest
Les Nicolles
La Villette
La Fosse
Jerbourg
Torteval
Les Villets
Le Bigard
German Occupation Museum
Petit Bot Bay
Moulin Huet Bay
St Martins Point
Point de la Moye
Icart Point

Jersey

Grosnez Point
Plemont Point
Sorel Point
Ronez Point
Belle Hougue Point
Ville la Bas
Plemont
Portinfer
Mourier Valley
St John's Bay
Fremont Point
La Colombière
La Grève de Lecq
Rouge Nez
North Coast Information Centre
La Mare
St John
Hautes Croix
Vicard Point
Bouley Bay
Millais
Battle of the Flowers
Grève de Lecq Valley
Leoville
St Mary
Trinity
Nez du Guet
Rozel Bay
La Coupe Point
L'Etacq
St Ouen
Six Rues
Carrefour
Handois Reservoir
Durrell Wildlife Conservation Trust
Rozel
Fliquet Bay
Verclut Point
Kempt Tower
The Living Legend
Hamptonne Country Life
Trois Bois
Steam / Automobile
St Martin
Archirondel
St Peter
St Lawrence
Becquet Vincent
St Catherine's Bay
St Ouen's Bay
Le Moulin de Quetivel
Grand Chemins
Maufant
Faldouët
Les Quennevais
Jersey War Tunnels
Millbrook
La Hougue Bie
Mont Orgueil
La Pulente
St Brelade
Beaumont
St Saviour
Five Oaks
Queen's Valley Reservoir
Gorey
Corbière Point
St Aubin
Longueville
Swiss Valley
Royal Bay of Grouville
Corbière
St Brelade's Bay
St Aubin's Bay
St Helier
Samarès Manor
Grouville
St Clement
Point La Moye
St Brelade's Bay
Belcroute Bay
Elizabeth Castle
Fort Regent
Les Haguais
St Clement
La Rocque
Point La Fret
Portelet Bay
Normont Command Bunker
Le Hocq
Le Bourg
Pontac
La Rocque Point
Poole
Weymouth via Guernsey
Le Croc
Plat Rocque Point
Guernsey, Portsmouth
St Clement's Bay
St-Malo

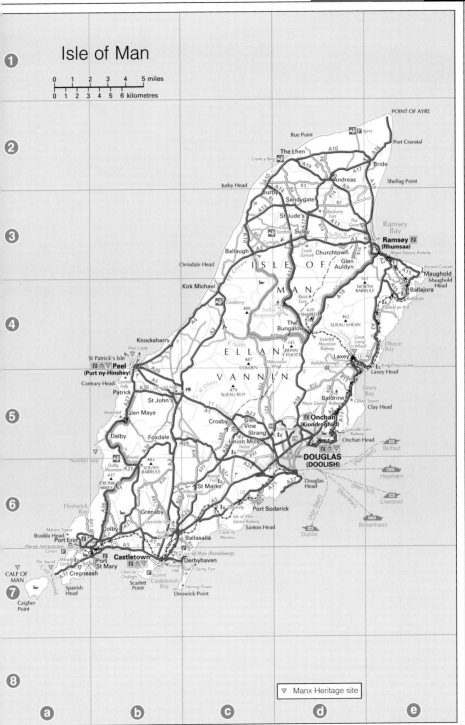

Isle of Man

0   1   2   3   4   5 miles
0   1   2   3   4   5   6 kilometres

POINT OF AYRE

Rue Point
Ayres
The Lhen
Port Cranstal
Cronk y Bing
A10
Bride
A17
Jurby Head
Andreas
Shellag Point
A9
Jurby
Sandygate
B7
St Jude's
A13
B3
Ballachurry
Fort
The
Grove
Ramsey
Bay
Close ny
Sulby
Carrefula
Ramsey
(Rhumsaa)
Manx Electric Railway
Ballaugh
Churchtown
Cronk
Sumark
Ancient Crosses
Glen
Auldyn
Maughold
Maughold
Head
Orrisdale Head
A18
561
NORTH
BARRULE
Ballajora
Kirk Michael
Ballafoyle
Cashtal yn Ard
Cooildarry
488
Block
Eary
620
SNAEFELL
462
SLIEAU LHEAN
The
Bungalow
Sulby
Reservoir
B10
545
Snaefell
Mountain
Railway
Great
Laxey
Big Wheel
Dhoon
Bay
Knocksharry
R.Neblo
BEINN
Y PHOTT
Ballachannagh
King Orry's Grave
Peel Castle
St Patrick's Isle
Peel
(Purt ny-Hinshey)
A20
487
COLDEN
Millennium
Way
Laxey
Laxey Head
Contrary Head
Corins
Folly
A1
479
SLIEAU RUY
TT Circuit
Laxey
Bay
Patrick
A30
Tynwald Hill
R.Dhoo
Cloven Stones
St John's
Manx Electric Railway
Baldrine
Clay Head
Waterfall
Glen Maye
A1
A23
Crosby
Glen
Vine
Groudle Glen
Railway
Dalby
Foxdale
Strang
Onchan
(Kiondroghad)
Onchan Head
Round
Table
483
Union Mills
Norse
House
Belfast
Niarbyl Bay
Dalby
Mountain
427
SOUTH
BARRULE
A24
(Apr-Sept)
437
CRONK Y
ARREY LAA
Brough
Fort
DOUGLAS
(DOOLISH)
Heysham
Fleshwick
Bay
A36
St Marks
10
Isle of Man
Steam Railway
Douglas
Head
Liverpool
Grenaby
Port Soderick
Santon Head
(Apr-Sept)
Milners Tower
Bradda Head
Port Erin
Colby
Riverdale Fally
Cronk ny
Merreu
Dublin
Birkenhead
Marine Interpretation
Centre
A5
Isle of Man (Ronaldsway)
A7
Meayll
Circle
Castletown
Derbyhaven
The Sound
Port
St Mary
Close ny
Chollagh
Hango
Hill
Derby Fort
CALF OF
MAN
Cregneash
Scarlett
Castletown
Bay
Spanish
Head
Scarlett
Point
Herring Tower
Caigher
Point
Dreswick Point

▽ Manx Heritage site

Restricted Junctions

Motorway and Primary Route junctions which have access or exit restrictions are shown on the map pages thus:

M1 London - Leeds

Junction	Northbound	Southbound
2	Access only from A1 *(northbound)*	Exit only to A1 *(southbound)*
4	Access only from A41 *(northbound)*	Exit only to A41 *(southbound)*
6A	Access only from M25 (no link from A405)	Exit only to M25 (no link from A405)
7	Access only from A414	Exit only to A414
17	Exit only to M45	Access only from M45
19	Exit only to M6 *(northbound)*	Access only from M6
21A	Exit only, no access	Access only, no exit
23A	Access only from A42	No restriction
24A	Access only, no exit	Exit only, no access
35A	Exit only, no access	Access only, no exit
43	Exit only to M621	Access only from M621
48	Exit only to A1(M) *(northbound)*	Access only from A1(M) *(southbound)*

M2 Rochester - Faversham

Junction	Westbound	Eastbound
1	No exit to A2 *(eastbound)*	No access from A2 *(westbound)*

M3 Sunbury - Southampton

Junction	Northeastbound	Southwestbound
8	Access only from A303, no exit	Exit only to A303, no access
10	Exit only, no access	Access only, no exit
14	Access from M27 only, no exit	No access to M27 *(westbound)*

M4 London - South Wales

Junction	Westbound	Eastbound
1	Access only from A4 *(westbound)*	Exit only to A4 *(eastbound)*
21	Exit only to M48	Access only from M48
23	Access only from M48	Exit only to M48
25	Exit only, no access	Access only, no exit
25A	Exit only, no access	Access only, no exit
29	Exit only to A48(M)	Access only from A48(M)
38	Exit only, no access	No restriction
39	Access only, no exit	No access or exit

M5 Birmingham - Exeter

Junction	Northeastbound	Southwestbound
10	Access only, no exit	Exit only, no access
11A	Access only from A417 *(westbound)*	Exit only to A417 *(eastbound)*
18A	Exit only to M49	Access only from M49
18	Exit only, no access	Access only, no exit
29	No restriction	Access only from A30 *(westbound)*

M6 Toll Motorway

Junction	Northwestbound	Southeastbound
T1	Access only, no exit	No access or exit
T2	No access or exit	Exit only, no access
T3	Staggered junction, follow signs - access only from A38 *(northbound)*	Staggered junction, follow signs - access only from A38 *(southbound)*
T5	Access only, no exit	Exit only to A5148 *(northbound)*, no access
T7	Exit only, no access	Access only, no exit
T8	Exit only, no access	Access only, no exit

M6 Rugby - Carlisle

Junction	Northbound	Southbound
3A	Exit only to M6 Toll	Access only from M6 Toll
4A	Access only from M42 *(southbound)*	Exit only to M42
5	Exit only, no access	Access only, no exit
10A	Exit only to M54	Access only from M54
11A	Access only from M6 Toll	Exit only to M6 Toll
with M56 (jct 20A)	No restriction	Access only from M56 *(eastbound)*
20	Access only, no exit	No restriction
24	Access only, no exit	Exit only, no access
25	Exit only, no access	Access only, no exit
29	No direct access, use adjacent slip road to jct 29A	No direct exit, use adjacent slip road from jct 29A
29A	Access only, no exit	Exit only, no access
30	Access only from M61	Exit only to M61
31A	Exit only, no access	Access only, no exit
45	Exit only, no access	Access only, no exit

M8 Edinburgh - Bishopton

Junction	Westbound	Eastbound
8	No access from M73 *(southbound)* or from A8 *(eastbound)* & A89	No exit to M73 *(northbound)* or to A8 *(westbound)* & A89
9	Access only, no exit	Exit only, no access
13	Access only from M80 *(southbound)*	Exit only to M80 *(northbound)*
14	Access only, no exit	Exit only, no access
16	Exit only to A804	Access only from A879
17	Exit only to A82	No restriction
18	Access only from A82 *(eastbound)*	Exit only to A814
19	No access from A814 *(westbound)*	Exit only to A814 *(westbound)*
20	Exit only, no access	Access only, no exit
21	Access only, no exit	Exit only to A8
22	Exit only to M77 *(southbound)*	Access only from M77 *(northbound)*
23	Exit only to B768	Access only from B768
25	No access or exit from or to A8	No access or exit from or to A8
25A	Exit only, no access	Access only, no exit
28	Exit only, no access	Access only, no exit
28A	Exit only to A737	Access only from A737

M9 Edinburgh - Dunblane

Junction	Northwestbound	Southeastbound
1A	Exit only to M9 spur	Access only from M9 spur
2	Access only, no exit	Exit only, no access
3	Exit only, no access	Access only, no exit
6	Access only, no exit	Exit only to A905
8	Exit only to M876 *(southwestbound)*	Access only from M876 *(northeastbound)*

M11 London - Cambridge

Junction	Northbound	Southbound
4	Access only from A406 *(eastbound)*	Exit only to A406
5	Exit only, no access	Access only, no exit
9	Exit only to A11	Access only from A11
13	Exit only, no access	Access only, no exit
14	Exit only, no access	Access only, no exit

M20 Swanley - Folkestone

Junction	Northwestbound	Southeastbound
2	Staggered junction; follow signs - access only	Staggered junction; follow signs - exit only
3	Exit only to M26 *(westbound)*	Access only from M26 *(eastbound)*
5	Access only from A20	For access follow signs - exit only to A20
6	No restriction	For exit follow signs
11A	Access only, no exit	Exit only, no access

M23 Hooley - Crawley

Junction	Northbound	Southbound
7	Exit only to A23 *(northbound)*	Access only from A23 *(southbound)*
10A	Access only, no exit	Exit only, no access

M25 London Orbital Motorway

Junction	Clockwise	Anticlockwise
1B	No direct access, use slip road to Jct 2. Exit only	Access only, no exit
5	No exit to M26 *(eastbound)*	No access from M26
19	Exit only, no access	Access only, no exit
21	Access only from M1 *(southbound)*. Exit only to M1 *(northbound)*	Access only from M1 *(southbound)*. Exit only to M1 *(northbound)*
31	No exit (use slip road via jct 30), access only	No access (use slip road via jct 30), exit only

M26 Sevenoaks - Wrotham

Junction	Westbound	Eastbound
with M25 (jct 5)	Exit only to clockwise M25 *(westbound)*	Access only from anticlockwise M25 *(eastbound)*
with M20 (jct 3)	Access only from M20 *(northwestbound)*	Exit only to M20 *(southeastbound)*

M27 Cadnam - Portsmouth

Junction	Westbound	Eastbound
4	Staggered junction; follow signs - access only from M3 *(southbound)*. Exit only to M3 *(northbound)*	Staggered junction; follow signs - access only from M3 *(southbound)*. Exit only to M3 *(northbound)*
10	Exit only, no access	Access only, no exit
12	Staggered junction; follow signs - exit only to M275 *(southbound)*	Staggered junction; follow signs - access only from M275 *(northbound)*

M40 London - Birmingham

Junction	Northwestbound	Southeastbound
3	Exit only, no access	Access only, no exit
7	Exit only, no access	Access only, no exit
8	Exit only to M40/A40	Access only from M40/A40
13	Exit only, no access	Access only, no exit
14	Access only, no exit	Exit only, no access
16	Access only, no exit	Exit only, no access

M42 Bromsgrove - Measham

Junction	Northeastbound	Southwestbound
1	Access only, no exit	Exit only, no access
7	Exit only to M6 *(northwestbound)*	Access only from M6 *(northwestbound)*
7A	Exit only to M6 *(southeastbound)*	No access or exit
8	Access only from M6 *(southeastbound)*	Exit only to M6 *(northwestbound)*

M45 Coventry - M1

Junction	Westbound	Eastbound
Dunchurch (unnumbered)	Access only from A45	Exit only, no access
with M1 (jct 17)	Access only from M1 *(northbound)*	Exit only to M1 *(southbound)*

M53 Mersey Tunnel - Chester

Junction	Northbound	Southbound
11	Access only from M56 *(westbound)*. Exit only to M56 *(eastbound)*	Access only from M56 *(westbound)*. Exit only to M56 *(eastbound)*

M54 Telford

Junction	Westbound	Eastbound
with M6 (jct 10A)	Access only from M6 *(northbound)*	Exit only to M6 *(southbound)*

M56 North Cheshire

Junction	Westbound	Eastbound
1	Access only from M60 (westbound)	Exit only to M60 (eastbound) & A34 (northbound)
2	Exit only, no access	Access only, no exit
3	Access only, no exit	Exit only, no access
4	Exit only, no access	Access only, no exit
7	Exit only, no access	No restriction
8	Access only, no exit	No access or exit
15	Exit only to M53	Access only from M53
16	No access or exit	No restrictions

M57 Liverpool Outer Ring Road

Junction	Northwestbound	Southeastbound
3	Access only, no exit	Exit only, no access
5	Access only from A580 (westbound)	Exit only, no access

M58 Liverpool - Wigan

Junction	Westbound	Eastbound
1	Exit only, no access	Access only, no exit

M60 Manchester Orbital

Junction	Clockwise	Anticlockwise
2	Access only, no exit	Exit only, no access
3	No access from M56	Access only from A34 (northbound)
4	Access only from A34 (northbound). Exit only to M56	Access only from M56 (eastbound). Exit only to A34 (southbound)
5	Access and exit only from and to A5103 (northbound)	Access and exit only from and to A5103 (southbound)
7	No direct access, use slip road to jct 8. Exit only to A56	Access only from A56. No exit - use jct 8
14	Access from A580 (eastbound)	Exit only to A580 (westbound)
16	Access only, no exit	Exit only, no access
20	Exit only, no access	Access only, no exit
22	No restriction	Exit only, no access
25	No restriction	No restriction
26	No restriction	Exit only, no access
27	Access only, no exit	Exit only, no access

M61 Manchester - Preston

Junction	Northwestbound	Southeastbound
3	No access or exit	Exit only, no access
with M6 (jct 30)	Exit only to M6 (northbound)	Access only from M6 (southbound)

M62 Liverpool - Kingston upon Hull

Junction	Westbound	Eastbound
23	Access only, no exit	Exit only, no access
32A	No access to A1(M) (southbound)	No restriction

M65 Preston - Colne

Junction	Northeastbound	Southwestbound
9	Exit only, no access	Access only, no exit
11	Access only, no exit	Exit only, no access

M66 Bury

Junction	Northbound	Southbound
with A56	Exit only to A56 (northbound)	Access only from A56 (southbound)
1	Exit only, no access	Access only, no exit

M67 Hyde Bypass

Junction	Westbound	Eastbound
1	Access only, no exit	Exit only, no access
2	Exit only, no access	Access only, no exit
3	Exit only, no access	No restriction

M69 Coventry - Leicester

Junction	Northbound	Southbound
2	Access only, no exit	Exit only, no access

M73 East of Glasgow

Junction	Northbound	Southbound
2	No access from or exit to A89. No access from M8 (eastbound).	No access from or exit to A89. No exit to M8 (westbound)

M74 and A74(M) Glasgow - Gretna

Junction	Northbound	Southbound
3	Access only, no exit	Exit only, no access
3A	Access only, no exit	Exit only, no access
7	Access only, no exit	Exit only, no access
9	No access or exit	Exit only, no access
10	No restrictions	Access only, no exit
11	Access only, no exit	Exit only, no access
12	Access only, no exit	Access only, no exit
18	Exit only, no access	Access only, no exit

M77 South of Glasgow

Junction	Northbound	Southbound
with M8 (jct 22)	No exit to M8 (westbound)	No access from M8 (eastbound)
4	Access only, no exit	Exit only, no access
6	Access only, no exit	Exit only, no access
7	Access only, no exit	No restriction

M80 Glasgow - Stirling

Junction	Northbound	Southbound
4A	Exit only, no access	Access only, no exit
6A	Access only, no exit	Exit only, no access
8	Exit only to M876 (northeastbound)	Access only from M876 (southwestbound)

M90 Forth Road Bridge - Perth

Junction	Northbound	Southbound
2A	Exit only to A92 (eastbound)	Access only from A92 (westbound)
7	Access only, no exit	Exit only, no access
8	Exit only, no access	Access only, no exit
10	No access from A912. No exit to A912 (southbound)	Access only from A912 (northbound). No exit to A912

M180 Doncaster - Grimsby

Junction	Westbound	Eastbound
1	Access only, no exit	Exit only, no access

M606 Bradford Spur

Junction	Northbound	Southbound
2	Exit only, no access	No restriction

M621 Leeds - M1

Junction	Clockwise	Anticlockwise
2A	Access only, no exit	Exit only, no access
4	No exit or access	No restriction
5	Access only, no exit	Exit only, no access
6	Exit only, no access	Access only, no exit
with M1 (jct 43)	Exit only to M1 (southbound)	Access only from M1 (northbound)

M876 Bonnybridge - Kincardine Bridge

Junction	Northeastbound	Southwestbound
with M80 (jct 5)	Access only from M80 (northbound)	Exit only to M80 (southbound)
with M9 (jct 8)	Exit only to M9 (eastbound)	Access only from M9 (westbound)

A1(M) South Mimms - Baldock

Junction	Northbound	Southbound
2	Exit only, no access	Access only, no exit
3	No restriction	Exit only, no access
5	Access only, no exit	No access or exit

A1(M) Pontefract - Bedale

Junction	Northbound	Southbound
41	No access to M62 (eastbound)	No restriction
43	Access only from M1 (northbound)	Exit only to M1 (southbound)

A1(M) Scotch Corner - Newcastle upon Tyne

Junction	Northbound	Southbound
57	Exit only to A66(M) (eastbound)	Access only from A66(M) (westbound)
65	No access Exit only to A194(M) & A1 (northbound)	No exit Access only from A194(M) & A1 (southbound)

A3(M) Horndean - Havant

Junction	Northbound	Southbound
1	Access only from A3	Exit only to A3
4	Exit only, no access	Access only, no exit

A48(M) Cardiff Spur

Junction	Westbound	Eastbound
29	Access only from M4 (westbound)	Exit only to M4 (eastbound)
29A	Exit only to A48 (westbound)	Access only from A48 (eastbound)

A66(M) Darlington Spur

Junction	Westbound	Eastbound
with A1(M) (jct 57)	Exit only to A1(M) (southbound)	Access only from A1(M) (northbound)

A194(M) Newcastle upon Tyne

Junction	Northbound	Southbound
with A1(M) (jct 65)	Access only from A1(M) (northbound)	Exit only to A1(M) (southbound)

A12 M25 - Ipswich

Junction	Northeastbound	Southwestbound
13	Access only, no exit	No restriction
14	Exit only, no access	Access only, no exit
20A	Exit only, no access	Access only, no exit
20B	Access only, no exit	Exit only, no access
21	No restriction	Access only, no exit
23	Exit only, no access	Access only, no exit
24	Access only, no exit	Exit only, no access
27	Exit only, no access	Access only, no exit
Dedham & Stratford St Mary (unnumbered)	Exit only	Access only

A14 M1 - Felixstowe

Junction	Westbound	Eastbound
With M1/M6 (jct 19)	Exit only to M6 and M1 (northbound)	Access only from M6 and M1 (southbound)
4	Exit only, no access	Access only, no exit
31	Access only from A1307	Exit only to A1307
34	Access only, no exit	Access only, no exit
36	Exit only to A11, access only from A1303	Access only from A11
38	Access only from A11	Exit only to A11
39	Exit only, no access	Access only, no exit
61	Access only, no exit	Exit only, no access

A55 Holyhead - Chester

Junction	Westbound	Eastbound
8A	Exit only, no access	Access only, no exit
23A	Access only, no exit	Exit only, no access
24A	Exit only, no access	No access or exit
33A	Access only, no exit	No access or exit
33B	Exit only, no access	Access only, no exit
36A	Exit only to A5104	Access only from A5104

Index to place names

This index lists places appearing in the main-map section of the atlas in alphabetical order. The reference following each name gives the atlas page number and grid reference of the square in which the place appears. The map shows counties and administrative areas, together with a list of the abbreviated name forms used in the index. The top 100 places of tourist interest are indexed in **red** (or **green** if a World Heritage site), motorway service areas in **blue**, airports in blue *italic* and National Parks in green *italic*.

Scotland

Abers	**Aberdeenshire**
Ag & B	**Argyll and Bute**
Angus	**Angus**
Border	**Scottish Borders**
C Aber	**City of Aberdeen**
C Dund	**City of Dundee**
C Edin	**City of Edinburgh**
C Glas	**City of Glasgow**
Clacks	**Clackmannanshire (1)**
D & G	**Dumfries & Galloway**
E Ayrs	**East Ayrshire**
E Duns	**East Dunbartonshire (2)**
E Loth	**East Lothian**
E Rens	**East Renfrewshire (3)**
Falk	**Falkirk**
Fife	**Fife**
Highld	**Highland**
Inver	**Inverclyde (4)**
Mdloth	**Midlothian (5)**
Moray	**Moray**
N Ayrs	**North Ayrshire**
N Lans	**North Lanarkshire (6)**
Ork	**Orkney Islands**
P & K	**Perth & Kinross**
Rens	**Renfrewshire (7)**
S Ayrs	**South Ayrshire**
Shet	**Shetland Islands**
S Lans	**South Lanarkshire**
Stirlg	**Stirling**
W Duns	**West Dunbartonshire (8)**
W Isls	**Western Isles**
	(Na h-Eileanan an Iar)
W Loth	**West Lothian**

Wales

Blae G	**Blaenau Gwent (9)**
Brdgnd	**Bridgend (10)**
Caerph	**Caerphilly (11)**
Cardif	**Cardiff**
Carmth	**Carmarthenshire**
Cerdgn	**Ceredigion**
Conwy	**Conwy**
Denbgs	**Denbighshire**
Flints	**Flintshire**
Gwynd	**Gwynedd**
IoA	**Isle of Anglesey**
Mons	**Monmouthshire**
Myr Td	**Merthyr Tydfil (12)**
Neath	**Neath Port Talbot (13)**
Newpt	**Newport (14)**
Pembks	**Pembrokeshire**
Powys	**Powys**
Rhondd	**Rhondda Cynon Taff (15)**
Swans	**Swansea**
Torfn	**Torfaen (16)**
V Glam	**Vale of Glamorgan (17)**
Wrexhm	**Wrexham**

Channel Islands & Isle of Man

Guern	**Guernsey**
Jersey	**Jersey**
IoM	**Isle of Man**

England

BaNES	**Bath & N E Somerset (18)**
Barns	**Barnsley (19)**
Bed	**Bedford**
Birm	**Birmingham**
Bl w D	**Blackburn with Darwen (20)**
Bmouth	**Bournemouth**
Bolton	**Bolton (21)**
Bpool	**Blackpool**
Br & H	**Brighton & Hove (22)**
Br For	**Bracknell Forest (23)**
Bristl	**City of Bristol**
Bucks	**Buckinghamshire**
Bury	**Bury (24)**
C Beds	**Central Bedfordshire**
C Brad	**City of Bradford**
C Derb	**City of Derby**
C KuH	**City of Kingston upon Hull**
C Leic	**City of Leicester**
C Nott	**City of Nottingham**
C Pete	**City of Peterborough**
C Plym	**City of Plymouth**
C Port	**City of Portsmouth**
C Sotn	**City of Southampton**
C Stke	**City of Stoke-on-Trent**
C York	**City of York**
Calder	**Calderdale (25)**
Cambs	**Cambridgeshire**
Ches E	**Cheshire East**
Ches W	**Cheshire West and Chester**
Cnwll	**Cornwall**
Covtry	**Coventry**
Cumb	**Cumbria Darltn**
Derbys	**Derbyshire**
Devon	**Devon**
Donc	**Doncaster (27)**
Dorset	**Dorset**
Dudley	**Dudley (28)**
Dur	**Durham**
E R Yk	**East Riding of Yorkshire**
E Susx	**East Sussex**
Essex	**Essex**
Gatesd	**Gateshead (29)**
Gloucs	**Gloucestershire**
Gt Lon	**Greater London**
Halton	**Halton (30)**
Hants	**Hampshire**
Hartpl	**Hartlepool (31)**
Herefs	**Herefordshire**
Herts	**Hertfordshire**
IoS	**Isles of Scilly**
IoW	**Isle of Wight**
Kent	**Kent**
Kirk	**Kirklees (32)**
Knows	**Knowsley (33)**
Lancs	**Lancashire**
Leeds	**Leeds**
Leics	**Leicestershire**
Lincs	**Lincolnshire**
Lpool	**Liverpool**
Luton	**Luton**
M Keyn	**Milton Keynes**
Manch	**Manchester**
Medway	**Medway**

Middsb	**Middlesbrough**
NE Lin	**North East Lincolnshire**
N Linc	**North Lincolnshire**
N Som	**North Somerset (34)**
N Tyne	**North Tyneside (35)**
N u Ty	**Newcastle upon Tyne**
N York	**North Yorkshire**
Nhants	**Northamptonshire**
Norfk	**Norfolk**
Notts	**Nottinghamshire**
Nthumb	**Northumberland**
Oldham	**Oldham (36)**
Oxon	**Oxfordshire**
Poole	**Poole**
R & Cl	**Redcar & Cleveland**
Readg	**Reading**
Rochdl	**Rochdale (37)**
Rothm	**Rotherham (38)**
Rutlnd	**Rutland**
S Glos	**South Gloucestershire (39)**
S on T	**Stockton-on-Tees (40)**
S Tyne	**South Tyneside (41)**
Salfd	**Salford (42)**
Sandw	**Sandwell (43)**
Sefton	**Sefton (44)**
Sheff	**Sheffield**
Shrops	**Shropshire**
Slough	**Slough (45)**
Solhll	**Solihull (46)**
Somset	**Somerset**
St Hel	**St Helens (47)**
Staffs	**Staffordshire**
Sthend	**Southend-on-Sea**
Stockp	**Stockport (48)**
Suffk	**Suffolk**
Sundld	**Sunderland**
Surrey	**Surrey**
Swindn	**Swindon**
Tamesd	**Tameside (49)**
Thurr	**Thurrock (50)**
Torbay	**Torbay**
Traffd	**Trafford (51)**
W & M	**Windsor and Maidenhead (52)**
W Berk	**West Berkshire**
W Susx	**West Sussex**
Wakefd	**Wakefield (53)**
Warrtn	**Warrington (54)**
Warwks	**Warwickshire**
Wigan	**Wigan (55)**
Wilts	**Wiltshire**
Wirral	**Wirral (56)**
Wokham	**Wokingham (57)**
Wolves	**Wolverhampton (58)**
Worcs	**Worcestershire**
Wrekin	**Telford & Wrekin (59)**
Wsall	**Walsall (60)**

ORKNEY ISLANDS

SHETLAND ISLANDS

WESTERN ISLES (Na h-Eileanan an Iar)

HIGHLAND

MORAY

S C O T L A N D

Aberdeen

ABERDEENSHIRE

ANGUS

PERTH & KINROSS

Dundee

FIFE

ARGYLL & BUTE

STIRLING

1

FALK

8 2
4 6 W
3 7 LOTH
Glasgow
5

Edinburgh

E LOTH

NORTH AYRSHIRE

S LANS

SCOTTISH BORDERS

E AYRS

S AYRS

DUMFRIES & GALLOWAY

NORTHUMBERLAND

Newcastle upon Tyne 35
29 41
Sunderland

CUMBRIA

DURHAM

31
26 40 R & CL
Middlesbrough

IoM

NORTH YORKSHIRE

Blackpool

LANCASHIRE

Bradford

York

EAST RIDING OF YORKSHIRE

Kingston upon Hull

Leeds

25

32 53

N LINCS

N E LINCS

20

55 37
21 24 36
47 42 49
Liverpool 33 54 51 48
56 30

19 27

Manchester

38

Sheffield

IoA

CONWY

FLINTS

CHES W

CHES E

DERBYS

NOTTS

LINCOLNSHIRE

DENBGS

WREXHAM

Stoke-on-Trent

Derby

Nottingham

GWYNEDD

59

STAFFS

LEICS

RUTLAND

NORFOLK

Leicester

Peterborough

SHROPSHIRE

58 60
28 43
46

Birmingham
Coventry

NHANTS

CAMBS

SUFFOLK

POWYS

WORCS

WARWKS

Milton Keynes

BED

CERDGN

HEREFS

W A L E S E N G L A N D

PEMBKS

CARMTH

MONS

GLOUCS

OXON

BUCKS

BEDS
Luton

HERTS

ESSEX

Southend-on-Sea

13 9
12
15 11 16
10 14
Cardiff 39
17 34 18

Swansea

Bristol

Swindon

Reading

52 45
57 23

W BERKS

GREATER LONDON

50

MEDWAY

SURREY

KENT

WILTSHIRE

HAMPSHIRE

W SUSX

E SUSX

SOMERSET

Southampton
Portsmouth

22

DEVON

DORSET

Bournemouth

IoW

Poole

CORNWALL

Plymouth

Torbay

CHANNEL ISLANDS

Guernsey

Jersey

IoS

A

Abbas Combe Somset 27 G6
Abberley Worcs 70 D2
Abberley Common
  Worcs 70 D2
Abberton Essex 62 B4
Abberton Worcs 71 H4
Abbess Roding Essex.....60 F5
Abbeydale Sheff..........114 F6
Abbey Dore Herefs 54 B3
Abbey Green Staffs 99 L2
Abbey St Bathans
  Border 178 F6
Abbeystead Lancs........130 B8
Abbey Town Cumb........147 L5
Abbey Village Lancs......121 J6
Abbey Wood Gt Lon 45 J4
Abbotrule Border........167 J6
Abbots Bickington
  Devon 9 K3
Abbots Bromley
  Staffs 100 B7
Abbotsbury Dorset 14 B5
Abbots Deuglie P & K...186 B5
Abbotsham Devon.........22 F6
Abbotskerswell
  Devon 7 K3
Abbots Langley Herts.....59 H7
Abbots Leigh N Som......38 D5
Abbotsley Cambs..........75 J3
Abbots Morton Worcs....71 H4
Abbots Ripton Cambs.....89 J7
Abbot's Salford
  Warwks 71 J4
Abbots Worthy Hants.....29 J5
Abbotts Ann Hants 29 G3
Abbott Street Dorset.......15 J3
Abdon Shrops 83 L6
Aberaeron Cerdgn 66 B3
Aberaman Rhondd 52 F7
Aberangell Gwynd.........81 J2
Aberarder Highld 202 F1
Aberargie P & K..........186 B4
Aberarth Cerdgn 66 B2
Aberavon Neath............51 L7
Abercanaid Myr Td........53 G7
Abercarn Caerph 37 K2
Abercastle Pembks........64 B7
Abercegir Powys 81 H3
Aberchalder Lodge
  Highld 202 B5
Aberchirder Abers 216 C4
Abercraf Powys 52 C5
Abercregan Neath.........36 D2
Abercwmboi Rhondd.....52 F7
Abercynon Rhondd 37 G2
Aberdalgie P & K........185 M4
Aberdare Rhondd 52 F7
Aberdaron Gwynd.........94 C7
Aberdeen C Aber........207 H4
Aberdeen Airport
  C Aber 207 G3
Aberdeen
  Crematorium
  C Aber 207 G4
Aberdour Fife 177 G2
Aberdulais Neath..........52 B7
Aberdyfi Gwynd............80 E4
Aberedw Powys 68 C5
Abereiddy Pembks........48 D2
Abererch Gwynd............95 G5
Aberfan Myr Td.............53 G7
Aberfeldy P & K..........194 D6
Aberffraw IoA..............108 D7
Aberford Leeds...........124 C3
Aberfoyle Stirlg..........184 C7
Abergavenny Mons........53 L5
Abergele Conwy...........110 C6
Abergorlech Carmth......66 D7
Abergwesyn Powys........67 J4
Abergwili Carmth..........50 F2
Abergwynfi Neath..........36 D2
Abergwyngregyn
  Gwynd 109 J6

Abergynolwyn
  Gwynd 80 F3
Aberkenfig Brdgnd........36 D4
Aberlady E Loth..........178 B3
Aberlemno Angus........196 E5
Aberllefenni Gwynd.......81 G2
Aberllynfi Powys 68 D6
Aberlour Moray 215 G5
Abermule Powys 82 D5
Abernant Carmth..........50 D2
Aber-nant Rhondd........52 F7
Abernethy P & K..........186 C4
Abernyte P & K............186 D2
Aberporth Cerdgn 65 J4
Abersoch Gwynd...........94 E6
Abersychan Torfn 53 K7
Aberthin V Glam 36 F5
Abertillery Blae G 53 K7
Abertridwr Caerph.........37 H3
Abertridwr Powys 97 G8
Aberuthven P & K........185 K4
Aberystwyth Cerdgn.....80 D6
Aberystwyth
  Crematorium
  Cerdgn 80 E6
Abingdon-on-
  Thames Oxon..............41 J2
Abinger Common
  Surrey 31 J3
Abinger Hammer
  Surrey 31 H2
Abington Nhants 73 L3
Abington S Lans..........165 H5
Abington Pigotts
  Cambs 75 K5
Abington Services
  S Lans 165 H4
Abingworth W Susx 18 F3
Ab Kettleby Leics........102 B7
Ablington Gloucs..........56 C6
Abney Derbys..............114 D5
Aboyne Abers 205 L5
Abram Wigan 112 E2
Abriachan Highld 212 E7
Abridge Essex 45 J2
Abronhill N Lans..........175 K3
Abson S Glos................39 G5
Abthorpe Nhants 73 J5
Aby Lincs...................118 F5
Acaster Malbis C York...124 E2
Acaster Selby N York....124 E3
Accrington Lancs.........121 L5
Accrington
  Crematorium
  Lancs 121 L5
Acha Ag & B...............188 F5
Achahoish Ag & B........172 D3
Achalader P & K..........195 H7
Achaleven Ag & B........182 D1
Acha Mor W Isls..........232 f3
Achanalt Highld 211 K3
Achandunie Highld 222 E6
Achany Highld 222 D2
Acharacle Highld 190 D3
Acharn Highld 190 E6
Acharn P & K..............194 B7
Achavanich Highld 231 H6
Achduart Highld 224 C7
Achfary Highld 228 D7
A'Chill Highld 198 D4
Achiltibuie Highld 224 C6
Achina Highld 229 L4
Achinhoan Ag & B 161 J6
Achintee Highld 210 E6
Achintraid Highld 210 C6
Achmelvich Highld 224 C4
Achmore Highld 210 D7
Achmore W Isls..........232 f3
Achnacarnin Highld 224 C3
Achnacarry Highld 201 J7
Achnacloich Highld 199 J4
Achnaconeran Highld ...202 C2
Achnacroish Ag & B 191 G7
Achnadrish House
  Ag & B 189 L6
Achnafauld P & K........185 J1
Achnagarron Highld 222 F7

Achnaha Highld 189 L3
Achnahaird Highld 224 B5
Achnairn Highld 225 L6
Achnalea Highld 191 G4
Achnamara Ag & B......172 D2
Achnasheen Highld......211 J3
Achnashellach Lodge
  Highld 210 F5
Achnastank Moray.......215 G7
Achosnich Highld 189 K3
Achranich Highld 190 E6
Achreamie Highld 230 E3
Achriabhach Highld 192 B3
Achriesgill Highld 228 C5
Achtoty Highld 229 K3
Achurch Nhants............88 E6
Achvaich Highld 222 F3
Achvarasdal Highld 230 C3
Ackergill Highld 231 L5
Acklam Middsb 141 L4
Acklam N York 134 B7
Ackleton Shrops 84 D4
Acklington Nthumb 159 G2
Ackton Wakefd 124 C6
Ackworth Moor Top
  Wakefd 124 C7
Acle Norfk 93 J2
Acock's Green Birm 85 K6
Acol Kent 35 J2
Acomb C York 124 E1
Acomb Nthumb..........150 B2
Aconbury Herefs 54 D2
Acton Ches E................98 F2
Acton Gt Lon 44 D4
Acton Staffs.................99 J4
Acton Suffk 77 K5
Acton Beauchamp
  Herefs.......................70 C4
Acton Bridge Ches W...112 E6
Acton Burnell Shrops 83 K3
Acton Green Herefs 70 C4
Acton Park Wrexhm 97 M3
Acton Round Shrops 84 B4
Acton Scott Shrops 83 J5
Acton Trussell Staffs 99 L8
Acton Turville S Glos 39 J4
Adbaston Staffs............99 H6
Adber Dorset................26 E7
Adbolton Notts 101 L5
Adderbury Oxon 72 F7
Adderley Shrops 98 F4
Addiewell W Loth........176 D5
Addingham C Brad.......123 G1
Addington Bucks 58 C3
Addington Gt Lon.........45 G7
Addington Kent............33 H2
Addiscombe Gt Lon 45 G6
Addlestone Surrey 43 H7
Addlethorpe Lincs........119 H7
Adeyfield Herts 59 H6
Adfa Powys..................82 B4
Adforton Herefs 69 H1
Adisham Kent...............35 G4
Adlestrop Gloucs..........56 E3
Adlingfleet E R Yk........125 K6
Adlington Lancs...........121 J7
Admaston Staffs..........100 B7
Admaston Wrekin..........84 B2
Adpar Cerdgn 65 J6
Adsborough Somset......25 L5
Adscombe Somset........25 J4
Adstock Bucks 58 C3
Adstone Nhants............73 H4
Adversane W Susx........31 H6
Advie Highld 214 D7
Adwick Le Street
  Donc 124 E8
Adwick upon Dearne
  Donc 115 J2
Ae D & G 155 H4
Ae Bridgend D & G 155 H5
Afan Forest Park
  Neath 36 D2
Affleck Abers 216 B6
Affpuddle Dorset 14 F4
Affric Lodge Highld.....201 J2
Afon-wen Flints..........110 F6

Afton IoW 16 D5
Agecroft
  Crematorium
  Salfd 113 J2
Agglethorpe N York.....131 K3
Aigburth Lpool 111 L4
Aike E R Yk 126 C2
Aiketgate Cumb 148 E5
Aikton Cumb..............148 B4
Ailsworth C Pete 89 G4
Ainderby Quernhow
  N York 132 E4
Ainderby Steeple
  N York 132 E2
Aingers Green Essex 62 D4
Ainsdale Sefton 120 D7
Ainstable Cumb...........148 F5
Ainsworth Bury 121 L5
Ainthorpe N York........142 E5
Ainville W Loth...........176 F5
Aird Ag & B 181 M7
Aird D & G 144 D3
Aird W Isls 232 g2
Aird a Mhulaidh W Isls..232 e3
Aird Asaig W Isls 232 e4
Aird Dhubh Highld 209 L6
Airdeny Ag & B 182 E2
Aird of Kinloch
  Ag & B 181 H2
Aird of Sleat Highld.....199 J5
Airdrie N Lans.............175 K5
Airdriehill N Lans 175 K5
Airds of Kells D & G 154 B7
Aird Uig W Isls 232 d2
Airidh a bhruaich
  W Isls 232 e3
Airieland D & G 146 D2
Airlie Angus...............195 L6
Airmyn E R Yk 125 H5
Airntully P & K............186 A1
Airor Highld 199 L4
Airth Falk 176 B2
Airton N York 131 G7
Aisby Lincs 103 G5
Aisby Lincs 116 E3
Aish Devon 7 G4
Aish Devon 7 J4
Aisholt Somset............25 J4
Aiskew N York 132 D2
Aislaby N York 134 B3
Aislaby N York 143 H5
Aislaby S on T............141 J5
Aisthorpe Lincs...........116 F5
Aith Shet...................235 c5
Akeld Nthumb 168 E4
Akeley Bucks 73 K6
Albaston Cnwll 6 B2
Alberbury Shrops 83 G1
Albourne W Susx 19 H3
Albrighton Shrops........84 E3
Albrighton Shrops........98 C8
Alburgh Norfk..............92 F6
Albury Herts 60 C3
Albury Surrey 31 H2
Albury Heath Surrey 31 H3
Alcaig Highld 212 E3
Alcaston Shrops 83 J6
Alcester Warwks 71 K3
Alciston E Susx............20 B5
Alcombe Somset..........24 F3
Alconbury Cambs.........89 H7
Alconbury Weston
  Cambs 89 H7
Aldborough N York......132 F6
Aldborough Norfk 106 E5
Aldbourne Wilts............40 E5
Aldbrough E R Yk 127 G3
Aldbrough St John
  N York 140 F5
Aldbury Herts 58 F5
Aldcliffe Lancs...........129 K7
Aldclune P & K............194 E4
Aldeburgh Suffk 79 K3
Aldeby Norfk 93 J5
Aldenham Herts 43 J2
Alderbury Wilts............28 D6
Alderford Norfk..........106 D8

Alderholt Dorset.............28 C8
Alderley Gloucs.............39 H3
Alderley Edge Ches E ...113 J5
Aldermans Green
   Covtry.....................86 D6
Aldermaston W Berk 41 L7
Alderminster Warwks 72 B5
Aldershot Hants..............30 E2
Alderton Gloucs.............55 M2
Alderton Nhants.............73 K5
Alderton Suffk................79 H6
Alderton Wilts.................39 J4
Aldfield N York..............132 D5
Aldford Ches W................98 B2
Aldgate Rutlnd................88 E3
Aldham Essex..................61 L3
Aldham Suffk...................78 C5
Aldingbourne W Susx 18 C5
Aldingham Cumb..........129 G5
Aldington Kent................34 E7
Aldington Worcs..............71 J5
Aldington Corner
   Kent.........................34 E7
Aldivalloch Moray.........205 H1
Aldochlay Ag & B..........174 C1
Aldreth Cambs.................90 C8
Aldridge Wsall.................85 J4
Aldringham Suffk............79 J3
Aldsworth Gloucs............56 D6
Aldunie Moray...............215 H8
Aldwark Derbys.............100 E2
Aldwark N York.............133 G6
Aldwick W Susx..............18 C6
Aldwincle Nhants............88 E6
Aldworth W Berk.............41 K4
Alexandria W Duns........174 D3
Aley Somset.....................25 J4
Alfington Devon...............12 E3
Alfold Surrey....................31 H5
Alfold Crossways
   Surrey.....................31 H4
Alford Abers..................206 B3
Alford Lincs...................118 F6
Alford Somset..................26 E5
Alford Crematorium
   Lincs.....................118 F6
Alfreton Derbys.............101 M2
Alfrick Worcs...................70 D4
Alfrick Pound Worcs.......70 D4
Alfriston E Susx...............20 B5
Algarkirk Lincs.............103 M5
Alhampton Somset..........26 F4
Alkborough N Linc.........125 K6
Alkham Kent....................35 H6
Alkmonton Derbys.........100 D5
Allaleigh Devon.................7 J5
Allanaquoich Abers.......204 D6
Allanbank N Lans...........175 L6
Allanton Border.............179 H7
Allanton N Lans.............175 L6
Allanton S Lans..............175 K7
Allaston Gloucs...............54 F6
Allbrook Hants.................29 J7
All Cannings Wilts...........40 B7
Allendale Nthumb..........149 L4
Allen End Warwks...........85 L4
Allenheads Nthumb.......149 L6
Allen's Green Herts.........60 D5
Allensmore Herefs...........69 J7
Allenton C Derb.............101 G6
Aller Devon......................24 B6
Aller Somset.....................26 B5
Allerby Cumb.................147 J4
Allercombe Devon...........12 D4
Allerford Somset.............24 D3
Allerston N York.............134 D3
Allerthorpe E R Yk.........125 J2
Allerton C Brad.............123 G4
Allerton Highld..............213 H2
Allerton Lpool...............111 L4
Allerton Bywater
   Leeds...................124 C5
Allerton Mauleverer
   N York..................132 F7
Allesley Covtry................86 C7
Allestree C Derb.............101 G5
Allexton Leics.................88 B4

Allgreave Ches E 113 L7
Allhallows Medway.........46 D4
Alligin Shuas Highld.....210 C3
Allington Dorset..............13 L4
Allington Lincs..............102 E4
Allington Wilts.................28 D4
Allington Wilts.................39 K5
Allington Wilts.................40 B7
Allithwaite Cumb...........129 J4
Alloa Clacks...................185 J8
Allonby Cumb................147 J6
Alloway S Ayrs..............163 J5
Allowenshay Somset.......26 B8
All Stretton Shrops.........83 J4
Alltchaorunn Highld......192 C6
Alltwalis Carmth..............66 B7
Alltwen Neath..................51 K5
Alltyblaca Cerdgn............66 C5
Allweston Dorset.............26 F8
Almeley Herefs................69 G4
Almington Staffs.............99 G5
Almondbank P & K.........185 M3
Almondbury Kirk...........123 H7
Almondsbury S Glos........38 E4
Alne N York....................133 G6
Alness Highld.................222 E7
Alnham Nthumb.............168 E7
Alnmouth Nthumb.........169 J7
Alnwick Nthumb.............169 J6
Alperton Gt Lon...............44 D4
Alphamstone Essex........77 K7
Alpheton Suffk................77 K4
Alphington Devon............11 L6
Alport Derbys.................114 E8
Alpraham Ches E.............98 E1
Alresford Essex................62 C4
Alrewas Staffs.................85 L1
Alsager Ches E................99 H2
Alsop en le Dale
   Derbys.................100 D2
Alston Cumb...................149 J5
Alston Devon...................13 H2
Alstone Gloucs................55 M2
Alstonefield Staffs.........100 C2
Alston Sutton Somset......26 B2
Alswear Devon.................23 L6
Altandhu Highld............224 B6
Altarnun Cnwll..................9 G8
Altass Highld.................222 L2
Altcreich Ag & B............190 D8
Altgaltraig Ag & B..........173 H4
Althorne Essex................61 L7
Althorpe N Linc.............125 K8
Altnabreac Station
   Highld..................230 E6
Altnaharra Highld..........225 M2
Alton Derbys..................115 G8
Alton Hants......................30 B4
Alton Staffs....................100 B4
Alton Barnes Wilts...........40 C7
Alton Pancras Dorset......14 D3
Alton Priors Wilts............40 C7
Alton Towers Staffs.......100 B4
Altrincham Traffd...........113 H4
Altrincham
   Crematorium
   Traffd...................113 G4
Altskeith Hotel Stirlg ...184 B6
Alva Clacks....................185 J7
Alvanley Ches W.............112 D6
Alvaston C Derb............101 H5
Alvechurch Worcs............85 J8
Alvecote Warwks.............86 B3
Alvediston Wilts..............27 L6
Alveley Shrops.................84 D6
Alverdiscott Devon.........23 H6
Alverstoke Hants.............17 H3
Alverstone IoW................17 H5
Alverthorpe Wakefd......123 L6
Alverton Notts...............102 C4
Alves Moray...................214 E3
Alvescot Oxon.................56 F6
Alveston S Glos................38 F3
Alveston Warwks..............72 B3
Alvingham Lincs............118 E4
Alvington Gloucs.............54 E7
Alwalton C Pete...............89 G4

Alwinton Nthumb..........168 D7
Alwoodley Leeds...........123 K3
Alyth P & K....................195 K6
Ambergate Derbys.........101 G3
Amberley Gloucs.............55 J7
Amberley W Susx 18 D3
Amble Nthumb...............159 G2
Amblecote Dudley...........84 F6
Ambler Thorn C Brad.....123 G5
Ambleside Cumb............137 K6
Ambleston Pembks..........49 G3
Ambrosden Oxon.............57 L4
Amcotts N Linc..............125 K7
Amersham Bucks............42 F2
Amersham Common
   Bucks.....................42 F2
Amersham Old Town
   Bucks.....................42 F2
Amersham on the
   Hill Bucks................58 F7
Amesbury Wilts................28 D3
Amhuinnsuidhe W Isls..232 d4
Amington Staffs...............86 B3
Amisfield Town D & G...155 H5
Amlwch IoA....................108 F3
Ammanford Carmth.........51 J3
Amotherby N York..........134 B5
Ampfield Hants................29 H6
Ampleforth N York.........133 J4
Ampney Crucis
   Gloucs....................56 B7
Ampney St Mary
   Gloucs....................56 C7
Ampney St Peter
   Gloucs....................56 B7
Amport Hants...................28 F3
Ampthill C Beds................74 F6
Ampton Suffk...................77 J1
Amroth Pembks................49 K6
Amulree P & K...............185 J1
Amwell Herts...................59 K5
Anaheilt Highld..............191 G4
Ancaster Lincs...............103 G4
Ancroft Nthumb.............168 E1
Ancrum Border..............167 K4
Anderby Lincs.................119 G6
Andover Hants.................29 G3
Andoversford Gloucs......56 A4
Andreas IoM...................237 d2
Anerley Gt Lon................45 G6
Anfield Lpool.................111 K3
Anfield Crematorium
   Lpool....................111 K3
Angarrack Cnwll................3 G4
Angelbank Shrops............83 L7
Angle Pembks...................48 E6
Anglesey IoA.................108 E5
Angmering W Susx..........18 E5
Angram N York...............124 D2
Ankerville Highld...........223 H6
Anlaby E R Yk................126 C5
Anmer Norfk..................105 H6
Anmore Hants..................17 J1
Annan D & G..................147 L2
Annandale Water
   Services D & G 155 J4
Annat Highld..................210 D4
Annathill N Lans.............175 J4
Anna Valley Hants...........29 G3
Annbank S Ayrs.............163 K5
Anne Hathaway's
   Cottage Warwks 71 L4
Annesley Notts...............101 J2
Annesley
   Woodhouse Notts ..101 J2
Annfield Plain Dur........150 F5
Anniesland C Glas..........174 F5
Ansdell Lancs................120 D5
Ansford Somset...............26 F5
Ansley Warwks.................86 C5
Anslow Staffs.................100 E7
Anslow Gate Staffs........100 D7
Anstey Herts....................60 C2
Anstey Leics....................87 G2
Anstruther Fife...............187 J6
Ansty W Susx...................19 J2
Ansty Warwks..................86 E6

Ansty Wilts......................27 L6
Anthorn Cumb...............147 L4
Antingham Norfk...........106 F5
An t-ob W Isls................232 d5
Anton's Gowt Lincs.......103 M3
Antony Cnwll.....................6 B5
Antrobus Ches W 112 F5
Anwick Lincs..................103 J3
Anwoth D & G................145 M4
Aperfield Gt Lon..............32 D2
Apethorpe Nhants...........88 E4
Apley Lincs....................117 J6
Apperknowle Derbys......115 G5
Apperley Gloucs...............55 K3
Appin Ag & B..................191 J6
Appleby N Linc..............126 B7
Appleby-in-
   Westmorland
   Cumb...................139 G3
Appleby Magna Leics......86 C2
Appleby Parva Leics........86 C2
Applecross Highld.........209 L5
Appledore Devon.............23 G5
Appledore Devon.............25 G8
Appledore Kent................34 C8
Appleford Oxon................41 K2
Applegarth Town
   D & G...................155 J5
Appleshaw Hants.............28 F3
Appleton Halton.............112 D4
Appleton Oxon.................57 H7
Appleton Warrtn............112 F5
Appleton-le-Moors
   N York..................133 L3
Appleton-le-Street
   N York..................134 B5
Appleton Roebuck
   N York..................124 E3
Appleton Thorn
   Warrtn.................112 F5
Appleton Wiske
   N York..................141 J6
Appletreehall Border....167 H6
Appletreewick N York...131 K7
Appley Somset.................25 G6
Appley Bridge Lancs......121 G8
Apse Heath IoW...............17 G5
Apsley End C Beds...........59 J2
Apuldram W Susx............18 A5
Arabella Highld...............223 H6
Arbirlot Angus...............196 F7
Arboll Highld..................223 J5
Arborfield Wokham..........42 C6
Arborfield Cross
   Wokham.................42 C6
Arbroath Angus..............197 G7
Arbuthnott Abers...........197 K2
Archddu Carmth..............50 F5
Archdeacon Newton
   Darltn..................141 G4
Archencarroch
   W Duns.................174 D3
Archiestown Moray.......214 F5
Arclid Green Ches E........99 H1
Ardallie Abers................217 J6
Ardanaiseig Hotel
   Ag & B.................182 F3
Ardaneaskan Highld......210 C7
Ardarroch Highld..........210 C6
Ardbeg Ag & B................160 D1
Ardbeg Ag & B................173 J5
Ardbeg Ag & B................173 K2
Ardcharnich Highld........220 F4
Ardchiavaig Ag & B.......180 E4
Ardchonnel Ag & B.........182 D5
Ardchullarie More
   Stirlg...................184 D5
Arddarroch Ag & B.........183 J7
Ardechive Highld...........201 H7
Ardeer N Ayrs.................163 H2
Ardeley Herts...................60 A3
Ardelve Highld...............210 D8
Arden Ag & B..................174 C1
Ardens Grafton
   Warwks..................71 K4
Ardentallen Ag & B........182 B3
Ardentinny Ag & B.........173 L2

Ardentraive Ag & B........173 H4
Ardeonaig Stirlg..........184 E1
Ardersier Highld..........213 J4
Ardessie Highld...........220 D4
Ardfern Ag & B...........182 A6
Ardfernal Ag & B.........171 K4
Ardgay Highld.............222 D4
Ardgour Highld............191 K4
Ardgowan Inver...........173 L4
Ardhallow Ag & B.........173 K4
Ardhasig W Isls...........232 e4
Ardheslaig Highld.........210 B3
Ardindrean Highld........220 F4
Ardingly W Susx............32 C7
Ardington Oxon............41 H3
Ardlamont Ag & B.........173 G5
Ardleigh Essex.............62 C3
Ardleigh Heath Essex.....62 C2
Ardler P & K..............195 L7
Ardley Oxon...............57 K3
Ardlui Ag & B.............183 K4
Ardlussa Ag & B...........172 B2
Ardmair Highld............220 E2
Ardmaleish Ag & B........173 J5
Ardminish Ag & B.........172 B8
Ardmolich Highld..........190 E3
Ardmore Ag & B...........174 C3
Ardmore Highld............222 F4
Ardnadam Ag & B.........173 K3
Ardnagrask Highld.........212 E4
Ardnarff Highld............210 D7
Ardnastang Highld........190 F4
Ardpatrick Ag & B.........172 C6
Ardrishaig Ag & B.........172 E2
Ardross Highld.............222 E6
Ardrossan N Ayrs..........163 G2
Ardsley East Leeds........123 K5
Ardslignish Highld.........190 B4
Ardtalla Ag & B............171 J7
Ardtoe Highld.............190 C3
Arduaine Ag & B..........182 A5
Ardullie Highld............212 E2
Ardvasar Highld...........199 K5
Ardvorlich P & K..........184 D3
Ardvourlie W Isls..........232 e3
Ardwell D & G............144 D5
Ardwick Manch............113 J3
Areley Kings Worcs.........70 E1
Arevegaig Highld..........190 D3
Arford Hants...............30 D4
Argoed Caerph.............53 J7
Argyll Forest Park
    Ag & B.................183 J6
Aribruach W Isls..........232 e3
Aridhglas Ag & B..........180 D3
Arileod Ag & B............188 F5
Arinagour Ag & B.........189 G5
Ariogan Ag & B...........182 C3
Arisaig Highld.............199 K7
Arisaig House Highld......199 L7
Arkendale N York..........132 F7
Arkesden Essex.............76 C7
Arkholme Lancs...........130 B5
Arkleton D & G............156 C4
Arkley Gt Lon..............44 E2
Arksey Donc...............115 L1
Arkwright Town
    Derbys.................115 H7
Arle Gloucs................55 L4
Arlecdon Cumb...........136 E4
Arlesey C Beds.............75 H7
Arleston Wrekin............84 B2
Arley Ches E..............112 F5
Arley Warwks..............86 C5
Arlingham Gloucs..........55 G6
Arlington Devon............23 K4
Arlington E Susx...........20 B4
Armadale Highld..........199 K5
Armadale Highld..........230 A3
Armadale W Loth.........176 C5
Armathwaite Cumb.......148 E5
Arminghall Norfk..........92 F3
Armitage Staffs.............85 J1
Armley Leeds..............123 K4
Armscote Warwks..........72 B5
Armthorpe Donc..........115 L1
Arnabost Ag & B..........188 F4

Arncliffe N York...........131 H5
Arncroach Fife............187 H6
Arndilly House
    Moray.................215 G5
Arne Dorset................15 H5
Arnesby Leics..............87 H5
Arngask P & K............186 B5
Arnisdale Highld..........200 C3
Arnish Highld.............209 J5
Arniston Mdloth...........177 K6
Arnol W Isls...............232 f1
Arnold E R Yk.............126 E3
Arnold Notts..............101 L4
Arnprior Stirlg............184 D7
Arnside Cumb.............129 K4
Aros Ag & B...............190 B7
Arrad Foot Cumb..........129 G4
Arram E R Yk.............126 C2
Arran N Ayrs..............162 B3
Arrathorne N York........132 C2
Arreton IoW...............17 G5
Arrina Highld.............210 B3
Arrington Cambs...........75 K4
Arrochar Ag & B..........183 K6
Arrow Warwks..............71 J3
Arscott Shrops.............83 J2
Artafallie Highld...........212 F4
Arthington Leeds..........123 K2
Arthingworth Nhants......87 L2
Arthrath Abers............217 H6
Arthrocie Abers...........217 J7
Arundel W Susx...........18 D4
Asby Cumb................136 E3
Ascog Ag & B.............173 J5
Ascot W & M..............42 F6
Ascott-under-
    Wychwood Oxon......56 F4
Asenby N York............132 F4
Asfordby Leics............102 B8
Asfordby Hill Leics........102 B8
Asgarby Lincs.............103 J4
Ash Kent..................35 H3
Ash Kent..................45 L6
Ash Somset................26 C7
Ash Surrey.................30 E2
Ashampstead W Berk......41 K5
Ashbocking Suffk..........78 E4
Ashbourne Derbys.........100 D3
Ashbrittle Somset..........25 G6
Ashburton Devon...........7 H2
Ashbury Devon.............10 D5
Ashbury Oxon..............40 E4
Ashby N Linc.............125 L8
Ashby by Partney
    Lincs..................118 F7
Ashby cum Fenby
    NE Lin.................118 C2
Ashby de la Launde
    Lincs..................103 H2
Ashby-de-la-Zouch
    Leics....................86 D1
Ashby Folville Leics........87 K2
Ashby Magna Leics........87 H5
Ashby Parva Leics.........87 G5
Ashby Puerorum
    Lincs..................118 D7
Ashby St Ledgers
    Nhants..................73 H2
Ashby St Mary Norfk......93 G3
Ashchurch Gloucs..........55 L2
Ashcombe Devon...........11 L8
Ashcombe N Som..........37 M7
Ashcott Somset............26 C4
Ashdon Essex..............76 E6
Ashe Hants.................29 K2
Asheldham Essex...........62 A7
Ashen Essex................77 H6
Ashendon Bucks...........58 B5
Asheridge Bucks...........58 F6
Ashfield Stirlg.............185 G6
Ashfield cum Thorpe
    Suffk....................78 E3
Ashfield Green Suffk.......92 F8
Ashford Devon..............7 G6
Ashford Devon.............23 H4
Ashford Kent...............34 D6
Ashford Surrey.............43 H6

Ashford Bowdler
    Shrops..................69 K1
Ashford Carbonell
    Shrops..................69 K1
Ashford Hill Hants.........41 K7
Ashford in the Water
    Derbys.................114 D7
Ashgill S Lans.............175 K7
Ash Green Surrey..........30 E2
Ash Green Warwks.........86 D6
Ashill Devon................12 E1
Ashill Norfk................91 K3
Ashill Somset..............25 L7
Ashingdon Essex...........46 E2
Ashington Nthumb........159 G5
Ashington Somset..........26 E6
Ashington W Susx..........18 F3
Ashkirk Border............167 G5
Ashleworth Gloucs.........55 J3
Ashleworth Quay
    Gloucs..................55 J3
Ashley Cambs..............77 G3
Ashley Ches E.............113 H5
Ashley Devon...............10 F3
Ashley Gloucs..............39 L2
Ashley Hants...............16 B4
Ashley Hants...............29 G5
Ashley Kent................35 J5
Ashley Nhants..............87 L5
Ashley Staffs...............99 H5
Ashley Wilts................39 J6
Ashley Green Bucks........58 F6
Ash Magna Shrops.........98 E4
Ashmansworth Hants......41 H8
Ashmansworthy
    Devon...................22 E7
Ash Mill Devon.............24 C6
Ashmore Dorset............27 K7
Ashmore Green
    W Berk..................41 J6
Ashorne Warwks...........72 C3
Ashover Derbys...........115 G8
Ashow Warwks.............72 C1
Ashperton Herefs..........70 B6
Ashprington Devon..........7 J4
Ash Priors Somset..........25 J5
Ashreigney Devon..........10 F3
Ash Street Suffk............78 B5
Ashtead Surrey.............44 D8
Ash Thomas Devon........12 C1
Ashton Ches W...........112 D7
Ashton Cnwll................3 G5
Ashton Devon..............11 K7
Ashton Herefs..............69 K2
Ashton Inver..............173 L3
Ashton Nhants.............73 L3
Ashton Nhants.............88 F5
Ashton Common
    Wilts....................39 K8
Ashton-in-Makerfield
    Wigan..................112 E2
Ashton Keynes Wilts........40 B2
Ashton under Hill
    Worcs....................71 H6
Ashton-under-Lyne
    Tamesd.................113 L2
Ashurst Hants..............16 D1
Ashurst Kent...............32 F5
Ashurst Lancs.............121 G8
Ashurst W Susx............19 G3
Ashurstwood W Susx......32 D5
Ash Vale Surrey............30 E2
Ashwater Devon.............9 K5
Ashwell Herts..............75 J6
Ashwell Rutlnd.............88 C2
Ashwell End Herts..........75 J6
Ashwellthorpe Norfk.......92 D4
Ashwick Somset............26 F2
Ashwicken Norfk..........105 H8
Askam in Furness
    Cumb..................128 F4
Askern Donc..............124 E7
Askerswell Dorset..........14 A4
Askett Bucks...............58 D6
Askham Cumb.............138 D3
Askham Notts.............116 C6
Askham Bryan C York.....124 E2

Askham Richard
    C York.................124 E2
Asknish Ag & B...........172 F1
Askrigg N York............131 H2
Askwith N York............123 H2
Aslackby Lincs.............103 H6
Aslacton Norfk..............92 D5
Aslockton Notts...........102 C4
Aspatria Cumb............147 K6
Aspenden Herts............60 B3
Aspley Guise C Beds........74 D7
Aspley Heath C Beds.......74 D7
Aspull Wigan..............121 J8
Asselby E R Yk.............125 H5
Assington Suffk............77 L2
Assington Green
    Suffk....................77 H4
Astbury Ches E.............99 J3
Astcote Nhants.............73 J4
Asterby Lincs..............118 C5
Asterley Shrops............83 H3
Asterton Shrops............83 H5
Asthall Oxon...............56 F5
Asthall Leigh Oxon.........56 F5
Astle Highld...............223 G4
Astley Shrops...............98 D8
Astley Warwks.............86 C5
Astley Wigan..............113 G2
Astley Worcs...............70 D2
Astley Abbots Shrops......84 C4
Astley Bridge Bolton.....121 K7
Astley Cross Worcs.........70 E1
Aston Ches E...............98 E3
Aston Ches W.............112 E5
Aston Derbys..............114 C5
Aston Flints..............111 J7
Aston Herts................59 L4
Aston Oxon................57 G7
Aston Rothm...............115 J4
Aston Shrops...............84 E5
Aston Shrops...............98 D6
Aston Staffs...............99 H4
Aston Staffs...............99 K7
Aston Wokham............42 C4
Aston Wrekin..............84 B2
Aston Abbotts Bucks.......58 D4
Aston Botterell
    Shrops..................84 B6
Aston-by-Stone
    Staffs...................99 K6
Aston Cantlow
    Warwks..................71 K3
Aston Clinton Bucks........58 E5
Aston Crews Herefs........54 F4
Aston End Herts............59 L3
Aston Fields Worcs.........71 G1
Aston Flamville Leics.......86 F5
Aston Ingham Herefs.......55 G4
Aston le Walls Nhants......72 F4
Aston Magna Gloucs........71 L7
Aston Munslow
    Shrops..................83 K6
Aston on Clun Shrops......83 H5
Aston Pigott Shrops........83 G3
Aston Rogers Shrops.......83 G3
Aston Rowant Oxon.........58 B7
Aston Somerville
    Worcs....................71 J6
Aston-sub-Edge
    Gloucs....................71 K6
Aston Tirrold Oxon.........41 K3
Aston-upon-Trent
    Derbys.................101 H6
Aston Upthorpe Oxon......41 K3
Astwick C Beds.............75 J4
Astwood M Keyn...........74 D5
Astwood Worcs.............71 G2
Astwood Bank Worcs.......71 J3
Astwood
    Crematorium
    Worcs....................70 F3
Aswarby Lincs.............103 H4
Aswardby Lincs............118 E7
Atcham Shrops.............83 K2
Athelhampton Dorset......14 E4
Athelington Suffk..........78 E1
Athelney Somset............25 M4

Athelstaneford
E Loth 178 C3
Atherington Devon..........23 J6
Atherstone Warwks 86 C4
Atherstone on Stour
Warwks.......................72 B4
Atherton Wigan 113 G2
Atlow Derbys 100 E3
Attadale Highld 210 E6
Atterby Lincs...................117 G3
Attercliffe Sheff 115 G4
Atterton Leics 86 D4
Attleborough Norfk 92 C4
Attleborough Warwks 86 D5
Attlebridge Norfk 92 D1
Attleton Green Suffk 77 G4
Atwick E R Yk.................126 F1
Atworth Wilts 39 J7
Aubourn Lincs...............116 F8
Auchbreck Moray 214 F8
Auchedly Abers 217 G7
Auchenblae Abers.........197 H1
Auchenbowie Stirlg 175 L2
Auchencairn D & G.......146 D5
Auchencairn D & G.......155 G5
Auchencairn N Ayrs......162 D4
Auchencrow Border 179 H6
Auchendinny Mdloth.....177 H6
Auchengray S Lans 176 D7
Auchenhalrig Moray 215 J3
Auchenheath S Lans.....164 F2
Auchenhessnane
D & G...........................154 E3
Auchenlochan Ag & B..173 G4
Auchenmade N Ayrs....174 C8
Auchenmalg D & G........144 F4
Auchentiber N Ayrs......174 C8
Auchindrain Ag & B......182 E6
Auchindrean Highld......221 G5
Auchininna Abers.........216 C5
Auchinleck E Ayrs.........164 B5
Auchinloch N Lans.......175 H4
Auchinstarry N Lans.....175 J3
Auchintore Highld.........191 L2
Auchiries Abers 217 K6
Auchlean Highld 203 K5
Auchlee Abers...............207 G6
Auchleven Abers 206 C1
Auchlochan S Lans 164 F3
Auchlossan Abers 206 B5
Auchlyne Stirlg 184 B2
Auchmillan E Ayrs 164 A4
Auchmithie Angus 197 G7
Auchmuirbridge Fife....186 C6
Auchnacree Angus 196 D4
Auchnagatt Abers.........217 H6
Auchnarrow Moray 204 F2
Auchnotteroch D & G...144 B3
Auchroisk Moray 215 H4
Auchterarder P & K 185 K5
Auchteraw Highld.........202 B4
Auchterblair Highld 203 L2
Auchtercairn Highld 219 J6
Auchterderran Fife........186 C7
Auchterhouse Angus ...196 B8
Auchterless Abers.........216 D6
Auchtermuchty Fife.......186 D5
Auchterneed Highld......212 D3
Auchtertool Fife.............177 H1
Auchtertyre Highld........210 C8
Auchtubh Stirlg 184 C4
Auckengill Highld 231 L3
Auckley Donc.................115 M2
Audenshaw Tamesd 113 K3
Audlem Ches E................98 F4
Audley Staffs 99 J3
Audley End Essex..........76 D6
Audley End House &
Gardens Essex.........76 D6
Aughton E R Yk.............125 G3
Aughton Lancs..............111 L1
Aughton Lancs..............129 L6
Aughton Rothm 115 J4
Aughton Wilts 28 E1
Aughton Park Lancs 112 B1
Auldearn Highld 213 L4
Aulden Herefs.................69 J4

Auldgirth D & G 154 F5
Auldhouse S Lans 175 H7
Ault a' chruinn Highld..200 E2
Aultbea Highld...............219 K4
Aultgrishin Highld.........219 H4
Aultguish Inn Highld.....221 J7
Ault Hucknall Derbys....115 J7
Aultmore Moray.............215 J4
Aultnagoire Highld........202 E2
Aultnamain Inn
Highld.........................222 F5
Aunsby Lincs..................103 H5
Aust S Glos.......................38 E3
Austendike Donc............116 A3
Austrey Warwks...............86 C3
Austwick N York.............130 E5
Authorpe Lincs...............118 E5
Avebury Wilts...................40 C6
Aveley Thurr.....................45 L4
Avening Gloucs...............39 K2
Averham Notts...............102 C2
Aveton Gifford Devon......7 G6
Aviemore Highld............203 L3
Avington W Berk..............41 G6
Avoch Highld..................213 G4
Avon Hants.......................15 L3
Avonbridge Falk............176 B4
Avon Dassett Warwks....72 E4
Avonmouth Bristl.............38 D5
Avonwick Devon................7 G4
Awbridge Hants...............28 F6
Awliscombe Devon..........12 E3
Awre Gloucs.....................55 G6
Awsworth Notts.............101 J4
Axbridge Somset............26 B1
Axford Hants.....................29 L3
Axford Wilts......................40 E6
Axminster Devon............13 H3
Axmouth Devon...............13 G4
Aycliffe Dur....................141 G3
Aydon Nthumb...............150 C2
Aylburton Gloucs............54 E7
Aylesbeare Devon...........12 D4
Aylesbury Bucks.............58 D5
Aylesby NE Lin...............126 F8
Aylesford Kent.................33 J2
Aylesham Kent................35 H4
Aylestone C Leic.............87 H4
Aylmerton Norfk............106 E5
Aylsham Norfk................106 E6
Aylton Herefs...................70 B6
Aylworth Gloucs..............56 C4
Aymestrey Herefs...........69 H2
Aynho Nhants...................57 K2
Ayot St Lawrence
Herts...........................59 K5
Ayr S Ayrs.......................163 J5
Aysgarth N York.............131 J2
Ayshford Devon...............25 G7
Ayside Cumb..................129 J3
Ayston Rutlnd...................88 C4
Ayton Border...................179 J6
Azerley N York................132 C5

Babbacombe Torbay 7 L3
Babbs Green Herts..........60 C5
Babcary Somset...............26 E5
Babraham Cambs............76 D4
Babworth Notts...............116 B5
Backaland Ork.................234 d4
Backfolds Abers..............217 J4
Backford Ches W............111 L6
Backies Highld................223 H2
Back of Keppoch
Highld.........................199 K7
Backwell N Som................38 C6
Baconsthorpe Norfk......106 D5
Bacton Herefs...................54 A2
Bacton Norfk..................107 H5
Bacton Suffk.....................78 C2
Bacup Lancs...................122 C6
Badachro Highld............219 J6
Badbury Swindn..............40 D4

Badby Nhants...................73 H3
Badcall Highld................228 B7
Badcall Highld................228 C4
Badcaul Highld...............220 D3
Baddesley Clinton
Warwks.........................86 B8
Baddesley Ensor
Warwks.........................86 C4
Baddidarrach Highld.....224 D4
Baddinsgill Border.........176 F7
Badenscoth Abers.........216 D6
Badenyon Abers.............205 H2
Badger Shrops..................84 D4
Badgeworth Gloucs........55 K4
Badgworth Somset..........26 B2
Badicaul Highld..............210 B8
Badingham Suffk.............79 G2
Badlesmere Kent.............34 D4
Badlieu Border................165 K5
Badlipster Highld...........231 J5
Badluachrach Highld.....220 C3
Badninish Highld...........223 G3
Badrallach Highld...........220 D3
Badsey Worcs...................71 J5
Badshot Lea Surrey.........30 E2
Badsworth Wakefd.........124 C7
Badwell Ash Suffk..........78 B2
Bagber Dorset...................27 H8
Bagby N York...................133 G4
Bag Enderby Lincs.........118 E6
Bagendon Gloucs............56 A6
Bagh a Chaisteil
W Isls...........................233 b9
Bagh a Tuath W Isls......233 b9
Bagillt Flints...................111 H6
Baginton Warwks............86 D8
Baglan Neath....................51 L6
Bagley Shrops..................98 B6
Bagley Somset.................26 C3
Bagnall Staffs...................99 L3
Bagot Shrops....................83 L8
Bagshot Surrey.................42 E7
Bagstone S Glos...............39 G3
Bagworth Leics................86 F2
Bagwy Llydiart
Herefs..........................54 C3
Baildon C Brad...............123 H3
Baildon Green C Brad...123 H3
Baile Ailein W Isls.........232 f3
Baile a Mhanaich
W Isls...........................233 b6
Baile Mor Ag & B...........180 D3
Baillieston C Glas...........175 J5
Bainbridge N York.........131 H2
Bainshole Abers.............216 B7
Bainton C Pete.................89 G3
Bainton E R Yk...............126 B1
Baintown Fife.................186 F6
Bairnkine Border............167 K6
Bakewell Derbys............114 E7
Bala Gwynd.......................96 E5
Balallan W Isls...............232 f3
Balbeg Highld.................212 C7
Balbeggie P & K.............186 C2
Balblair Highld...............212 D5
Balblair Highld...............213 G2
Balby Donc.....................115 K2
Balcary D & G.................146 E5
Balchraggan Highld.......212 E5
Balchreick Highld...........228 B4
Balcombe W Susx............32 B6
Balcomie Links Fife......187 K5
Baldersby N York...........132 E4
Baldersby St James
N York.........................132 E4
Balderstone Lancs.........121 J4
Balderton Notts.............102 D3
Baldinnie Fife.................187 G5
Baldinnies P & K...........185 L4
Baldock Herts...................75 J7
Baldock Services
Herts............................75 J6
Baldovie C Dund............187 G2
Baldrine IoM..................237 d5
Baldslow E Susx..............20 F3
Bale Norfk.......................106 B5
Baledgarno P & K..........186 D2

Balemartine Ag & B.......188 C7
Balerno C Edin...............177 G5
Balfarg Fife.....................186 D6
Balfield Angus................196 E3
Balfour Ork....................234 c5
Balfron Stirlg..................174 F1
Balgaveny Abers............216 C6
Balgonar Fife.................185 L8
Balgowan D & G............144 D6
Balgowan Highld...........202 F6
Balgown Highld.............218 B7
Balgracie D & G.............144 B3
Balgray S Lans...............165 H5
Balham Gt Lon.................44 F5
Balhary P & K.................195 L6
Balholmie P & K............186 B1
Baligill Highld................230 C3
Balintore Angus.............195 L5
Balintore Highld............223 J6
Balintraid Highld...........223 G7
Balivanich W Isls...........233 b6
Balkeerie Angus............196 B7
Balkholme E R Yk..........125 J5
Ballachulish Highld.......191 L5
Ballajora IoM.................237 e4
Ballanlay Ag & B............173 H6
Ballantrae S Ayrs..........152 C5
Ballasalla IoM................237 b6
Ballater Abers................205 J6
Ballaugh IoM..................237 c3
Ballchraggan Highld......223 G6
Ballencrieff E Loth.........178 B3
Ballevullin Ag & B..........188 B6
Ballidon Derbys.............100 D2
Balliekine N Ayrs...........161 L2
Balliemore Ag & B.........182 F7
Balligmorrie S Ayrs.......152 F4
Ballimore Stirlg.............184 C4
Ballindalloch Moray.......214 E6
Ballindean P & K............186 D2
Ballinger Common
Bucks...........................58 E7
Ballingham Herefs..........54 E2
Ballingry Fife.................186 C7
Ballinluig P & K.............194 F6
Ballinshoe Angus...........196 C5
Ballintuim P & K............195 H5
Balloch Highld...............213 H5
Balloch N Lans...............175 K4
Balloch P & K.................185 H4
Balloch S Ayrs...............153 G3
Balloch W Duns.............174 D3
Balls Cross W Susx........31 G6
Balls Green E Susx.........32 E6
Ballygown Ag & B..........189 K7
Ballygrant Ag & B..........171 G5
Ballyhaugh Ag & B.........188 F5
Balmacellan D & G.........154 B6
Balmae D & G.................146 C6
Balmaha Stirlg...............174 D1
Balmalcolm Fife............186 E5
Balmangan D & G..........146 B5
Balmedie Abers..............207 H2
Balmerino Fife...............186 F3
Balmichael N Ayrs.........162 B3
Balmoral Castle
Grounds Abers.........205 G6
Balmore E Duns.............175 G4
Balmuchy Highld...........223 J5
Balmule Fife...................177 G2
Balmullo Fife.................187 G4
Balnacoil Lodge
Highld.........................226 E6
Balnacra Highld.............210 F5
Balnacroft Abers............205 G6
Balnafoich Highld..........213 G7
Balnaguard P & K..........194 E6
Balnahard Ag & B..........180 F1
Balnahard Ag & B..........180 F7
Balnain Highld...............212 C7
Balnakeil Highld............228 F2
Balne N York..................124 F6
Balquharn P & K............185 L1
Balquhidder Stirlg.........184 C3
Balsall Common Solhll...86 B7
Balsall Heath Birm.........85 J6
Balscote Oxon..................72 E6

Balsham Cambs..............76 E4
Baltasound Shet 235 e1
Baltersan D & G............145 J3
Baltonsborough
  Somset.....................26 D4
Balvicar Ag & B..........181 M4
Balvraid Highld..........200 C3
Balvraid Highld..........213 K7
Bamber Bridge Lancs...121 H5
Bamber's Green
  Essex......................60 F4
Bamburgh Nthumb......169 H3
Bamburgh Castle
  Nthumb...................169 H3
Bamford Derbys..........114 E5
Bampton Cumb...........138 D4
Bampton Devon............24 E6
Bampton Oxon.............56 F7
Bampton Grange
  Cumb......................138 D4
Banavie Highld...........191 L2
Banbury Oxon..............72 F6
Banbury
  Crematorium
  Oxon.......................72 F6
Bancffosfelen
  Carmth.....................50 F3
Banchory Abers..........206 D6
Banchory-Devenick
  Abers......................207 G5
Bancycapel Carmth......50 E3
Bancyfelin Carmth.......50 D2
Bandirran P & K..........186 C2
Banff Abers................216 D2
Bangor Gwynd............109 H6
Bangor Crematorium
  Gwynd....................109 H6
Bangor-is-y-coed
  Wrexhm....................98 B4
Bangors Cnwll...............9 G5
Banham Norfk.............92 C6
Bank Hants..................16 C2
Bankend D & G...........147 H2
Bankfoot P & K...........185 M1
Bankglen E Ayrs.........164 C6
Bankhead C Aber........207 G4
Bankhead S Lans........165 J1
Banknock Falk............175 K3
Banks Lancs...............120 E6
Bankshill D & G..........155 L5
Banningham Norfk......106 F6
Bannister Green
  Essex......................61 H4
Bannockburn Stirlg 175 L1
Banstead Surrey..........44 E7
Bantham Devon.............6 F6
Banton N Lans...........175 K3
Banwell N Som............38 B8
Bapchild Kent..............34 C3
Bapton Wilts................27 M4
Barabhas W Isls.........232 f1
Barassie S Ayrs..........163 J3
Barbaraville Highld.....223 G6
Barbieston S Ayrs.......163 K5
Barbon Cumb.............130 C3
Barbrook Devon..........23 L2
Barby Nhants...............73 G1
Barcaldine Ag & B......191 J7
Barcombe E Susx.........19 L3
Barcombe Cross
  E Susx.....................19 L3
Barden Park Kent.........33 G4
Bardfield End Green
  Essex......................61 G2
Bardfield Saling Essex...61 G3
Bardney Lincs............117 J7
Bardon Leics...............86 F2
Bardon Mill Nthumb...149 K3
Bardowie E Duns.......175 G4
Bardrainney Inver......174 C4
Bardsea Cumb............129 G5
Bardsey Leeds...........124 B2
Bardsey Island Gwynd...94 B7
Bardwell Suffk............91 L8
Bare Lancs................129 K6
Barfad D & G.............145 G2
Barford Norfk.............92 D3

Barford Warwks...........72 C3
Barford St John Oxon...57 H2
Barford St Martin
  Wilts.......................28 B5
Barford St Michael
  Oxon.......................57 H2
Barfrestone Kent..........35 H5
Bargeddie N Lans......175 J5
Bargoed Caerph..........53 J7
Bargrennan D & G.....153 H6
Barham Cambs............89 G7
Barham Kent...............35 G5
Barham Suffk..............78 D4
Barham
  Crematorium
  Kent........................35 G5
Bar Hill Cambs............75 L2
Barholm Lincs.............88 F2
Barkby Leics...............87 J2
Barkby Thorpe Leics...87 J2
Barkestone-le-Vale
  Leics......................102 C5
Barkham Wokham........42 C6
Barking Gt Lon............45 H3
Barking Suffk...............78 C4
Barkingside Gt Lon......45 H3
Barking Tye Suffk........78 C4
Barkisland Calder.......122 F6
Barkla Shop Cnwll.........3 J2
Barkston Lincs...........102 F4
Barkston Ash N York...124 D4
Barkway Herts............75 L7
Barlanark C Glas........175 H5
Barlaston Staffs...........99 K5
Barlavington W Susx....18 C3
Barlborough Derbys...115 J6
Barlby N York............124 F4
Barlestone Leics..........86 E3
Barley Herts................76 B6
Barley Lancs.............122 B3
Barleythorpe Rutlnd....88 B2
Barling Essex..............46 F3
Barlings Lincs............117 H6
Barlochan D & G........146 E4
Barlow Derbys...........115 G6
Barlow Gatesd...........150 E3
Barlow N York...........124 F5
Barmby Moor E R Yk...125 J2
Barmby on the
  Marsh E R Yk.........125 G5
Barmollack Ag & B......161 K1
Barmouth Gwynd.........80 E1
Barmpton Darltn.......141 H4
Barmston E R Yk........135 J7
Barnacarry Ag & B......182 E8
Barnack C Pete............88 F3
Barnard Castle Dur...140 D4
Barnard Gate Oxon......57 H6
Barnardiston Suffk......77 G5
Barnbarroch D & G.....146 E4
Barnburgh Donc........115 J2
Barnby Suffk...............93 K5
Barnby Dun Donc......124 F8
Barnby in the
  Willows Notts........102 E3
Barnby Moor Notts....116 A5
Barncorkrie D & G.....144 D7
Barnes Gt Lon.............44 E5
Barnes Street Kent......33 H4
Barnet Gt Lon..............44 E2
Barnetby le Wold
  N Linc....................126 C8
Barney Norfk.............106 B6
Barnham Suffk............91 K7
Barnham W Susx.........18 C5
Barnham Broom
  Norfk......................92 C3
Barnhead Angus.......197 G5
Barnhill C Dund..........187 H2
Barnhill Moray...........214 E3
Barnhills D & G..........152 B7
Barningham Dur........140 D5
Barningham Suffk.......91 L7
Barnoldby le Beck
  NE Lin....................118 C2
Barnoldswick Lancs...122 C2
Barns Green W Susx....31 J6

Barnsley Barns..........115 G1
Barnsley Gloucs..........56 B6
Barnsley
  Crematorium
  Barns.....................115 G1
Barnstaple Devon........23 J5
Barnston Essex............61 G4
Barnston Wirral..........111 J5
Barnstone Notts.........102 B5
Barnt Green Worcs......85 H8
Barnton C Edin...........177 G4
Barnton Ches W.........112 F6
Barnwell All Saints
  Nhants.....................88 F6
Barnwell St Andrew
  Nhants.....................88 F6
Barnwood Gloucs.......55 K4
Barr S Ayrs................153 G4
Barra W Isls..............233 b9
Barra Airport W Isls...233 b9
Barrachan D & G........145 J3
Barraigh W Isls..........233 b9
Barrapoll Ag & B........188 B7
Barrasford Nthumb....158 A4
Barrhead E Rens........174 F6
Barrhill S Ayrs...........152 F5
Barrington Cambs........76 B5
Barrington Somset.......26 B7
Barripper Cnwll............3 H4
Barrmill N Ayrs...........174 C7
Barrock Highld...........231 J2
Barrow Gloucs...........55 K3
Barrow Lancs.............121 L3
Barrow Rutlnd.............88 C1
Barrow Somset...........27 G5
Barrow Suffk..............77 H2
Barrowby Lincs.........102 E5
Barrowden Rutlnd.......88 D4
Barrowford Lancs......122 C3
Barrow Gurney
  N Som.....................38 D6
Barrow Haven
  N Linc....................126 D6
Barrow-in-Furness
  Cumb....................128 E5
Barrow Island Cumb...128 E5
Barrow-upon-
  Humber N Linc.......126 D6
Barrow upon Soar
  Leics......................101 L8
Barrow upon Trent
  Derbys...................101 G6
Barry Angus..............187 J1
Barry V Glam.............37 H6
Barry Island V Glam....37 H6
Barsby Leics..............87 K2
Barsham Suffk............93 H5
Barston Solhll.............86 B7
Bartestree Herefs.......69 L6
Barthol Chapel Abers...216 F7
Bartholomew Green
  Essex......................61 H4
Barthomley Ches E.....99 H3
Bartley Hants..............28 F8
Bartley Green Birm.....85 H6
Bartlow Cambs...........76 E5
Barton Cambs.............76 B4
Barton Ches W...........98 C2
Barton Gloucs............56 C3
Barton Lancs............120 E8
Barton Lancs............121 G3
Barton N York...........141 G5
Barton Oxon..............57 K6
Barton Torbay..............7 K3
Barton Bendish Norfk...91 G3
Barton End Gloucs......39 J2
Barton Hartshorn
  Bucks......................57 M2
Barton in Fabis Notts...101 K6
Barton in the Beans
  Leics......................86 E3
Barton-le-Clay C Beds...59 H2
Barton-le-Street
  N York...................133 L5
Barton-le-Willows
  N York...................133 L6
Barton Mills Suffk.......91 G8

Barton-on-Sea Hants......16 B4
Barton-on-the-Heath
  Warwks...................56 E2
Barton St David
  Somset.....................26 D5
Barton Seagrave
  Nhants.....................88 C7
Barton Stacey Hants...29 H3
Barton Town Devon.....23 L4
Barton Turf Norfk......107 H7
Barton-under-
  Needwood Staffs....100 D8
Barton-upon-Humber
  N Linc....................126 C6
Barton Waterside
  N Linc....................126 C6
Barvas W Isls............232 f1
Barway Cambs............90 D7
Barwell Leics..............86 F4
Barwick Devon............10 E4
Barwick Somset..........26 E8
Barwick in Elmet
  Leeds....................124 B3
Baschurch Shrops......98 B7
Bascote Warwks.........72 E2
Bashall Eaves Lancs...121 K2
Basildon Essex...........46 B3
Basildon & District
  Crematorium
  Essex......................46 C3
Basingstoke Hants.....29 M2
Basingstoke
  Crematorium
  Hants.......................29 K3
Baslow Derbys..........114 E6
Bason Bridge Somset...25 M3
Bassaleg Newpt.........37 L3
Bassendean Border...167 K1
Bassenthwaite Cumb...137 H2
Bassett C Sotn...........29 H7
Bassingbourn Cambs...75 K5
Bassingham Lincs.....102 E3
Bassingthorpe Lincs...102 F6
Bassus Green Herts.....60 A3
Baston Lincs...............89 G2
Bastwick Norfk.........107 J8
Batchworth Herts.......43 H2
Batcombe Dorset........14 C2
Batcombe Somset.......27 G4
Batford Herts..............59 J5
Bath BaNES...............39 H7
Bathampton BaNES....39 H7
Bathealton Somset......25 G6
Batheaston BaNES.....39 H6
Bathford BaNES.........39 H6
Bathgate W Loth........176 D5
Bathley Notts............102 C2
Bathpool Cnwll............5 L2
Bathpool Somset........25 K6
Bath Side Essex.........62 F2
Bathville W Loth........176 C5
Bathway Somset.........26 E2
Batley Kirk................123 J5
Batsford Gloucs..........71 J7
Battersby N York.......142 D5
Battersea Gt Lon........44 F5
Battisford Tye Suffk....78 B4
Battle E Susx.............20 F3
Battle Powys...............52 F2
Battledykes Angus....196 D5
Battle of Britain
  Memorial Flight
  Visitor Centre
  Lincs.....................103 L2
Battlesbridge Essex....46 C2
Battleton Somset.........24 E6
Baughton Worcs.........70 F6
Baughurst Hants.........41 L7
Baulds Abers............206 B6
Baulking Oxon............40 F3
Baumber Lincs..........117 L6
Baunton Gloucs..........56 A6
Baverstock Wilts.........28 B5
Bawburgh Norfk.........92 D2
Bawdeswell Norfk.....106 C7
Bawdrip Somset.........25 M4
Bawdsey Suffk............79 H6

Bawtry Donc................115 M3
Baxenden Lancs..........122 B5
Baxterley Warwks.........86 C4
Bay Highld.................208 D4
Bayble W Isls..............232 g2
Baybridge Hants..........29 K6
Baycliff Cumb.............129 G5
Baydon Wilts................40 F5
Bayford Herts...............60 A6
Bayford Somset............27 G5
Bayhead W Isls...........233 b6
Baylham Suffk...............78 D4
Baysham Herefs...........54 E3
Bayston Hill Shrops......83 J2
Baythorne End Essex....77 G6
Bayton Worcs...............84 C8
Bayworth Oxon.............57 J7
Beachampton Bucks......73 L6
Beachamwell Norfk.......91 H3
Beachy Head E Susx....20 C6
Beacon Devon...............12 F2
Beacon End Essex........62 A3
Beacon Hill Surrey.......30 E4
Beacon's Bottom
    Bucks......................42 C2
Beaconsfield Bucks......42 F3
Beaconsfield
    Services Bucks........42 F3
Beadlam N York..........133 K3
Beadlow C Beds...........75 G6
Beadnell Nthumb.........169 J4
Beaford Devon..............10 E2
Beal N York................124 E5
Beal Nthumb...............169 G2
Bealsmill Cnwll...............6 A1
Beaminster Dorset.........13 L3
Beamish Dur...............150 F4
Beamsley N York.........131 K8
Beanacre Wilts.............39 K7
Beanley Nthumb.........169 G5
Beardon Devon.............10 D7
Beare Green Surrey......31 K4
Bearley Warwks...........71 L3
Bearpark Dur..............151 G6
Bearsden E Duns.........174 F4
Bearsted Kent..............33 K3
Bearstone Shrops........99 G5
Bearwood Birm.............85 H6
Bearwood Herefs.........69 H4
Bearwood Poole...........15 K3
Beattock D & G...........155 J2
Beauchamp Roding
    Essex.....................60 F6
Beaufort Blae G............53 J5
Beaulieu Hants.............16 E3
Beauly Highld.............212 D5
Beaumaris IoA.............109 H6
Beaumont Cumb.........148 C3
Beaumont Essex...........62 E3
Beaumont Jersey........236 C7
Beausale Warwks.........72 B1
Beauworth Hants.........29 L6
Beazley End Essex.......61 H3
Bebington Wirral........111 K5
Beccles Suffk...............93 J5
Becconsall Lancs........120 F6
Beckbury Shrops..........84 D3
Beckenham Gt Lon......45 G6
Beckenham
    Crematorium
    Gt Lon....................45 G6
Beckermet Cumb........136 E6
Beckfoot Cumb...........147 J5
Beckford Worcs............71 H7
Beckhampton Wilts......40 C6
Beckingham Lincs......102 E2
Beckingham Notts......116 C4
Beckington Somset.......27 J2
Beckjay Shrops............83 H7
Beckley E Susx............21 G2
Beckley Oxon...............57 K5
Beck Row Suffk............91 G7
Beck Side Cumb.........128 F3
Beckwithshaw N York..132 D8
Becontree Gt Lon........45 J3

Bedale N York............132 D2
Bedchester Dorset........27 J7
Beddau Rhondd...........37 G4
Beddgelert Gwynd........95 K3
Beddingham E Susx.....19 L4
Beddington Gt Lon......44 F6
Beddington Corner
    Gt Lon....................44 F6
Bedfield Suffk...............78 F2
Bedford Bed................74 F5
Bedford
    Crematorium Bed....75 G4
Bedhampton Hants.......17 K2
Bedingfield Suffk..........78 E2
Bedlam N York............132 D7
Bedlington Nthumb.....159 G5
Bedlinog Myr Td...........53 H7
Bedminster Bristl.........38 E6
Bedminster Down
    Bristl.....................38 E6
Bedmond Herts............59 J7
Bednall Staffs...............99 L8
Bedrule Border...........167 J5
Bedstone Shrops..........83 G7
Bedwas Caerph...........37 J3
Bedwellty Caerph........53 J7
Bedworth Warwks........86 D6
Beeby Leics.................87 J2
Beech Hants.................30 B4
Beech Staffs.................99 J5
Beech Hill W Berk........42 B7
Beechingstoke Wilts.....40 C8
Beedon W Berk............41 J5
Beeford E R Yk...........135 H8
Beeley Derbys.............114 E7
Beelsby NE Lin...........117 K2
Beenham W Berk.........41 L6
Beer Devon..................13 G5
Beer Somset.................26 B5
Beercrocombe
    Somset...................25 L7
Beer Hackett Dorset.....14 B1
Beesands Devon.............7 J7
Beesby Lincs...............118 F5
Beeson Devon................7 J7
Beeston C Beds...........75 H5
Beeston Ches W...........98 D2
Beeston Leeds............123 K4
Beeston Norfk..............91 K1
Beeston Notts.............101 K5
Beeston Regis Norfk...106 E4
Beeswing D & G..........146 F2
Beetham Cumb...........129 K4
Beetham Somset..........25 L8
Beetley Norfk..............106 A8
Begbroke Oxon............57 J5
Begelly Pembks............49 J6
Beguildy Powys............82 D7
Beighton Norfk............93 H2
Beighton Sheff...........115 H5
Beinn Na Faoghla
    W Isls....................233 c7
Beith N Ayrs...............174 C7
Bekesbourne Kent........35 G4
Belaugh Norfk............107 G8
Belbroughton Worcs.....85 G7
Belchalwell Dorset.......14 E1
Belchamp Otten
    Essex.....................77 J6
Belchamp St Paul
    Essex.....................77 H6
Belchamp Walter
    Essex.....................77 J6
Belchford Lincs..........118 D6
Belford Nthumb.........169 G3
Belgrave C Leic............87 H3
Belhaven E Loth.........178 E3
Belhelvie Abers..........207 H2
Belhinnie Abers..........215 K8
Bellabeg Abers...........205 H3
Bellanoch Ag & B.......182 A8
Bellaty Angus............195 K4
Bell Busk N York.........131 G7
Belleau Lincs..............118 E5
Bell End Worcs.............85 G7
Bellerby N York...........131 L2
Belle Vue Cumb..........148 C4

Belle Vue Wakefd.......123 L6
Bellfield S Lans...........164 F3
Bellfield S Lans...........165 J5
Bellingdon Bucks.........58 F6
Bellingham Nthumb....157 L5
Belloch Ag & B...........161 H2
Bellochantuy Ag & B....161 H3
Bell o' th' Hill Ches W...98 D4
Bellshill N Lans...........175 J6
Bellside N Lans...........175 L6
Bellsquarry W Loth.....176 E5
Bells Yew Green
    E Susx....................33 G6
Belluton BaNES............38 E7
Belmaduthy Highld.....213 G3
Belmont Bl w D...........121 K7
Belmont Gt Lon............44 E7
Belmont S Ayrs...........163 J5
Belmont Shet..............235 d2
Belnacraig Abers........205 J3
Belper Derbys.............101 G3
Belsay Nthumb...........158 D6
Belses Border.............167 J4
Belsford Devon..............7 H4
Belsize Herts................59 G7
Belstead Suffk..............78 D6
Belstone Devon............10 F6
Belthorn Lancs...........121 L5
Beltinge Kent...............47 K6
Beltingham Nthumb....149 K3
Beltoft N Linc.............116 D1
Belton Leics...............101 H7
Belton Lincs...............102 F4
Belton Lincs...............116 C1
Belton Norfk................93 K3
Belton Rutlnd...............88 B3
Belvedere Gt Lon.........45 J4
Belvoir Leics..............102 D5
Belvoir Castle Leics...102 D5
Bembridge IoW............17 J5
Bemerton Wilts............28 C5
Bempton E R Yk.........135 J5
Benacre Suffk...............93 K6
Benbecula W Isls.......233 c7
Benbecula Airport
    W Isls....................233 c6
Benbuie D & G...........154 C3
Benderloch Ag & B.....191 H8
Benenden Kent.............33 K6
Benfieldside Dur.........150 D4
Bengeo Herts...............60 A5
Bengeworth Worcs.......71 J5
Benhall Green Suffk.....79 H3
Benhall Street Suffk.....79 H3
Benholm Abers...........197 K3
Beningbrough N York..133 H7
Benington Herts...........59 M4
Benington Lincs..........104 C3
Benllech IoA...............109 G5
Benmore Ag & B.........173 K2
Bennan N Ayrs...........162 C5
Ben Nevis Highld.......192 B3
Benniworth Lincs........117 K5
Benover Kent...............33 J4
Ben Rhydding C Brad..123 H2
Benslie N Ayrs............163 J2
Benson Oxon................41 L3
Benthoul C Aber.........206 F5
Bentley Donc..............115 K1
Bentley E R Yk...........126 C4
Bentley Hants..............30 C3
Bentley Suffk...............78 D6
Bentley Warwks...........86 C4
Bentley
    Crematorium
    Essex.....................45 L2
Bentpath D & G..........156 B4
Bentwichen Devon........24 B5
Bentworth Hants..........30 A4
Benvie Angus.............186 E2
Benville Dorset.............14 A2
Benwick Cambs...........89 L5
Beoley Worcs...............71 J1
Beoraidbeg Highld.....199 L6
Bepton W Susx............18 B3
Berden Essex...............60 D3
Berea Pembks..............48 D2

Bere Alston Devon.........6 C3
Bere Ferrers Devon........6 C3
Bere Regis Dorset........14 F4
Bergh Apton Norfk.......93 G4
Berinsfield Oxon..........41 L2
Berkeley Gloucs..........55 G7
Berkhamsted Herts.......59 G6
Berkley Somset............27 J2
Berkswell Solihll..........86 B7
Bermondsey Gt Lon.....45 G4
Bernera Highld...........200 C2
Bernisdale Highld.......208 F4
Berrick Prior Oxon.......41 L2
Berrick Salome Oxon....41 L2
Berriedale Highld.......227 K4
Berrier Cumb.............137 L2
Berriew Powys.............82 D4
Berrington Shrops........83 K3
Berrington Worcs.........69 L2
Berrington Green
    Worcs....................69 L2
Berrow Somset.............25 L2
Berrow Green Worcs.....70 D3
Berryhillock Moray.....215 L3
Berryhillock Moray.....215 L4
Berrynarbor Devon.......23 J3
Berry Pomeroy
    Devon......................7 J4
Bersham Wrexhm.........97 L3
Berwick E Susx............20 B5
Berwick Bassett Wilts...40 C5
Berwick Hill Nthumb...158 F6
Berwick St James
    Wilts.....................28 B4
Berwick St John Wilts...27 L6
Berwick St Leonard
    Wilts.....................27 L5
Berwick-upon-
    Tweed Nthumb......179 K7
Bescar Lancs..............120 E7
Besford Worcs..............71 G5
Bessacarr Donc..........115 L2
Bessingby E R Yk.......135 J6
Bessingham Norfk......106 E5
Besthorpe Norfk...........92 C4
Besthorpe Notts..........116 D8
Bestwood Village
    Notts....................101 K3
Beswick E R Yk...........126 C2
Betchworth Surrey.......31 K2
Bethel Gwynd.............109 G7
Bethel IoA..................108 E7
Bethersden Kent...........34 C6
Bethesda Gwynd.........109 J7
Bethesda Pembks.........49 J4
Bethlehem Carmth.......51 K1
Bethnal Green Gt Lon...45 G4
Betley Staffs.................99 H3
Betsham Kent...............45 L5
Betteshanger Kent........35 J4
Bettiscombe Dorset......13 K3
Bettisfield Wrexhm.......98 C5
Bettws Newpt...............37 L3
Bettws Bledrws
    Cerdgn...................66 D4
Bettws Cedewain
    Powys....................82 C4
Bettws Evan Cerdgn.....65 J5
Bettws-Newydd
    Mons.....................54 A6
Bettyhill Highld..........229 L3
Betws Brdgnd.............36 D3
Betws Gwerfil Goch
    Denbgs...................97 G3
Betws-y-Coed Conwy...96 C2
Betws-yn-Rhos
    Conwy...................110 C6
Beulah Cerdgn............65 J5
Beulah Powys..............67 K4
Bevercotes Notts........116 B6
Beverley E R Yk.........126 C3
Beverston Gloucs.........39 K2
Bewcastle Cumb.........156 F7
Bewdley Worcs............84 D7
Bewerley N York.........132 B6
Bewholme E R Yk.......126 E1
Bexhill E Susx.............20 E4

Bexley Gt Lon................45 J5
Bexleyheath Gt Lon......45 J5
Bexwell Norfk................90 F3
Beyton Suffk.................77 L2
Beyton Green Suffk......77 L2
Bhaltos W Isls.............232 d2
Bhatarsaigh W Isls....233 b10
Bibury Gloucs...............56 C6
Bicester Oxon..............57 L4
Bickenhill Solhll...........85 L6
Bicker Lincs...............103 L5
Bickerstaffe Lancs......112 C2
Bickerton N York.......124 C1
Bickford Staffs............84 F2
Bickington Devon...........7 J2
Bickington Devon........23 H5
Bickleigh Devon.............6 D4
Bickleigh Devon..........12 B2
Bickley Ches W............98 D3
Bickley Gt Lon............45 H6
Bickley N York...........134 E2
Bicknacre Essex..........61 J7
Bicknoller Somset........25 H4
Bicknor Kent...............33 L2
Bicton Shrops..............82 F6
Bicton Shrops..............83 J1
Bidborough Kent..........32 F5
Biddenden Kent...........33 L5
Biddenham Bed...........74 E4
Biddestone Wilts.........39 K5
Biddisham Somset.......26 B2
Biddlesden Bucks........73 J6
Biddulph Staffs............99 K2
Biddulph Moor Staffs....99 K2
Bideford Devon............23 G6
Bidford-on-Avon
   Warwks......................71 K4
Bielby E R Yk.............125 J2
Bieldside C Aber........207 G5
Bierley IoW..................17 G6
Bierton Bucks..............58 D5
Big Balcraig D & G.....145 H6
Bigbury Devon...............6 F6
Bigbury-on-Sea
   Devon.........................6 F6
Bigby Lincs................117 H1
Big Carlae D & G........154 B3
Biggar S Lans............165 K2
Biggin Derbys............100 D2
Biggin Hill Gt Lon........32 D2
Biggin Hill Airport
   Gt Lon.......................45 H7
Biggleswade C Beds....75 H5
Bigholms D & G..........156 B6
Bighouse Highld.........230 C3
Bighton Hants.............29 L4
Biglands Cumb...........148 A4
Bignor W Susx.............18 D3
Big Pit Blaenavon
   (WHS) Torfn...............53 K6
Bigrigg Cumb.............136 D5
Big Sand Highld.........219 H5
Bigton Shet...............235 c7
Bilborough C Nott......101 K4
Bilbrook Somset..........25 G3
Bilbrough N York........124 E2
Bilbster Highld...........231 K5
Bildershaw Dur.........140 F3
Bildeston Suffk...........78 B5
Billericay Essex..........46 B2
Billesdon Leics...........87 K3
Billesley Warwks.........71 K3
Billingborough Lincs..103 J5
Billinge St Hel..........112 D2
Billingford Norfk..........92 E7
Billingford Norfk........106 B7
Billingham S on T......141 K3
Billinghay Lincs.........103 J2
Billingley Barns.........115 H1
Billingshurst W Susx...31 H6
Billingsley Shrops........84 C6
Billington C Beds........58 F4
Billington Lancs.........121 L4
Billockby Norfk............93 J2
Billy Row Dur.............150 E7
Bilsborrow Lancs.......121 G3
Bilsby Lincs..............119 G6

Bilsham W Susx...........18 D5
Bilsington Kent...........34 D7
Bilsthorpe Notts........101 M1
Bilston Mdloth............177 H5
Bilston Wolves............85 G4
Bilstone Leics.............86 D3
Bilton E R Yk............126 E4
Bilton N York............124 D1
Bilton N York............132 D7
Bilton Warwks............86 F8
Binbrook Lincs...........117 K3
Bincombe Dorset.........14 D5
Binegar Somset...........26 E2
Binfield Br For............42 D6
Binfield Heath Oxon.....42 C5
Bingfield Nthumb.......158 B7
Bingham Notts...........102 B4
Bingley C Brad...........123 G3
Binham Norfk.............106 B5
Binley Covtry...............86 E7
Binley Hants................29 H2
Binley Woods Warwks...86 E7
Binnegar Dorset..........15 G5
Binniehill Falk............176 B4
Binscombe Surrey........30 F3
Binstead IoW...............17 H4
Binsted Hants..............30 C3
Binsted W Susx...........18 D4
Binton Warwks.............71 K4
Bintree Norfk.............106 B7
Birch Essex.................61 M4
Bircham Newton
   Norfk.......................105 J5
Bircham Tofts Norfk...105 J6
Birchanger Essex........60 E4
Birchanger Green
   Services Essex..........60 E4
Birch Cross Staffs......100 C6
Bircher Herefs.............69 J2
Birch Green Essex.......61 M4
Birchgrove Cardif........37 J4
Birchgrove Swans........51 K5
Birchgrove W Susx......32 D7
Birchington Kent..........35 J2
Birchley Heath
   Warwks......................86 C5
Birchover Derbys.......100 E1
Birch Services Rochdl..122 C8
Birch Vale Derbys......114 A4
Birchwood Lincs.........116 F7
Birch Wood Somset.....25 K8
Birchwood Warrtn......112 F4
Bircotes Notts...........115 M3
Birdbrook Essex..........77 G6
Birdforth N York.........133 G4
Birdham W Susx..........17 M3
Birdingbury Warwks.....72 E2
Birdlip Gloucs..............55 L5
Birdsall N York..........134 C6
Birds Edge Kirk.........123 J8
Birds Green Essex.......60 F6
Birdsgreen Shrops.......84 D6
Birdsmoorgate
   Dorset.......................13 K3
Birdwell Barns..........115 G2
Birgham Border..........168 B2
Birichin Highld..........223 G3
Birkby N York............141 H6
Birkdale Sefton..........120 D7
Birkenbog Abers........215 L2
Birkenhead Wirral......111 K4
Birkenhills Abers........216 E5
Birkenshaw Kirk........123 J5
Birkhall Abers............205 H6
Birkhill Angus...........186 F1
Birkhill D & G............166 B6
Birkin N York............124 E5
Birley Herefs...............69 J4
Birley Carr Sheff.......115 G3
Birling Kent.................46 B7
Birlingham Worcs........71 G5
Birmingham Birm........85 J6
Birmingham Airport
   Solhll........................85 L6
Birnam P & K............195 G7
Birness Abers............217 J7
Birse Abers...............206 B6

Birsemore Abers.......205 L5
Birstall Kirk..............123 J5
Birstall Leics..............87 H2
Birstwith N York........132 C7
Birtley Gatesd...........151 G4
Birtley Herefs.............69 G2
Birtley Nthumb..........157 L6
Birtley Crematorium
   Gatesd.....................151 G4
Birts Street Worcs.......70 D7
Bisbrooke Rutlnd........88 C4
Biscathorpe Lincs.....118 C5
Bisham W & M.............42 D4
Bishampton Worcs.......71 H4
Bish Mill Devon...........24 B6
Bishop Auckland Dur..140 F2
Bishopbridge Lincs....117 G4
Bishopbriggs E Duns..175 G4
Bishop Burton E R Yk..126 B3
Bishop Middleham
   Dur...........................141 H2
Bishopmill Moray.......214 D2
Bishop Monkton
   N York.....................132 E6
Bishop Norton Lincs...117 G3
Bishopsbourne Kent....35 G4
Bishops Cannings
   Wilts..........................40 B7
Bishop's Castle
   Shrops.......................83 G5
Bishop's Caundle
   Dorset.......................27 G8
Bishop's Cleeve
   Gloucs........................55 L3
Bishop's Frome
   Herefs........................70 B5
Bishop's Green Essex...61 G4
Bishops Hull Somset....25 J6
Bishop's Itchington
   Warwks......................72 E3
Bishops Lydeard
   Somset.......................25 J5
Bishop's Norton
   Gloucs........................55 J3
Bishop's Nympton
   Devon........................24 B6
Bishop's Offley Staffs..99 H6
Bishop's Stortford
   Herts..........................60 D4
Bishop's Sutton
   Hants.........................29 L5
Bishop's Tachbrook
   Warwks......................72 C3
Bishop's Tawton
   Devon........................23 J5
Bishopsteignton
   Devon..........................7 K2
Bishopstoke Hants......29 J7
Bishopston Swans.......51 H7
Bishopstone Bucks......58 D6
Bishopstone E Susx....19 M5
Bishopstone Herefs.....69 H5
Bishopstone Kent........47 K6
Bishopstone Swindn....40 E4
Bishopstone Wilts.......28 B6
Bishopstrow Wilts.......27 K3
Bishop Sutton BaNES...38 E7
Bishop's Waltham
   Hants.........................29 K7
Bishopswood Somset...25 K8
Bishop's Wood Staffs...84 E2
Bishopsworth Bristl.....38 E6
Bishop Thornton
   N York.....................132 D6
Bishopthorpe C York..124 F2
Bishopton Darltn.......141 J3
Bishopton Rens.........174 E4
Bishop Wilton E R Yk..134 C7
Bishton Newpt............38 B3
Bishton Staffs...........100 A7
Bisley Gloucs...............55 K6
Bisley Surrey...............42 F8
Bissoe Cnwll.................3 K3
Bisterne Hants............15 L3
Bitchfield Lincs.........103 G6
Bittadon Devon...........23 J3
Bittaford Devon.............6 F4

Bitterley Shrops..........83 L7
Bitterne C Sotn...........29 J8
Bitteswell Leics...........87 G6
Bitton S Glos...............39 G6
Bix Oxon.....................42 B4
Bixter Shet................235 C5
Blaby Leics..................87 H4
Blackadder Border......179 H7
Blackawton Devon.........7 J5
Blackborough Devon....12 E1
Blackborough End
   Norfk..........................90 F1
Black Bourton Oxon....56 F6
Blackboys E Susx........20 B2
Blackbrook Derbys.....101 G3
Blackbrook St Hel.....112 D3
Blackbrook Staffs........99 H5
Blackburn Abers.........206 F3
Blackburn Bl w D........121 K5
Blackburn W Loth......176 D5
Blackburn with
   Darwen Services
   Bl w D......................121 K5
Black Callerton N u Ty..150 F2
Blackcraig E Ayrs.......164 C7
Black Crofts Ag & B...182 D1
Blackdog Abers..........207 H3
Black Dog Devon.........11 J3
Blackdown Dorset.......13 K2
Blacker Hill Barns......115 G2
Blackfen Gt Lon..........45 J5
Blackfield Hants..........16 E3
Blackford P & K.........185 J3
Blackford Somset........26 B2
Blackford Somset........26 F8
Blackfordby Leics......101 G8
Blackhall C Edin.......177 G4
Blackhall Colliery Dur..151 K6
Blackhall Mill Gatesd..150 E4
Blackhaugh Border....166 F3
Blackheath Gt Lon......45 G5
Blackheath Sandw.......85 H6
Blackheath Suffk.........93 J8
Blackheath Surrey......31 G3
Blackhill Abers..........217 K3
Blackhill Abers..........217 K5
Blackhill Dur.............150 D4
Blackhill of
   Clackriach Abers....217 H5
Blackhorse Devon.......12 C4
Blacklaw D & G.........165 K4
Blackley Manch.........113 J3
Blackley
   Crematorium
   Manch......................113 J2
Blacklunans P & K.....195 J4
Blackmarstone
   Herefs........................69 K6
Blackmill Brdgnd.........36 E3
Blackmoor Hants........30 C5
Blackmoor N Som........38 C7
Blackmoorfoot Kirk....123 G7
Blackmore Essex.........60 F7
Blackmore End Essex...61 H2
Blackness Falk...........176 E3
Blacknest Hants...........30 D3
Black Notley Essex......61 J4
Blacko Lancs.............122 C3
Black Pill Swans..........51 J7
Blackpool Bpool........120 D4
Blackpool Devon...........7 J5
Blackpool Airport
   Lancs......................120 D4
Blackridge W Loth.....176 B5
Blackrod Bolton.........121 J7
Blacksboat Moray......214 E6
Blackshaw D & G.......147 J2
Blackshaw Head
   Calder.....................122 E5
Blackstone W Susx......19 H3
Black Street Suffk........93 K6
Blackthorn Oxon.........57 L4
Blackthorpe Suffk.......77 K2
Blacktoft E R Yk........125 J5
Blacktop C Aber........207 G4
Black Torrington
   Devon........................10 C4

Blackwall Derbys...........100 E3
Blackwater Cnwll...............3 J3
Blackwater Hants..........42 D7
Blackwater IoW...............17 G5
Blackwater Somset........25 K7
Blackwaterfoot
N Ayrs.......................162 A4
Blackwell Cumb............148 D4
Blackwell Derbys...........101 H2
Blackwell Derbys...........114 C6
Blackwell Warwks...........72 B5
Blackwell Worcs.............71 H1
Blackwood Caerph..........37 J2
Blackwood D & G.........154 F5
Blackwood S Lans.........164 F1
Blacon Ches W..............111 L2
Bladnoch D & G............145 J4
Bladon Oxon...................57 J5
Blaenannerch Cerdgn....65 H5
Blaenau Ffestiniog
Gwynd.........................96 A4
Blaenavon Torfn.............53 K6
Blaenffos Pembks...........65 H6
Blaengarw Brdgnd..........36 D2
Blaengwrach Neath.........52 D6
Blaengwynfi Neath..........36 D2
Blaenpennal Cerdgn......66 E2
Blaenplwyf Cerdgn.........80 D7
Blaenporth Cerdgn.........65 J5
Blaenrhondda
Rhondd......................52 E7
Blaenwaun Carmth.........50 B1
Blaen-y-Coed Carmth.....50 D1
Blaen-y-cwm Rhondd.....52 E7
Blagdon N Som..............38 D8
Blagdon Somset.............25 K7
Blagdon Torbay.................7 K4
Blagdon Hill Somset.......25 K7
Blaich Highld.................191 K2
Blain Highld..................190 D3
Blaina Blae G.................53 J6
Blair Atholl P & K.........194 D4
Blair Drummond
Stirlg.........................184 F7
Blairgowrie P & K.........195 J7
Blairhall Fife.................176 D2
Blairingone P & K..........185 K7
Blairlogie Stirlg.............185 H7
Blairmore Ag & B..........173 L2
Blairmore Highld...........228 C4
Blair's Ferry Ag & B......173 G4
Blaisdon Gloucs..............55 G5
Blakebrook Worcs...........84 E7
Blakedown Worcs...........84 F7
Blake End Essex.............61 H4
Blakemere Ches W........112 D7
Blakemere Herefs............69 G6
Blakenall Heath Wsall.....85 H3
Blakeney Gloucs..............54 F6
Blakeney Norfk.............106 B4
Blakenhall Ches E............99 G3
Blakenhall Wolves...........85 G4
Blakesley Nhants.............73 J4
Blanchland Nthumb.......150 B5
Blandford Forum
Dorset........................15 G2
Blandford St Mary
Dorset........................15 G2
Blanefield Stirlg.............174 F3
Blankney Lincs.............103 H1
Blantyre S Lans.............175 J6
Blar a' Chaorainn
Highld......................191 L3
Blargie Highld...............202 F6
Blarmachfoldach
Highld......................191 L3
Blaston Leics..................88 B4
Blatherwycke Nhants......88 D4
Blawith Cumb................129 G2
Blawquhairn D & G.......154 B5
Blaxhall Suffk.................79 H3
Blaxton Donc................116 A2
Blaydon Gatesd.............150 F3
Bleadney Somset............26 C3
Bleadon N Som..............25 M1
Blean Kent......................47 H6
Bleasby Notts...............102 B3

Blebocraigs Fife............187 G4
Bleddfa Powys................68 E2
Bledington Gloucs..........56 E4
Bledlow Bucks................58 C7
Bledlow Ridge Bucks......58 C7
Blegbie E Loth..............178 B6
Blencarn Cumb..............138 F2
Blencogo Cumb.............147 L5
Blendworth Hants...........30 B8
Blennerhasset Cumb......147 L6
Bletchingdon Oxon.........57 J4
Bletchingley Surrey.........32 B3
Bletchley M Keyn............58 E2
Bletchley Shrops.............98 F5
Bletherston Pembks........49 H4
Bletsoe Bed.....................74 E3
Blewbury Oxon...............41 K4
Blickling Norfk..............106 E6
Blidworth Notts.............101 L2
Blidworth Bottoms
Notts........................101 L2
Blindcrake Cumb...........147 K7
Blindley Heath Surrey.....32 C4
Blisland Cnwll...................5 H2
Blissford Hants................28 D8
Bliss Gate Worcs............84 D8
Blisworth Nhants.............73 K4
Blithbury Staffs.............100 B8
Blockley Gloucs...............71 L7
Blofield Norfk..................93 G2
Blofield Heath Norfk.......93 G2
Blo Norton Norfk.............92 B7
Bloomfield Border.........167 J4
Blore Staffs....................100 C3
Bloxham Oxon................72 E7
Bloxholm Lincs.............103 H2
Bloxwich Wsall...............85 H3
Bloxworth Dorset............15 G4
Blubberhouses
N York......................132 B7
Blue Anchor Somset.......24 F3
Blue Bell Hill Kent..........46 C7
Blue John Cavern
Derbys.....................114 C5
Blundellsands Sefton.....111 J2
Blundeston Suffk............93 L4
Blunham C Beds.............75 H4
Blunsdon St Andrew
Swindn........................40 C3
Bluntington Worcs..........84 F8
Bluntisham Cambs..........89 L8
Blyborough Lincs..........116 F3
Blyford Suffk...................93 J7
Blymhill Staffs.................84 E2
Blyth Notts....................115 L4
Blyth Nthumb.................159 H5
Blyth Bridge Border.......165 M1
Blythburgh Suffk.............93 J7
Blyth Crematorium
Nthumb.....................159 H5
Blythe Border................178 D7
Blyton Lincs..................116 D3
Boarhills Fife.................187 J5
Boarhunt Hants...............17 H2
Boarstall Bucks...............57 L5
Boath Highld.................222 D6
Boat of Garten Highld...203 L2
Bobbing Kent..................46 E6
Bobbington Staffs...........84 E5
Bocking Essex.................61 J4
Bocking
Churchstreet
Essex..........................61 J3
Boddam Abers...............217 L6
Boddam Shet.................235 C7
Boddington Gloucs.........55 K3
Bodedern IoA................108 D5
Bodelwyddan
Denbgs.....................110 D6
Bodenham Herefs............69 K4
Bodenham Wilts.............28 D6
Bodenham Moor
Herefs.........................69 K4
Bodewryd IoA...............108 E4
Bodfari Denbgs.............110 F7
Bodffordd IoA................108 F6
Bodfuan Gwynd..............94 F5

Bodham Norfk..............106 D4
Bodiam E Susx................33 K7
Bodiam Castle E Susx.....33 K7
Bodicote Oxon................72 F6
Bodinnick Cnwll................5 H5
Bodle Street Green
E Susx.........................20 D3
Bodmin Cnwll....................5 G3
Bodmin Moor Cnwll..........5 J1
Bodnant Garden NT
Conwy.......................109 M6
Bodsham Kent.................34 E5
Bodwen Cnwll....................5 G4
Bogallan Highld.............212 F4
Bogbrae Abers...............217 J7
Bogend S Ayrs...............163 K3
Boggs Holdings
E Loth........................177 L4
Boghall Mdloth.............177 H5
Boghall W Loth.............176 D5
Boghead S Lans.............164 F2
Bogmoor Moray............215 H2
Bogmuir Abers...............197 G3
Bogniebrae Abers..........216 B5
Bognor Regis W Susx.....18 C6
Bogroy Highld................203 L2
Bogue D & G..................154 B6
Bohortha Cnwll.................3 L5
Bohuntine Highld...........201 L8
Bolam Dur.....................140 F3
Bolberry Devon.................7 G7
Boldmere Birm................85 K5
Boldre Hants...................16 C3
Boldron Dur...................140 C4
Bole Notts.....................116 C4
Bolehill Derbys..............100 F2
Bolham Devon.................24 E7
Bolham Water Devon.......25 J8
Bolingey Cnwll..................3 K1
Bollington Ches E...........113 L6
Bolney W Susx.................31 L6
Bolnhurst Bed.................74 F3
Bolshan Angus...............197 G6
Bolsover Derbys.............115 J7
Bolsterstone Sheff..........114 F3
Boltby N York.................133 G3
Boltenstone Abers.........205 J3
Bolton Bolton................121 L8
Bolton Cumb...................138 F3
Bolton E Loth.................178 B4
Bolton E R Yk................125 J1
Bolton Nthumb...............169 G6
Bolton Abbey N York.....131 K8
Bolton by Bowland
Lancs.........................122 B1
Boltonfellend Cumb......148 E2
Boltongate Cumb..........147 M6
Bolton le Sands Lancs...129 K6
Bolton Low Houses
Cumb........................147 M6
Bolton-on-Swale
N York......................141 G7
Bolton Percy N York.....124 E3
Bolton Upon Dearne
Barns.........................115 J2
Bolventor Cnwll................5 J1
Bomere Heath Shrops.....98 C8
Bonar Bridge Highld......222 E3
Bonawe Ag & B..............182 E2
Bonby N Linc................126 C7
Boncath Pembks.............65 H6
Bonchester Bridge
Border......................167 J6
Bondleigh Devon.............10 F4
Bonds Lancs..................121 G2
Bo'ness Falk.................176 D3
Boney Hay Staffs.............85 J2
Bonhill W Duns.............174 D3
Boningale Shrops............84 E3
Bonjedward Border........167 K5
Bonkle N Lans...............175 L6
Bonnington Angus.........196 F7
Bonnington Kent.............34 E7
Bonnybank Fife..............186 F6
Bonnybridge Falk..........175 L3
Bonnykelly Abers...........217 G4
Bonnyrigg Mdloth.........177 J5

Bonnyton Angus............196 B8
Bonsall Derbys..............100 F2
Bonshaw Tower
D & G.......................155 M7
Bont-Dolgadfan
Powys..........................81 J4
Bont-goch or Elerch
Cerdgn.......................80 F6
Bontnewydd Cerdgn......66 E2
Bontnewydd Gwynd........95 H1
Bontuchel Denbgs...........97 G2
Bonvilston V Glam...........37 G5
Boode Devon...................23 H4
Booker Bucks..................42 D3
Boon Border..................167 J1
Boosbeck R & Cl...........142 E4
Boose's Green Essex......61 K2
Boot Cumb....................137 G6
Booth Calder.................122 F5
Boothby Graffoe
Lincs.........................103 G2
Boothby Pagnell
Lincs.........................102 F6
Boothferry E R Yk........125 H5
Boothstown Salfd..........113 G2
Bootle Cumb..................128 D2
Bootle Sefton................111 K3
Boraston Shrops.............70 B1
Bordeaux Guern............236 e2
Borden Kent....................34 B3
Border Forest Park......157 G5
Borders
Crematorium
Border......................167 H3
Boreham Essex................61 J6
Boreham Wilts................27 K3
Boreham Street
E Susx.........................20 D4
Borehamwood Herts......44 D2
Boreland D & G.............155 L4
Boreraig Highld.............208 C4
Borgh W Isls..................232 f1
Borgh W Isls..................233 b9
Borgie Highld................229 K4
Borgue D & G................146 B5
Borgue Highld...............227 K4
Borley Essex....................77 J6
Borneskitaig Highld.......218 B7
Borness D & G...............146 A5
Boroughbridge
N York......................132 F6
Borough Green Kent.......33 G2
Borrowash Derbys..........101 H5
Borrowby N York...........132 F2
Borrowstoun Falk..........176 D3
Borstal Medway...............46 B6
Borth Cerdgn...................80 E5
Borthwickbrae
Border......................166 F6
Borthwickshiels
Border......................166 F6
Borth-y-Gest Gwynd......95 K5
Borve Highld.................209 G5
Borve W Isls..................232 d4
Borve W Isls..................232 f1
Borve W Isls..................233 b9
Borwick Lancs...............129 L5
Bosbury Herefs...............70 C5
Boscastle Cnwll................8 E6
Boscombe Bmouth..........15 L4
Boscombe Wilts..............28 D4
Bosham W Susx...............17 L2
Bosherston Pembks.........49 G8
Bosley Ches E................113 K7
Bossall N York................133 L7
Bossiney Cnwll..................8 E6
Bossingham Kent............34 F5
Bossington Somset..........24 D2
Bostock Green
Ches W......................112 F7
Boston Lincs..................104 B4
Boston Crematorium
Lincs.........................104 A4
Boston Spa Leeds.........124 C2
Boswinger Cnwll...............4 F7
Botallack Cnwll.................2 C5
Botany Bay Gt Lon..........59 M7

Botesdale Suffk..............92 C7
Bothal Nthumb...........159 G5
Bothamsall Notts.........116 A6
Bothel Cumb...............147 L6
Bothenhampton
  Dorset 13 L4
Bothwell S Lans 175 J6
Bothwell Services
  S Lans 175 J6
Botley Bucks 59 G7
Botley Hants 29 K8
Botley Oxon 57 J6
Botolph Claydon
  Bucks 58 B3
Botolphs W Susx...........19 G4
Bottesford Leics.........102 D5
Bottesford N Linc........116 E1
Bottisham Cambs..........76 D3
Bottomcraig Fife.........186 F3
Bottoms Calder 122 D6
Botusfleming Cnwll..........6 B4
Botwnnog Gwynd 94 E6
Bough Beech Kent..........32 E4
Boughrood Powys 68 C6
Boughton Nhants 73 L2
Boughton Norfk............91 G3
Boughton Notts..........116 B7
Boughton Aluph Kent......34 D5
Boughton Green
  Kent 33 K3
Boughton
  Monchelsea Kent......33 K3
Boughton Street
  Kent 34 E3
Bouldon Shrops............83 K6
Boulmer Nthumb..........169 K6
Boultham Lincs...........116 F7
Bourn Cambs 75 K3
Bourne Lincs 103 H7
Bournebridge Essex 45 J2
Bournebrook Birm 85 J6
Bourne End Bucks..........42 E3
Bourne End C Beds........74 D5
Bourne End Herts 59 G6
Bournemouth
  Bmouth 15 K4
Bournemouth
  Airport Dorset...........15 L3
Bournemouth
  Crematorium
  Bmouth 15 L4
Bournes Green
  Sthend.......................46 E3
Bournheath Worcs..........85 G8
Bournmoor Dur 151 H5
Bournville Birm 85 J7
Bourton Dorset 27 H5
Bourton Oxon 40 E3
Bourton Shrops............83 L4
Bourton Wilts...............40 B7
Bourton on
  Dunsmore Warwks....72 E1
Bourton-on-the-Hill
  Gloucs........................56 D2
Bourton-on-the-
  Water Gloucs.............56 D4
Bousd Ag & B 189 G4
Bouth Cumb................129 H3
Bouthwaite N York.......131 L5
Boveridge Dorset..........28 B7
Bovey Tracey Devon........7 J1
Bovingdon Herts 59 G7
Bow Devon 11 G4
Bow Gt Lon 45 G4
Bow Ork......................234 b7
Bow Brickhill M Keyn.....74 C7
Bowbridge Gloucs..........55 J6
Bowburn Dur...............151 H7
Bowcombe IoW..............16 F5
Bowd Devon 12 E4
Bowden Border 167 H4
Bowden Hill Wilts 39 L6
Bowdon Traffd............113 H4
Bower Highld...............231 J3
Bowerchalke Wilts 28 A6
Bowermadden Highld...231 J3
Bowers Staffs................99 J5

Bowers Gifford Essex.....46 C3
Bowershall Fife...........176 F1
Bower's Row Leeds 124 B5
Bowes Dur 140 C4
Bowgreave Lancs.........121 G2
Bowhouse D & G 147 H2
Bowland Border 167 G2
Bowley Herefs 69 K4
Bowlhead Green
  Surrey.......................30 E4
Bowling C Brad...........123 H4
Bowling W Duns 174 E4
Bowmanstead Cumb.....137 J7
Bowmore Ag & B..........170 F6
Bowness-on-Solway
  Cumb 147 L3
Bowness-on-
  Windermere
  Cumb 137 L7
Bow of Fife Fife...........186 E5
Bowriefauld Angus......196 E6
Bowsden Nthumb........168 E2
Bow Street Cerdgn 80 E6
Box Gloucs...................55 K7
Box Wilts......................39 J6
Boxford Suffk................77 L6
Boxford W Berk 41 H6
Boxgrove W Susx 18 B4
Boxley Kent...................33 K2
Boxmoor Herts..............59 H6
Boxted Essex.................62 B2
Boxted Essex.................62 B2
Boxted Suffk.................77 J4
Boxted Cross Essex........62 B2
Boxworth Cambs............75 L2
Boyden Gate Kent..........47 L6
Boylestone Derbys.......100 D5
Boyndie Abers 216 C2
Boyndlie Abers 217 G2
Boynton E R Yk...........135 H6
Boysack Angus 197 G6
Boyton Cnwll..................9 J6
Boyton Suffk.................79 H5
Boyton Wilts.................27 L4
Boyton Cross Essex........61 G6
Boyton End Suffk..........77 G5
Bozeat Nhants 74 C3
Brabourne Kent 34 E6
Brabourne Lees
  Kent 34 E6
Brabstermire Highld....231 K2
Bracadale Highld........208 E6
Braceborough Lincs 88 F2
Bracebridge Heath
  Lincs 117 G7
Bracebridge Low
  Fields Lincs.............116 F7
Braceby Lincs..............103 G5
Bracewell Lancs..........122 C2
Brackenfield Derbys....101 G2
Brackenhirst N Lans 175 K5
Bracklesham W Susx 17 L3
Brackletter Highld......201 J8
Brackley Nhants...........73 H6
Bracknell Br For 42 E6
Braco P & K 185 H5
Bracobrae Moray 215 L4
Bracon Ash Norfk..........92 E4
Bracora Highld............199 L6
Bracorina Highld........199 L6
Bradbourne Derbys......100 D3
Bradbury Dur 141 H2
Bradden Nhants 73 J5
Bradenham Bucks..........42 D2
Bradenstoke Wilts.........39 M4
Bradfield Devon 12 D1
Bradfield Essex.............62 D2
Bradfield Norfk...........106 F5
Bradfield Sheff...........114 F3
Bradfield W Berk 41 L6
Bradfield Combust
  Suffk.........................77 K3
Bradfield Green
  Ches E.......................99 G2
Bradfield Heath Essex...62 D3
Bradfield St Clare
  Suffk.........................77 K3

Bradfield St George
  Suffk.........................77 K3
Bradford C Brad..........123 H4
Bradford Devon 9 L4
Bradford Abbas
  Dorset 26 E8
Bradford Leigh Wilts 39 J7
Bradford-on-Avon
  Wilts..........................39 J7
Bradford-on-Tone
  Somset 25 J6
Bradford Peverell
  Dorset 14 C4
Bradiford Devon 23 J5
Brading IoW..................17 H5
Bradley Derbys............100 E4
Bradley Hants 29 M3
Bradley NE Lin 118 C1
Bradley Staffs...............99 K8
Bradley Wolves.............85 G4
Bradley Worcs 71 H3
Bradley Green Worcs.....71 H3
Bradley in the Moors
  Staffs.......................100 B4
Bradley Stoke S Glos.....38 E4
Bradmore Notts...........101 L6
Bradninch Devon 12 C2
Bradnop Staffs............100 A2
Bradpole Dorset 13 L4
Bradshaw Calder 123 G4
Bradstone Devon 9 K8
Bradwall Green
  Ches E.......................113 H8
Bradwell Derbys..........114 D5
Bradwell Essex 61 J4
Bradwell M Keyn 74 B6
Bradwell Norfk.............93 K3
Bradwell
  Crematorium
  Staffs.........................99 J3
Bradwell-on-Sea
  Essex.........................62 B6
Bradwell Waterside
  Essex.........................62 B6
Bradworthy Devon...........9 J3
Brae Highld................213 G2
Brae Shet....................235 c4
Braeface Falk..............175 K3
Braehead Angus 197 H5
Braehead D & G 145 J4
Braehead S Lans 176 C7
Braemar Abers 204 E6
Braemore Highld.........221 G5
Braemore Highld.........227 J3
Brae Roy Lodge
  Highld......................201 L6
Braeside Inver 173 L4
Braes of Coul Angus....195 L5
Braes of Enzie Moray ...215 J3
Braeswick Ork 234 d4
Braevallich Ag & B 182 D6
Brafferton Darltn.........141 H3
Brafferton N York.........132 F5
Brafield-on-the-
  Green Nhants 74 B3
Bragar W Isls 232 f2
Bragbury End Herts......59 L4
Braidwood S Lans 175 L8
Brailsford Derbys........100 E4
Braintree Essex............61 J4
Braiseworth Suffk.........78 D1
Braishfield Hants..........29 G6
Braithwaite Cumb.......137 H3
Braithwell Donc.........115 K3
Bramber W Susx...........19 G4
Bramcote Warwks..........86 E5
Bramcote
  Crematorium
  Notts........................101 J5
Bramdean Hants 29 L5
Bramerton Norfk..........93 G3
Bramfield Herts............59 M5
Bramfield Suffk.............93 H8
Bramford Suffk.............78 D5
Bramhall Stockp..........113 K5
Bramham Leeds...........124 C2
Bramhope Leeds..........123 K2

Bramley Hants 41 M8
Bramley Leeds.............123 K4
Bramley Rothm............115 J3
Bramley Surrey..............31 G3
Bramley Corner
  Hants........................41 M8
Bramling Kent 35 G4
Brampford Speke
  Devon 11 L5
Brampton Cambs..........75 J3
Brampton Cumb...........138 F3
Brampton Cumb...........148 F3
Brampton Lincs............116 D5
Brampton Norfk...........106 F7
Brampton Rothm..........115 H2
Brampton Suffk.............93 J3
Brampton Abbotts
  Herefs.......................54 E3
Brampton Ash
  Nhants.......................87 L5
Brampton Bryan
  Herefs.......................83 G8
Brampton-en-le-
  Morthen Rothm 115 J4
Bramshall Staffs..........100 B6
Bramshaw Hants...........28 F7
Bramshott Hants...........30 D5
Bramwell Somset 26 B5
Branault Highld...........190 B3
Brancaster Norfk.........105 J6
Brancaster Staithe
  Norfk........................105 J6
Brancepeth Dur 150 F2
Branchill Moray 214 D4
Branderburgh Moray ...214 F4
Brandesburton E R Yk...126 E2
Brandeston Suffk..........78 F2
Brandiston Norfk.........106 D7
Brandon Dur...............151 G7
Brandon Lincs.............102 E3
Brandon Suffk..............91 H6
Brandon Warwks 86 E2
Brandon Parva Norfk....92 C2
Brandsby N York..........133 J7
Brandy Wharf Lincs......117 G2
Bran End Essex............61 G3
Branksome Poole 15 K4
Branksome Park
  Poole.........................15 K4
Bransbury Hants 29 H4
Bransby Lincs..............116 E5
Branscombe Devon 12 F4
Bransford Worcs...........70 E4
Bransgore Hants 16 A4
Bransholme C KuH......126 D7
Bransley Shrops 84 B3
Branston Leics............102 D7
Branston Lincs.............117 G7
Branston Staffs............100 E6
Branston Booths
  Lincs 117 H7
Branstone IoW..............17 G7
Brant Broughton
  Lincs 102 E3
Brantham Suffk.............78 D7
Branthwaite Cumb.......136 E4
Branthwaite Cumb.......148 B5
Brantingham E R Yk.....125 L5
Branton Donc..............115 M3
Branton Nthumb.........168 F7
Branton Green N York...132 F7
Branxton Nthumb........168 D7
Brassington Derbys.....100 E2
Brasted Kent.................32 E3
Brasted Chart Kent........32 E3
Brathens Abers 206 D5
Bratoft Lincs................119 G6
Brattleby Lincs............116 F7
Bratton Wilts.................27 K3
Bratton Wrekin.............84 B1
Bratton Clovelly
  Devon 10 C3
Bratton Fleming
  Devon 23 K5
Bratton Seymour
  Somset 26 F7
Braughing Herts............60 C3

Braunston Nhants........73 G2
Braunston Rutlnd........88 B3
Braunstone Leics........87 G3
Braunton Devon..........23 H4
Brawby N York..........134 B4
Brawl Highld...........230 B3
Bray W & M.............42 E4
Braybrooke Nhants.......87 L6
Brayford Devon..........23 L4
Bray Shop Cnwll..........5 M2
Brayton N York.........124 F4
Braywick W & M.........42 E4
Breachwood Green
  Herts................59 J4
Breadsall Derbys.......101 G5
Breadstone Gloucs......55 G7
Breage Cnwll............3 G5
Breakachy Highld......212 D5
Breakspear
  Crematorium
  Gt Lon...............43 H3
Brealangwell Lodge
  Highld...............222 C3
Bream Gloucs...........54 E6
Breamore Hants.........28 D7
Brean Somset...........25 L1
Breanais W Isls.......232 d3
Brearton N York.......132 E7
Breascleit W Isls.....232 e2
Breasclete W Isls.....232 e2
Breaston Derbys.......101 J5
Brechfa Carmth.........66 C7
Brechin Angus.........196 F4
Breckles Norfk.........91 L5
Brecon Powys...........53 G3
Brecon Beacons
  National Park
  Powys................52 F3
Bredbury Stockp.......113 L3
Brede E Susx...........21 G3
Bredenbury Herefs......69 L3
Bredfield Suffk........78 F4
Bredgar Kent...........34 B3
Bredhurst Kent.........46 D7
Bredon Worcs...........71 G6
Bredon's Hardwick
  Worcs................71 G7
Bredon's Norton
  Worcs................71 G6
Bredwardine Herefs.....69 G5
Breedon on the Hill
  Leics...............101 H7
Breich W Loth.........176 C6
Breightmet Bolton....121 L8
Breighton E R Yk.....125 G4
Breinton Herefs........69 J6
Bremhill Wilts.........39 L5
Brenchley Kent.........33 H5
Brendon Devon..........24 B2
Brenfield Ag & B......172 E2
Brenish W Isls........232 d3
Brent Eleigh Suffk.....77 L5
Brentford Gt Lon.......44 D5
Brentingby Leics......102 C8
Brent Knoll Somset.....25 M2
Brent Mill Devon........7 G4
Brent Pelham Herts.....60 C2
Brentwood Essex........45 L2
Brenzett Kent..........21 K1
Brenzett Green Kent....34 D8
Brereton Staffs........85 J1
Brereton Green
  Ches E..............113 H8
Bressay Shet..........235 d6
Bressingham Norfk......92 C7
Bretby Derbys.........100 F7
Bretby Crematorium
  Derbys..............100 F7
Bretford Warwks........86 E7
Bretforton Worcs.......71 K5
Bretherton Lancs.....121 G6
Brettabister Shet.....235 d5
Brettenham Norfk.......91 L6
Brettenham Suffk.......77 L4
Bretton Flints........111 K8
Brewood Staffs.........84 F2
Briantspuddle Dorset...14 F4

Brickendon Herts.......60 A6
Bricket Wood Herts.....59 J7
Brick Houses Sheff....114 F5
Bricklehampton
  Worcs................71 H6
Bride IoM.............237 e2
Bridekirk Cumb........147 K7
Bridestowe Devon.......10 D6
Brideswell Abers......216 B6
Bridford Devon.........11 J7
Bridge Kent............35 G4
Bridgehampton
  Somset...............26 E6
Bridge Hewick N York..132 E5
Bridgehill Dur........150 D5
Bridgemary Hants.......17 H2
Bridgend Abers........215 L7
Bridgend Ag & B.......161 K2
Bridgend Ag & B.......171 G6
Bridgend Angus........196 E3
Bridgend Brdgnd........36 E4
Bridgend D & G........165 L7
Bridgend Devon..........6 E6
Bridgend Fife.........186 F5
Bridgend Moray........215 J7
Bridgend P & K........186 B3
Bridgend W Loth.......176 E3
Bridgend of
  Lintrathen Angus....195 L5
Bridge of Alford
  Abers...............206 B2
Bridge of Allan Stirlg..185 G7
Bridge of Avon Moray..204 E2
Bridge of Avon Moray..214 E7
Bridge of Balgie
  P & K...............193 J6
Bridge of Brewlands
  Angus...............195 J4
Bridge of Brown
  Highld..............204 D2
Bridge of Cally P & K..195 J6
Bridge of Canny
  Abers...............206 C6
Bridge of Craigisla
  Angus...............195 K5
Bridge of Dee D & G...146 C3
Bridge of Don C Aber..207 H4
Bridge of Dulsie
  Highld..............213 L6
Bridge of Dye Abers...206 C7
Bridge of Earn P & K..186 B4
Bridge of Ericht
  P & K...............193 H5
Bridge of Feugh
  Abers...............206 D6
Bridge of Forss
  Highld..............230 F2
Bridge of Gairn Abers..205 H6
Bridge of Gaur P & K..193 H5
Bridge of Marnoch
  Abers...............216 B4
Bridge of Orchy
  Ag & B..............192 E7
Bridge of Tilt P & K..194 D4
Bridge of Tynet
  Moray...............215 J3
Bridge of Walls Shet..235 b5
Bridge of Weir Rens...174 D5
Bridgerule Devon........9 H4
Bridge Sollers Herefs..69 H6
Bridge Street Suffk....77 K5
Bridgetown Somset......24 E5
Bridge Trafford
  Ches W..............112 C7
Bridgham Norfk.........91 L6
Bridgnorth Shrops......84 C5
Bridgwater Somset......25 L4
Bridgwater Services
  Somset...............25 L4
Bridlington E R Yk....135 J6
Bridport Dorset........13 L4
Bridstow Herefs........54 E3
Brierfield Lancs......122 C3
Brierley Barns........124 C7
Brierley Gloucs........54 F5
Brierley Hill Dudley...85 G6
Brigg N Linc..........117 G1

Briggate Norfk........107 G6
Briggswath N York.....143 H5
Brigham Cumb..........136 F2
Brigham E R Yk........135 G8
Brighouse Calder.....123 H6
Brighstone IoW.........16 E5
Brighthampton Oxon.....57 G7
Brightley Devon........10 E5
Brightling E Susx......20 D2
Brightlingsea Essex....62 C5
Brighton Br & H........19 J5
Brighton le Sands
  Sefton..............111 J2
Brightons Falk........176 C3
Brightwalton W Berk....41 H5
Brightwell Suffk.......78 F5
Brightwell Baldwin
  Oxon................41 M2
Brightwell-cum-
  Sotwell Oxon........41 L3
Brightwell Upperton
  Oxon................42 A2
Brignall Dur..........140 D5
Brig o'Turk Stirlg....184 C6
Brigsley NE Lin.......118 C2
Brigsteer Cumb........129 K2
Brigstock Nhants.......88 D6
Brill Bucks............58 A5
Brill Cnwll............3 J5
Brilley Herefs.........68 F5
Brimfield Herefs.......69 K2
Brimfield Cross
  Herefs...............69 K2
Brimington Derbys.....115 H6
Brimley Devon...........7 J1
Brimpsfield Gloucs.....55 L5
Brimpton W Berk........41 K7
Brimscombe Gloucs......55 K7
Brimstage Wirral......111 J5
Brincliffe Sheff.....114 F4
Brind E R Yk..........125 H4
Brindister Shet.......235 C5
Brindle Lancs.........121 J5
Brineton Staffs........84 E2
Bringhurst Leics.......88 B5
Bringsty Common
  Herefs...............70 C4
Brington Cambs.........88 F7
Briningham Norfk......106 C5
Brinkhill Lincs.......118 E6
Brinkley Cambs.........76 F4
Brinklow Warwks........86 E7
Brinkworth Wilts.......40 A4
Brinscall Lancs.......121 J6
Brinsley Notts........101 J3
Brinsworth Rothm.....115 H4
Brinton Norfk.........106 C5
Brinyan Ork...........234 c5
Brisley Norfk.........105 M7
Brislington Bristl.....38 F6
Brissenden Green
  Kent.................34 C6
Bristol Bristl.........38 E5
Bristol Airport N Som..38 D7
Bristol Zoo Gardens
  Bristl...............38 E5
Briston Norfk.........106 C6
Britford Wilts.........28 D5
Brithdir Caerph........53 J7
Brithdir Gwynd.........96 B8
British Legion Village
  Kent.................33 J2
Briton Ferry Neath.....51 L6
Britwell Salome Oxon...42 A2
Brixham Torbay.........7 L5
Brixton Devon..........6 E5
Brixton Gt Lon.........44 F5
Brixton Deverill Wilts..27 K4
Brixworth Nhants.......73 L1
Brize Norton Oxon......56 F6
Brize Norton Airport
  Oxon................56 F6
Broad Alley Worcs......70 F2
Broad Blunsdon
  Swindn...............40 D3
Broadbottom Tamesd...113 M3
Broadbridge W Susx.....17 M2

Broadbridge Heath
  W Susx...............31 J5
Broad Campden
  Gloucs...............71 L6
Broad Carr Calder....123 G6
Broad Chalke Wilts.....28 B6
Broadclyst Devon.......12 C3
Broadfield Inver......174 C4
Broadford Highld......199 K2
Broadford Bridge
  W Susx...............31 H6
Broadgairhill Border..166 C7
Broad Green Worcs......70 D4
Broadhaugh Border.....179 H7
Broad Haven Pembks.....48 E5
Broadheath Traffd....113 H4
Broadhembury
  Devon................12 E2
Broadhempston
  Devon.................7 J3
Broad Hinton Wilts.....40 C5
Broadland Row
  E Susx...............21 G2
Broad Layings Hants....41 H7
Broadley Moray........215 J3
Broad Marston Worcs....71 K5
Broadmayne Dorset......14 D5
Broadmoor Pembks.......49 J6
Broadoak Dorset........13 K3
Broad Oak E Susx.......20 C2
Broad Oak E Susx.......21 G2
Broad Oak Herefs.......54 C4
Broad Oak Kent.........35 G3
Broad Oak St Hel......112 D3
Broad's Green Essex....61 H5
Broadstairs Kent.......35 K2
Broadstone Poole.......15 J4
Broadstone Shrops......83 K5
Broad Street E Susx....21 H3
Broad Street Kent......33 L2
Broad Town Wilts.......40 C5
Broadwas Worcs.........70 D4
Broadwater Herts.......59 L4
Broadwater W Susx......18 F5
Broadwaters Worcs......84 E7
Broadway Pembks........48 E5
Broadway Somset........25 L7
Broadway Worcs.........71 K6
Broadwell Gloucs.......54 E5
Broadwell Gloucs.......56 D3
Broadwell Oxon.........56 E6
Broadwell Warwks.......72 F2
Broadwindsor Dorset....13 K2
Broadwood Kelly
  Devon................10 F4
Broadwoodwidger
  Devon.................9 K6
Brochel Highld........209 J5
Brochroy Ag & B.......182 E2
Brockamin Worcs........70 D4
Brockbridge Hants......29 L7
Brockdish Norfk........92 E7
Brockenhurst Hants.....16 C3
Brocketsbrae S Lans...164 F2
Brockford Street
  Suffk................78 D2
Brockhall Nhants.......73 J3
Brockham Surrey........31 K2
Brockhampton
  Gloucs...............56 B4
Brockhampton Hants.....17 K2
Brockhampton
  Herefs...............54 E2
Brockhampton
  Estate NT Herefs.....70 C4
Brockholes Kirk......123 H7
Brocklesby Lincs......126 E7
Brockley N Som.........38 C6
Brockley Suffk.........77 J1
Brockley Green Suffk...77 G5
Brockley Green Suffk...77 J4
Brockton Shrops........83 G3
Brockton Shrops........83 G6
Brockton Shrops........83 L5
Brockweir Gloucs.......54 D7
Brockworth Gloucs......55 K5
Brocton Staffs.........99 L8

Brodick N Ayrs 162 C3
Brodie Moray 214 B3
Brodsworth Donc 115 J1
Brogaig Highld 218 C7
Brokenborough Wilts 39 K3
Broken Cross Ches E 113 K6
Brokerswood Wilts 27 J2
Bromborough Wirral 111 K5
Brome Suffk 92 D7
Brome Street Suffk 92 D7
Bromeswell Suffk 79 G4
Bromfield Cumb 147 L5
Bromfield Shrops 83 J7
Bromham Bed 74 E4
Bromham Wilts 39 L7
Bromley Gt Lon 45 H6
Bromley Shrops 84 D4
Brompton Medway 46 C6
Brompton N York 141 J7
Brompton-by-
  Sawdon N York 134 E3
Brompton-on-Swale
  N York 140 F7
Brompton Ralph
  Somset 25 G5
Brompton Regis
  Somset 24 E5
Bromsberrow Gloucs 70 D7
Bromsberrow Heath
  Gloucs 55 G2
Bromsgrove Worcs 71 G1
Bromyard Herefs 70 B4
Bronant Cerdgn 66 E2
Brongest Cerdgn 65 K5
Bronington Wrexhm 98 C4
Bronllys Powys 68 D7
Bronwydd Carmth 50 E2
Bronygarth Shrops 97 K5
Bron-y-Nant
  Crematorium
  Conwy 110 A5
Brook Hants 28 F8
Brook IoW 16 E5
Brook Kent 34 E6
Brook Surrey 30 F4
Brooke Norfk 93 G4
Brooke Rutlnd 88 B3
Brookenby Lincs 117 K3
Brookfield Rens 174 D5
Brookhampton
  Somset 26 F5
Brook Hill Hants 28 F8
Brookhouse Lancs 129 L6
Brookhouse Rothm 115 K4
Brookhouse Green
  Ches E 99 J1
Brookhouses Derbys 114 B4
Brookland Kent 21 K1
Brooklands Traffd 113 H4
Brookmans Park
  Herts 59 L7
Brook Street Essex 45 L2
Brook Street Kent 34 C7
Brookthorpe Gloucs 55 J5
Brookwood Surrey 42 F8
Broom C Beds 75 H6
Broom Rothm 115 H3
Broom Warwks 71 K4
Broome Norfk 93 H5
Broome Shrops 83 H7
Broome Worcs 84 F7
Broomedge Warrtn 113 G4
Broomfield Essex 61 H5
Broomfield Kent 33 L3
Broomfield Kent 47 K6
Broomfield Somset 25 K5
Broomfleet E R Yk 125 K5
Broomhaugh
  Nthumb 150 C3
Broom Hill Barns 115 H2
Broom Hill Notts 101 K3
Broomhill Nthumb 159 G3
Broompark Dur 151 G6
Brora Highld 226 F7
Broseley Shrops 84 C3
Brotherlee Dur 150 A7
Brotherton N York 124 D5

Brotton R & Cl 142 E4
Broubster Highld 230 F4
Brough Cumb 139 H4
Brough E R Yk 125 L5
Brough Highld 231 J2
Brough Notts 102 D2
Brough Shet 235 d4
Broughall Shrops 98 E4
Brough Lodge Shet 235 d2
Brough Sowerby
  Cumb 139 H5
Broughton Border 165 L3
Broughton Cambs 89 K7
Broughton Flints 111 K8
Broughton Hants 28 F5
Broughton Lancs 121 G4
Broughton M Keyn 74 C6
Broughton N Linc 126 B8
Broughton N York 122 D1
Broughton N York 134 B5
Broughton Nhants 88 B7
Broughton Oxon 72 E6
Broughton Salfd 113 J2
Broughton V Glam 36 E6
Broughton Astley
  Leics 87 G5
Broughton Gifford
  Wilts 39 K7
Broughton Green
  Worcs 71 G3
Broughton Hackett
  Worcs 71 G4
Broughton-in-
  Furness Cumb 128 F3
Broughton Mains
  D & G 145 J6
Broughton Mills
  Cumb 128 F2
Broughton Moor
  Cumb 147 J7
Broughton Poggs
  Oxon 56 E7
Broughty Ferry
  C Dund 187 H2
Brown Candover
  Hants 29 L4
Brown Edge Staffs 99 K2
Brownhill Abers 217 G6
Brownhills Fife 187 H4
Brownhills Wsall 85 J3
Browninghill Green
  Hants 41 L7
Brown Lees Staffs 99 K2
Brownsea Island
  Dorset 15 J5
Browns Hill Gloucs 55 K7
Brownston Devon 7 G5
Broxa N York 134 E2
Broxbourne Herts 60 B6
Broxburn E Loth 178 E3
Broxburn W Loth 176 E4
Broxted Essex 60 F3
Bruan Highld 231 K7
Bruar P & K 194 C3
Brucefield Highld 223 K4
Bruchag Ag & B 173 J6
Bruichladdich Ag & B ..170 E6
Bruisyard Suffk 79 G2
Bruisyard Street
  Suffk 79 G2
Brumby N Linc 125 K8
Brund Staffs 100 C1
Brundall Norfk 93 G2
Brundish Suffk 78 F1
Brundish Street Suffk 78 F1
Brunery Highld 190 E3
Brunswick Village
  N u Ty 159 G7
Brunthwaite C Brad 122 F2
Bruntingthorpe Leics 87 H5
Brunton Fife 186 E3
Brunton Wilts 28 E1
Brushford Devon 11 G4
Brushford Somset 24 E6
Bruton Somset 27 G4
Bryan's Green Worcs 70 F2
Bryanston Dorset 15 G2

Brydekirk D & G 155 L7
Bryher IoS 2 a1
Brympton Somset 26 D7
Bryn Carmth 51 G5
Bryn Neath 36 C3
Brynamman Carmth 51 K3
Brynberian Pembks 64 F7
Bryncir Gwynd 95 H4
Bryn-coch Neath 51 L5
Bryncroes Gwynd 94 D6
Bryncrug Gwynd 80 E3
Bryneglwys Denbgs 97 H3
Brynford Flints 111 G6
Bryn Gates Wigan 112 E2
Bryngwran IoA 108 D6
Bryngwyn Mons 54 B6
Bryngwyn Powys 68 D5
Bryn-Henllan Pembks 64 E6
Brynhoffnant Cerdgn 65 K4
Brynmawr Blae G 53 J5
Bryn-mawr Gwynd 94 D5
Brynmenyn Brdgnd 36 D4
Brynmill Swans 51 J6
Brynna Rhondd 36 F4
Brynrefail Gwynd 109 H8
Brynsadler Rhondd 37 G4
Bryn Saith Marchog
  Denbgs 97 G3
Brynsiencyn IoA 108 F7
Brynteg IoA 109 G5
Bryn-y-Maen Conwy 110 B6
Bualintur Highld 198 F2
Bubbenhall Warwks 86 D8
Bubwith E R Yk 125 H4
Buccleuch Border 166 E6
Buchanan Smithy
  Stirlg 174 E1
Buchanhaven Abers 217 L5
Buchanty P & K 185 J2
Buchany Stirlg 184 F6
Buchlyvie Stirlg 184 C8
Buckabank Cumb 148 C5
Buckden Cambs 75 H2
Buckden N York 131 H4
Buckenham Norfk 93 H3
Buckerell Devon 12 E3
Buckfast Devon 7 H3
Buckfastleigh Devon 7 H3
Buckhaven Fife 186 F7
Buckholt Mons 54 D5
Buckhorn Weston
  Dorset 27 H6
Buckhurst Hill Essex 45 H2
Buckie Moray 215 J2
Buckingham Bucks 73 K7
Buckland Bucks 58 E5
Buckland Devon 7 G6
Buckland Gloucs 71 J7
Buckland Herts 75 L7
Buckland Kent 35 J6
Buckland Oxon 41 G2
Buckland Surrey 31 K2
Buckland Brewer
  Devon 22 F7
Buckland Common
  Bucks 58 F6
Buckland Dinham
  Somset 27 H2
Buckland Filleigh
  Devon 10 C3
Buckland in the
  Moor Devon 7 G2
Buckland
  Monachorum
  Devon 6 D3
Buckland Newton
  Dorset 14 D2
Buckland Ripers
  Dorset 14 C6
Buckland St Mary
  Somset 25 L8
Buckland-Tout-
  Saints Devon 7 H6
Bucklebury W Berk 41 K6
Bucklers Hard Hants 16 E3
Bucklesham Suffk 78 F6
Buckley Flints 111 J8

Bucklow Hill Ches E 113 G5
Buckminster Leics 102 E7
Bucknall C Stke 99 K3
Bucknall Lincs 117 K7
Bucknell Oxon 57 K3
Bucknell Shrops 83 G8
Buckpool Moray 215 J2
Bucksburn C Aber 207 G4
Buck's Cross Devon 22 E6
Bucks Green W Susx 31 H5
Buckshaw Village
  Lancs 121 H6
Bucks Horn Oak
  Hants 30 D3
Buck's Mills Devon 22 E6
Buckton E R Yk 135 J3
Buckton Nthumb 169 G2
Buckworth Cambs 89 G7
Budby Notts 115 L2
Bude Cnwll 9 G4
Budge's Shop Cnwll 5 M4
Budleigh Salterton
  Devon 12 D6
Budock Water Cnwll 3 K5
Buerton Ches E 99 G4
Bugbrooke Nhants 73 J3
Bugle Cnwll 4 F4
Bugley Dorset 27 H6
Bugthorpe E R Yk 134 B7
Buildwas Shrops 84 B3
Builth Wells Powys 68 B4
Bulbridge Wilts 28 C5
Bulford Wilts 28 D3
Bulkeley Ches E 98 D2
Bulkington Warwks 86 E6
Bulkington Wilts 39 L8
Bulkworthy Devon 9 K3
Bullbrook Br For 42 E6
Bullington Hants 29 J3
Bullington Lincs 117 H6
Bulmer Essex 77 J4
Bulmer N York 133 K6
Bulmer Tye Essex 77 J6
Bulphan Thurr 45 M2
Bulwark Abers 217 H5
Bulwell C Nott 101 K4
Bulwick Nhants 88 D5
Bumble's Green
  Essex 60 C6
Bunacaimb Highld 199 K7
Bunarkaig Highld 201 J7
Bunbury Ches E 98 E2
Bunchrew Highld 212 F5
Bundalloch Highld 210 D8
Bunessan Ag & B 180 E3
Bungay Suffk 93 G5
Bunnahabhain
  Ag & B 171 J4
Bunny Notts 101 L6
Buntait Highld 212 C7
Buntingford Herts 60 B3
Bunwell Norfk 92 D5
Burbage Leics 86 F5
Burbage Wilts 40 E7
Burchett's Green
  W & M 42 D4
Burcombe Wilts 28 B5
Burcott Bucks 58 E4
Bures Essex 77 K7
Burford Oxon 56 E5
Burford Shrops 69 L2
Burg Ag & B 189 J7
Burgates Hants 30 C5
Burgess Hill W Susx 19 J2
Burgh Suffk 78 F4
Burgh by Sands
  Cumb 148 B3
Burgh Castle Norfk 93 K3
Burghclere Hants 41 J7
Burghead Moray 214 D1
Burghfield W Berk 41 L6
Burghfield Common
  W Berk 42 A6
Burgh Heath Surrey 44 E7
Burghill Herefs 69 J5
Burgh Island Devon 6 F6
Burgh le Marsh Lincs ..119 G7

Burgh next Aylsham
Norfk 106 F7
Burgh on Bain Lincs ... 117 L4
Burgh St Margaret
Norfk 93 J2
Burgh St Peter Norfk 93 K5
Burghwallis Donc 124 E7
Burham Kent 46 B7
Buriton Hants 30 C7
Burland Ches E 98 E2
Burlawn Cnwll 4 F2
Burleigh Gloucs 55 K7
Burlescombe Devon 25 G7
Burleston Dorset 14 E4
Burley Hants 16 B2
Burley Rutlnd 88 C2
Burleydam Ches E 98 E4
Burley Gate Herefs 69 L5
Burley in Wharfedale
C Brad 123 H2
Burley Street Hants 16 B2
Burley Wood Head
C Brad 123 H2
Burlton Shrops 98 C7
Burmarsh Kent 34 E7
Burmington Warwks 72 C6
Burn N York 124 F5
Burnage Manch 113 K3
Burnaston Derbys 100 F6
Burnbrae N Lans 176 B6
Burnby E R Yk 125 K2
Burneside Cumb 138 D7
Burneston N York 132 D3
Burnett BaNES 38 F7
Burnfoot Border 166 F6
Burnfoot Border 167 H6
Burnfoot D & G 155 G4
Burnfoot D & G 156 C3
Burnfoot D & G 156 C3
Burnfoot P & K 185 K6
Burnham Bucks 42 F4
Burnham Deepdale
Norfk 105 J4
Burnham Market
Norfk 105 K4
Burnham Norton
Norfk 105 K4
Burnham-on-Crouch
Essex 46 F2
Burnham-on-Sea
Somset 25 L2
Burnham Overy
Norfk 105 K4
Burnham Overy
Staithe Norfk 105 K4
Burnham Thorpe
Norfk 105 K4
Burnhaven Abers 217 L5
Burnhead D & G. 154 E3
Burnhervie Abers 206 D2
Burnhill Green Staffs ... 84 E4
Burnhope Dur 150 F5
Burnhouse N Ayrs 174 D7
Burniston N York 134 F2
Burnley Lancs 122 C4
Burnley
Crematorium
Lancs 122 B4
Burnmouth Border 179 K6
Burn of Cambus
Stirlg 184 F6
Burnopfield Dur 150 F4
Burnsall N York 131 J7
Burnside Angus 196 C4
Burnside Angus 196 E6
Burnside Fife 186 B5
Burnside Moray 214 E1
Burnside W Loth 176 E3
Burnside of
Duntrune Angus 187 G1
Burntisland Fife 177 H2
Burntwood Staffs 85 J2
Burntwood Green
Staffs 85 J2
Burnt Yates N York ... 132 C7
Burnworthy Somset ... 25 J7
Burpham Surrey 31 G2

Burpham W Susx 18 E4
Burradon Nthumb 168 E7
Burrafirth Shet. 235 e1
Burravoe Shet 235 d3
Burrells Cumb 138 F4
Burrelton P & K 195 K8
Burridge Devon 13 H2
Burridge Hants 17 G1
Burrill N York 132 C3
Burringham N Linc 125 K8
Burrington Devon 10 F2
Burrington Herefs. ... 69 J1
Burrington N Som 38 C8
Burrough Green
Cambs 76 F4
Burrough on the Hill
Leics 87 L2
Burrow Lancs 130 C4
Burrow Somset 24 E3
Burrow Bridge
Somset 26 A5
Burrowhill Surrey 42 F7
Burry Green Swans 50 F7
Burry Port Carmth 50 F5
Burscough Lancs 120 F7
Burscough Bridge
Lancs 120 F7
Bursea E R Yk 125 J4
Bursledon Hants. 16 F1
Burslem C Stke 99 K3
Burstall Suffk 78 D5
Burstock Dorset 13 K2
Burston Norfk 92 D6
Burstow Surrey 32 B5
Burstwick E R Yk 126 F5
Burtersett N York 131 G2
Burtholme Cumb 148 F3
Burthorpe Green
Suffk 77 H2
Burtoft Lincs 103 L5
Burton Ches W 111 K6
Burton Ches W 112 D8
Burton Dorset 15 M4
Burton Lincs 116 F6
Burton Pembks 49 G6
Burton Somset 25 J3
Burton Wilts 39 J4
Burton Agnes E R Yk .. 135 H6
Burton Bradstock
Dorset 13 L4
Burton Coggles Lincs .. 103 G7
Burton Constable
Hall E R Yk 126 F4
Burton End Essex 60 E4
Burton Fleming
E R Yk 135 G5
Burton Hastings
Warwks 86 E5
Burton-in-Kendal
Cumb 129 L4
Burton-in-Kendal
Services Cumb 129 L4
Burton in Lonsdale
N York 130 C5
Burton Joyce Notts ... 101 M4
Burton Latimer
Nhants 88 C8
Burton Lazars Leics ... 87 L1
Burton Leonard
N York 132 E6
Burton on the Wolds
Leics 101 L7
Burton Overy Leics ... 87 J4
Burton Pedwardine
Lincs 103 J4
Burton Pidsea E R Yk .. 127 G4
Burton Salmon
N York 124 D5
Burton's Green Essex .. 61 K3
Burton upon Stather
N Linc 125 K6
Burton upon Trent
Staffs 100 E7
Burton Waters Lincs ... 116 F6
Burtonwood Warrtn ... 112 E3
Burtonwood
Services Warrtn 112 E4

Burwardsley Ches W ... 98 D2
Burwarton Shrops 84 B6
Burwash E Susx 33 H7
Burwash Common
E Susx 20 D2
Burwash Weald
E Susx 20 D2
Burwell Cambs 76 E2
Burwell Lincs 118 E5
Burwen IoA 108 E3
Burwick Ork 234 c8
Bury Bury 122 B7
Bury Cambs 89 K6
Bury Somset 24 E6
Bury W Susx 18 D3
Bury Green Herts 60 D4
Bury St Edmunds
Suffk 77 J2
Burythorpe N York 134 C6
Busby E Rens 175 G6
Buscot Oxon 40 E2
Bush Abers 197 J4
Bush Bank Herefs 69 J4
Bushbury Wolves 85 G3
Bushbury
Crematorium
Wolves 85 G3
Bushey Herts 43 J2
Bushey Heath Herts ... 43 J2
Bush Hill Park
Gt Lon 45 G2
Bushley Worcs 70 F7
Bushmoor Shrops 83 J6
Bushton Wilts 40 B5
Bussage Gloucs 55 K7
Bussex Somset 26 A4
Butcombe N Som 38 D7
Bute Ag & B. 173 H4
Butleigh Somset 26 D5
Butleigh Wootton
Somset 26 D4
Butlers Marston
Warwks 72 D4
Butley Suffk 79 H4
Buttercrambe
N York 133 L7
Butterdean Border ... 179 G5
Butterknowle Dur 140 E3
Butterleigh Devon 12 C2
Buttermere Cumb 137 G4
Buttershaw C Brad ... 123 H5
Butterstone P & K 195 G2
Butterton Staffs 99 J4
Butterton Staffs 100 B2
Butterwick Lincs 104 C4
Butterwick N York 133 L4
Butterwick N York 134 F5
Buttington Powys 82 E2
Buttonoak Shrops 84 D7
Buxhall Suffk 78 B3
Buxted E Susx 20 A2
Buxton Derbys 114 B6
Buxton Norfk 106 F7
Buxton Heath Norfk .. 106 E7
Bwlch Powys 53 J4
Bwlchgwyn Wrexhm .. 97 K2
Bwlchllan Cerdgn 66 D3
Bwlchtocyn Gwynd ... 94 E7
Bwlch-y-cibau Powys .. 97 J8
Bwlch-y-ffridd Powys .. 82 B4
Bwlch-y-groes
Pembks 65 H7
Bwlch-y-sarnau
Powys 82 B8
Byers Green Dur 150 F7
Byfield Nhants 73 G4
Byfleet Surrey 43 H7
Byford Herefs 69 H6
Byker N u Ty 151 G3
Bylchau Conwy 110 D8
Byley Ches W 113 G7
Byrness Nthumb 157 K2
Bystock Devon 12 D5
Bythorn Cambs 88 F7
Byton Herefs 69 G2
Bywell Nthumb 150 D3
Byworth W Susx 31 G7

C

Cabourne Lincs 117 J2
Cabrach Ag & B. 171 J5
Cabrach Moray 215 J8
Cabus Lancs 121 G2
Cadbury Devon 11 L4
Cadder E Duns 175 G4
Caddington C Beds ... 59 H4
Caddonfoot Border ... 167 G3
Cadeby Donc 115 K2
Cadeby Leics 86 E3
Cadeleigh Devon 11 L4
Cade Street E Susx ... 20 C2
Cadgwith Cnwll 3 J7
Cadham Fife 186 D6
Cadishead Salfd 113 G3
Cadle Swans 51 J6
Cadley Lancs 121 G4
Cadley Wilts 28 E2
Cadley Wilts 40 E6
Cadmore End Bucks ... 42 C3
Cadnam Hants 28 F8
Cadney N Linc 117 G2
Cadoxton V Glam 37 H6
Cadoxton
Juxta-Neath
Neath 51 L5
Caeathro Gwynd 95 J1
Caenby Lincs 117 G4
Caeo Carmth 66 F6
Caerau Brdgnd 36 D2
Caerau Cardif 37 H5
Caer Farchell Pembks .. 48 D3
Caergeiliog IoA 108 D5
Caergwrle Flints 97 L2
Caerlanrig Border 156 D2
Caerleon Newpt 37 M3
Caerleon Roman
Fortress & Baths
Newpt 37 M3
Caernarfon Gwynd ... 108 F8
Caernarfon Castle
WHS Gwynd 108 F8
Caerphilly Caerph 37 J3
Caersws Powys 82 B5
Caerwedros Cerdgn ... 65 L4
Caerwent Mons 38 C3
Caerwys Flints 110 F6
Cairinis W Isls 233 c6
Cairnbaan Ag & B. ... 172 E1
Cairnbulg Abers 217 J2
Cairncross Border 179 J5
Cairncurran Inver 174 C4
Cairndow Ag & B. 183 H5
Cairneyhill Fife 176 E2
Cairngarroch D & G .. 144 C5
Cairngorms
National Park
Moray 204 C5
Cairnie Abers 215 K5
Cairnorrie Abers 217 G6
Cairnryan D & G 144 C2
Cairnty Moray 215 H4
Caister-on-Sea Norfk .. 93 L2
Caistor Lincs 117 J2
Caistor St Edmund
Norfk 92 F3
Calanais W Isls 232 e2
Calbourne IoW 16 E5
Calcot Flints 111 G6
Calcot Gloucs 56 C6
Calcot Row W Berk ... 42 A6
Calcots Moray 215 G2
Caldbeck Cumb 148 B6
Caldecote Cambs 75 L3
Caldecote Cambs 89 G5
Caldecote Highfields
Cambs 75 L3
Caldecott Nhants 74 E2
Caldecott Oxon 41 J2
Caldecott Rutlnd 88 C5
Calderbank N Lans ... 175 K5
Calder Bridge Cumb .. 136 E6
Caldercruix N Lans ... 175 L5
Calder Grove Wakefd .. 123 L6

Caldermill S Lans 164 D2
Calder Vale Lancs 121 G2
Calderwood S Lans 175 H7
Caldey Island Pembks .. 49 K7
Caldicot Mons................ 38 C3
Caldmore Wsall.............. 85 H4
Caldwell N York 140 E5
Calf of Man IoM............ 237 a7
Calfsound Ork............... 234 d4
Calgary Ag & B............ 189 J6
Califer Moray............... 214 D3
California Falk............. 176 B3
California Norfk............ 93 K1
Calke Derbys 101 G7
Callakille Highld 209 L4
Callander Stirlg 184 D5
Callanish W Isls 232 e2
Callestick Cnwll............. 3 K2
Calligarry Highld......... 199 K5
Callington Cnwll.............. 6 A3
Callow Herefs............... 69 J7
Callow End Worcs 70 E4
Callow Hill Wilts 40 B4
Calmore Hants 29 G7
Calmsden Gloucs 56 B6
Calne Wilts................ 39 M6
Calshot Hants.............. 16 F3
Calstock Cnwll................ 6 C3
Calstone Wellington
  Wilts.................... 40 B6
Calthorpe Norfk 106 E6
Calthorpe Street
  Norfk................... 107 J7
Calthwaite Cumb........ 148 E6
Calton Staffs.............. 100 C3
Calveley Ches E 98 E2
Calver Derbys............. 114 E6
Calverhall Shrops 98 E5
Calverleigh Devon....... 11 L3
Calverton M Keyn......... 73 L6
Calverton Notts.......... 101 L3
Calvine P & K 194 C3
Calzeat Border............ 165 L3
Cam Gloucs................. 55 H7
Camasachoirce
  Highld................. 190 F4
Camasine Highld 190 F4
Camas Luinie Highld .. 210 E8
Camastianavaig
  Highld................. 209 H6
Camault Muir Highld.... 212 D6
Camber E Susx..... 21 J2
Camberley Surrey 42 E7
Camberwell Gt Lon 44 F5
Camblesforth N York... 124 F5
Cambo Nthumb............ 158 C5
Camborne Cnwll.............. 3 H4
Cambourne Cambs 75 K3
Cambridge Cambs 76 C3
Cambridge Gloucs....... 55 H7
Cambridge Airport
  Cambs................... 76 C3
Cambridge City
  Crematorium
  Cambs................... 76 B3
Cambrose Cnwll............. 3 H3
Cambus Clacks 185 H8
Cambusavie
  Platform Highld.... 223 G3
Cambusbarron Stirlg... 185 G8
Cambuskenneth
  Stirlg................. 185 G8
Cambuslang S Lans...... 175 H6
Cambus o' May Abers... 205 J5
Cambuswallace
  S Lans................ 165 K2
Camden Town Gt Lon.... 44 F4
Cameley BaNES.............. 38 E8
Camelford Cnwll............... 8 E7
Camelon Falk.............. 176 B3
Camerory Highld......... 214 C7
Camerton BaNES........... 39 G8
Camerton Cumb.......... 136 E2
Camghouran P & K 193 J5
Camieston Border....... 167 J4
Cammachmore Abers... 207 G6
Cammeringham Lincs.. 116 F5

Camore Highld............. 223 G4
Campbeltown Ag & B... 161 J5
Campbeltown Airport
  Ag & B................. 161 H5
Cample D & G................ 154 F4
Campmuir P & K 195 K8
Camps W Loth............. 176 E5
Campsall Donc............ 124 E7
Campsea Ash Suffk 79 G4
Campton C Beds............ 75 G6
Camptown Border....... 167 K6
Camrose Pembks 48 F4
Camserney P & K......... 194 C6
Camusnagaul Highld ... 191 L2
Camusnagaul Highld... 220 D4
Camusteel Highld....... 209 L6
Camusterrach Highld... 209 L6
Canada Hants............... 28 F7
Candacraig Abers........ 205 H5
Candlesby Lincs.......... 118 F7
Candy Mill Border...... 165 L2
Cane End Oxon............ 42 B4
Canewdon Essex........... 46 E2
Canford Cliffs Poole ... 15 K5
Canford
  Crematorium
  Bristl................... 38 E5
Canford Heath Poole ... 15 J4
Canisbay Highld......... 231 L2
Canley Covtry.............. 86 C7
Canley Crematorium
  Covtry.................. 86 C7
Cann Dorset............... 27 K7
Canna Highld............. 198 C4
Cannich Highld........... 211 L7
Cannington Somset..... 25 K4
Canning Town Gt Lon... 45 H4
Cannock Staffs............ 85 H2
Cannock Chase Staffs... 99 M8
Cannon Bridge Herefs... 69 H6
Canonbie D & G.......... 156 C6
Canon Frome Herefs.... 70 B5
Canon Pyon Herefs...... 69 J5
Canons Ashby Nhants... 73 H4
Canonstown Cnwll.......... 2 F3
Canterbury Kent......... 34 F3
Canterbury
  Cathedral Kent...... 34 F3
Cantley Norfk.............. 93 H3
Canton Cardif.............. 37 J5
Cantraywood Highld... 213 J5
Cantsfield Lancs......... 130 C5
Canvey Island Essex.... 46 D4
Canwick Lincs............ 117 G7
Canworthy Water
  Cnwll..................... 9 G6
Caol Highld............... 191 L2
Caolas Scalpaigh
  W Isls................. 232 e4
Caoles Ag & B............ 188 D6
Caonich Highld........... 201 G6
Capel Kent................. 33 H4
Capel Surrey.............. 31 K4
Capel Bangor Cerdgn.... 80 E7
Capel Coch IoA........... 108 F5
Capel Curig Conwy........ 96 A2
Capel Dewi Carmth....... 50 F2
Capel Dewi Cerdgn...... 66 B6
Capel-Dewi Cerdgn...... 80 E6
Capel Garmon Conwy.... 96 C2
Capel Hendre Carmth.... 51 H4
Capel Iwan Carmth....... 65 J7
Capel le Ferne Kent..... 35 H6
Capel Parc IoA............ 108 F4
Capel St Andrew
  Suffk.................... 79 H5
Capel St Mary Suffk.... 78 C6
Capel Seion Cerdgn..... 80 E7
Capelulo Conwy.......... 109 L6
Capenhurst Ches W..... 111 K6
Capheaton Nthumb..... 158 C6
Caplaw E Rens........... 174 E6
Cappercleuch Border... 166 C5
Capton Devon................ 7 J5
Caputh P & K............. 195 H7
Carbis Bay Cnwll........... 2 F4

Carbost Highld........... 208 F5
Carbost Highld........... 208 F7
Carbrook Sheff........... 115 G4
Carbrooke Norfk.......... 91 L3
Car Colston Notts........ 102 B4
Carcroft Donc............ 124 E8
Cardenden Fife.......... 186 C7
Cardhu Moray............ 214 F5
Cardiff Cardif............. 37 J5
Cardiff Airport V Glam... 37 G6
Cardiff Gate Services
  Cardif................... 37 K4
Cardiff West Services
  Cardif................... 37 H4
Cardigan Cerdgn.......... 65 G5
Cardington Bed............ 74 F5
Cardington Shrops....... 83 K4
Cardinham Cnwll............. 5 H3
Cardrain D & G........... 144 D8
Cardrona Border........ 166 D2
Cardross Ag & B.......... 174 C3
Cardross
  Crematorium
  Ag & B................. 174 C3
Cardryne D & G.......... 144 D7
Cardurnock Cumb....... 147 L3
Careby Lincs............... 88 E1
Careston Angus.......... 196 E4
Carew Pembks............ 49 H6
Carew Cheriton
  Pembks................. 49 H6
Carew Newton
  Pembks................. 49 H6
Carey Herefs.............. 54 E2
Carfin N Lans............. 175 K6
Carfraemill Border..... 178 B7
Cargate Green Norfk.... 93 H2
Cargenbridge D & G.... 155 G6
Cargill P & K............. 195 J8
Cargo Cumb.............. 148 C3
Cargreen Cnwll............... 6 C4
Carham Nthumb......... 168 B2
Carhampton Somset.... 24 F3
Carharrack Cnwll........... 3 J3
Carie P & K............... 193 K5
Carinish W Isls.......... 233 c6
Carisbrooke IoW........ 16 F5
Cark Cumb................ 129 H4
Carkeel Cnwll................ 6 B4
Carlabhagh W Isls...... 232 e2
Carlbury Darltn......... 140 F4
Carlby Lincs............... 88 F2
Carleen Cnwll............... 3 G5
Carleton N York......... 122 E1
Carleton
  Crematorium
  Bpool.................. 120 D3
Carleton Forehoe
  Norfk.................... 92 C3
Carleton Rode Norfk.... 92 D5
Carleton St Peter
  Norfk.................... 93 H3
Carlincraig Abers....... 216 D5
Carlingcott BaNES....... 39 G8
Carlisle Cumb............ 148 D4
Carlisle Airport
  Cumb.................... 148 E3
Carlisle Crematorium
  Cumb.................... 148 C4
Carlops Border.......... 177 G6
Carloway W Isls......... 232 e2
Carlton Barns........... 124 B7
Carlton Bed.............. 74 D4
Carlton Cambs........... 76 F4
Carlton Leeds........... 123 L5
Carlton Leics............ 86 E3
Carlton N York.......... 124 F5
Carlton N York.......... 131 K3
Carlton N York.......... 133 J3
Carlton Notts........... 101 L4
Carlton S on T.......... 141 J3
Carlton Suffk............ 79 H2
Carlton Colville Suffk... 93 K5
Carlton Curlieu Leics... 87 K4
Carlton Green Cambs... 76 F4
Carlton Husthwaite
  N York.................. 133 G4

Carlton-in-Cleveland
  N York.................. 142 B6
Carlton in Lindrick
  Notts................... 115 L5
Carlton-le-Moorland
  Lincs................... 102 E2
Carlton Miniott
  N York.................. 132 F4
Carlton-on-Trent
  Notts................... 116 D8
Carlton Scroop Lincs.... 102 F4
Carluke S Lans........... 175 L7
Carmacoup S Lans...... 164 F4
Carmarthen Carmth..... 50 F2
Carmel Carmth............ 51 H3
Carmel Flints............ 111 G6
Carmel Gwynd............ 95 H2
Carmichael S Lans...... 165 K2
Carmountside
  Crematorium
  C Stke.................. 99 K3
Carmunnock C Glas..... 175 G6
Carmyle C Glas........... 175 H6
Carmyllie Angus........ 196 E7
Carnaby E R Yk.......... 135 H4
Carnbee Fife............. 187 J6
Carnbo P & K............ 185 L6
Carn Brea Cnwll............. 3 H3
Carnbrogie Abers....... 216 F8
Carndu Highld........... 210 D3
Carnduff S Lans......... 164 D1
Carnell E Ayrs........... 163 L3
Carnforth Lancs......... 129 K5
Carn-gorm Highld...... 200 E2
Carnhell Green Cnwll...... 3 G4
Carnie Abers............. 206 F4
Carnkie Cnwll................ 3 H4
Carnkie Cnwll................ 3 J4
Carno Powys.............. 81 K4
Carnock Fife............. 176 E1
Carnon Downs Cnwll....... 4 C7
Carnousie Abers........ 216 C4
Carnoustie Angus....... 187 J1
Carnwath S Lans........ 165 J3
Carol Green Solhll....... 86 C7
Carperby N York........ 131 J2
Carradale Ag & B....... 161 K2
Carrbridge Highld...... 203 L2
Carrefour Jersey........ 236 c6
Carreglefn IoA........... 108 E4
Carr Gate Wakefd...... 123 L5
Carrhouse N Linc....... 116 C1
Carrick Ag & B........... 172 F2
Carrick Castle Ag & B.. 183 H8
Carriden Falk............ 176 D3
Carrington Mdloth..... 177 J6
Carrington Traffd...... 113 H3
Carrog Denbgs........... 97 H4
Carron Falk............... 176 B2
Carron Moray............ 214 F6
Carronbridge D & G.... 154 F3
Carron Bridge Stirlg... 175 K2
Carronshore Falk....... 176 B2
Carr Shield Nthumb.... 149 K5
Carrutherstown
  D & G................... 155 J7
Carruth House Inver... 174 C5
Carrville Dur............ 151 H4
Carsaig Ag & B.......... 181 H3
Carseriggan D & G...... 145 G2
Carsethorn D & G....... 147 H3
Carshalton Gt Lon...... 44 F6
Carsington Derbys..... 100 E3
Carskey Ag & B.......... 161 H7
Carsluith D & G......... 145 K4
Carsphairn D & G....... 153 L4
Carstairs S Lans........ 165 H1
Carstairs Junction
  S Lans.................. 165 J1
Carterton Oxon.......... 56 F6
Carthew Cnwll.............. 4 F5
Carthorpe N York....... 132 D3
Cartland S Lans......... 165 G1
Cartmel Cumb........... 129 H4
Carway Carmth........... 50 F4
Cashe's Green Gloucs... 55 J6
Cassington Oxon........ 57 J5

Cassop Colliery Dur 151 J7
Castel Guern. 236 c3
Casterton Cumb. 130 C4
Castle Acre Norfk 91 J1
Castle Ashby Nhants 74 C3
Castlebay W Isls 233 b9
Castle Bolton N York 131 J2
Castle Bromwich
Solhll 85 K5
Castle Bytham Lincs 103 G8
Castlebythe Pembks 49 H2
Castle Caereinion
Powys 82 D3
Castle Camps Cambs 76 F6
Castle Carrock Cumb 148 F4
Castlecary Falk 175 K3
Castle Cary Somset 26 F5
Castle Combe Wilts 39 J5
Castle Donington
Leics 101 H6
Castle Douglas D & G 146 D3
Castle Eaton Swindn 40 C2
Castle Eden Dur 151 K7
Castleford Wakefd 124 C5
Castle Frome Herefs 70 C5
Castle Gresley Derbys 100 F8
Castle Hedingham
Essex 77 H7
Castlehill Border 166 C3
Castlehill Highld. 231 H2
Castle Hill Suffk 78 D5
Castlehill W Duns 174 D3
Castle Kennedy D & G 144 D3
Castle Lachlan Ag & B 182 E7
Castlemartin Pembks 48 F7
Castlemilk C Glas 175 G6
Castlemorton Worcs 70 E6
Castlemorton
Common Worcs 70 E6
Castle O'er D & G 156 A4
Castle Pulverbatch
Shrops 83 H3
Castlerigg Stone
Circle Cumb 137 J3
Castle Rising Norfk 105 G7
Castleside Dur 150 D5
Castle Stuart Highld 213 H4
Castlethorpe M Keyn 74 B5
Castleton Border 156 E4
Castleton Derbys 114 D5
Castleton N York 142 E5
Castleton Newpt 37 K4
Castleton Rochdl 122 D7
Castletown Highld 231 H3
Castletown IoM 237 b7
Castletown Sundld 151 J4
Castley N York 123 K2
Caston Norfk 91 L4
Castor C Pete 89 G4
Catacol N Ayrs 172 F7
Catcliffe Rothm 115 H4
Catcomb Wilts 40 A5
Catcott Somset 26 B4
Catcott Burtle
Somset 26 B3
Caterham Surrey 32 C3
Catfield Norfk 107 H7
Catford Gt Lon 45 G5
Catforth Lancs 121 G4
Cathcart C Glas 175 G6
Cathedine Powys 53 H3
Catherington Hants 30 B8
Catherston
Leweston Dorset 13 J4
Catisfield Hants 17 G2
Catlodge Highld 202 F6
Catmere End Essex 76 C6
Catmore W Berk 41 J4
Caton Lancs 129 L6
Caton Green Lancs 129 L6
Catrine E Ayrs 164 B4
Catsfield E Susx 20 E3
Catsgore Somset 26 D6
Catshill Worcs 85 G8
Cattadale Ag & B 161 H7
Cattal N York 133 G8
Cattawade Suffk 62 D2

Catterall Lancs 121 G3
Catterick N York 141 G7
Catterick Bridge
N York 141 G7
Catterlen Cumb 148 E7
Catterline Abers 197 L2
Catterton N York 124 D2
Catteshall Surrey 31 G3
Catthorpe Leics 87 G7
Cattistock Dorset 14 B3
Catton N York 132 E4
Catton Nthumb 149 L4
Catwick E R Yk 126 E2
Catworth Cambs 88 F8
Caudle Green Gloucs 55 L6
Caulcott Oxon 57 K3
Cauldcots Angus 197 G6
Cauldhame Stirlg 184 E8
Cauldmill Border 167 H6
Cauldon Staffs 100 B3
Cauldwell Derbys 86 B1
Caulkerbush D & G 147 G4
Caulside D & G 156 D6
Caundle Marsh
Dorset 27 G8
Caunton Notts 102 C1
Causeway End D & G 145 J3
Causeway End Essex 61 G4
Causewayend S Lans 165 K3
Causewayhead Stirlg 185 G7
Causeyend Abers 207 H2
Causey Park Bridge
Nthumb 158 F3
Cavendish Suffk 77 J5
Cavenham Suffk 77 H1
Caversfield Oxon 57 L3
Caversham Readg 42 B5
Caverswall Staffs 99 L4
Caverton Mill Border 167 M4
Cawdor Highld 213 K4
Cawood N York 124 E3
Cawsand Cnwll 6 C5
Cawston Norfk 106 D7
Cawthorne Barns 123 K8
Caxton Cambs 75 K3
Caynham Shrops 83 K8
Caythorpe Lincs 102 F3
Caythorpe Notts 102 B4
Cayton N York 135 G3
Ceann a Bhaigh W Isls 233 b6
Ceannacroc Lodge
Highld 201 K3
Cearsiadar W Isls 232 f3
Cefn Newpt 37 L3
Cefn-brith Conwy 96 E3
Cefn-bryn-brain
Carmth 51 L3
Cefn Cribwr Brdgnd 36 D4
Cefneithin Carmth 51 G3
Cefngorwydd Powys 67 J5
Cefn-mawr Wrexhm 97 L4
Cefn-y-pant Carmth 49 K3
Cellardyke Fife 187 J6
Cellarhead Staffs 99 L3
Cemaes IoA 108 E3
Cemmaes Powys 81 H3
Cemmaes Road
Powys 81 H3
Cenarth Cerdgn 65 J6
Ceres Fife 186 F5
Cerne Abbas Dorset 14 C3
Cerney Wick Gloucs 40 B2
Cerrigydrudion
Conwy 96 E3
Ceunant Gwynd 95 J1
Chaceley Gloucs 55 J2
Chacewater Cnwll 3 K3
Chackmore Bucks 73 K7
Chacombe Nhants 72 F5
Chadbury Worcs 71 H5
Chadderton Oldham 113 K1
Chaddesden C Derb 101 G5
Chaddesley Corbett
Worcs 84 F8
Chaddlehanger
Devon 6 C1
Chaddleworth W Berk 41 H5

Chadlington Oxon 57 G4
Chadshunt Warwks 72 D4
Chadwell Leics 102 C7
Chadwell Heath
Gt Lon 45 J3
Chadwell St Mary
Thurr 45 M4
Chadwick Worcs 70 E2
Chadwick End Solhll 86 B8
Chaffcombe Somset 13 J1
Chagford Devon 11 G7
Chailey E Susx 19 K2
Chainhurst Kent 33 J4
Chaldon Surrey 32 B3
Chale IoW 16 F6
Chale Green IoW 16 F6
Chalfont Common
Bucks 43 G3
Chalfont St Giles
Bucks 43 G2
Chalfont St Peter
Bucks 43 G3
Chalford Gloucs 55 K7
Chalford Wilts 27 K2
Chalgrove Oxon 41 M2
Chalk Kent 46 A5
Chalkwell Kent 34 B2
Challacombe Devon 23 L3
Challoch D & G 145 H2
Challock Kent 34 D5
Chalton C Beds 59 G3
Chalton Hants 30 B7
Chalvey Slough 42 F4
Chalvington E Susx 20 B4
Chandler's Cross
Herts 43 H2
Chandler's Ford
Hants 29 H7
Chanterlands
Crematorium
C KuH 126 D4
Chantry Somset 27 G3
Chantry Suffk 78 D5
Chapel Fife 186 D8
Chapel Allerton Leeds 123 L3
Chapel Allerton
Somset 26 B2
Chapel Amble Cnwll 4 F2
Chapel Brampton
Nhants 73 K2
Chapel Chorlton
Staffs 99 J5
Chapelend Way Essex 77 G6
Chapel-en-le-Frith
Derbys 114 B5
Chapel Green Warwks 72 F3
Chapel Haddlesey
N York 124 E5
Chapelhall N Lans 175 K5
Chapel Hill Abers 217 K7
Chapel Hill Lincs 103 K2
Chapel Hill Mons 54 D7
Chapel Hill N York 123 L2
Chapelhope Border 166 C5
Chapelknowe D & G 156 B7
Chapel Lawn Shrops 82 F7
Chapel le Dale N York 130 E4
Chapel Leigh Somset 25 H5
Chapel of Garioch
Abers 206 D1
Chapel Rossan D & G 144 D6
Chapel Row W Berk 41 L6
Chapel St Leonards
Lincs 119 H6
Chapel Stile Cumb 137 K6
Chapelton Angus 197 G6
Chapelton Devon 23 J6
Chapelton S Lans 175 J8
Chapeltown Bl w D 121 L7
Chapeltown Moray 204 F2
Chapeltown Sheff 115 G3
Chapmanslade Wilts 27 J2
Chapmans Well
Devon 9 J6
Chapmore End Herts 60 B5
Chappel Essex 61 L3
Chard Somset 13 H2

Chard Junction
Somset 13 J2
Chardleigh Green
Somset 13 H1
Chardstock Devon 13 H2
Charfield S Glos 39 G3
Charing Kent 34 C5
Charing
Crematorium
Kent 34 C5
Charingworth Gloucs 71 L6
Charlbury Oxon 57 G4
Charlcombe BaNES 39 H6
Charlcutt Wilts 39 M5
Charlecote Warwks 72 C3
Charlemont Sandw 85 H5
Charles Devon 23 L5
Charleston Angus 196 C7
Charlestown C Aber 207 H5
Charlestown C Brad 123 H3
Charlestown Calder 122 E5
Charlestown Cnwll 5 G5
Charlestown Fife 176 E2
Charlestown Highld 213 G5
Charlestown Highld 219 J6
Charlestown Salfd 113 J2
Charles Tye Suffk 78 B4
Charlesworth Derbys 114 A3
Charlinch Somset 25 K4
Charlottetown Fife 186 E5
Charlton Gt Lon 45 H4
Charlton Nhants 73 G7
Charlton Nthumb 157 K5
Charlton Oxon 41 H3
Charlton Somset 25 L6
Charlton Somset 27 G2
Charlton W Susx 18 B3
Charlton Wilts 27 K6
Charlton Wilts 39 L3
Charlton Worcs 71 H5
Charlton Wrekin 83 L2
Charlton Abbots
Gloucs 56 B3
Charlton Adam
Somset 26 D5
Charlton All Saints
Wilts 28 D6
Charlton Down
Dorset 14 D4
Charlton Horethorne
Somset 26 F6
Charlton Kings Gloucs 55 L4
Charlton Mackrell
Somset 26 D5
Charlton Marshall
Dorset 15 G2
Charlton Musgrove
Somset 27 G5
Charlton-on-Otmoor
Oxon 57 K5
Charlton on the Hill
Dorset 15 G2
Charlton St Peter
Wilts 28 C1
Charlwood Hants 30 A5
Charlwood Surrey 31 L3
Charminster Dorset 14 D4
Charmouth Dorset 13 J4
Charndon Bucks 58 A3
Charney Bassett
Oxon 41 G2
Charnock Richard
Lancs 121 H7
Charnock Richard
Crematorium
Lancs 121 H6
Charnock Richard
Services Lancs 121 H7
Charsfield Suffk 78 F3
Charter Alley Hants 41 L8
Charterhall Border 179 G8
Charterhouse Somset 26 D1
Chartershall Stirlg 175 K1
Chartham Kent 34 E4
Chartham Hatch Kent 34 E4
Chartridge Bucks 58 F7
Chart Sutton Kent 33 K4

Charvil Wokham 42 C5
Charwelton Nhants 73 G4
Chase Terrace Staffs 85 J2
Chasetown Staffs..........85 J2
Chastleton Oxon 56 E3
Chasty Devon..................9 J4
Chatburn Lancs 121 L2
Chatcull Staffs................99 H5
Chatham Medway 46 C6
Chatham Green Essex 61 H5
Chathill Nthumb..........169 J4
Chatsworth House
    Derbys 114 E7
Chattenden Medway 46 C5
Chatteris Cambs............90 B6
Chatterton Lancs 122 B6
Chattisham Suffk..........78 C6
Chatto Border 168 B5
Chatton Nthumb..........168 F4
Chawleigh Devon 11 G3
Chawton Hants..............30 B4
Cheadle Staffs..............100 A4
Cheadle Stockp............113 K4
Cheadle Hulme
    Stockp 113 K4
Cheam Gt Lon 44 E7
Chearsley Bucks 58 B6
Chebsey Staffs 99 J6
Checkendon Oxon 42 A4
Checkley Ches E 99 G4
Checkley Staffs............100 B5
Chedburgh Suffk............77 H3
Cheddar Somset............26 C2
Cheddington Bucks 58 F4
Cheddleton Staffs..........99 L3
Cheddon Fitzpaine
    Somset 25 K6
Chedgrave Norfk 93 H4
Chedington Dorset 13 L2
Chediston Suffk............93 H7
Chedworth Gloucs 56 B5
Chedzoy Somset............25 M4
Cheetham Hill
    Manch 113 J2
Cheldon Devon 11 H3
Chelford Ches E 113 J6
Chellaston C Derb 101 G6
Chellington Bed 74 D4
Chelmarsh Shrops..........84 C5
Chelmondiston Suffk 78 E6
Chelmorton Derbys 114 C7
Chelmsford Essex 61 H6
Chelmsford
    Crematorium
    Essex 61 H6
Chelmsley Wood
    Solhll 85 L6
Chelsea Gt Lon 44 F4
Chelsfield Gt Lon 45 J7
Chelsworth Suffk..........77 L5
Cheltenham Gloucs......55 L4
Cheltenham
    Crematorium
    Gloucs 55 L4
Chelveston Nhants 74 E1
Chelvey N Som 38 C6
Chelwood BaNES..........38 F7
Chelwood Gate
    E Susx 32 D6
Cheney Longville
    Shrops 83 H6
Chenies Bucks 43 G2
Chepstow Mons 38 D2
Cherhill Wilts 40 B6
Cherington Gloucs 55 K7
Cherington Warwks 72 C6
Cheriton Hants 29 L5
Cheriton Kent 35 G7
Cheriton Swans 50 F6
Cheriton Bishop
    Devon 11 H6
Cheriton Fitzpaine
    Devon 11 K4
Cheriton or
Stackpole Elidor
    Pembks 49 G7
Cherrington Wrekin 98 F8

Cherry Burton E R Yk....126 B3
Cherry Hinton Cambs....76 C3
Cherry Orchard
    Worcs 70 F4
Cherry Willingham
    Lincs 117 G6
Chertsey Surrey............43 H6
Cherwell Valley
    Services Oxon............57 K3
Cheselbourne Dorset 14 E3
Chesham Bucks 58 F7
Chesham Bury 122 B7
Chesham Bois Bucks 58 F7
Cheshunt Herts 60 B7
Chesil Beach Dorset......14 B6
Cheslyn Hay Staffs........85 H3
Chessetts Wood
    Warwks 85 L8
Chessington Gt Lon 44 D7
Chessington World
    of Adventures
    Gt Lon 44 D7
Chester Ches W 112 B7
Chesterblade Somset....26 F3
Chester Cathedral
    Ches W 112 B7
Chester
    Crematorium
    Ches W 111 L7
Chesterfield Derbys....115 G7
Chesterfield
    Crematorium
    Derbys 115 H6
Chesterfield Services
    Derbys 101 H1
Chesterhill Mdloth 177 K5
Chester-le-Street Dur..151 G5
Chester Moor Dur 151 G5
Chesters Border 167 J5
Chesters Border 167 K7
Chester Services
    Ches W 112 C6
Chesterton Cambs 76 C3
Chesterton Cambs 89 G4
Chesterton Gloucs 56 A7
Chesterton Oxon 57 K4
Chesterton Shrops 84 D4
Chesterton Green
    Warwks 72 D3
Chesterwood
    Nthumb 149 L2
Chester Zoo Ches W....112 B7
Chestfield Kent..............47 J6
Cheston Devon 7 G4
Cheswardine Shrops 99 G6
Cheswick Nthumb........168 F1
Chetnole Dorset............14 B2
Chettisham Cambs........90 D6
Chettle Dorset................27 L8
Chetton Shrops 84 B5
Chetwynd Wrekin..........99 G7
Chetwynd Aston
    Wrekin 99 H8
Cheveley Cambs............76 F3
Chevening Kent............32 E2
Chevington Suffk..........77 H3
Cheviot Hills 168 A7
Chevithorne Devon 24 F7
Chew Magna BaNES......38 E7
Chew Stoke BaNES........38 E7
Chewton Keynsham
    BaNES 38 F6
Chewton Mendip
    Somset 26 E2
Chicheley M Keyn..........74 C5
Chichester W Susx........18 B5
Chichester
    Crematorium
    W Susx 18 B4
Chickerell Dorset..........14 C6
Chicklade Wilts 27 K4
Chidden Hants 30 A7
Chiddingfold Surrey 30 F4
Chiddingly E Susx........20 B3
Chiddingstone Kent 32 E4
Chiddingstone
    Causeway Kent 32 F4

Chideock Dorset............13 K4
Chidham W Susx............17 L2
Chidswell Kirk 123 K6
Chieveley W Berk 41 J5
Chignall St James
    Essex 61 G6
Chignall Smealy Essex....61 G5
Chigwell Essex..............45 H2
Chigwell Row Essex......45 J2
Chilbolton Hants 29 H4
Chilcomb Hants 29 J5
Chilcombe Dorset 13 M4
Chilcompton Somset....26 F2
Chilcote Leics 86 C2
Childer Thornton
    Ches W 111 K6
Child Okeford Dorset....27 J8
Childrey Oxon 41 G3
Child's Ercall Shrops....98 F7
Childswickham Worcs....71 J6
Childwall Lpool 112 B4
Chilfrome Dorset..........14 B3
Chilgrove W Susx..........18 A3
Chilham Kent 34 E4
Chillaton Devon 10 C8
Chillenden Kent............35 H4
Chillerton IoW..............16 F5
Chillesford Suffk..........79 H4
Chillington Devon 7 J7
Chillington Somset........13 K1
Chilmark Wilts 27 L5
Chilmington Green
    Kent 34 C6
Chilson Oxon 56 F4
Chilsworthy Cnwll..........6 B2
Chilsworthy Devon 9 J4
Chiltern Hills 42 C2
Chilterns
    Crematorium
    Bucks 42 F2
Chilthorne Domer
    Somset 26 D7
Chilton Bucks 58 B5
Chilton Dur..................141 H2
Chilton Oxon 41 J4
Chilton Candover
    Hants 29 L4
Chilton Cantelo
    Somset 26 E6
Chilton Foliat Wilts 40 F6
Chilton Polden
    Somset 26 B4
Chilton Street Suffk......77 H5
Chilton Trinity
    Somset 25 L4
Chilwell Notts 101 K5
Chilworth Hants 29 H7
Chilworth Surrey..........31 G3
Chimney Oxon 57 G7
Chineham Hants 30 A1
Chingford Gt Lon..........45 G2
Chinley Derbys 114 B5
Chinnor Oxon 58 C7
Chipnall Shrops............99 G6
Chippenham Cambs......76 F1
Chippenham Wilts........39 L5
Chipperfield Herts 59 H7
Chipping Herts 60 B2
Chipping Lancs 121 J2
Chipping Campden
    Gloucs 71 L6
Chipping Norton
    Oxon 56 F3
Chipping Ongar
    Essex 60 E7
Chipping Sodbury
    S Glos 39 G4
Chipping Warden
    Nhants 72 F5
Chipstable Somset........25 G6
Chipstead Kent............32 E3
Chipstead Surrey..........32 B2
Chirbury Shrops 82 F4
Chirk Wrexhm 97 L5
Chirnside Border 179 H6
Chirnsidebridge
    Border 179 H7

Chirton Wilts 40 B8
Chisbury Wilts 40 F6
Chiselborough
    Somset 26 C8
Chiseldon Swindn........40 D4
Chiselhampton Oxon 57 L7
Chisholme Border 166 F6
Chislehurst Gt Lon........45 H6
Chislet Kent..................47 L6
Chisley Calder 122 F5
Chiswell Green Herts....59 J6
Chiswick Gt Lon............44 E4
Chisworth Derbys 113 M3
Chithurst W Susx..........30 D6
Chittering Cambs..........76 C1
Chitterne Wilts..............27 M3
Chittlehamholt
    Devon 23 K7
Chittlehampton
    Devon 23 K6
Chittoe Wilts..................39 L6
Chivelstone Devon..........7 H7
Chivenor Devon............23 H4
Chlenry D & G..............144 D3
Chobham Surrey 42 F7
Cholderton Wilts 28 E3
Cholesbury Bucks 58 F6
Chollerton Nthumb 158 B5
Cholsey Oxon 41 L3
Cholstrey Herefs 69 J3
Chop Gate N York 142 C7
Choppington
    Nthumb 159 G5
Chopwell Gatesd 150 E4
Chorley Ches E 98 D3
Chorley Lancs 121 H6
Chorley Shrops 84 C6
Chorleywood Herts 43 H2
Chorleywood West
    Herts 43 G2
Chorlton Ches E 99 G3
Chorlton-cum-Hardy
    Manch 113 J3
Chorlton Lane Ches W....98 C3
Choulton Shrops 83 H5
Chrishall Essex 76 C6
Chrisswell Inver 173 L4
Christchurch Cambs......90 C4
Christchurch Dorset 15 M4
Christchurch Newpt....37 M3
Christian Malford
    Wilts 39 L5
Christleton Ches W......112 C7
Christon N Som 38 B8
Christon Bank
    Nthumb 169 J5
Christow Devon............11 J7
Chudleigh Devon..........11 J6
Chudleigh Knighton
    Devon 7 J1
Chulmleigh Devon 11 G3
Church Lancs 121 L5
Churcham Gloucs 55 H4
Church Aston Wrekin....99 G6
Church Brampton
    Nhants 73 K2
Church Broughton
    Derbys 100 D5
Church Cove Cnwll..........3 J8
Church Crookham
    Hants 30 D2
Churchdown Gloucs....55 K4
Church Eaton Staffs......99 J8
Church End C Beds 59 G4
Church End C Beds 75 H6
Churchend Essex..........47 G2
Church End Essex 61 H3
Church End Gt Lon 44 E3
Church Enstone Oxon....57 G3
Church Fenton
    N York 124 D3
Churchfield Sandw........85 H5
Church Green Devon 12 F3
Church Hanborough
    Oxon 57 H5
Church Houses
    N York 142 E7

Churchill Devon 13 H3
Churchill N Som 38 C7
Churchill Oxon 56 F3
Churchill Worcs 71 G4
Churchill Worcs 84 F7
Churchinford Somset 25 K8
Church Knowle
  Dorset 15 H6
Church Langton Leics 87 K5
Church Lawford
  Warwks 86 F7
Church Leigh Staffs 100 A5
Church Lench Worcs 71 H4
Church Mayfield
  Staffs 100 D4
Church Minshull
  Ches E 98 F1
Church Norton
  W Susx 18 B6
Churchover Warwks 87 G7
Church Preen Shrops 83 K4
Church Pulverbatch
  Shrops 83 H3
Churchstanton
  Somset 25 J8
Churchstoke Powys 82 F5
Churchstow Devon 7 G6
Church Stowe Nhants 73 J3
Church Street Kent 46 B5
Church Stretton
  Shrops 83 J5
Churchtown Cnwll 5 H1
Churchtown Derbys 114 E8
Churchtown IoM 237 d3
Churchtown Lancs 121 G2
Church Village
  Rhondd 37 G3
Church Warsop Notts 115 K7
Churston Ferrers
  Torbay 7 K5
Churt Surrey 30 D4
Churton Ches W 98 B2
Churwell Leeds 123 K5
Chwilog Gwynd 95 G5
Chyandour Cnwll 2 E5
Chysauster Cnwll 2 E4
Cilcain Flints 111 G7
Cilcennin Cerdgn 66 C3
Cilfrew Neath 52 B7
Cilfynydd Rhondd 37 G3
Cilgerran Pembks 65 H6
Cilmaengwyn Neath 51 L4
Cilmery Powys 67 L4
Cilsan Carmth 51 H2
Ciltalgarth Gwynd 96 D4
Cilycwm Carmth 67 G6
Cimla Neath 36 B2
Cinderford Gloucs 54 F5
Cippenham Slough 42 F4
Cirencester Gloucs 56 A7
City Gt Lon 45 G4
City Airport Gt Lon 45 H4
City of Bath BaNES 39 H7
City of London
  Crematorium
  Gt Lon 45 H3
Clabhach Ag & B 188 F5
Clachaig Ag & B 173 J3
Clachan Ag & B 172 C6
Clachan Ag & B 182 A4
Clachan Ag & B 191 G7
Clachan Highld 209 H6
Clachan-a-Luib W Isls 233 C6
Clachan Mor Ag & B 188 C6
Clachan na Luib W Isls 233 C6
Clachan of Campsie
  E Duns 175 G3
Clachan-Seil Ag & B 181 M4
Clachnaharry Highld 213 J5
Clachtoll Highld 224 C3
Clackavoid P & K 195 J4
Clacket Lane
  Services Surrey 32 D3
Clackmannan Clacks 185 J8
Clackmarras Moray 214 F3
Clacton-on-Sea Essex 62 E5
Cladich Ag & B 182 F3

Cladswell Worcs 71 J3
Claggan Highld 190 E6
Claigan Highld 208 C4
Clanfield Hants 30 B7
Clanfield Oxon 56 F7
Clanville Hants 28 F2
Clanville Somset 26 F5
Claonaig Ag & B 172 E6
Clapgate Herts 60 C3
Clapham Bed 74 F4
Clapham Gt Lon 44 F5
Clapham N York 130 E5
Clapham W Susx 18 F4
Clapton Somset 13 K2
Clapton Somset 26 F2
Clapton-in-Gordano
  N Som 38 C5
Clapton-on-the-Hill
  Gloucs 56 D4
Claravale Gatesd 150 E3
Clarbeston Pembks 49 H3
Clarbeston Road
  Pembks 49 H4
Clarborough Notts 116 B5
Clare Suffk 77 H5
Clarebrand D & G 146 D2
Clarencefield D & G 147 J2
Clarilaw Border 167 H5
Clarkston E Rens 175 G6
Clashmore Highld 223 G4
Clashmore Highld 224 C3
Clashnessie Highld 224 C3
Clashnoir Moray 204 F2
Clathy P & K 185 K4
Clathymore P & K 185 L3
Clatt Abers 205 L1
Clatter Powys 81 L5
Clatworthy Somset 25 G5
Claughton Lancs 121 G3
Claughton Lancs 130 B6
Claughton Wirral 111 J4
Claverdon Warwks 71 L2
Claverham N Som 38 C6
Clavering Essex 60 D2
Claverley Shrops 84 E5
Claverton BaNES 39 H7
Clawdd-coch V Glam 37 G5
Clawdd-newydd
  Denbgs 97 G3
Clawton Devon 9 J5
Claxby Lincs 117 J3
Claxton N York 133 L7
Claxton Norfk 93 H3
Claybrooke Magna
  Leics 86 F5
Clay Coton Nhants 87 H7
Clay Cross Derbys 115 H8
Claydon Oxon 72 F4
Claydon Suffk 78 D5
Claygate D & G 156 D6
Claygate Kent 33 J4
Claygate Surrey 44 D7
Clayhall Gt Lon 45 H3
Clayhanger Devon 24 F6
Clayhidon Devon 25 J7
Clayhill E Susx 21 G2
Clayock Highld 231 H4
Claypits Gloucs 55 H6
Claypole Lincs 102 D3
Clayton C Brad 123 G4
Clayton Donc 124 C8
Clayton W Susx 19 J3
Clayton-le-Moors
  Lancs 121 L4
Clayton-le-Woods
  Lancs 121 H6
Clayton West Kirk 123 K7
Clayworth Notts 116 B4
Cleadale Highld 199 G3
Cleadon S Tyne 151 J3
Clearbrook Devon 6 D3
Clearwell Gloucs 54 E6
Cleasby N York 141 G5
Cleat Ork 234 C8
Cleatlam Dur 140 E4
Cleator Cumb 136 D4
Cleator Moor Cumb 136 E4

Cleckheaton Kirk 123 J5
Cleehill Shrops 83 L7
Cleekhimin N Lans 175 K6
Clee St Margaret
  Shrops 83 L6
Cleethorpes NE Lin 127 H8
Cleeton St Mary
  Shrops 84 B7
Cleeve N Som 38 C7
Cleeve Oxon 41 L4
Cleeve Hill Gloucs 55 M3
Cleeve Prior Worcs 71 J5
Cleghornie E Loth 178 D2
Clehonger Herefs 69 J6
Cleish P & K 186 A7
Cleland N Lans 175 L6
Clenamacrie Ag & B 182 C2
Clenchwarton Norfk 104 F7
Clenerty Abers 216 E3
Clent Worcs 85 G7
Cleobury Mortimer
  Shrops 84 C7
Cleobury North
  Shrops 84 B6
Cleongart Ag & B 161 H3
Clephanton Highld 213 J4
Clerkhill D & G 156 A3
Cleuch-head D & G 154 E3
Clevancy Wilts 40 B5
Clevedon N Som 38 B6
Cleveleys Lancs 120 D2
Cleverton Wilts 39 L4
Clewer Somset 26 C2
Cley next the Sea
  Norfk 106 C4
Cliburn Cumb 138 E3
Cliddesden Hants 29 M2
Cliffe Medway 46 C5
Cliffe N York 125 G4
Cliff End E Susx 21 H3
Cliffe Woods Medway 46 C5
Clifford Herefs 68 E5
Clifford Leeds 124 C2
Clifford Chambers
  Warwks 71 L4
Clifford's Mesne
  Gloucs 55 G4
Clifton Bristl 38 E5
Clifton C Beds 75 H6
Clifton C Nott 101 K5
Clifton C York 133 J8
Clifton Calder 123 H6
Clifton Cumb 138 D2
Clifton Derbys 100 D4
Clifton Devon 23 J3
Clifton Donc 115 K3
Clifton Lancs 120 F4
Clifton N York 123 J2
Clifton Oxon 57 J2
Clifton Worcs 70 F5
Clifton Campville
  Staffs 86 B2
Clifton Hampden
  Oxon 41 K2
Clifton Reynes
  M Keyn 74 C4
Clifton upon
  Dunsmore Warwks 87 G7
Clifton upon Teme
  Worcs 70 C3
Cliftonville Kent 35 K1
Climping W Susx 18 D5
Clink Somset 27 H2
Clint N York 132 D7
Clinterty C Aber 206 F3
Clint Green Norfk 92 B2
Clintmains Border 167 J3
Clippesby Norfk 93 J2
Clipsham Rutlnd 88 D1
Clipston Nhants 87 K7
Clipston Notts 101 M5
Clipstone C Beds 58 F3
Clipstone Notts 115 L8
Clitheroe Lancs 121 L3
Clive Shrops 98 D7
Clixby Lincs 117 J2
Cloatley Wilts 39 M3

Clocaenog Denbgs 97 G2
Clochan Moray 215 J3
Clodock Herefs 53 L3
Clola Abers 217 J5
Clophill C Beds 74 F6
Clopton Nhants 88 F7
Clopton Suffk 78 F4
Clopton Corner
  Suffk 78 F4
Clos du Valle Guern 236 d2
Closeburn D & G 154 F4
Closeburnmill D & G 154 F3
Closworth Somset 14 B1
Clothall Herts 59 L2
Clotton Ches W 112 D8
Clough Foot Calder 122 D5
Clough Head Calder 123 G6
Cloughton N York 143 K7
Clousta Shet 235 C5
Clova Angus 196 B2
Clovelly Devon 22 E6
Clovenfords Border 167 G3
Clovulin Highld 191 K4
Clowne Derbys 115 J6
Clows Top Worcs 70 C1
Cluanie Inn Highld 201 G3
Cluanie Lodge Highld 201 G3
Clugston D & G 145 H4
Clun Shrops 82 F7
Clunas Highld 213 K5
Clunbury Shrops 83 G7
Clunderwen Carmth 49 J4
Clune Highld 203 J1
Clunes Highld 201 J7
Clungunford Shrops 83 H7
Clunie P & K 195 H7
Clunton Shrops 83 G7
Cluny Fife 186 D7
Clutton BaNES 38 F8
Clutton Ches W 98 C2
Clutton Hill BaNES 38 F8
Clydach Mons 53 K5
Clydach Swans 51 K5
Clydach Vale Rhondd 36 F2
Clydebank W Duns 174 F4
Clydebank
  Crematorium
  W Duns 174 E4
Clyffe Pypard Wilts 40 B5
Clynder Ag & B 174 A2
Clyne Neath 52 C7
Clynnog-fawr Gwynd 95 G3
Clyro Powys 68 E5
Clyst Honiton Devon 12 C4
Clyst Hydon Devon 12 D3
Clyst St George
  Devon 12 C5
Clyst St Lawrence
  Devon 12 D3
Clyst St Mary Devon 12 C4
Cnoc W Isls 232 g2
Cnwch Coch Cerdgn 80 F8
Coad's Green Cnwll 5 L1
Coalburn S Lans 164 F3
Coalburns Gatesd 150 E3
Coaley Gloucs 55 H7
Coalhill Essex 61 J7
Coalpit Heath S Glos 38 F4
Coalport Wrekin 84 C3
Coalsnaughton Clacks 185 J7
Coaltown of
  Balgonie Fife 186 E7
Coaltown of Wemyss
  Fife 186 E7
Coalville Leics 86 E2
Coanwood Nthumb 149 H3
Coat Somset 26 C7
Coatbridge N Lans 175 J5
Coatdyke N Lans 175 K5
Coate Swindn 40 D4
Coate Wilts 40 B7
Coates Cambs 89 K4
Coates Gloucs 55 L5
Coates Lincs 116 E5
Coates W Susx 18 D3
Cobbaton Devon 23 K6
Coberley Gloucs 55 L5

Cobham Kent.................46 A6
Cobham Surrey.............43 J7
Cobham Services
   Surrey.......................43 J8
Cobnash Herefs..............69 J3
Cobo Guern..................236 c2
Coburby Abers.............217 H2
Cockayne Hatley
   C Beds.......................75 J5
Cock Bridge Abers......205 G4
Cockburnspath
   Border......................179 G4
Cock Clarks Essex........61 K7
Cockenzie and Port
   Seton E Loth.........177 L4
Cockerham Lancs........120 F1
Cockermouth Cumb....136 F2
Cockernhoe Herts.......59 J4
Cockett Swans..............51 J6
Cockfield Dur..............140 E3
Cockfield Suffk............77 K4
Cockfosters Gt Lon......44 F2
Cock Green Essex.........61 H4
Cocking W Susx............18 B3
Cocking Causeway
   W Susx.......................18 B2
Cockington Torbay........7 K3
Cocklake Somset...........26 C2
Cockley Cley Norfk........91 H2
Cock Marling E Susx.....21 H2
Cockpole Green
   Wokham....................42 D4
Cockshutt Shrops.........98 B6
Cockthorpe Norfk.......106 B4
Cockwood Devon..........12 C6
Cockyard Derbys.........114 B5
Coddenham Suffk.........78 D4
Coddington Herefs.......70 C6
Coddington Notts.......102 D2
Codford St Mary Wilts...27 L4
Codford St Peter
   Wilts.........................27 L4
Codicote Herts..............59 K4
Codmore Hill W Susx....31 H7
Codnor Derbys............101 H3
Codrington S Glos........39 G5
Codsall Staffs...............84 F3
Codsall Wood Staffs....84 F3
Coedpoeth Wrexhm......97 L3
Coed Talon Flints..........97 L2
Coed-y-paen Mons........53 M7
Coffinswell Devon...........7 K3
Cofton Devon................12 C6
Cofton Hackett
   Worcs.......................85 H7
Cogan V Glam...............37 J6
Cogenhoe Nhants.........74 B3
Coggeshall Essex..........61 K4
Coignafearn Highld....203 H2
Coilacriech Abers........205 H6
Coillore Highld............208 E6
Coity Brdgnd.................36 E4
Col W Isls....................232 g2
Colaboll Highld...........225 L6
Colan Cnwll....................4 D4
Colaton Raleigh
   Devon.......................12 D5
Colbost Highld............208 C5
Colburn N York...........140 F7
Colby Cumb.................138 F3
Colby IoM...................237 b6
Colchester Essex..........62 B3
Colchester
   Crematorium
   Essex.......................62 B4
Cold Ash W Berk..........41 K6
Cold Ashby Nhants......87 J7
Cold Ashton S Glos......39 H6
Cold Aston Gloucs........56 C4
Coldbackie Highld......229 J4
Cold Brayfield M Keyn..74 D4
Coldean Br & H.............19 J4
Coldeast Devon..............7 J2
Colden Calder.............122 E5
Colden Common
   Hants.......................29 J6

Cold Hanworth Lincs....117 G5
Coldharbour Surrey......31 J3
Cold Higham Nhants....73 J4
Coldingham Border....179 J5
Cold Kirby N York.......133 H3
Coldmeece Staffs.........99 J6
Cold Norton Essex........61 K7
Cold Overton Leics.......88 B2
Coldred Kent................35 H5
Coldridge Devon...........11 G4
Coldstream Border.....168 C2
Coldwaltham W Susx....18 D3
Coldwell Herefs............69 H7
Coldwells Abers..........217 H6
Cole Somset.................26 F5
Colebatch Shrops.........83 G6
Colebrook Devon...........12 C2
Colebrooke Devon........11 H5
Coleby Lincs...............102 F1
Coleby N Linc.............125 L6
Coleford Devon.............11 H5
Coleford Gloucs............54 E6
Coleford Somset...........27 G2
Colegate End Norfk......92 E6
Colehill Dorset.............15 J3
Coleman's Hatch
   E Susx.......................32 D6
Colemere Shrops..........98 B6
Colemore Hants............30 B5
Colenden P & K...........186 B2
Colerne Wilts...............39 J6
Colesbourne Gloucs......56 A5
Coleshill Bucks.............42 F2
Coleshill Oxon..............40 E2
Coleshill Warwks..........85 L5
Coley BaNES.................26 E1
Colgate W Susx............31 L5
Colinsburgh Fife.........187 H6
Colinton C Edin...........177 H5
Colintraive Ag & B......173 H4
Colkirk Norfk..............105 L7
Coll Ag & B................189 G5
Collace P & K..............186 C2
Collafirth Shet............235 C3
Collaton Devon..............7 G7
Collaton St Mary
   Torbay........................7 K4
College of Roseisle
   Moray......................214 E2
College Town Br For......42 D7
Collessie Fife..............186 E5
Collier Row Gt Lon......45 J2
Collier's End Herts.......60 B4
Collier Street Kent.......33 J4
Collieston Abers........217 K8
Collin D & G................155 H6
Collingbourne Ducis
   Wilts.........................28 E2
Collingbourne
   Kingston Wilts.......28 E1
Collingham Leeds......124 B2
Collingham Notts.......102 D1
Collington Herefs.........70 B3
Collingtree Nhants......73 L4
Collins Green Warrtn..112 E3
Colliston Angus.........196 F7
Colliton Devon.............12 E2
Collyweston Nhants....88 E3
Colmonell S Ayrs.......152 D5
Colmworth Bed...........75 G3
Colnbrook Slough........43 G5
Colne Cambs................89 L7
Colne Lancs................122 C3
Colne Engaine Essex....61 K3
Colney Norfk................92 E3
Colney Heath Herts.....59 K6
Coln Rogers Gloucs......56 B6
Coln St Aldwyns
   Gloucs.......................56 C6
Coln St Dennis
   Gloucs.......................56 B5
Colonsay Ag & B........180 E7
Colonsay Airport
   Ag & B....................180 E8
Colpy Abers................216 C7
Colquhar Border.........166 E2

Colsterworth Lincs.....102 F7
Colston Bassett
   Notts.......................102 B5
Coltfield Moray..........214 D2
Coltishall Norfk..........106 F8
Colton Cumb...............129 G3
Colton Leeds..............124 B4
Colton N York.............124 E2
Colton Norfk................92 D2
Colton Staffs..............100 B7
Colt's Hill Kent............33 H4
Colvend D & G...........146 F4
Colwall Herefs..............70 D6
Colwell Nthumb.........158 B6
Colwich Staffs............100 A7
Colwinston V Glam......36 E5
Colworth W Susx..........18 C5
Colwyn Bay Conwy....110 B5
Colyford Devon.............13 G4
Colyton Devon..............13 G4
Combe Oxon.................57 H5
Combe W Berk.............41 G7
Combe Down BaNES....39 H7
Combe Fishacre
   Devon.........................7 J3
Combe Florey Somset...25 J5
Combe Hay BaNES........39 G7
Combeinteignhead
   Devon.........................7 K2
Combe Martin Devon...23 J3
Combe Raleigh
   Devon.......................12 F3
Comberbach Ches W...112 F6
Comberford Staffs........85 L3
Comberton Cambs........75 L4
Comberton Herefs........69 K2
Combe St Nicholas
   Somset......................13 H1
Combrook Warwks........72 C4
Combs Derbys............114 B6
Combs Suffk.................78 C3
Combs Ford Suffk.........78 C3
Combwich Somset........25 K3
Comers Abers.............206 D4
Comhampton Worcs.....70 E2
Commins Coch Powys...81 J3
Commondale N York...142 E5
Common End Cumb....136 D3
Common Moor Cnwll......5 K2
Compstall Stockp.......113 L4
Compstonend D & G...146 B4
Compton Devon.............7 K3
Compton Hants.............29 J6
Compton Staffs............84 E6
Compton Surrey...........30 F3
Compton W Berk..........41 K4
Compton W Susx..........30 C7
Compton Wilts.............28 C2
Compton Abbas
   Dorset......................27 K7
Compton Abdale
   Gloucs.......................56 B5
Compton Bassett
   Wilts.........................40 B6
Compton
   Beauchamp Oxon....40 F3
Compton Bishop
   Somset......................26 B1
Compton
   Chamberlayne
   Wilts.........................28 B5
Compton Dando
   BaNES.......................38 F7
Compton Dundon
   Somset......................26 C5
Compton Durville
   Somset......................26 B7
Compton Greenfield
   S Glos......................38 E4
Compton Martin
   BaNES.......................38 D8
Compton
   Pauncefoot
   Somset......................26 F6
Compton Valence
   Dorset......................14 B4
Comrie Fife................176 D1

Comrie P & K..............185 G3
Conaglen House
   Highld.....................191 K3
Conchra Highld...........210 D8
Concraigie P & K........195 H7
Conderton Worcs.........71 G6
Condicote Gloucs.........56 D3
Condorrat N Lans.......175 K4
Condover Shrops..........83 J3
Coney Hill Gloucs..........55 J4
Coneyhurst Common
   W Susx.......................31 J6
Coneysthorpe N York..133 L3
Coney Weston Suffk.....91 L7
Congerstone Leics........86 D3
Congham Norfk...........105 H7
Congleton Ches E.......113 J8
Congresbury N Som......38 C7
Conheath D & G..........147 H2
Conicavel Moray.........214 B4
Coningsby Lincs..........103 L2
Conington Cambs.........75 K2
Conington Cambs.........89 H6
Conisbrough Donc......115 K2
Conisholme Lincs.......118 E3
Coniston Cumb...........137 J7
Coniston E R Yk..........126 E4
Coniston Cold N York..131 G8
Conistone N York.......131 J6
Connah's Quay Flints..111 J7
Connel Ag & B...........182 C1
Connel Park E Ayrs....164 C6
Connor Downs Cnwll.....3 G4
Conon Bridge Highld..212 E4
Cononley N York.........122 E2
Consall Staffs..............99 M3
Consett Dur................150 E5
Constable Burton
   N York....................132 B2
Constable Lee Lancs...122 B5
Constantine Cnwll..........3 J5
Constantine Bay
   Cnwll..........................4 D2
Contin Highld.............212 D3
Conwy Conwy............109 L6
Conyer's Green Suffk...77 K2
Cooden E Susx.............20 E4
Cookbury Devon............9 K4
Cookham W & M..........42 E4
Cookham Dean
   W & M.......................42 E4
Cookham Rise W & M...42 E4
Cookhill Worcs.............71 J3
Cookley Suffk...............93 H7
Cookley Worcs.............84 E7
Cookley Green Oxon....42 B3
Cookney Abers...........207 G6
Cook's Green Essex......62 E4
Cooks Green Suffk........77 L4
Cooksmill Green
   Essex.......................61 G6
Coolham W Susx..........31 J6
Cooling Medway...........46 C5
Coombe Cnwll................4 E5
Coombe Devon...............7 L2
Coombe Devon.............12 E4
Coombe Gloucs............39 H2
Coombe Hants.............30 A4
Coombe Bissett Wilts...28 C6
Coombe Cellars
   Devon.........................7 K2
Coombe Hill Gloucs......55 K3
Coombe Keynes
   Dorset......................14 F5
Coombe Pafford
   Torbay........................7 L3
Coombes W Susx..........19 G4
Coombes-Moor
   Herefs.......................69 G2
Coopersale Common
   Essex.......................60 D7
Copdock Suffk..............78 D6
Copford Green Essex....61 L4
Copgrove N York.........132 E6
Copister Shet..............235 d3
Cople Bed....................75 G5
Copley Dur.................140 D3

Copmanthorpe
C York 124 E2
Compere End Staffs....99 J6
Copp Lancs.................120 F3
Coppenhall Staffs........99 K8
Copperhouse Cnwll........2 F4
Coppingford Cambs....89 H7
Copplestone Devon......11 H4
Coppull Lancs.............121 H7
Copsale W Susx............31 K6
Copster Green Lancs...121 K4
Copston Magna
Warwks 86 F5
Cop Street Kent.............35 J3
Copt Hewick N York....132 E5
Copthorne W Susx.........32 B5
Copt Oak Leics.............86 F2
Copythorne Hants.........28 F8
Corbets Tey Gt Lon......45 K3
Corbiere Jersey...........236 a7
Corbridge Nthumb......150 C3
Corby Nhants..............88 C5
Corby Glen Lincs........103 G7
Cordon N Ayrs............162 D4
Coreley Shrops...........84 B8
Corfe Somset...............25 K7
Corfe Castle Dorset......15 H6
Corfe Mullen Dorset.....15 J3
Corfton Shrops............83 J6
Corgarff Abers............205 G4
Corhampton Hants........29 L7
Corley Warwks............86 C6
Corley Services
Warwks 86 C6
Cormuir Angus...........195 L3
Cornard Tye Suffk........77 K6
Cornforth Dur.............151 H7
Cornhill Abers............216 B3
Cornhill-on-Tweed
Nthumb 168 C2
Cornholme Calder.......122 D5
Cornoigmore Ag & B...188 C6
Cornsay Dur...............150 E6
Cornsay Colliery Dur...150 F6
Corntown Highld.........212 E3
Corntown V Glam.........36 E5
Cornwell Oxon.............56 F3
Cornwood Devon............6 E4
Cornworthy Devon..........7 J5
Corpach Highld..........191 L2
Corpusty Norfk..........106 D6
Corrachree Abers.......205 K4
Corran Highld............191 K4
Corran Highld............200 C4
Corrie D & G..............155 L5
Corrie N Ayrs.............162 C2
Corriecravie N Ayrs....162 B5
Corriegills N Ayrs......162 D3
Corriegour Lodge
Hotel Highld...........201 K6
Corriemoille Highld....212 B2
Corrimony Highld.......212 B7
Corringham Lincs.......116 E4
Corringham Thurr........46 B4
Corris Gwynd...............81 G2
Corris Uchaf Gwynd.....81 G2
Corrow Ag & B............183 H1
Corry Highld..............199 K1
Corscombe Devon........10 F5
Corscombe Dorset.......13 M2
Corse Gloucs...............55 H3
Corse Lawn Gloucs.......55 J2
Corsham Wilts.............39 K6
Corsindae Abers.........206 D4
Corsley Wilts..............27 J3
Corsley Heath Wilts.....27 J3
Corsock D & G............154 D6
Corston BaNES............39 G7
Corston Wilts..............39 L4
Corstorphine C Edin...177 G4
Cortachy Angus..........196 C4
Corton Suffk...............93 L4
Corton Wilts...............27 L4
Corton Denham
Somset 26 F6
Coruanan Highld........191 L3
Corwen Denbgs............97 G4

Coryton Devon.............10 C7
Coryton Thurr.............46 C4
Cosby Leics................87 G4
Coseley Dudley...........85 G5
Cosgrove Nhants.........73 L6
Cosham C Port.............17 J2
Cosheston Pembks.......49 G6
Coshieville P & K.......194 C6
Cossall Notts.............101 J4
Cossington Leics........87 H2
Cossington Somset.......26 A4
Costessey Norfk...........92 E2
Costock Notts.............101 L7
Coston Leics..............102 D7
Coston Norfk...............92 C3
Cote Oxon...................57 G7
Cotebrook Ches W......112 E7
Cotehill Cumb............148 E5
Cotes Leics...............101 K7
Cotesbach Leics...........87 G6
Cotford St Luke
Somset 25 J6
Cotgrave Notts...........101 M5
Cothal Abers..............207 G3
Cotham Notts.............102 C3
Cotherstone Dur.........140 C4
Cothill Oxon...............57 J7
Cotleigh Devon............13 G3
Cotmanhay Derbys......101 J4
Coton Cambs...............76 B3
Coton Nhants..............73 J1
Coton Staffs................99 J3
Coton Clanford Staffs...99 K7
Coton Hill Shrops........83 J2
Coton in the Elms
Derbys 86 B1
Cotswolds 55 M6
Cott Devon....................7 H4
Cottam Lancs.............121 G4
Cottam Notts.............116 D5
Cottenham Cambs........76 C2
Cottered Herts............60 A3
Cotterstock Nhants......88 F5
Cottesbrooke Nhants....87 K8
Cottesmore Rutlnd......88 C2
Cottingham E R Yk......126 C4
Cottingham Nhants.......88 B5
Cottingley C Brad......123 G3
Cottingley Hall
Crematorium
Leeds 123 K4
Cottisford Oxon...........57 L2
Cotton Suffk................78 C2
Cottown Abers............206 E3
Cottown Abers............215 L8
Cottown of Gight
Abers 216 F6
Cotts Devon...................6 C3
Coughton Warwks........71 J3
Coulaghailtro Ag & B...172 C5
Coulags Highld...........210 D3
Coull Abers...............205 L5
Coulport Ag & B..........173 L2
Coulsdon Gt Lon..........32 B2
Coulston Wilts.............27 L2
Coulter S Lans...........165 K3
Coulton N York...........133 K5
Coultra Fife...............186 F3
Cound Shrops..............83 L3
Coundon Dur..............141 G2
Countersett N York.....131 H2
Countess Wear
Devon 12 B4
Countesthorpe Leics....87 H4
Countisbury Devon.......24 B2
Coupar Angus P & K....195 K7
Coupland Nthumb.......168 D3
Cour Ag & B...............172 D8
Courteachan Highld....199 L6
Courteenhall Nhants....73 L4
Court Henry Carmth......51 H2
Courtsend Essex..........47 G2
Courtway Somset..........25 J5
Cousland Mdloth.........177 K5
Cousley Wood E Susx....33 H6
Cove Ag & B...............173 L2
Cove Border...............179 G4

Cove Devon.................24 E7
Cove Hants..................30 E1
Cove Highld...............219 J3
Cove Bay C Aber.........207 H5
Covehithe Suffk...........93 L6
Coven Staffs................85 G3
Coveney Cambs............90 C6
Covenham St
Bartholomew
Lincs 118 D3
Covenham St Mary
Lincs 118 D3
Coventry Covtry...........86 D7
Coventry Airport
Warwks 86 D8
Coverack Cnwll............3 K7
Coverack Bridges
Cnwll 3 H5
Coverham N York........131 L3
Covington Cambs........74 F1
Covington S Lans........165 J2
Cowan Bridge Lancs...130 C4
Cowbeech E Susx.........20 C3
Cowbit Lincs..............103 L8
Cowbridge V Glam........36 F5
Cowden Kent................32 E5
Cowdenbeath Fife.......177 G1
Cowers Lane Derbys....100 F3
Cowes IoW...................16 F3
Cowesby N York.........133 G2
Cowfold W Susx...........31 K6
Cowhill S Glos.............38 E3
Cowie Stirlg..............175 L1
Cowley Devon...............11 K5
Cowley Gloucs.............55 L5
Cowley Gt Lon.............43 H4
Cowley Oxon................57 K7
Cowling Lancs...........121 H6
Cowling N York...........122 E2
Cowling N York...........132 C3
Cowlinge Suffk............77 G4
Cowpen Nthumb..........159 H5
Cowplain Hants............17 K1
Cowshill Dur.............149 L6
Cowslip Green N Som....38 C7
Cowthorpe N York.......132 F8
Coxbank Ches E...........98 F4
Coxbench Derbys........101 G4
Coxford Cnwll...............8 F5
Coxford Norfk............105 K6
Coxheath Kent.............33 J3
Coxhoe Dur...............151 H7
Coxley Somset.............26 D3
Coxley Wick Somset......26 D3
Coxtie Green Essex......45 K2
Coxwold N York..........133 H4
Coychurch Brdgnd........36 E4
Coychurch
Crematorium
Brdgnd 36 E4
Coylton S Ayrs...........163 K5
Coylumbridge Highld...203 L3
Coytrahen Brdgnd........36 D4
Crabbs Cross Worcs......71 J2
Crabtree W Susx...........31 K6
Crackenthorpe Cumb...138 F3
Crackington Haven
Cnwll 8 F5
Crackleybank Shrops....84 D2
Cracoe N York............131 J7
Craddock Devon...........25 G8
Cradley Dudley...........85 G6
Cradley Herefs............70 D5
Cradley Heath Sandw....85 G6
Cradoc Powys..............52 F2
Crafthole Cnwll.............6 B5
Craggan Highld..........204 C1
Craghead Dur.............150 F5
Crai Powys.................52 D3
Craibstone Moray.......215 L3
Craichie Angus...........196 E6
Craig Angus...............197 H5
Craig Highld..............211 G4
Craigbank E Ayrs.......164 C6
Craigburn Border.......177 H7
Craigcleuch D & G......156 C5
Craigdam Abers..........216 F7

Craigdhu Ag & B.........182 B6
Craigearn Abers.........206 D3
Craigellachie Moray...215 G5
Craigend P & K..........186 B4
Craigend Rens............174 E4
Craigendoran Ag & B...174 C3
Craigends Rens...........174 D5
Craighlaw D & G..........145 G3
Craighouse Ag & B......171 K5
Craigie P & K.............195 H7
Craigie S Ayrs............163 K3
Craigiefold Abers.......217 H2
Craigley D & G............146 D4
Craig Llangiwg Neath....51 K4
Craiglockhart C Edin...177 H4
Craigmillar C Edin......177 J4
Craigneston D & G......154 D3
Craigneuk N Lans........175 K5
Craigneuk N Lans........175 K6
Craignure Ag & B........190 E8
Craigo Angus.............197 H4
Craigrothie Fife.........186 F5
Craigruie Stirlg.........184 B4
Craigton Angus..........196 E8
Craigton C Aber..........206 F5
Craigton E Rens..........174 F7
Craigton
Crematorium
C Glas 174 F5
Craigton of Airlie
Angus 196 B6
Crail Fife.................187 K5
Crailing Border..........167 L4
Craiselound N Linc.....116 C2
Crakehall N York.........132 C2
Crambe N York...........133 L6
Cramlington Nthumb...159 G6
Cramond C Edin..........177 G3
Cramond Bridge
C Edin 177 G4
Cranage Ches E..........113 H7
Cranberry Staffs..........99 J5
Cranborne Dorset........28 B8
Cranbourne Br For........42 F5
Cranbrook Kent............33 K6
Cranfield C Beds..........74 D6
Cranford Gt Lon...........43 J5
Cranford St Andrew
Nhants 88 D7
Cranford St John
Nhants 88 D7
Cranham Gloucs..........55 K5
Crank St Hel..............112 D2
Cranleigh Surrey..........31 H4
Cranmore Somset.........26 F3
Cranoe Leics...............87 L4
Cransford Suffk...........79 G2
Cranshaws Border.......178 E6
Crantock Cnwll.............4 C4
Cranwell Lincs...........103 G3
Cranwich Norfk............91 H4
Cranworth Norfk..........92 B3
Craobh Haven Ag & B...182 A6
Crarae Ag & B............182 E7
Crask Inn Highld........225 L4
Crask of Aigas Highld...212 D6
Craster Nthumb..........169 K5
Cratfield Suffk............93 G7
Crathes Abers............206 E6
Crathes Castle Abers...206 D6
Crathie Abers............205 G6
Crathie Highld...........202 E6
Crathorne N York........141 K5
Craven Arms Shrops......83 H6
Crawcrook Gatesd......150 E3
Crawford S Lans..........165 J5
Crawfordjohn S Lans...165 G5
Crawley Hants.............29 H4
Crawley Oxon..............57 G5
Crawley W Susx............31 L4
Crawley Down
W Susx 32 C5
Crawshawbooth
Lancs 122 B5
Crawton Abers...........197 L1
Cray N York...............131 H4
Crayford Gt Lon...........45 K5

Crayke N York 133 H5
Crays Hill Essex 46 B2
Creacombe Devon 24 C7
Creagan Inn Ag & B........191 J7
Creag Ghoraidh W Isls ..233 C7
Creagorry W Isls 233 C7
Creaguaineach
 Lodge Highld............192 E3
Creaton Nhants 73 K1
Creca D & G 155 M7
Credenhill Herefs 69 J5
Crediton Devon 11 J5
Creebank D & G 153 H6
Creebridge D & G 145 J2
Creech Heathfield
 Somset 25 L6
Creech St Michael
 Somset 25 L6
Creed Cnwll..................4 E6
Creekmouth Gt Lon 45 J4
Creeting St Mary
 Suffk 78 D3
Creeton Lincs 103 G8
Creetown D & G 145 K3
Cregneash IoM 237 a7
Creich Fife 186 E3
Creigiau Cardif 37 G4
Cremyll Cnwll................6 C5
Cressage Shrops..........83 L3
Cressbrook Derbys......114 D6
Cresselly Pembks 49 H6
Cressex Bucks 42 D3
Cressing Essex 61 J4
Cresswell Nthumb 159 H4
Cresswell Pembks 49 H6
Cresswell Staffs 99 L5
Creswell Derbys 115 K6
Cretingham Suffk........78 F3
Cretshengan Ag & B....172 C5
Crewe Ches E 99 G2
Crewe Ches W 98 B2
Crewe Crematorium
 Ches E 99 G2
Crewe Green Ches E......99 G2
Crew Green Powys........83 G1
Crewkerne Somset 13 K1
Crewton C Derb 101 G5
Crianlarich Stirlg.........183 L3
Cribyn Cerdgn 66 C4
Criccieth Gwynd 95 J5
Crich Derbys 101 G2
Crichton Mdloth 177 K6
Crick Nhants 87 H8
Crickadarn Powys 68 C6
Cricket St Thomas
 Somset 13 J2
Crickhowell Powys 53 K4
Cricklade Wilts 40 C2
Cricklewood Gt Lon 44 E3
Crieff P & K 185 H3
Criggion Powys............82 F1
Crigglestone Wakefd ...123 L7
Crimond Abers 217 K3
Crimplesham Norfk 90 F3
Crimscote Warwks........72 B5
Crinaglack Highld 212 C6
Crinan Ag & B 182 A8
Crindledyke N Lans 175 L6
Cringleford Norfk 92 E3
Crinow Pembks 49 J5
Croachy Highld 213 G8
Crockenhill Kent...........45 J6
Crocker End Oxon........42 B3
Crockernwell Devon......11 H6
Crockerton Wilts 27 K3
Crocketford D & G 154 E7
Crockham Hill Kent.......32 D3
Croeserw Neath 36 D2
Croes-goch Pembks......48 D2
Croes-lan Cerdgn 65 L5
Croesor Gwynd 95 L4
Croesyceiliog Carmth....50 E3
Croesyceiliog Torfn 37 L2
Croft Leics 87 G4
Croft Lincs 104 E1
Croft Warrtn 112 F3
Croftamie Stirlg...........174 E2

Crofton Wakefd 124 B6
Croft-on-Tees N York....141 H5
Croftown Highld 220 F5
Crofts Moray 215 G4
Crofts of Dipple
 Moray 215 H3
Crofts of Savoch
 Abers 217 K3
Crofty Swans...............51 G6
Croggan Ag & B..........181 L3
Croglin Cumb..............148 F5
Croick Highld..............222 B3
Cromarty Highld..........223 H7
Crombie Fife 176 E2
Cromdale Highld 214 D8
Cromer Herts 59 M3
Cromer Norfk..............106 F4
Cromford Derbys 100 F2
Cromhall S Glos............39 G3
Cromor W Isls.............232 f3
Cromwell Notts 102 D1
Cronberry E Ayrs.........164 C5
Crondall Hants 30 C2
Cronton Knows...........112 C4
Crook Cumb................138 C7
Crook Dur..................150 E7
Crookedholm E Ayrs.....163 L3
Crookham Nthumb.......168 D2
Crookham W Berk 41 K7
Crookham Village
 Hants 30 C2
Crook Inn Border.........165 L4
Crooklands Cumb 129 L3
Crook of Devon P & K ..185 L7
Cropredy Oxon.............72 F5
Cropston Leics 87 G2
Cropthorne Worcs........71 H5
Cropton N York...........134 B2
Cropwell Bishop
 Notts 102 B5
Cropwell Butler Notts ..102 B5
Cros W Isls.................232 g1
Crosbost W Isls 232 f3
Crosby Cumb...............147 J7
Crosby IoM 237 c5
Crosby N Linc..............125 K7
Crosby Sefton 111 J2
Crosby Garret Cumb ...139 G5
Crosby Ravensworth
 Cumb 138 F4
Croscombe Somset.......26 E3
Cross Somset 26 B3
Crossaig Ag & B...........172 E7
Crossapol Ag & B........188 C7
Cross Ash Mons 54 B4
Cross-at-Hand Kent......33 K4
Crosscanonby Cumb....147 J6
Crossdale Street
 Norfk 106 F5
Cross Flatts C Brad......123 G3
Crossford Fife..............176 E2
Crossford S Lans.........175 L8
Crossgatehall E Loth ...177 K5
Crossgates E Ayrs........163 J1
Crossgates Fife 176 F1
Cross Gates Leeds 124 B4
Crossgates N York.......134 F3
Crossgill Lancs 129 L6
Cross Green Leeds.......123 L4
Cross Green Suffk........77 K4
Cross Green Suffk........78 B4
Cross Hands Carmth.....51 H3
Crosshands E Ayrs.......163 L4
Crosshill Fife 186 C7
Crosshill S Ayrs...........163 J7
Crosshouse E Ayrs.......163 K2
Cross Houses Shrops....83 K3
Cross in Hand E Susx ...20 B2
Cross Inn Cerdgn..........65 L3
Cross Keys Ag & B......174 C2
Crosskeys Caerph..........37 K3
Crosskirk Highld..........230 F2
Cross Lane IoW 17 G4
Cross Lane Head
 Shrops 84 C4
Crosslee Rens 174 D5
Crossmichael D & G 146 C2

Cross of Jackston
 Abers 216 E7
Cross o' th' hands
 Derbys 100 F4
Crossroads Abers 206 B4
Crossroads Abers 206 E6
Cross Street Suffk.........92 E7
Crosston Angus...........196 E5
Cross Town Ches E.......113 H5
Crossway Green
 Worcs 70 E2
Crossways Dorset 14 E5
Crosswell Pembks 64 F6
Crosthwaite Cumb 129 J2
Croston Lancs 121 G6
Crostwick Norfk............92 F1
Crouch End Gt Lon........44 F3
Croucheston Wilts 28 B6
Crouch Hill Dorset........14 D1
Croughton Nhants.........73 G7
Crovie Abers 216 F2
Crowan Cnwll.................3 H4
Crowborough E Susx......32 F6
Crowcombe Somset 25 H4
Crowdecote Derbys......114 C7
Crowden Derbys...........114 B2
Crow Edge Barns.........114 D2
Crowell Oxon................58 C7
Crowfield Suffk.............78 D3
Crowhill E Loth 178 F4
Crow Hill Herefs...........54 F3
Crowhurst E Susx..........20 F3
Crowhurst Surrey..........32 D4
Crowland Lincs 89 J2
Crowland Suffk.............78 B1
Crowlas Cnwll.................2 F5
Crowle N Linc..............125 J7
Crowle Worcs................71 G4
Crowle Green Worcs......71 G3
Crowmarsh Gifford
 Oxon 41 L3
Crown Corner Suffk.......78 F1
Crownhill C Plym............6 C4
Crownhill
 Crematorium
 M Keyn 74 B6
Crownthorpe Norfk........92 C3
Crowntown Cnwll...........3 H5
Crows-an-Wra Cnwll.......2 D5
Crowthorne Wokham.....42 D7
Crowton Ches W..........112 E6
Croxdale Dur...............151 G7
Croxden Staffs 100 B5
Croxley Green Herts......43 H2
Croxteth Lpool 111 L3
Croxton Cambs.............75 J3
Croxton N Linc............126 D7
Croxton Norfk...............91 K6
Croxton Norfk.............106 B6
Croxton Staffs..............99 H6
Croxton Kerrial Leics....102 D6
Croy Highld 213 J4
Croy N Lans................175 J3
Croyde Devon 23 G4
Croydon Cambs............75 K5
Croydon Gt Lon 44 F6
Croydon
 Crematorium
 Gt Lon 44 F6
Crubenmore Highld 203 G7
Cruckmeole Shrops.......83 H2
Cruckton Shrops...........83 H2
Cruden Bay Abers 217 K6
Crudgington Wrekin.......98 F8
Crudwell Wilts..............39 L2
Crumlin Caerph............37 K2
Crumplehorn Cnwll.........5 K5
Crumpsall Manch 113 J2
Crundale Kent...............34 E5
Crunwear Pembks 49 K5
Crux Easton Hants.........29 H1
Crwbin Carmth.............50 F3
Cryers Hill Bucks..........42 E2
Crymmych Pembks........65 G7
Crynant Neath..............52 C6
Crystal Palace Gt Lon....45 G5
Cuaig Highld 209 L3

Cuan Ag & B 181 L4
Cubbington Warwks.....72 E2
Cubert Cnwll..................4 C4
Cublington Bucks..........58 D4
Cublington Herefs.........69 H6
Cuckfield W Susx..........32 B7
Cucklington Somset.......27 H6
Cuckney Notts..............115 K7
Cuddesdon Oxon...........57 L7
Cuddington Bucks..........58 C5
Cuddington Ches W......112 E7
Cuddington Heath
 Ches W 98 C5
Cudham Gt Lon............32 D2
Cudliptown Devon.........10 D8
Cudnell Bmouth 15 K3
Cudworth Barns 124 B8
Cudworth Somset 13 J1
Cuffley Herts................59 M7
Cuil Highld 191 J5
Culbokie Highld 212 E3
Culburnie Highld 212 D6
Culcabock Highld 213 G5
Culcharry Highld 213 K4
Culcheth Warrtn 112 F3
Culdrain Abers 215 L7
Culduie Highld 209 L6
Culford Suffk.................77 J1
Culgaith Cumb 138 E2
Culham Oxon................41 J2
Culkein Highld 224 C2
Culkein Drumbeg
 Highld 224 D2
Culkerton Gloucs...........39 L2
Cullen Moray 215 L2
Cullercoats N Tyne........159 J7
Cullerlie Abers 206 E5
Cullicudden Highld 213 G2
Cullingworth C Brad.....123 G3
Cuillin Hills Highld........199 G3
Cullipool Ag & B...........181 L5
Cullivoe Shet...............235 d2
Culloden Highld 213 H5
Cullompton Devon.........12 C2
Cullompton Services
 Devon 12 D2
Culm Davy Devon.........25 H7
Culmington Shrops........83 J6
Culmstock Devon..........25 H8
Culnacraig Highld.........224 C7
Culnaightrie D & G 146 D3
Culnaknock Highld........209 H2
Culrain Highld 222 D3
Culross Fife 176 D2
Culroy S Ayrs...............163 H6
Culsalmond Abers 216 C7
Culscadden D & G 145 K5
Culshabbin D & G 145 G5
Culswick Shet..............235 b6
Cultercullen Abers 207 H1
Cults C Aber................207 G5
Culverstone Green
 Kent 45 M7
Culverthorpe Lincs 103 G4
Culworth Nhants 73 G5
Culzean Castle &
 Country Park
 S Ayrs 163 G7
Cumbernauld N Lans....175 K4
Cumbernauld Village
 N Lans.................175 K3
Cumberworth Lincs......119 G6
Cuminestown Abers.....216 F4
Cumledge Border.........179 G6
Cummersdale Cumb......148 D4
Cummertrees D & G.....147 K2
Cummingston Moray.....214 E1
Cumnock E Ayrs..........164 B5
Cumnor Oxon...............57 J7
Cumrew Cumb 148 F4
Cumrue D & G 155 J3
Cumwhinton Cumb.......148 D4
Cumwhitton Cumb........148 E4
Cundall N York.............132 F5
Cunninghamhead
 N Ayrs..................163 J2
Cunningsburgh Shet....235 d4

Cupar Fife....................186 F4
Cupar Muir Fife.............186 F5
Curbar Derbys..............114 E6
Curbridge Hants.............17 G1
Curbridge Oxon.............57 G6
Curdridge Hants.............29 K8
Curdworth Warwks.........85 L5
Curland Somset..............25 L7
Curridge W Berk............41 J6
Currie C Edin................177 G5
Curry Mallet Somset......25 L6
Curry Rivel Somset.........26 B6
Curtisden Green Kent.....33 J5
Curtisknowle Devon.........7 H5
Cury Cnwll......................3 H6
Cushnie Abers...............205 L3
Cutcloy D & G...............145 J7
Cutcombe Somset..........24 E4
Cuthill Highld................223 G4
Cutnall Green Worcs......70 F2
Cutsdean Gloucs............56 C3
Cutthorpe Derbys..........115 G6
Cuxham Oxon................42 A2
Cuxton Medway.............46 B6
Cuxwold Lincs...............117 K2
Cwm Denbgs.................110 E6
Cwmafan Neath..............36 B3
Cwmaman Rhondd.........52 F7
Cwmbâch Powys.............68 D6
Cwmbach Carmth...........50 B1
Cwmbach Rhondd..........52 F7
Cwmbach Llechrhyd
Powys.........................68 B4
Cwmbran Torfn.............37 L2
Cwmcarn Caerph...........37 K2
Cwmcarvan Mons...........54 C6
Cwm-cou Cerdgn...........65 J6
Cwm Crawnon Powys....53 H4
Cwmdare Rhondd..........52 F7
Cwmdu Powys...............53 J4
Cwmdu Swans...............51 J6
Cwmduad Carmth...........65 L7
Cwmfelin Brdgnd...........36 D3
Cwmfelin Myr Td...........53 H7
Cwmfelin Boeth
Carmth.......................49 K4
Cwmfelinfach Caerph.....37 J3
Cwmffrwd Carmth...........50 E3
Cwmgiedd Powys...........52 C5
Cwmgorse Carmth..........51 K4
Cwmgwili Carmth............51 H4
Cwmhiraeth Carmth........65 K6
Cwm Llinau Powys..........81 J2
Cwmllynfell Neath...........51 L3
Cwmmawr Carmth...........51 G3
Cwmparc Rhondd............36 E2
Cwmpengraig
Carmth.......................65 K6
Cwmtillery Blae G............53 K6
Cwm-twrch Isaf
Powys.........................52 B6
Cwm-twrch Uchaf
Powys.........................51 L4
Cwm-y-glo Gwynd.........109 H8
Cwmystwyth Cerdgn.......81 H8
Cwrt-newydd Cerdgn......66 C5
Cylibebyll Neath..............51 L5
Cymer Neath..................36 D2
Cymmer Rhondd.............36 F3
Cynghordy Carmth...........67 H6
Cynonville Neath..............36 C2
Cynwyd Denbgs................97 G4
Cynwyl Elfed Carmth......65 L8

D

Daccombe Devon..............7 K3
Dacre Cumb...................138 C2
Dacre N York.................132 B7
Dacre Banks N York.......132 B6
Daddry Shield Dur.........149 M7
Dadford Bucks.................73 J6
Dadlington Leics..............86 E4
Dagenham Gt Lon............45 J3
Daglingworth Gloucs......55 M6

Dagnall Bucks.................59 G5
Dailly S Ayrs.................152 F2
Dairsie Fife...................187 G4
Dalabrog W Isls.............233 b8
Dalavich Ag & B.............182 D5
Dalbeattie D & G...........146 E3
Dalby IoM.....................237 b5
Dalby N York.................133 K5
Dalcapon P & K..............194 F5
Dalchalm Highld.............226 F7
Dalchreichart Highld......201 L3
Dalchruin P & K.............184 F4
Dalcrue P & K................185 L2
Dalditch Devon................12 D5
Daldowie
Crematorium
C Glas......................175 J6
Dale Derbys..................101 H5
Dale Pembks....................48 D6
Dalelia Highld................190 E3
Dalgarven N Ayrs..........163 H1
Dalgety Bay Fife............177 G2
Dalgig E Ayrs................164 B6
Dalginross P & K...........185 G3
Dalguise P & K..............194 F6
Dalhalvaig Highld...........230 C5
Dalham Suffk...................77 G3
Daliburgh W Isls............233 b8
Dalkeith Mdloth..............177 K5
Dallas Moray.................214 D4
Dallinghoo Suffk.............78 F4
Dallington E Susx...........20 D2
Dallington Nhants............73 K3
Dalmally Ag & B.............183 H3
Dalmary Stirlg...............184 C7
Dalmellington E Ayrs.....153 K2
Dalmeny C Edin.............176 F3
Dalmore Highld..............222 F7
Dalmuir W Duns.............174 E4
Dalnabreck Highld..........190 E3
Dalnacardoch P & K......194 B3
Dalnahaitnach Highld.....203 K2
Dalnaspidal P & K..........193 K2
Dalnawillan Lodge
Highld.......................230 F7
Daloist P & K.................194 C5
Dalqueich P & K.............186 A6
Dalquhairn S Ayrs.........153 G3
Dalreavoch Lodge
Highld.......................226 D6
Dalry N Ayrs..................174 B7
Dalrymple E Ayrs...........163 J6
Dalserf S Lans...............175 L7
Dalsmeran Ag & B.........161 G6
Dalston Cumb................148 C5
Dalswinton D & G..........155 G5
Dalton D & G.................155 K7
Dalton N York...............132 F4
Dalton N York................140 E5
Dalton Nthumb...............158 E7
Dalton-in-Furness
Cumb.......................128 F5
Dalton-le-Dale Dur........151 K5
Dalton-on-Tees
N York......................141 H5
Dalton Piercy Hartpl......141 L2
Dalveich Stirlg...............184 D3
Dalwhinnie Highld..........202 F7
Dalwood Devon................13 G3
Damerham Hants.............28 C7
Damgate Norfk.................93 J2
Danbury Essex.................61 J6
Danby N York................142 F5
Danby Wiske N York......141 H7
Dandaleith Moray...........215 G5
Danderhall Mdloth..........177 J4
Danebridge Ches E........114 B8
Dane End Herts...............60 B4
Danehill E Susx...............32 D7
Dane Hills C Leic.............87 H3
Dane Street Kent.............34 E4
Danshillock Abers..........216 D3
Danskine E Loth.............178 C5
Darenth Kent...................45 K5
Daresbury Halton...........112 E5
Darfield Barns...............115 H1

Dargate Kent...................34 E3
Darite Cnwll......................5 K3
Darlaston Wsall...............85 H4
Darlaston Green Wsall....85 H4
Darley N York.................132 C7
Darley Abbey C Derb....101 G5
Darley Bridge Derbys....100 E1
Darley Dale Derbys........114 F8
Darley Green Solhll.........85 L8
Darleyhall Herts..............59 J4
Darley Head N York.......132 B7
Darlingscott Warwks......72 B6
Darlington Darltn...........141 H4
Darlington
Crematorium
Darltn.......................141 G4
Darlton Notts................116 C6
Darnick Border..............167 H3
Darowen Powys...............81 H3
Darra Abers..................216 E5
Darracott Devon...............9 G2
Darracott Devon..............23 G4
Darras Hall Nthumb......158 E7
Darrington Wakefd........124 D6
Darsham Suffk................79 J1
Darshill Somset...............26 E3
Dartford Kent..................45 K5
Dartington Devon.............7 H4
Dartmoor
National Park
Devon.......................11 G8
Dartmouth Devon.............7 K5
Darton Barns................123 L7
Darvel E Ayrs................164 B2
Darwen Bl w D..............121 K6
Datchet W & M................43 G5
Datchworth Herts............59 L4
Daubhill Bolton..............121 K8
Daugh of Kinermony
Moray.......................214 F6
Dauntsey Wilts................39 M4
Dava Highld...................214 C6
Davenham Ches W.........112 F7
Daventry Nhants..............73 H3
Davidson's Mains
C Edin......................177 G4
Davidstow Cnwll...............8 F7
Davington D & G...........155 M2
Davington Hill Kent.........34 D3
Daviot Abers.................216 E8
Daviot Highld................213 H6
Daviot House Highld......213 H6
Davoch of Grange
Moray.......................215 K4
Dawesgreen Surrey........31 K3
Dawley Wrekin................84 C2
Dawlish Devon................12 B6
Dawlish Warren
Devon.......................12 C6
Daybrook Notts.............101 L4
Daylesford Gloucs..........56 E3
Deal Kent.......................35 K4
Dean Cumb...................136 E3
Dean Devon......................7 H3
Dean Devon....................23 L2
Dean Hants.....................29 K7
Dean Oxon......................57 G4
Dean Somset...................26 F3
Dean Bottom Kent..........45 L6
Deanburnhaugh
Border.......................166 F6
Deancombe Devon............7 G3
Dean Court Oxon............57 J6
Deane Bolton................121 K8
Deane Hants...................29 K2
Deanhead Kirk..............122 F7
Deanland Dorset.............27 M7
Dean Prior Devon.............7 H3
Deanraw Nthumb...........149 L3
Deans W Loth................176 D5
Deanscales Cumb..........136 F2
Deanshanger
Nhants.......................73 L6
Deanshaugh Moray.......215 H4
Deanston Stirlg..............184 F6
Dearham Cumb..............147 J7
Debach Suffk...................78 F4
Debden Essex................45 H2
Debden Essex.................60 E2
Debenham Suffk..............78 E2
Deblin's Green Worcs....70 E5
Dechmont W Loth.........176 E4
Dechmont Road
W Loth......................176 D4
Deddington Oxon............57 J2
Dedham Essex................62 C2
Dedworth W & M............42 F5
Deene Nhants.................88 D5
Deenethorpe Nhants......88 D5
Deepcar Sheff...............114 F3
Deeping Gate C Pete......89 G2
Deeping St James
Lincs.........................89 H2
Deeping St Nicholas
Lincs.........................89 J1
Deerhurst Gloucs............55 K3
Defford Worcs.................71 G5
Defynnog Powys.............52 E3
Deganwy Conwy............109 L5
Degnish Ag & B.............182 A5
Deighton C York............124 F2
Deighton N York............141 J6
Deiniolen Gwynd...........109 H8
Delabole Cnwll..................8 E7
Delamere Ches W..........112 E7
Delfrigs Abers...............207 H2
Delliefure Highld............214 D7
Dell Quay W Susx..........18 A5
Delnabo Moray..............204 E3
Delnashaugh Inn
Moray.......................214 E7
Delny Highld..................223 G6
Delph Oldham................122 E8
Delves Dur....................150 E5
Dembleby Lincs.............103 H5
Denaby Donc.................115 J2
Denbigh Denbgs............110 E7
Denbrae Fife.................186 F4
Denbury Devon..................7 J3
Denby Derbys................101 H4
Denby Dale Kirk............123 J8
Denchworth Oxon...........41 G3
Dendron Cumb..............128 F5
Denfield P & K...............185 K4
Denford Nhants..............88 E7
Dengie Essex..................62 B7
Denham Bucks................43 H3
Denham Suffk.................77 H3
Denham Suffk.................92 E8
Denham Green Bucks.....43 H3
Denhead Abers..............217 J4
Denhead Fife.................187 G5
Denhead of Gray
C Dund......................186 F2
Denholm Border............167 J3
Denholme C Brad..........123 G4
Denmead Hants..............30 A8
Denmore C Aber............207 H3
Dennington Suffk............79 G2
Denny Falk.....................175 L2
Dennyloanhead Falk......175 L3
Den of Lindores Fife......186 D4
Denshaw Oldham...........122 E7
Denside Abers...............206 F6
Densole Kent...................35 G6
Denston Suffk.................77 H4
Denstone Staffs............100 C4
Denstroude Kent.............34 E3
Dent Cumb....................130 D3
Denton Cambs.................89 G6
Denton Darltn................140 F4
Denton E Susx.................19 L5
Denton Kent....................35 G5
Denton Lincs.................102 E6
Denton N York...............123 H2
Denton Nhants................74 B3
Denton Norfk...................93 G5
Denton Tamesd.............113 L3
Denver Norfk...................90 E3
Denwick Nthumb...........169 J6
Deopham Norfk...............92 C4
Deopham Green
Norfk.........................92 C4
Depden Suffk..................77 H3

Deptford Gt Lon 45 G4
Deptford Wilts...............28 A4
Derby C Derb 101 G5
Derby Devon 23 J5
Derbyhaven IoM 237 b7
Derculich P & K...........194 D5
Dereham Norfk 92 B2
Deri Caerph 53 H7
Derringstone Kent.........35 G5
Derrington Staffs...........99 K7
Derry Hill Wilts 39 L6
Derrythorpe N Linc 125 J8
Dersingham Norfk 105 H6
Dervaig Ag & B 189 K6
Derwen Denbgs............97 G3
Derwenlas Powys..........80 F4
Derwent Water
  Cumb 137 J3
Desborough Nhants 88 B6
Desford Leics 86 F3
Deskford Moray............215 L3
Detling Kent...................33 K2
Devauden Mons 54 C7
Devil's Bridge Cerdgn....81 G7
Devizes Wilts.................40 A7
Devonport C Plym 6 C5
Devonside Clacks 185 J7
Devoran Cnwll 4 C7
Dewarton Mdloth 177 K5
Dewlish Dorset 14 E3
Dewsbury Kirk.............123 K6
Dewsbury Moor
  Crematorium Kirk 123 J6
Deytheur Powys............97 K8
Dial Post W Susx 18 F2
Dibden Hants 16 E2
Dibden Purlieu Hants ...16 E2
Dickleburgh Norfk.........92 E6
Didbrook Gloucs 56 B2
Didcot Oxon 41 K3
Didcot Railway
  Centre Oxon..............41 K3
Diddington Cambs 75 H2
Diddlebury Shrops 83 K6
Didling W Susx 18 A3
Didmarton Gloucs 39 J3
Didsbury Manch 113 J3
Digby Lincs 103 H2
Digg Highld 218 C7
Diggle Oldham 122 F8
Digmoor Lancs............112 C1
Dihewyd Cerdgn...........66 C4
Dilham Norfk 107 G7
Dilhorne Staffs..............99 L4
Dill Hall Lancs 121 L4
Dillington Cambs 75 G2
Dilston Nthumb 150 B3
Dilton Wilts 27 K2
Dilton Marsh Wilts.........27 J2
Dilwyn Herefs 69 H4
Dinas Gwynd 94 E5
Dinas Pembks 64 E6
Dinas-Mawddwy
  Gwynd.......................81 J1
Dinas Powys V Glam 37 J6
Dinder Somset 26 E3
Dinedor Herefs 69 K6
Dingestow Mons 54 C6
Dingle Lpool 111 K4
Dingley Nhants 87 L6
Dingwall Highld 212 E3
Dinnet Abers 205 K5
Dinnington N u Ty.........158 F7
Dinnington Rothm........115 K4
Dinnington Somset........26 B8
Dinorwic Gwynd............95 K1
Dinton Bucks 58 C5
Dinton Wilts 28 A5
Dinwoodie D & G.........155 K4
Dinworthy Devon 9 J2
Dipford Somset 25 J6
Dippen Ag & B.............161 K2
Dippen N Ayrs 162 D5
Dippertown Devon 10 C7
Dipple Moray...............215 H3
Dipple S Ayrs 152 E2
Diptford Devon 7 G4

Dipton Dur 150 E4
Dirleton E Loth 178 B2
Dirt Pot Nthumb 149 L5
Diseworth Leics...........101 J7
Dishforth N York 132 F5
Disley Ches E 113 L5
Diss Norfk....................92 D7
Distington Cumb 136 D3
Distington Hall
  Crematorium
  Cumb 136 E3
Ditchampton Wilts.........28 C5
Ditcheat Somset 26 F4
Ditchingham Norfk.........93 G5
Ditchling E Susx 19 J3
Ditherington Shrops......83 K2
Ditteridge Wilts 39 J6
Dittisham Devon 7 K5
Ditton Kent...................33 J2
Ditton Green Cambs 76 F3
Ditton Priors Shrops......83 L5
Dixton Mons 54 D5
Dobcross Oldham........113 M1
Dobwalls Cnwll...............5 K3
Doccombe Devon 11 H7
Dochgarroch Highld.....212 F6
Docking Norfk 105 J5
Docklow Herefs.............69 L3
Dockray Cumb 137 L3
Doddinghurst Essex 60 F7
Doddington Cambs 90 B5
Doddington Kent............34 C4
Doddington Lincs.........116 E7
Doddington Nthumb.....168 E3
Doddington Shrops 84 B7
Doddiscombsleigh
  Devon 11 K7
Dodd's Green Ches E 98 E4
Dodford Nhants 73 H3
Dodford Worcs 85 G8
Dodington S Glos 39 H4
Dodington Somset..........25 J4
Dodleston Ches W..........98 A1
Dodside E Rens............174 F7
Dods Leigh Staffs.........100 A5
Dodworth Barns...........114 F1
Dogdyke Lincs.............103 K2
Dogmersfield Hants 30 C2
Dolanog Powys..............82 B2
Dolbenmaen Gwynd.......95 J4
Dolfach Powys...............81 K3
Dolfor Powys.................82 C6
Dolgarrog Conwy.........109 L7
Dolgellau Gwynd 96 B8
Doll Highld 226 F7
Dollar Clacks...............185 K7
Dollarfield Clacks........185 K7
Dolphin Flints..............111 H6
Dolphinholme Lancs....129 L8
Dolphinton S Lans........176 F8
Dolton Devon.................10 E3
Dolwen Conwy 110 B6
Dolwyddelan Conwy......96 B3
Domgay Powys..............97 L8
Doncaster Donc 115 L2
Doncaster North
  Services Donc...........125 G7
Donhead St Andrew
  Wilts..........................27 K6
Donhead St Mary
  Wilts..........................27 K6
Donibristle Fife 177 G2
Doniford Somset...........25 G3
Donington Lincs...........103 K5
Donington on Bain
  Lincs........................118 C5
Donington Park
  Services Leics...........101 J7
Donisthorpe Leics.........86 C2
Donnington Gloucs 56 D3
Donnington Shrops 83 L2
Donnington W Berk 41 J6
Donnington W Susx 18 B5
Donnington Wrekin 84 C2
Donnington Wood
  Wrekin......................84 C2
Donyatt Somset 25 M8

Doonfoot S Ayrs 163 H5
Dorback Lodge
  Highld 204 D3
Dorchester Dorset 14 D4
Dorchester Oxon...........41 L2
Dordon Warwks 86 C4
Dore Sheff 114 F5
Dores Highld 212 F7
Dorking Surrey..............31 K2
Dormans Land Surrey....32 D5
Dormanstown Herefs 69 L6
Dormston Worcs 71 H3
Dorney Bucks................42 F5
Dornie Highld...............200 D1
Dornoch Highld 223 H4
Dornock D & G.............147 M2
Dorrery Highld 230 F5
Dorridge Solhll 85 L8
Dorrington Lincs...........103 H2
Dorrington Shrops..........83 J3
Dorrington Shrops..........99 G4
Dorsington Warwks 71 K4
Dorstone Herefs............69 G6
Dorton Bucks.................58 B5
Douglas IoM 237 d6
Douglas S Lans............165 G4
Douglas and Angus
  C Dund 187 G2
Douglas Borough
  Crematorium IoM 237 d5
Douglas Pier Ag & B 183 H7
Douglastown Angus......196 C6
Douglas Water S Lans..165 G3
Douglas West S Lans...164 F3
Doulting Somset 26 F3
Dounby Ork 234 b5
Doune Highld 221 L2
Doune Stirlg 184 F6
Dounepark S Ayrs........152 E3
Dounie Highld 222 D4
Dousland Devon 6 D3
Dove Holes Derbys......114 B6
Dovenby Cumb 147 J7
Dover Kent...................35 J6
Dover Castle Kent 35 J6
Dovercourt Essex..........62 F2
Doverdale Worcs 70 F2
Doveridge Derbys.......100 C5
Doversgreen Surrey.......31 L2
Dowally P & K 194 F6
Dowdeswell Gloucs 55 M4
Dowlais Myr Td.............53 G6
Dowland Devon 10 E3
Dowlish Wake
  Somset 26 A8
Down Ampney Gloucs....40 C2
Downderry Cnwll............5 L5
Downe Gt Lon...............45 H7
Downend Gloucs 39 J2
Downend S Glos 38 F5
Downfield C Dund 186 F2
Downgate Cnwll..............6 A2
Downham Essex............46 B2
Downham Gt Lon 45 H5
Downham Lancs...........122 B2
Downham Market
  Norfk.........................90 E3
Down Hatherley
  Gloucs 55 K4
Downhead Somset 26 E6
Downhead Somset 27 G3
Downhill P & K 186 A2
Downholme N York 140 E7
Downies Abers 207 H6
Downley Bucks..............42 D2
Down St Mary Devon 11 H4
Downs Crematorium
  Br & H 19 J4
Downside Surrey...........43 J8
Down Thomas Devon 6 D6
Downton Wilts...............28 D6
Dowsby Lincs 103 J3
Doynton S Glos.............39 G5
Draethen Caerph...........37 K3
Draffan S Lans.............164 F1
Drakeholes Notts.........116 B4
Drakemyre N Ayrs.......174 B7

Drakes Broughton
  Worcs 71 G5
Draughton N York.........131 K8
Draughton Nhants.........87 L7
Drax N York 125 G5
Draycote Warwks 72 F1
Draycott Derbys...........101 H6
Draycott Gloucs.............71 L7
Draycott Somset 26 C2
Draycott in the Clay
  Staffs.......................100 D6
Draycott in the
  Moors Staffs..............99 M4
Drayton C Port 17 J2
Drayton Leics 88 B5
Drayton Norfk 92 E2
Drayton Oxon 41 J2
Drayton Oxon 72 E6
Drayton Somset 26 B6
Drayton Worcs 85 G7
Drayton Bassett
  Staffs.........................85 L4
Drayton Beauchamp
  Bucks........................58 E5
Drayton Manor Park
  Staffs.........................85 L4
Drayton Parslow
  Bucks........................58 D3
Drayton St Leonard
  Oxon..........................41 L2
Dreen Hill Pembks 48 F5
Drefach Carmth..............51 G3
Drefach Carmth..............65 K6
Drefach Cerdgn..............66 C5
Dreghorn N Ayrs...........163 J2
Drellingore Kent............35 H6
Drem E Loth 178 B3
Drewsteignton
  Devon 11 H6
Driffield E R Yk............134 F7
Driffield Gloucs.............56 B7
Drift Cnwll.....................2 D5
Drigg Cumb 136 E7
Drighlington Leeds 123 J5
Drimnin Highld 190 B5
Drimpton Dorset 13 K2
Drimsallie Highld 191 J1
Dringhouses C York 124 E2
Drinkstone Suffk 77 L3
Drinkstone Green
  Suffk.........................77 L3
Droitton Staffs.............100 A6
Droitwich Worcs 70 F2
Dron P & K..................186 B4
Dronfield Derbys..........115 G5
Drongan E Ayrs............163 K5
Dronley Abers..............186 L1
Droop Dorset................14 E2
Droxford Hants 29 L7
Droylsden Tamesd.......113 K2
Druid Denbgs................97 G4
Druidston Pembks.........48 E4
Druimarbin Highld 191 L3
Druimavuic Ag & B.......191 K7
Druimdrishaig Ag & B...172 C4
Druimindarroch
  Highld 199 L7
Drum Ag & B 172 F3
Drum P & K.................185 L7
Drumalbin S Lans.........165 K2
Drumbeg Highld...........224 D3
Drumblade Abers 216 B6
Drumbreddon D & G....144 C6
Drumbuie Highld 210 B7
Drumburgh Cumb 148 A3
Drumburn D & G...........146 F4
Drumchapel C Glas......174 F4
Drumchastle P & K.......193 L5
Drumclog S Lans..........164 C2
Drumeldrie Fife 187 G6
Drumelzier Border 165 M3
Drumfearn Highld.........199 L3
Drumfrennie Abers.......206 D5
Drumgley Angus..........196 C6
Drumguish Highld 203 J5
Drumin Moray..............214 E7
Drumjohn D & G 153 L3

Drumlamford S Ayrs.....153 G6
Drumlasie Abers.........206 C4
Drumleaning Cumb......148 A5
Drumlemble Ag & B.....161 H5
Drumlithie Abers.......197 J1
Drummoddie D & G......145 H6
Drummore D & G........144 D7
Drummuir Moray........215 J5
Drumnadrochit
  Highld...............212 D7
Drumnaglaur D & G.....144 D7
Drumnagorrach
  Moray................215 L4
Drumpark D & G........154 F6
Drumrunie Lodge
  Highld...............224 D2
Drumshang S Ayrs......163 G6
Drumuie Highld........209 G5
Drumuillie Highld.....204 B2
Drumvaich Stirlg......184 E6
Drunzie P & K.........186 B5
Drybeck Cumb..........138 F4
Drybridge Moray.......215 K2
Drybridge N Ayrs......163 J3
Drybrook Gloucs.......54 F4
Dryburgh Border.......167 J3
Dry Doddington Lincs..102 D3
Dry Drayton Cambs.....75 L3
Drymen Stirlg.........174 E2
Drymuir Abers.........217 G5
Drynoch Highld........208 F7
Dubford Abers.........216 F2
Duchally Highld.......225 J5
Ducklington Oxon......57 G6
Duddenhoe End
  Essex................76 C7
Duddingston C Edin....177 J4
Duddington Nhants.....88 E4
Duddlestone Somset....25 K7
Duddo Nthumb..........168 D2
Duddon Ches W.........112 D8
Dudleston Shrops......97 M5
Dudleston Heath
  Shrops...............98 A5
Dudley Dudley.........85 G5
Dudley N Tyne.........159 G7
Dudley Port Sandw.....85 G5
Dudsbury Dorset.......15 K3
Duffield Derbys.......101 G4
Duffryn Neath.........36 C2
Dufftown Moray........215 H6
Duffus Moray..........214 E2
Dufton Cumb...........139 G3
Duggleby N York.......134 D6
Duirinish Highld......210 B7
Duisdalemore Highld...199 L3
Duisky Highld.........191 K2
Duke Street Suffk.....78 C6
Dukinfield Tamesd.....113 L2
Dukinfield
  Crematorium
  Tamesd..............113 L2
Dulcote Somset........26 E3
Dulford Devon.........12 D2
Dull P & K............194 C6
Dullatur N Lans.......175 K3
Dullingham Cambs......76 F3
Duloe Beds............75 H3
Duloe Cnwll...........5 K4
Dulverton Somset......24 E5
Dulwich Gt Lon........45 G5
Dumbarton W Duns......174 D4
Dumbleton Gloucs......71 H7
Dumfries D & G........155 G6
Dumgoyne Stirlg.......174 F2
Dummer Hants..........29 L3
Dumpton Kent..........35 K2
Dun Angus.............197 G4
Dunalastair P & K.....193 L5
Dunan Ag & B..........173 K4
Dunan Highld..........209 J8
Dunan P & K...........193 G5
Dunaverty Ag & B......161 H7
Dunball Somset........25 L3
Dunbar E Loth.........178 E3
Dunbeath Highld.......227 L3

Dunbeg Ag & B.........182 C2
Dunblane Stirlg.......185 G6
Dunbog Fife...........186 E4
Duncanston Highld.....212 F3
Duncanstone Abers.....216 B8
Dunchideock Devon.....11 K7
Dunchurch Warwks......72 F1
Duncow D & G..........155 G5
Duncrievie P & K......186 B5
Duncton W Susx........18 C3
Dundee C Dund.........186 F2
Dundee Airport
  C Dund..............186 F2
Dundee
  Crematorium
  C Dund..............186 F2
Dundon Somset.........26 C5
Dundonald S Ayrs......163 J3
Dundonnell Highld.....220 E4
Dundraw Cumb..........147 L5
Dundreggan Highld.....201 L3
Dundrennan D & G......146 D5
Dundry N Som..........38 E6
Dunecht Abers.........206 E4
Dunfermline Fife......176 F2
Dunfermline
  Crematorium Fife....176 F2
Dunfield Gloucs.......40 C2
Dungavel S Lans.......164 D3
Dungeness Kent........21 L3
Dunham Notts..........116 D6
Dunham-on-the-Hill
  Ches W...............112 C6
Dunhampton Worcs......70 F2
Dunham Town Traffd....113 H4
Dunham
  Woodhouses
  Traffd...............113 G4
Dunholme Lincs........117 G5
Dunino Fife...........187 J5
Dunipace Falk.........175 L2
Dunkeld P & K.........195 G7
Dunkerton BaNES.......39 G8
Dunkeswell Devon......12 E2
Dunkeswick N York.....123 L2
Dunkirk Kent..........34 E3
Dunkirk S Glos........39 H4
Dunk's Green Kent.....33 G3
Dunlappie Angus.......196 F3
Dunley Worcs..........70 E2
Dunlop E Ayrs.........174 D8
Dunmaglass Highld.....202 F2
Dunmore Falk..........176 B1
Dunnet Highld.........231 J2
Dunnichen Angus.......196 E6
Dunning P & K.........185 L4
Dunnington C York.....133 K8
Dunnington E R Yk.....126 E1
Dunnington Warwks.....71 J4
Dunoon Ag & B.........173 K3
Dunphail Moray........214 C5
Dunragit D & G........144 E4
Duns Border...........179 G7
Dunsby Lincs..........103 J6
Dunscore D & G........154 F5
Dunscroft Donc........124 F8
Dunsdale R & Cl.......142 D4
Dunsden Green Oxon....42 C5
Dunsdon Devon.........9 J3
Dunsfold Surrey.......31 G4
Dunsford Devon........11 J6
Dunshalt Fife.........186 D5
Dunshillock Abers.....217 J3
Dunsill Notts.........101 J1
Dunsley N York........143 H5
Dunsley Staffs........84 F6
Dunsmore Bucks........58 E6
Dunsop Bridge Lancs...121 K1
Dunstable C Beds......59 G4
Dunstall Staffs.......100 D7
Dunstan Nthumb........169 K5
Dunster Somset........24 F3
Duns Tew Oxon.........57 J3
Dunston Gatesd........151 G3
Dunston Lincs.........117 H8
Dunston Norfk.........92 F3
Dunston Staffs........99 L8

Dunstone Devon........6 E5
Dunstone Devon........7 G2
Dunsville Donc........124 F8
Dunswell E R Yk.......126 D4
Dunsyre S Lans........176 E8
Dunterton Devon.......6 B1
Duntisbourne
  Abbots Gloucs.......55 L6
Duntisbourne Rouse
  Gloucs...............55 M6
Duntish Dorset........14 D2
Duntocher W Duns......174 E4
Dunton Bucks..........58 D3
Dunton C Beds.........75 J5
Dunton Norfk..........105 L6
Dunton Bassett Leics..87 G5
Dunton Green Kent.....32 F2
Duntulm Highld........218 C6
Dunure S Ayrs.........163 G6
Dunvant Swans.........51 H6
Dunvegan Highld.......208 D5
Dunwich Suffk.........79 K1
Durgan Cnwll..........3 K5
Durham Dur............151 G6
Durham Cathedral
  Dur.................151 G6
Durham
  Crematorium Dur....151 G6
Durham Services Dur..151 H7
Durham Tees Valley
  Airport S on T......141 J5
Durisdeer D & G.......154 F2
Durisdeermill D & G...154 F2
Durleigh Somset.......25 L4
Durley Hants..........29 K7
Durley Wilts..........40 E7
Durley Street Hants...29 K7
Durlock Kent..........35 H3
Durlock Kent..........35 J2
Durness Highld........228 F3
Durno Abers...........216 D8
Duror Highld..........191 K5
Durran Ag & B.........182 D5
Durrington W Susx.....18 F5
Durrington Wilts......28 D3
Durris Abers..........206 E6
Dursley Gloucs........39 H2
Dursley Cross Gloucs..55 G4
Durston Somset........25 L5
Durweston Dorset......15 G2
Duston Nhants.........73 K3
Duthil Highld.........203 L1
Dutton Ches W.........112 E5
Duxford Cambs........76 C5
Duxford Oxon.........57 G7
Dwygyfylchi Conwy.....109 L6
Dwyran IoA...........108 F7
Dyce C Aber..........207 G3
Dyffryn Ardudwy
  Gwynd...............95 K7
Dyffryn Cellwen
  Neath...............52 D6
Dyke Lincs...........103 J7
Dyke Moray...........214 B3
Dykehead Angus.......195 K5
Dykehead Angus.......196 C4
Dykehead N Lans......176 B6
Dykehead Stirlg......184 D7
Dykelands Abers......197 H3
Dykends Angus........195 K5
Dykeside Abers.......216 D5
Dymchurch Kent.......34 E8
Dymock Gloucs........55 G2
Dyrham S Glos........39 H5
Dysart Fife..........186 E8
Dyserth Denbgs.......110 E5

E

Eagland Hill Lancs...120 F2
Eagle Lincs..........116 E7
Eaglescliffe S on T..141 K4
Eaglesfield Cumb.....136 F2
Eaglesfield D & G....155 M7
Eaglesham E Rens.....175 G7

Eagley Bolton........121 L7
Eakring Notts........102 A1
Ealand N Linc........125 J7
Ealing Gt Lon........44 D4
Eals Nthumb..........149 H4
Eamont Bridge Cumb...138 D2
Earby Lancs..........122 D2
Eardington Shrops....84 C5
Eardisland Herefs....69 H3
Eardisley Herefs.....68 F5
Eardiston Shrops.....98 A7
Eardiston Worcs......70 C2
Earith Cambs.........89 L8
Earlestown St Hel....112 E3
Earley Wokham........42 C6
Earlham Norfk........92 E2
Earlham
  Crematorium
  Norfk...............92 E2
Earlish Highld.......208 F3
Earls Barton Nhants..74 C2
Earls Colne Essex....61 K3
Earls Common Worcs...71 G3
Earl's Croome Worcs..70 F6
Earlsdon Covtry......86 D7
Earlsferry Fife......187 H7
Earlsfield Gt Lon....44 E5
Earlsford Abers......216 F7
Earlsheaton Kirk.....123 K6
Earl Shilton Leics...86 F4
Earl Soham Suffk.....78 F2
Earl Sterndale
  Derbys..............114 C7
Earlston Border......167 J3
Earlston E Ayrs......163 K3
Earlswood Surrey.....32 B4
Earlswood Warwks.....85 K8
Earnley W Susx.......17 M3
Earsdon N Tyne.......159 H7
Earsham Norfk........93 G5
Eartham W Susx.......18 C4
Easby N York.........142 C5
Easdale Ag & B.......181 L4
Easebourne W Susx....30 E6
Easenhall Warwks.....86 F7
Eashing Surrey.......30 F3
Easington Bucks......58 B6
Easington Dur........151 K6
Easington E R Yk.....127 J6
Easington R & Cl.....142 F4
Easington Colliery
  Dur.................151 K6
Easington Lane
  Sundld..............151 J5
Easingwold N York....133 H5
Eassie and Nevay
  Angus...............196 B7
East Aberthaw
  V Glam..............37 G6
East Allington Devon..7 H6
East Anstey Devon....24 D6
East Ashey IoW.......17 H5
East Ashling W Susx..17 M2
East Ayton N York....134 F3
East Barkwith Lincs..117 K5
East Barming Kent....33 J3
East Barnby N York...143 G5
East Barnet Gt Lon...44 F2
East Barns E Loth....178 F3
East Barsham Norfk...105 L5
East Beckham Norfk...106 E4
East Bedfont Gt Lon..43 H5
East Bergholt Suffk..78 C7
East Bilney Norfk....106 A8
East Blatchington
  E Susx..............20 A5
East Boldon S Tyne...151 J3
East Boldre Hants....16 D3
Eastbourne Darltn....141 H4
Eastbourne E Susx....20 C5
Eastbourne
  Crematorium
  E Susx..............20 D5
East Bradenham
  Norfk...............91 L2
East Brent Somset....25 M2
Eastbridge Suffk.....79 J2

East Bridgford Notts......102 B4
East Buckland Devon 23 L5
East Budleigh Devon 12 D5
Eastburn C Brad 122 F2
Eastbury Herts 43 J2
Eastbury W Berk 41 G5
East Butterwick
    N Linc 116 D1
Eastby N York 131 J8
East Calder W Loth........176 E5
East Carleton Norfk......92 E3
East Carlton Leeds........123 J2
East Carlton Nhants........88 B5
East Chaldon
    (Chaldon Herring)
    Dorset 14 E5
East Challow Oxon....... 41 G3
East Charleton Devon 7 H7
East Chelborough
    Dorset 14 A2
East Chiltington
    E Susx 19 K3
East Chinnock
    Somset 26 C8
East Chisenbury Wilts ... 28 C2
Eastchurch Kent 47 G5
East Clandon Surrey 31 H2
East Claydon Bucks 58 C3
East Coker Somset........ 26 D8
Eastcombe Gloucs 55 K6
East Compton
    Somset 26 E3
East Cornworthy
    Devon 7 J5
Eastcote Gt Lon 43 J3
Eastcote Nhants............. 73 K4
Eastcote Solhll 85 L7
Eastcott Wilts 28 A1
East Cottingwith
    E R Yk 125 G3
Eastcourt Wilts 40 E7
East Cowes IoW............ 16 F4
East Cowick E R Yk......125 G6
East Cowton N York......141 H6
East Cranmore
    Somset 27 G3
East Dean E Susx 20 B6
East Dean Gloucs......... 54 F4
East Dean Hants 28 F6
East Dean W Susx 18 B3
East Devon
    Crematorium
    Devon 12 D4
East Drayton Notts......116 C6
East Dulwich Gt Lon 45 G5
East Dundry N Som....... 38 E7
East Ella C KuH.............126 C5
Eastend Essex............... 46 F2
East End Hants 16 D3
East End Hants 41 H7
East End Kent 33 L6
East End Oxon 57 H5
East End Somset 26 F3
Easter Balmoral
    Abers 205 G6
Easter Compton
    S Glos 38 E4
Easter Dalziel Highld ...213 H4
Eastergate W Susx........ 18 C5
Easterhouse C Glas 175 J5
Easter Howgate
    Mdloth........................177 H5
Easter Kinkell Highld ...212 E4
Easter Moniack
    Highld 212 E5
Eastern Green Covtry ... 86 C7
Easter Ord Abers 206 F4
Easter Pitkierie Fife.....187 J6
Easter Skeld Shet 235 c6
Easter Softlaw
    Border 168 A3
Easterton Wilts 28 A1
East Everleigh Wilts...... 28 D2
East Farleigh Kent 33 J3
East Farndon Nhants......87 K6
East Ferry Lincs 116 D2
Eastfield N Lans 176 B5

Eastfield N York 135 G3
East Fortune E Loth......178 C3
East Garston W Berk..... 41 G5
Eastgate Dur 150 B7
Eastgate Norfk 106 D7
East Goscote Leics........ 87 J2
East Grafton Wilts......... 40 E7
East Grimstead Wilts 28 E5
East Grinstead
    W Susx 32 D5
East Guldeford
    E Susx 21 J2
East Haddon Nhants...... 73 J2
East Hagbourne
    Oxon 41 K3
East Halton N Linc......126 E6
East Ham Gt Lon 45 H4
Easthampstead Park
    Crematorium
    Br For 42 D6
Easthampton Herefs...... 69 H2
East Hanney Oxon 41 H2
East Hanningfield
    Essex 61 J7
East Hardwick
    Wakefd 124 C6
East Harling Norfk........ 92 B6
East Harlsey N York 141 K7
East Harnham Wilts...... 28 C5
East Harptree BaNES... 26 E1
East Hartburn S on T....141 K4
East Harting W Susx 30 D7
East Hatch Wilts 27 L5
East Hatley Cambs....... 75 K4
East Hauxwell N York ..132 B2
East Haven Angus.......187 J1
East Heckington
    Lincs 103 K4
East Hedleyhope
    Dur 150 E6
East Helmsdale
    Highld 227 H5
East Hendred Oxon 41 J3
East Heslerton N York ..134 E4
East Hoathly E Susx 20 B3
East Holme Dorset........ 15 G5
Easthope Shrops.......... 83 L4
Easthorpe Essex........... 61 L4
East Horrington
    Somset 26 E3
East Horsley Surrey 31 H2
East Howe Bmouth....... 15 K4
East Huntspill Somset ... 25 M3
East Ilsley W Berk 41 J4
Eastington Devon 11 H3
Eastington Gloucs 55 H6
Eastington Gloucs........ 56 C5
East Keal Lincs 118 E8
East Kennett Wilts........ 40 C6
East Keswick Leeds 124 B2
East Kilbride S Lans 175 H7
East Kirkby Lincs 118 D8
East Knighton Dorset.... 14 F5
East Knoyle Wilts 27 K5
East Lambrook
    Somset 26 B7
East Lancashire
    Crematorium
    Bury 122 B8
Eastlands D & G...........154 E7
East Langdon Kent 35 J3
East Langton Leics........ 87 K5
East Lavant W Susx...... 18 B4
East Lavington
    W Susx 18 C3
East Layton N York 140 E5
Eastleach Martin
    Gloucs 56 D6
Eastleach Turville
    Gloucs 56 D6
East Leake Notts..........101 K7
Eastleigh Devon 23 H5
Eastleigh Hants 29 J7
East Lexham Norfk......105 K8
Eastling Kent 34 C4
East Linton E Loth........178 D3
East Lockinge Oxon......41 H3

East London
    Crematorium
    Gt Lon 45 H4
East Lound N Linc 116 C2
East Lulworth Dorset..... 15 G6
East Lutton N York........134 E5
East Lydford Somset...... 26 E5
East Malling Kent........... 33 J2
East Marden W Susx..... 30 D8
East Markham Notts......116 C6
East Martin Hants 28 B7
East Marton N York......122 D1
East Meon Hants 30 B6
East Mersea Essex....... 62 C5
East Midlands Airport
    Leics 101 J7
East Molesey Surrey 43 J6
East Morden Dorset....... 15 G4
East Morton C Brad 123 G3
East Morton D & G 154 F3
East Ness N York 133 L4
Eastney C Port.............. 17 J3
Eastnor Herefs.............. 70 D6
East Norton Leics.......... 87 L4
East Oakley Hants 29 K5
East Ogwell Devon........ 7 J2
Easton Cambs............... 75 G1
Easton Devon 11 G6
Easton Dorset 14 D7
Easton Hants 29 K5
Easton Lincs 102 F6
Easton Norfk................. 92 D2
Easton Somset............. 26 D3
Easton Suffk................. 79 G3
Easton Wilts 39 K6
Easton Grey Wilts......... 39 K3
Easton-in-Gordano
    N Som 38 D5
Easton Maudit
    Nhants........................ 74 C3
Easton-on-the-Hill
    Nhants........................ 88 E3
Easton Royal Wilts........ 40 D7
East Orchard Dorset..... 27 J7
East Peckham Kent....... 33 H4
East Pennar Pembks..... 49 G6
East Pennard Somset.... 26 E4
East Perry Cambs......... 75 G2
East Portlemouth
    Devon 7 H7
East Prawle Devon 7 H8
East Preston W Susx..... 18 E5
East Putford Devon........ 9 K2
East Quantoxhead
    Somset 25 H3
East Rainton Sundld 151 H5
East Ravendale
    NE Lin 118 C2
East Raynham Norfk....105 L7
Eastrea Cambs............. 89 K4
East Riding
    Crematorium
    E R Yk 134 F5
Eastriggs D & G...........147 M2
East Rigton Leeds........124 B2
Eastrington E R Yk......125 J4
Eastrop Swindn 40 D2
East Rounton N York....141 K6
East Rudham Norfk......105 K6
East Runton Norfk........106 E4
East Ruston Norfk........107 H6
Eastry Kent 35 J4
East Saltoun E Loth......178 B5
East Sheen Gt Lon........ 44 D5
East Shefford W Berk.... 41 H5
East Stockwith Lincs 116 C3
East Stoke Dorset......... 15 G5
East Stoke Notts..........102 C3
East Stour Dorset......... 27 J6
East Stourmouth
    Kent 35 H3
East Stowford Devon.... 23 K6
East Stratton Hants 29 K4
East Studdal Kent......... 35 J5
East Taphouse Cnwll..... 5 J3
East-the-Water
    Devon 23 G6

East Thirston
    Nthumb 158 F3
East Tilbury Thurr 46 B5
East Tisted Hants 30 B5
East Torrington Lincs ...117 J3
East Tuddenham
    Norfk.......................... 92 C2
East Tytherley Hants..... 28 F5
East Tytherton Wilts...... 39 L5
East Village Devon 11 J4
Eastville Bristl 38 E5
Eastville Lincs 104 C2
East Walton Norfk........ 91 G1
East Week Devon 10 F6
Eastwell Leics 102 C6
East Wellow Hants 28 F7
East Wemyss Fife........186 E7
East Whitburn W Loth...176 C5
Eastwick Herts 60 C5
East Wickham Gt Lon... 45 J3
East Williamston
    Pembks 49 J6
East Winch Norfk......... 91 G1
East Winterslow Wilts ... 28 E5
East Wittering W Susx... 17 L3
East Witton N York....... 131 L3
Eastwood Notts 101 J3
Eastwood Sthend 46 D3
East Woodburn
    Nthumb 158 A5
East Woodhay Hants..... 41 H7
East Worldham Hants ... 30 C4
East Wretham Norfk..... 91 K5
East Youlstone Devon..... 9 H2
Eathorpe Warwks........ 72 E2
Eaton Ches E...............113 K7
Eaton Ches W..............112 E8
Eaton Leics 102 D6
Eaton Norfk................. 92 E3
Eaton Notts.................116 B6
Eaton Oxon 57 H7
Eaton Shrops 83 K5
Eaton Bray C Beds...... 58 F4
Eaton Constantine
    Shrops 83 L3
Eaton Green C Beds..... 58 F4
Eaton Hastings Oxon ... 56 E7
Eaton Mascott
    Shrops 83 K3
Eaton Socon Cambs..... 75 H3
Eaton upon Tern
    Shrops 98 F7
Ebberston N York........134 D3
Ebbesborne Wake
    Wilts........................... 27 M6
Ebbw Vale Blae G........ 53 J6
Ebchester Dur 150 D4
Ebford Devon 12 C5
Ebley Gloucs............... 55 J6
Ebnal Ches W............. 98 C3
Ebrington Gloucs 71 L6
Ecchinswell Hants........ 41 J8
Ecclaw Border 178 F5
Ecclefechan D & G......155 L7
Eccles Border 168 A2
Eccles Kent.................. 46 B7
Eccles Salfd 113 H2
Ecclesall Sheff............114 F5
Eccles Crematorium
    Salfd 113 H3
Ecclesfield Sheff..........115 G3
Eccleshall Staffs........... 99 J6
Eccleshill C Brad 123 H4
Ecclesmachan W Loth..176 E4
Eccles Road Norfk........ 92 B5
Eccleston Ches W........112 B8
Eccleston Lancs 121 G6
Eccleston St Hel..........112 C3
Echt Abers 206 E4
Eckford Border 167 L4
Eckington Derbys.........115 H5
Eckington Worcs.......... 71 G6
Ecton Nhants 74 B2
Edale Derbys 114 C4
Eday Ork 234 d4
Eday Airport Ork 234 d4
Edburton W Susx......... 19 H4

Edderton Highld..........222 F4
Eddleston Border..........177 H8
Eddlewood S Lans..........175 J7
Edenbridge Kent..........32 D4
Edenfield Lancs..........122 B6
Edenhall Cumb..........138 E2
Edenham Lincs..........103 H7
Eden Park Gt Lon..........45 G6
Eden Project Cnwll..........5 G3
Edensor Derbys..........114 E7
Edentaggart Ag & B..........183 K8
Edenthorpe Donc..........115 L1
Edern Gwynd..........94 E5
Edgbaston Birm..........85 J6
Edgcott Bucks..........58 B4
Edgcott Somset..........24 D4
Edge Gloucs..........55 J6
Edgefield Norfk..........106 C5
Edgefield Green
  Norfk..........106 D5
Edgerton Kirk..........123 H6
Edgeworth Gloucs..........55 L6
Edgmond Wrekin..........99 G8
Edgton Shrops..........83 H6
Edgware Gt Lon..........44 D2
Edgworth Bl w D..........121 L6
Edinbane Highld..........208 E4
Edinburgh C Edin..........177 H4
Edinburgh Airport
  C Edin..........176 F4
Edinburgh Castle
  C Edin..........177 H4
Edinburgh Royal
  Botanic Gardens
  C Edin..........177 H4
Edinburgh Zoo
  C Edin..........177 G4
Edingale Staffs..........86 B2
Edingham D & G..........146 E3
Edingley Notts..........102 A2
Edingthorpe Norfk..........107 G6
Edingthorpe Green
  Norfk..........107 G6
Edington Border..........179 J7
Edington Nthumb..........158 E5
Edington Somset..........26 B4
Edington Wilts..........27 L2
Edington Burtle
  Somset..........26 B3
Edingworth Somset..........26 A2
Edithmead Somset..........25 L2
Edith Weston Rutlnd..........88 D3
Edlesborough Bucks..........58 F4
Edlingham Nthumb..........169 G7
Edlington Lincs..........118 C7
Edmondsham Dorset..........15 K1
Edmondsley Dur..........151 G5
Edmondthorpe Leics..........102 E8
Edmonton Gt Lon..........45 G2
Edmundbyers Dur..........150 C5
Ednam Border..........167 L2
Edradynate P & K..........194 D6
Edrom Border..........179 H7
Edstaston Shrops..........98 D6
Edstone Warwks..........71 L3
Edwalton Notts..........101 L5
Edwinstowe Notts..........115 L7
Edworth C Beds..........75 J6
Edwyn Ralph Herefs..........70 B3
Edzell Angus..........196 F3
Edzell Woods Abers..........197 G3
Efail-fach Neath..........36 B2
Efail Isaf Rhondd..........37 G4
Efailnewydd Gwynd..........94 F5
Efailwen Carmth..........49 K3
Efenechtyd Denbgs..........97 H2
Effgill D & G..........156 B4
Effingham Surrey..........31 J2
Efford Crematorium
  C Plym..........6 D4
Egerton Bolton..........121 K7
Egerton Kent..........34 B5
Eggborough N York..........124 E5
Eggbuckland C Plym..........6 D4
Eggesford Devon..........11 G3
Eggington C Beds..........58 F3
Egginton Derbys..........100 E6

Egglescliffe S on T..........141 K4
Eggleston Dur..........140 C3
Egham Surrey..........43 G6
Egleton Rutlnd..........88 C3
Eglingham Nthumb..........169 G5
Egloshayle Cnwll..........4 F2
Egloskerry Cnwll..........9 H7
Eglwysbach Conwy..........109 M7
Eglwys Cross Wrexhm..........98 C4
Eglwyswrw Pembks..........65 G6
Egmanton Notts..........116 B7
Egremont Cumb..........136 D5
Egremont Wirral..........111 K3
Egton N York..........143 G6
Egton Bridge N York..........143 G6
Egypt Bucks..........42 F3
Eigg Highld..........199 G7
Eight Ash Green
  Essex..........61 M3
Eilanreach Highld..........200 C2
Elan Valley Powys..........67 J2
Elan Village Powys..........67 K2
Elberton S Glos..........38 E3
Elburton C Plym..........6 D5
Elcombe Swindn..........40 C4
Eldersfield Worcs..........55 H2
Elderslie Rens..........174 E5
Eldon Dur..........141 G2
Elfhill Abers..........206 F7
Elford Staffs..........85 L2
Elgin Moray..........214 F2
Elgol Highld..........199 H3
Elham Kent..........35 G6
Elie Fife..........187 H7
Elim IoA..........108 D4
Eling Hants..........29 G8
Elkesley Notts..........116 B6
Elkstone Gloucs..........55 L5
Ella Abers..........216 C3
Ellacombe Torbay..........7 L3
Elland Calder..........123 G6
Ellary Ag & B..........172 C3
Ellastone Staffs..........100 C4
Ellel Lancs..........129 K7
Ellemford Border..........178 F6
Ellenabeich Ag & B..........181 L4
Ellenhall Staffs..........99 J7
Ellen's Green Surrey..........31 H4
Ellerbeck N York..........141 K7
Ellerby N York..........143 G4
Ellerdine Heath
  Wrekin..........98 F7
Elleric Ag & B..........191 K6
Ellerker E R Yk..........125 L5
Ellerton E R Yk..........125 G3
Ellerton N York..........141 G7
Ellesborough Bucks..........58 D6
Ellesmere Shrops..........98 B5
Ellesmere Port
  Ches W..........111 L6
Ellingham Norfk..........93 H5
Ellingham Nthumb..........169 H4
Ellingstring N York..........132 B3
Ellington Cambs..........75 H1
Ellington Nthumb..........159 G4
Elliots Green Somset..........27 J3
Ellisfield Hants..........29 M3
Ellishader Highld..........209 H2
Ellistown Leics..........86 E2
Ellon Abers..........217 H7
Ellonby Cumb..........148 D7
Elloughton E R Yk..........126 B5
Ellwood Gloucs..........54 E6
Elm Cambs..........90 C3
Elmbridge Worcs..........70 F2
Elmdon Essex..........76 C6
Elmdon Solhll..........85 L6
Elmers End Gt Lon..........45 G6
Elmer's Green Lancs..........112 D1
Elmesthorpe Leics..........86 F4
Elmhurst Staffs..........85 K2
Elmley Castle Worcs..........71 H6
Elmley Lovett Worcs..........70 F1
Elmore Gloucs..........55 H5
Elmore Back Gloucs..........55 H5
Elm Park Gt Lon..........45 K3
Elmsett Suffk..........78 C5

Elmstead Market
  Essex..........62 C3
Elmsted Kent..........34 F5
Elmstone Kent..........35 H3
Elmstone Hardwicke
  Gloucs..........55 K3
Elmswell E R Yk..........134 F7
Elmswell Suffk..........78 B2
Elmton Derbys..........115 J6
Elphin Highld..........224 F6
Elphinstone E Loth..........177 K4
Elrick Abers..........206 F4
Elrig D & G..........145 G5
Elrington Nthumb..........149 L3
Elsdon Nthumb..........158 B4
Elsenham Essex..........60 E3
Elsfield Oxon..........57 K6
Elsham N Linc..........126 C7
Elsing Norfk..........92 C1
Elslack N York..........122 D2
Elson Hants..........17 H3
Elsrickle S Lans..........165 K2
Elstead Surrey..........30 E3
Elsted W Susx..........30 D7
Elsthorpe Lincs..........103 H7
Elston Notts..........102 C3
Elstow Bed..........74 F5
Elstree Herts..........44 D2
Elstronwick E R Yk..........126 F4
Elswick Lancs..........120 F3
Elsworth Cambs..........75 K2
Elterwater Cumb..........137 K6
Eltham Gt Lon..........45 H5
Eltham Crematorium
  Gt Lon..........45 J5
Eltisley Cambs..........75 J3
Elton Cambs..........88 F5
Elton Ches W..........112 C6
Elton Derbys..........100 E1
Elton Herefs..........69 J1
Elton Notts..........102 C5
Elton S on T..........141 J4
Eltringham Nthumb..........150 D3
Elvanfoot S Lans..........165 J6
Elvaston Derbys..........101 H6
Elveden Suffk..........91 J7
Elvetham Heath
  Hants..........30 D1
Elvingston E Loth..........178 A4
Elvington C York..........125 G2
Elvington Kent..........35 H5
Elwick Hartpl..........141 K2
Elworth Ches E..........99 H1
Elworthy Somset..........25 G4
Ely Cambs..........90 D7
Ely Cardif..........37 H5
Emberton M Keyn..........74 C5
Embleton Cumb..........137 G2
Embleton Nthumb..........169 J5
Embo Highld..........223 H3
Emborough Somset..........26 E2
Embo Street Highld..........223 H3
Embsay N York..........131 J8
Emery Down Hants..........16 C2
Emley Kirk..........123 K7
Emmington Oxon..........58 C7
Emneth Norfk..........90 C2
Emneth Hungate
  Norfk..........90 D3
Empingham Rutlnd..........88 D2
Empshott Hants..........30 C5
Emstrey
  Crematorium
  Shrops..........83 K2
Emsworth Hants..........17 K2
Enborne W Berk..........41 H7
Enborne Row
  W Berk..........41 H7
Enderby Leics..........87 G4
Endmoor Cumb..........129 L3
Endon Staffs..........99 L2
Endon Bank Staffs..........99 L2
Enfield Gt Lon..........60 B7
Enfield Crematorium
  Gt Lon..........60 B7
Enfield Lock Gt Lon..........60 B7

Enfield Wash Gt Lon..........60 B7
Enford Wilts..........28 C2
Engine Common
  S Glos..........39 G4
Englefield W Berk..........41 L6
Englefield Green
  Surrey..........43 G6
English Bicknor
  Gloucs..........54 E5
Englishcombe BaNES..........39 G7
English Frankton
  Shrops..........98 C6
Enham-Alamein
  Hants..........29 G2
Enmore Somset..........25 K4
Enmore Green
  Dorset..........27 J6
Ennerdale Bridge
  Cumb..........136 E4
Enochdhu P & K..........195 G4
Ensay Ag & B..........189 J6
Ensbury Bmouth..........15 K3
Ensdon Shrops..........83 H1
Enstone Oxon..........57 G3
Enterkinfoot D & G..........154 E2
Enville Staffs..........84 E6
Eolaigearraidh W Isls..........233 b9
Epney Gloucs..........55 H5
Epperstone Notts..........101 M3
Epping Essex..........60 D7
Epping Green Essex..........60 C6
Epping Upland Essex..........60 C6
Eppleby N York..........140 F5
Epsom Surrey..........44 E7
Epwell Oxon..........72 D6
Epworth N Linc..........116 C2
Erbistock Wrexhm..........97 M4
Erdington Birm..........85 K5
Eridge Green E Susx..........32 E5
Erines Ag & B..........172 E4
Eriska Ag & B..........191 H7
Eriskay W Isls..........233 c9
Eriswell Suffk..........91 G7
Erith Gt Lon..........45 K4
Erlestoke Wilts..........27 L2
Ermington Devon..........6 F5
Erpingham Norfk..........106 E6
Errogie Highld..........202 E2
Errol P & K..........186 D3
Erskine Rens..........174 E4
Ervie D & G..........144 B2
Erwarton Suffk..........78 F7
Erwood Powys..........68 C6
Eryholme N York..........141 H5
Eryrys Denbgs..........97 J2
Escomb Dur..........140 F2
Escrick N York..........124 F2
Esgairgeiliog Powys..........81 G3
Esh Dur..........150 F6
Esher Surrey..........43 J7
Eshott Nthumb..........158 F3
Esh Winning Dur..........150 F6
Eskadale Highld..........212 C6
Eskbank Mdloth..........177 J5
Eskdale Green
  Cumb..........137 G6
Eskdalemuir D & G..........156 A3
Esprick Lancs..........120 E3
Essendine Rutlnd..........88 F2
Essendon Herts..........59 L6
Essich Highld..........213 G6
Essington Staffs..........85 G3
Esslemont Abers..........217 H7
Eston R & Cl..........142 C4
Etal Nthumb..........168 D2
Etchilhampton Wilts..........40 B7
Etchingham E Susx..........33 J7
Etchinghill Kent..........34 F6
Etchinghill Staffs..........100 B8
Eton W & M..........42 F5
Eton Wick W & M..........42 F5
Etruria C Stke..........99 K3
Etteridge Highld..........203 G6
Ettersgill Dur..........139 K2
Ettiley Heath Ches E..........99 G1
Ettingshall Wolves..........85 G4
Ettington Warwks..........72 C5

Etton C Pete....89 G3
Etton E R Yk....126 B2
Ettrick Border....166 D6
Ettrickbridge Border..166 F4
Ettrickhill Border....166 C6
Etwall Derbys....100 F6
Euston Suffk....91 K7
Euxton Lancs....121 H6
Evanton Highld....212 F2
Evedon Lincs....103 H3
Evelix Highld....223 G4
Evenjobb Powys....68 F3
Evenley Nhants....73 H7
Evenlode Gloucs....56 E3
Evenwood Dur....140 E3
Evercreech Somset....26 F4
Everingham E R Yk..125 J3
Everleigh Wilts....28 D2
Eversholt C Beds....59 G2
Evershot Dorset....14 B2
Eversley Hants....42 C7
Eversley Cross
  Hants....42 C7
Everthorpe E R Yk..125 L4
Everton C Beds....75 H4
Everton Hants....16 C4
Everton Lpool....111 K3
Everton Notts....116 B4
Evertown D & G....156 C6
Evesbatch Herefs....70 C5
Evesham Worcs....71 J5
Evington C Leic....87 J3
Ewden Village Sheff..114 F3
Ewell Surrey....44 E7
Ewell Minnis Kent....35 H6
Ewelme Oxon....41 M3
Ewen Gloucs....40 A2
Ewenny V Glam....36 D5
Ewerby Lincs....103 J3
Ewhurst Surrey....31 H4
Ewhurst Green
  E Susx....20 F2
Ewhurst Green
  Surrey....31 H4
Ewloe Flints....111 J7
Eworthy Devon....10 C6
Ewshot Hants....30 D2
Ewyas Harold Herefs..54 B3
Exbourne Devon....10 E4
Exbridge Somset....24 E6
Exbury Hants....16 E3
Exelby N York....132 D3
Exeter Devon....11 L6
Exeter Airport Devon..12 C4
Exeter & Devon
  Crematorium
  Devon....12 B4
*Exeter Services
  Devon....12 C4*
Exford Somset....24 D4
Exfordsgreen Shrops..83 J3
Exhall Warwks....71 K4
Exhall Warwks....86 D6
Exlade Street Oxon....42 A4
Exminster Devon....12 B5
*Exmoor National Park
  Somset....24 D4*
Exmouth Devon....12 C6
Exning Suffk....76 E2
Exton Devon....12 C5
Exton Hants....29 L7
Exton Rutlnd....88 D2
Exton Somset....24 E5
Exwick Devon....11 K6
Eyam Derbys....114 E6
Eydon Nhants....73 G4
Eye C Pete....89 J3
Eye Herefs....69 J2
Eye Suffk....92 D8
Eyemouth Border....179 K5
Eyeworth C Beds....75 J5
Eyhorne Street Kent..33 L3
Eyke Suffk....79 G4
Eynesbury Cambs....75 H3
Eynsford Kent....45 K6
Eynsham Oxon....57 H6
Eype Dorset....13 L4

Eyre Highld....208 F4
Eythorne Kent....35 H5
Eyton Herefs....69 J3
Eyton Shrops....98 C7
Eyton on Severn
  Shrops....83 L3
Eyton upon the
  Weald Moors
  Wrekin....84 B1

F

Faccombe Hants....41 H8
Faceby N York....141 L6
Fachwen Powys....82 B1
Faddiley Ches E....98 E3
Fadmoor N York....133 K2
Faerdre Swans....51 K5
Faifley W Duns....174 F4
Failand N Som....38 D6
Failford S Ayrs....163 L4
Failsworth Oldham....113 K2
Fairbourne Gwynd....80 E2
Fairburn N York....124 D5
Fairfield Derbys....114 B6
Fairfield Worcs....85 G7
Fairford Gloucs....56 D7
Fairgirth D & G....146 F4
Fair Green Norfk....90 F1
Fairhaven Lancs....120 D5
Fair Isle Shet....235 e7
Fairlands Surrey....30 F2
Fairlie N Ayrs....173 L7
Fairlight E Susx....21 G4
Fairmile Devon....12 E3
Fairmile Surrey....43 J7
Fairnilee Border....167 G3
Fair Oak Hants....29 J7
Fairoak Staffs....99 H6
Fair Oak Green Hants..42 A7
Fairseat Kent....45 L7
Fairstead Essex....61 J5
Fairstead Norfk....105 G8
Fairwarp E Susx....32 E7
Fairwater Cardif....37 H5
Fairy Cross Devon....22 F6
Fakenham Norfk....105 L6
Fakenham Magna
  Suffk....91 K7
Fala Mdloth....177 L6
Fala Dam Mdloth....177 L6
Faldingworth Lincs....117 H5
Faldouet Jersey....236 e7
Falfield S Glos....39 G2
Falkenham Suffk....79 G6
Falkirk Falk....176 B3
Falkirk Crematorium
  Falk....176 B3
Falkland Fife....186 D6
Fallburn S Lans....165 J2
Fallin Stirlg....185 H8
Fallodon Nthumb....169 J5
Fallowfield Manch....113 J3
Fallowfield Nthumb....150 B2
Falls of Blarghour
  Ag & B....182 E5
Falmer E Susx....19 K4
Falmouth Cnwll....3 K5
Falnash Border....156 D2
Falsgrave N York....134 F2
Falstone Nthumb....157 J5
Fanagmore Highld....228 B5
Fancott C Beds....59 G3
Fanellan Highld....212 D5
Fangdale Beck N York..142 C7
Fangfoss E R Yk....134 B8
Fanmore Ag & B....189 K7
Fannich Lodge Highld..211 K2
Fans Border....167 J2
Far Bletchley M Keyn..74 C7
Farcet Cambs....89 H5
Far Cotton Nhants....73 L3
Fareham Hants....17 H2
Far End Cumb....137 J7
Farewell Staffs....85 J2

Faringdon Oxon....40 F2
Farington Lancs....121 H5
Farlam Cumb....148 F3
Farleigh N Som....38 D6
Farleigh Surrey....32 C2
Farleigh Hungerford
  Somset....39 J8
Farleigh Wallop
  Hants....29 L3
Farlesthorpe Lincs....119 G6
Farleton Cumb....129 L4
Farleton Lancs....130 B6
Farley Staffs....100 B4
Farley Wilts....28 E5
Farley Green Surrey....31 H3
Farley Hill Wokham....42 C7
Farleys End Gloucs....55 H5
Farlington C Port....17 J2
Farlington N York....133 J6
Farlow Shrops....84 B7
Farmborough BaNES....38 F7
Farmcote Gloucs....56 B3
Farmers Carmth....66 E5
Farmington Gloucs....56 C5
Farmoor Oxon....57 J6
Far Moor Wigan....112 D2
Farmtown Moray....215 L4
Farnborough Gt Lon....45 H7
Farnborough Hants....30 E2
Farnborough W Berk....41 H4
Farnborough Warwks..72 E5
Farnborough Park
  Hants....30 E1
Farnborough Street
  Hants....30 E1
Farncombe Surrey....31 G3
Farndish Bed....74 D2
Farndon Ches W....98 B2
Farndon Notts....102 C3
Farne Islands
  Nthumb....169 K2
Farnell Angus....197 G5
Farnham Dorset....27 L7
Farnham Essex....60 D3
Farnham N York....132 E7
Farnham Suffk....79 H3
Farnham Surrey....30 D3
Farnham Common
  Bucks....42 F4
Farnham Royal Bucks..42 F4
Farningham Kent....45 K6
Farnley Leeds....123 K4
Farnley N York....123 J2
Farnley Tyas Kirk....123 H7
Farnsfield Notts....101 M2
Farnworth Bolton....113 G1
Farnworth Halton....112 D4
Far Oakridge Gloucs....55 L7
Farr Highld....203 K5
Farr Highld....213 G7
Farr Highld....229 L3
Farraline Highld....202 E2
Farringdon Devon....12 C4
Farrington Gurney
  BaNES....26 F1
Far Sawrey Cumb....137 K7
Farthinghoe Nhants....73 G6
Farthingstone
  Nhants....73 H4
Fartown Kirk....123 H6
Fartown Leeds....123 J4
Fasnacloich Ag & B....191 K6
Fasnakyle Highld....211 L8
Fassfern Highld....191 K2
Fatfield Sundld....151 H4
Fauldhouse W Loth....176 C6
Faulkbourne Essex....61 J5
Faulkland Somset....27 H1
Fauls Shrops....98 E6
Faversham Kent....34 D3
Fawdington N York....132 F5
Fawdon N u Ty....151 G2
Fawkham Green Kent..45 L6
Fawler Oxon....57 G4
Fawley Bucks....42 C3
Fawley Hants....16 F2
Fawley W Berk....41 H4

Faxfleet E R Yk....125 K5
Faygate W Susx....31 K5
Fazakerley Lpool....111 K3
Fazeley Staffs....85 L3
Fearby N York....132 B4
Fearn Highld....223 H6
Fearnan P & K....194 B7
Fearnbeg Highld....210 B3
Fearnhead Warrtn....209 L3
Fearnmore Highld....209 L3
Fearnoch Ag & B....172 F3
Featherstone Staffs....85 G3
Featherstone Wakefd..124 C6
Feckenham Worcs....71 H3
Feering Essex....61 L4
Feetham N York....140 C7
Felbridge Surrey....32 C5
Felbrigg Norfk....106 E5
Felcourt Surrey....32 C5
Felindre Carmth....51 G2
Felindre Carmth....65 K6
Felindre Powys....82 D7
Felindre Swans....51 J5
Felindre Farchog
  Pembks....64 F6
Felingwm Isaf
  Carmth....51 G2
Felingwm Uchaf
  Carmth....51 G1
Felixkirk N York....133 G3
Felixstowe Suffk....79 G7
Felling Gatesd....151 G3
Felmersham Bed....74 E3
Felmingham Norfk....106 F6
Felpham W Susx....18 C5
Felsham Suffk....77 L3
Felsted Essex....61 G4
Feltham Gt Lon....43 J5
Felthamhill Surrey....43 H6
Felthorpe Norfk....106 E8
Felton Herefs....69 L5
Felton N Som....38 D7
Felton Nthumb....158 F5
Felton Butler Shrops....98 B8
Feltwell Norfk....91 G5
Fence Lancs....122 C3
Fence Rothm....115 H4
Fencott Oxon....57 L5
Fendike Corner Lincs..104 D1
Fen Ditton Cambs....76 C3
Fen Drayton Cambs....75 L2
Feniscowles Bl w D....121 J5
Feniton Devon....12 E3
Fenland
  Crematorium
  Cambs....90 B5
Fenn Green Shrops....84 D6
Fenn Street Medway....46 D5
Fenny Bentley Derbys..100 D3
Fenny Bridges Devon..12 E3
Fenny Compton
  Warwks....72 E4
Fenny Drayton Leics....86 D4
Fenstanton Cambs....75 K2
Fen Street Norfk....92 B4
Fenton C Stke....99 K4
Fenton Cambs....89 K7
Fenton Cumb....148 E4
Fenton Lincs....102 E3
Fenton Lincs....116 D6
Fenton Notts....116 C5
Fenton Nthumb....169 G2
Fenton Barns E Loth..178 B3
Fenwick Donc....124 F7
Fenwick E Ayrs....163 L2
Fenwick Nthumb....158 D7
Fenwick Nthumb....169 G2
Feock Cnwll....4 C7
Feolin Ferry Ag & B....171 H4
Fergushill N Ayrs....163 J2
Feriniquarrie Highld....208 B4
Fern Angus....196 D4
Ferndale Rhondd....36 F2
Ferndown Dorset....15 K3
Ferness Highld....214 B5
Fernham Oxon....40 F3
Fernhill Heath Worcs..70 F3
Fernhurst W Susx....30 E5

Fernie Fife......................186 E4
Ferniegair S Lans........175 K7
Fernilea Highld.............208 F2
Fernilee Derbys............114 A5
Fernwood Notts...........102 D3
Ferrensby N York..........132 E7
Ferrindonald Highld.....199 K4
Ferring W Susx................18 F5
Ferrybridge Services
  Wakefd......................124 D6
Ferryden Angus............197 H5
Ferryhill Dur..................141 H2
Ferry Point Highld........223 G4
Ferryside Carmth............50 D4
Ferrytown Highld..........223 G4
Fersfield Norfk................92 C6
Fersit Highld.................192 F2
Feshiebridge Highld......203 K4
Fetcham Surrey...............31 J1
Fetlar Shet...................235 e2
Fetterangus Abers........217 J4
Fettercairn Abers.........197 G2
Fewston N York.............132 B8
Ffairfach Carmth............51 J2
Ffair Rhos Cerdgn..........67 G2
Ffestiniog Gwynd............96 A4
Ffestiniog Railway
  Gwynd.........................95 L4
Fforest Carmth................51 H5
Fforest Fach Swans........51 J6
Ffostrasol Cerdgn...........65 L5
Ffrith Flints.....................97 L2
Ffynnongroyw Flints.....111 L6
Fiag Lodge Highld.........225 K3
Ficklesole Surrey............32 C2
Fiddington Somset..........25 K4
Fiddleford Dorset............27 J8
Fiddlers Green Cnwll.........4 C5
Field Staffs...................100 A5
Field Dalling Norfk........106 B5
Field Head Leics.............86 F2
Fifehead Magdalen
  Dorset.........................27 H6
Fifehead Neville
  Dorset.........................14 E1
Fifehead St Quintin
  Dorset.........................14 E1
Fife Keith Moray...........215 J4
Fifield Oxon....................56 E4
Fifield W & M..................42 E5
Figheldean Wilts............28 D3
Filby Norfk.....................93 K2
Filey N York..................135 H4
Filgrave M Keyn..............74 C5
Filkins Oxon....................56 E6
Filleigh Devon.................23 K5
Fillingham Lincs............116 F4
Fillongley Warwks...........86 C6
Filton S Glos...................38 E5
Fimber E R Yk...............134 D7
Finavon Angus...............196 D5
Fincham Norfk................91 G3
Finchampstead
  Wokham......................42 D7
Fincharn Ag & B............182 C6
Finchdean Hants.............30 C8
Finchingfield Essex.........61 G2
Finchley Gt Lon..............44 F2
Findern Derbys..............100 F6
Findhorn Moray.............214 C2
Findhorn Bridge
  Highld........................213 J8
Findochty Moray............215 K2
Findo Gask P & K..........185 L4
Findon Abers.................207 H6
Findon W Susx.................18 F4
Findon Mains Highld......212 F3
Findrack House
  Abers........................206 B4
Finedon Nhants...............74 D1
Fingask P & K...............186 C4
Fingest Bucks.................42 C3
Finghall N York..............132 B2
Fingland D & G..............164 E6
Finglesham Kent.............35 J4
Fingringhoe Essex...........62 B4
Finlarig Stirlg................184 C1
Finmere Oxon..................57 M2
Finnart P & K................193 H5
Finningham Suffk............78 C1
Finningley Donc.............116 A2
Finsbay W Isls..............232 d5
Finstall Worcs................71 H1
Finsthwaite Cumb..........129 H2
Finstock Oxon.................57 G5
Finstown Ork................234 b6
Fintry Abers..................216 E4
Fintry Stirlg..................175 H2
Finzean Abers...............206 B6
Fionnphort Ag & B........180 D3
Fionnsbhagh W Isls......232 d5
Firbank Cumb...............130 C2
Firbeck Rothm...............115 K4
Firby N York..................132 D3
Firby N York..................134 B6
Firle E Susx....................19 M4
Firsby Lincs..................118 F8
Fir Tree Dur..................150 E7
Fishbourne IoW...............17 G4
Fishbourne W Susx..........18 A5
Fishbourne Roman
  Palace W Susx..............18 A5
Fishburn Dur.................141 J2
Fishcross Clacks............185 J7
Fisherford Abers............216 C7
Fisherrow E Loth...........177 K4
Fisher's Pond Hants........29 J7
Fisherton Highld............213 H4
Fisherton S Ayrs............163 H6
Fisherton de la Mere
  Wilts...........................27 M4
Fishguard Pembks..........64 D6
Fishlake Donc...............125 G7
Fishnish Pier Ag & B.....190 D7
Fishponds Bristl.............38 F5
Fishtoft Lincs................104 B4
Fishtoft Drove Lincs......104 A3
Fiskavaig Highld............208 E7
Fiskerton Lincs..............117 H6
Fiskerton Notts.............102 C3
Fittleton Wilts................28 D2
Fittleworth W Susx..........18 D2
Fitz Shrops....................98 C8
Fitzhead Somset.............25 H5
Fitzwilliam Wakefd........124 C7
Five Ash Down E Susx.....19 M2
Five Ashes E Susx...........32 F7
Fivehead Somset............26 A6
Fivelanes Cnwll.................9 G8
Five Oak Green Kent.......33 H4
Five Oaks Jersey............236 d7
Five Oaks W Susx...........31 H5
Five Roads Carmth..........50 F4
Flackwell Heath
  Bucks.........................42 E3
Fladbury Worcs..............71 H5
Fladdabister Shet..........235 c6
Flagg Derbys.................114 C7
Flamborough E R Yk......135 K5
Flamborough Head
  E R Yk........................135 K5
Flamingo Land
  Theme Park
  N York........................134 B4
Flamstead Herts.............59 H5
Flansham W Susx............18 C5
Flanshaw Wakefd..........123 L6
Flasby N York................131 H7
Flash Staffs..................114 A7
Flashader Highld...........208 E4
Flaunden Herts...............59 G7
Flawborough Notts........102 C4
Flawith N York..............133 G6
Flax Bourton N Som........38 D6
Flaxby N York................132 F7
Flaxley Gloucs................55 G5
Flaxpool Somset.............25 H4
Flaxton N York..............133 K6
Fleckney Leics................87 J5
Flecknoe Warwks............73 G2
Fledborough Notts........116 D6
Fleet Dorset....................14 C6
Fleet Hants....................30 D2
Fleet Lincs....................104 C7
Fleet Air Arm
  Museum Somset.........26 D6
Fleet Hargate Lincs.......104 C7
Fleet Services Hants......30 D1
Fleetwood Lancs...........120 D2
Flemingston V Glam........36 F6
Flemington S Lans.........175 H6
Flempton Suffk...............77 J1
Fletchertown Cumb.......147 L6
Fletching E Susx.............19 L2
Flexbury Cnwll..................9 G4
Flexford Surrey...............30 F2
Flimby Cumb.................147 H7
Flimwell E Susx..............33 J6
Flint Flints...................111 H6
Flintham Notts..............102 C4
Flinton E R Yk...............126 F4
Flitcham Norfk..............105 H6
Flitton C Beds................74 F7
Flitwick C Beds...............74 F7
Flixborough N Linc.......125 K7
Flixborough Stather
  N Linc........................125 K7
Flixton N York...............135 G4
Flixton Suffk...................93 G6
Flixton Traffd................113 H3
Flockton Kirk................123 J7
Flockton Green Kirk......123 K7
Flodigarry Highld..........218 C6
Flookburgh Cumb..........129 H4
Flordon Norfk..................92 E4
Flore Nhants...................73 J3
Flowton Suffk..................78 C5
Flushing Cnwll...................3 L4
Fluxton Devon................12 E4
Flyford Flavell Worcs......71 H4
Fobbing Thurr................46 B4
Fochabers Moray...........215 H3
Fochriw Caerph...............53 H6
Fockerby N Linc............125 K6
Foddington Somset.........26 E5
Foel Powys.....................81 L2
Foggathorpe E R Yk......125 J7
Fogo Border..................179 G8
Fogwatt Moray..............214 F3
Foindle Highld...............228 B5
Folda Angus..................195 J4
Fole Staffs....................100 B5
Foleshill Covtry...............86 D6
Folke Dorset....................26 F8
Folkestone Kent..............35 H7
Folkingham Lincs..........103 H5
Folkington E Susx............20 B5
Folksworth Cambs...........89 G5
Folkton N York...............135 G4
Folla Rule Abers............216 D7
Follifoot N York.............132 E8
Folly Gate Devon.............10 E5
Fonthill Bishop Wilts.......27 L5
Fonthill Gifford Wilts......27 L5
Fontmell Magna
  Dorset.........................27 K7
Fontmell Parva
  Dorset.........................27 J8
Fontwell W Susx.............18 C4
Foolow Derbys..............114 D6
Forbestown Abers.........205 H3
Forcett N York...............140 F5
Ford Ag & B..................182 C6
Ford Bucks.....................58 C6
Ford Derbys..................115 H5
Ford Devon.....................22 F6
Ford Gloucs....................56 C3
Ford Nthumb................168 E2
Ford Somset...................25 H5
Ford Staffs...................100 B2
Ford W Susx....................18 D5
Ford Wilts......................39 J5
Fordcombe Kent.............32 F5
Fordell Fife...................177 G2
Forden Powys.................82 E4
Ford End Essex...............61 G5
Forder Green Devon..........7 H3
Fordham Cambs...............76 F1
Fordham Essex................61 L3
Fordham Norfk................90 E4
Fordingbridge Hants.......28 D8
Fordon E R Yk...............135 G4
Fordoun Abers...............197 J2
Fordstreet Essex..............61 L3
Ford Street Somset..........25 J7
Fordwich Kent................35 G3
Fordyce Abers...............216 B2
Forebridge Staffs............99 L7
Forest Guern.................236 C4
Forest Chapel Ches E.....113 L6
Forest Gate Gt Lon..........45 H3
Forest Green Surrey........31 J3
Forest Hall N Tyne..........151 G2
Forest Hill Gt Lon............45 G5
Forest Hill Oxon..............57 L6
Forest Lane Head
  N York........................132 E7
Forest Mill Clacks..........185 K8
Forest of Dean
  Gloucs........................54 F5
Forest Park
  Crematorium
  Gt Lon..........................45 J2
Forest Row E Susx...........32 D6
Forestside W Susx...........30 C8
Forfar Angus.................196 D6
Forgandenny P & K........186 A4
Forge Hammer
  Torfn...........................37 L2
Forgie Moray.................215 J4
Forgieside Moray...........215 J4
Forgue Abers.................216 B5
Formby Sefton..............111 J1
Forncett End Norfk..........92 D5
Forncett St Mary
  Norfk..........................92 E5
Forncett St Peter
  Norfk..........................92 E5
Fornham All Saints
  Suffk...........................77 J2
Fornham St Martin
  Suffk...........................77 J2
Fornighty Highld...........213 L4
Forres Moray.................214 C3
Forsbrook Staffs.............99 L4
Forse Highld.................227 M2
Forsinard Highld...........230 C6
Fort Augustus Highld....202 B4
Forteviot P & K.............185 L4
Forth S Lans..................176 C7
Forthampton Gloucs.......55 K2
Fortingall P & K............194 B6
Forton Hants..................29 H3
Forton Lancs.................121 G1
Forton Shrops.................83 H1
Forton Somset................13 J2
Forton Staffs...................99 H7
Fortrie Abers.................216 C5
Fortrose Highld.............213 H3
Fortuneswell Dorset.......14 D7
Fort William Highld......191 L2
Forty Hill Gt Lon.............60 B7
Fosbury Wilts..................40 F8
Foscot Oxon....................56 E4
Fosdyke Lincs...............104 A5
Foss P & K....................194 C5
Fossebridge Gloucs........56 B5
Foster Street Essex.........60 D6
Foston Derbys...............100 D6
Foston Leics...................87 H4
Foston Lincs.................102 E4
Foston N York...............133 L6
Foston on the Wolds
  E R Yk........................135 H7
Fotherby Lincs...............118 D3
Fotheringhay Nhants......88 F5
Foula Shet....................235 a6
Foulden Border..............179 J7
Foulden Norfk.................91 H4
Foul End Warwks............86 B4
Foulness Island Essex......47 G2
Foulon Vale
  Crematorium
  Guern........................236 d3
Foulridge Lancs............122 D3
Foulsham Norfk.............106 B7
Fountainhall Border......177 L8
Four Ashes Suffk.............78 B1

Four Crosses Powys......97 K8
Four Elms Kent............32 E4
Four Forks Somset......25 A4
Four Gotes Cambs........90 C1
Four Lanes Cnwll...........3 J4
Four Marks Hants........30 A4
Four Mile Bridge IoA..108 C5
Four Oaks Solhll..........86 B7
Fourpenny Highld......223 H3
Four Roads Carmth......50 F4
Fourstones Nthumb....149 M2
Four Throws Kent........33 K7
Fovant Wilts................28 A5
Foveran Abers...........207 H2
Fowey Cnwll.................5 H5
Fowlhall Kent..............33 J4
Fowlis Angus.............186 E2
Fowlis Wester P & K...185 J3
Fowlmere Cambs.........76 B5
Fownhope Herefs........69 L7
Foxbar Rens...............174 E6
Foxcote Somset...........27 G1
Foxdale IoM...............237 b5
Foxearth Essex...........77 J5
Foxfield Cumb...........128 F3
Foxhole Cnwll...............4 F5
Foxholes N York.........134 F5
Foxley Norfk..............106 C7
Foxt Staffs................100 B3
Foxton Cambs.............76 B5
Foxton Leics..............87 K5
Foxton N York...........141 K7
Foxwood Shrops.........84 B7
Foy Herefs.................54 E3
Foyers Highld............202 D2
Foynesfield Highld......213 L4
Fraddon Cnwll..............4 E4
Fradley Staffs.............85 L2
Fradswell Staffs..........99 M6
Fraisthorpe E R Yk....135 J7
Framfield E Susx.........20 A2
Framingham Earl
  Norfk......................92 F3
Framingham Pigot
  Norfk......................92 F3
Framlingham Suffk......79 G2
Frampton Dorset........14 C4
Frampton Lincs.........104 B5
Frampton Cotterell
  S Glos......................38 F4
Frampton Mansell
  Gloucs.....................55 L7
Frampton on Severn
  Gloucs.....................55 H6
Framsden Suffk...........78 E3
Framwellgate Moor
  Dur........................151 G2
Franche Worcs............84 E7
Frankby Wirral...........111 H4
Frankley Worcs...........85 H7
Frankley Services
  Worcs......................85 H7
Frankton Warwks........72 E1
Frant E Susx...............33 G6
Fraserburgh Abers.....217 J2
Frating Essex.............62 C4
Frating Green Essex....62 C4
Fratton C Port............17 J3
Freathy Cnwll...............6 B5
Freckenham Suffk.......76 F1
Freckleton Lancs.......120 F5
Freeby Leics.............102 D7
Freefolk Hants...........29 J2
Freeland Oxon............57 H5
Freethorpe Norfk........93 J3
Freethorpe Common
  Norfk......................93 J3
Freiston Lincs...........104 B4
Fremington Devon.......23 H5
Fremington N York.....140 D7
Frenchay S Glos.........38 F5
Frenich P & K...........194 C5
Frensham Surrey........30 D3
Freshfield Sefton.......120 C8
Freshford Wilts...........39 H7
Freshwater IoW..........16 D5
Fressingfield Suffk......92 F7

Freston Suffk..............78 E6
Freswick Highld.........231 L3
Fretherne Gloucs........55 G6
Frettenham Norfk......106 F8
Freuchie Fife.............186 E6
Freystrop Pembks........49 G5
Friar Park Sandw.........85 H4
Friday Bridge Cambs....90 C3
Friday Street Suffk......79 H3
Fridaythorpe E R Yk..134 D7
Friern Barnet Gt Lon...44 F2
Friesthorpe Lincs.......117 H5
Frieston Lincs...........102 F3
Frieth Bucks..............42 D3
Frilford Oxon.............41 H2
Frilsham W Berk.........41 K5
Frimley Surrey............42 E8
Frindsbury Medway.....46 C6
Fring Norfk..............105 H5
Fringford Oxon..........57 L3
Frinsted Kent............34 B4
Frinton-on-Sea Essex..62 F4
Friockheim Angus.....196 F6
Frisby on the
  Wreake Leics..........102 B8
Friskney Lincs..........104 D2
Friston E Susx...........20 B6
Friston Suffk............79 J3
Fritchley Derbys........101 G3
Fritham Hants............28 E8
Frithelstock Devon......23 G7
Frithelstock Stone
  Devon......................23 G7
Frithville Lincs.........104 A3
Frittenden Kent.........33 K5
Frittiscombe Devon......7 J6
Fritton Norfk............92 F5
Fritton Norfk............93 K4
Fritwell Oxon............57 K3
Frizinghall C Brad.....123 H4
Frizington Cumb........136 E4
Frocester Gloucs........55 H7
Frodesley Shrops........83 K3
Frodsham Ches W......112 D6
Frogden Border........168 B4
Frog End Cambs.........76 B5
Froggatt Derbys........114 E6
Froghall Staffs..........100 A3
Frogmore Devon..........7 H7
Frognall Lincs...........89 H2
Frog Pool Worcs........70 E2
Frogwell Cnwll............6 A3
Frolesworth Leics.......87 G5
Frome Somset...........27 H2
Frome St Quintin
  Dorset.....................14 B2
Fromes Hill Herefs......70 C5
Froncysyllte Denbgs....97 K4
Fron-goch Gwynd........96 D5
Fron Isaf Wrexhm........97 L4
Frosterley Dur..........150 C7
Froxfield Wilts...........40 F6
Froxfield Green Hants..30 B6
Fryern Hill Hants........29 H7
Fryerning Essex.........61 G7
Fuinary Highld..........190 C6
Fulbeck Lincs...........102 F3
Fulbourn Cambs.........76 D4
Fulbrook Oxon..........56 E5
Fulflood Hants...........29 J5
Fulford C York..........124 F2
Fulford Somset...........25 K5
Fulford Staffs...........99 L5
Fulham Gt Lon...........44 E5
Fulking W Susx..........19 H4
Fullarton N Ayrs.......163 H2
Fuller Street Essex......61 H5
Fullerton Hants..........29 G4
Fulletby Lincs..........118 D6
Fullready Warwks........72 C5
Full Sutton E R Yk....134 B7
Fullwood E Ayrs.......174 E7
Fulmer Bucks............43 G4
Fulmodeston Norfk....106 B6
Fulnetby Lincs..........117 H5
Fulney Lincs............103 L7
Fulstow Lincs..........118 D3

Fulwell Sundld.........151 J3
Fulwood Lancs.........121 H4
Fulwood Sheff..........114 F4
Fundenhall Norfk........92 D4
Funtington W Susx......17 L2
Funtullich P & K.......184 F3
Furley Devon............13 H2
Furnace Ag & B.........182 E7
Furnace Carmth.........51 G5
Furness Vale Derbys..114 A5
Furneux Pelham
  Herts.......................60 C3
Furzley Hants............28 F7
Fyfield Essex............60 F6
Fyfield Hants............28 F3
Fyfield Oxon.............57 H7
Fyfield Wilts.............40 C6
Fyfield Wilts.............40 D7
Fylingthorpe N York..143 J6
Fyning W Susx...........30 D6
Fyvie Abers..............216 E6

G

Gabroc Hill E Ayrs....174 E7
Gaddesby Leics..........87 K2
Gaddesden Row
  Herts.......................59 H5
Gadgirth S Ayrs.......163 K5
Gaer-llwyd Mons........38 C2
Gaerwen IoA............108 F7
Gailes N Ayrs...........163 H3
Gailey Staffs.............85 G2
Gainford Dur...........140 F4
Gainsborough Lincs...116 D4
Gainsford End Essex....77 G7
Gairloch Highld........219 J6
Gairlochy Highld.......201 J8
Gairneybridge P & K..186 B7
Gaitsgill Cumb..........148 C5
Galashiels Border......167 G3
Galgate Lancs...........121 G6
Galhampton Somset....26 F5
Gallanachbeg Ag & B..182 B2
Gallanachmore
  Ag & B...................182 B3
Gallatown Fife.........186 E8
Galleywood Essex......61 H7
Gallovie Highld........202 E7
Galloway Forest
  Park......................153 J5
Gallowfauld Angus....196 D7
Gallowhill P & K.......186 B1
Galltair Highld.........200 C2
Galmpton Devon.........7 G7
Galmpton Torbay........7 K5
Galphay N York........132 C5
Galston E Ayrs.........163 L3
Gamblesby Cumb.......149 G6
Gamlingay Cambs.......75 J4
Gamlingay Great
  Heath Cambs............75 J4
Gamrie Abers............216 F2
Gamston Notts..........101 L5
Gamston Notts..........116 B6
Ganavan Bay Ag & B..182 B2
Ganllwyd Gwynd........96 B7
Gannachy Angus.......196 F3
Ganstead E R Yk.......126 E4
Ganthorpe N York.....133 L5
Ganton N York..........134 F4
Garbity Moray..........215 H4
Garboldisham Norfk....92 B7
Garbole Highld.........203 H1
Garchory Abers.........205 G4
Gardeners Green
  Wokham...................42 D6
Gardenstown Abers...216 F2
Garden Village Sheff..114 E2
Garderhouse Shet.....235 c5
Gare Hill Somset........27 H4
Garelochhead Ag & B..173 L1
Garford Oxon............41 H2
Garforth Leeds.........124 B4
Gargrave N York.......131 H8

Gargunnock Stirlg....184 F8
Garlic Street Norfk.....92 E6
Garlieston D & G.......145 K5
Garlinge Kent...........35 J2
Garlinge Green Kent....34 F4
Garlogie Abers.........206 E4
Garmond Abers.........216 F4
Garmouth Moray.......215 H2
Garmston Shrops........83 L3
Garn-Dolbenmaen
  Gwynd.....................95 J3
Garnkirk N Lans.......175 J5
Garrabost W Isls.......232 g2
Garrallan E Ayrs.......164 B5
Garras Cnwll..............3 J6
Garreg Gwynd............95 K4
Garrigill Cumb.........149 J6
Garroch D & G.........153 M6
Garrochtrie D & G....144 D7
Garrochty Ag & B......173 J7
Garros Highld..........209 H2
Garsdale Head Cumb..130 E2
Garsdon Wilts...........39 L3
Garshall Green Staffs..99 L5
Garsington Oxon........57 J7
Garstang Lancs........121 G2
Garston Herts............59 J7
Garston Lpool..........112 B5
Gartachossan Ag & B..171 G6
Gartcosh N Lans.......175 J5
Garth Powys.............67 G5
Garth Wrexhm...........97 K4
Garthamlock C Glas..175 H4
Garthmyl Powys.........82 E4
Garthorpe Leics.......102 D7
Garthorpe N Linc.....125 K6
Garth Penrhyncoch
  Cerdgn.....................80 E7
Garth Row Cumb.......138 D7
Gartly Abers............215 L7
Gartmore Stirlg.......184 C7
Gartness N Lans.......175 K5
Gartness Stirlg........174 F2
Gartocharn W Duns..174 D2
Garton-on-the-Wolds
  E R Yk....................134 F7
Gartymore Highld....227 M5
Garvald E Loth........178 D4
Garvan Highld..........191 J2
Garvard Ag & B........171 G1
Garve Highld...........212 B3
Garvellachs Ag & B...181 K5
Garvestone Norfk.......92 B3
Garvock Inver..........174 B4
Garway Herefs..........54 C4
Garyvard W Isls.......232 F3
Gasper Wilts............27 H5
Gastard Wilts...........39 K6
Gasthorpe Norfk........91 L7
Gaston Green Essex....60 D5
Gatcombe IoW..........16 F5
Gate Burton Lincs.....116 D5
Gateford Notts.........124 E5
Gateforth N York......124 E5
Gatehead E Ayrs.......163 K5
Gate Helmsley N York.133 L7
Gatehouse Nthumb....157 K4
Gatehouse of Fleet
  D & G....................145 M4
Gateley Norfk..........106 A7
Gatenby N York........132 E3
Gateshaw Border......168 B5
Gateshead Gatesd.....151 G3
Gateside Angus........196 D7
Gateside E Rens.......174 E6
Gateside Fife..........186 C5
Gateside N Ayrs.......174 C7
Gateslack D & G......154 F2
Gatley Stockp..........113 J4
Gattonside Border....167 H3
Gatwick Airport
  W Susx....................32 B5
Gaulby Leics............87 K4
Gauldry Fife...........186 F3
Gauldswell P & K.....195 K6
Gautby Lincs...........117 K6
Gavinton Border......179 G7
Gawcott Bucks..........58 B2

Gawsworth Ches E **113** K7
Gawthrop Cumb **130** D3
Gawthwaite Cumb **129** G3
Gaydon Warwks **72** D4
Gayhurst M Keyn **74** B5
Gayle N York **131** G2
Gayles N York **140** E5
Gayton Nhants **73** K4
Gayton Norfk **105** H8
Gayton Staffs **99** M6
Gayton le Marsh Lincs..**118** F5
Gayton Thorpe Norfk...**105** H8
Gaywood Norfk............**105** G7
Gazeley Suffk **77** G2
Gearraidh Bhaird
    W Isls **232** f3
Geary Highld **208** D3
Gedding Suffk **77** L3
Geddington Nhants **88** C6
Gedling Notts................**101** L4
Gedney Lincs................**104** C7
Gedney Broadgate
    Lincs **104** C7
Gedney Drove End
    Lincs **104** D6
Gedney Dyke Lincs......**104** C7
Gedney Hill Lincs **89** L2
Geeston Rutlnd...............**88** E3
Geldeston Norfk.............**93** H5
Gellifor Denbgs............**110** F8
Gelligaer Caerph............**37** H2
Gellilydan Gwynd...........**95** M4
Gellinudd Neath **51** K5
Gellyburn P & K...........**195** H8
Gellywen Carmth **50** C2
Gelston D & G **146** D3
Gelston Lincs................**102** E4
Gembling E R Yk..........**135** H7
Gentleshaw Staffs..........**85** J2
Georgefield D & G **156** B4
George Green Bucks **43** G4
Georgeham Devon..........**23** G4
Georgemas Junction
    Station Highld..........**231** H4
George Nympton
    Devon **23** L6
Georth Ork **234** b5
Germansweek Devon......**10** C6
Gerrans Cnwll.................**4** D8
Gerrards Cross Bucks **43** G3
Gerrick R & Cl..............**142** E5
Gestingthorpe Essex **77** J2
Geuffordd Powys..........**82** E2
Gidea Park Gt Lon **45** K3
Giffnock E Rens **175** G6
Gifford E Loth **178** C5
Giffordtown Fife..........**186** E5
Giggleswick N York **130** F6
Gigha Ag & B **171** L7
Gilberdyke E R Yk........**125** K5
Gilchriston E Loth........**178** B5
Gilcrux Cumb...............**147** K7
Gildersome Leeds.........**123** K5
Gildingwells Rothm **115** K4
Gilesgate Moor Dur......**151** H6
Gileston V Glam **36** F6
Gilfach Caerph...............**53** J7
Gilfach Goch Brdgnd **36** F3
Gilfachrheda Cerdgn.....**65** L3
Gilgarran Cumb............**136** E3
Gillamoor N York **133** K2
Gillen Highld................**208** D3
Gillesbie D & G **155** K4
Gilling East N York.......**133** J4
Gillingham Dorset **27** J6
Gillingham Medway........**46** C6
Gillingham Norfk...........**93** J5
Gilling West N York.....**140** F6
Gillock Highld...............**231** J4
Gills Highld...................**231** K2
Gilmanscleuch Border...**166** E5
Gilroes Crematorium
    C Leic..........................**87** H3

Gilsland Nthumb..........**149** G2
Gilston Border..............**177** L6
Gilston Herts **60** D5
Gilwern Mons................**53** K5
Gimingham Norfk.........**107** G5
Gipping Suffk **78** C2
Gipsey Bridge Lincs......**103** M3
Girdle Toll N Ayrs.........**163** J2
Girlsta Shet.................**235** c5
Girsby N York **141** J5
Girthon D & G **146** A4
Girton Cambs **76** B3
Girton Notts................**116** D7
Girvan S Ayrs **152** E3
Gisburn Lancs..............**122** C2
Gisleham Suffk...............**93** K5
Gislingham Suffk............**78** C1
Gissing Norfk **92** D6
Gittisham Devon **12** E3
Gladestry Powys............**68** E4
Gladsmuir E Loth **177** M4
Glais Swans **51** K5
Glaisdale N York...........**143** G6
Glamis Angus...............**196** C6
Glanaman Carmth..........**51** J3
Glandford Norfk...........**106** C4
Glandwr Pembks...........**49** K2
Glandyfi Cerdgn.............**80** F4
Glanllynfi Brdgnd...........**36** D3
Glan-rhyd Powys............**52** B6
Glanton Nthumb...........**169** G6
Glanvilles Wootton
    Dorset **14** D2
Glan-y-don Flints..........**111** G5
Glapthorn Nhants **88** E5
Glapwell Derbys............**115** J7
Glasbury Powys.............**68** D6
Glascwm Powys.............**68** D4
Glasfryn Conwy.............**96** E3
Glasgow C Glas **175** G5
Glasgow Airport Rens ..**174** E5
Glasgow Science
    Centre C Glas............**175** G5
Glasinfryn Gwynd..........**109** H7
Glasnacardoch Bay
    Highld **199** L6
Glasnakille Highld.........**199** H3
Glassford S Lans **175** J8
Glasshouse Gloucs **55** G4
Glasshouses N York.....**132** B6
Glasson Cumb..............**148** A3
Glasson Lancs...............**129** K7
Glassonby Cumb...........**149** G3
Glasterlaw Angus.........**196** F6
Glaston Rutlnd...............**88** C4
Glastonbury Somset......**26** D4
Glatton Cambs **89** H6
Glazebrook Warrtn **113** G3
Glazebury Warrtn **112** F3
Glazeley Shrops.............**84** C5
Gleaston Cumb.............**128** F5
Glebe Highld................**202** D2
Gledhow Leeds.............**123** L3
Gledpark D & G **146** B5
Gledrid Shrops...............**97** L5
Glemsford Suffk.............**77** J5
Glenallachie Moray.......**215** G6
Glenancross Highld......**199** K6
Glenaros House
    Ag & B **190** B7
Glen Auldyn IoM..........**237** d3
Glenbarr Ag & B..........**161** H3
Glenbarry Abers **216** B4
Glenbeg Highld **190** C4
Glenbervie Abers.........**197** J1
Glenboig N Lans..........**175** J5
Glenborrodale Highld...**190** C4
Glenbranter Ag & B.....**183** G7
Glenbreck Border.........**165** K5
Glenbrittle House
    Highld **198** F2
Glenbuck E Ayrs..........**164** E4
Glencally Angus...........**196** B4
Glencaple D & G **147** H2
Glencarron Lodge
    Highld **211** G4
Glencarse P & K...........**186** C3

Glen Clunie Lodge
    Abers **204** E8
Glencoe Highld **191** L5
Glencothe Border.........**165** L4
Glencraig Fife...............**186** C7
Glencrosh D & G **154** D4
Glendale Highld **208** B4
Glendaruel Ag & B.......**173** G2
Glendevon P & K **185** K6
Glendoe Lodge Highld.**202** C4
Glendoick P & K...........**186** C3
Glenduckie Fife............**186** D4
Glenegedale Ag & B.....**170** F7
Glenelg Highld.............**200** C2
Glenerney Moray..........**214** C5
Glenfarg P & K **186** B5
Glenfield Leics...............**87** G3
Glenfinnan Highld........**191** H1
Glenfintaig Lodge
    Highld **201** K7
Glenfoot P & K **186** C4
Glenfyne Lodge
    Ag & B **183** H4
Glengarnock N Ayrs.....**174** C7
Glengolly Highld..........**231** G3
Glengorm Castle
    Ag & B **189** K5
Glengrasco Highld........**209** G5
Glenholm Border..........**165** L3
Glenhoul D & G **154** A5
Glenisla Angus.............**195** K4
Glenkin Ag & B **173** K3
Glenkindie Abers.........**205** K3
Glenlivet Moray...........**214** F8
Glenlochar D & G **146** C3
Glenlomond P & K........**186** C6
Glenluce D & G **144** E4
Glenmassen Ag & B.....**173** J2
Glenmavis N Lans........**175** K5
Glen Maye IoM **237** b5
Glenmore Highld **209** G6
Glenmore Lodge
    Highld **204** B4
Glen Nevis House
    Highld **192** B3
Glenochil Clacks..........**185** H7
Glen Parva Leics............**87** H4
Glenquiech Angus........**196** C4
Glenralloch Ag & B......**172** E4
Glenridding Cumb........**137** L4
Glenrothes Fife............**186** D7
Glenshero Lodge
    Highld **202** E6
Glenstriven Ag & B......**173** J3
Glentham Lincs............**117** G4
Glen Trool Lodge
    D & G **153** J6
Glentrool Village
    D & G **153** H6
Glentruim House
    Highld **203** G6
Glentworth Lincs..........**116** F4
Glenuig Highld.............**190** D2
Glenvarragill Highld.....**209** G6
Glen Vine IoM..............**237** c5
Glenwhilly D & G..........**152** E7
Glespin S Lans **164** F4
Glewstone Herefs..........**54** E3
Glinton C Pete...............**89** H3
Glooston Leics...............**87** L4
Glossop Derbys............**114** B3
Gloster Hill Nthumb.....**159** G2
Gloucester Gloucs **55** J4
Gloucester
    Crematorium
    Gloucs **55** J5
Gloucestershire
    Airport Gloucs **55** K4
Glusburn N York **122** F2
Glutt Lodge Highld.......**227** L2
Glympton Oxon **57** H4
Glynarthen Cerdgn........**65** K5
Glyn Ceiriog Wrexhm....**97** H4
Glyncorrwg Neath **52** D7
Glynde E Susx **19** L4
Glyndyfrdwy Denbgs.....**97** J4
Glynneath Neath...........**52** D6

Glynn Valley
    Crematorium
    Cnwll **5** H3
Glyntaff
    Crematorium
    Rhondd **37** H3
Glyntawe Powys............**52** D5
Glynteg Carmth.............**65** K6
Gnosall Staffs **99** J7
Gnosall Heath Staffs **99** J7
Goadby Leics.................**87** L4
Goadby Marwood
    Leics.........................**102** C7
Goatacre Wilts **40** A5
Goathill Dorset...............**26** F7
Goathland N York.........**143** H6
Goathurst Somset..........**25** K5
Gobowen Shrops............**97** L5
Godalming Surrey **30** F3
Goddard's Green
    Kent............................**33** L6
Godmanchester
    Cambs **75** J1
Godmanstone Dorset....**14** C3
Godmersham Kent **34** E5
Godney Somset **26** C3
Godolphin Cross
    Cnwll **3** G5
Godre'r-graig Neath **51** L4
Godshill IoW **17** G6
Godstone Surrey **32** C3
Goetre Mons **53** L6
Goff's Oak Herts **60** B7
Gofilon Mons **53** L6
Gogar C Edin **177** G4
Goginan Cerdgn **80** F7
Golan Gwynd **95** J4
Golant Cnwll...................**5** H5
Golberdon Cnwll.............**5** M2
Golborne Wigan...........**112** E3
Golcar Kirk **123** G7
Goldcliff Newpt **38** A4
Golden Green Kent **33** H4
Golden Pot Hants **30** B3
Golders Green Gt Lon ...**44** E3
Golders Green
    Crematorium
    Gt Lon **44** E3
Goldhanger Essex **61** L6
Goldington Bed.............**74** F4
Goldsborough N York..**132** F7
Goldsborough N York...**143** H4
Goldsithney Cnwll..........**2** F5
Goldsworth Park
    Surrey **43** G8
Goldthorpe Barns.........**115** J2
Goldworthy Devon **22** F6
Gollanfield Highld **213** J4
Golspie Highld.............**223** H2
Gomeldon Wilts **28** D4
Gomshall Surrey **31** H2
Gonalston Notts............**102** B3
Gonerby Hill Foot
    Lincs.........................**102** E5
Gonfirth Shet..............**235** c4
Good Easter Essex **60** F5
Gooderstone Norfk **91** H3
Goodleigh Devon **23** J5
Goodmanham E R Yk...**125** K2
Goodmayes Gt Lon **45** J3
Goodnestone Kent **34** D3
Goodnestone Kent **35** H4
Goodrich Herefs............**54** E4
Goodrich Castle
    Herefs **54** E4
Goodrington Torbay **7** K4
Goodshaw Lancs **122** B5
Goodwick Pembks.........**64** C6
Goodworth Clatford
    Hants **29** G3
Goole E R Yk................**125** H5
Goom's Hill Worcs **71** H4
Goonbell Cnwll...............**3** J2
Goonhavern Cnwll..........**3** K1
Goonvrea Cnwll..............**3** J2
Goosecruives Abers......**206** E8
Gooseford Devon..........**11** G6

Goose Green Essex........62 D3
Goose Green S Glos.......38 F5
Gooseham Cnwll............9 G2
Goosey Oxon..............41 G3
Goosnargh Lancs.........121 H3
Goostrey Ches E..........113 H7
Gordano Services
  N Som.....................38 D5
Gordon Border............167 K2
Gordon Arms Hotel
  Border...................166 D4
Gordonstown Abers......216 B3
Gordonstown Abers......216 D6
Gorebridge Mdloth.......177 K6
Gorefield Cambs..........90 B2
Gores Wilts................40 C8
Gorey Jersey.............236 e7
Goring Oxon...............41 L4
Goring-by-Sea W Susx....18 F5
Gorleston on Sea
  Norfk.....................93 L3
Gornal Wood
Crematorium
  Dudley....................85 G5
Gorrachie Abers.........216 E3
Gorran Churchtown
  Cnwll......................4 F7
Gorran Haven Cnwll.......4 F7
Gorsedd Flints...........111 G6
Gorse Hill Swindn........40 D3
Gorseinon Swans.........51 H5
Gorsgoch Cerdgn.........66 C4
Gorslas Carmth...........51 H3
Gorsley Gloucs...........55 G3
Gorsley Common
  Herefs....................54 F3
Gorstan Highld..........212 B2
Gorsty Hill Staffs.......100 C6
Gorten Ag & B............181 L2
Gorthleck Highld........202 E2
Gorton Manch............113 K3
Gosbeck Suffk...........78 D4
Gosberton Lincs.........103 L6
Gosfield Essex...........61 J3
Gosforth Cumb...........136 E6
Gosforth N u Ty.........151 G2
Gospel End Staffs.......84 F5
Gosport Hants...........17 H3
Gossington Gloucs.......55 H7
Gotham Notts...........101 K6
Gotherington Gloucs.....55 L3
Cotton Somset...........25 K5
Goudhurst Kent..........33 J5
Goulceby Lincs.........118 C5
Gourdas Abers..........216 E6
Gourdie C Dund..........186 F2
Gourdon Abers..........197 K3
Gourock Inver..........173 L3
Govan C Glas...........174 F5
Goveton Devon............7 H6
Gowdall E R Yk..........124 F6
Gower Highld............212 D3
Gower Swans.............51 G7
Gowerton Swans.........51 H6
Gowkhall Fife...........176 E1
Goxhill E R Yk..........126 F2
Goxhill N Linc..........126 D6
Grabhair W Isls.........232 f3
Graffham W Susx.........18 C3
Grafham Cambs...........75 H2
Grafham Surrey...........31 G3
Grafton N York..........132 F6
Grafton Oxon............56 F7
Grafton Shrops...........98 B8
Grafton Worcs............71 H6
Grafton Flyford
  Worcs.....................71 G4
Grafton Regis
  Nhants....................73 L5
Grafton Underwood
  Nhants....................88 D7
Grafty Green Kent........34 B5
Graig Conwy.............109 M6
Graig-fechan Denbgs.....97 J2
Grain Medway............46 E5
Grainsby Lincs.........118 C2
Grainthorpe Lincs.......118 E3

Grampound Cnwll..........4 E6
Grampound Road
  Cnwll......................4 E5
Gramsdal W Isls.........233 c6
Gramsdale W Isls........233 c6
Granborough Bucks.......58 C3
Granby Notts...........102 C5
Grandborough
  Warwks....................72 F2
Grand Chemins
  Jersey...................236 d7
Grandes Rocques
  Guern....................236 c2
Grand Prix Collection
  Donington Leics.........101 H7
Grandtully P & K........194 E5
Grange Cumb............137 H4
Grange Medway...........46 D6
Grange P & K...........186 D3
Grange Crossroads
  Moray....................215 K4
Grange Hall Moray.......214 C3
Grangehall S Lans.......165 J2
Grange Hill Essex........45 H2
Grangemill Derbys.......100 E2
Grange Moor Kirk.......123 J7
Grangemouth Falk.......176 C3
Grange of Lindores
  Fife.....................186 D4
Grange-over-Sands
  Cumb.....................129 J4
Grangepans Falk........176 D3
Grangetown R & Cl......142 C3
Grangetown Sundld......151 K4
Grange Villa Dur........151 G4
Gransmoor E R Yk.......135 H7
Granston Pembks.........64 C7
Grantchester Cambs......76 B4
Grantham Lincs.........102 E5
Grantham
Crematorium
  Lincs....................102 F5
Granton C Edin.........177 H3
Grantown-on-Spey
  Highld...................214 C8
Grantshouse Border.....179 G5
Grasby Lincs...........117 H1
Grasmere Cumb..........137 K5
Grasscroft Oldham......113 L1
Grassendale Lpool......111 L4
Grassington N York.....131 J6
Grassmoor Derbys.......115 H7
Grassthorpe Notts......116 C7
Grateley Hants..........28 F3
Graveley Cambs..........75 J2
Graveley Herts..........59 L3
Graveney Kent...........34 E3
Gravesend Kent..........46 A5
Gravir W Isls...........232 f3
Grayingham Lincs.......116 F3
Grayrigg Cumb..........138 E7
Grays Thurr.............45 L4
Grayshott Hants.........30 E4
Grayswood Surrey........30 E4
Greasbrough Rothm......115 H3
Greasby Wirral.........111 H4
Great Abington
  Cambs.....................76 D5
Great Addington
  Nhants....................88 D7
Great Alne Warwks.......71 K3
Great Altcar Lancs......111 K1
Great Amwell Herts......60 B5
Great Asby Cumb........138 F5
Great Ashfield Suffk.....78 B2
Great Ayton N York.....142 C5
Great Baddow Essex......61 H6
Great Badminton
  S Glos....................39 J4
Great Bardfield Essex....61 G2
Great Barford Bed.......75 G4
Great Barr Sandw........85 J4
Great Barrington
  Gloucs....................56 E5
Great Barrow Ches W....112 C7
Great Barton Suffk.......77 K2
Great Barugh N York....134 B4

Great Bavington
  Nthumb...................158 C6
Great Bealings Suffk.....78 F5
Great Bedwyn Wilts......40 F7
Great Bentley Essex......62 D4
Great Billing Nhants......74 B3
Great Bircham Norfk....105 J6
Great Blakenham
  Suffk.....................78 D4
Great Blencow Cumb.....138 C2
Great Bolas Wrekin.......98 F7
Great Bookham
  Surrey....................31 J1
Great Bourton Oxon......72 F5
Great Bowden Leics......87 L5
Great Bradley Suffk......76 F4
Great Braxted Essex......61 K5
Great Bricett Suffk......78 C4
Great Brickhill Bucks.....58 E3
Great Bridgeford
  Staffs....................99 K6
Great Brington
  Nhants....................73 J2
Great Bromley Essex......62 C3
Great Broughton
  Cumb.....................136 E2
Great Broughton
  N York...................142 C6
Great Budworth
  Ches W...................112 F6
Great Burdon Darltn.....141 H4
Great Burstead Essex.....46 B2
Great Busby N York.....142 B6
Great Carlton Lincs.....118 E4
Great Casterton
  Rutlnd....................88 E2
Great Chalfield Wilts.....39 K7
Great Chart Kent.........34 C6
Great Chatwell Staffs.....84 E1
Great Chesterford
  Essex.....................76 D6
Great Cheverell Wilts.....27 M1
Great Chishill Cambs.....76 B6
Great Clacton Essex......62 E5
Great Clifton Cumb......136 E2
Great Coates NE Lin.....126 F8
Great Comberton
  Worcs.....................71 G6
Great Corby Cumb.......148 E4
Great Cornard Suffk......77 K6
Great Cowden E R Yk....126 F3
Great Coxwell Oxon......40 F2
Great Cransley
  Nhants....................88 B7
Great Cressingham
  Norfk.....................91 J3
Great Crosthwaite
  Cumb.....................137 J3
Great Cubley Derbys.....100 D5
Great Cumbrae
  Island N Ayrs...........173 K6
Great Dalby Leics........87 L2
Great Doddington
  Nhants....................74 C2
Great Dunham Norfk......91 K1
Great Dunmow Essex......61 G4
Great Durnford Wilts.....28 C4
Great Easton Essex......60 F3
Great Easton Leics.......88 B5
Great Eccleston Lancs...120 F3
Great Ellingham
  Norfk.....................92 B4
Great Elm Somset........27 H2
Great Everdon
  Nhants....................73 H3
Great Eversden
  Cambs.....................75 L4
Great Fencote N York...132 D2
Great Finborough
  Suffk.....................78 B3
Greatford Lincs..........88 F2
Great Fransham
  Norfk.....................91 K2
Great Gaddesden
  Herts.....................59 G5
Greatgate Staffs........100 B4
Great Gidding Cambs......89 G6

Great Givendale
  E R Yk...................134 C8
Great Glemham Suffk.....79 H3
Great Glen Leics.........87 J4
Great Gonerby Lincs....102 E5
Great Gransden
  Cambs.....................75 J4
Great Green Cambs........75 K5
Great Green Suffk........77 K4
Great Habton N York....134 B4
Great Hale Lincs........103 J4
Great Hallingbury
  Essex.....................60 E4
Greatham Hants..........30 C5
Greatham Hartpl........142 D2
Greatham W Susx.........18 E3
Great Hampden
  Bucks.....................58 D7
Great Harrowden
  Nhants....................74 C1
Great Harwood Lancs....121 L4
Great Haseley Oxon......57 M7
Great Hatfield E R Yk...126 F3
Great Haywood Staffs.....99 M7
Great Heck N York.......124 E6
Great Henny Essex........77 K6
Great Hinton Wilts.......39 K8
Great Hockham Norfk.....91 L5
Great Holland Essex......62 E4
Great Hollands Br For....42 E4
Great Horkesley
  Essex.....................62 B2
Great Hormead Herts.....60 C3
Great Horton C Brad....123 H4
Great Horwood Bucks.....58 C2
Great Houghton
  Barns....................115 H1
Great Houghton
  Nhants....................73 L3
Great Hucklow
  Derbys...................114 D6
Great Kelk E R Yk.......135 H7
Great Kimble Bucks.......58 D6
Great Kingshill Bucks....42 E2
Great Langdale Cumb....137 J6
Great Langton N York...141 H4
Great Leighs Essex.......61 H4
Great Limber Lincs......126 E8
Great Linford M Keyn....74 C6
Great Livermere Suffk....77 K1
Great Longstone
  Derbys...................114 D6
Great Lumley Dur........151 H5
Great Malvern Worcs......70 D5
Great Maplestead
  Essex.....................77 J7
Great Marton Bpool.....120 D4
Great Massingham
  Norfk....................105 J7
Great Milton Oxon........57 L7
Great Missenden
  Bucks.....................58 E7
Great Mitton Lancs......121 K3
Great Mongeham
  Kent......................35 K4
Great Moulton Norfk......92 E5
Great Musgrave
  Cumb.....................139 H4
Great Ness Shrops........98 B8
Great Notley Essex.......61 H4
Great Oak Mons..........54 B6
Great Oakley Essex.......62 D3
Great Oakley Nhants......88 C6
Great Offley Herts........59 J3
Great Ormside Cumb.....139 G4
Great Orton Cumb.......148 B4
Great Ouseburn
  N York...................133 G6
Great Oxendon
  Nhants....................87 K6
Great Oxney Green
  Essex.....................61 G6
Great Paxton Cambs......75 H2
Great Plumpton
  Lancs....................120 E4
Great Plumstead
  Norfk.....................93 G2

Great Ponton Lincs......102 F6
Great Preston Leeds......124 B5
Great Raveley Cambs......89 J7
Great Rissington
  Gloucs......56 D5
Great Rollright Oxon......56 F2
Great Ryburgh
  Norfk......106 A6
Great Ryton Shrops......83 J3
Great Saling Essex......61 H3
Great Salkeld Cumb......148 F7
Great Sampford
  Essex......76 F7
Great Saughall
  Ches W......111 K7
Great Shefford
  W Berk......41 G5
Great Shelford Cambs......76 C4
Great Smeaton
  N York......141 H6
Great Snoring Norfk......105 M5
Great Somerford
  Wilts......39 L4
Great Soudley Shrops......99 G6
Great Stainton Darltn......141 H3
Great Stambridge
  Essex......46 E2
Great Staughton
  Cambs......75 G2
Great Steeping Lincs......118 F8
Great Stoke S Glos......38 F4
Greatstone-on-Sea
  Kent......21 L2
Great Strickland
  Cumb......138 D3
Great Stukeley
  Cambs......89 J8
Great Sturton Lincs......117 K6
Great Swinburne
  Nthumb......158 B6
Great Tew Oxon......57 H3
Great Tey Essex......61 L3
Great Thurlow Suffk......76 F4
Great Torrington
  Devon......23 H7
Great Tosson Nthumb......158 C3
Great Totham Essex......61 K5
Great Totham Essex......61 L5
Great Urswick Cumb......129 G5
Great Wakering Essex......46 F3
Great Waldingfield
  Suffk......77 K5
Great Walsingham
  Norfk......105 M5
Great Waltham Essex......61 H5
Great Warley Essex......45 L2
Great Washbourne
  Gloucs......71 H7
Great Weeke Devon......11 G7
Great Weldon Nhants......88 D5
Great Wenham Suffk......78 C6
Great Whittington
  Nthumb......158 C7
Great Wigborough
  Essex......62 A5
Great Wilbraham
  Cambs......76 D3
Great Wishford Wilts......28 B4
Great Witcombe
  Gloucs......55 K5
Great Witley Worcs......70 D2
Great Wolford
  Warwks......72 B7
Greatworth Nhants......73 G6
Great Wratting Suffk......77 G5
Great Wymondley
  Herts......59 K3
Great Wyrley Staffs......85 H3
Great Yarmouth
  Norfk......93 L3
Great Yarmouth
  Crematorium
  Norfk......93 K3
Great Yeldham Essex......77 H6
Greenburn W Loth......176 C6
Green End Herts......60 B2
Green End Herts......60 B4

Greenfield Ag & B......173 M1
Greenfield C Beds......74 F7
Greenfield Flints......111 H6
Greenfield Highld......201 J5
Greenfield Oldham......113 M2
Greenford Gt Lon......43 J4
Greengairs N Lans......175 K4
Greengates C Brad......123 J3
Greenham Somset......25 G7
Green Hammerton
  N York......133 G7
Greenhaugh Nthumb......157 K5
Greenhead Nthumb......149 H3
Green Heath Staffs......85 H2
Greenhill D & G......155 J6
Greenhill Falk......175 L3
Greenhill Kent......47 K6
Greenhill S Lans......165 H3
Greenhithe Kent......45 L5
Greenholm E Ayrs......164 B3
Greenhouse Border......167 H5
Greenhow Hill N York......131 L6
Greenland Highld......231 J3
Greenland Sheff......115 H4
Greenlaw Border......167 L1
Greenlea D & G......155 H6
Greenloaning P & K......185 H6
Greenmount Bury......122 B7
Greenock Inver......174 B3
Greenock
  Crematorium
  Inver......174 B3
Greenodd Cumb......129 G3
Green Ore Somset......26 E2
Green Quarter Cumb......138 C6
Greenshields S Lans......165 K2
Greenside Gatesd......150 E3
Greenside Kirk......123 H7
Greens Norton
  Nhants......73 J4
Greenstead Essex......62 B3
Greenstead Green
  Essex......61 K3
Green Street Herts......59 K7
Green Street Herts......60 D4
Green Street Green
  Kent......45 L6
Green Tye Herts......60 C4
Greenway Somset......25 L6
Greenwich Gt Lon......45 G4
Greet Gloucs......56 B3
Greete Shrops......69 L1
Greetham Lincs......118 D7
Greetham Rutlnd......88 D2
Greetland Calder......123 G6
Greinton Somset......26 B4
Grenaby IoM......237 b6
Grendon Nhants......74 C3
Grendon Warwks......86 C4
Grendon Underwood
  Bucks......58 B4
Grenoside Sheff......115 G3
Grenoside
  Crematorium
  Sheff......114 F3
Greosabhagh W Isls......232 e4
Gresford Wrexhm......97 M2
Gresham Norfk......106 E5
Greshornish House
  Hotel Highld......208 E4
Gressenhall Norfk......91 L1
Gressenhall Green
  Norfk......91 L1
Gressingham Lancs......130 B5
Greta Bridge Dur......140 D5
Gretna D & G......148 B2
Gretna Green D & G......148 B2
Gretna Services D & G......148 B2
Gretton Gloucs......56 A2
Gretton Nhants......88 C5
Gretton Shrops......83 K4
Grewelthorpe N York......132 D4
Greyrigg D & G......155 J4
Greys Green Oxon......42 B4
Greysouthen Cumb......136 E2
Greystoke Cumb......138 B2
Greystone Angus......196 E7

Greywell Hants......30 B2
Griff Warwks......86 D5
Griffithstown Torfn......53 L7
Grimeford Village
  Lancs......121 J7
Grimesthorpe Sheff......115 G4
Grimethorpe Barns......124 C8
Grimley Worcs......70 E3
Grimmet S Ayrs......163 H7
Grimoldby Lincs......118 E4
Grimpo Shrops......98 A7
Grimsargh Lancs......121 H4
Grimsby NE Lin......127 G7
Grimsby
  Crematorium
  NE Lin......118 C1
Grimscote Nhants......73 J4
Grimscott Cnwll......9 H4
Grimshader W Isls......232 f3
Grimsthorpe Lincs......103 H7
Grimston Leics......102 B7
Grimston Norfk......105 H7
Grimstone Dorset......14 C4
Grimstone End Suffk......77 L2
Grindale E R Yk......135 H5
Grindleford Derbys......114 E6
Grindleton Lancs......121 L2
Grindley Brook
  Shrops......98 D4
Grindlow Derbys......114 D6
Grindon Staffs......100 B2
Gringley on the Hill
  Notts......116 C4
Grinsdale Cumb......148 C4
Grinshill Shrops......98 D7
Grinton N York......140 D7
Griomaisiader W Isls......232 f3
Griomsaigh W Isls......233 c6
Grishipoll Ag & B......188 F4
Gristhorpe N York......135 H3
Griston Norfk......91 L4
Gritley Ork......234 d6
Grittenham Wilts......40 B4
Grittleton Wilts......39 K4
Grizebeck Cumb......128 F3
Grizedale Cumb......137 K7
Groby Leics......87 G3
Groes Conwy......110 D8
Groes-faen Rhondd......37 G4
Groeslon Gwynd......95 H2
Groes-Wen Caerph......37 H3
Grogarry W Isls......233 b7
Grogport Ag & B......161 K1
Groigearraidh W Isls......233 b7
Gronant Flints......110 F5
Groombridge E Susx......32 F5
Grosebay W Isls......232 e4
Grosmont Mons......54 B3
Grosmont N York......143 H6
Groton Suffk......77 L6
Grouville Jersey......236 e7
Grove Notts......116 C5
Grove Oxon......41 H3
Grove Green Kent......33 K3
Grove Park Gt Lon......45 H5
Grovesend Swans......51 H5
Gruinard Highld......219 L4
Gruinart Ag & B......170 F5
Grula Highld......208 F8
Gruline Ag & B......190 B7
Grundisburgh Suffk......78 F4
Gruting Shet......235 c5
Gualachulain Highld......192 B7
Guardbridge Fife......187 G4
Guarlford Worcs......70 E5
Guay P & K......194 F6
Guernsey Guern......236 c3
Guernsey Airport
  Guern......236 c3
Guestling Green
  E Susx......21 G3
Guestling Thorn
  E Susx......21 G3
Guestwick Norfk......106 C6
Guide Post Nthumb......159 G5
Guilden Morden
  Cambs......75 K5

Guilden Sutton
  Ches W......112 C7
Guildford Surrey......31 G2
Guildford
  Crematorium
  Surrey......31 G3
Guildtown P & K......186 B2
Guilsborough Nhants......87 J8
Guilsfield Powys......82 E2
Guiltreehill S Ayrs......163 J7
Guineaford Devon......23 J4
Guisborough R & Cl......142 D4
Guiseley Leeds......123 J3
Guist Norfk......106 B7
Guiting Power Gloucs......56 C3
Gullane E Loth......178 B2
Gulval Cnwll......2 E5
Gulworthy Devon......6 C2
Gumfreston Pembks......49 J7
Gumley Leics......87 K5
Gunby Lincs......102 E7
Gunby Lincs......118 F7
Gundleton Hants......29 L5
Gun Hill E Susx......20 C3
Gunn Devon......23 K5
Gunnerside N York......139 L7
Gunnerton Nthumb......158 A7
Gunness N Linc......125 K7
Gunnislake Cnwll......6 C2
Gunnista Shet......235 d6
Gunthorpe N Linc......116 D3
Gunthorpe Norfk......106 B5
Gunthorpe Notts......102 B4
Gunwalloe Cnwll......3 H6
Gurnard IoW......16 F4
Gurney Slade Somset......26 F2
Gurnos Powys......52 B6
Gussage All Saints
  Dorset......15 J1
Gussage St Andrew
  Dorset......27 L8
Gussage St Michael
  Dorset......15 J1
Guston Kent......35 J5
Gutcher Shet......235 d2
Guthrie Angus......196 F6
Guyhirn Cambs......90 B3
Guyzance Nthumb......158 F2
Gwaenysgor Flints......110 F5
Gwalchmai IoA......108 E6
Gwaun-Cae-Gurwen
  Carmth......51 K3
Gweek Cnwll......3 J6
Gwenddwr Powys......68 B6
Gwennap Cnwll......3 J4
Gwent Crematorium
  Mons......37 L2
Gwernaffield Flints......111 H7
Gwernesney Mons......54 B7
Gwernogle Carmth......66 C7
Gwernymynydd
  Flints......111 H8
Gwespyr Flints......110 F5
Gwinear Cnwll......3 G4
Gwithian Cnwll......3 G3
Gwyddelwern
  Denbgs......97 G3
Gwyddgrug Carmth......66 B7
Gwytherin Conwy......96 D1

H

Habberley Shrops......83 H3
Habberley Worcs......84 E7
Habergham Lancs......122 B4
Habertoft Lincs......119 G7
Habrough NE Lin......126 E7
Hacconby Lincs......103 J7
Haceby Lincs......103 G5
Hacheston Suffk......79 G3
Hackbridge Gt Lon......44 F6
Hackenthorpe Sheff......115 H5
Hackford Norfk......92 C3
Hackforth N York......132 C2
Hackland Ork......234 c5

Hackleton Nhants 74 B4
Hacklinge Kent.............35 J4
Hackness N York........134 F2
Hackney Gt Lon.............45 G3
Hackthorn Lincs...........117 G5
Hackthorpe Cumb.......138 D3
Hadden Border............168 B3
Haddenham Bucks......58 C6
Haddenham Cambs.....90 C7
Haddington E Loth.....178 B4
Haddington Lincs.......116 E8
Haddiscoe Norfk........93 J4
Haddo Abers................216 F6
Haddon Cambs.............89 G5
Hadfield Derbys.........114 A3
Hadham Ford Herts......60 C4
Hadleigh Essex............46 D3
Hadleigh Suffk.............78 B6
Hadley Worcs................70 F2
Hadley Wrekin.............84 C2
Hadley End Staffs......100 C7
Hadley Wood Gt Lon....44 E1
Hadlow Kent..................33 H3
Hadlow Down E Susx...20 B2
Hadnall Shrops.............98 D7
Hadrian's Wall
  Nthumb......................150 B2
Hadstock Essex............76 D5
Hadzor Worcs...............71 G3
Haggersta Shet..........235 c5
Haggerston Nthumb...168 F2
Haggs Falk...................175 L3
Hagley Herefs..............69 L6
Hagley Worcs................85 G7
Hagworthingham
  Lincs..........................118 D7
Haile Cumb..................136 E5
Hailey Oxon..................57 G5
Hailsham E Susx...........20 C4
Hainault Gt Lon............45 J2
Hainford Norfk...........106 F8
Hainton Lincs..............117 K5
Haisthorpe E R Yk......135 H6
Hakin Pembks...............48 F6
Halam Notts................102 B2
Halbeath Fife..............176 F1
Halberton Devon.........24 F8
Halcro Highld.............231 J4
Hale Cumb...................129 K4
Hale Halton.................112 C5
Hale Hants...................28 D7
Hale Surrey..................30 D2
Hale Traffd.................113 H4
Halebarns Traffd.......113 H4
Hales Norfk...................93 H4
Hales Staffs..................99 G5
Hales Place Kent.........34 F3
Hale Street Kent.........33 H4
Halesowen Dudley......85 G6
Halesworth Suffk........93 H7
Halewood Knows........112 C4
Halford Devon................7 J2
Halford Warwks............72 C5
Halfpenny Green
  Staffs..........................84 E5
Halfway House
  Shrops.........................83 G2
Halfway Houses Kent...46 F5
Halifax Calder............123 G5
Halket E Ayrs..............174 D7
Halkirk Highld...........231 G4
Halkyn Flints...............111 H7
Hall E Rens..................174 D7
Halland E Susx.............20 A3
Hallaton Leics.............87 L4
Hallatrow BaNES..........38 F8
Hallbankgate Cumb...149 G3
Hall Dunnerdale
  Cumb...........................137 H7
Hallen S Glos................38 D4
Hallgarth Dur.............151 H6
Hall Glen Falk............176 B3
Hall Green Birm...........85 K7
Hallin Highld..............208 D3
Halling Medway............46 B7
Hallington Lincs.........118 D4

Hallington Nthumb....158 C6
Halliwell Bolton.........121 K7
Halloughton Notts.....102 B3
Hallow Worcs................70 E3
Hall's Green Herts........59 L3
Hallyne Border...........166 B2
Halmore Gloucs...........55 G7
Halnaker W Susx...........18 B4
Halsall Lancs...............120 E7
Halse Nhants................73 H6
Halse Somset.................25 H5
Halsetown Cnwll.............2 E4
Halsham E R Yk...........127 G5
Halstead Essex.............61 K2
Halstead Kent...............45 J7
Halstead Leics..............87 L3
Halstock Dorset...........14 A2
Haltemprice
  Crematorium
  E R Yk.........................126 C4
Haltham Lincs.............118 C8
Halton Bucks................58 E6
Halton Halton..............112 D5
Halton Lancs...............129 K6
Halton Leeds...............123 L4
Halton Nthumb...........150 C2
Halton Wrexhm............97 L4
Halton East N York......131 K8
Halton Gill N York......131 G4
Halton Holegate Lincs..118 F7
Halton Lea Gate
  Nthumb......................149 H4
Halton Shields
  Nthumb......................150 C2
Halton West N York.....130 F8
Haltwhistle Nthumb...149 J3
Halvergate Norfk..........93 J3
Halwell Devon..................7 H5
Halwill Devon...............10 C5
Halwill Junction
  Devon..........................10 C5
Ham Devon.....................13 G3
Ham Gloucs...................55 G7
Ham Gt Lon...................44 D5
Ham Kent......................35 J4
Ham Somset..................25 L6
Ham Wilts.....................41 G7
Hambleden Bucks.........42 C3
Hambledon Hants.........29 M7
Hambledon Surrey.......30 F4
Hamble-le-Rice Hants..16 F2
Hambleton Lancs.........120 E3
Hambleton N York......124 E4
Hambridge Somset.......26 B6
Hambrook W Susx..........17 L2
Hameringham Lincs....118 D7
Hamerton Cambs..........89 G7
Ham Green Worcs........71 H2
Hamilton S Lans...........175 J7
Hamilton Services
  S Lans........................175 J6
Hamlet Dorset...............14 B2
Hammersmith Gt Lon...44 E4
Hammerwich Staffs......85 J3
Hammoon Dorset..........27 J8
Hamnavoe Shet...........235 c6
Hampden Park E Susx...20 C5
Hampnett Gloucs.........56 C5
Hampole Donc............124 D7
Hampreston Dorset......15 K3
Hampstead Gt Lon........44 E3
Hampstead Norreys
  W Berk.........................41 K5
Hampsthwaite
  N York.........................132 C7
Hampton C Pete............89 H5
Hampton Gt Lon...........43 J6
Hampton Kent...............47 K6
Hampton Shrops...........84 D6
Hampton Swindn...........40 D3
Hampton Worcs.............71 H5
Hampton Bishop
  Herefs..........................69 L6
Hampton Court
  Palace Gt Lon............44 D6
Hampton Heath
  Ches W...........................98 D3

Hampton in Arden
  Solhll............................86 B7
Hampton Lovett
  Worcs...........................70 F2
Hampton Lucy
  Warwks.........................72 B3
Hampton Magna
  Warwks.........................72 C2
Hampton Poyle Oxon....57 J5
Hampton Wick Gt Lon...44 D6
Hamptworth Wilts........28 E7
Hamsey E Susx...............19 L3
Hamstall Ridware
  Staffs.........................100 C8
Hamstead Marshall
  W Berk..........................41 H7
Hamsterley Dur...........140 E2
Hamsterley Dur...........150 E4
Hamstreet Kent.............34 D7
Ham Street Somset.......26 D4
Hamworthy Poole..........15 J4
Hanbury Staffs............100 D6
Hanbury Worcs..............71 G2
Hanchurch Staffs..........99 J4
Handa Island Highld...228 A6
Hand and Pen Devon....12 D4
Handbridge Ches W......112 B7
Handcross W Susx..........31 L5
Handforth Ches E.........113 J5
Handley Ches W.............98 C2
Handley Derbys............101 G1
Handsworth Birm..........85 J5
Handsworth Sheff.......115 H4
Hanging Heaton
  Kirk............................123 K6
Hanging Houghton
  Nhants..........................87 L8
Hanging Langford
  Wilts.............................28 B4
Hangleton Br & H...........19 H4
Hanham S Glos...............38 F6
Hankelow Ches E...........98 F4
Hankerton Wilts............39 L3
Hanley C Stke...............99 K3
Hanley Castle Worcs.....70 E6
Hanley Child Worcs.......70 E6
Hanley Swan Worcs.......70 E6
Hanley William Worcs...70 C2
Hanlith N York.............131 G7
Hanmer Wrexhm............98 C4
Hannaford Devon..........23 J5
Hannington Hants.........29 K1
Hannington Nhants.......74 B1
Hannington Swindn.......40 D2
Hannington Wick
  Swindn..........................40 D2
Hanslope M Keyn...........74 B5
Hanthorpe Lincs..........103 H7
Hanwell Gt Lon.............44 D4
Hanwell Oxon................72 E5
Hanwood Shrops...........83 J2
Hanworth Gt Lon...........43 J6
Hanworth Norfk...........106 E5
Happendon S Lans......165 G3
Happisburgh Norfk.....107 H6
Happisburgh
  Common Norfk.........107 H6
Hapsford Ches W.........112 C6
Hapton Lancs...............122 B4
Hapton Norfk.................92 E4
Harberton Devon.............7 H4
Harbertonford Devon.....7 H5
Harbledown Kent..........34 F3
Harborne Birm..............85 H6
Harborough Magna
  Warwks.........................86 F7
Harbottle Nthumb......158 B2
Harbourneford
  Devon.............................7 G4
Harbury Warwks...........72 D3
Harby Leics..................102 C6
Harby Notts.................116 E7
Harcombe Devon...........11 K8
Harcombe Devon...........12 F4
Harcombe Bottom
  Devon............................13 J4
Harden C Brad.............123 G3

Harden Wsall.................85 H4
Hardenhuish Wilts........39 K5
Hardgate Abers...........206 E5
Hardgate D & G...........146 E2
Hardgate W Duns.........174 F4
Hardham W Susx............18 E3
Hardingham Norfk........92 C3
Hardingstone Nhants....73 L3
Hardington Somset.......27 H2
Hardington
  Mandeville
  Somset..........................13 M1
Hardington Marsh
  Somset..........................13 M1
Hardington Moor
  Somset..........................26 D8
Hardisworthy Devon.....22 C7
Hardley Hants................16 E2
Hardley Street Norfk....93 H4
Hardraw N York...........131 G2
Hardstoft Derbys.........115 H8
Hardway Hants...............17 H3
Hardway Somset............27 G5
Hardwick Bucks.............58 D4
Hardwick Cambs............75 L3
Hardwick Nhants...........74 B1
Hardwick Norfk..............92 F5
Hardwick Oxon...............57 G6
Hardwick Oxon...............57 L3
Hardwicke Gloucs..........55 H5
Hardwicke Gloucs..........55 K3
Hardy's Green Essex.....61 M4
Hare Croft C Brad.......123 G4
Harefield Gt Lon............43 H3
Hare Green Essex..........62 D3
Hare Hatch Wokham......42 D5
Harehill Derbys...........100 D5
Harehills Leeds............123 L4
Harelaw Border............167 H5
Harelaw D & G..............156 D6
Harescombe Gloucs......55 J6
Haresfield Gloucs.........55 J6
Harestock Hants............29 J5
Hare Street Essex.........60 C5
Hare Street Herts.........60 C3
Harewood Leeds..........123 L2
Harewood End
  Herefs..........................54 D3
Harford Devon..................6 F5
Hargrave Ches W............98 C1
Hargrave Nhants............74 F1
Hargrave Suffk..............77 H3
Harkstead Suffk............78 E7
Harlaston Staffs............86 B2
Harlaxton Lincs...........102 E6
Harlech Gwynd...............95 K6
Harlescott Shrops.........83 K1
Harlesden Gt Lon..........44 E4
Harlesthorpe Derbys...115 J6
Harleston Devon..............7 J6
Harleston Norfk.............92 F6
Harleston Suffk.............78 B3
Harlestone Nhants........73 K2
Harle Syke Lancs.........122 C4
Harley Rothm...............115 G2
Harley Shrops................83 L3
Harlington C Beds.........59 G2
Harlington Donc..........115 J2
Harlington Gt Lon.........43 H5
Harlosh Highld............208 D5
Harlow Essex.................60 D6
Harlow Hill Nthumb....150 D2
Harlthorpe E R Yk.......125 H3
Harlton Cambs...............76 B4
Harlyn Cnwll....................4 D2
Harman's Cross
  Dorset............................15 J6
Harmby N York.............131 K2
Harmer Green Herts......59 L5
Harmer Hill Shrops.......98 C7
Harmston Lincs...........116 F8
Harnage Shrops..............83 L3
Harnhill Gloucs..............56 B7
Harold Hill Gt Lon..........45 K2
Haroldston West
  Pembks..........................48 E4
Haroldswick Shet.......235 e1

Harold Wood Gt Lon 45 K3
Harome N York 133 K3
Harpenden Herts 59 J5
Harpford Devon 12 E4
Harpham E R Yk 135 H7
Harpley Norfk 105 J7
Harpley Worcs 70 C3
Harpole Nhants 73 K3
Harpsdale Highld 231 G4
Harpswell Lincs 116 F4
Harpurhey Manch 113 K2
Harraby Cumb 148 D4
Harracott Devon 23 J6
Harrapool Highld 199 K2
Harrietfield P & K 185 K2
Harrietsham Kent 33 L3
Harringay Gt Lon 44 F3
Harrington Cumb 136 D3
Harrington Lincs 118 E6
Harrington Nhants 87 L7
Harringworth Nhants 88 D4
Harris W Isls 232 d4
Harrogate N York 132 D8
Harrogate
  Crematorium
  N York 132 E8
Harrold Bed 74 D3
Harrow Gt Lon 44 D3
Harrowbarrow Cnwll 6 B2
Harrow Green Suffk 77 J4
Harrow on the Hill
  Gt Lon 44 D3
Harrow Weald
  Gt Lon 44 D2
Harston Cambs 76 B4
Harston Leics 102 D6
Harswell E R Yk 125 J3
Hart Hartpl 151 L7
Hartburn Nthumb 158 D5
Hartest Suffk 77 J4
Hartfield E Susx 32 E6
Hartford Cambs 89 J8
Hartford Ches W 112 F6
Hartfordbridge Hants 42 C8
Hartford End Essex 61 G4
Harthill N York 140 F6
Hartgrove Dorset 27 J7
Harthill Ches W 98 D2
Harthill N Lans 176 B5
Harthill Rothm 115 J3
Hartington Derbys 100 C1
Hartland Devon 22 D6
Hartland Quay Devon 22 C6
Hartlebury Worcs 70 E1
Hartlepool Hartpl 151 L7
Hartlepool
  Crematorium
  Hartpl 142 B2
Hartley Cumb 139 H5
Hartley Kent 33 K6
Hartley Kent 45 L6
Hartley Wespall
  Hants 42 B8
Hartley Wintney
  Hants 30 C1
Hartlip Kent 46 D7
Harton N York 133 L6
Harton S Tyne 151 J2
Hartpury Gloucs 55 J3
Hartshead Kirk 123 J6
Hartshead Moor
  Services Calder 123 H5
Hartshill C Stke 99 K4
Hartshill Warwks 86 D5
Hartshorne Derbys 100 F7
Hartwell Nhants 73 L4
Hartwith N York 132 C6
Hartwood N Lans 175 L6
Hartwoodmyres
  Border 166 F4
Harvel Kent 46 A7
Harvington Worcs 71 J5
Harvington Worcs 84 F8
Harwell Notts 116 B3
Harwell Oxon 41 J3
Harwich Essex 62 F2
Harwood Dale N York ...143 K7

Harwood Park
  Crematorium
  Herts 59 L4
Harworth Notts 115 L3
Hasbury Dudley 85 G6
Hascombe Surrey 31 G4
Haselbech Nhants 87 K7
Haselbury Plucknett
  Somset 13 L1
Haseley Warwks 72 B2
Haselor Warwks 71 K3
Hasfield Gloucs 55 J3
Haskayne Lancs 120 E8
Hasketon Suffk 78 F4
Haslemere Surrey 30 E5
Haslingden Lancs 122 B6
Haslingfield Cambs 76 B4
Haslington Ches E 99 G2
Hassingham Norfk 93 H3
Hassocks W Susx 19 J3
Hassop Derbys 114 E6
Haster Highld 231 K5
Hastingleigh Kent 34 E5
Hastings E Susx 21 G4
Hastings Borough
  Crematorium
  E Susx 21 G3
Hastingwood Essex 60 D6
Hastoe Herts 58 F6
Haswell Dur 151 J6
Haswell Plough Dur 151 J6
Hatch Beauchamp
  Somset 25 L7
Hatch End Gt Lon 43 J3
Hatchmere Ches W 112 D6
Hatcliffe NE Lin 117 K2
Hatfield Donc 125 G8
Hatfield Herefs 69 L3
Hatfield Herts 59 L6
Hatfield Broad Oak
  Essex 60 E5
Hatfield Heath Essex 60 E5
Hatfield Peverel
  Essex 61 J5
Hatfield Woodhouse
  Donc 125 G8
Hatford Oxon 41 G2
Hatherden Hants 29 G2
Hatherleigh Devon 10 D4
Hathern Leics 101 J7
Hatherop Gloucs 56 D6
Hathersage Derbys 114 E5
Hathersage Booths
  Derbys 114 E5
Hatherton Ches E 99 G3
Hatherton Staffs 85 G2
Hatley St George
  Cambs 75 K4
Hatt Cnwll 6 B4
Hattersley Tamesd 113 M3
Hatton Abers 217 K6
Hatton Angus 196 D7
Hatton Derbys 100 E6
Hatton Gt Lon 43 J5
Hatton Lincs 117 K6
Hatton Shrops 83 J5
Hatton Warrtn 112 E5
Hatton Warwks 72 B2
Hatton of Fintray
  Abers 206 F3
Haugh E Ayrs 163 L4
Haugham Lincs 118 D5
Haughhead E Duns 175 G3
Haughley Suffk 78 B3
Haughley Green Suffk 78 B2
Haugh of Glass
  Moray 215 J6
Haugh of Urr D & G 146 E2
Haughs of Kinnaird
  Angus 197 G5
Haughton Shrops 98 B6
Haughton Staffs 99 K7
Haughton le Skerne
  Darltn 141 H4
Haughton Moss
  Ches E 98 E2
Haultwick Herts 60 B4

Haunton Staffs 86 B2
Hauxton Cambs 76 B4
Havant Hants 17 K2
Havenstreet IoW 17 G4
Havercroft Wakefd 124 B7
Haverfordwest
  Pembks 48 F4
Haverhill Suffk 76 F5
Haverigg Cumb 128 E4
Havering-atte-
  Bower Gt Lon 45 K2
Haversham M Keyn 74 B6
Haverthwaite Cumb 129 H3
Havyat N Som 38 C7
Hawarden Flints 111 J7
Hawbush Green
  Essex 61 J4
Hawen Cerdgn 65 K5
Hawes N York 131 G2
Hawe's Green Norfk 92 F4
Hawford Worcs 70 E3
Hawick Border 167 G6
Hawkchurch Devon 13 J3
Hawkedon Suffk 77 H4
Hawkeridge Wilts 27 K2
Hawkesbury S Glos 39 H3
Hawkesbury Upton
  S Glos 39 H3
Hawkhurst Kent 33 K6
Hawkinge Kent 35 G6
Hawkinge
  Crematorium
  Kent 35 G6
Hawkley Hants 30 C5
Hawkridge Somset 24 D5
Hawkshead Cumb 137 K7
Hawkshead Hill
  Cumb 137 K7
Hawksland S Lans 165 G2
Hawkstone Shrops 98 E6
Hawkswick N York 131 H5
Hawksworth Leeds 123 H3
Hawksworth Notts 102 C4
Hawkwell Essex 46 E2
Hawley Hants 42 E8
Hawling Gloucs 56 B4
Hawnby N York 133 H2
Haworth C Brad 122 F3
Hawstead Suffk 77 J3
Hawthorn Dur 151 K5
Hawthorn Hill Lincs 103 K2
Hawton Notts 102 C3
Haxby C York 133 J7
Haxey N Linc 116 C2
Haycombe
  Crematorium
  BaNES 39 G7
Haydock St Hel 112 E3
Haydon Bridge
  Nthumb 149 L3
Haydon Wick Swindn 40 C3
Hayes Gt Lon 43 J4
Hayes Gt Lon 45 H6
Hayes End Gt Lon 43 H4
Hayfield Ag & B 182 E5
Hayfield Derbys 114 B4
Hayhillock Angus 196 E7
Hayle Cnwll 2 F4
Hayley Green Dudley 85 G6
Hayling Island Hants 17 K3
Hayne Devon 11 H7
Haynes (Church End)
  C Beds 74 F6
Haynes (Northwood
  End) C Beds 75 G6
Haynes (Silver End)
  C Beds 75 G6
Haynes (West End)
  C Beds 74 F6
Hay-on-Wye Powys 68 G6
Hayscastle Pembks 48 F3
Hayscastle Cross
  Pembks 48 F3
Hay Street Herts 60 C3
Hayton Cumb 147 K6
Hayton Cumb 148 E4
Hayton E R Yk 125 J2

Hayton Notts 116 B5
Haytor Vale Devon 7 H1
Haytown Devon 9 K3
Haywards Heath
  W Susx 19 J2
Haywood Donc 124 E7
Hazelbank S Lans 165 G1
Hazelbury Bryan
  Dorset 14 E2
Hazeleigh Essex 61 K7
Hazel Grove Stockp 113 L4
Hazelton Walls Fife 186 E3
Hazelwood Derbys 101 G4
Hazlemere Bucks 42 E2
Hazlerigg N u Ty 159 G7
Hazleton Gloucs 56 B4
Heacham Norfk 105 G5
Headbourne Worthy
  Hants 29 J5
Headcorn Kent 33 L4
Headingley Leeds 123 K4
Headington Oxon 57 K6
Headlam Dur 140 F4
Headlesscross
  N Lans 176 B6
Headless Cross Worcs 71 J2
Headley Hants 30 D4
Headley Hants 41 K7
Headley Surrey 31 K1
Headley Down Hants 30 D4
Headon Notts 116 C6
Heads Nook Cumb 148 E4
Heage Derbys 101 G3
Healaugh N York 124 D2
Healaugh N York 140 C7
Heald Green Stockp 113 J4
Heale Somset 25 K7
Heale Somset 26 B6
Healey N York 132 B4
Healeyfield Dur 150 D5
Healing NE Lin 126 F7
Heamoor Cnwll 2 E5
Heanor Derbys 101 H3
Heanton
  Punchardon
  Devon 23 H4
Heapham Lincs 116 E4
Heart of England
  Crematorium
  Warwks 86 E5
Heart of Scotland
  Services N Lans 176 B5
Heasley Mill Devon 24 B5
Heast Highld 199 K2
Heath Derbys 115 J7
Heath Wakefd 123 L6
Heath and Reach
  C Beds 58 F3
Heathcote Derbys 100 D1
Heather Leics 86 E2
Heathfield E Susx 20 C2
Heathfield Somset 25 J6
Heath Green Worcs 71 J1
Heath Hall D & G 155 H6
Heath Hayes &
  Wimblebury Staffs 85 H2
Heath Hill Shrops 84 D2
Heathrow Airport
  Gt Lon 43 H5
Heathton Shrops 84 E5
Heath Town Wolves 85 G4
Heatley Warrtn 113 G4
Heaton C Brad 123 H4
Heaton N u Ty 151 G2
Heaton Staffs 113 L8
Heaton's Bridge
  Lancs 120 E7
Heaverham Kent 33 G2
Heavitree Devon 12 B4
Hebburn S Tyne 151 H3
Hebden N York 131 J6
Hebden Bridge Calder ..122 E5
Hebing End Herts 60 A4
Hebron Carmth 49 K3
Hebron Nthumb 158 F4
Heckfield Hants 42 B7
Heckfield Green Suffk ...92 E7

Heckfordbridge
Essex 61 M4
Heckington Lincs 103 J4
Heckmondwike Kirk 123 J5
Heddington Wilts 39 M6
Heddon-on-the-Wall
Nthumb 150 E2
Hedenham Norfk 93 G5
Hedge End Hants 29 J8
Hedgerley Bucks 42 F3
Hedging Somset 25 L5
Hedley on the Hill
Nthumb 150 D3
Hednesford Staffs 85 H2
Hedon E R Yk 126 F5
Hedsor Bucks 42 E3
Heglibister Shet 235 C5
Heighington Darltn 141 G3
Heighington Lincs 117 G7
Heightington Worcs 70 D1
Heiton Border 167 L4
Hele Devon 12 C2
Hele Devon 23 H3
Helensburgh Ag & B ...174 B2
Helenton S Ayrs 163 K3
Helford Cnwll 3 K6
Helford Passage
Cnwll 3 K6
Helhoughton Norfk 105 K7
Helions Bumpstead
Essex 76 F6
Helland Cnwll 5 G2
Hellescott Cnwll 9 H6
Hellesdon Norfk 92 E2
Hellidon Nhants 73 G3
Hellifield N York 131 G7
Hellingly E Susx 20 C4
Helmdon Nhants 73 H5
Helme Kirk 123 G7
Helmingham Suffk 78 E3
Helmsdale Highld 227 H5
Helmshore Lancs 122 B6
Helmsley N York 133 J3
Helperby N York 133 G5
Helperthorpe N York ..134 E5
Helpringham Lincs 103 J4
Helpston C Pete 89 G3
Helsby Ches W 112 C6
Helston Cnwll 3 H5
Helstone Cnwll 8 E8
Helton Cumb 138 D3
Hemel Hempstead
Herts 59 H6
Hemerdon Devon 6 E4
Hemingbrough
N York 125 G4
Hemingby Lincs 118 C6
Hemingford Abbots
Cambs 75 K1
Hemingford Grey
Cambs 75 K1
Hemingstone Suffk 78 D4
Hemington Leics 101 J4
Hemington Nhants 88 F6
Hemington Somset 27 G2
Hemley Suffk 79 G6
Hemlington Middsb 142 B4
Hempnall Norfk 92 F5
Hempnall Green
Norfk 92 F5
Hempriggs Moray 214 D2
Hempstead Essex 76 F6
Hempstead Norfk 106 D5
Hempstead Norfk 107 J6
Hempton Norfk 105 L6
Hempton Oxon 57 H2
Hemsby Norfk 107 K8
Hemswell Lincs 116 F4
Hemswell Cliff Lincs ..116 F4
Hemsworth Wakefd 124 C7
Hemyock Devon 25 H8
Hendon Gt Lon 44 E3
Hendon Sundld 151 K4
Hendon
Crematorium
Gt Lon 44 E2
Hendy Carmth 51 H5

Henfield W Susx 19 G3
Hengoed Caerph 37 J2
Hengoed Powys 68 E4
Hengrave Suffk 77 J2
Henham Essex 60 E3
Heniarth Powys 82 C2
Henlade Somset 25 L6
Henley Dorset 14 D2
Henley Somset 26 B5
Henley Suffk 78 E4
Henley W Susx 30 E6
Henley-in-Arden
Warwks 71 L2
Henley-on-Thames
Oxon 42 C4
Henley's Down E Susx ..20 E3
Henllan Cerdgn 65 K6
Henllan Denbgs 110 E7
Henllys Torfn 37 K3
Henlow C Beds 75 H6
Hennock Devon 11 J8
Henny Street Essex 77 K6
Henryd Conwy 109 L6
**Henry's Moat (Castell
Hendre)** Pembks 49 H3
Hensall N York 124 F5
Henshaw Nthumb 149 K3
Hensingham Cumb 136 D4
Henstead Suffk 93 K6
Hensting Hants 29 J6
Henstridge Somset 27 G7
Henstridge Ash
Somset 27 G7
Henton Oxon 58 C7
Henton Somset 26 C3
Henwick Worcs 70 E4
Henwood Cnwll 5 L2
Heol-y-Cyw Brdgnd 36 E4
Hepple Nthumb 158 C2
Hepscott Nthumb 158 F5
Heptonstall Calder 122 E5
Hepworth Kirk 114 D1
Hepworth Suffk 92 B8
Herbrandston
Pembks 48 E6
Hereford Herefs 69 K6
Hereford
Crematorium
Herefs 69 J6
Hereson Kent 35 K2
Heribusta Highld 218 B7
Heriot Border 177 L7
Hermiston C Edin 177 G4
Hermitage Border 156 E3
Hermitage Dorset 14 C2
Hermitage W Berk 41 J5
Hermon Carmth 65 K7
Hermon Pembks 49 L2
Herne Kent 47 K6
Herne Bay Kent 47 K6
Herne Hill Gt Lon 44 F5
Herne Pound Kent 33 H3
Hernhill Kent 34 E3
Herodsfoot Cnwll 5 K4
Heronsford S Ayrs 152 D5
Herriard Hants 30 A3
Herringfleet Suffk 93 K4
Herringswell Suffk 77 G1
Herringthorpe Rothm...115 J3
Herrington Sundld 151 J4
Hersden Kent 35 G3
Hersham Surrey 43 J7
Herstmonceux E Susx ..20 D3
Herston Ork 234 c7
Hertford Herts 60 B5
Hertford Heath Herts ...60 B5
Hertingfordbury
Herts 60 A5
Hesketh Bank Lancs ...120 F5
Hesketh Lane Lancs ...121 J3
Hesket Newmarket
Cumb 148 C7
Hesleden Dur 151 K7
Heslington C York 124 F1
Hessay C York 133 H8
Hessenford Cnwll 5 L4
Hessett Suffk 77 L3

Hessle E R Yk 126 C5
Hessle Wakefd 124 C6
Hest Bank Lancs 129 K6
Heston Gt Lon 43 J5
Heston Services
Gt Lon 43 J5
Hestwall Ork 234 b5
Heswall Wirral 111 J5
Hethe Oxon 57 L3
Hethersett Norfk 92 D3
Hethersgill Cumb 148 E2
Hett Dur 151 G7
Hetton N York 131 H7
Hetton-le-Hole
Sundld 151 J5
Heugh Nthumb 158 D7
Heughhead Abers 205 J3
Heugh Head Border ...179 H6
Heveningham Suffk 93 G8
Hever Kent 32 E4
Heversham Cumb 129 K3
Hevingham Norfk 106 E7
Hewas Water Cnwll 4 F6
Hewelsfield Gloucs 54 E7
Hewish Somset 13 K2
Hewood Dorset 13 J2
Hexham Nthumb 150 B3
Hextable Kent 45 K6
Hexthorpe Donc 115 K2
Hexton Herts 59 J2
Hexworthy Cnwll 9 K8
Hexworthy Devon 6 F2
Heybridge Essex 61 G7
Heybridge Essex 61 K6
Heybrook Bay Devon 6 D6
Heydon Cambs 76 B6
Heydon Norfk 106 D6
Heydour Lincs 103 G5
Heylipoll Ag & B 188 C7
Heylor Shet 235 c3
Heysham Lancs 129 J7
Heyshott W Susx 18 B3
Heytesbury Wilts 27 L3
Heythrop Oxon 57 G3
Heywood Rochdl 122 C7
Heywood Wilts 27 K2
Hibaldstow N Linc 116 F2
Hickleton Donc 115 J1
Hickling Norfk 107 J7
Hickling Notts 102 B6
Hickling Green Norfk ..107 J7
Hickstead W Susx 31 L7
Hidcote Bartrim
Gloucs 71 L6
Hidcote Boyce Gloucs ..71 L6
High Ackworth
Wakefd 124 C6
Higham Barns 114 F1
Higham Derbys 101 H2
Higham Kent 33 G4
Higham Kent 46 B5
Higham Lancs 122 B3
Higham Suffk 77 H2
Higham Suffk 78 B7
Higham Ferrers
Nhants 74 D2
Higham Gobion
C Beds 59 J2
Higham Hill Gt Lon 45 G3
Higham on the Hill
Leics 86 E4
Highampton Devon 10 C4
Highams Park Gt Lon ...45 H2
High Ardwell D & G ...144 C6
High Auldgirth D & G ..154 F5
High Bankhill Cumb ...148 F6
High Beach Essex 60 C7
High Bentham N York ..130 C5
High Bickington
Devon 23 J7
High Biggins Cumb 130 B4
High Blantyre S Lans ..175 J6
High Bonnybridge
Falk 175 L3
High Bray Devon 23 L5
Highbridge Somset 25 L3
Highbrook W Susx 32 C7

High Brooms Kent 33 G5
Highburton Kirk 123 J7
Highbury Gt Lon 44 F3
Highbury Somset 27 G6
High Casterton
Cumb 130 C4
High Catton E R Yk 133 L8
Highclere Hants 41 H8
Highcliffe Dorset 16 B4
High Coniscliffe
Darltn 141 G4
High Crosby Cumb 148 E3
High Cross E Ayrs 163 K1
High Cross Hants 30 B6
High Cross Herts 60 B4
High Cross Warwks 71 L2
High Drummore
D & G 144 D7
High Easter Essex 60 F5
High Ellington N York ..132 B3
Higher Ansty Dorset 14 E2
Higher Bartle Lancs ...121 G4
Higher
Bockhampton
Dorset 14 D4
Higher Brixham
Torbay 7 L5
Higher Chillington
Somset 13 K1
Higher Folds Wigan ...113 G2
Higher Gabwell
Devon 7 L3
Higher Heysham
Lancs 129 J7
Higher Irlam Salfd 113 G3
Higher Kinnerton
Flints 97 L1
Higher Muddiford
Devon 23 J4
Higher Penwortham
Lancs 121 G5
Higher Prestacott
Devon 9 K5
Higher Town Cnwll 4 C6
Higher Town Cnwll 4 F4
Higher Town IoS 2 b1
Higher Walton Lancs ..121 J1
Higher Walton Warrtn..112 E4
Higher Wambrook
Somset 13 H2
Higher Waterston
Dorset 14 D4
Higher Wheelton
Lancs 121 J6
Higher Whitley
Ches W 112 F5
Higher Wincham
Ches W 113 G6
Higher Wraxall
Dorset 14 B3
Higher Wych Ches W 98 C4
High Etherley Dur 140 F2
Highfield Gatesd 150 E3
Highfield N Ayrs 174 C7
Highgate Gt Lon 44 F3
High Grantley N York ..132 C5
High Green Norfk 92 D3
High Green Norfk 92 E5
High Green Sheff 115 G3
High Halden Kent 34 B7
High Halstow
Medway 46 C5
High Ham Somset 26 B5
High Harrogate
N York 132 D7
High Hatton Shrops 98 E7
High Hauxley
Nthumb 159 H6
High Hawsker N York ..143 J5
High Hesket Cumb 148 E6
High Hoyland Barns ...123 K8
High Hurstwood
E Susx 32 E7
High Hutton N York 134 B5
High Ireby Cumb 147 M7

High Kilburn N York 133 H4
High Lands Dur..............140 E3
Highland Wildlife
 Park Highld 203 J4
Highlane Derbys 115 H5
High Lane Stockp 113 L4
High Lanes Cnwll 3 G4
Highleadon Gloucs 55 H4
High Legh Ches E 113 G5
Highleigh W Susx............18 A6
High Leven S on T 141 K5
Highley Shrops 84 D6
High Littleton BaNES 38 F8
High Lorton Cumb 137 G3
High Marnham Notts 116 D7
High Melton Donc..........115 K2
High Mickley Nthumb 150 D3
Highmoor Oxon...............42 B4
Highmoor Cross Oxon......42 B4
Highnam Gloucs 55 H4
High Newport Sundld....151 J4
High Newton Cumb........129 J3
High Nibthwaite
 Cumb 129 G2
High Offley Staffs 99 H7
High Ongar Essex............60 E7
High Onn Staffs...............84 E1
High Park Corner
 Essex 62 C4
High Pennyvenie
 E Ayrs 163 L7
High Roding Essex...........60 F4
High Salvington
 W Susx 18 F4
High Spen Gatesd..........150 E3
Highsted Kent................34 B3
Highstreet Kent..............34 E3
Highstreet Green
 Surrey 31 G4
Hightae D & G 155 J6
Hightown Sefton 111 J2
Hightown Green
 Suffk 77 L4
High Toynton Lincs 118 C7
High Valleyfield Fife 176 D2
Highweek Devon 7 J2
Highwood Hill Gt Lon 44 E2
Highworth Swindn 40 D4
High Wray Cumb...........137 K7
High Wych Herts 60 D5
High Wycombe Bucks 42 E2
Hilborough Norfk............91 J4
Hilcott Wilts 40 C8
Hildenborough Kent 32 F4
Hilden Park Kent............33 G4
Hildersham Cambs..........76 D5
Hilderstone Staffs...........99 L5
Hilderthorpe E R Yk 135 J6
Hilgay Norfk...................90 E4
Hill S Glos 38 F2
Hill Warwks 72 F2
Hillam N York 124 D5
Hill Brow Hants 30 C6
Hillbutts Dorset 15 J3
Hill Chorlton Staffs..........99 H5
Hillclifflane Derbys 100 F3
Hill Common Somset......25 H6
Hilldyke Lincs 104 B3
Hillend Fife 176 F2
Hill End Fife 185 L7
Hill End Gloucs 70 F6
Hillend Mdloth 177 H5
Hillend N Lans 175 L5
Hillesden Bucks 58 B3
Hillesley Gloucs 39 H3
Hillfarrance Somset..........25 J6
Hill Green Kent...............46 D7
Hillhead Abers 216 B7
Hill Head Hants 17 G2
Hillhead S Lans 165 J2
Hillhead of Cocklaw
 Abers 217 K5
Hilliclay Highld 231 H3
Hillingdon Gt Lon 43 H4
Hillington C Glas 174 F5
Hillington Norfk 105 H7

Hillmorton Warwks 87 G8
Hill of Beath Fife 176 F1
Hill of Fearn Highld........223 H5
Hillowton D & G 146 D3
Hill Ridware Staffs........100 B8
Hillside Abers 207 H5
Hillside Angus 197 H4
Hill Side Kirk 123 H6
Hills Town Derbys 115 J7
Hillstreet Hants..............29 G7
Hillswick Shet 235 C3
Hill Top Wakefd 123 L7
Hillwell Shet 235 C8
Hilmarton Wilts 40 A5
Hilperton Wilts................39 K8
Hilsea C Port 17 J2
Hilston E R Yk 127 G4
Hilton Border 179 H7
Hilton Cambs 75 K2
Hilton Cumb..................139 G3
Hilton Derbys 100 E6
Hilton Dorset..................14 E2
Hilton Dur 140 F3
Hilton Highld 223 J6
Hilton S on T 141 K5
Hilton Shrops 84 D4
Hilton Park Services
 Staffs 85 G3
Himbleton Worcs 71 G3
Himley Staffs 84 F5
Hincaster Cumb 129 L3
Hinchley Wood
 Surrey 44 D6
Hinckley Leics 86 E5
Hinderclay Suffk..............92 B7
Hinderwell N York 143 G4
Hindhead Surrey 30 E4
Hindley Wigan 112 F1
Hindlip Worcs 70 F3
Hindolveston Norfk 106 C6
Hindon Wilts 27 K5
Hindringham Norfk 106 B5
Hingham Norfk...............92 B3
Hinstock Shrops 99 G7
Hintlesham Suffk 78 C5
Hinton Herefs 69 G6
Hinton S Glos 39 G5
Hinton Shrops 83 H2
Hinton Ampner Hants 29 L6
Hinton Blewett
 BaNES 26 E1
Hinton Charterhouse
 BaNES 39 H8
Hinton-in-the-
 Hedges Nhants 73 H6
Hinton Martell Dorset 15 J2
Hinton on the Green
 Worcs 71 H6
Hinton Parva Swindn......40 E4
Hinton St George
 Somset 26 B8
Hinton St Mary
 Dorset 27 H7
Hinton Waldrist Oxon.....57 G7
Hints Staffs 85 L3
Hinwick Bed...................74 D3
Hinxhill Kent 34 D6
Hinxton Cambs...............76 C5
Hinxworth Herts 75 J6
Hipperholme Calder 123 H5
Hipswell N York 140 F7
Hirn Abers 206 D5
Hirnant Powys 97 G7
Hirst Nthumb 159 G5
Hirst Courtney N York . 124 F5
Hirwaun Rhondd.............52 E6
Hiscott Devon.................23 J6
Histon Cambs..................76 B2
Hitcham Suffk 78 B4
Hitcham Causeway
 Suffk 78 B4
Hitcham Street Suffk......78 B4
Hitchin Herts..................59 K3
Hither Green Gt Lon 45 H5
Hittisleigh Devon 11 H5
Hive E R Yk 125 J4
Hixon Staffs..................100 A7

Hoaden Kent..................35 H3
Hoar Cross Staffs..........100 C7
Hoarwithy Herefs 54 D3
Hoath Kent.....................47 K7
Hobarris Shrops..............82 F7
Hobkirk Border 167 J7
Hobson Dur...................150 F4
Hoby Leics 102 A8
Hockering Norfk 92 C2
Hockerton Notts 102 B2
Hockley Essex.................46 D2
Hockley Heath Solhll 85 L8
Hockwold cum
 Wilton Norfk 91 G6
Hockworthy Devon 25 G7
Hoddesdon Herts............60 B6
Hoddlesden Bl w D........121 L6
Hoddom Cross D & G 155 L7
Hoddom Mains D & G ...155 K7
Hodgeston Pembks 49 H7
Hodnet Shrops.................98 E6
Hodsock Notts...............115 L4
Hodsoll Street Kent 45 M7
Hodson Swindn 40 D4
Hodthorpe Derbys 115 K6
Hoe Norfk 92 B1
Hogben's Hill Kent..........34 D4
Hoggeston Bucks.............58 D3
Hoggrill's End Warwks.....86 B5
Hoghton Lancs 121 J5
Hognaston Derbys 100 E3
Hogsthorpe Lincs 119 H6
Holbeach Lincs 104 B7
Holbeach Bank Lincs 104 B6
Holbeach Clough
 Lincs 104 B6
Holbeach Drove Lincs 89 K2
Holbeach Hurn Lincs 104 C6
Holbeach St Johns
 Lincs 104 B8
Holbeach St Mark's
 Lincs 104 B6
Holbeach St
 Matthew Lincs 104 C6
Holbeck Notts...............115 K6
Holberrow Green
 Worcs 71 H3
Holbeton Devon 6 F5
Holborn Gt Lon 44 F4
Holbrook Derbys 101 G4
Holbrook Suffk................78 E6
Holbrooks Covtry 86 D6
Holbury Hants.................16 E2
Holcombe Devon 12 B7
Holcombe Somset...........26 F2
Holcombe Rogus
 Devon 25 G7
Holcot Nhants 73 L1
Holden Lancs 122 B1
Holdenby Nhants 73 K2
Holder's Green Essex 61 G3
Holdgate Shrops 83 L5
Holdingham Lincs 103 H3
Holditch Dorset 13 J2
Holemoor Devon 10 B4
Holford Somset 25 J3
Holgate C York 124 E1
Holker Cumb.................129 H4
Holkham Norfk..............105 L4
Holkham Hall Norfk 105 L4
Hollacombe Devon 9 K4
Holland Fen Lincs 103 L3
Holland-on-Sea Essex.....62 E5
Hollandstoun Ork 234 e3
Hollee D & G 148 A2
Hollesley Suffk................79 H5
Hollicombe Torbay 7 K4
Hollingbourne Kent.........33 L3
Hollingbury Br & H........19 J4
Hollingdon Bucks............58 E3
Hollington Derbys 100 E5
Hollington Staffs............100 B5
Hollingworth Tamesd....114 A3
Hollinsclough Staffs.......114 B7
Hollins End Sheff 115 G5
Hollins Green Warrtn 113 G4

Hollinswood Wrekin 84 C2
Hollinwood
 Crematorium
 Oldham....................113 K2
Hollocombe Devon 10 F3
Holloway Derbys 100 F2
Holloway Gt Lon 44 F3
Hollowell Nhants 73 K1
Hollowmoor Heath
 Ches W 112 C7
Hollows D & G 156 C6
Hollybush Caerph...........53 J7
Hollybush E Ayrs...........163 K6
Hollybush Herefs............70 D6
Hollym E R Yk 127 H5
Holmbridge Kirk 114 C1
Holmbury St Mary
 Surrey 31 J3
Holmbush Cnwll 5 G5
Holmcroft Staffs..............99 K7
Holme Cambs..................89 H6
Holme Cumb.................129 L4
Holme Kirk 114 C1
Holme N York 132 E3
Holme Notts 102 D2
Holme Chapel Lancs 122 C5
Holme Hale Norfk 91 K3
Holme Lacy Herefs 69 L7
Holme Marsh Herefs 69 G4
Holme next the Sea
 Norfk 105 H4
Holme on the Wolds
 E R Yk 126 B2
Holme Pierrepont
 Notts 101 L5
Holmer Herefs 69 K6
Holmer Green Bucks.......42 E2
Holme St Cuthbert
 Cumb 147 J5
Holmes Chapel
 Ches E 113 H7
Holmesfield Derbys 114 F6
Holmeswood Lancs 120 F6
Holmethorpe Surrey.......32 B3
Holme upon
 Spalding Moor
 E R Yk 125 J3
Holmewood Derbys 115 H7
Holmfirth Kirk 123 H8
Holmhead E Ayrs...........164 B5
Holmpton E R Yk 127 J5
Holmrook Cumb 136 E7
Holmsford Bridge
 Crematorium
 N Ayrs 163 J2
Holmside Dur................150 F5
Holne Devon 7 G3
Holnicote Somset............24 E3
Holsworthy Devon............9 J4
Holsworthy Beacon
 Devon 9 K3
Holt Dorset 15 J2
Holt Norfk....................106 C5
Holt Wilts 39 K7
Holt Worcs 70 E3
Holt Wrexhm 98 B2
Holtby C York 133 K8
Holt End Worcs 71 J1
Holt Heath Worcs 70 E2
Holton Oxon....................57 L6
Holton Somset 27 G6
Holton Suffk 93 J7
Holton cum
 Beckering Lincs 117 J5
Holton le Clay Lincs 118 C2
Holton le Moor Lincs 117 H3
Holton St Mary Suffk 78 C6
Holwell Dorset 14 D1
Holwell Herts 59 K2
Holwell Leics 102 B7
Holwell Oxon 56 E6
Holwick Dur 139 K2
Holybourne Hants 30 B4
Holyhead IoA 108 C5
Holy Island IoA 108 C5
Holy Island Nthumb......169 H2
Holymoorside Derbys...115 G7

Holyport W & M..............42 E5
Holystone Nthumb......158 B2
Holytown N Lans.........175 K6
Holytown
  Crematorium
  N Lans.....................175 K6
Holywell C Beds............59 G5
Holywell Cambs............75 L1
Holywell Cnwll................4 B4
Holywell Dorset............14 B2
Holywell Flints.............111 G6
Holywell Green
  Calder....................123 G6
Holywell Lake Somset....25 H7
Holywell Row Suffk......91 G7
Holywood D & G..........155 G6
Holywood Village
  D & G....................155 G6
Homer Shrops...............84 B3
Homer Green Sefton....111 K2
Homersfield Suffk.........93 G6
Homington Wilts............28 C6
Honeybourne Worcs......71 K5
Honeychurch Devon......10 F4
Honeystreet Wilts..........40 C7
Honey Tye Suffk...........77 L7
Honiley Warwks............86 B8
Honing Norfk...............107 G6
Honingham Norfk..........92 D2
Honington Lincs..........102 F4
Honington Suffk............91 K8
Honington Warwks.......72 C6
Honiton Devon..............12 F3
Honley Kirk.................123 H7
Honor Oak
  Crematorium
  Gt Lon.....................45 G5
Hooe C Plym...................6 D5
Hooe E Susx.................20 E4
Hoo Green Ches E.......113 G5
Hoohill Bpool..............120 D3
Hook E R Yk................125 H5
Hook Gt Lon.................44 D7
Hook Hants...................30 B1
Hook Pembks................49 G5
Hook Wilts.....................40 B4
Hooke Dorset................14 A3
Hook Green Kent...........33 H6
Hook Green Kent...........45 L6
Hook Norton Oxon........57 G2
Hookway Devon.............11 K5
Hooley Surrey................32 B3
Hoo St Werburgh
  Medway....................46 C5
Hooton Levitt Rothm....115 K3
Hooton Pagnell Donc...124 D8
Hooton Roberts
  Rothm....................115 J3
Hope Derbys................114 D5
Hope Devon....................7 G7
Hope Flints...................97 L2
Hope Shrops..................83 L8
Hope Staffs.................100 C2
Hope Bowdler Shrops....83 J5
Hopehouse Border........166 D6
Hopeman Moray...........214 E1
Hope Mansell Herefs....54 F4
Hopesay Shrops............83 H6
Hope under Dinmore
  Herefs......................69 K4
Hopgrove C York.........133 K8
Hopperton N York........132 F7
Hopstone Shrops...........84 D5
Hopton Derbys.............100 E2
Hopton Staffs................99 L7
Hopton Suffk.................92 B7
Hopton Cangeford
  Shrops.....................83 K7
Hopton Castle Shrops....83 G7
Hoptonheath Shrops......83 H7
Hopton on Sea Norfk....93 L4
Hopton Wafers
  Shrops.....................84 B7
Hopwas Staffs...............85 L3
Hopwood Worcs............85 J7
Hopwood Park
  Services Worcs.....85 J8

Horam E Susx...............20 C3
Horbling Lincs.............103 J5
Horbury Wakefd.........123 K6
Horden Dur.................151 K6
Hordle Hants.................16 C4
Hordley Shrops.............98 B6
Horfield Bristl...............38 E5
Horham Suffk................92 E8
Horkesley Heath
  Essex.......................62 B3
Horkstow N Linc.........126 B6
Horley Oxon..................72 E5
Horley Surrey................32 B5
Hornblotton Green
  Somset.....................26 E5
Hornby Lancs..............130 B5
Hornby N York.............132 C2
Hornby N York.............141 J6
Horncastle Lincs.........118 C7
Hornchurch Gt Lon.......45 K3
Horncliffe Nthumb.......179 J7
Horndean Border.........179 J8
Horndean Hants............30 B8
Horndon Devon.............10 D8
Horndon on the Hill
  Thurr........................46 A4
Horne Surrey.................32 C4
Horner Somset..............24 D3
Horning Norfk.............107 H8
Horninghold Leics.........88 B4
Horninglow Staffs.......100 E7
Horningsea Cambs........76 C3
Horningsham Wilts........27 J3
Horningtoft Norfk........105 M7
Horns Cross Devon........22 F6
Hornsea E R Yk...........126 F2
Hornsey Gt Lon.............44 F3
Hornton Oxon................72 E5
Horra Shet...................235 d2
Horrabridge Devon..........6 D2
Horringer Suffk.............77 J3
Horrocksford
  Lancs......................121 L2
Horsebridge Devon.........6 B2
Horsebridge E Susx......20 C4
Horsebridge Hants........29 G5
Horsehay Wrekin...........84 C3
Horseheath Cambs........76 E5
Horsehouse N York......131 K4
Horsell Surrey...............43 G8
Horseman's Green
  Wrexhm....................98 C4
Horsey Norfk...............107 K7
Horsey Somset..............25 L4
Horsford Norfk..............92 E1
Horsforth Leeds...........123 J3
Horsham W Susx...........31 K5
Horsham Worcs..............70 D3
Horsham St Faith
  Norfk........................92 E1
Horsington Lincs.........117 K7
Horsington Somset.......27 G6
Horsley Derbys...........101 G4
Horsley Gloucs..............39 J2
Horsley Nthumb..........150 D2
Horsley Nthumb..........157 L3
Horsleycross Street
  Essex.......................62 D3
Horsleyhill Border........167 H5
Horsley Woodhouse
  Derbys....................101 H4
Horsmonden Kent.........33 J5
Horspath Oxon..............57 L6
Horstead Norfk............106 F8
Horsted Keynes
  W Susx.....................32 C7
Horton Bucks................58 F4
Horton Dorset...............15 J2
Horton Lancs...............122 C1
Horton Nhants..............74 B4
Horton S Glos................39 H4
Horton Somset..............25 L7
Horton Staffs.................99 L2
Horton Swans................50 F7
Horton W & M...............43 G5
Horton Wilts..................40 B7
Horton Wrekin...............84 C1

Horton-cum-Studley
  Oxon........................57 L5
Horton Green Ches W...98 C3
Horton in
  Ribblesdale
  N York....................130 F5
Horton Kirby Kent.........45 K6
Horwich Bolton...........121 J7
Horwood Devon.............23 H6
Hoscote Border...........166 F6
Hose Leics..................102 B6
Hosh P & K..................185 H3
Hoswick Shet...............235 C7
Hotham E R Yk............125 L4
Hothfield Kent...............34 C5
Hoton Leics.................101 L7
Hough Ches E...............99 G3
Hougham Lincs............102 E4
Hough Green Halton....112 C4
Hough-on-the-Hill
  Lincs......................102 F3
Houghton Cambs...........75 K1
Houghton Hants............29 G5
Houghton Pembks.........49 G6
Houghton W Susx.........18 D4
Houghton Conquest
  C Beds.....................74 F6
Houghton Green
  E Susx......................21 H2
Houghton-le-Spring
  Sundld....................151 H5
Houghton on the Hill
  Leics........................87 J3
Houghton Regis
  C Beds.....................59 G4
Houghton St Giles
  Norfk......................105 L5
Hound Green Hants.......42 B8
Houndslow Border.......178 D8
Houndwood Border......179 H5
Hounslow Gt Lon..........43 J5
Househill Highld..........213 L4
Houses Hill Kirk..........123 J6
Housieside Abers........207 G1
Houston Rens..............174 D5
Houstry Highld............227 K2
Houton Ork..................234 b6
Hove Br & H..................19 J5
Hoveringham Notts.....102 B3
Hoveton Norfk.............107 G8
Hovingham N York......133 K4
How Caple Herefs........54 E3
Howden E R Yk...........125 H5
Howden-le-Wear
  Dur........................150 E7
Howe Highld...............231 K3
Howe N York...............132 E4
Howe Norfk...................92 F4
Howe Bridge
  Crematorium
  Wigan....................112 F2
Howe Green Essex........61 J7
Howegreen Essex..........61 K7
Howell Lincs................103 J4
Howe of Teuchar
  Abers.....................216 E5
Howes D & G..............147 L2
Howe Street Essex........61 H5
Howe Street Essex........77 G7
Howey Powys................68 B3
Howgate Cumb............136 D3
Howgate Mdloth..........177 H6
Howick Nthumb..........169 K5
Howlett End Essex........76 E7
Howley Somset.............13 H1
How Mill Cumb...........148 E4
Howmore W Isls..........233 b7
Hownam Border..........168 B5
Howsham N Linc.........117 H2
Howsham N York.........133 L6
Howtel Nthumb............168 D3
Howwood Rens............174 D6
Hoxne Suffk..................92 E7
Hoy Ork......................234 b7
Hoylake Wirral............111 H4
Hoyland Nether
  Barns......................115 G2

Hoyland Swaine
  Barns......................114 E1
Hubberston Pembks.....48 E6
Huby N York................123 K2
Huby N York................133 J6
Hucclecote Gloucs.......55 K4
Hucking Kent................33 L2
Hucknall Notts............101 K3
Huddersfield Kirk.......123 H7
Huddersfield
  Crematorium Kirk...123 H6
Huddington Worcs........71 G3
Hudswell N York.........140 E7
Huggate E R Yk..........134 D7
Hughenden Valley
  Bucks.......................42 E2
Hughley Shrops............83 L4
Hugh Town IoS...............2 b2
Huish Devon..................10 D3
Huish Wilts...................40 C7
Huish Champflower
  Somset.....................25 G3
Huish Episcopi
  Somset.....................26 B6
Hulcott Bucks...............58 D5
Hulham Devon..............12 C5
Hulland Derbys...........100 E3
Hulland Ward Derbys...100 E3
Hullavington Wilts.......39 K4
Hullbridge Essex...........46 D2
Hull, Kingston upon
  C KuH.....................126 D5
Hulme Manch..............113 J3
Hulme Staffs.................99 L4
Hulme Warrtn..............112 E4
Hulme End Staffs........100 C2
Hulme Walfield
  Ches E....................113 J7
Hulverstone IoW...........16 E5
Hulver Street Suffk.......93 K6
Humberside Airport
  N Linc...................126 D7
Humberston NE Lin....118 D1
Humberstone C Leic.....87 J3
Humbie E Loth...........178 B5
Humbleton E R Yk......126 F4
Humby Lincs...............103 G6
Hume Border...............167 L2
Humshaugh Nthumb...158 A7
Huna Highld................231 L2
Huncote Leics...............87 G4
Hundalee Border..........167 K5
Hunderthwaite Dur.....140 F4
Hundleby Lincs............118 E7
Hundleton Pembks.......49 G7
Hundon Suffk................77 G5
Hundred House
  Powys......................68 C4
Hungarton Leics...........87 K3
Hungerford Somset......25 G4
Hungerford W Berk......41 G6
Hungerford
  Newtown W Berk....41 G6
Hungerstone Herefs......69 J7
Hunmanby N York......135 M4
Hunningham Warwks....72 D2
Hunsbury Hill Nhants...73 K3
Hunsdon Herts..............60 C5
Hunsingore N York.....132 F8
Hunslet Leeds.............123 L4
Hunsonby Cumb..........149 G7
Hunstanton Norfk.......105 G4
Hunstanworth Dur......150 B5
Hunsterson Ches E.......99 G4
Hunston Suffk...............77 L2
Hunston W Susx...........18 B5
Hunstrete BaNES..........38 F7
Hunter's Quay Ag & B...173 K4
Huntham Somset..........25 M6
Hunthill Lodge
  Angus.....................196 C2
Huntingdon Cambs.......89 J8
Huntingfield Suffk........93 G8
Huntington C York......133 J7
Huntington Ches W....112 B8
Huntington E Loth.......178 B4

Huntington Herefs........68 E4
Huntington Staffs 85 H2
Huntley Gloucs 55 G4
Huntly Abers 215 L6
Hunton Kent 33 J4
Hunton N York 132 B2
Huntscott Somset..........24 E3
Huntsham Devon 24 F7
Huntshaw Devon 23 H6
Huntspill Somset............25 L3
Huntstile Somset............25 K5
Huntworth Somset..........25 L4
Hunwick Dur.................140 F2
Hunworth Norfk 106 C5
Hurdcott Wilts 28 D5
Hurdsfield Ches E.........113 L6
Hurley W & M 42 D4
Hurley Warwks 86 B4
Hurley Common
  Warwks......................86 B4
Hurlford E Ayrs 163 L3
Hurn Dorset....................15 L3
Hursley Hants 29 H6
Hurst Wokham 42 C5
Hurstbourne Priors
  Hants 29 H3
Hurstbourne Tarrant
  Hants 29 G2
Hurst Green E Susx 33 J7
Hurst Green Essex 62 C5
Hurst Green Lancs........121 K3
Hurst Green Surrey 32 D3
Hurstpierpoint
  W Susx.........................19 J3
Hurstwood Lancs 122 C4
Hurtiso Ork..................234 c6
Hurworth-on-Tees
  Darltn 141 H5
Hurworth Place
  Darltn 141 H5
Husbands Bosworth
  Leics...........................87 J6
Husborne Crawley
  C Beds 74 D7
Husthwaite N York.......133 H4
Hutcliffe Wood
  Crematorium
  Sheff 115 G5
Huthwaite Notts 101 J2
Huttoft Lincs 119 G6
Hutton Border 179 J7
Hutton E R Yk...............134 F8
Hutton Essex...................45 M2
Hutton Lancs 121 G5
Hutton N Som 37 M8
Hutton Buscel N York ...134 F3
Hutton Conyers
  N York......................132 E5
Hutton Cranswick
  E R Yk.......................126 C1
Hutton End Cumb.........148 D7
Hutton Henry Dur........151 K7
Hutton-le-Hole
  N York......................133 L2
Hutton Lowcross
  R & Cl.......................142 D4
Hutton Magna Dur 140 E5
Hutton Roof Cumb........130 B4
Hutton Roof Cumb........148 C7
Hutton Rudby N York....141 K6
Hutton Sessay N York...133 G4
Hutton Wandesley
  N York......................124 D1
Huxham Devon 12 B3
Huxley Ches W................98 D1
Huyton Knows 112 C4
Hycemoor Cumb...........128 D2
Hyde Tamesd................113 L3
Hyde Heath Bucks..........58 F7
Hyde Lea Staffs..............99 K8
Hyndford Bridge
  S Lans 165 H2
Hynish Ag & B...............188 C8
Hyssington Powys..........82 F5
Hythe Hants 16 E2
Hythe Kent 34 F7
Hythe End W & M 43 G6

Ibberton Dorset..............14 E2
Ible Derbys...................100 E2
Ibsley Hants...................15 L1
Ibstock Leics 86 E2
Ibstone Bucks 42 C2
Ibthorpe Hants 29 G2
Iburndale N York 143 H5
Ibworth Hants 29 K1
Ichrachan Ag & B 182 E2
Ickburgh Norfk...............91 J4
Ickenham Gt Lon 43 H3
Ickford Bucks.................57 M6
Ickham Kent...................35 G3
Ickleford Herts 59 K2
Icklesham E Susx 21 H3
Ickleton Cambs..............76 C5
Icklingham Suffk............91 H8
Ickornshaw N York 122 E2
Ickwell Green C Beds......75 G5
Ickworth Suffk 77 J3
Icomb Gloucs 56 E4
Idbury Oxon 56 E4
Iddesleigh Devon 10 E3
Ide Devon 11 K6
Ide Hill Kent...................32 E3
Iden E Susx 21 H2
Iden Green Kent 33 J5
Iden Green Kent 33 K6
Idle C Brad 123 H3
Idless Cnwll.....................4 C6
Idlicote Warwks 72 C5
Idmiston Wilts 28 D4
Idole Carmth 50 E3
Idridgehay Derbys 100 F3
Idrigill Highld...............208 F2
Idstone Oxon 40 E4
Iffley Oxon.....................57 K7
Ifield W Susx 31 L4
Ifold W Susx...................31 G5
Iford Bmouth 15 L4
Iford E Susx 19 L4
Ifton Mons 38 C3
Ightfield Shrops.............98 E5
Ightham Kent 33 G2
Ilam Staffs....................100 C3
Ilchester Somset 26 D6
Ilderton Nthumb..........168 F5
Ilford Gt Lon 45 H3
Ilford Somset.................26 A7
Ilfracombe Devon 23 H2
Ilkeston Derbys.............101 J4
Ilketshall St Andrew
  Suffk 93 H6
Ilketshall St
  Margaret Suffk 93 H6
Ilkley C Brad 123 G2
Illand Cnwll.....................5 L1
Illey Dudley 85 H7
Illogan Cnwll...................3 H3
Illston on the Hill
  Leics...........................87 K4
Ilmer Bucks....................58 C6
Ilmington Warwks 72 B5
Ilminster Somset............26 A8
Ilsington Devon 7 H2
Ilston Swans 51 H7
Ilton N York 132 B4
Ilton Somset 25 M7
Imachar N Ayrs.............161 L2
Immingham NE Lin 126 F7
Immingham Dock
  NE Lin 126 F7
Impington Cambs...........76 C2
Ince Ches W..................112 C6
Ince Blundell Sefton 111 K2
Ince-in-Makerfield
  Wigan 112 E1
Inchbae Lodge Hotel
  Highld 221 K7
Inchbare Angus.............196 F4
Inchberry Moray...........215 G4
Incheril Highld 211 G3
Inchinnan Rens 174 E5

Inchlaggan Highld.........201 J5
Inchmichael P & K........186 D3
Inchnacardoch Hotel
  Highld 202 B3
Inchnadamph Highld....224 F4
Inchture P & K 186 D2
Inchvuilt Highld 211 K6
Inchyra P & K 186 C4
Indian Queens Cnwll.......4 E4
Ingatestone Essex 61 G7
Ingbirchworth Barns....114 E1
Ingestre Staffs 99 L7
Ingham Lincs................116 F5
Ingham Norfk 107 H7
Ingham Suffk 77 J1
Ingham Corner Norfk...107 H6
Ingleby Derbys..............101 G6
Ingleby Arncliffe
  N York......................141 K6
Ingleby Barwick
  S on T 141 K4
Ingleby Greenhow
  N York......................142 C6
Ingleigh Green Devon 10 E4
Inglesbatch BaNES.........39 G7
Inglesham Swindn..........56 D7
Ingleston D & G 147 G2
Ingleton Dur 140 F3
Ingleton N York 130 D5
Inglewhite Lancs 121 H3
Ingoe Nthumb 158 C7
Ingol Lancs 121 G4
Ingoldisthorpe Norfk...105 G6
Ingoldmells Lincs 119 H7
Ingoldsby Lincs.............103 G6
Ingram Nthumb 168 F6
Ingrave Essex..................45 M2
Ingrow C Brad..............122 F3
Ings Cumb 138 C7
Ingst S Glos....................38 E3
Ingthorpe RutInd 88 E2
Ingworth Norfk 106 E6
Inkberrow Worcs 71 H3
Inkhorn Abers...............217 H6
Inkpen W Berk 41 G7
Inkstack Highld 231 J2
Innellan Ag & B 173 K4
Innerleithen Border 166 E3
Innerleven Fife.............186 F7
Innermessan D & G 144 C3
Innerwick E Loth 178 F4
Innesmill Moray 215 G2
Insch Abers 216 C8
Insh Highld 203 J5
Inskip Lancs 120 F3
Instow Devon 23 G5
Intake Sheff 115 H5
Inver Abers 204 F6
Inver Highld 223 J5
Inver P & K 194 F7
Inverailort Highld.........190 F1
Inverallochy Abers........217 K2
Inveran Highld 222 D2
Inveraray Ag & B 182 F5
Inverarish Highld..........209 J7
Inverarity Angus...........196 D7
Inverarnan Stirlg 183 K4
Inverasdale Highld........219 J4
Inverbeg Ag & B 183 K7
Inverbervie Abers 197 K2
Inver-boyndie Abers.....216 C2
Invercreran House
  Hotel Ag & B 191 K6
Inverdruie Highld 203 L3
Inveresk E Loth.............177 K4
Inveresragan Ag & B 182 E1
Inverewe Garden
  Highld 219 K5
Inverey Abers 204 D7
Inverfarigaig Highld.....202 D2
Inverfolla Ag & B 191 J7
Invergarry Highld.........201 L5
Invergeldie P & K 184 F2
Invergloy Highld...........201 K7
Invergordon Highld......222 F7
Invergowrie P & K 186 F2

Inverguseran Highld....200 B4
Inverhadden P & K.......193 L5
Inverherive Hotel
  Stirlg 183 L3
Inverie Highld 200 B5
Inverinan Ag & B 182 E4
Inverinate Highld 200 E2
Inverkeilor Angus 197 G6
Inverkeithing Fife........176 F2
Inverkeithny Abers.......216 C5
Inverkip Inver...............173 L4
Inverkirkaig Highld......224 C4
Inverlael Highld............220 F4
Inverlair Highld............192 E1
Inverliever Lodge
  Ag & B 182 C6
Inverlochy Ag & B 183 H2
Invermark Angus..........196 D1
Invermoriston Highld...202 C3
Invernaver Highld........229 L4
Inverness Highld 213 G5
Inverness
  Crematorium
  Highld 212 F5
Inverness Dalcross
  Airport Highld..........213 J4
Invernoaden Ag & B 183 G7
Inveroran Hotel
  Ag & B 192 D7
Inverquharity Angus....196 C5
Inverquhomery
  Abers........................217 J5
Inverroy Highld 201 K8
Inversanda Highld........191 J4
Invershiel Highld..........200 E2
Invershin Highld 222 D3
Invershore Highld 231 J8
Inversnaid Hotel
  Stirlg 183 K5
Inverugie Abers 217 L5
Inveruglas Ag & B 183 K5
Inveruglass Highld 203 J5
Inverurie Abers 206 E2
Inwardleigh Devon 10 E5
Inworth Essex.................61 L4
Iochdar W Isls 233 b7
Iona Ag & B..................180 D3
Iping W Susx 30 D6
Ipplepen Devon 7 J3
Ipsden Oxon...................41 M4
Ipstones Staffs..............100 A3
Ipswich Suffk 78 E5
Ipswich
  Crematorium
  Suffk 78 E5
Irby Wirral 111 J5
Irby in the Marsh
  Lincs.........................118 F8
Irby upon Humber
  NE Lin 117 K1
Irchester Nhants 74 D2
Ireby Cumb 147 M7
Ireby Lancs 130 C4
Ireleth Cumb 128 F4
Ireshopeburn Dur........149 L7
Irlam Salfd 113 G3
Irnham Lincs 103 G7
Iron Acton S Glos...........39 G4
Ironbridge Wrekin..........84 C3
Ironbridge Gorge
  Shrops 84 C3
Ironmacannie D & G....154 B6
Ironville Derbys............101 H3
Irstead Norfk 107 H7
Irthington Cumb..........148 E3
Irthlingborough
  Nhants.......................74 D1
Irton N York 134 F3
Irvine N Ayrs................163 H2
Irvine Maritime
  Centre N Ayrs...........163 H2
Isauld Highld 230 E3
Isbister Shet 235 c2
Isbister Shet 235 d4
Isfield E Susx 19 L3
Isham Nhants................88 C8
Isington Hants 30 C3

Islay Ag & B 171 G4
Islay Airport Ag & B..... 170 F7
Isle Abbotts Somset....... 26 A7
Isle Brewers Somset...... 26 A7
Isleham Cambs 90 F8
Isle of Dogs Gt Lon...... 45 G4
Isle of Grain Medway... 46 E5
Isle of Lewis W Isls 232 f2
Isle of Man IoM............237 C4
Isle of Man
   Ronaldsway
   Airport IoM.............237 b7
Isle of Mull Ag & B.......181 J1
Isle of Purbeck
   Dorset 15 J5
Isle of Sheppey Kent 46 F6
Isle of Skye Highld 208 F6
Isle of Thanet Kent 35 J2
Isle of Walney Cumb ..128 E6
Isle of Whithorn
   D & G 145 K7
Isle of Wight IoW 17 G5
Isle of Wight
   Crematorium IoW... 17 G4
Isleornsay Highld 199 L3
Isles of Scilly St
   Mary's Airport IoS...... 2 b2
Islesteps D & G.............155 G7
Isleworth Gt Lon............ 44 D5
Isley Walton Leics.........101 H7
Islibhig W Isls................232 d3
Islington Gt Lon.............. 44 F3
Islington
   Crematorium
   Gt Lon...................... 44 F2
Islip Nhants................... 88 E7
Islip Oxon...................... 57 K5
Islivig W Isls..................232 d3
Isombridge Wrekin....... 83 L2
Itchen Abbas Hants 29 K5
Itchen Stoke Hants 29 K5
Itchingfield W Susx....... 31 J5
Itteringham Norfk 106 D6
Itton Mons...................... 38 C2
Itton Common Mons..... 38 C2
Ivegill Cumb.................148 D6
Iver Bucks...................... 43 G4
Iver Heath Bucks 43 G4
Iveston Dur...................150 E5
Ivinghoe Bucks 58 F5
Ivinghoe Aston Bucks ..58 F4
Ivington Herefs 69 J3
Ivybridge Devon............. 6 F5
Ivychurch Kent.............. 21 K1
Ivy Hatch Kent............... 33 G3
Iwade Kent.................... 46 E6
Iwerne Courtney or
   Shroton Dorset........ 27 K8
Iwerne Minster
   Dorset 27 K8
IWM Duxford Cambs ..76 C5
Ixworth Suffk................. 77 L1
Ixworth Thorpe Suffk...91 K8

Jack-in-the-Green
   Devon..................... 12 C4
Jackton S Lans 175 G7
Jacobstow Cnwll............. 9 G5
Jacobstowe Devon........ 10 E4
Jameston Pembks........ 49 H7
Jamestown Highld........212 D3
Jamestown W Duns....174 D3
Janetstown Highld........227 L3
Janets-town Highld.......231 L5
Jardine Hall D & G 155 J5
Jarrow S Tyne................151 H3
Jasper's Green Essex 61 H3
Jawcraig Falk................175 L4
Jaywick Essex................. 62 D5
Jedburgh Border...........167 K5
Jeffreyston Pembks..... 49 J6
Jemimaville Highld........213 H2
Jerbourg Guern 236 d4

Jersey Jersey.................236 c6
Jersey Airport Jersey 236 b7
Jersey Crematorium
   Jersey.....................236 C7
Jesmond N u Ty 151 G2
Jevington E Susx............ 20 B5
Jockey End Herts 59 H5
Johnby Cumb.................148 D7
John Lennon Airport
   Lpool........................112 B5
John o' Groats Highld...231 L2
Johnshaven Abers........197 J3
Johnston Pembks.......... 48 F5
Johnstone D & G 155 M3
Johnstone Rens 174 D5
Johnstonebridge
   D & G 155 J4
Johnstown Carmth....... 50 E2
Johnstown Wrexhm..... 97 L4
Joppa C Edin.................177 J4
Joppa Cerdgn................. 66 D2
Joppa S Ayrs.................163 K5
Jordanston Pembks..... 64 C7
Joyden's Wood Kent 45 K5
Juniper Nthumb............150 B3
Juniper Green C Edin....177 G5
Jura Ag & B....................171 J2
Jurby IoM......................237 C2

K

Kaber Cumb...................139 H5
Kaimend S Lans 165 J1
Kames Ag & B 173 G4
Kames E Ayrs................164 D4
Kea Cnwll........................ 4 C7
Keadby N Linc................125 K7
Keal Cotes Lincs...........104 B1
Kearsley Bolton............113 H1
Kearsney Kent................ 35 H6
Kearstwick Cumb 130 B4
Kedington Suffk............. 77 G5
Kedleston Derbys..........100 F4
Keelby Lincs..................126 E8
Keele Staffs................... 99 J4
Keele Services Staffs..... 99 J4
Keelham C Brad............123 G4
Keeston Pembks........... 48 F4
Keevil Wilts.................... 39 L8
Kegworth Leics..............101 J7
Kehelland Cnwll............. 3 G3
Keig Abers.....................206 B2
Keighley C Brad 122 F3
Keighley
   Crematorium
   C Brad.....................122 F3
Keilarsbrae Clacks.......185 J8
Keillour P & K...............185 K3
Keiloch Abers...............204 E6
Keils Ag & B...................171 K5
Keinton Mandeville
   Somset..................... 26 D5
Keir Mill D & G..............154 E4
Keisley Cumb.................139 G3
Keiss Highld...................231 L4
Keith Moray....................215 J4
Keithick P & K................195 K8
Keithock Angus.............196 F4
Keithtown Highld...........212 E3
Kelbrook Lancs.............122 D2
Kelby Lincs....................103 G4
Keld N York....................139 K6
Kelfield N York...............124 F3
Kelham Notts.................102 C2
Kelhead D & G...............147 K2
Kellamergh Lancs.........120 E5
Kellas Angus.................187 G1
Kellas Moray..................214 E4
Kellaton Devon............... 7 J7
Kelling Norfk..................106 C4
Kellington N York...........124 E5
Kelloe Dur......................151 J7
Kelloholm D & G............164 E6
Kelly Devon...................... 9 K8
Kelmarsh Nhants...........87 K7

Kelmscott Oxon 56 E7
Kelsale Suffk................... 79 H2
Kelsall Ches W...............112 D7
Kelshall Herts................. 75 K7
Kelsick Cumb.................147 L5
Kelso Border..................167 L3
Kelstedge Derbys..........115 G8
Kelstern Lincs................118 C4
Kelston BaNES................ 39 G6
Keltneyburn P & K.........194 B6
Kelton D & G..................155 H7
Kelty Fife.......................186 B8
Kelvedon Essex.............. 61 K4
Kelvedon Hatch
   Essex....................... 60 F7
Kelynack Cnwll............... 2 C5
Kemback Fife.................187 G4
Kemberton Shrops........ 84 D3
Kemble Gloucs............... 39 M2
Kemerton Worcs........... 71 G6
Kemeys Commander
   Mons 53 M6
Kemnay Abers...............206 E3
Kempley Gloucs............. 54 F3
Kempley Green
   Gloucs...................... 55 G3
Kempsey Worcs............. 70 F5
Kempsford Gloucs......... 40 D2
Kempshott Hants........... 29 L2
Kempston Bed............... 74 F5
Kempton Shrops............ 83 G6
Kemp Town Br & H........ 19 J5
Kemsing Kent................. 32 F2
Kenardington Kent......... 34 C7
Kenchester Herefs........ 69 J6
Kencot Oxon................... 56 E6
Kendal Cumb.................129 L2
Kenfig Brdgnd................ 36 C4
Kenilworth Warwks....... 72 C1
Kenley Gt Lon................. 32 B2
Kenley Shrops................ 83 L4
Kenmore Highld............210 B3
Kenmore P & K..............194 B7
Kenn Devon.................... 11 L7
Kenn N Som................... 38 B6
Kennacraig Ag & B........172 D5
Kennerleigh Devon........ 11 J4
Kennessee Green
   Sefton.....................111 L2
Kennet Clacks...............176 C1
Kennethmont Abers.....215 L8
Kennett Cambs.............. 77 G2
Kennford Devon............. 11 L7
Kenninghall Norfk......... 92 C6
Kennington Kent........... 34 D5
Kennington Oxon........... 57 K7
Kennoway Fife...............186 F6
Kenny Somset............... 25 L7
Kennyhill Suffk............... 90 F7
Kennythorpe N York......134 C6
Kenovay Ag & B.............188 C6
Kensaleyre Highld.........208 F4
Kensington Gt Lon........ 44 E4
Kensworth Common
   C Beds...................... 59 G4
Kentallen Highld...........191 K5
Kent and Sussex
   Crematorium
   Kent.......................... 33 G5
Kentchurch Herefs........ 54 B3
Kentford Suffk................ 77 G2
Kent International
   Airport Kent............. 35 J2
Kentisbeare Devon........ 12 D2
Kentisbury Devon.......... 23 K3
Kentish Town Gt Lon..... 44 F3
Kentmere Cumb............138 C6
Kenton Devon................ 12 B5
Kenton Gt Lon............... 44 D3
Kenton N u Ty...............150 F2
Kenton Suffk.................. 78 E2
Kentra Highld................190 D3
Kent's Green Gloucs..... 55 H4
Kent's Oak Hants.......... 28 F6
Kenwyn Cnwll................. 4 C6
Keoldale Highld.............228 F3
Keppoch Highld.............200 D1

Kepwick N York 133 G2
Keresley Covtry 86 D6
Kerrera Ag & B...............182 B2
Kerris Cnwll.................... 2 D5
Kerry Powys................... 82 D5
Kerrycroy Ag & B...........173 J6
Kersall Notts.................116 B8
Kersbrook Devon........... 12 D5
Kersey Suffk................... 78 B5
Kershader W Isls............232 f3
Kerswell Devon.............. 12 D2
Kerswell Green Worcs... 70 F5
Kesgrave Suffk............... 78 F5
Kessingland Suffk.......... 93 L6
Kestle Cnwll.................... 4 F6
Kestle Mill Cnwll............. 4 D4
Keston Gt Lon................ 45 H7
Keswick Cumb...............137 J3
Keswick Norfk................ 92 E3
Kettering Nhants............ 88 C7
Kettering
   Crematorium
   Nhants....................... 88 C7
Ketteringham Norfk....... 92 E3
Kettins P & K.................195 K8
Kettlebaston Suffk......... 77 L4
Kettlebridge Fife............186 E6
Kettlebrook Staffs.......... 86 B3
Kettleburgh Suffk........... 78 F3
Kettleholm D & G 155 K6
Kettleshulme Ches E....113 M5
Kettlesing N York...........132 C7
Kettlesing Bottom
   N York......................132 C7
Kettlestone Norfk..........106 A6
Kettlethorpe Lincs........116 D6
Kettletoft Ork................234 d4
Kettlewell N York...........131 H5
Ketton Rutlnd................. 88 E3
Kew Gt Lon..................... 44 D5
Kewstoke N Som 37 M7
Kexby C York..................125 G1
Kexby Lincs....................116 E4
Key Green Ches E..........113 K8
Keyham Leics.................. 87 J3
Keyhaven Hants............. 16 C4
Keyingham E R Yk..........127 G5
Keymer W Susx.............. 19 J3
Keynsham BaNES........... 38 F6
Keysoe Bed.................... 74 F3
Keysoe Row Bed............ 74 F3
Keyston Cambs.............. 88 F7
Keyworth Notts..............101 L6
Kibblesworth Gatesd....151 G4
Kibworth
   Beauchamp Leics....87 K5
Kibworth Harcourt
   Leics......................... 87 K5
Kidbrooke Gt Lon........... 45 H5
Kidderminster Worcs..... 84 E7
Kidlington Oxon.............. 57 J5
Kidmore End Oxon......... 42 B5
Kidsdale D & G...............145 J7
Kidsgrove Staffs............. 99 J2
Kidwelly Carmth............. 50 E4
Kiel Crofts Ag & B..........191 H8
Kielder Nthumb.............157 G4
Kiells Ag & B..................171 H5
Kilbarchan Rens............174 D5
Kilbeg Highld.................199 K4
Kilberry Ag & B..............172 C5
Kilbirnie N Ayrs.............174 C7
Kilbride Ag & B...............172 C3
Kilbride Ag & B...............173 H5
Kilbuiack Moray.............214 D3
Kilburn Derbys...............101 G4
Kilburn Gt Lon................ 44 E4
Kilburn N York...............133 H4
Kilby Leics...................... 87 J4
Kilchamaig Ag & B.........172 D6
Kilchattan Ag & B...........173 J7
Kilchattan Ag & B...........180 E7
Kilcheran Ag & B............191 G8
Kilchoan Highld.............189 L4
Kilchoman Ag & B...........170 D5
Kilchrenan Ag & B..........182 E3
Kilconquhar Fife............187 H6

Kilcot Gloucs 55 G3
Kilcoy Highld 212 E4
Kilcreggan Ag & B..........173 L3
Kildale N York................142 D5
Kildalloig Ag & B.............161 J5
Kildary Highld.................223 G6
Kildavaig Ag & B.............173 G5
Kildavanan Ag & B..........173 H5
Kildonan Highld...............227 G4
Kildonan N Ayrs..............162 D5
Kildonan Lodge
   Highld..........................226 F4
Kildonnan Highld.............199 G7
Kildrochet House
   D & G............................144 C4
Kildrummy Abers 205 K2
Kildwick N York..............122 F2
Kilfinan Ag & B...............172 F3
Kilfinnan Highld..............201 K6
Kilgetty Pembks...............49 J6
Kilgrammie S Ayrs..........152 F2
Kilgwrrwg Common
   Mons.............................38 C2
Kilham E R Yk.................135 G6
Kilkenneth Ag & B...........188 B7
Kilkenzie Ag & B.............161 H4
Kilkerran Ag & B.............161 J5
Kilkhampton Cnwll............9 H3
Killamarsh Derbys..........115 J3
Killay Swans....................51 H6
Killearn Stirlg 174 F2
Killen Highld...................213 G3
Killerby Darltn................140 F3
Killerton Devon...............12 C3
Killichonan P & K............193 J5
Killiechonate Highld........192 D1
Killiechronan Ag & B......190 B7
Killiecrankie P & K..........194 E4
Killilan Highld.................210 E7
Killimster Highld.............231 K4
Killin Stirlg 184 C2
Killinghall N York............132 D7
Killington Cumb...............130 C2
Killington Lake
   Services Cumb.............130 B2
Killingworth N Tyne.........159 G7
Killochyett Border...........167 G1
Kilmacolm Inver..............174 C4
Kilmahog Stirlg...............184 D5
Kilmahumaig Ag & B......182 A8
Kilmaluag Highld.............218 C6
Kilmany Fife....................186 F3
Kilmarnock E Ayrs...........163 K2
Kilmartin Ag & B.............182 B7
Kilmaurs E Ayrs...............163 K2
Kilmelford Ag & B...........182 B5
Kilmersdon Somset.........27 G2
Kilmeston Hants..............29 L6
Kilmichael Ag & B...........161 H5
Kilmichael Glassary
   Ag & B 182 B8
Kilmichael of
   Inverlussa Ag & B........172 D2
Kilmington Devon.............13 H3
Kilmington Wilts..............27 H4
Kilmington Common
   Wilts.............................27 H4
Kilmington Street
   Wilts.............................27 H4
Kilmorack Highld.............212 D5
Kilmore Ag & B................182 C3
Kilmore Highld................199 K4
Kilmory Ag & B................172 C4
Kilmory Highld.................190 B3
Kilmory N Ayrs................162 B5
Kilmuir Highld.................208 D5
Kilmuir Highld.................213 G4
Kilmuir Highld.................218 B7
Kilmuir Highld.................223 G6
Kilmun Ag & B.................173 K3
Kilnave Ag & B................170 F4
Kilncadzow S Lans...........176 B8
Kilndown Kent.................33 J6
Kilninver Ag & B.............182 B3
Kilnsea E R Yk.................127 J7
Kilnsey N York.................131 H6
Kilnwick E R Yk...............126 C1

Kiloran Ag & B................180 E7
Kilpatrick N Ayrs.............162 A4
Kilpeck Herefs.................54 C3
Kilpin E R Yk...................125 J5
Kilrenny Fife...................187 J6
Kilsby Nhants..................73 H1
Kilspindie P & K..............186 C3
Kilstay D & G..................144 D7
Kilsyth N Lans.................175 J3
Kiltarlity Highld...............212 D6
Kilton R & Cl...................142 E4
Kilton Thorpe R & Cl.......142 E4
Kilvaxter Highld...............218 B7
Kilve Somset....................25 H3
Kilvington Notts..............102 D4
Kilwinning N Ayrs............163 H2
Kimberley Norfk..............92 C3
Kimberley Notts..............101 J4
Kimberworth Rothm........115 H3
Kimblesworth Dur...........151 G5
Kimbolton Cambs............75 G2
Kimbolton Herefs............69 K3
Kimcote Leics.................87 H6
Kimmeridge Dorset.........15 H6
Kimpton Hants.................28 F3
Kimpton Herts.................59 K4
Kinbrace Highld...............226 F3
Kinbuck Stirlg.................185 G6
Kincaple Fife...................187 G4
Kincardine Fife...............176 C2
Kincardine Highld............222 E4
Kincardine O'Neil
   Abers.............................206 B5
Kinclaven P & K..............195 J8
Kincorth C Aber...............207 H5
Kincorth House
   Moray............................214 C3
Kincraig Highld................203 K4
Kincraigie P & K..............194 F6
Kindallachan P & K..........194 F6
Kinerarach Ag & B...........172 B7
Kineton Gloucs................56 C3
Kineton Warwks...............72 D4
Kinfauns P & K................186 C3
Kingarth Ag & B..............173 J6
King Arthur's
   Labyrinth Gwynd...........81 G3
Kingcausie Abers.............207 G5
Kingcoed Mons................54 B6
Kingerby Lincs................117 H3
Kingham Oxon..................56 E3
Kingholm Quay D & G......155 G7
Kinghorn Fife..................177 H2
Kinglassie Fife................186 D7
Kingoldrum Angus...........196 B5
Kingoodie P & K..............186 E2
Kingsand Cnwll.................6 C5
Kingsbarns Fife...............187 K5
Kingsbridge Devon............7 H6
Kingsbridge Somset........24 F4
King's Bromley Staffs......85 K1
Kingsburgh Highld...........208 F4
Kingsbury Gt Lon............44 D3
Kingsbury Warwks...........86 B4
Kingsbury Episcopi
   Somset...........................26 B7
King's Caple Herefs.........54 E3
Kingsclere Hants.............41 K8
King's Cliffe Nhants.........88 E4
Kingscote Gloucs.............39 J2
Kingscott Devon................23 H7
King's Coughton
   Warwks...........................71 J3
Kingscross N Ayrs............162 D4
Kingsdon Somset.............26 D6
Kingsdown Kent...............35 K5
Kingsdown Swindn...........40 D3
Kingsdown Wilts..............39 J6
Kingsdown
   Crematorium
   Swindn...........................40 D3
Kingseat Fife..................176 F1
Kingsey Bucks.................58 C6
Kingsfold W Susx.............31 K4
Kingsford C Aber.............206 F4
Kingsford E Ayrs..............174 E8
Kingsgate Kent................35 K1

Kingshall Street Suffk.....77 K3
King's Heath Birm............85 J7
Kings Hill Kent.................33 H3
King's Hill Wsall..............85 H4
Kings House Hotel
   Highld............................192 D5
Kingshouse Hotel
   Stirlg............................184 C4
Kingskerswell Devon.........7 K3
Kingskettle Fife...............186 E5
Kingsland Herefs.............69 J3
Kingsland IoA..................108 C5
Kings Langley Herts........59 H7
Kingsley Ches W..............112 D6
Kingsley Hants.................30 C4
Kingsley Staffs................100 A3
Kingsley Green
   W Susx..........................30 E5
Kingsley Park Nhants.......73 L3
King's Lynn Norfk............104 F8
Kings Meaburn Cumb.......138 E3
King's Mills Guern...........236 c3
Kingsmuir Angus.............196 D6
Kings Muir Border...........166 C2
Kingsmuir Fife................187 J5
Kingsnorth Kent..............34 D6
King's Norton Birm..........85 J7
King's Norton Leics.........87 K4
Kings Nympton
   Devon.............................23 L7
King's Pyon Herefs..........69 J4
Kings Ripton Cambs........89 J7
King's Somborne
   Hants.............................29 G5
King's Stag Dorset..........14 D1
King's Stanley Gloucs......55 J7
King's Sutton Nhants.......72 F7
Kingstanding Birm...........85 J5
Kingsteignton Devon.........7 K2
Kingsthorne Herefs.........54 D2
Kingsthorpe Nhants.........73 L2
Kingston Cambs..............75 L4
Kingston Cnwll..................6 A2
Kingston Devon.................6 F6
Kingston Dorset...............14 E1
Kingston Dorset...............15 H6
Kingston E Loth..............178 C3
Kingston IoW...................16 F6
Kingston Kent.................35 G4
Kingston Bagpuize
   Oxon..............................57 H7
Kingston Blount
   Oxon..............................58 C7
Kingston Deverill
   Wilts..............................27 J4
Kingstone Herefs.............69 H7
Kingstone Somset............26 B8
Kingstone Staffs..............100 B6
Kingston Lisle Oxon.........40 F3
Kingston near Lewes
   E Susx............................19 K4
Kingston on Soar
   Notts.............................101 J6
Kingston on Spey
   Moray............................215 H2
Kingston Russell
   Dorset...........................14 B4
Kingston St Mary
   Somset...........................25 K5
Kingston Seymour
   N Som.............................38 B6
Kingston upon Hull
   C KuH............................126 D5
Kingston upon
   Thames Gt Lon.............44 D6
Kingston upon
   Thames
   Crematorium
   Gt Lon...........................44 D6
King's Walden Herts.......59 K4
Kingswear Devon...............7 K5
Kingswells C Aber...........207 G4
Kings Weston Bristl........38 D5
Kingswinford Dudley........84 F5
Kingswood Bucks.............58 B4
Kingswood Gloucs............39 H3
Kingswood S Glos............38 F5

Kingswood Somset...........25 H4
Kingswood Surrey............31 L1
Kingswood Warwks..........71 L1
Kingswood Common
   Staffs.............................84 E3
Kings Worthy Hants.........29 J5
Kingthorpe Lincs............117 J6
Kington Herefs................68 F3
Kington S Glos.................38 F3
Kington Worcs.................71 H4
Kington Langley Wilts.....39 L5
Kington Magna
   Dorset...........................27 H6
Kington St Michael
   Wilts..............................39 K5
Kingussie Highld.............203 H5
Kingweston Somset.........26 D5
Kinharrachie Abers..........217 H7
Kinharvie D & G..............147 G2
Kinkell Bridge P & K........185 J4
Kinknockie Abers............217 J6
Kinleith C Edin...............177 G5
Kinlet Shrops..................84 C7
Kinloch Highld.................198 F5
Kinloch Highld.................225 H2
Kinloch Highld.................229 H5
Kinloch P & K..................195 J7
Kinlochard Stirlg.............184 B6
Kinlochbervie Highld.......228 C4
Kinlocheil Highld.............191 J1
Kinlochewe Highld...........210 E4
Kinloch Hourn Highld......200 E4
Kinlochlaggan Highld......202 E7
Kinlochleven Highld.........192 C4
Kinlochmoidart
   Highld............................190 E2
Kinlochnanuagh
   Highld............................200 B8
Kinloch Rannoch
   P & K.............................193 L5
Kinloss Moray.................214 C3
Kinmel Bay Conwy...........110 D5
Kinmuck Abers................206 F2
Kinmundy Abers..............207 G2
Kinnabus Ag & B.............160 B2
Kinnadie Abers................217 H5
Kinnaird P & K................194 F5
Kinneff Abers..................197 K2
Kinnelhead D & G............155 H2
Kinnell Angus.................196 F6
Kinnerley Shrops.............97 M7
Kinnersley Herefs............69 G5
Kinnersley Worcs............70 F5
Kinnerton Powys.............68 E2
Kinnesswood P & K.........186 C6
Kinnordy Angus...............196 B5
Kinoulton Notts...............102 B6
Kinross P & K..................186 B6
Kinrossie P & K...............186 C2
Kinross Services
   P & K.............................186 B6
Kinsham Herefs...............69 G2
Kinsham Worcs................71 G7
Kinsley Wakefd...............124 C7
Kinson Bmouth................15 K3
Kintail Highld..................200 F2
Kintbury W Berk..............41 G6
Kintessack Moray............214 B3
Kintillo P & K..................186 B4
Kinton Herefs..................83 H8
Kinton Shrops..................98 A8
Kintore Abers..................206 E3
Kintour Ag & B................171 H7
Kintra Ag & B..................170 F8
Kintra Ag & B..................180 D3
Kintraw Ag & B...............182 B6
Kintyre Ag & B................161 J2
Kinveachy Highld.............203 L2
Kinver Staffs...................84 E6
Kippax Leeds...................124 C4
Kippen Stirlg...................184 E7
Kippford or Scaur
   D & G............................146 E4
Kipping's Cross Kent.......33 H5
Kirbister Ork...................234 b6
Kirby Bedon Norfk...........93 G3
Kirby Bellars Leics..........102 B8

Kirby Cane Norfk............93 H5
Kirby Cross Essex..........62 E4
Kirby Fields Leics..........87 G3
Kirby Grindalythe
N York.......................134 D6
Kirby Hill N York...........132 F5
Kirby Hill Nthumb.........140 E6
Kirby Knowle N York.....133 G3
Kirby le Soken Essex.....62 F4
Kirby Misperton
N York.......................134 B4
Kirby Muxloe Leics........87 G3
Kirby Underdale
E R Yk........................134 C7
Kirby Wiske N York.......132 E3
Kirdford W Susx...........31 G6
Kirk Highld.................231 K4
Kirkabister Shet..........235 d6
Kirkandrews D & G......146 A5
Kirkandrews upon
Eden Cumb................148 C4
Kirkbampton Cumb.....148 B4
Kirkbean D & G...........147 G3
Kirk Bramwith Donc....124 F7
Kirkbuddo Angus........196 E7
Kirkburn Border.........166 D2
Kirkburn E R Yk..........134 F7
Kirkburton Kirk...........123 J7
Kirkby Knows..............111 L2
Kirkby Lincs...............117 H3
Kirkby N York.............142 C6
Kirkby Fleetham
N York.......................141 G7
Kirkby Green Lincs......103 H2
Kirkby in Ashfield
Notts.........................101 J2
Kirkby-in-Furness
Cumb.........................128 F3
Kirkby la Thorpe
Lincs.........................103 J4
Kirkby Lonsdale
Cumb.........................130 B4
Kirkby Malham
N York.......................131 G7
Kirkby Mallory Leics......86 F4
Kirkby Malzeard
N York.......................132 C5
Kirkbymoorside
N York.......................133 L3
Kirkby on Bain Lincs....118 C8
Kirkby Overblow
N York.......................123 L2
Kirkby Stephen
Cumb.........................139 H5
Kirkby Thore Cumb......138 F3
Kirkby Underwood
Lincs.........................103 H6
Kirkby Wharf N York....124 D3
Kirkcaldy Fife.............186 D8
Kirkcaldy
Crematorium Fife....186 D8
Kirkcambeck Cumb.....148 F2
Kirkchrist D & G..........146 B5
Kirkcolm D & G...........144 B2
Kirkconnel D & G........164 E6
Kirkconnell D & G.......147 G2
Kirkcowan D & G........145 G3
Kirkcudbright D & G....146 B5
Kirkdale Lpool............111 K3
Kirk Deighton N York...124 B1
Kirk Ella E R Yk...........126 C5
Kirkfieldbank S Lans...165 G2
Kirkgunzeon D & G......146 F2
Kirk Hallam Derbys.....101 J4
Kirkham Lancs............120 F4
Kirkham N York...........134 B6
Kirkhamgate Wakefd...123 K6
Kirk Hammerton
N York.......................133 G7
Kirkhaugh Nthumb......149 H5
Kirkheaton Kirk...........123 H6
Kirkheaton Nthumb.....158 C6
Kirkhill Highld............212 E5
Kirkhope S Lans..........165 J7
Kirkibost Highld..........199 H2
Kirkinch P & K............195 L7

Kirkinner D & G...........145 J5
Kirkintilloch E Duns....175 H4
Kirk Ireton Derbys......100 E3
Kirkland Cumb............136 E4
Kirkland D & G............154 E4
Kirkland D & G............155 H4
Kirkland D & G............164 E6
Kirk Langley Derbys....100 F5
Kirkleatham R & Cl......142 D3
Kirklevington S on T....141 K5
Kirkley Suffk...............93 L5
Kirklington N York.......132 D4
Kirklington Notts........102 B2
Kirklinton Cumb.........148 D2
Kirkliston C Edin.........176 F4
Kirkmabreck D & G......145 K4
Kirkmaiden D & G.......144 D7
Kirk Merrington Dur....141 G2
Kirk Michael IoM.........237 c4
Kirkmichael P & K.......195 H4
Kirkmichael S Ayrs.....163 J7
Kirkmuirhill S Lans.....164 F2
Kirknewton Nthumb....168 D4
Kirknewton W Loth.....176 F5
Kirkney Abers............215 L7
Kirk of Shotts N Lans...175 L5
Kirkoswald Cumb........148 F6
Kirkoswald S Ayrs.......163 G7
Kirkpatrick D & G........154 F4
Kirkpatrick Durham
D & G.......................154 D7
Kirkpatrick-Fleming
D & G.......................156 B7
Kirk Sandall Donc.......124 F8
Kirksanton Cumb........128 D4
Kirk Smeaton N York...124 D7
Kirkstall Leeds...........123 K4
Kirkstead Lincs...........103 K1
Kirkstile Abers............215 L7
Kirkstile D & G............156 C4
Kirkstyle Highld..........231 L2
Kirkthorpe Wakefd.....124 B6
Kirkton Abers.............206 C1
Kirkton D & G.............155 G6
Kirkton Fife................186 F3
Kirkton Highld............210 C3
Kirkton Highld............210 D6
Kirkton P & K..............185 K4
Kirkton Manor Border..166 C2
Kirkton of Airlie
Angus.......................195 L6
Kirkton of
Auchterhouse
Angus.......................196 B8
Kirkton of Barevan
Highld.......................213 K5
Kirkton of Collace
P & K.........................186 C2
Kirkton of
Glenbuchat Abers....205 J3
Kirkton of Logie
Buchan Abers...........217 J7
Kirkton of Menmuir
Angus.......................196 E4
Kirkton of Monikie
Angus.......................196 E8
Kirkton of Rayne
Abers........................216 D7
Kirkton of Skene
Abers........................206 F4
Kirkton of
Strathmartine
Angus.......................186 F1
Kirkton of Tealing
Angus.......................196 C8
Kirkton of Tough
Abers........................206 C3
Kirktown Abers...........217 J2
Kirktown Abers...........217 K4
Kirktown of Alvah
Abers........................216 D3
Kirktown of Bourtie
Abers........................206 F1
Kirktown of
Fetteresso Abers.....206 F7
Kirktown of
Mortlach Moray.......215 H6

Kirktown of Slains
Abers........................217 K8
Kirkurd Border...........165 M1
Kirkwall Ork...............234 c6
Kirkwall Airport Ork....234 c6
Kirkwhelpington
Nthumb....................158 C5
Kirk Yetholm Border...168 C4
Kirmington N Linc.......126 D7
Kirmond le Mire Lincs..117 K3
Kirn Ag & B.................173 K3
Kirriemuir Angus........196 C5
Kirstead Green Norfk...93 G4
Kirtlebridge D & G......155 M7
Kirtling Cambs...........77 G3
Kirtling Green Cambs...76 F4
Kirtlington Oxon.........57 J4
Kirtomy Highld...........229 M3
Kirton Lincs...............104 A5
Kirton Notts...............116 B7
Kirton Suffk...............78 F6
Kirtonhill W Duns.......174 D4
Kirton in Lindsey
N Linc.......................116 F2
Kirwaugh D & G..........145 J4
Kishorn Highld...........210 C6
Kislingbury Nhants.....73 K3
Kittisford Somset........25 G6
Kittybrewster C Aber...207 H4
Kivernoll Herefs.........54 C2
Kiveton Park Rothm....115 J5
Knaith Lincs...............116 D5
Knap Corner Dorset....27 J6
Knaphill Surrey..........42 F8
Knapp Somset............25 L6
Knapton C York..........124 E1
Knapton N York..........134 D4
Knapton Norfk...........107 G5
Knapwell Cambs.........75 K2
Knaresborough
N York.......................132 E7
Knarsdale Nthumb......149 H4
Knaven Abers.............217 G5
Knayton N York..........132 F2
Knebworth Herts........59 L4
Knedlington E R Yk.....125 H5
Kneesall Notts...........116 B8
Kneesworth Cambs.....75 L5
Kneeton Notts............102 B4
Knelston Swans.........50 F7
Knenhall Staffs...........99 L5
Knightcote Warwks.....72 E4
Knightley Staffs..........99 J7
Knighton C Leic..........87 H4
Knighton Dorset.........14 C1
Knighton Powys.........82 F8
Knighton Somset........25 J3
Knighton Staffs..........99 G4
Knighton Staffs..........99 H6
Knighton on Teme
Worcs.......................70 B1
Knightwick Worcs.......70 D4
Knill Herefs...............68 F3
Knipton Leics.............102 D6
Kniveton Derbys.........100 E3
Knock Cumb...............138 F2
Knock Highld..............199 K4
Knock Moray.............215 L4
Knock W Isls..............232 g2
Knockally Highld.........227 K3
Knockan Highld..........224 F6
Knockando Moray.......214 F6
Knockbain Highld........212 E5
Knockbain Highld........212 F3
Knock Castle N Ayrs....173 L5
Knockdee Highld.........231 H4
Knockdow Ag & B........173 J4
Knockdown Wilts........39 J3
Knockeen S Ayrs.........153 G3
Knockenkelly N Ayrs...162 D4
Knockentiber E Ayrs...163 K2
Knockholt Kent...........32 E2
Knockholt Pound Kent..32 E2
Knockin Shrops..........97 M7
Knockinlaw E Ayrs......163 K2
Knocknain D & G.........144 B3
Knockrome Ag & B......171 K4

Knocksharry IoM........237 b4
Knocksheen D & G......153 M5
Knockvennie Smithy
D & G.......................154 D7
Knodishall Suffk.........79 J3
Knodishall Common
Suffk........................79 J3
Knole Somset.............26 C6
Knolls Green Ches E....113 J5
Knolton Wrexhm........98 B5
Knook Wilts...............27 L3
Knossington Leics......88 B2
Knott End-on-Sea
Lancs.......................120 E2
Knotting Bed.............74 E2
Knotting Green Bed....74 E2
Knottingley Wakefd....124 D5
Knotty Ash Lpool........112 B3
Knowbury Shrops.......83 L7
Knowe D & G..............153 G2
Knowehead D & G......154 A4
Knoweside S Ayrs.......163 G6
Knowle Bristl.............38 E6
Knowle Devon...........11 H5
Knowle Devon...........12 C2
Knowle Devon...........12 D6
Knowle Devon...........23 H4
Knowle Shrops...........83 L8
Knowle Solhll............85 L7
Knowle Somset..........24 E3
Knowlefield Cumb......148 D4
Knowle Green Lancs...121 J3
Knowle St Giles
Somset.....................13 J1
Knowl Hill W & M........42 D4
Knowsley Knows........112 C3
Knowsley Safari Park
Knows.......................112 C3
Knowstone Devon.......24 C4
Knox Bridge Kent.......33 K5
Knucklas Powys.........82 F8
Knuston Nhants.........74 D2
Knutsford Ches E........113 H5
Knutsford Services
Ches E......................113 G6
Krumlin Calder..........122 F6
Kuggar Cnwll.............3 J7
Kyleakin Highld..........200 B1
Kyle of Lochalsh
Highld.......................210 B8
Kylerhea Highld..........200 B2
Kylesku Highld...........224 F2
Kylesmorar Highld.....200 C6
Kyles Scalpay W Isls...232 e4
Kylestrome Highld......224 F2
Kynnersley Wrekin.....84 C1
Kyrewood Worcs........69 L2

L

Lacasaigh W Isls........232 f3
Lacasdal W Isls..........232 g2
Laceby NE Lin............117 K1
Lacey Green Bucks.....58 D7
Lach Dennis Ches W....113 G6
Lackford Suffk...........77 H1
Lackford Green Suffk...77 H1
Lacock Wilts..............39 K6
Ladbroke Warwks.......72 E3
Laddingford Kent.......33 J4
Ladock Cnwll.............4 D5
Lady Ork...................234 d4
Ladybank Fife............186 E5
Ladygill S Lans...........165 H4
Lady Hall Cumb..........128 E3
Ladykirk Border.........179 J8
Ladywood Birm..........85 J6
Ladywood Worcs........70 F3
La Fontenelle Guern...236 e1
Lag D & G..................154 F5
Laga Highld...............190 D4
Lagavulin Ag & B........160 C1
Lagg N Ayrs...............162 B5
Laggan Highld............201 L6
Laggan Highld............202 F6

Lagganlia Highld 203 K5
La Greve de Lecq
  Jersey.......................236 b5
Laid Highld....................228 F4
Laide Highld...................219 L3
Laig Highld.....................199 G3
Laigh Clunch E Ayrs.....174 E8
Laigh Fenwick E Ayrs....163 L2
Laigh Glenmuir E Ayrs..164 C5
Laighstonehall S Lans...175 J7
Laindon Essex.................46 B3
Lairg Highld...................225 M7
Laisterdyke C Brad.......123 J4
Lake IoW.........................17 H5
Lake Poole......................15 J4
Lake Wilts.......................28 C4
Lake District
  National Park
  Cumb..........................137 H5
Lakenheath Suffk...........91 G6
Lakesend Norfk...............90 D4
Laleston Brdgnd.............36 D4
Lamarsh Essex................77 K7
Lamas Norfk..................106 F7
Lambden Border............167 L2
Lamberhurst Kent...........33 H6
Lamberhurst Down
  Kent..............................33 H6
Lamberton Border.........179 K6
Lambeth Gt Lon..............44 F4
Lambeth
  Crematorium
  Gt Lon...........................44 F5
Lambfair Green Suffk.....77 G4
Lambley Notts...............101 M4
Lambley Nthumb...........149 H4
Lambourn W Berk...........40 F5
Lambourne End
  Essex.............................45 J2
Lambs Green W Susx.......31 L4
Lamerton Devon...............6 C1
Lamesley Gatesd...........151 G4
Lamington S Lans..........165 J3
Lamlash N Ayrs.............162 C3
Lamonby Cumb..............148 D7
Lamorna Cnwll..................2 E6
Lamorran Cnwll.................4 D7
Lampeter Cerdgn............66 D5
Lampeter Velfrey
  Pembks..........................49 K5
Lamphey Pembks............49 H7
Lamplugh Cumb.............136 F3
Lamport Nhants..............87 L8
Lamyatt Somset..............26 F4
Lanark S Lans................165 G2
Lancaster Lancs............129 K7
Lancaster &
  Morecambe
  Crematorium
  Lancs............................129 K6
Lancaster Services
  (Forton) Lancs.............121 G1
Lanchester Dur..............150 F5
Lancing W Susx...............19 G5
L'Ancresse Guern..........236 d1
Landbeach Cambs...........76 C2
Landcross Devon.............23 G6
Landerberry Abers.........206 E4
Landford Wilts.................28 E7
Land-hallow Highld.......227 L2
Landican
  Crematorium
  Wirral...........................111 J4
Landimore Swans...........50 F6
Landkey Devon................23 J5
Landore Swans................51 J6
Landrake Cnwll.................6 B4
Land's End Cnwll..............2 C6
Land's End Airport
  Cnwll..............................2 C6
Landulph Cnwll.................6 C4
Lane Cnwll........................4 C4
Laneast Cnwll...................9 G7
Lane End Bucks...............42 D3
Lane End Wilts................27 J3
Lane Ends Derbys..........100 E5
Laneham Notts..............116 D6

Lane Head Dur...............140 E5
Lanehead Dur................149 L6
Langaller Somset............25 K6
Langar Notts..................102 B5
Langbank Rens...............174 D4
Langbar N York..............123 G1
Langcliffe N York...........130 F6
Langdale End N York.....134 E2
Langdown Hants..............16 E2
Langdyke Fife.................186 E6
Langenhoe Essex.............62 B4
Langford C Beds...............75 H6
Langford Devon................12 D2
Langford Essex................61 K6
Langford Notts................102 D2
Langford Oxon................56 E7
Langford Budville
  Somset..........................25 H6
Langham Essex................62 B2
Langham Norfk..............106 B4
Langham Rutlnd..............88 B2
Langham Suffk................77 L1
Langho Lancs.................121 K4
Langholm D & G.............156 C5
Langlee Border...............167 H3
Langley Hants..................16 F3
Langley Herts...................59 K4
Langley Kent....................33 K3
Langley Nthumb.............149 L3
Langley Slough................43 G5
Langley Somset................25 G5
Langley W Susx...............30 D5
Langley Warwks..............71 L3
Langley Burrell Wilts......39 L5
Langley Green Essex........61 L4
Langley Marsh
  Somset..........................25 G5
Langley Park Dur...........150 F6
Langley Street Norfk......93 H3
Langley Upper Green
  Essex.............................76 C7
Langney E Susx...............20 D5
Langold Notts.................115 L4
Langore Cnwll....................9 J7
Langport Somset.............26 B6
Langrick Lincs...............103 L3
Langridge BaNES............39 H6
Langrigg Cumb...............147 K5
Langrish Hants................30 B6
Langsett Barns..............114 E2
Langside P & K...............185 G5
Langstone Hants.............17 K2
Langthorne N York........132 C2
Langthorpe N York........132 F6
Langthwaite N York.......140 C6
Langtoft E R Yk.............134 F6
Langtoft Lincs.................89 G2
Langton Dur...................140 F4
Langton Lincs................118 C7
Langton Lincs................118 E7
Langton N York..............134 C6
Langton by Wragby
  Lincs............................117 J6
Langton Green Kent........32 F5
Langton Herring
  Dorset...........................14 C6
Langton Matravers
  Dorset...........................15 J6
Langtree Devon...............10 C2
Langwathby Cumb.........148 F7
Langwell House
  Highld..........................227 K4
Langwith Derbys............115 K7
Langwith Junction
  Derbys..........................115 K7
Langworth Lincs............117 H6
Lanhydrock House &
  Gardens Cnwll................5 H3
Lanivet Cnwll....................5 G3
Lanlivery Cnwll.................5 G4
Lanner Cnwll.....................3 J4
Lanreath Cnwll.................5 J5
Lansallos Cnwll.................5 J5
Lanteglos Cnwll................8 E7
Lanteglos Highway
  Cnwll..............................5 J5
Lanton Border................167 J5

Lanton Nthumb..............168 D3
Lapford Devon..................11 H3
Laphroaig Ag & B..........160 C1
Lapley Staffs....................84 F2
Lapworth Warwks...........71 L1
Larachbeg Highld..........190 E6
Larbert Falk...................176 B3
Largie Abers...................216 B7
Largiemore Ag & B........172 F2
Largoward Fife...............187 H5
Largs N Ayrs..................173 L6
Largybeg N Ayrs............162 D5
Largymore N Ayrs..........162 D4
Larkfield Inver...............173 L4
Larkfield Kent.................33 J2
Larkhall S Lans..............175 K7
Larkhill Wilts...................28 C3
Larling Norfk....................92 B5
La Rocque Jersey..........236 e8
Lartington Dur...............140 C4
Lasham Hants.................30 A3
Lasswade Mdloth...........177 J5
Lastingham N York........133 L2
Latchingdon Essex..........61 L7
Latchley Cnwll...................6 B2
Lathbury M Keyn.............74 C5
Latheron Highld.............227 L2
Latheronwheel
  Highld..........................227 L3
Lathones Fife.................187 H5
Latimer Bucks.................59 G7
Latteridge S Glos............38 F4
Lattiford Somset..............27 G6
Latton Wilts.....................40 C2
Lauder Border................178 C8
Laugharne Carmth..........50 C4
Laughterton Lincs..........116 D6
Laughton E Susx.............20 A3
Laughton Leics................87 J5
Laughton Lincs..............103 H6
Laughton Lincs..............116 D3
Laughton-en-le-
  Morthen Rothm...........115 K4
Launcells Cnwll................9 H4
Launceston Cnwll.............9 J7
Launton Oxon..................57 L4
Laurencekirk Abers.......197 H3
Laurieston D & G...........146 B3
Laurieston Falk..............176 B3
Lavendon M Keyn............74 D4
Lavenham Suffk...............77 K5
Lavernock V Glam...........37 J6
Laversdale Cumb...........148 E3
Laverstock Wilts..............28 D5
Laverstoke Hants............29 J2
Laverton Gloucs..............71 J7
Laverton N York.............132 C5
Laverton Somset..............27 H2
La Villette Guern...........236 d4
Lavister Wrexhm.............98 A2
Law S Lans.....................175 L7
Lawers P & K..................193 L7
Lawford Essex.................62 C2
Lawford Somset..............25 H4
Law Hill S Lans..............175 L7
Lawhitton Cnwll................9 J7
Lawkland N York...........130 E6
Lawns Wood
  Crematorium
  Leeds...........................123 K3
Lawrenny Pembks...........49 H6
Lawshall Suffk.................77 K4
Laxay W Isls..................232 f3
Laxdale W Isls...............232 f2
Laxey IoM.......................237 d4
Laxfield Suffk..................93 G8
Laxford Bridge Highld...228 C6
Laxo Shet......................235 d4
Laxton E R Yk................125 J5
Laxton Nhants.................88 D4
Laxton Notts..................116 C7
Laycock C Brad..............122 F3
Layer Breton Essex.........61 M4
Layer-de-la-Haye
  Essex.............................62 A4
Layer Marney Essex........61 L4
Layham Suffk...................78 B6

Laymore Dorset..............13 K2
Laytham E R Yk..............125 H3
Lazonby Cumb...............148 F6
Lea Derbys....................101 G2
Lea Herefs.......................54 F4
Lea Lincs.......................116 D4
Lea Shrops......................83 G5
Lea Wilts.........................39 L3
Leachkin Highld............212 F5
Leadburn Border............177 H7
Leadenham Lincs...........102 F3
Leaden Roding Essex......60 F5
Leadgate Dur.................150 E5
Leadhills S Lans.............165 G6
Leafield Oxon..................56 F5
Leagrave Luton...............59 H4
Leake Common Side
  Lincs............................104 C3
Lealholm N York............142 F5
Lealt Highld...................209 H3
Lea Marston Warwks......86 B5
Leamington Hastings
  Warwks..........................72 F2
Leamington Spa
  Warwks..........................72 D2
Leap Cross E Susx..........20 C4
Leasgill Cumb................129 K3
Leasingham Lincs..........103 H3
Leasingthorne Dur........141 G2
Leatherhead Surrey........31 K1
Leathley N York.............123 J2
Leaton Shrops.................98 C8
Leaveland Kent...............34 D4
Leavenheath Suffk..........77 L6
Leavening N York..........134 C6
Leaves Green Gt Lon.......45 H7
Lebberston N York.........135 G3
Le Bourg Guern.............236 d3
Lechlade on Thames
  Gloucs...........................56 E7
Lecht Gruinart Ag & B...170 E5
Leck Lancs.....................130 C4
Leckbuie P & K..............193 L7
Leckford Hants...............29 G4
Leckhampstead
  Bucks............................73 K6
Leckhampstead
  W Berk...........................41 H5
Leckhampstead
  Thicket W Berk...............41 H5
Leckhampton Gloucs......55 L4
Leckmelm Highld...........220 F4
Leconfield E R Yk..........126 C2
Ledaig Ag & B................191 H8
Ledburn Bucks.................58 E4
Ledbury Herefs................70 C6
Ledgemoor Herefs...........69 H4
Ledmore Junction
  Highld..........................224 F6
Ledsham Leeds..............124 C4
Ledston Leeds................124 C5
Ledwell Oxon..................57 H3
Lee Devon......................23 H3
Lee Gt Lon......................45 H5
Leebotwood Shrops.........83 J4
Leece Cumb...................128 F5
Lee Chapel Essex...........46 B3
Lee Clump Bucks............58 E6
Leeds Kent.....................33 L3
Leeds Leeds..................123 K4
Leeds Bradford
  Airport Leeds...............123 J3
Leeds Castle Kent...........33 L3
Leedstown Cnwll..............3 G4
Leek Staffs.....................99 M2
Leek Wootton
  Warwks..........................72 C2
Lee Mill Devon.................6 E5
Leeming N York.............132 D2
Leeming Bar N York.......132 D2
Lee-on-the-Solent
  Hants.............................17 G3
Lees Derbys..................100 E5
Lees Oldham.................113 L2
Lees Green Derbys........100 E5

Leesthorpe Leics 87 L2
Leeswood Flints 97 K1
Leetown P & K................186 C3
Leftwich Ches W............112 F6
Legbourne Lincs............118 E5
Legerwood Border 167 J2
Legoland W & M................42 F5
Legsby Lincs..................117 J4
Leicester C Leic..............87 H3
Leicester Forest East
   Leics..........................87 G3
Leicester Forest East
   Services Leics............87 G3
Leigh Dorset....................14 C2
Leigh Gloucs...................55 K3
Leigh Kent.......................32 F4
Leigh Surrey....................31 L3
Leigh Wigan...................112 F2
Leigh Wilts........................40 B3
Leigh Worcs.....................70 D4
Leigh Beck Essex............46 D4
Leigh Delamere Wilts ...39 K5
Leigh Delamere
   Services Wilts............39 K5
Leigh Green Kent............34 B7
Leigh Knoweglass
   S Lans.......................175 H7
Leigh-on-Sea Sthend......46 D3
Leigh Park Dorset............15 J3
Leigh Sinton Worcs.........70 D4
Leighswood Wsall............85 J3
Leighterton Gloucs..........39 J3
Leighton Powys................82 E3
Leighton Shrops...............84 B3
Leighton Bromswold
   Cambs........................89 G7
Leighton Buzzard
   C Beds.......................58 F3
Leigh upon Mendip
   Somset......................27 G3
Leigh Woods N Som.........38 E6
Leinthall Earls Herefs ...69 J2
Leinthall Starkes
   Herefs........................69 J1
Leintwardine Herefs......83 H8
Leire Leics........................87 G5
Leiston Suffk....................79 J3
Leith C Edin...................177 H3
Leitholm Border.............168 B1
Lelant Cnwll........................2 F4
Lelley E R Yk...................126 F4
Lempitlaw Border..........168 B3
Lemreway W Isls...........232 f3
Lemsford Herts................59 L5
Lenchwick Worcs.............71 J5
Lendalfoot S Ayrs..........152 D4
Lendrick Stirlg................184 C6
Lendrum Terrace
   Abers.........................217 L6
Lenham Kent....................34 B4
Lenham Heath Kent........34 B5
Lenie Highld...................202 D1
Lennel Border.................168 C2
Lennox Plunton
   D & G.........................146 A5
Lennoxtown E Duns......175 H3
Lenton C Nott.................101 K5
Lenton Lincs...................103 G6
Lenwade Norfk...............106 D8
Lenzie E Duns................175 H4
Leochel-Cushnie
   Abers.........................205 L4
Leominster Herefs.........69 K3
Leonard Stanley
   Gloucs.......................55 J7
Lephin Highld.................208 B4
Leppington N York.........134 B7
Lepton Kirk.....................123 J7
Lerags Ag & B................182 B3
L'Eree Guern.................236 b3
Lerryn Cnwll.......................5 J4
Lerwick Shet..................235 d6
Lesbury Nthumb............169 J6
Leslie Abers...................206 B1
Leslie Fife......................186 D6
Lesmahagow S Lans.....164 F2
Lesnewth Cnwll.................8 F6

Les Quartiers Guern....236 d2
Les Quennevais
   Jersey.......................236 b7
Lessingham Norfk.........107 H6
Lessonhall Cumb...........147 L5
Leswalt D & G.................144 B3
L'Etacq Jersey...............236 a6
Letchmore Heath
   Herts..........................43 J2
Letchworth Garden
   City Herts.................59 L2
Letcombe Bassett
   Oxon..........................41 G4
Letcombe Regis Oxon....41 G3
Letham Angus................196 E6
Letham Border...............167 K7
Letham Falk...................176 B2
Letham Fife...................186 E4
Letham Grange
   Angus.......................197 G7
Lethendy P & K..............195 H7
Lethenty Abers...............206 B2
Lethenty Abers...............216 F6
Letheringham Suffk.......78 F3
Letheringsett Norfk......106 C5
Letterewe Highld..........219 L7
Letterfearn Highld........200 D2
Letterfinlay Lodge
   Hotel Highld.............201 K6
Lettermorar Highld.......199 M7
Letters Highld................220 F4
Lettershaw S Lans.........165 H5
Letterston Pembks.........48 F2
Lettoch Highld...............204 C2
Lettoch Highld...............214 D7
Letton Herefs...................69 G5
Letty Green Herts...........59 M5
Letwell Rothm................115 K4
Leuchars Fife.................187 G3
Leumrabhagh
   W Isls.......................232 f3
Leurbost W Isls..............232 f3
Levedale Staffs................84 F1
Leven E R Yk..................126 D2
Leven Fife......................186 F7
Levens Cumb..................129 K3
Levens Green Herts........60 B4
Levenshulme Manch.....113 K3
Levenwick Shet..............235 C7
Leverburgh W Isls.........232 d5
Leverington Cambs.........90 C2
Leverstock Green
   Herts..........................59 H6
Leverton Lincs...............104 C3
Le Villocq Guern...........236 c2
Levington Suffk...............78 F6
Levisham N York............134 C2
Lew Oxon..........................56 F6
Lewannick Cnwll................9 H8
Lewdown Devon...............10 C7
Lewes E Susx...................19 L4
Leweston Pembks...........48 F3
Lewisham Gt Lon.............45 G5
Lewisham
   Crematorium
   Gt Lon.......................45 H5
Lewiston Highld.............212 D8
Lewistown Brdgnd...........36 E3
Lewknor Oxon...................42 B2
Lewson Street Kent........34 C3
Lewtrenchard Devon.......10 C7
Lexden Essex....................62 A3
Lexworthy Somset...........25 K4
Leybourne Kent................33 H2
Leyburn N York...............131 L2
Leygreen Herts.................59 K3
Ley Hill Bucks...................59 G7
Leyland Lancs.................121 H6
Leylodge Abers..............206 E3
Leys Abers.....................217 J4
Leys P & K......................195 K8
Leysdown-on-Sea
   Kent..........................47 G6
Leysmill Angus...............196 F6
Leys of Cossans
   Angus.......................196 C6
Leysters Herefs...............69 L2

Leyton Gt Lon...................45 G3
Leytonstone Gt Lon.........45 H3
Lezant Cnwll.......................5 M1
Lhanbryde Moray...........215 G3
Libanus Powys..................52 F3
Libberton S Lans............165 J2
Liberton C Edin..............177 J4
Lichfield Staffs.................85 K2
Lickey Worcs.....................85 H7
Lickey End Worcs............85 H8
Lickfold W Susx................30 F6
Liddesdale Highld..........190 F4
Liddington Swindn...........40 E4
Lidgate Suffk....................77 G3
Lidlington C Beds............74 E6
Liff Angus.......................186 E2
Lifford Birm......................85 J7
Lifton Devon........................9 K7
Liftondown Devon..............9 K7
Lighthorne Warwks..........72 D4
Lighthorne Heath
   Warwks......................72 D4
Lightwater Surrey............42 F7
Lilbourne Nhants.............87 H7
Lilleshall Wrekin.............84 D1
Lilley Herts........................59 J3
Lilliesleaf Border...........167 H4
Lillingstone Dayrell
   Bucks.........................73 K6
Lillingstone Lovell
   Bucks.........................73 K6
Lillington Dorset.............26 F8
Lilliput Poole....................15 K4
Lilstock Somset...............25 J3
Limbury Luton..................59 H3
Limekilnburn S Lans.....175 J7
Limekilns Fife................176 E2
Limerigg Falk.................176 B4
Limerstone IoW................16 E6
Lime Street Worcs...........55 J2
Limington Somset............26 D6
Limmerhaugh E Ayrs.....164 C4
Limpenhoe Norfk.............93 H3
Limpley Stoke Wilts.........39 H7
Limpsfield Surrey.............32 D3
Limpsfield Chart
   Surrey.......................32 D3
Linby Notts....................101 K3
Linchmere W Susx...........30 E5
Lincluden D & G..............155 G6
Lincoln Lincs..................116 F7
Lincoln Crematorium
   Lincs.........................117 G7
Lincomb Worcs.................70 E2
Lindale Cumb..................129 J4
Lindal in Furness
   Cumb........................128 F4
Lindfield W Susx..............32 C7
Lindford Hants.................30 D4
Lindley Kirk....................123 G6
Lindridge Worcs...............70 C2
Lindsell Essex..................61 G3
Lindsey Suffk....................77 L5
Lindsey Tye Suffk............78 B5
Lingdale R & Cl...............142 E4
Lingen Herefs...................69 G2
Lingfield Surrey................32 C4
Lingwood Norfk................93 H2
Linicro Highld.................218 B7
Linkend Worcs..................55 J2
Linkenholt Hants.............41 G8
Linkinhorne Cnwll.............5 L2
Linktown Fife.................177 J1
Linkwood Moray.............214 F3
Linley Shrops...................83 G5
Linley Green Herefs........70 C4
Linlithgow W Loth.........176 D3
Linsidemore Highld.......222 D2
Linslade C Beds...............58 E3
Linstead Parva Suffk......93 G7
Linstock Cumb................148 D4
Linthurst Worcs...............85 H8
Linthwaite Kirk..............123 G7
Lintlaw Border................179 H6
Lintmill Moray................215 L2
Linton Border..................168 B4
Linton Cambs...................76 E5

Linton Derbys...................86 C1
Linton Herefs....................54 F3
Linton Kent........................33 K3
Linton Leeds....................124 B2
Linton N York..................131 J6
Linton Hill Herefs............54 F3
Linton-on-Ouse
   N York.......................133 G7
Linwood Lincs.................117 G5
Linwood Rens.................174 E5
Lionacleit W Isls.............233 b7
Lional W Isls...................232 g1
Liphook Hants...................30 D5
Liscard Wirral..................111 J3
Liscombe Somset.............24 D5
Liskeard Cnwll....................5 J3
Lismore Ag & B...............191 G7
Liss Hants.........................30 C5
Lissett E R Yk..................135 H7
Lissington Lincs.............117 J5
Lisvane Cardif..................37 J4
Liswerry Newpt................37 M3
Litcham Norfk.................105 L8
Litchborough Nhants......73 J4
Litchfield Hants...............29 J2
Litherland Sefton...........111 K2
Litlington Cambs.............75 K6
Litlington E Susx.............20 B5
Little Abington
   Cambs........................76 D5
Little Addington
   Nhants........................88 D8
Little Airies D & G..........145 J3
Little Alne Warwks..........71 K3
Little Altcar Sefton........111 J1
Little Amwell Herts.........60 B5
Little Aston Staffs...........85 K4
Little Ayton N York........142 C5
Little Baddow Essex........61 J6
Little Badminton
   S Glos........................39 J4
Little Bampton Cumb ...148 A4
Little Bardfield Essex......61 G2
Little Barford Bed...........75 H3
Little Barningham
   Norfk.........................106 D5
Little Barrington
   Gloucs........................56 D5
Little Barrow Ches W....112 C7
Little Bavington
   Nthumb.....................158 C6
Little Bedwyn Wilts.........40 F7
Little Bentley Essex.........62 D3
Little Berkhamsted
   Herts..........................59 M6
Little Billing Nhants........74 B3
Little Billington
   C Beds.......................58 F4
Little Birch Herefs...........54 E2
Little Blakenham
   Suffk..........................78 D5
Little Blencow Cumb.....148 E7
Little Bognor W Susx......31 G7
Little Bollington
   Ches E.......................113 G4
Little Bookham
   Surrey.......................31 J1
Littleborough Notts........116 D5
Littleborough Rochdl....122 D7
Littlebourne Kent............35 G3
Little Bourton Oxon.........72 E5
Little Braxted Essex.........61 K5
Little Brechin Angus......196 F4
Littlebredy Dorset...........14 B5
Little Brickhill M Keyn.....58 E2
Little Brington
   Nhants........................73 J2
Little Bromley Essex........62 C3
Little Budworth
   Ches W......................112 E7
Littleburn Highld............212 F4
Little Burstead Essex......46 A2
Littlebury Essex................76 D6
Littlebury Green
   Essex.........................76 C6
Little Bytham Lincs.......103 G8
Little Carlton Lincs.......118 E4

Little Casterton
 Rutlnd 88 E2
Little Cawthorpe
 Lincs 118 E5
Little Chalfont Bucks 43 G2
Little Chart Kent.......34 C5
Little Chesterford
 Essex 76 D6
Little Cheverell Wilts....27 M2
Little Chishill Cambs 76 B6
Little Clacton Essex......62 E4
Little Clifton Cumb 136 E2
Little Comberton
 Worcs 71 G5
Little Common E Susx 20 E4
Little Compton
 Warwks 56 E3
Little Cornard Suffk 77 K6
Little Cowarne Herefs 69 L4
Little Coxwell Oxon 40 F2
Little Crakehall
 N York 132 C2
Little Cressingham
 Norfk 91 K4
Little Crosby Sefton......111 K2
Little Cubley Derbys....100 D5
Little Dalby Leics 87 L2
Littledean Gloucs 54 F5
Little Dewchurch
 Herefs 54 D2
Little Ditton Cambs....76 F3
Little Downham
 Cambs 90 D6
Little Driffield E R Yk....134 F7
Little Dunham Norfk 91 K2
Little Dunkeld P & K....195 G7
Little Dunmow Essex....61 G4
Little Durnford Wilts....28 C5
Little Easton Essex....60 F3
Little Eaton Derbys......101 L4
Little Ellingham Norfk....92 B4
Little Everdon Nhants....73 H3
Little Eversden
 Cambs 75 L4
Little Faringdon Oxon....56 E7
Little Fencote N York....132 D2
Little Fenton N York 124 D4
Little Fransham
 Norfk 91 K2
Little Gaddesden
 Herts 59 G5
Little Glemham Suffk....79 H3
Little Gorsley Herefs....55 G3
Little Gransden
 Cambs 75 J4
Little Green Somset 27 G2
Little Hadham Herts....60 C4
Little Hale Lincs 103 J4
Little Hallam Derbys....101 J4
Little Hallingbury
 Essex 60 D4
Littleham Devon....12 D6
Littleham Devon....23 G6
Littlehampton W Susx....18 D5
Little Harrowden
 Nhants..................74 C1
Little Haseley Oxon....57 M7
Little Haven Pembks......48 E5
Littlehaven W Susx 31 K5
Little Hay Staffs 85 K3
Little Haywood Staffs....100 A7
Littlehempston
 Devon..................7 J4
Little Hereford Herefs....69 K2
Little Horkesley Essex....62 A2
Little Hormead Herts....60 C3
Little Horsted E Susx....19 M3
Little Horton C Brad....123 H4
Little Horwood Bucks....58 C2
Little Houghton
 Barns 115 H1
Little Houghton
 Nhants..................74 B3
Little Hucklow Derbys....114 D5
Little Hutton N York......133 G4
Little Irchester
 Nhants..................74 C2

Little Keyford Somset 27 H3
Little Kimble Bucks 58 D6
Little Kineton Warwks 72 D4
Little Kingshill Bucks 58 E7
Little Knox D & G 146 E3
Little Langdale Cumb...137 J6
Little Langford Wilts.......28 B4
Little Leigh Ches W 112 F6
Little Leighs Essex.........61 H5
Little Lever Bolton......121 L8
Little Linford M Keyn....74 B5
Little Load Somset............26 C6
Little London E Susx....20 C2
Little London Hants....29 G2
Little London Hants....41 L8
Little Longstone
 Derbys..................114 D6
Little Maplestead
 Essex 77 J7
Little Marcle Herefs 70 C7
Little Marlow Bucks........42 E3
Little Massingham
 Norfk 105 J7
Little Melton Norfk 92 E3
Littlemill Abers....205 H6
Littlemill Highld....213 L4
Little Mill Mons....53 L7
Little Milton Oxon....57 L7
Little Missenden
 Bucks..................58 F7
Littlemore Oxon....57 K7
Little Musgrave
 Cumb 139 H5
Little Ness Shrops..........98 B8
Little Newcastle
 Pembks..................49 G2
Little Newsham Dur....140 E4
Little Norton Somset....26 C7
Little Oakley Essex........62 F3
Little Oakley Nhants.......88 C6
Little Orton Cumb....148 C4
Littleover C Derb..........101 G5
Little Packington
 Warwks..................86 B6
Little Paxton Cambs......75 H3
Little Petherick Cnwll....4 E2
Little Plumstead
 Norfk..................93 G2
Little Ponton Lincs......102 F6
Littleport Cambs............90 E6
Little Preston Nhants.......73 H4
Little Raveley Cambs.......89 J7
Little Reedness E R Yk....125 J6
Little Ribston N York.....132 F8
Little Rissington
 Gloucs..................56 D4
Little Rollright Oxon........56 F3
Little Ryburgh Norfk....106 A6
Little Salkeld Cumb......148 F7
Little Sampford Essex....76 F7
Little Saughall
 Ches W..................111 K7
Little Saxham Suffk 77 H2
Little Scatwell Highld....212 B3
Little Shelford Cambs....76 C4
Little Singleton Lancs....120 E3
Little Skipwith N York....125 G3
Little Smeaton N York....124 D6
Little Snoring Norfk....106 A6
Little Sodbury S Glos....39 H4
Little Somborne
 Hants..................29 G5
Little Somerford
 Wilts..................39 L4
Little Soudley Shrops....99 G6
Little Stainton Darltn....141 J3
Little Stanney Ches W....112 B6
Little Staughton Bed....75 G2
Little Steeping Lincs....118 F8
Little Stoke Staffs............99 K6
Littlestone-on-Sea
 Kent..................21 L2
Little Stonham Suffk 78 E3
Little Stretton Leics......87 J4
Little Stretton Shrops....83 J5
Little Strickland
 Cumb..................138 E4

Little Stukeley Cambs....89 H7
Little Sugnall Staffs........99 J6
Little Swinburne
 Nthumb..................158 B6
Little Sypland D & G....146 C4
Little Tew Oxon....57 G3
Little Tey Essex....61 L4
Little Thetford Cambs....90 D7
Little Thorpe Dur....151 K6
Littlethorpe Leics..........87 G4
Littlethorpe N York....132 E5
Little Thurlow Suffk....76 F4
Little Thurrock Thurr....45 L4
Littleton Angus..........196 B6
Littleton Ches W....112 C7
Littleton D & G....146 B4
Littleton Hants....29 J5
Littleton Somset..............26 C5
Littleton Surrey....43 H6
Littleton Drew Wilts....39 J4
Littleton-on-Severn
 S Glos..................38 E3
Littleton Pannell
 Wilts..................27 M2
Little Torrington
 Devon..................10 D2
Littletown Dur....151 H6
Little Town Lancs....121 K4
Little Urswick Cumb....128 F5
Little Wakering Essex....46 F3
Little Walden Essex....76 D6
Little Waldingfield
 Suffk..................77 K5
Little Walsingham
 Norfk..................105 M5
Little Waltham Essex....61 H5
Little Weighton
 E R Yk..................126 B4
Little Weldon Nhants....88 D5
Little Wenlock Wrekin....84 B3
Little Weston Somset....26 F6
Little Whitefield IoW....17 H4
Littlewick Green
 W & M..................42 D4
Little Wilbraham
 Cambs..................76 D3
Little Witcombe
 Gloucs..................55 K5
Little Witley Worcs....70 D2
Little Wittenham
 Oxon..................41 K2
Little Wolford Warwks....72 C7
Little Woodcote
 Gt Lon..................44 F7
Littleworth Oxon....40 F2
Littleworth Staffs....99 L7
Littleworth Worcs....70 F4
Little Wymington
 Bed..................74 D2
Little Wymondley
 Herts..................59 K3
Little Wyrley Staffs....85 H3
Little Yeldham Essex....77 H6
Littley Green Essex....61 H4
Litton Derbys..............114 D6
Litton N York....131 G5
Litton Somset....26 E1
Litton Cheney Dorset....14 A4
Liurbost W Isls..........232 f3
Liverpool Lpool..........111 K4
Liversedge Kirk....123 J5
Liverton Devon..............7 J2
Liverton R & Cl....142 F4
Livingston W Loth....176 E5
Livingston Village
 W Loth..................176 E5
Lixwm Flints....111 G7
Lizard Cnwll..................3 J8
Llanaelhaearn Gwynd....95 G4
Llanafan Cerdgn..........66 F1
Llanafan-Fawr
 Powys..................67 L4
Llanaligo IoA....109 G4
Llanarmon Dyffryn
 Ceiriog Wrexhm....97 J6
Llanarmon-yn-Ial
 Denbgs..................97 J2

Llanarth Cerdgn 65 L3
Llanarth Mons....54 B5
Llanarthne Carmth....51 G2
Llanasa Flints..................110 F5
Llanbadarn Fawr
 Cerdgn..................80 E7
Llanbadarn Fynydd
 Powys..................82 C7
Llanbadoc Mons....54 B7
Llanbeder Newpt....38 B3
Llanbedr Gwynd....95 K7
Llanbedr Powys....53 K4
Llanbedr-Dyffryn-
 Clwyd Denbgs....97 H2
Llanbedrgoch IoA........109 G5
Llanbedrog Gwynd......94 F6
Llanbedr-y-Cennin
 Conwy..................109 L7
Llanberis Gwynd............95 K1
Llanbethery V Glam....37 G6
Llanbister Powys............82 C8
Llanblethian V Glam....36 F5
Llanboidy Carmth....49 L3
Llanbradach Caerph....37 J3
Llancadle V Glam....37 G6
Llancarfan V Glam....37 G6
Llancloudy Herefs....54 D4
Llandaff Cardif....37 J5
Llandanwg Gwynd....95 K6
Llanddaniel Fab IoA....109 G7
Llanddarog Carmth....51 G3
Llanddeiniol Cerdgn....66 D1
Llanddeiniolen
 Gwynd..................109 H7
Llandderfel Gwynd....96 F5
Llanddeusant IoA........108 D4
Llanddew Powys....53 G2
Llanddewi Swans....50 F7
Llanddewi Brefi
 Cerdgn..................66 F4
Llanddewi
 Rhydderch Mons....53 M5
Llanddewi Velfrey
 Pembks..................49 K4
Llanddewi
 Ystradenni Powys....68 C2
Llanddoget Conwy....109 M8
Llanddona IoA....109 H5
Llanddowror Carmth....50 B3
Llanddulas Conwy....110 C6
Llanddwywe Gwynd....95 K7
Llanddyfnan IoA....109 G5
Llandefaelog-Tre'r-
 Graig Powys....53 H3
Llandefalle Powys....68 C7
Llandegfan IoA....109 H6
Llandegla Denbgs....97 J3
Llandegley Powys....68 D2
Llandegveth Mons....37 M2
Llandeilo Carmth....51 J2
Llandeilo Graban
 Powys..................68 C5
Llandeloy Pembks....48 E3
Llandenny Mons....54 B7
Llandevaud Newpt....38 B3
Llandevenny Mons....38 B3
Llandinam Powys....82 B5
Llandissilio Pembks....49 J3
Llandogo Mons....54 D7
Llandough V Glam....36 F6
Llandough V Glam....37 J5
Llandovery Carmth....67 G7
Llandow V Glam....36 E5
Llandre Carmth....66 F6
Llandre Cerdgn....80 E6
Llandre Isaf Pembks....49 J2
Llandrillo Denbgs....97 G5
Llandrillo-yn-Rhos
 Conwy..................110 B5
Llandrindod Wells
 Powys..................68 B3
Llandrinio Powys....97 L8
Llandudno Conwy....109 L5
Llandudno Junction
 Conwy..................109 M6
Llandulas Powys....67 J6

Llandwrog Gwynd............95 H2
Llandybie Carmth.............51 J3
Llandyfaelog Carmth 50 E3
Llandyfriog Cerdgn 65 K6
Llandygai Gwynd........109 H7
Llandygwydd Cerdgn....65 H5
Llandyrnog Denbgs....110 F8
Llandyssil Powys..........82 E4
Llandysul Cerdgn 65 L6
Llanedeyrn Cardif 37 K4
Llaneglwys Powys...........68 B6
Llanegryn Gwynd...........80 D3
Llanegwad Carmth 51 G2
Llaneilian IoA 108 F3
Llanelian-yn-Rhôs
   Conwy.......................110 B6
Llanelidan Denbgs 97 H3
Llanelieu Powys...............68 D7
Llanellen Mons..............53 L5
Llanelli Carmth................51 G5
Llanelli Crematorium
   Carmth 51 G5
Llanelltyd Gwynd............96 A8
Llanelwedd Powys...........68 B4
Llanenddwyn Gwynd......95 K7
Llanengan Gwynd 94 E6
Llanerchymedd IoA 108 E5
Llanerfyl Powys..............82 B2
Llanfachraeth IoA 108 D5
Llanfachreth Gwynd......96 B7
Llanfaelog IoA 108 D6
Llanfaelrhys Gwynd......94 D6
Llanfaethlu IoA 108 D4
Llanfair Gwynd...............95 K6
Llanfair Caereinion
   Powys.........................82 C3
Llanfair Clydogau
   Cerdgn 66 E4
Llanfair Dyffryn
   Clwyd Denbgs............97 H2
Llanfairfechan Conwy...109 K6
Llanfair P G IoA...........109 G6
Llanfair Talhaiarn
   Conwy.......................110 C7
Llanfair Waterdine
   Shrops.......................82 E7
Llanfairynghornwy
   IoA 108 D4
Llanfair-yn-Neubwll
   IoA 108 C6
Llanfallteg Carmth.........49 K4
Llanfallteg West
   Carmth 49 K4
Llanfarian Cerdgn 80 D7
Llanfechain Powys..........97 J7
Llanfechell IoA 108 E3
Llanferres Denbgs.........97 J1
Llanfihangel-ar-arth
   Carmth 66 B6
Llanfihangel Glyn
   Myfyr Conwy...............96 F3
Llanfihangel Nant
   Bran Powys.................67 K7
Llanfihangel
   Rhydithon Powys....68 D2
Llanfihangel Rogiet
   Mons 38 C3
Llanfihangel-y-
   Creuddyn Cerdgn....80 F7
Llanfihangel-yng-
   Ngwynfa Powys.....82 C1
Llanfihangel yn
   Nhowyn IoA 108 D6
Llanfihangel-y-
   traethau Gwynd......95 K5
Llanfilo Powys.................53 H2
Llanfoist Mons................53 L5
Llanfor Gwynd.................96 E5
Llanfrechfa Torfn............37 L2
Llanfrynach Powys..........53 G3
Llanfwrog Denbgs..........97 H2
Llanfwrog IoA 108 C5
Llanfyllin Powys..............97 H8
Llanfynydd Carmth.........66 D8
Llanfynydd Flints.............97 J1
Llanfyrnach Pembks.......49 L2
Llangadfan Powys...........81 L2

Llangadog Carmth 66 F8
Llangadwaladr IoA 108 E7
Llangaffo IoA 108 F7
Llangammarch Wells
   Powys.........................67 K5
Llangan V Glam...............36 E5
Llangarron Herefs..........54 D4
Llangathen Carmth..........51 H2
Llangattock Powys...........53 K4
Llangattock Lingoed
   Mons 54 A4
Llangedwyn Powys..........97 J7
Llangefni IoA 108 F6
Llangeinor Brdgnd..........36 E3
Llangeitho Cerdgn..........66 E3
Llangeler Carmth 65 L6
Llangelynin Gwynd 80 D3
Llangendeirne
   Carmth 50 F3
Llangennech Carmth.......51 H5
Llangennith Swans..........50 E7
Llangenyw Conwy........110 B7
Llangian Gwynd...............94 E6
Llangloffan Pembks........64 C7
Llanglydwen Carmth.......49 K3
Llangoed IoA 109 J5
Llangollen Denbgs.........97 K4
Llangolman Pembks........49 J3
Llangors Powys...............53 H3
Llangower Gwynd............96 D6
Llangranog Cerdgn.........65 K4
Llangristiolus IoA..........108 F6
Llangrove Herefs............54 D4
Llangunllo Powys.............68 E1
Llangunnor Carmth 50 E2
Llangurig Powys...............81 K7
Llangwm Conwy.............96 F4
Llangwm Mons................54 B7
Llangwm Pembks............49 G5
Llangwnnadl Gwynd.......94 D6
Llangwyryfon Cerdgn.....66 D1
Llangybi Cerdgn 66 E4
Llangybi Gwynd...............95 G4
Llangybi Mons.................38 A2
Llangynhafal Denbgs....110 F8
Llangynidr Powys.............53 J4
Llangynin Carmth 50 B2
Llangynog Carmth 50 D3
Llangynog Powys.............97 G7
Llangynwyd Brdgnd........36 D3
Llanhamlach Powys.........53 H3
Llanharan Rhondd..........36 F4
Llanharry Rhondd...........36 F4
Llanhennock Mons..........38 A2
Llanhilleth Blae G............53 K7
Llanidloes Powys.............81 K6
Llaniestyn Gwynd............94 E5
Llanigon Powys................68 E6
Llanilar Cerdgn 80 E8
Llanilid Rhondd...............36 F4
Llanina Cerdgn 65 L3
Llanishen Cardif..............37 J4
Llanishen Mons...............54 C7
Llanllechid Gwynd........109 J7
Llanllowell Mons..............54 B7
Llanllugan Powys.............82 B3
Llanllwch Carmth.............50 E2
Llanllwchaiarn Powys.....82 C5
Llanllwni Carmth..............66 C6
Llanllyfni Gwynd..............95 H3
Llanmadoc Swans...........50 F6
Llanmaes V Glam............36 F6
Llanmartin Newpt...........38 B3
Llanmiloe Carmth............50 B4
Llannefydd Conwy.........110 D7
Llannon Carmth...............51 G4
Llannor Gwynd.................94 F5
Llanon Cerdgn 66 C2
Llanover Mons.................53 L6
Llanpumsaint
   Carmth 65 L8
Llanrhaeadr-ym-
   Mochnant Powys....97 H7
Llanrhian Pembks...........48 D2
Llanrhidian Swans..........50 F6
Llanrhychwyn Conwy.....96 B1
Llanrhyddlad IoA 108 D4

Llanrhystud Cerdgn........66 C1
Llanrug Gwynd.............109 G8
Llanrumney Cardif 37 K4
Llanrwst Conwy...............96 C1
Llansadurnen Carmth 50 C4
Llansadwrn Carmth 66 F7
Llansadwrn IoA 109 H6
Llansaint Carmth.............50 E4
Llansamlet Swans...........51 K6
Llansanffraid Glan
   Conwy Conwy.........109 M6
Llansannan Conwy........110 C7
Llansantffraed Powys....53 H4
Llansantffraed-
   Cwmdeuddwr
   Powys.........................67 L2
Llansantffraed-in-
   Elvel Powys...............68 C4
Llansantffraid
   Cerdgn 66 C2
Llansantffraid-ym-
   Mechain Powys.......97 K7
Llansawel Carmth 66 E7
Llansilin Powys................97 K6
Llansoy Mons..................54 C7
Llanspyddid Powys..........53 F3
Llanstadwell Pembks......48 F6
Llansteffan Carmth..........50 D4
Llantarnam Torfn............37 L2
Llanteg Pembks...............49 K5
Llanthewy Skirrid
   Mons 53 M5
Llanthony Mons...............53 L3
Llantilio-Crossenny
   Mons 54 B5
Llantilio Pertholey
   Mons 53 L5
Llantrisant Mons..............38 B2
Llantrisant Rhondd.........37 G4
Llantrithyd V Glam..........37 G6
Llantwit Fardre
   Rhondd.......................37 G3
Llantwit Major V Glam....36 F6
Llanuwchllyn Gwynd......96 D6
Llanvaches Newpt..........38 B3
Llanvair Discoed
   Mons 38 C3
Llanvapley Mons.............54 A5
Llanvetherine Mons........54 A5
Llanvihangel
   Crucorney Mons 53 L4
Llanwddyn Powys............96 F8
Llanwenog Cerdgn 66 C5
Llanwern Newpt..............38 A3
Llanwinio Carmth............50 C1
Llanwnda Gwynd.............95 H2
Llanwnda Pembks...........64 C6
Llanwnnen Cerdgn 66 C5
Llanwnog Powys..............82 B5
Llanwrda Carmth.............66 F7
Llanwrin Powys................81 H3
Llanwrthwl Powys............67 L2
Llanwrtyd Wells
   Powys.........................67 J5
Llanwyddelan
   Powys.........................82 C4
Llanyblodwel Shrops......97 K7
Llanybri Carmth...............50 D3
Llanybydder Carmth 66 C5
Llanycefn Pembks...........49 J3
Llanychaer Bridge
   Pembks.......................64 D7
Llanymawddwy
   Gwynd.......................96 D8
Llanymynech Powys........97 K7
Llanynghenedl IoA 108 D5
Llanynys Denbgs..........110 F8
Llanyre Powys.................68 B3
Llanystumdwy
   Gwynd.......................95 H5
Llanywern Powys.............53 H3
Llawhaden Pembks.........49 H4
Llawryglyn Powys............81 K5
Llay Wrexhm..................97 M2
Llechrhyd Caerph...........53 H6
Llechryd Cerdgn.............65 H5
Lledrod Cerdgn...............66 E1

Lleyn Peninsula
   Gwynd.......................94 E5
Lithfaen Gwynd...............94 F4
Lloc Flints.....................111 G6
Llowes Powys..................68 D6
Llwydcoed Rhondd.........52 F6
Llwydcoed
   Crematorium
   Rhondd.......................52 F6
Llwydiarth Powys.............82 B1
Llwyncelyn Cerdgn.........66 B3
Llwyndafydd Cerdgn 65 L4
Llwyngwril Gwynd...........80 D2
Llwynmawr Wrexhm........97 K5
Llwynypia Rhondd...........36 F2
Llynclys Shrops...............97 L7
Llynfaes IoA 108 E5
Llysfaen Conwy..............110 B6
Llyswen Powys..................68 C6
Llysworney V Glam..........36 E5
Llys-y-frân Pembks.........49 H3
Llywel Powys....................52 D3
Loan Falk......................176 C3
Loanhead Mdloth............177 J5
Loaningfoot D & G 147 G4
Loans S Ayrs..................163 J3
Lobhillcross Devon 10 C7
Lochailort Highld...........200 B8
Lochaline Highld............190 D7
Lochans D & G...............144 C4
Locharbriggs D & G......155 H6
Lochavich Ag & B...........182 D4
Lochawe Ag & B............183 G2
Loch Baghasdail
   W Isls.......................233 c8
Lochboisdale W Isls......233 c8
Lochbuie Ag & B...........181 J3
Lochcarron Highld 210 D6
Lochdon Ag & B............181 L2
Lochdonhead Ag & B....181 L2
Lochead Ag & B.............172 D3
Lochearnhead Stirlg 184 D3
Lochee C Dund..............186 F2
Locheilside Station
   Highld.......................191 K2
Lochend Highld............212 F6
Lochgair Ag & B.............172 F1
Lochgelly Fife................186 C8
Lochgilphead Ag & B....172 E2
Lochgoilhead Ag & B....183 H6
Lochieheads Fife...........186 D5
Lochill Moray.................215 G2
Lochindorb Lodge
   Highld.......................214 B7
Lochinver Highld 224 D4
Loch Lomond and
   The Trossachs
   National Park
   Stirlg.........................184 A5
Lochluichart Highld 211 L2
Lochmaben D & G 155 J5
Lochmaddy W Isls.........233 c6
Loch Maree Hotel
   Highld.......................219 L7
Loch nam Madadh
   W Isls.......................233 c6
Loch Ness Highld..........202 E1
Lochore Fife..................186 C7
Lochranza N Ayrs..........172 F7
Lochside Abers..............197 H4
Lochside D & G.............155 G6
Lochside Highld 213 J4
Lochslin Highld..............223 J5
Lochton S Ayrs..............152 F6
Lochty Angus.................196 E4
Lochty Fife....................187 H5
Lochuisge Highld...........190 F5
Lochwinnoch Rens.........174 C6
Lochwood D & G 155 J3
Lockengate Cnwll 5 G4
Lockerbie D & G.............155 K5
Lockeridge Wilts.............40 C6
Lockerley Hants..............28 D4

Locking N Som 38 A8
Locking Stumps
  Warrtn 112 F3
Lockington E R Yk 126 B2
Lockleywood Shrops....99 G6
Locksbottom Gt Lon 45 H6
Locks Heath Hants 17 G2
Lockton N York 134 C2
Loddington Leics..........87 L3
Loddington Nhants.......88 B7
Loddiswell Devon...........7 G6
Loddon Norfk 93 H4
Lode Cambs...................76 D3
Lode Heath Solhll 85 L7
Loders Dorset 13 L4
Lodge Hill
  Crematorium
  Birm.........................85 H6
Lodsworth W Susx 30 F6
Lofthouse Leeds..........123 L5
Lofthouse N York 131 L5
Lofthouse Gate
  Wakefd.....................123 L5
Loftus R & Cl 142 F4
Logan E Ayrs................164 C5
Loganlea W Loth 176 C6
Loggerheads Staffs.......99 G5
Logie Angus................197 H4
Logie Fife.....................186 F4
Logie Moray................214 C4
Logie Coldstone
  Abers.......................205 K4
Logie Newton Abers....216 C6
Logie Pert Angus........197 G4
Logierait P & K 194 F6
Logierieve Abers 217 H8
Login Carmth 49 K3
Lolworth Cambs............75 L2
Lonbain Highld 209 L4
Londesborough
  E R Yk 125 K2
London Gt Lon 44 F4
London Apprentice
  Cnwll.........................4 F6
London Colney Herts....11 G6
Londonderry N York....132 D3
London Gateway
  Services Gt Lon 44 D2
Londonthorpe Lincs 102 F5
Londubh Highld 219 K5
Lonemore Highld 219 J6
Long Ashton N Som......38 D6
Long Bank Worcs 84 D8
Long Bennington
  Lincs 102 D4
Longbenton N Tyne 151 G2
Longborough Gloucs.....56 D2
Long Bredy Dorset 14 B4
Longbridge Birm.........85 H7
Longbridge Deverill
  Wilts.........................27 K4
Long Buckby Nhants....73 J2
Longburton Dorset.......26 F8
Long Clawson Leics ...102 B6
Longcliffe Derbys.......100 E2
Longcombe Devon 7 J4
Long Compton
  Staffs 99 J7
Long Compton
  Warwks.....................56 F2
Longcot Oxon 40 F3
Long Crendon Bucks 58 B6
Long Crichel Dorset 15 J1
Longden Shrops 83 J3
Long Ditton Surrey 44 D6
Longdon Staffs 85 J2
Longdon Worcs 70 E7
Longdon Green Staffs...85 J2
Longdon upon Tern
  Wrekin 84 B1
Longdown Devon 11 K6
Longdowns Cnwll 3 J4
Long Duckmanton
  Derbys 115 H7
Long Eaton Derbys 101 J5
Longfield Kent..............45 L6
Longford Covtry 86 D6

Longford Derbys..........100 E5
Longford Gloucs...........55 J4
Longford Shrops 98 F5
Longford Wrekin 99 G8
Longforgan P & K 186 E2
Longformacus
  Border 178 E6
Longframlington
  Nthumb 158 E3
Long Green Ches W.....112 C7
Longham Dorset 15 K3
Longham Norfk 91 L1
Long Hanborough
  Oxon 57 H5
Longhaven Abers........217 L6
Longhirst Nthumb 158 F4
Longhope Gloucs 55 G4
Longhope Ork..............234 b7
Longhorsley Nthumb...158 E4
Longhoughton
  Nthumb 169 J6
Long Itchington
  Warwks.....................72 E2
Longlane Derbys.........100 E5
Long Lawford
  Warwks.....................86 F7
Longleat Safari &
  Adventure Park
  Wilts.........................27 J3
Longlevens Gloucs.......55 J4
Longleys P & K...........195 L7
Long Load Somset 26 C6
Longmanhill Abers......216 E3
Long Marston Herts......58 E5
Long Marston N York..124 D1
Long Marston Warwks...71 L5
Long Marton Cumb.....138 F3
Long Melford Suffk.......77 J5
Longmoor Camp
  Hants 30 C5
Longmorn Moray 214 F3
Longmoss Ches E.......113 K6
Long Newton Gloucs....39 K3
Longnewton Border 167 J4
Long Newton E Loth....178 B5
Longnewton S on T.....141 J4
Longney Gloucs............55 H5
Longniddry E Loth 177 L3
Longnor Shrops............83 J4
Longnor Staffs 114 C8
Longparish Hants.........29 H3
Long Preston N York...130 F7
Longridge Lancs 121 J3
Longridge W Loth 176 C5
Longriggend N Lans....175 L4
Long Riston E R Yk.....126 E3
Longrock Cnwll..............2 E5
Longsdon Staffs 99 L2
Longside Abers 217 K5
Longstanton Cambs.....76 B2
Longstock Hants...........29 G4
Longstowe Cambs........75 K4
Long Stratton Norfk.....92 E5
Long Street M Keyn 74 B5
Longstreet Wilts...........28 C2
Long Sutton Hants........30 C3
Long Sutton Lincs 104 C7
Long Sutton Somset....26 C6
Longthorpe C Pete 89 H4
Long Thurlow Suffk 78 B2
Longthwaite Cumb......138 B3
Longton C Stke 99 K4
Longton Lancs 121 G5
Longtown Cumb...........148 C2
Longtown Herefs 53 L3
Longueville Jersey 236 d7
Longville in the Dale
  Shrops 83 K5
Long Waste Wrekin 84 B1
Long Whatton Leics....101 J7
Longwick Bucks 58 C6
Long Wittenham
  Oxon 41 K2
Longwitton Nthumb....158 D4
Longwood D & G........146 C3
Longworth Oxon...........57 G7
Longyester E Loth 178 C5

Lonmay Abers..............217 J3
Lonmore Highld..........208 D5
Looe Cnwll......................5 K5
Loose Kent 33 K3
Loosley Row Bucks.......58 D7
Lootcherbrae Abers 216 B4
Lopen Somset 26 B8
Loppington Shrops 98 C6
Lords Wood Medway 46 C7
Lornty P & K 195 J6
Loscoe Derbys.............101 H3
Lossiemouth Moray 214 F1
Lost Gardens of
  Heligan Cnwll...............4 F6
Lostock Gralam
  Ches W....................113 G6
Lostock Green
  Ches W....................113 G6
Lostwithiel Cnwll............5 H4
Lothbeg Highld...........227 G6
Lothersdale N York 122 E2
Lothmore Highld.........227 G6
Loudwater Bucks 42 E3
Loughborough Leics...101 K8
Loughborough
  Crematorium
  Leics.......................101 K8
Loughor Swans.............51 H6
Loughton Essex 45 H2
Loughton M Keyn 74 B6
Lound Lincs 103 H8
Lound Notts 116 B4
Lound Suffk..................93 K4
Lount Leics 101 G8
Louth Lincs 118 D4
Lovedean Hants 30 B8
Lover Wilts 28 E7
Loversall Donc............115 L2
Loves Green Essex 61 G6
Loveston Pembks..........49 J5
Lovington Somset.........26 E5
Low Ackworth
  Wakefd....................124 C6
Low Barbeth D & G.....144 B2
Low Bentham N York ..130 C5
Low Biggins Cumb......130 B4
Low Borrowbridge
  Cumb 138 E6
Low Bradfield Sheff.....114 E3
Low Bradley N York....122 F2
Low Burnham N Linc..116 C2
Lowca Cumb...............136 D3
Low Catton E R Yk.....133 L8
Low Crosby Cumb......148 D3
Lowdham Notts..........102 A3
Low Dinsdale Darltn...141 J5
Lower Aisholt Somset...25 J4
Lower Ansty Dorset......14 E2
Lower Apperley
  Gloucs.......................55 J3
Lower Ashton Devon....11 J7
Lower Assendon
  Oxon 42 C4
Lower Bartle Lancs 121 G4
Lower Basildon
  W Berk......................41 L5
Lower Beeding
  W Susx......................31 L6
Lower Benefield
  Nhants......................88 E5
Lower Bentley Worcs....71 H2
Lower Boddington
  Nhants......................72 F4
Lower Bourne Surrey....30 D3
Lower Brailes Warwks...72 C6
Lower Breakish
  Highld.....................199 L2
Lower Broadheath
  Worcs........................70 E3
Lower Broxwood
  Herefs........................69 G4
Lower Bullingham
  Herefs........................69 K6
Lower Burgate Hants....28 D7
Lower Caldecote
  C Beds 75 H5
Lower Chapel Powys 68 B7

Lower Chicksgrove
  Wilts..........................27 L5
Lower Chute Wilts........28 F2
Lower Clapton Gt Lon ...45 G3
Lower Clent Worcs........85 G7
Lower Cumberworth
  Kirk 123 J8
Lower Dean Bed 74 F2
Lower Diabaig Highld...210 C3
Lower Dicker E Susx 20 B4
Lower Down Shrops......83 G6
Lower Dunsforth
  N York 133 G6
Lower Egleton Herefs ...70 B5
Lower End M Keyn 74 D6
Lower Eythorne Kent.....35 H5
Lower Failand N Som....38 D5
Lower Farringdon
  Hants 30 B4
Lower Feltham
  Gt Lon 43 H6
Lower Froyle Hants 30 C3
Lower Gabwell Devon 7 L2
Lower Gledfield
  Highld.....................222 D4
Lower Godney
  Somset......................26 C3
Lower Gravenhurst
  C Beds 75 G7
Lower Green Kent.........32 F5
Lower Green Kent.........33 G5
Lower Halliford
  Surrey 43 H6
Lower Halstow Kent......46 E6
Lower Hamworthy
  Poole 15 J4
Lower Hardres Kent 34 F4
Lower Hartwell Bucks....58 C5
Lower Hergest Herefs....68 F4
Lower Heyford Oxon......57 J3
Lower Houses Kirk......123 H7
Lower Irlam Salfd........113 G3
Lower Killeyan Ag & B..160 A2
Lower Langford
  N Som 38 C7
Lower Largo Fife.........187 G6
Lower Leigh Staffs......100 A5
Lower Loxhore
  Devon........................23 K4
Lower Lydbrook
  Gloucs.......................54 E5
Lower Lye Herefs 69 H2
Lower Machen Newpt....37 K3
Lower Merridge
  Somset......................25 J4
Lower Middleton
  Cheney Nhants 73 G6
Lower Moor Worcs 71 H5
Lower Morton S Glos 38 F3
Lower Nazeing Essex 60 C6
Lower Penarth
  V Glam 37 J6
Lower Penn Staffs.........84 F4
Lower Peover Ches E ...113 H6
Lower Quinton
  Warwks.......................71 L5
Lower Raydon Suffk......78 C6
Lower Roadwater
  Somset......................25 G4
Lower Seagry Wilts 39 L4
Lower Shelton C Beds....74 F6
Lower Shiplake Oxon 42 C4
Lower Shuckburgh
  Warwks.......................72 F3
Lower Slaughter
  Gloucs.......................56 D4
Lower Standen Kent 35 H6
Lower Stanton St
  Quintin Wilts 39 L4
Lower Stoke Medway 46 D5
Lower Stone Gloucs.......38 F3
Lower Stow Bedon
  Norfk.........................91 L5
Lower Street Norfk......106 F5
Lower Street Suffk........78 D4
Lower Swanwick
  Hants 16 F1

Lower Swell Gloucs........56 D3
Lower Tean Staffs........100 A5
Lower Town Devon.......7 G2
Lower Town Pembks......64 D6
Lower Upcott Devon.....11 K8
Lower Upham Hants....29 K7
Lower Weare Somset.....26 B2
Lower Welson Herefs....68 F4
Lower Westmancote
Worcs..................71 G6
Lower Whatley
Somset.................27 H3
Lower Whitley
Ches W................112 E5
Lower Wield Hants....29 M4
Lower Willingdon
E Susx.................20 C5
Lower Withington
Ches E................113 J7
Lower Woodford
Wilts..................28 C4
Lower Wraxhall
Dorset................14 B3
Lowesby Leics...........87 K3
Lowestoft Suffk.........93 L5
Loweswater Cumb....137 G3
Low Fell Gatesd.......151 G3
Lowfield Heath
W Susx................31 L4
Low Gartachorrans
Stirlg.................174 E2
Low Grantley N York...132 C5
Low Ham Somset........26 B5
Low Harrogate
N York................132 D7
Low Hesket Cumb.....148 E5
Low Hutton N York....134 B6
Lowick Nhants..........88 E7
Lowick Nthumb.......168 F2
Lowick Green Cumb....129 G3
Low Lorton Cumb.....137 G3
Low Marnham Notts...116 D7
Low Mill N York.......142 E7
Low Moorsley Sundld..151 H5
Low Moresby Cumb...136 D3
Low Newton Cumb....129 J3
Low Row Cumb.......149 G3
Low Row N York.......140 B7
Low Salchrie D & G...144 B2
Low Santon N Linc....125 L7
Lowsonford Warwks....71 L2
Low Tharston Norfk....92 E4
Lowther Cumb.........138 D3
Lowthorpe E R Yk....135 G7
Lowton Somset.........25 J7
Low Torry Fife.........176 D2
Low Worsall N York...141 J5
Low Wray Cumb......137 K6
Loxbeare Devon.........11 L2
Loxhill Surrey...........31 G4
Loxhore Devon.........23 K4
Loxley Warwks.........72 C4
Loxton N Som..........26 A1
Loxwood W Susx.......31 H5
Loyal Lodge Highld...229 J6
Lubenham Leics........87 K6
Luccombe Somset.....24 E3
Luccombe Village
IoW....................17 H6
Lucker Nthumb.......169 H4
Luckett Cnwll............6 B2
Lucking Street Essex...77 J7
Luckington Wilts.......39 J4
Lucklawhill Fife......187 G3
Luckwell Bridge
Somset.................24 E4
Lucton Herefs..........69 J2
Ludag W Isls..........233 b9
Ludborough Lincs....118 D3
Ludbrook Devon.........6 F5
Ludchurch Pembks....49 K5
Luddenden Calder....122 F5
Luddenden Foot
Calder................122 F5
Luddesdown Kent.....46 A6
Luddington N Linc...125 J7
Luddington Warwks...71 L4

Luddington in the
Brook Nhants........89 G6
Ludford Lincs.........117 K4
Ludford Shrops........83 K8
Ludgershall Bucks....58 A4
Ludgershall Wilts......28 E2
Ludgvan Cnwll...........2 E5
Ludham Norfk.......107 H8
Ludlow Shrops.........83 K7
Ludney Somset.........26 B8
Ludwell Wilts..........27 K6
Ludworth Dur.........151 J6
Luffness E Loth.......178 B3
Lugar E Ayrs..........164 C5
Luggate Burn E Loth..178 D4
Luggiebank N Lans...175 K4
Lugton E Ayrs........174 D7
Lugwardine Herefs....69 K6
Luib Highld...........209 J8
Luing Ag & B.........181 L5
Lulham Herefs.........69 H6
Lullington Derbys......86 B2
Lullington Somset.....27 H2
Lulsgate Bottom
N Som.................38 D7
Lulsley Worcs..........70 D4
Lumb Calder..........122 F6
Lumby N York........124 D4
Lumloch E Duns.....175 H4
Lumphanan Abers....206 B4
Lumphinnans Fife....186 C8
Lumsden Abers.......205 K2
Lunan Angus.........197 H6
Lunanhead Angus....196 D6
Luncarty P & K......186 A2
Lund E R Yk.........126 B2
Lund N York.........125 G4
Lundie Angus.........186 E1
Lundin Links Fife....187 G6
Lundin Mill Fife.....187 G6
Lundy Devon...........22 B3
Lunga Ag & B.........181 L5
Lunna Shet..........235 d4
Lunsford Kent..........33 J2
Lunsford's Cross
E Susx.................20 E4
Lunt Sefton...........111 K2
Luppitt Devon..........12 F2
Lupset Wakefd.......123 L6
Lupton Cumb.........129 L4
Lurgashall W Susx.....30 F6
Lurley Devon...........11 L2
Luscombe Devon........7 J4
Luss Ag & B..........183 L8
Lussagiven Ag & B...171 L2
Lusta Highld.........208 D3
Lustleigh Devon.......11 H8
Luston Herefs.........69 J2
Luthermuir Abers....197 G3
Luthrie Fife.........186 E4
Luton Devon............7 K1
Luton Devon...........12 D2
Luton Luton...........59 H4
Luton Medway.........46 C6
Luton Airport Luton...59 J4
Lutterworth Leics.....87 G6
Lutton Devon............6 E4
Lutton Devon............7 G4
Lutton Lincs.........104 C7
Lutton Nhants.........89 G6
Luxborough Somset...24 F4
Luxulyan Cnwll.........5 G4
Lybster Highld.......231 J7
Lydbury North Shrops..83 G6
Lydd Kent.............21 K2
Lydd Airport Kent....21 L2
Lydden Kent..........35 H5
Lydden Kent..........35 K2
Lyddington Rutlnd....88 C4
Lydeard St Lawrence
Somset.................25 H5
Lydford Devon.........10 D7
Lydford on Fosse
Somset.................26 E5
Lydgate Calder......122 D5
Lydham Shrops........83 G5
Lydiard Millicent Wilts..40 C3

Lydiard Tregoze
Swindn................40 C4
Lydiate Sefton........111 K2
Lydiate Ash Worcs....85 H7
Lydlinch Dorset........27 H8
Lydney Gloucs.........54 F7
Lydstep Pembks.......49 J7
Lye Dudley...........85 G6
Lye Green E Susx......32 F6
Lye Green Warwks.....71 L2
Lye's Green Wilts......27 J3
Lyford Oxon...........41 H2
Lymbridge Green
Kent...................34 F4
Lyme Regis Dorset....13 J4
Lyminge Kent.........34 F6
Lymington Hants......16 C4
Lyminster W Susx.....18 D5
Lymm Warrtn........113 G4
Lympne Kent..........34 F7
Lympsham Somset....25 M1
Lympstone Devon.....12 C5
Lynchat Highld.......203 J5
Lynch Green Norfk....92 D3
Lyndhurst Hants......16 C2
Lyndon Rutlnd........88 C3
Lyne Border.........166 B2
Lyne Surrey...........43 G7
Lyneal Shrops.........98 C6
Lyneham Oxon........56 F4
Lyneham Wilts.........40 A5
Lyneham Airport Wilts..40 A5
Lynemouth Nthumb..159 H4
Lyne of Skene Abers..206 E4
Lyness Ork..........234 b7
Lyng Norfk..........106 C8
Lyng Somset..........25 M5
Lynmouth Devon......23 L2
Lynsted Kent..........34 C3
Lynton Devon..........23 L2
Lyon's Gate Dorset....14 C2
Lyonshall Herefs......69 G4
Lytchett Matravers
Dorset................15 H4
Lytchett Minster
Dorset................15 H4
Lyth Highld.........231 K3
Lytham Lancs.......120 E5
Lytham St Anne's
Lancs................120 D5
Lythe N York.........143 H5
Lythmore Highld....230 F3

M

Mabe Burnthouse
Cnwll...................3 K4
Mablethorpe Lincs...119 G4
Macclesfield Ches E...113 K6
Macclesfield
Crematorium
Ches E................113 K6
Macduff Abers.......216 D2
Macharioch Ag & B...161 J7
Machen Caerph........37 K3
Machrie N Ayrs......162 A3
Machrihanish Ag & B.161 G5
Machrins Ag & B....180 E8
Machynlleth Powys....81 G4
Machynys Carmth.....51 G5
Mackworth Derbys...100 F5
Macmerry E Loth....177 L4
Madderty P & K......185 K3
Maddiston Falk......176 C3
Madeley Staffs.........99 H4
Madeley Wrekin........84 C3
Madingley Cambs.....76 B3
Madley Herefs.........69 H6
Madresfield Worcs....70 E5
Madron Cnwll...........2 E5
Maenclochog Pembks..49 J3
Maendy V Glam.......36 F5
Maentwrog Gwynd....95 L4
Maen-y-groes Cerdgn..65 L3
Maer Staffs...........99 H5

Maerdy Rhondd.........36 F2
Maesbrook Shrops....97 L7
Maesbury Shrops......97 L7
Maesbury Marsh
Shrops................97 L7
Maesllyn Cerdgn.......65 K5
Maesteg Brdgnd........36 D3
Maesybont Carmth.....51 H3
Maesycwmmer
Caerph.................37 J2
Maggieknockater
Moray................215 H5
Magham Down
E Susx.................20 C4
Maghull Sefton......111 K2
Magna Park Leics.....87 G6
Magor Mons...........38 B3
Magor Services Mons...38 B3
Maidenbower W Susx..31 L3
Maiden Bradley Wilts..27 J4
Maidencombe Torbay...7 L3
Maidenhayne Devon...13 H4
Maiden Head N Som...38 E6
Maidenhead W & M...42 E4
Maiden Newton
Dorset................14 B3
Maidens S Ayrs......163 G3
Maiden's Green
Br For.................42 E5
Maiden Wells Pembks..49 G7
Maidford Nhants......73 H4
Maids Moreton Bucks..73 K7
Maidstone Kent.......33 K3
Maidstone Services
Kent...................33 L3
Maidwell Nhants......87 L7
Mail Shet...........235 d6
Maindee Newpt.......37 L3
Mainland Ork........234 c6
Mainland Shet......235 c5
Mainsforth Dur......141 H2
Mains of Balhall
Angus................196 E4
Mains of Balnakettle
Abers................197 G2
Mains of Dalvey
Highld................214 D7
Mains of Haulkerton
Abers................197 H2
Mains of Lesmoir
Abers................215 K8
Mains of Melgunds
Angus................196 E5
Mainsriddle D & G...147 G4
Mainstone Shrops.....82 F6
Maisemore Gloucs.....55 J4
Malborough Devon......7 G7
Maldon Essex.........61 K6
Malham N York......131 G6
Maligar Highld.......209 G2
Mallaig Highld.......199 L6
Mallaigvaig Highld...199 L5
Malleny Mills C Edin..177 G5
Malltraeth IoA.......108 E7
Mallwyd Gwynd........81 J2
Malmesbury Wilts.....39 L3
Malmsmead Devon....24 C2
Malpas Ches W........98 C3
Malpas Cnwll...........4 D7
Malpas Newpt.........37 L3
Maltby Rothm.......115 K3
Maltby S on T........141 L5
Maltby le Marsh
Lincs................118 F5
Maltman's Hill Kent...34 B6
Malton N York......134 C5
Malvern Hills.........70 D5
Malvern Link Worcs...70 E5
Malvern Wells Worcs..70 D6
Mamble Worcs.........70 C1
Mamhilad Mons........53 L7
Manaccan Cnwll........3 K6
Manafon Powys........82 C3
Manais W Isls.......232 d5
Manaton Devon........11 H8
Manby Lincs.........118 E4
Mancetter Warwks.....86 D4

Manchester Manch...... 113 J3
Manchester Airport
  Manch 113 J5
Mancot Flints 111 K7
Mandally Highld 201 L5
Manderston House
  Border 179 G7
Manea Cambs 90 C5
Maney Birm............. 85 K4
Manfield N York 140 F4
Mangotsfield S Glos...... 38 F5
Manish W Isls............ 232 d5
Manley Ches W 112 D7
Manmoel Caerph 53 J7
Mannel Ag & B 188 C7
Manningford
  Bohune Wilts...... 40 C8
Manningford Bruce
  Wilts.................. 40 C8
Manningham C Brad..... 123 H4
Manning's Heath
  W Susx................. 31 K5
Mannington Dorset 15 K2
Manningtree Essex 62 D2
Mannofield C Aber...... 207 H4
Manorbier Pembks 49 H7
Manorbier Newton
  Pembks 49 H7
Manorhill Border....... 167 K3
Manorowen Pembks 64 C7
Manor Park Gt Lon..... 45 H3
Manor Park
  Crematorium
  Gt Lon.............. 45 H3
Mansell Gamage
  Herefs............... 69 H5
Mansell Lacy Herefs...... 69 H5
Mansfield E Ayrs 164 C6
Mansfield Notts......... 101 K1
Mansfield & District
  Crematorium
  Notts.................. 101 K2
Mansfield
  Woodhouse Notts .. 115 K8
Manston Dorset.......... 27 J7
Manston Kent............. 35 J2
Manston Leeds 124 B4
Manswood Dorset 15 J2
Manthorpe Lincs 88 F1
Manton N Linc 116 F2
Manton Rutlnd............. 88 C3
Manton Wilts............. 40 D6
Manuden Essex 60 D3
Maperton Somset 26 F6
Maplebeck Notts......... 102 B1
Mapledurham Oxon 42 A5
Mapledurwell Hants 30 B2
Maplehurst W Susx 31 K6
Maplescombe Kent....... 45 K7
Mapleton Derbys......... 100 D3
Mapperley Derbys......... 101 H4
Mapperley Park
  C Nott................. 101 L4
Mapperton Dorset 13 L3
Mappleborough
  Green Warwks..... 71 J2
Mappleton E R Yk...... 126 F2
Mapplewell Barns 123 L7
Mappowder Dorset 14 E2
Marazanvose Cnwll...... 4 C5
Marazion Cnwll............ 2 F5
Marbury Ches E 98 E4
March Cambs............. 90 B4
March S Lans 165 J6
Marcham Oxon............ 41 J2
Marchamley Shrops..... 98 E6
Marchington Staffs...... 100 C6
Marchros Gwynd......... 94 F7
Marchwiel Wrexhm...... 98 A3
Marchwood Hants........ 16 D1
Marcross V Glam........ 36 E6
Marden Herefs............ 69 K5
Marden Kent............. 33 J4
Marden Wilts............. 40 C8
Marden Thorn Kent 33 K5
Mardy Mons............. 53 L5
Mareham le Fen Lincs .. 103 L1

Mareham on the Hill
  Lincs 118 C7
Marehill W Susx 18 E3
Maresfield E Susx....... 19 M2
Marfleet C KuH 126 E5
Marford Wrexhm......... 98 A2
Margam Neath 36 B3
Margam
  Crematorium
  Neath 36 C4
Margaret Marsh
  Dorset 27 J7
Margaretting Essex 61 G7
Margaretting Tye
  Essex 61 G7
Margate Kent............. 35 K1
Margnaheglish N Ayrs.. 162 D3
Margrie D & G 145 M5
Margrove Park R & Cl... 142 E4
Marham Norfk............ 91 G2
Marhamchurch Cnwll..... 9 G4
Marholm C Pete........... 89 G3
Mariansleigh Devon..... 24 B6
Marine Town Kent 46 F5
Marionburgh Abers 206 D4
Marishader Highld 209 H2
Maristow Devon............ 6 C3
Marjoriebanks D & G ... 155 J5
Mark Somset............. 26 B2
Markbeech Kent.......... 32 E5
Markby Lincs............ 119 G5
Mark Cross E Susx 33 G6
Markeaton
  Crematorium
  C Derb 100 F5
Market Bosworth
  Leics................. 86 E3
Market Deeping Lincs... 89 G2
Market Drayton
  Shrops............... 98 F5
Market Harborough
  Leics................. 87 K6
Market Lavington
  Wilts................. 28 A1
Market Overton
  Rutlnd.............. 88 C1
Market Rasen Lincs...... 117 J4
Market Stainton Lincs... 118 C5
Market Warsop Notts... 115 K7
Market Weighton
  E R Yk.............. 125 K3
Market Weston Suffk ... 92 B7
Markfield Leics........... 86 F2
Markham Caerph 53 J7
Markham Moor Notts .. 116 B6
Markinch Fife.......... 186 E6
Markington N York 132 D6
Markle E Loth........... 178 C3
Marksbury BaNES........ 38 F7
Marks Tey Essex......... 61 L4
Markyate Herts........... 59 H5
Marlborough Wilts........ 40 D6
Marlcliff Warwks........ 71 K4
Marldon Devon............. 7 K3
Marlesford Suffk........ 79 G3
Marlingford Norfk........ 92 D2
Marloes Pembks.......... 48 D5
Marlow Bucks 42 D3
Marlow Bottom
  Bucks................. 42 D3
Marlpit Hill Kent........ 32 D4
Marnhull Dorset.......... 27 H7
Marple Stockp........... 113 L4
Marr Donc.............. 115 K1
Marrick N York......... 140 D7
Marsden Kirk............ 122 F7
Marsden S Tyne........ 151 J3
Marshalswick Herts..... 59 K6
Marsham Norfk.......... 106 E7
Marsh Baldon Oxon..... 57 K7
Marshborough Kent...... 35 J1
Marshbrook Shrops...... 83 J5
Marshchapel Lincs 118 E2
Marsh Farm Luton...... 59 H3
Marshfield Newpt....... 37 K4
Marshfield S Glos....... 39 H5
Marshgate Cnwll 8 F6

Marsh Gibbon Bucks...... 57 M4
Marsh Green Devon...... 12 D4
Marsh Green Kent...... 32 D4
Marshland St James
  Norfk.................. 90 D2
Marsh Lane Derbys 115 H5
Marsh Street Somset..... 24 F3
Marshwood Dorset...... 13 J3
Marske N York.......... 140 D6
Marske-by-the-Sea
  R & Cl............... 142 D3
Marston Herefs......... 69 G3
Marston Lincs.......... 102 E4
Marston Oxon........... 57 K6
Marston Staffs........... 99 L6
Marston Wilts........... 27 L1
Marston Green Solhll.... 85 L6
Marston Magna
  Somset 26 E6
Marston Meysey Wilts... 40 C2
Marston
  Montgomery
  Derbys............... 100 C5
Marston Moretaine
  C Beds............... 74 E6
Marston on Dove
  Derbys............... 100 E6
Marston St Lawrence
  Nhants............... 73 G6
Marston Trussell
  Nhants............... 87 K6
Marstow Herefs.......... 54 D4
Marsworth Bucks........ 58 F5
Marten Wilts............ 40 F7
Martham Norfk.......... 107 J8
Martin Hants............ 28 B7
Martin Kent............. 35 J5
Martin Lincs............ 103 J1
Martinhoe Devon........ 23 L2
Martin Hussingtree
  Worcs................. 70 F3
Martinstown Dorset...... 14 C5
Martlesham Suffk........ 78 F5
Martlesham Heath
  Suffk................. 78 F5
Martletwy Pembks 49 H5
Martley Worcs........... 70 D3
Martock Somset......... 26 C7
Marton Ches E........... 113 J7
Marton E R Yk.......... 126 F3
Marton Lincs............ 116 D5
Marton Middsb.......... 142 B4
Marton N York.......... 132 F6
Marton N York.......... 134 B3
Marton Shrops.......... 82 F3
Marton Warwks.......... 72 E2
Marton-le-Moor
  N York............... 132 E5
Martyr Worthy Hants 29 K5
Marwick Ork............ 234 b5
Marwood Devon.......... 23 H4
Marybank Highld........ 212 D4
Maryburgh Highld....... 212 E3
Maryculter Abers....... 207 G5
Marygold Border........ 179 G6
Maryhill C Glas......... 175 G4
Maryhill
  Crematorium
  C Glas............... 175 G4
Marykirk Abers......... 197 H3
Marylebone Gt Lon..... 44 F4
Marylebone Wigan..... 121 H8
Marypark Moray........ 214 F6
Maryport Cumb......... 147 H7
Maryport D & G......... 144 D7
Marystow Devon.......... 10 C7
Mary Tavy Devon......... 6 D1
Maryton Angus......... 197 H5
Marywell Abers......... 206 B6
Marywell Abers......... 207 H5
Marywell Angus........ 197 G5
Masham N York......... 132 C4
Masongill N York....... 130 C4
Masonhill
  Crematorium
  S Ayrs............... 163 J3
Mastin Moor Derbys ... 115 J6

Matching Green
  Essex 60 E5
Matching Tye Essex..... 60 E5
Matfen Nthumb 158 C7
Matfield Kent............ 33 H5
Mathern Mons........... 38 D3
Mathon Herefs........... 70 D5
Mathry Pembks.......... 48 E2
Matlask Norfk........... 106 D5
Matlock Derbys.......... 100 F1
Matlock Bath Derbys.... 100 F2
Matson Gloucs........... 55 J5
Mattersey Notts......... 116 B4
Mattingley Hants........ 42 B8
Mattishall Norfk........ 92 C2
Mattishall Burgh
  Norfk.................. 92 C2
Mauchline E Ayrs....... 163 L4
Maud Abers............. 217 H5
Maufant Jersey......... 236 d6
Maugersbury Gloucs 56 D3
Maughold IoM........... 237 e3
Mauld Highld........... 212 C6
Maulden C Beds......... 74 F6
Maulds Meaburn
  Cumb................. 138 F4
Maunby N York......... 132 E3
Maundown Somset 25 G5
Mautby Norfk........... 93 K2
Mavesyn Ridware
  Staffs................. 85 J1
Mavis Enderby Lincs.... 118 E7
Mawbray Cumb......... 147 J5
Mawdesley Lancs....... 121 G7
Mawdlam Brdgnd....... 36 C4
Mawgan Cnwll............. 3 J6
Mawgan Porth Cnwll...... 4 D3
Mawla Cnwll.............. 3 J3
Mawnan Cnwll............. 3 K5
Mawnan Smith Cnwll 3 K5
Mawsley Nhants......... 88 B7
Maxey C Pete........... 89 G2
Maxstoke Warwks...... 86 B6
Maxton Border.......... 167 J4
Maxton Kent............ 35 J6
Maxwell Town D & G... 155 G6
Maxworthy Cnwll.......... 9 H6
May Bank Staffs......... 99 J3
Maybole S Ayrs......... 163 H7
Maybury Surrey......... 43 G8
Mayfield E Susx......... 33 G7
Mayfield Mdloth........ 177 K5
Mayfield Staffs......... 100 D4
Mayford Surrey......... 31 G1
May Hill Gloucs......... 55 G4
Mayland Essex.......... 61 L7
Maylandsea Essex...... 61 L7
Maynard's Green
  E Susx................ 20 C3
Maypole Green Norfk.... 93 J4
Maypole Green Suffk.... 77 K3
Meadgate BaNES........ 39 G8
Meadle Bucks........... 58 D6
Meadowfield Dur....... 151 G6
Meadwell Devon.......... 9 K8
Meanwood Leeds....... 123 K3
Meare Somset........... 26 C3
Meare Green Somset 25 L6
Meare Green Somset ... 25 M6
Mearns E Rens.......... 174 F7
Mears Ashby Nhants.... 74 B2
Measham Leics......... 86 D2
Meathop Cumb......... 129 J4
Meavy Devon............. 6 D3
Medbourne Leics....... 88 B5
Meddon Devon............ 9 H2
Meden Vale Notts...... 115 L7
Mednenham Bucks...... 42 D4
Medomsley Dur........ 150 E4
Medstead Hants......... 30 A4
Medway
  Crematorium
  Kent................. 46 C7
Medway Services
  Medway............. 46 D7
Meerbrook Staffs........ 99 M1
Meesden Herts......... 60 C2

Meeth Devon	10	E3
Meeting House Hill		
Norfk	107	G6
Meidrim Carmth	50	C2
Meifod Powys	82	D2
Meigle P & K	195	L7
Meikle Carco D & G	164	F6
Meikle Earnock S Lans	175	J7
Meikle Kilmory		
Ag & B	173	H6
Meikle Obney P & K	195	G8
Meikleour P & K	195	J7
Meikle Wartle Abers	216	D7
Meinciau Carmth	50	F4
Meir C Stke	99	L4
Melbourn Cambs	75	L5
Melbourne Derbys	101	G7
Melbourne E R Yk	125	H2
Melbury Abbas		
Dorset	27	K7
Melbury Bubb Dorset	14	B2
Melbury Osmond		
Dorset	14	B2
Melchbourne Bed	74	E2
Melcombe Bingham		
Dorset	14	B2
Meldon Devon	10	E6
Meldon Nthumb	158	E6
Meldreth Cambs	75	L5
Meldrum Stirlg	184	F7
Melfort Ag & B	182	B5
Meliden Denbgs	110	E5
Melin-y-wig Denbgs	97	G3
Melkinthorpe Cumb	138	D3
Melkridge Nthumb	149	J3
Melksham Wilts	39	K7
Melling Lancs	130	B5
Melling Sefton	111	L2
Mellis Suffk	92	C8
Mellon Charles		
Highld	219	K3
Mellon Udrigle Highld	219	K3
Mellor Lancs	121	J4
Mellor Stockp	113	M4
Mellor Brook Lancs	121	J4
Mells Somset	27	G2
Melmerby Cumb	149	G7
Melmerby N York	131	K3
Melmerby N York	132	E4
Melness Highld	229	J3
Melplash Dorset	13	L3
Melrose Border	167	H3
Melsetter Ork	234	b7
Melsonby N York	140	F5
Meltham Kirk	123	G7
Melton E R Yk	126	B5
Melton Suffk	79	G4
Melton Constable		
Norfk	106	C6
Melton Mowbray		
Leics	102	C8
Melton Ross N Linc	126	D7
Melvaig Highld	219	H4
Melverley Shrops	83	G1
Melvich Highld	230	C3
Membury Devon	13	H2
Membury Services		
W Berk	40	F5
Memsie Abers	217	H2
Memus Angus	196	C5
Menai Bridge IoA	109	H6
Mendham Suffk	92	F6
Mendip Crematorium		
Somset	26	E3
Mendip Hills	26	D2
Mendlesham Suffk	78	D2
Mendlesham Green		
Suffk	78	D2
Menheniot Cnwll	5	L4
Mennock D & G	164	F7
Menston C Brad	123	H2
Menstrie Clacks	185	H7
Mentmore Bucks	58	E4
Meoble Highld	200	C7
Meole Brace Shrops	83	J2
Meonstoke Hants	29	L7
Meopham Kent	45	M6

Mepal Cambs	90	B7
Meppershall C Beds	75	G7
Mere Ches E	113	G5
Mere Wilts	27	J5
Mere Brow Lancs	120	F6
Mereclough Lancs	122	C4
Mereworth Kent	33	H3
Meriden Solhll	86	B6
Merkadale Highld	208	F7
Merley Poole	15	J3
Merrion Pembks	48	F7
Merriott Somset	26	C8
Merrow Surrey	31	G2
Merry Hill Herts	43	J2
Merryhill Wolves	84	F4
Merrymeet Cnwll	5	L3
Mersea Island Essex	62	B5
Mersham Kent	34	E6
Merstham Surrey	32	B3
Merston W Susx	18	B5
Merstone IoW	17	G5
Merthyr Cynog		
Powys	67	L6
Merthyr Mawr		
Brdgnd	36	D5
Merthyr Tydfil Myr Td	53	G6
Merthyr Vale Myr Td	53	G7
Merton Devon	10	D3
Merton Gt Lon	44	E6
Merton Norfk	91	K4
Merton Oxon	57	L4
Meshaw Devon	24	B7
Messing Essex	61	L4
Messingham N Linc	116	E2
Metfield Suffk	93	G7
Metherell Cnwll	6	B3
Metheringham Lincs	103	H1
Methil Fife	186	F7
Methilhill Fife	186	F7
Methlick Abers	217	G6
Methven P & K	185	L3
Methwold Norfk	91	G4
Methwold Hythe		
Norfk	91	G4
Mettingham Suffk	93	H5
Metton Norfk	106	E5
Mevagissey Cnwll	4	F6
Mexborough Donc	115	J2
Mey Highld	231	K2
Meyllteyrn Gwynd	94	D6
Meysey Hampton		
Gloucs	56	C7
Miabhig W Isls	232	d2
Miavaig W Isls	232	d2
Michaelchurch Herefs	54	D3
Michaelchurch		
Escley Herefs	69	G7
Michaelstone-y-		
Fedw Newpt	37	K4
Michaelston-le-Pit		
V Glam	37	J5
Michaelstow Cnwll	5	G1
Michaelwood		
Services Gloucs	39	G2
Micheldever Hants	29	K4
Micheldever Station		
Hants	29	K3
Michelmersh Hants	29	G6
Mickfield Suffk	78	D3
Micklebring Donc	115	K3
Mickleby N York	143	G5
Micklefield Leeds	124	C4
Mickleham Surrey	31	K2
Mickleover C Derb	100	F5
Mickleton Dur	140	B3
Mickleton Gloucs	71	L5
Mickletown Leeds	124	B5
Mickle Trafford		
Ches W	112	C7
Mickley N York	132	C4
Mickley Square		
Nthumb	150	D3
Mid Ardlaw Abers	217	H2
Midbea Ork	234	c4
Mid Beltie Abers	206	C5
Mid Calder W Loth	176	E5
Mid Clyth Highld	231	K7

Mid Culbeuchly Abers	216	C3
Middle Aston Oxon	57	J2
Middle Barton Oxon	57	H3
Middlebie D & G	155	L6
Middlebridge P & K	194	D3
Middle Chinnock		
Somset	26	C8
Middle Claydon		
Bucks	58	B3
Middleham N York	131	L3
Middle Handley		
Derbys	115	H6
Middlehill Wilts	39	J6
Middlehope Shrops	83	K5
Middle Kames Ag & B	172	F1
Middle Littleton		
Worcs	71	J5
Middlemarsh Dorset	14	C2
Middle Mayfield		
Staffs	100	C4
Middle Rasen Lincs	117	H4
Middle Rocombe		
Devon	7	K2
Middlesbrough		
Middsb	141	L4
Middleshaw Cumb	129	L2
Middlesmoor N York	131	K5
Middle Stoke Medway	46	D5
Middlestone Dur	141	G2
Middlestown Wakefd	123	K6
Middlethird Border	167	K2
Middleton Ag & B	188	B7
Middleton Derbys	100	F2
Middleton Derbys	114	D8
Middleton Essex	77	K6
Middleton Hants	29	H3
Middleton Herefs	69	K1
Middleton Leeds	123	L5
Middleton N York	123	G2
Middleton N York	134	B3
Middleton Nhants	88	B5
Middleton Norfk	90	F1
Middleton Nthumb	158	D5
Middleton P & K	186	B6
Middleton Rochdl	113	K1
Middleton Shrops	83	K7
Middleton Suffk	79	J2
Middleton Swans	50	E7
Middleton Warwks	85	L4
Middleton Cheney		
Nhants	73	G6
Middleton		
Crematorium		
Rochdl	113	K1
Middleton-in-		
Teesdale Dur	139	L3
Middleton Moor Suffk	79	J2
Middleton One Row		
Darltn	141	J5
Middleton-on-Sea		
W Susx	18	C5
Middleton on the Hill		
Herefs	69	K2
Middleton on the		
Wolds E R Yk	125	L2
Middleton Park		
C Aber	207	H3
Middleton		
Quernhow N York	132	E4
Middleton St George		
Darltn	141	J5
Middleton Scriven		
Shrops	84	C6
Middleton Stoney		
Oxon	57	K4
Middleton Tyas		
N York	141	G6
Middle Town IoS	2	a2
Middletown Powys	82	F2
Middle Tysoe Warwks	72	D5
Middle Wallop Hants	28	F4
Middlewich Ches E	113	G7
Middle Winterslow		
Wilts	28	E5
Middlewood Cnwll	5	L2
Middle Woodford		
Wilts	28	C4

Middlewood Green		
Suffk	78	D3
Middleyard E Ayrs	163	M3
Middlezoy Somset	26	B5
Midford BaNES	39	H7
Midgham W Berk	41	K6
Midgley Calder	122	F5
Midgley Wakefd	123	K7
Midhopestones Sheff	114	E2
Midhurst W Susx	30	E6
Mid Lavant W Susx	18	B4
Midlem Border	167	H4
Mid Mains Highld	212	C6
Midpark Ag & B	173	H6
Midsomer Norton		
BaNES	26	F1
Midtown Highld	229	J4
Mid Warwickshire		
Crematorium		
Warwks	72	C3
Mid Yell Shet	235	d3
Migvie Abers	205	K4
Milborne Port Somset	26	F7
Milborne St Andrew		
Dorset	14	F3
Milborne Wick		
Somset	26	F7
Milbourne Nthumb	158	E6
Milburn Cumb	138	F2
Milbury Heath S Glos	38	F3
Milby N York	132	F6
Milcombe Oxon	72	E7
Milden Suffk	77	L5
Mildenhall Suffk	91	G8
Mildenhall Wilts	40	E6
Mileham Norfk	105	L8
Mile Oak Br & H	19	H4
Milesmark Fife	176	E2
Miles Platting Manch	113	J2
Mile Town Kent	46	F5
Milfield Nthumb	168	D3
Milford Derbys	101	G4
Milford Devon	22	C6
Milford Staffs	99	L7
Milford Surrey	30	F3
Milford Haven		
Pembks	48	F6
Milford on Sea Hants	16	C4
Milkwall Gloucs	54	E6
Milland W Susx	30	D5
Mill Bank Calder	122	F6
Millbreck Abers	217	J5
Millbridge Surrey	30	D3
Millbrook C Beds	74	E6
Millbrook C Sotn	29	G8
Millbrook Cnwll	6	B5
Millbrook Jersey	236	c7
Mill Brow Stockp	113	L4
Millbuie Abers	206	F4
Millbuie Highld	212	E4
Millcorner E Susx	21	G2
Millcraig Highld	222	E7
Milldale Staffs	100	C2
Mill End Bucks	42	C4
Mill End Herts	60	B2
Millerhill Mdloth	177	J4
Miller's Dale Derbys	114	C6
Millerston C Glas	175	H5
Mill Green Cambs	76	F5
Mill Green Essex	61	G7
Mill Green Lincs	103	L7
Mill Green Suffk	77	L6
Mill Green Suffk	78	B3
Mill Green Suffk	78	D3
Millhalf Herefs	68	F5
Millheugh S Lans	175	K7
Mill Hill Gt Lon	44	E2
Millhouse Ag & B	173	G4
Millhousebridge		
D & G	155	K5
Millhouse Green		
Barns	114	E2
Millhouses Sheff	115	G5
Milliken Park Rens	174	D6
Millington E R Yk	125	J1
Millmeece Staffs	99	J5

Mill of Drummond
P & K......................185 H4
Mill of Haldane
W Duns..................174 D2
Millom Cumb................128 E4
Millport N Ayrs............173 K7
Mill Street Suffk..........78 C1
Millthrop Cumb.............130 C2
Milltimber C Aber.........207 G5
Milltown Abers............205 G4
Milltown Abers............205 K3
Milltown D & G.............156 C6
Milltown Devon..............23 J4
Milltown of
Campfield Abers.....206 C5
Milltown of Edinvillie
Moray.....................215 G6
Milltown of Learney
Abers....................206 C5
Milnathort P & K..........186 B6
Milngavie E Duns.........175 G4
Milnrow Rochdl...........122 D7
Milnthorpe Cumb..........129 K3
Milovaig Highld...........208 B4
Milson Shrops..............84 B8
Milstead Kent...............34 B3
Milston Wilts..............28 D3
Milthorpe Nhants...........73 H5
Milton Cambs...............76 C2
Milton Cumb...............148 F3
Milton D & G..............144 F4
Milton D & G..............154 E7
Milton Derbys.............100 F7
Milton Highld.............209 L5
Milton Highld.............212 D7
Milton Highld.............212 E4
Milton Highld.............223 G6
Milton Highld.............231 L5
Milton Inver..............174 C5
Milton Kent................46 A5
Milton Moray..............204 E2
Milton Moray..............215 L2
Milton N Som...............37 M7
Milton Notts..............116 B6
Milton Oxon................41 J3
Milton Oxon................72 F7
Milton P & K..............195 G4
Milton Pembks..............49 H6
Milton Somset..............26 C6
Milton Stirlg.............184 B6
Milton W Duns.............174 D4
Milton Abbas Dorset........14 F3
Milton Abbot Devon..........9 K8
Milton Bridge Mdloth.....177 H5
Milton Bryan C Beds........58 F3
Milton Clevedon
Somset....................26 F4
Milton Combe Devon..........6 D3
Milton Damerel
Devon......................9 K3
Milton Ernest Bed..........74 E4
Milton Green Ches W........98 C2
Milton Hill Oxon...........41 J3
Milton Keynes M Keyn.......74 C6
Milton Lilbourne Wilts.....40 D7
Milton Malsor Nhants.......73 K4
Milton Morenish
P & K....................184 D1
Milton of
Auchinhove** Abers...206 B5
Milton of Balgonie
Fife.....................186 E7
Milton of Buchanan
Stirlg...................174 E1
Milton of Campsie
E Duns...................175 H3
Milton of Leys Highld....213 G6
Milton of Murtle
C Aber...................207 G5
Milton of Tullich
Abers....................205 J6
Milton on Stour
Dorset....................27 J5
Milton Regis Kent..........46 E6
Milton-under-
Wychwood** Oxon........56 E4
Milverton Somset...........25 H6

Milverton Warwks...........72 C2
Milwich Staffs.............99 L6
Minard Ag & B.............182 D7
Minchinhampton
Gloucs....................55 K7
Minehead Somset...........24 F3
Minera Wrexhm..............97 L3
Minety Wilts...............40 A3
Minffordd Gwynd............95 K5
Mingarrypark Highld......190 D3
Miningsby Lincs...........118 D8
Minions Cnwll...............5 L2
Minishant S Ayrs..........163 J6
Minllyn Gwynd..............81 J2
Minnigaff D & G...........145 J2
Minnonie Abers............216 E3
Minskip N York............132 F6
Minstead Hants.............16 C1
Minsted W Susx.............30 D7
Minster Kent...............35 J2
Minster Kent...............46 F5
Minsterley Shrops..........83 G3
Minster Lovell Oxon........56 F5
Minsterworth Gloucs........55 H5
Minterne Magna
Dorset....................14 C2
Minting Lincs.............117 K6
Mintlaw Abers.............217 J5
Mintlyn
Crematorium
Norfk....................105 G8
Minto Border..............167 H5
Minton Shrops..............83 H5
Mirehouse Cumb............136 D4
Mireland Highld...........231 K4
Mirfield Kirk.............123 J6
Miserden Gloucs............55 L6
Miskin Rhondd..............37 G4
Misson Notts..............116 B3
Misterton Leics............87 G6
Misterton Notts...........116 C3
Misterton Somset...........13 L2
Mistley Essex..............62 D2
Mitcham Gt Lon.............44 F6
Mitcheldean Gloucs.........54 F4
Mitchell Cnwll..............4 D5
Mitchellslacks D & G......155 G3
Mitchel Troy Mons..........54 C6
Mitford Nthumb............158 F5
Mithian Cnwll...............3 J2
Mixbury Oxon...............73 H7
Mobberley Ches E..........113 H5
Mobberley Staffs..........100 A4
Mochdre Powys..............82 B5
Mochrum D & G.............145 H5
Mockbeggar Kent............33 J4
Mockerkin Cumb............136 F3
Modbury Devon...............6 F5
Moddershall Staffs.........99 L5
Moelfre IoA...............109 G4
Moelfre Powys..............97 J6
Moffat D & G..............155 J2
Moggerhanger
C Beds....................75 G5
Moira Leics................86 C1
Molash Kent................34 D4
Mol-chlach Highld.........199 G3
Mold Flints...............111 H8
Moldgreen Kirk............123 H7
Molehill Green Essex.......60 E3
Molescroft E R Yk.........126 C3
Molesworth Cambs...........88 F7
Molland Devon..............24 C5
Mollington Ches W.........111 L7
Mollington Oxon............72 F5
Mollinsburn N Lans........175 J4
Mondynes Abers............197 J1
Monewden Suffk.............78 F3
Moneydie P & K............185 M2
Moniaive D & G............154 D4
Monifieth Angus...........187 H2
Monikie Angus.............196 E8
Monimail Fife.............186 E5
Monken Hadley
Gt Lon....................44 E1
Monk Fryston N York.......124 D5
Monkhide Herefs............70 B5

Monkhill Cumb.............148 C3
Monkhopton Shrops..........84 B5
Monkland Herefs............69 J3
Monkleigh Devon............23 G7
Monknash V Glam............36 E6
Monkokehampton
Devon.....................10 E4
Monkseaton N Tyne.........159 H7
Monks Eleigh Suffk.........77 L5
Monk's Gate W Susx.........31 K6
Monks Heath Ches E........113 J6
Monk Sherborne
Hants.....................29 L1
Monksilver Somset..........25 G4
Monks Kirby Warwks.........86 F6
Monk Soham Suffk...........78 E2
Monks Risborough
Bucks.....................58 D6
Monksthorpe Lincs.........118 F7
Monk Street Essex..........60 F3
Monkswood Mons.............53 M7
Monkton Devon..............12 F2
Monkton Kent...............47 M6
Monkton S Ayrs............163 J4
Monkton S Tyne............151 H3
Monkton Combe
BaNES.....................39 H7
Monkton Deverill
Wilts.....................27 J4
Monkton Farleigh
Wilts.....................39 J7
Monkton Heathfield
Somset....................25 K6
Monkton Wyld Dorset........13 J3
Monkwearmouth
Sundld...................151 J4
Monkwood Hants.............30 A5
Monmore Green
Wolves....................85 G4
Monmouth Mons..............54 D5
Monnington on Wye
Herefs....................69 G5
Monreith D & G............145 H6
Montacute Somset...........26 D7
Montford Shrops............83 H1
Montford Bridge
Shrops....................83 H1
Montgarrie Abers..........206 B2
Montgomery Powys...........82 E4
Montrose Angus............197 H5
Mont Saint Guern..........236 b3
Monxton Hants..............28 F3
Monyash Derbys............114 D7
Monymusk Abers............206 D3
Monzie P & K..............185 H3
Moodiesburn N Lans........175 J4
Moonzie Fife..............186 E4
Moor Allerton Leeds.......123 K4
Moorby Lincs..............118 D8
Moor Crichel Dorset........15 J2
Moordown Bmouth............15 K4
Moore Halton.............112 E5
Moor End Calder..........122 F5
Moorends Donc.............125 G7
Moorhead C Brad...........123 H3
Moorhouse Cumb............148 B4
Moorhouse Notts...........116 C7
Moorhouse Bank
Surrey....................32 D3
Moorlinch Somset...........26 B4
Moor Monkton
N York...................133 H7
Moorsholm R & Cl..........142 E4
Moorside Dorset............27 H7
Moorswater Cnwll............5 K3
Moorthorpe Wakefd.........124 B7
Moortown Leeds............123 K3
Moortown Lincs............117 H2
Morangie Highld...........223 G5
Morar Highld..............199 L6
Moray Crematorium
Moray....................215 J3
Morborne Cambs.............89 G5
Morchard Bishop
Devon.....................11 H4
Morcombelake
Dorset....................13 K4

Morcott Rutlnd.............88 D4
Morda Shrops...............97 L6
Morden Dorset..............15 H4
Morden Gt Lon..............44 E6
Mordiford Herefs...........69 L6
Mordon Dur...............141 H2
More Shrops................83 G5
Morebath Devon.............24 E6
Morebattle Border.........168 B4
Morecambe Lancs...........129 J6
Moredon Swindn.............40 C3
Morefield Highld..........220 E3
Morehall Kent..............35 G7
Moreleigh Devon.............7 H5
Morenish P & K............184 D1
Morestead Hants............29 K6
Moreton Dorset.............14 F4
Moreton Essex..............60 E6
Moreton Herefs.............69 K2
Moreton Oxon...............58 B6
Moreton Wirral............111 J4
Moreton Corbet
Shrops....................98 E7
Moretonhampstead
Devon.....................11 H7
Moreton-in-Marsh
Gloucs....................56 D2
Moreton Jeffries
Herefs....................69 L5
Moreton Morrell
Warwks....................72 C4
Moreton on Lugg
Herefs....................69 K5
Moreton Pinkney
Nhants....................73 H5
Moreton Say Shrops.........98 F5
Moreton Valence
Gloucs....................55 H6
Morfa Nefyn Gwynd..........94 E4
Morham E Loth.............178 C4
Morland Cumb..............138 E3
Morley Ches E.............113 J5
Morley Derbys.............101 H4
Morley Leeds..............123 K5
Morley Green Ches E.......113 J5
Morley St Botolph
Norfk.....................92 C4
Morningside C Edin........177 H4
Morningside N Lans........175 L7
Morningthorpe Norfk........92 F5
Morpeth Nthumb............158 F5
Morphie Abers.............197 H4
Morrey Staffs.............100 C8
Morriston Swans............51 J6
Morston Norfk.............106 B4
Mortehoe Devon.............23 G3
Morthen Rothm.............115 J4
Mortimer W Berk............41 M7
Mortimer West End
Hants.....................41 M7
Mortlake Gt Lon............44 E5
Mortlake
Crematorium
Gt Lon....................44 D5
Morton Cumb...............148 C4
Morton Derbys.............101 H1
Morton Lincs..............103 H7
Morton Lincs..............116 D3
Morton Notts..............102 B3
Morton Shrops..............97 L7
Mortonhall
Crematorium
C Edin...................177 H5
Morton-on-Swale
N York...................132 E2
Morton on the Hill
Norfk.....................92 D1
Morvah Cnwll...............2 D4
Morvich Highld............200 E2
Morville Shrops............84 C5
Morwellham Quay
Devon......................6 C3
Morwenstow Cnwll............9 G2
Mosborough Sheff..........115 H5
Moscow E Ayrs.............163 L2
Moseley Birm...............85 J6
Moseley Wolves.............85 G4

Moseley Worcs 70 E3
Moss Ag & B 188 B7
Moss Donc 124 F7
Mossat Abers 205 K2
Mossbank Shet 235 d4
Moss Bank St Hel 112 D3
Mossbay Cumb 136 D2
Mossblown S Ayrs 163 K4
Mossburnford Border ..167 K6
Mossdale D & G 154 B7
Mossdale E Ayrs 153 K2
Moss Edge Lancs 120 F2
Mossend N Lans 175 K6
Mossley Tamesd 113 L2
Mosspaul Hotel
    Border 156 D3
Moss-side Highld 213 K4
Mosstodloch Moray 215 H3
Mossyard D & G 145 L5
Mossy Lea Lancs 121 H7
Mosterton Dorset 13 L2
Moston Manch 113 K2
Mostyn Flints 111 G5
Motcombe Dorset 27 J6
Mothecombe Devon 6 F6
Motherby Cumb 138 B2
Motherwell N Lans 175 K6
Motspur Park Gt Lon 44 E6
Mottingham Gt Lon 45 H5
Mottisfont Hants 28 F6
Mottistone IoW 16 E5
Mottram in
    Longdendale
    Tamesd 113 M3
Mottram St Andrew
    Ches E 113 K5
Mouldsworth Ches W...112 D7
Moulin P & K 194 E4
Moulsecoomb Br & H 19 J4
Moulsford Oxon 41 L4
Moulsoe M Keyn 74 C6
Moultavie Highld 222 E7
Moulton Ches W 112 F7
Moulton Lincs 104 A7
Moulton N York 141 G6
Moulton Nhants 73 L2
Moulton Suffk 77 G2
Moulton V Glam 37 G6
Moulton Chapel Lincs....103 M8
Moulton St Mary
    Norfk 93 H3
Moulton Seas End
    Lincs 104 A6
Mount Cnwll 5 J3
Mountain C Brad 123 G4
Mountain Ash
    Rhondd 53 G7
Mountain Cross
    Border 176 F8
Mount Ambrose
    Cnwll 3 J3
Mount Bures Essex 61 L2
Mountfield E Susx 20 E2
Mountgerald House
    Highld 212 E3
Mount Hawke Cnwll 3 J2
Mountjoy Cnwll 4 D4
Mount Lothian
    Mdloth 177 H6
Mountnessing Essex....60 F8
Mounton Mons...............38 D2
Mount Pleasant
    Derbys 101 G3
Mount Pleasant Suffk...77 G5
Mountsett
    Crematorium Dur ..150 E4
Mountsorrel Leics 87 H2
Mount Tabor Calder 122 F5
Mousehill Surrey...........30 F3
Mousehole Cnwll.............2 E6
Mouswald D & G 155 J7
Mow Cop Ches E............99 J2
Mowhaugh Border 168 B5
Mowsley Leics 87 J3
Moy Highld 202 C8
Moy Highld 213 J7
Moyle Highld 200 D2

Moylegrove Pembks....64 F5
Muasdale Ag & B 161 H2
Muchalls Abers 207 G6
Much Birch Herefs 54 D3
Much Cowarne
    Herefs 70 B5
Much Dewchurch
    Herefs 54 C2
Muchelney Somset 26 B6
Muchelney Ham
    Somset 26 C6
Much Hadham Herts 60 C4
Much Hoole Lancs 120 F6
Muchlarnick Cnwll 5 K5
Much Marcle Herefs.....54 F2
Much Wenlock
    Shrops 84 B4
Muck Highld 189 K1
Muckleburgh
    Collection Norfk 106 D4
Mucklestone Staffs......99 G5
Muckton Lincs 118 E5
Muddiford Devon 23 J4
Muddles Green E Susx ...20 B3
Mudeford Dorset 16 A4
Mudford Somset 26 E7
Mudford Sock
    Somset 26 E7
Mugdock Stirlg 175 G3
Mugeary Highld 209 G6
Mugginton Derbys 100 F4
Muirden Abers 216 D4
Muirdrum Angus 196 F8
Muiresk Abers 216 D5
Muirhead Angus 186 E1
Muirhead Fife 186 E6
Muirhead N Lans 175 J4
Muirkirk E Ayrs 164 D4
Muirmill Stirlg 175 J2
Muir of Fowlis Abers ...206 B3
Muir of Miltonduff
    Moray 214 E3
Muir of Ord Highld 212 E4
Muirshearlich Highld ...192 B1
Muirtack Abers 217 J6
Muirton P & K 185 J5
Muirton Mains
    Highld 212 C4
Muirton of Ardblair
    P & K 195 J7
Muker N York 139 K7
Mulbarton Norfk 92 E4
Mulben Moray 215 H4
Mull Ag & B 181 J1
Mullion Cnwll 3 H7
Mullion Cove Cnwll 3 H7
Mumby Lincs 119 G6
Munderfield Row
    Herefs 70 B4
Munderfield Stocks
    Herefs 70 B4
Mundesley Norfk 107 G5
Mundford Norfk............91 H5
Mundham Norfk............93 G4
Mundon Hill Essex........61 K7
Mungrisdale Cumb 137 K2
Munlochy Highld 213 G4
Munnoch N Ayrs 174 B8
Munsley Herefs.............70 B6
Munslow Shrops...........83 K6
Murchington Devon 11 G7
Murcott Oxon 57 L5
Murkle Highld 231 H2
Murlaggan Highld 200 F6
Murroes Angus 187 G1
Murrow Cambs..............89 L3
Mursley Bucks...............58 D3
Murthill Angus 196 D5
Murthly P & K 195 H8
Murton C York 133 K8
Murton Cumb 139 G3
Murton Dur 151 J5
Murton Nthumb 179 K8
Musbury Devon 14 H4
Musselburgh E Loth....177 K4
Muston Leics 102 D5
Muston N York 135 H4

Muswell Hill Gt Lon 44 F3
Mutehill D & G 146 C5
Mutford Suffk 93 K6
Muthill P & K 185 H4
Mybster Highld 231 H5
Myddfai Carmth 52 B3
Myddle Shrops 98 C7
Mydroilyn Cerdgn 66 B4
Mylor Cnwll 4 C8
Mylor Bridge Cnwll 4 C8
Mynachlog ddu
    Pembks 49 K2
Mynydd-bach Mons 38 C2
Mynydd-Bach Swans 51 J6
Mynyddgarreg
    Carmth 50 E4
Mynydd Isa Flints 111 J8
Myrebird Abers 206 E5
Myredykes Border 157 G3
Mytchett Surrey 30 E1
Mytholm Calder 122 E5
Mytholmroyd Calder ...122 F5
Myton-on-Swale
    N York 132 F6

N

Naast Highld 219 J5
Na Buirgh W Isls 232 d4
Naburn C York 124 F2
Nab Wood
    Crematorium
    C Brad 123 H3
Nackington Kent 34 F4
Nacton Suffk 78 F6
Nafferton E R Yk..........135 G7
Nailbourne Somset 25 K5
Nailsea N Som 38 C6
Nailstone Leics 86 E3
Nailsworth Gloucs 55 J7
Nairn Highld 213 K3
Nannerch Flints 111 G7
Nanpantan Leics 87 G1
Nanpean Cnwll 4 F5
Nanstallon Cnwll 5 G3
Nanternis Cerdgn 65 L3
Nantgaredig Carmth 50 F2
Nantglyn Denbgs 96 F1
Nantmel Powys 68 B2
Nantmor Gwynd 95 K4
Nant Peris Gwynd 95 K2
Nantwich Ches E 98 F3
Nantyglo Blae G 53 J6
Nant-y-moel Brdgnd 36 E2
Naphill Bucks 42 D2
Napton on the Hill
    Warwks 72 F3
Narberth Pembks 49 J4
Narborough Leics 87 G4
Narborough Norfk........91 H2
Nasareth Gwynd...........95 H3
Naseby Nhants 87 K7
Nash Bucks 73 L7
Nash Newpt 37 M4
Nash Shrops 69 L1
Nassington Nhants 88 F4
Nateby Cumb 139 H6
Nateby Lancs 120 F2
National Memorial
    Arboretum Staffs.....85 L1
National Motor
    Museum
    (Beaulieu) Hants ...16 E2
National Space
    Science Centre
    C Leic 87 H3
Natland Cumb 129 L2
Naughton Suffk 78 B5
Naunton Gloucs 56 C4
Naunton Worcs 70 F6
Naunton Beauchamp
    Worcs 71 G4
Navenby Lincs 103 G2
Navestock Essex 45 K1
Navestock Side Essex...60 E8

Navidale House
    Hotel Highld 227 J5
Navity Highld 213 J2
Nawton N York 133 K3
Nayland Suffk 77 L7
Nazeing Essex 60 C6
Neap Shet 235 d5
Near Cotton Staffs 100 B4
Near Sawrey Cumb 137 K7
Neasden Gt Lon 44 E3
Neasham Darltn 141 H4
Neath Neath 51 L6
Neatham Hants 30 C4
Neatishead Norfk........107 H7
Nebo Cerdgn 66 D2
Nebo Conwy 96 C2
Nebo Gwynd 95 H3
Nebo IoA 108 F4
Necton Norfk 91 K2
Nedd Highld 224 D4
Nedging Suffk 78 B5
Nedging Tye Suffk 78 B4
Needham Norfk.............92 F6
Needham Market
    Suffk 78 C4
Needingworth
    Cambs 75 L1
Neen Savage Shrops 84 C7
Neen Sollars Shrops 84 B8
Neenton Shrops 84 B5
Nefyn Gwynd 94 E4
Neilston E Rens............174 E6
Nelson Caerph 37 H2
Nelson Lancs 122 C3
Nemphlar S Lans 165 G1
Nempnett Thrubwell
    BaNES 38 D7
Nenthead Cumb 149 K6
Nenthorn Border 167 K2
Nercwys Flints 97 K1
Nereabolls Ag & B 170 E7
Nerston S Lans 175 H6
Nesbit Nthumb 168 E3
Nesfield N York 123 G1
Ness Botanic
    Gardens Ches W....111 J6
Nesscliffe Shrops 98 B8
Neston Ches W 111 J6
Neston Wilts 39 K6
Netchwood Shrops.......84 B5
Nether Alderley
    Ches E 113 J6
Netheravon Wilts 28 D2
Nether Blainslie
    Border 167 H2
Netherbrae Abers 216 F3
Nether Broughton
    Leics 102 B7
Netherburn S Lans 175 L8
Netherbury Dorset 13 L3
Netherby N York 123 L2
Nether Cerne Dorset 14 C3
Nethercleuch D & G 155 K5
Nether Compton
    Dorset 26 E7
Nether Crimond
    Abers 206 F2
Nether Dallachy
    Moray 215 H2
Netherend Gloucs 54 E7
Netherfield E Susx 20 E2
Nether Fingland
    S Lans 165 H7
Netherhampton Wilts ...28 C5
Nether Handwick
    Angus 196 B7
Nether Haugh Rothm...115 H3
Netherhay Dorset 13 K2
Nether Headon Notts...116 C6
Nether Heage Derbys...101 G3
Nether Heyford
    Nhants 73 J3
Nether Howcleugh
    S Lans 165 K6
Nether Kellet Lancs 129 K6
Nether Kinmundy
    Abers 217 K5

Nether Langwith
  Notts...........115 K7
Netherlaw D & G......146 C6
Netherley Abers..........207 G6
Nethermill D & G..........155 H5
Nethermuir Abers.......217 G5
Netherne-on-the-Hill
  Surrey................32 B3
Netheroyd Hill Kirk......123 H6
Nether Padley Derbys...114 E6
Netherplace E Rens....174 F7
Nether Poppleton
  C York...............133 J8
Netherseal Derbys.......86 C2
Nether Silton N York.....133 G2
Nether Stowey
  Somset................25 J4
Netherthong Kirk........123 H8
Netherton Angus.......196 E6
Netherton Devon.......7 K2
Netherton Dudley........85 G6
Netherton Kirk...........123 H7
Netherton N Lans.......175 K7
Netherton Nthumb......168 E7
Netherton P & K.......195 J6
Netherton Stirlg.......175 G3
Netherton Wakefd.....123 K6
Nethertown Cumb.....136 D5
Nethertown Highld.....231 L1
Nethertown Staffs.....100 C8
Netherurd Border......165 L1
Nether Wallop Hants...28 F4
Nether Wasdale
  Cumb..............136 F6
Nether Westcote
  Gloucs..............56 E4
Nether Whitacre
  Warwks..............86 B5
Nether Whitecleuch
  S Lans.............165 G5
Nether Winchendon
  Bucks................58 B5
Netherwitton
  Nthumb............158 D4
Nethy Bridge Highld...204 B2
Netley Hants..........16 F2
Netley Marsh Hants......29 G8
Nettlebed Oxon........42 B3
Nettlebridge Somset...26 F2
Nettlecombe Dorset....13 M4
Nettleden Herts.........59 G6
Nettleham Lincs.......117 G6
Nettlestead Kent.......33 H3
Nettlestead Green
  Kent................33 H3
Nettlestone IoW.......17 H4
Nettlesworth Dur......151 G5
Nettleton Lincs.......117 J2
Nettleton Wilts.......39 J5
Netton Wilts...........28 C4
Nevern Pembks.......64 F6
Nevill Holt Leics.......88 B5
New Abbey D & G...147 G2
New Aberdour Abers....217 G2
New Addington
  Gt Lon.............45 G7
Newall Leeds..........123 J2
New Alresford Hants...29 L5
New Alyth P & K.......195 K6
Newark Ork...........234 e4
Newark-on-Trent
  Notts..............102 D2
Newarthill N Lans.....175 K6
New Ash Green Kent....45 L6
New Balderton Notts...102 D3
New Barn Kent.......45 L6
New Barnet Gt Lon....44 F2
Newbattle Mdloth....177 J5
New Bewick Nthumb...169 G5
Newbie D & G.......147 L3
Newbiggin Cumb.....138 C2
Newbiggin Cumb.....138 F2
Newbiggin Cumb.....148 F5
Newbiggin Dur.......139 K2
Newbiggin N York....131 J3
Newbiggin-by-the-
  Sea Nthumb..........159 H5

Newbigging Angus......187 H1
Newbigging Angus......195 L7
Newbigging Angus......196 C8
Newbigging S Lans......165 K1
Newbiggin-on-Lune
  Cumb..............139 G6
New Bilton Warwks......86 F7
Newbold Derbys.......115 G6
Newbold on Avon
  Warwks..............86 F7
Newbold on Stour
  Warwks..............72 B5
Newbold Pacey
  Warwks..............72 C3
Newbold Verdon
  Leics................86 F3
New Bolingbroke
  Lincs..............104 A2
Newborough C Pete......89 H3
Newborough IoA.......108 E7
Newborough Staffs.....100 C7
New Boultham Lincs ...116 F7
Newbourne Suffk.......78 F6
New Bradwell M Keyn ...74 B6
New Brampton
  Derbys.............115 G6
New Brancepeth Dur...151 G6
Newbridge C Edin......176 F4
Newbridge Caerph.......37 K2
Newbridge Cnwll.......2 D5
Newbridge D & G.......155 G6
Newbridge Hants.......28 F7
Newbridge IoW.......16 E5
Newbridge Green
  Worcs..............70 E6
Newbridge on Wye
  Powys..............67 L3
New Brighton Wirral....111 J3
Newbrough Nthumb....149 L2
New Buckenham
  Norfk................92 C5
Newbuildings Devon....11 J4
Newburgh Abers.......207 J1
Newburgh Abers.......217 H3
Newburgh Fife.......186 D4
Newburgh Lancs.......121 G7
Newburgh Priory
  N York.............133 H4
Newburn N u Ty.......150 F2
Newbury Somset........27 G2
Newbury W Berk.......41 J6
Newbury Park Gt Lon....45 J3
Newby Cumb.........138 E3
Newby Lancs.........122 B2
Newby N York.......130 D5
Newby N York.......142 B5
Newby Bridge Cumb...129 H3
Newby East Cumb.....148 E4
New Byth Abers.......216 F4
Newby West Cumb.....148 C4
Newcastle Mons.......54 C5
Newcastle Shrops......82 E6
Newcastle Airport
  Nthumb...........158 F7
Newcastle Emlyn
  Carmth..............65 J6
Newcastleton Border...156 E5
Newcastle-under-
  Lyme Staffs..........99 J4
Newcastle upon
  Tyne N u Ty.......151 G3
Newchapel Pembks......65 H6
Newchapel Surrey......32 C5
Newchurch IoW.......17 G5
Newchurch Kent.......34 E7
Newchurch Mons.......38 C2
Newchurch Powys......68 E4
Newchurch Staffs......100 D7
New Costessey Norfk...92 D2
Newcraighall C Edin...177 J4
New Crofton Wakefd....124 B6
New Cross Gt Lon.......45 G5
New Cross Somset.......26 B7
New Cumnock E Ayrs ...164 C6
New Deer Abers.......217 G5
New Denham Bucks.....43 H4
Newdigate Surrey......31 K3

New Duston Nhants.....73 K3
New Earswick C York...133 J7
New Edlington Donc....115 K2
New Elgin Moray.........214 F3
New Ellerby E R Yk.....126 E3
Newell Green Br For....42 E6
New Eltham Gt Lon......45 H5
New End Worcs.......71 J3
Newenden Kent.......33 L7
New England C Pete.....89 H4
Newent Gloucs.......55 G3
Newfield Dur.........150 F7
Newfield Highld.......223 H6
New Fletton C Pete......89 H4
New Forest
  National Park
  Hants................16 C2
Newgale Pembks.......48 E3
New Galloway D & G ...154 B6
Newgate Street Herts...59 M6
New Gilston Fife.......187 G5
New Grimsby IoS.......2 a1
Newhall Ches E.......98 E4
New Hartley Nthumb...159 H6
Newhaven C Edin......177 H3
Newhaven E Susx.......19 L5
New Haw Surrey........43 H7
New Hedges Pembks....49 J6
New Holland N Linc....126 D5
Newholm N York.......143 H5
New Houghton
  Derbys.............115 J7
New Houghton Norfk ...105 J6
Newhouse N Lans.....175 L6
New Hutton Cumb.....130 B2
Newick E Susx.........19 L2
Newington Kent.........35 G7
Newington Kent.......46 E6
Newington Oxon.......41 L2
New Inn Carmth.......66 B6
New Inn Torfn.........53 L7
New Invention
  Shrops.............82 F7
New Lakenham Norfk...92 F3
New Lanark S Lans....165 G2
Newland C KuH.......126 D4
Newland Gloucs.......54 D6
Newland N York.......125 G5
Newland Somset.......24 C4
Newland Worcs.......70 E5
Newlandrig Mdloth....177 K6
Newlands Border.......156 E4
Newlands Nthumb....150 D4
Newlands of
  Dundurcas Moray...215 G4
New Langholm D & G ...156 C5
New Leake Lincs.......104 C2
New Leeds Abers.......217 J4
New Lodge Barns......123 L8
New Longton Lancs....121 G5
New Luce D & G.......144 E3
Newlyn Cnwll.........2 E5
Newlyn East Cnwll.....4 C5
Newmachar Abers.....207 G2
Newmains N Lans.....175 L6
New Malden Gt Lon....44 E6
Newman's Green
  Suffk................77 K5
Newmarket Suffk.......76 F2
Newmarket W Isls......232 f2
New Marske R & Cl....142 D3
New Marston Oxon......57 K6
New Mill Abers.......206 E8
Newmill Border.......167 G7
New Mill Cnwll.........2 E4
New Mill Kirk.........123 H8
Newmill Moray.......215 K4
Newmillerdam
  Wakefd............123 L7
Newmill of Inshewan
  Angus.............196 C4
Newmills C Edin......177 G5
New Mills Derbys.....113 M4
Newmills Fife.........176 D2
Newmills Mons.......54 D6
New Mills Powys.......82 C4
Newmiln P & K.......186 B2

Newmilns E Ayrs.......164 B2
New Milton Hants.......16 B4
New Mistley Essex.......62 D2
New Moat Pembks.......49 H3
Newney Green Essex....61 G6
Newnham Gloucs.......55 G5
Newnham Hants.......30 B2
Newnham Herts.......75 J6
Newnham Kent.......34 C3
Newnham Nhants.......73 H3
Newnham Worcs.......70 B2
New Ollerton Notts....116 A7
New Pitsligo Abers....217 G3
Newport Cnwll.........9 J7
Newport E R Yk.......125 K4
Newport Essex.......76 D7
Newport Gloucs.......39 G2
Newport Highld.......227 K4
Newport IoW.........16 F5
Newport Newpt.......37 L3
Newport Pembks.......64 E6
Newport Wrekin.......99 H8
Newport-on-Tay Fife ...187 G2
Newport Pagnell
  M Keyn.............74 C5
Newport Pagnell
  Services M Keyn.....74 C5
New Prestwick S Ayrs...163 J4
New Quay Cerdgn......65 L3
Newquay Cnwll.........4 C4
Newquay Airport
  Cnwll................4 D3
New Rackheath
  Norfk................93 G2
New Radnor Powys.....68 E3
New Ridley Nthumb....150 D3
New Romney Kent......21 L2
New Rossington
  Donc..............115 L2
New Sauchie Clacks...185 J7
Newseat Abers.......216 D7
Newsham Lancs.......121 G4
Newsham N York......132 E3
Newsham N York......140 E5
Newsham Nthumb....159 H4
New Sharlston
  Wakefd............124 B6
Newsholme E R Yk....125 H5
New Silksworth
  Sundld............151 J4
Newsome Kirk.......123 H7
New Somerby Lincs...102 F5
New Southgate
  Crematorium
  Gt Lon.............44 F2
Newstead Border.......167 H3
Newstead Notts.......101 K3
Newstead Nthumb....169 H4
New Stevenston
  N Lans.............175 K6
Newthorpe Notts......101 J4
Newton Ag & B.......182 F7
Newton Border.......167 J5
Newton Brdgnd.......36 C5
Newton C Beds.......75 J5
Newton Cambs.......76 B5
Newton Cambs.......90 B1
Newton Ches W.......98 D1
Newton Ches W.......112 B7
Newton Cumb.......128 F5
Newton Derbys.......101 H2
Newton Herefs.......53 M2
Newton Herefs.......69 K4
Newton Highld.......212 F4
Newton Highld.......213 H5
Newton Highld.......213 J2
Newton Highld.......231 L5
Newton Lincs.......103 H5
Newton Mdloth.......177 J4
Newton Moray.......214 E2
Newton Moray.......215 H2
Newton Nhants.......88 C6
Newton Norfk.......91 J1
Newton Notts.......102 B4
Newton Nthumb....150 C3
Newton S Lans.......165 H3
Newton S Lans.......175 H6

Newton Staffs....100 B7
Newton Suffk....77 K6
Newton W Loth....176 E3
Newton Warwks....87 G7
Newton Abbot Devon....7 K2
Newton Arlosh Cumb..147 L4
Newton Aycliffe Dur...141 G3
Newton Bewley
Hartpl....141 K2
Newton Blossomville
M Keyn....74 D4
Newton Bromswold
Nhants....74 E2
Newton Burgoland
Leics....86 D2
Newton-by-the-Sea
Nthumb....169 J4
Newton by Toft Lincs...117 H4
Newton Ferrers Cnwll....6 A3
Newton Ferrers
Devon....6 E6
Newton Ferry W Isls....232 C5
Newton Flotman
Norfk....92 E4
Newtongrange
Mdloth....177 J5
Newton Green Mons....38 D3
Newton Harcourt
Leics....87 J4
Newton Heath Manch..113 K2
Newtonhill Abers....207 G6
Newton-in-Bowland
Lancs....121 K1
Newton Kyme N York..124 C2
Newton-le-Willows
N York....132 C2
Newton-le-Willows
St Hel....112 E3
Newtonloan Mdloth....177 J5
Newton Longville
Bucks....58 D2
Newton Mearns
E Rens....174 F7
Newtonmill Angus....196 F4
Newtonmore Highld....203 H5
Newton Morrell
N York....141 G5
Newton of
Balcanquhal P & K..186 B5
Newton of Balcormo
Fife....187 H6
Newton on Ouse
N York....133 H7
Newton-on-
Rawcliffe N York..134 C2
Newton-on-the-
Moor Nthumb....158 F2
Newton on Trent
Lincs....116 D6
Newton Poppleford
Devon....12 E4
Newton Purcell Oxon...57 L3
Newton Regis
Warwks....86 C3
Newton Reigny
Cumb....138 C2
Newton St Cyres
Devon....11 K5
Newton St Faith
Norfk....92 F1
Newton St Loe BaNES..39 G7
Newton St Petrock
Devon....9 K3
Newton Solney
Derbys....100 F7
Newton Stacey Hants...29 H4
Newton Stewart
D & G....145 J3
Newton Tony Wilts....28 E4
Newton Tracey
Devon....23 H6
Newton under
Roseberry R & Cl..142 C5
Newton upon
Derwent E R Yk..125 H2
Newton Valence
Hants....30 B5

Newton Wamphray
D & G....155 K3
Newton with Scales
Lancs....120 F4
Newtown Cumb....147 J5
Newtown Cumb....148 E3
Newtown D & G....164 F7
Newtown Devon....12 D3
Newtown Devon....24 B6
New Town Dorset....27 L7
New Town Dorset....27 M7
New Town E Susx....19 M2
Newtown Gloucs....54 F7
Newtown Hants....29 L8
Newtown Herefs....70 B5
Newtown Herefs....70 C6
Newtown Highld....202 B4
Newtown IoW....16 E4
Newtown Nthumb....168 F4
Newtown Poole....15 K4
Newtown Powys....82 C5
Newtown Shrops....98 B7
Newtown Shrops....98 C6
Newtown Somset....25 L8
Newtown Staffs....99 K1
Newtown Wigan....112 E1
Newtown Worcs....70 F4
Newtown Linford
Leics....87 G2
Newtown of
Beltrees Rens....174 D6
Newtown St
Boswells Border....167 J3
New Tredegar Caerph....53 H7
New Trows S Lans....164 F2
Newtyle Angus....195 L7
New Walsoken
Cambs....90 C2
New Waltham NE Lin....118 C1
New Winton E Loth....177 L4
Newyork Ag & B....182 D5
New York Lincs....103 L2
Neyland Pembks....49 G6
Nicholashayne Devon...25 H7
Nicholaston Swans....51 G7
Nidd N York....132 D7
Nigg C Aber....207 H5
Nigg Highld....223 H6
Nigg Ferry Highld....223 H7
Ninebanks Nthumb....149 K4
Nine Elms Swindn....40 C3
Ninfield E Susx....20 E3
Ningwood IoW....16 E5
Nisbet Border....167 K4
Nisbet Hill Border....179 G7
Niton IoW....17 F6
Nitshill C Glas....174 F6
Nocton Lincs....117 H8
Noke Oxon....57 K5
Nolton Pembks....48 E4
Nolton Haven
Pembks....48 E4
No Man's Heath
Ches W....98 D3
No Man's Heath
Warwks....86 C2
Nomansland Devon....11 J3
Nomansland Wilts....28 E7
Noneley Shrops....98 C6
Nonington Kent....35 H4
Nook Cumb....129 L3
Norbiton Gt Lon....44 D6
Norbury Ches E....98 E3
Norbury Derbys....100 C4
Norbury Gt Lon....44 F6
Norbury Shrops....83 G5
Norbury Staffs....99 H7
Norchard Worcs....70 F2
Nordelph Norfk....90 D4
Nordley Shrops....84 C4
Norfolk Broads Norfk...93 K2
Norham Nthumb....179 J8
Norley Ches W....112 E6
Norleywood Hants....16 D3
Normanby Lincs....117 G4
Normanby N Linc....125 K7
Normanby N York....134 B3

Normanby R & Cl....142 C4
Normanby le Wold
Lincs....117 J3
Normandy Surrey....30 F2
Norman's Green
Devon....12 D2
Normanton C Derb....101 G5
Normanton Leics....102 D4
Normanton Lincs....102 F4
Normanton Notts....102 B2
Normanton Wakefd....124 B6
Normanton le Heath
Leics....86 D2
Normanton on Soar
Notts....101 K7
Normanton on the
Wolds Notts....101 L6
Normanton on Trent
Notts....116 C7
Norris Green Lpool....111 L3
Norris Hill Leics....86 D1
Norristhorpe Kirk....123 J6
Northall Bucks....58 F4
Northallerton N York...141 J7
Northam C Sotn....29 H8
Northam Devon....23 G5
Northampton Nhants....73 L3
Northampton Worcs....70 E2
North Anston Rothm....115 K5
North Ascot Br For....42 E6
North Aston Oxon....57 J3
Northaw Herts....59 L7
Northay Somset....13 H1
North Baddesley
Hants....29 H7
North Ballachulish
Highld....191 L4
North Barrow Somset....26 E5
North Barsham Norfk..105 L5
North Benfleet Essex....46 C3
North Bersted W Susx...18 C5
North Berwick E Loth..178 C2
North Boarhunt
Hants....17 H1
Northborough C Pete...89 H3
Northbourne Kent....35 J4
North Bovey Devon....11 H7
North Bradley Wilts....27 J1
North Brentor Devon....10 C8
North Brewham
Somset....27 G4
Northbrook Hants....29 K4
North Buckland
Devon....23 G4
North Burlingham
Norfk....93 H2
North Cadbury
Somset....26 F6
North Carlton Lincs....116 F6
North Carlton Notts....115 L4
North Cave E R Yk....125 K4
North Cerney Gloucs....56 A6
North Chailey E Susx....19 K2
Northchapel W Susx....30 F5
North Charford Hants...28 D7
North Charlton
Nthumb....169 H5
North Cheam Gt Lon....44 E6
North Cheriton
Somset....27 G6
North Chideock
Dorset....13 K4
Northchurch Herts....58 F6
North Cliffe E R Yk....125 K3
North Clifton Notts....116 D6
North Cockerington
Lincs....118 E4
North Connel Ag & B....182 C1
North Cornelly
Brdgnd....36 C4
North Cotes Lincs....118 E2
Northcott Devon....9 J6
Northcourt Oxon....57 J7
North Cove Suffk....93 K5
North Cowton N York..141 G6
North Crawley
M Keyn....74 D5

North Creake Norfk....105 K5
North Curry Somset....25 L6
North Dalton E R Yk...125 L1
North Deighton
N York....124 B1
North Devon
Crematorium
Devon....23 H5
Northdown Kent....35 K2
North Downs....34 B4
North Duffield N York..125 G3
North Duntulm
Highld....218 C6
North East Surrey
Crematorium
Gt Lon....44 E6
North Elmham Norfk..106 B7
North Elmsall Wakefd..124 D7
North End C Port....17 J3
North End Essex....61 G4
North End Hants....28 C7
North End Nhants....74 D2
North End W Susx....18 D5
Northend Warwks....72 E4
Northenden Manch....113 J4
North Erradale Highld..219 H5
North Evington C Leic...87 J3
North Fambridge
Essex....61 K7
North Ferriby E R Yk..126 B5
Northfield Birm....85 H7
Northfield C Aber....207 G4
Northfield E R Yk....126 C5
Northfields Lincs....88 E2
Northfleet Kent....45 M5
North Frodingham
E R Yk....135 H8
North Gorley Hants....15 M1
North Green Suffk....79 G3
North Greetwell Lincs..117 G6
North Grimston
N York....134 C6
North Hayling Hants....17 K2
North Hill Cnwll....5 L1
North Hillingdon
Gt Lon....43 H4
North Hinksey
Village Oxon....57 J6
North Holmwood
Surrey....31 K3
North Huish Devon....7 G5
North Hykeham Lincs..116 F7
Northiam E Susx....21 G2
Northill C Beds....75 G5
Northington Hants....29 K4
North Kelsey Lincs....117 H2
North Kessock Highld..213 G5
North Killingholme
N Linc....126 E6
North Kilvington
N York....132 F3
North Kilworth Leics....87 H6
North Kyme Lincs....103 J3
North Landing E R Yk..135 K5
Northlands Lincs....104 B2
Northleach Gloucs....56 C5
North Lee Bucks....58 D6
Northleigh Devon....12 F3
North Leigh Oxon....57 H5
North Leverton with
Habblesthorpe
Notts....116 C5
Northlew Devon....10 D5
North Littleton Worcs...71 J3
North Lopham Norfk....92 C6
North Luffenham
Rutlnd....88 D3
North Marden W Susx...30 D7
North Marston Bucks....58 C4
North Middleton
Mdloth....177 K6
North Millbrook Abers..216 F5
North Milmain D & G....144 C4
North Molton Devon....24 B5
Northmoor Oxon....57 H7
North Moreton Oxon....41 K3
Northmuir Angus....196 C5

North Mundham
W Susx 18 B5
North Muskham
Notts 102 D2
North Newbald E R Yk .. 125 L3
North Newington
Oxon 72 E6
North Newton Wilts 40 C8
North Newton
Somset 25 L5
Northney Hants 17 K2
North Nibley Gloucs 39 H2
Northolt Gt Lon 43 J4
Northop Flints 111 H7
Northop Hall Flints 111 J7
North Ormesby
Middsb 142 B4
North Ormsby Lincs 118 C3
Northorpe Kirk 123 J6
Northorpe Lincs 103 K5
Northorpe Lincs 116 E3
North Otterington
N York 132 E2
North Owersby Lincs 117 H3
Northowram Calder 123 G5
North Perrott
Somset 13 L1
North Petherton
Somset 25 L5
North Petherwin
Cnwll 9 H6
North Pickenham
Norfk 91 J3
North Piddle Worcs 71 G4
North Poorton Dorset ... 13 M3
Northport Dorset 15 H5
North Queensferry
Fife 176 F3
North Rauceby Lincs 103 G3
Northrepps Norfk 106 F5
North Reston Lincs 118 E5
North Rigton N York 123 K1
North Rode Ches E 113 K7
North Ronaldsay Ork .. 234 e3
North Ronaldsay
Airport Ork 234 e3
North Runcton Norfk 90 F1
North Scarle Lincs 116 D7
North Shian Ag & B 191 H7
North Shields N Tyne 151 J2
North Shoebury
Sthend 46 F3
North Shore Bpool 120 D3
North Side C Pete 89 K4
North Somercotes
Lincs 118 F3
North Stainley
N York 132 D4
North Stifford Thurr 45 L4
North Stoke BaNES 39 G6
North Stoke Oxon 41 L3
North Stoke W Susx 18 D4
North Street Kent 34 D3
North Street W Berk 41 M6
North Sunderland
Nthumb 169 J3
North Tamerton
Cnwll 9 J5
North Tawton Devon 10 F4
North Third Stirlg 175 K1
North Thoresby Lincs ... 118 D2
Northton W Isls 232 d5
North Town Devon 10 D3
North Town Somset 26 E3
North Town W & M 42 E4
North Tuddenham
Norfk 92 C2
North Uist W Isls 233 b6
Northumberland
National Park
Nthumb 157 L3
North Walsham Norfk .. 107 G6
North Warnham Hants ... 29 K3
North Warnborough
Hants 30 B2
North Weald Bassett
Essex 60 D7

North Wheatley
Notts 116 C4
Northwich Ches W 112 F6
Northwick Worcs 70 E3
North Widcombe
BaNES 38 E8
North Willingham
Lincs 117 K4
North Wingfield
Derbys 115 H8
North Witham Lincs 102 F7
Northwold Norfk 91 H4
Northwood Gt Lon 43 H3
Northwood IoW 16 F4
Northwood Shrops 98 C6
Northwood Green
Gloucs 55 G5
North Wootton
Dorset 26 F8
North Wootton Norfk .. 105 G7
North Wootton
Somset 26 E3
North Wraxall Wilts 39 J5
North York Moors
National Park
N York 142 F6
Norton Donc 124 E7
Norton E Susx 19 M5
Norton Gloucs 55 J3
Norton Halton 112 D5
Norton N York 134 C5
Norton Nhants 73 H2
Norton Notts 115 L6
Norton Powys 68 F2
Norton S on T 141 K3
Norton Shrops 84 D4
Norton Suffk 77 L2
Norton W Susx 18 C4
Norton Wilts 39 K4
Norton Worcs 70 F4
Norton Worcs 71 J5
Norton Bavant Wilts 27 K3
Norton Bridge Staffs 99 K6
Norton Canes Staffs 85 H2
Norton Canes
Services Staffs 85 H3
Norton Canon Herefs 69 H5
Norton Disney Lincs 102 E2
Norton Fitzwarren
Somset 25 J6
Norton Green IoW 16 D5
Norton Hawkfield
BaNES 38 E7
Norton Heath Essex 60 F6
Norton in Hales
Shrops 99 G5
Norton-Juxta-
Twycross Leics 86 D3
Norton-le-Clay N York .. 132 F5
Norton Lindsey
Warwks 72 B2
Norton Little Green
Suffk 77 L2
Norton Malreward
BaNES 38 E7
Norton St Philip
Somset 27 H1
Norton Subcourse
Norfk 93 J4
Norton sub Hamdon
Somset 26 C7
Norwell Notts 102 C1
Norwell Woodhouse
Notts 116 B8
Norwich Norfk 92 F2
Norwich Airport Norfk .. 92 E2
Norwich Cathedral
Norfk 92 F2
Norwich (St Faith)
Crematorium
Norfk 92 F1
Norwick Shet 235 e1
Norwood Clacks 185 J8
Norwood Green
Gt Lon 43 J5
Norwood Hill Surrey 31 L3
Noss Mayo Devon 6 E6

Nosterfield N York 132 D4
Nostie Highld 210 D8
Notgrove Gloucs 56 C4
Nottage Brdgnd 36 C5
Nottingham C Nott 101 L5
Notton Wakefd 123 L7
Notton Wilts 39 K6
Noutard's Green
Worcs 70 E2
Nuffield Oxon 42 A3
Nunburnholme
E R Yk 125 K2
Nuneaton Warwks 86 D5
Nunhead Gt Lon 45 G5
Nun Monkton N York ... 133 H7
Nunney Somset 27 G3
Nunnington N York 133 K4
Nunsthorpe NE Lin 127 G8
Nunthorpe C York 124 F1
Nunthorpe Middsb 142 C4
Nunthorpe Village
Middsb 142 C5
Nunton Wilts 28 D6
Nunwick N York 132 E5
Nursling Hants 29 G7
Nutbourne W Susx 17 L2
Nutbourne W Susx 18 E3
Nutfield Surrey 32 B3
Nuthall Notts 101 K4
Nuthampstead Herts 76 B7
Nuthurst W Susx 31 K6
Nutley E Susx 32 D7
Nuttall Bury 122 B7
Nybster Highld 231 L3
Nyetimber W Susx 18 B6
Nyewood W Susx 30 D6
Nymet Rowland
Devon 11 G4
Nymet Tracey Devon 11 G5
Nympsfield Gloucs 55 J7
Nynehead Somset 25 H6
Nyton W Susx 18 C5

Oadby Leics 87 J4
Oad Street Kent 34 B3
Oakamoor Staffs 100 B4
Oakbank W Loth 176 E5
Oak Cross Devon 10 D5
Oakdale Caerph 37 J2
Oake Somset 25 J6
Oaken Staffs 84 F3
Oakenclough Lancs 121 H2
Oakengates Wrekin 84 C2
Oakenshaw Dur 150 F7
Oakenshaw Kirk 123 H5
Oakford Cerdgn 66 B3
Oakford Devon 24 E6
Oakham Rutlnd 88 C2
Oakhanger Hants 30 C4
Oakhill Somset 26 F3
Oakington Cambs 76 B2
Oakle Street Gloucs 55 H4
Oakley Bed 74 E4
Oakley Bucks 57 M5
Oakley Fife 176 D1
Oakley Hants 29 K2
Oakley Suffk 92 E7
Oakridge Gloucs 55 K7
Oaksey Wilts 39 M2
Oakthorpe Leics 86 D2
Oakwood C Derb 101 G5
Oakworth C Brad 122 F3
Oare Kent 34 D3
Oare Somset 24 C3
Oare Wilts 40 D7
Oasby Lincs 103 G5
Oath Somset 26 B6
Oathlaw Angus 196 C5
Oatlands Park Surrey 43 H7
Oban Ag & B 182 B2
Oban Airport Ag & B 182 C1
Obley Shrops 83 G7
Obney P & K 195 G8

Oborne Dorset 26 F7
Occold Suffk 78 D1
Occumster Highld 231 J7
Ochiltree E Ayrs 163 L5
Ockbrook Derbys 101 H5
Ockham Surrey 31 H1
Ockle Highld 190 B3
Ockley Surrey 31 J4
Ocle Pychard Herefs 69 L5
Odcombe Somset 26 D7
Odd Down BaNES 39 H7
Oddingley Worcs 71 G3
Oddington Gloucs 56 E3
Oddington Oxon 57 K5
Odell Bed 74 D3
Odiham Hants 30 C2
Odsal C Brad 123 H5
Odsey Cambs 75 K6
Odstock Wilts 28 D6
Odstone Leics 86 E3
Offchurch Warwks 72 D2
Offenham Worcs 71 J5
Offerton Stockp 113 K4
Offham E Susx 19 L3
Offham Kent 33 H2
Offham W Susx 18 D4
Offord Cluny Cambs 75 J2
Offord D'Arcy Cambs 75 J2
Offton Suffk 78 C5
Offwell Devon 12 F3
Ogbourne Maizey
Wilts 40 D6
Ogbourne St Andrew
Wilts 40 D6
Ogbourne St George
Wilts 40 D5
Ogle Nthumb 158 E6
Oglet Lpool 112 C5
Ogmore V Glam 36 D5
Ogmore-by-Sea
V Glam 36 D5
Ogmore Vale Brdgnd 36 E3
Okeford Fitzpaine
Dorset 14 F1
Okehampton Devon 10 E5
Oker Side Derbys 100 F1
Okewood Hill Surrey 31 J4
Old Nhants 87 L8
Old Aberdeen C Aber ... 207 H4
Old Alresford Hants 29 L5
Oldany Highld 224 D2
Old Auchenbrack
D & G 154 D3
Old Basford C Nott 101 K4
Old Basing Hants 30 A2
Old Beetley Norfk 106 A8
Oldberrow Warwks 71 K2
Old Bewick Nthumb 169 G5
Old Bolingbroke Lincs .. 118 E8
Old Bramhope Leeds ... 123 J2
Old Brampton Derbys .. 115 G6
Old Bridge of Urr
D & G 146 D2
Old Buckenham
Norfk 92 C5
Old Burghclere Hants ... 41 J8
Oldbury Sandw 85 H5
Oldbury Shrops 84 C5
Oldbury Warwks 86 C5
Oldbury-on-Severn
S Glos 38 E2
Oldbury on the Hill
Gloucs 39 J3
Old Byland N York 133 H3
Old Cantley Donc 115 L2
Oldcastle Mons 53 L3
Old Catton Norfk 92 F2
Old Clee NE Lin 127 G8
Old Cleeve Somset 25 G3
Old Clipstone Notts 115 L8
Old Colwyn Conwy 110 B6
Oldcotes Notts 115 L4
Old Dailly S Ayrs 152 F3
Old Dalby Leics 102 A7
Old Deer Abers 217 J5
Old Edlington Donc 115 K3
Old Ellerby E R Yk 126 E3

Old Felixstowe Suffk 79 G7
Oldfield Worcs 70 E2
Old Fletton C Pete 89 H4
Oldford Somset................27 H2
Old Forge Herefs 54 E4
Old Grimsby IoS.................2 a1
Old Hall Green Herts 60 B4
Oldham Oldham...............113 L1
Oldhamstocks E Loth ...178 F4
Old Harlow Essex 60 D5
Old Hunstanton
  Norfk 105 G4
Old Hurst Cambs 89 K7
Old Hutton Cumb.........130 B2
Old Kilpatrick W Duns...174 E4
Old Knebworth Herts 59 L4
Old Lakenham Norfk 92 F3
Oldland S Glos 38 F6
Old Langho Lancs.........121 K4
Old Leake Lincs 104 C3
Old Malton N York 134 C5
Oldmeldrum Abers 216 F8
Oldmill Cnwll 6 B2
Old Milverton Warwks ...72 C2
Oldmixon N Som 37 M8
Old Newton Suffk...........78 C3
Old Radnor Powys.........68 E3
Old Rayne Abers...........216 D8
Old Romney Kent 21 K2
Old Shoreham W Susx ...19 G4
Oldshoremore Highld....228 C4
Old Sodbury S Glos........39 H4
Old Somerby Lincs 102 F5
Oldstead N York...........133 H4
Old Stratford Nhants......73 L6
Old Struan P & K 194 C4
Old Swinford Dudley 84 F6
Old Thirsk N York 132 F3
Old Town Cumb............130 B3
Old Town E Susx 20 C5
Old Town IoS 2 b2
Old Trafford Traffd.......113 J3
Oldwall Cumb...............148 E3
Oldwalls Swans 50 F6
Old Warden C Beds 75 G5
Old Weston Cambs.........89 G7
Old Wick Highld............231 L5
Old Windsor W & M 43 G5
Old Wives Lees Kent 34 E4
Old Woking Surrey 43 G8
Olgrinmore Highld.........231 G5
Olive Green Staffs........100 C8
Oliver's Battery Hants....29 J6
Ollaberry Shet 235 C3
Ollach Highld................209 H6
Ollerton Ches E 113 H6
Ollerton Notts...............116 A7
Ollerton Shrops..............98 F7
Olney M Keyn 74 C4
Olrig House Highld........231 H3
Olton Solihll 85 K6
Olveston S Glos 38 E3
Ombersley Worcs............70 E2
Ompton Notts 116 B7
Onchan IoM..................237 d5
Onecote Staffs..............100 B2
Onibury Shrops...............83 J7
Onich Highld.................191 K4
Onllwyn Neath.................52 C6
Onneley Staffs.................99 H4
Onslow Green Essex 61 G4
Onslow Village Surrey 31 G2
Onston Ches W 112 E6
Opinan Highld................219 H6
Orbliston Moray.............215 G3
Orbost Highld................208 D5
Orby Lincs 119 G7
Orchard Portman
  Somset 25 K6
Orcheston Wilts 28 B3
Orcop Herefs...................54 C3
Orcop Hill Herefs............54 C3
Ord Abers.....................216 C3
Ordhead Abers 206 C3
Ordie Abers 205 K5
Ordiequish Moray..........215 H3
Ordsall Notts.................116 B5

Ore E Susx......................21 G4
Orford Suffk 79 J4
Orford Warrtn 112 E4
Organford Dorset 15 H4
Orkney Islands Ork 234 c6
Orlestone Kent 34 D7
Orleton Herefs................69 J2
Orleton Worcs.................70 C2
Orlingbury Nhants...........74 C1
Ormesby R & Cl.............142 C4
Ormesby St
  Margaret Norfk.............93 K1
Ormesby St Michael
  Norfk 93 K1
Ormiscaig Highld...........219 K4
Ormiston E Loth 177 L4
Ormsaigmore Highld 189 L4
Ormsary Ag & B 172 C4
Ormskirk Lancs.............120 F8
Oronsay Ag & B 171 G2
Orphir Ork 234 b6
Orpington Gt Lon 45 J6
Orrell Sefton.................111 K3
Orrell Wigan.................112 D2
Orroland D & G 146 D5
Orsett Thurr 45 M4
Orslow Staffs..................84 E1
Orston Notts.................102 C4
Orton Cumb 138 F5
Orton Nhants 88 B7
Orton Staffs...................84 F4
Orton Longueville
  C Pete 89 H4
Orton-on-the-Hill
  Leics 86 C3
Orton Waterville
  C Pete 89 H4
Orwell Cambs..................75 L4
Osbaldeston Lancs.......121 J4
Osbaldwick C York 124 F1
Osbaston Leics...............86 E3
Osbaston Shrops............97 L7
Osborne House IoW........17 G4
Osbournby Lincs...........103 H5
Oscroft Ches W 112 D7
Ose Highld 208 E6
Osgathorpe Leics 101 H8
Osgodby Lincs 117 H3
Osgodby N York 124 F4
Osgodby N York 135 G3
Oskaig Highld...............209 H6
Oskamull Ag & B..........189 L7
Osmaston Derbys.........100 D4
Osmington Dorset 14 D5
Osmington Mills
  Dorset 14 E6
Osmondthorpe Leeds ...123 L4
Osmotherley N York 141 K7
Osney Oxon....................57 J6
Ospringe Kent................34 D3
Ossett Wakefd...............123 K6
Ossington Notts............116 C8
Osterley Gt Lon 44 D5
Oswaldkirk N York 133 K4
Oswaldtwistle Lancs.....121 L5
Oswestry Shrops............97 L6
Otford Kent.....................32 F2
Otham Kent....................33 K3
Othery Somset................26 B5
Otley Leeds...................123 J2
Otley Suffk 78 E4
Otterbourne Hants 29 J6
Otterburn N York 131 G7
Otterburn Nthumb 157 M4
Otter Ferry Ag & B........172 F2
Otterham Cnwll 8 F6
Otterhampton
  Somset 25 K3
Otternish W Isls 232 c5
Ottershaw Surrey............43 G7
Otterswick Shet 235 d3
Otterton Devon 12 E5
Ottery St Mary Devon ...12 E4
Ottinge Kent 34 F6
Ottringham E R Yk 127 G5
Oughterside Cumb........147 K6
Oughtibridge Sheff........114 F3

Oughtrington
  Warrtn 113 G4
Oulston N York..............133 H5
Oulton Cumb.................147 M5
Oulton Norfk.................106 D6
Oulton Staffs..................99 K5
Oulton Suffk...................93 L5
Oulton Broad Suffk........93 L5
Oulton Street Norfk......106 D6
Oundle Nhants................88 F6
Ounsdale Staffs..............84 F5
Ousby Cumb 149 G7
Ousden Suffk..................77 G3
Ousefleet E R Yk 125 K6
Ouston Dur 151 G4
Outgate Cumb...............137 K7
Outhgill Cumb 139 H6
Outhill Warwks 71 K2
Outlane Kirk..................123 G6
Out Rawcliffe Lancs.....120 E3
Outwell Norfk 90 D3
Outwood Surrey.............32 B4
Outwoods Staffs.............99 H8
Ouzlewell Green
  Leeds 123 L5
Over Cambs 75 L1
Over Burrows Derbys......71 G6
Overcombe Dorset 14 D6
Over Compton Dorset.....26 E7
Overdale
  Crematorium
  Bolton 121 K8
Over Haddon Derbys 114 D7
Over Kellet Lancs.........129 L5
Over Kiddington
  Oxon 57 H4
Overleigh Somset...........26 C4
Over Norton Oxon...........56 F3
Over Peover Ches E 113 H6
Overpool Ches W..........111 L6
Overscaig Hotel
  Highld 225 J4
Overseal Derbys.............86 C1
Over Silton N York........133 G2
Oversland Kent...............34 E3
Overstone Nhants...........74 B2
Over Stowey Somset.......25 J4
Overstrand Norfk...........106 F4
Over Stratton
  Somset 26 B7
Overthorpe Nhants.........72 F6
Overton C Aber..............207 G3
Overton Hants.................29 K2
Overton Lancs...............129 J7
Overton N York..............133 H7
Overton Shrops...............69 K1
Overton Swans................50 F7
Overton Wakefd............123 K7
Overton Wrexhm.............98 A4
Overtown N Lans...........175 L7
Over Wallop Hants..........28 F4
Over Whitacre
  Warwks 86 B5
Over Worton Oxon...........57 H3
Oving Bucks....................58 C4
Oving W Susx.................18 B5
Ovingdean Br & H 19 K5
Ovingham Nthumb.........150 D3
Ovington Dur.................140 E4
Ovington Essex...............77 H6
Ovington Hants...............29 K5
Ovington Norfk...............91 K3
Ovington Nthumb..........150 D3
Ower Hants.....................28 F7
Owermoigne Dorset........14 E5
Owlerton Sheff..............115 G4
Owlsmoor Br For............42 D7
Owlswick Bucks..............58 C6
Owmby Lincs 117 G4
Owmby Lincs 117 H1
Owslebury Hants.............29 K6
Owston Donc.................124 E7
Owston Leics...................87 L3
Owston Ferry N Linc.....116 D2
Owstwick E R Yk 127 G4
Owthorne E R Yk 127 H5
Owthorpe Notts.............102 A5

Owton Manor Hartpl 141 L2
Oxborough Norfk 91 G3
Oxcombe Lincs 118 D6
Oxen End Essex............129 L2
Oxenhope C Brad.........122 F4
Oxen Park Cumb...........129 G3
Oxenpill Somset 26 C3
Oxenton Gloucs 55 L2
Oxenwood Wilts..............40 F8
Oxford Oxon...................57 K6
Oxford Airport Oxon 57 J5
Oxford Crematorium
  Oxon 57 K6
Oxford Services Oxon 57 L6
Oxhey Herts....................43 J2
Oxhill Warwks 72 C5
Oxley Wolves..................84 F3
Oxley Green Essex..........61 L5
Oxlode Cambs................90 C6
Oxnam Border 167 L5
Oxnead Norfk................106 F7
Oxshott Surrey................43 J7
Oxspring Barns..............114 F2
Oxted Surrey...................32 C3
Oxton Border 178 B7
Oxton N York................124 D2
Oxton Notts..................101 M3
Oxwich Swans.................51 G7
Oxwich Green Swans......50 F7
Oykel Bridge Hotel
  Highld 221 K2
Oyne Abers 206 D1
Oystermouth Swans.......51 H7

P

Pabail W Isls 232 g2
Packington Leics.............86 D1
Padanaram Angus.........196 C6
Padbury Bucks................58 B2
Paddington Gt Lon 44 F4
Paddlesworth Kent 35 G6
Paddlesworth Kent 46 B7
Paddock Wood Kent 33 H4
Padiham Lancs 122 B4
Padside N York..............132 B7
Padstow Cnwll...................4 E2
Padworth W Berk............41 L7
Pagham W Susx..............18 B6
Paglesham Essex 46 F2
Paignton Torbay...............7 K4
Pailton Warwks...............86 F6
Painscastle Powys 68 D5
Painshawfield
  Nthumb 150 D3
Painsthorpe E R Yk 134 C7
Painswick Gloucs 55 K6
Painter's Forstal Kent.....34 D3
Paisley Rens.................174 E5
Paisley Woodside
  Crematorium
  Rens 174 E5
Pakefield Suffk................93 L5
Pakenham Suffk..............77 L2
Paley Street W & M 42 E5
Palfrey Wsall..................85 H4
Palgrave Suffk.................92 D7
Pallington Dorset 14 E4
Palmerston E Ayrs.........163 L5
Palnackie D & G............146 E4
Palnure D & G...............145 J3
Palterton Derbys...........115 J7
Pamber End Hants.........41 L8
Pamber Green Hants......41 L8
Pamber Heath Hants......41 L7
Pamington Gloucs 55 L2
Pamphill Dorset..............15 J3
Pampisford Cambs..........76 C5
Panbride Angus.............187 J1
Pancrasweek Devon 9 H4
Pandy Mons...................53 M4
Pandy Tudur Conwy 110 B8
Panfield Essex.................61 H3
Pangbourne W Berk 41 M5
Pangdean W Susx 19 J4

Pannal N York 123 L1
Pannal Ash N York 132 D8
Pannanich Wells
　Hotel Abers 205 D6
Pant Shrops 97 L7
Pantasaph Flints 111 G6
Pant-ffrwyth Brdgnd 36 E4
Pant Glas Gwynd 95 H3
Pantglas Powys 81 G4
Panton Lincs 117 K5
Pant-y-dwr Powys 81 L8
Pant-y-mwyn Flints......111 H8
Panxworth Norfk...........93 H2
Papa Westray Airport
　Ork 234 c3
Papcastle Cumb............136 F2
Papigoe Highld.............231 L5
Papple E Loth...............178 D4
Papplewick Notts 101 K3
Papworth Everard
　Cambs 75 K3
Papworth St Agnes
　Cambs 75 J2
Par Cnwll.........................5 G5
Parbold Lancs 121 G7
Parbrook Somset...........26 E6
Parc Gwynd 96 D5
Parc Gwyn
　Crematorium
　Pembks 49 K5
Parc Seymour Newpt....38 B3
Pardshaw Cumb............136 F3
Parham Suffk..................79 G3
Park D & G 154 F4
Park Nthumb 149 H3
Park Corner Oxon 42 B3
Park Crematorium
　Lancs 120 E5
Parkend Gloucs 54 E6
Parkers Green Kent 33 G4
Park Farm Kent.............34 D6
Parkgate Ches W..........111 J4
Parkgate D & G...........155 H4
Park Gate Hants 17 G2
Park Gate Leeds 123 J3
Parkgate Surrey 31 K3
Parkgrove
　Crematorium
　Angus 196 F6
Parkhall W Duns 174 E4
Parkham Devon 22 F6
Parkmill Swans 51 G7
Park Royal Gt Lon 44 D4
Parkside Dur 151 K5
Parkside N Lans 175 L6
Parkstone Poole 15 J4
Park Street Herts 59 J6
Park Wood
　Crematorium
　Calder 123 G6
Parndon Essex...............60 C6
Parndon Wood
　Crematorium
　Essex.........................60 C6
Parracombe Devon 23 L3
Parson Drove Cambs......89 L2
Parson's Heath Essex....62 B3
Partick C Glas..............174 F5
Partington Traffd 113 G3
Partney Lincs 118 F7
Parton Cumb 136 D3
Partridge Green
　W Susx......................19 G2
Parwich Derbys 100 D2
Passenham Nhants.........73 L6
Paston Norfk 107 G5
Patcham Br & H.............19 J4
Patching W Susx............18 E4
Patchway S Glos............38 E4
Pateley Bridge
　N York 132 B6
Pathhead Fife...............186 E8
Pathhead Mdloth 177 K5
Path of Condie P & K....185 M5
Patna E Ayrs 163 K7
Patney Wilts 40 B8
Patrick IoM...................237 b5

Patrick Brompton
　N York 132 C2
Patricroft Salfd.............113 H2
Patrington E R Yk.........127 H6
Patrington Haven
　E R Yk 127 H6
Patrixbourne Kent.........35 G4
Patterdale Cumb...........137 L4
Pattingham Staffs..........84 E4
Pattishall Nhants...........73 J4
Pattiswick Green
　Essex.........................61 K3
Paul Cnwll.......................2 E5
Paulerspury Nhants.......73 K5
Paull E R Yk.................126 E5
Paul's Dene Wilts 28 C5
Paulton BaNES..............26 F1
Pauperhaugh
　Nthumb 158 D3
Pavenham Bed...............74 E4
Pawlett Somset..............25 L3
Paxford Gloucs 71 L6
Paxton Border 179 J7
Payhembury Devon........12 E3
Paythorne Lancs 122 C1
Peacehaven E Susx.......19 L5
Peak District
　National Park
　Sheff........................114 D3
Peak Forest Derbys 114 C5
Peakirk C Pete 89 H3
Peasedown St John
　BaNES 39 G8
Peaseland Green
　Norfk 92 C1
Peasemore W Berk 41 J5
Peasenhall Suffk 79 H2
Pease Pottage
　W Susx.......................31 L5
Peaslake Surrey.............31 H3
Peasley Cross St Hel ...112 D3
Peasmarsh E Susx.........21 H2
Peathill Abers 217 H2
Peat Inn Fife 187 G5
Peatling Magna Leics....87 H5
Peatling Parva Leics......87 H5
Pebmarsh Essex 77 J7
Pebworth Worcs 71 K5
Pecket Well Calder.......122 E5
Peckforton Ches E.........98 D2
Peckham Gt Lon 45 G5
Peckleton Leics 86 F4
Pedlinge Kent................34 F7
Pedmore Dudley 85 G6
Pedwell Somset.............26 B4
Peebles Border 166 C2
Peel IoM.......................237 b4
Peene Kent....................35 G6
Pegsdon C Beds 59 J2
Pegswood Nthumb 159 G5
Pegwell Kent 35 K2
Peinchorran Highld......209 H7
Peinlich Highld.............208 F3
Peldon Essex 62 B5
Pelsall Wsall..................85 H3
Pelton Dur...................151 G4
Pelynt Cnwll....................5 K5
Pemberton Carmth 51 G5
Pemberton Wigan........112 D2
Pembrey Carmth............50 E5
Pembridge Herefs 69 H3
Pembroke Pembks 49 G7
Pembroke Dock
　Pembks 49 G6
Pembrokeshire Coast
　National Park
　Pembks 48 E4
Pembury Kent 33 G5
Pen-allt Herefs..............54 E3
Penallt Mons..................54 D6
Penally Pembks 49 J7
Penarth V Glam 37 J6
Pen-bont
　Rhydybeddau
　Cerdgn 80 F6
Penbryn Cerdgn 65 J4
Pencader Carmth...........66 B7

Pencaitland E Loth 177 L5
Pencarnisiog IoA..........108 D6
Pencarreg Carmth 66 C5
Pencelli Powys...............53 H3
Penclawdd Swans..........51 G6
Pencoed Brdgnd 36 E4
Pencombe Herefs 69 L4
Pencraig Herefs.............54 E4
Pencraig Powys..............97 G6
Pendeen Cnwll.................2 C4
Penderyn Rhondd..........52 E6
Pendine Carmth 50 B4
Pendlebury Salfd 113 H2
Pendleton Lancs...........121 L3
Pendock Worcs 55 H2
Pendoggett Cnwll............8 D8
Pendomer Somset.........13 M1
Pendoylan V Glam.........37 G5
Penegoes Powys............81 G4
Pen-ffordd Pembks 49 J3
Pengam Caerph..............37 J2
Pengam Cardif...............37 K5
Penge Gt Lon 45 G6
Pengelly Cnwll.................8 E7
Penhallow Cnwll..............3 K2
Penhalvean Cnwll............3 J4
Penhill Swindn...............40 D3
Penhow Newpt 38 B3
Penicuik Mdloth 177 H6
Penifiler Highld............209 G6
Peninver Ag & B 161 J4
Penistone Barns............114 E2
Penkill S Ayrs...............152 F3
Penkridge Staffs............85 G2
Penley Wrexhm 98 B4
Penllyn V Glam...............36 F5
Penmachno Conwy 96 C3
Penmaen Caerph............37 J2
Penmaen Swans 51 G7
Penmaenmawr
　Conwy 109 K6
Penmaenpool Gwynd.....95 M8
Penmark V Glam............37 G6
Penmount
　Crematorium
　Cnwll...........................4 C6
Penmynydd IoA 109 G6
Penn Bucks 42 F2
Pennal Gwynd................80 F4
Pennan Abers 216 F2
Pennant Powys 81 J4
Pennerley Shrops...........83 G4
Pennines......................122 E4
Pennington Cumb 128 F4
Pennorth Powys.............53 H3
Penn Street Bucks 42 F2
Penny Bridge Cumb.......129 G3
Pennycross Ag & B 181 G3
Pennyghael Ag & B......181 H3
Pennyglen S Ayrs..........163 H7
Pennymoor Devon 11 K3
Pennywell Sundld.........151 J4
Penparc Cerdgn 65 H5
Penperlleni Mons...........53 L6
Penpoll Cnwll...................5 J5
Penponds Cnwll...............3 H4
Penpont D & G 154 E4
Pen-rhiw Pembks...........65 H6
Penrhiwceiber
　Rhondd 37 G2
Pen Rhiwfawr Neath.......51 L4
Penrhiw-llan Cerdgn.......65 K6
Penrhiw-pal Cerdgn 65 K5
Penrhos Gwynd 94 F5
Penrhos Mons.................54 B5
Penrhyn Bay Conwy 110 A5
Penrhyn Castle NT
　Gwynd 109 H6
Penrhyndeudraeth
　Gwynd 95 K5
Penrice Swans................50 F7
Penrioch N Ayrs............161 L1
Penrith Cumb 138 D2
Penrose Cnwll..................4 D2
Penruddock Cumb 138 B2
Penryn Cnwll....................3 K4
Pensarn Conwy 110 C5

Pensax Worcs 70 C2
Penselwood Somset........27 H5
Pensford BaNES 38 F7
Pensham Worcs 71 G5
Penshaw Sundld 151 H4
Penshurst Kent 32 F4
Pensilva Cnwll..................5 L2
Pentewan Cnwll...............4 F6
Pentir Gwynd 109 H7
Pentire Cnwll...................4 C4
Pentlow Essex 77 J5
Pentney Norfk 91 G2
Pentonbridge Cumb 156 D6
Penton Mewsey
　Hants 29 G3
Pentraeth IoA 109 G5
Pentre Mons 54 B7
Pentre Rhondd 36 F2
Pentre Shrops 98 A8
Pentrebach Myr Td 53 G7
Pentre-bach Powys 52 E2
Pentre Berw IoA 108 F6
Pentrebychan
　Crematorium
　Wrexhm.......................97 L3
Pentre-celyn Denbgs 97 J3
Pentre-celyn Powys 81 J3
Pentre-chwyth
　Swans 51 J6
Pentre-cwrt Carmth........65 L6
Pentredwr Denbgs 97 J3
Pentrefelin Gwynd..........95 J5
Pentrefoelas Conwy 96 D3
Pentregat Cerdgn 65 K4
Pentre-Gwenlais
　Carmth 51 H3
Pentre Hodrey
　Shrops 83 G7
Pentre Llanrhaeadr
　Denbgs 110 F8
Pentre Meyrick
　V Glam 36 E5
Pentre-tafarn-y-
　fedw Conwy.................96 C1
Pentrich Derbys............101 G3
Pentridge Dorset 28 B7
Pen-twyn Mons..............54 D6
Pentwynmaur
　Caerph........................37 J2
Pentyrch Cardif 37 H4
Penwithick Cnwll.............5 G5
Penybanc Carmth...........51 H2
Penybont Powys 68 C2
Pen-y-bont Powys 97 K7
Pen-y-bont-fawr
　Powys 97 G7
Pen-y-bryn Pembks........65 G6
Penycae Wrexhm 97 L4
Pen-y-clawdd Mons 54 C6
Pen-y-coedcae
　Rhondd 37 G3
Pen-y-cwn Pembks.........48 E3
Pen-y-felin Flints..........111 G7
Penyffordd Flints............97 L1
Pen-y-Garnedd
　Powys 97 H7
Pen-y-graig Gwynd........94 D5
Penygraig Rhondd 36 F3
Penygroes Carmth..........51 H3
Penygroes Gwynd...........95 H2
Pen-y-Mynydd
　Carmth 50 F5
Penymynydd Flints 97 L1
Penysarn IoA 108 F4
Pen-y-stryt Denbgs 97 J3
Penywaun Rhondd.........52 F6
Penzance Cnwll................2 E5
Peopleton Worcs 71 G4
Peplow Shrops 98 F7
Perceton N Ayrs 163 J2
Percyhorner Abers 217 H2
Perham Down Wilts 28 E2
Periton Somset...............24 E3
Perivale Gt Lon 44 D4
Perkins Village
　Devon 12 D4
Perlethorpe Notts 115 M7

Perranarworthal
Cnwll.............3 K4
Perranporth Cnwll.........3 K1
Perranuthnoe Cnwll.......2 F5
Perranwell Cnwll...........3 K4
Perranzabuloe Cnwll......3 K2
Perry Barr Birm.............85 J5
Perry Barr
Crematorium
Birm....................85 J5
Perry Green Wilts.........39 L3
Pershall Staffs.............99 J6
Pershore Worcs............71 G5
Pertenhall Bed.............74 F2
Perth P & K.................186 B3
Perth Crematorium
P & K.......................186 A3
Perthy Shrops.............98 A5
Perton Herefs.............69 L6
Perton Staffs...............84 F4
Peterborough C Pete...89 H4
Peterborough
Crematorium
C Pete..................89 H3
Peterborough
Services Cambs.....89 G5
Peterchurch Herefs....69 G6
Peterculter C Aber.....206 F5
Peterhead Abers.......217 L5
Peterlee Dur..............151 K6
Petersfield Hants........30 C6
Peter's Green Herts....59 J4
Petersham Gt Lon.......44 D5
Peters Marland
Devon.....................10 C3
Peterstone
Wentlooge Newpt..37 K4
Peterston-super-Ely
V Glam...................37 G5
Peterstow Herefs.......54 E3
Peter Tavy Devon........6 D1
Petham Kent..............34 F4
Petherwin Gate Cnwll...9 H6
Petrockstow Devon.....10 D3
Pett E Susx................21 H3
Pettaugh Suffk...........78 E3
Petterden Angus........196 C7
Pettinain S Lans.........165 J2
Pettistree Suffk...........79 G4
Petton Devon..............24 F6
Petts Wood Gt Lon.....45 J6
Pettycur Fife..............177 H2
Pettymuk Abers.........207 G1
Petworth W Susx.........31 G6
Pevensey E Susx..........20 D5
Pevensey Bay E Susx...20 D5
Pewsey Wilts..............40 D7
Phepson Worcs...........71 G3
Philham Devon............22 D6
Philiphaugh Border....166 F4
Phillack Cnwll...............2 F4
Philleigh Cnwll.............4 D7
Philpstoun W Loth.....176 E3
Phoenix Green Hants...30 C1
Phones Highld...........203 G6
Pibsbury Somset.........26 C6
Pickburn Donc...........115 K1
Pickering N York........134 C3
Pickford Covtry...........86 C6
Pickhill N York...........132 E3
Picklescott Shrops......83 J4
Pickmere Ches E........113 G6
Pickney Somset...........25 J5
Pickwell Leics.............87 L2
Pickworth Lincs.........103 H5
Pickworth Rutlnd.........88 E2
Picton Ches W............112 B7
Picton N York.............141 K5
Piddinghoe E Susx......19 L5
Piddington Nhants.......74 B4
Piddington Oxon..........57 M5
Piddlehinton Dorset....14 D3
Piddletrenthide
Dorset....................14 D3
Pidley Cambs..............89 K7
Piercebridge Darltn...140 F4
Pierowall Ork.............234 C3

Pilgrims Hatch Essex...45 L2
Pilham Lincs..............116 E3
Pillaton Cnwll...............6 A3
Pillerton Hersey
Warwks.................72 C5
Pillerton Priors
Warwks.................72 C5
Pilley Barns..............115 G2
Pilley Hants................16 D3
Pilling Lancs..............120 E2
Pilning S Glos.............38 D4
Pilsbury Derbys.........114 C8
Pilsdon Dorset............13 K3
Pilsley Derbys...........101 H1
Pilsley Derbys...........114 E7
Pilson Green Norfk......93 H2
Piltdown E Susx..........19 L2
Pilton Devon...............23 J5
Pilton Nhants..............88 E6
Pilton Rutlnd...............88 D3
Pilton Somset.............26 E3
Pimperne Dorset.........15 G1
Pinchbeck Lincs.........103 L7
Pin Green Herts..........59 L3
Pinhoe Devon.............12 C4
Pinley Green Warwks...72 B2
Pinminnoch S Ayrs....152 E4
Pinmore S Ayrs.........152 E4
Pinn Devon.................12 E5
Pinner Gt Lon.............43 J3
Pinner Green Gt Lon...43 J3
Pinvin Worcs..............71 G5
Pinwherry S Ayrs......152 E5
Pinxton Derbys.........101 J2
Pipe and Lyde Herefs..69 K5
Pipe Aston Herefs.......69 J1
Pipe Gate Shrops........99 G4
Piperhill Highld.........213 K4
Pipewell Nhants..........88 B6
Pirbright Surrey..........30 F1
Pirnie Border.............167 K4
Pirnmill N Ayrs..........161 L1
Pirton Herts...............59 J2
Pishill Oxon................42 B3
Pistyll Gwynd..............94 F4
Pitagowan P & K........194 C3
Pitblae Abers............217 J2
Pitcairngreen P & K...185 M3
Pitcalnie Highld........223 H6
Pitcaple Abers...........206 D1
Pitcarity Angus..........196 B4
Pitchcombe Gloucs.....55 J6
Pitchcott Bucks...........58 C4
Pitchford Shrops.........83 K3
Pitch Green Bucks.......58 C7
Pitchroy Moray..........214 E6
Pitcombe Somset........26 F5
Pitcox E Loth.............178 E4
Pitfichie Abers...........206 D3
Pitglassie Abers........216 D5
Pitgrudy Highld.........223 H3
Pitlessie Fife............186 E5
Pitlochry P & K..........194 E5
Pitmachie Abers........216 C8
Pitmain Highld..........203 H5
Pitmedden Abers.......217 G8
Pitmedden Garden
Abers.....................217 G8
Pitminster Somset......25 K7
Pitmuies Angus.........196 F6
Pitmunie Abers.........206 C3
Pitney Somset............26 C5
Pitroddie P & K..........186 C3
Pitscottie Fife............187 G5
Pitsea Essex...............46 C3
Pitsford Nhants...........73 L2
Pitstone Bucks............58 F5
Pittarrow Abers..........197 H2
Pittenweem Fife........187 J6
Pitteuchar Fife...........186 D7
Pittington Dur...........151 H6
Pittodrie House
Hotel Abers..........206 D1
Pitton Wilts................28 E5
Pittulie Abers............217 J2
Pity Me Dur..............151 G5
Pixham Surrey...........31 K2

Plains N Lans............175 L5
Plaish Shrops..............83 K4
Plaistow Gt Lon...........45 H4
Plaistow W Susx..........31 G5
Plaitford Hants............28 F7
Platt Kent...................33 G2
Plawsworth Dur.........151 G5
Plaxtol Kent................33 G3
Playden E Susx............21 H2
Playford Suffk.............78 F5
Play Hatch Oxon..........42 C5
Playing Place Cnwll......4 C7
Playley Green Gloucs...55 H2
Plealey Shrops.............83 H3
Plean Stirlg...............175 L2
Pleasance Fife...........186 D5
Pleasington
Crematorium
Bl w D...................121 J5
Pleasley Derbys.........115 J8
Plemstall Ches W........112 C7
Pleshey Essex.............61 G5
Plockton Highld.........210 C7
Plowden Shrops..........83 H6
Pluckley Kent..............34 B5
Pluckley Thorne Kent..34 B5
Plumbland Cumb........147 K6
Plumley Ches E..........113 G6
Plumpton Cumb.........148 E7
Plumpton E Susx.........19 K3
Plumpton Nhants.........73 H5
Plumpton Green
E Susx....................19 K3
Plumstead Gt Lon.......45 J4
Plumstead Norfk........106 D5
Plumtree Notts..........101 L6
Plungar Leics............102 C5
Plurenden Kent...........34 C7
Plush Dorset...............14 D3
Plwmp Cerdgn............65 K4
Plymouth C Plym..........6 C5
Plymouth Airport
C Plym.....................6 D4
Plympton C Plym..........6 D5
Plymstock C Plym.........6 D5
Plymtree Devon..........12 D2
Pockley N York..........133 K3
Pocklington E R Yk....125 J2
Podimore Somset........26 D6
Podington Bed...........74 D3
Podmore Staffs...........99 H5
Pointon Lincs............103 J6
Pokesdown Bmouth...15 L4
Polbain Highld..........224 B6
Polbathic Cnwll...........6 A4
Polbeth W Loth.........176 D5
Poldark Mine Cnwll......3 H5
Polebrook Nhants.......88 F6
Polegate E Susx..........20 C5
Polesworth Warwks....86 C3
Polglass Highld.........224 C6
Polgooth Cnwll............4 F5
Polgown D & G..........154 C2
Poling W Susx.............18 E5
Poling Corner W Susx..18 E5
Polkerris Cnwll.............5 H5
Pollington E R Yk.......124 F6
Polloch Highld...........190 F3
Pollokshaws C Glas....175 G6
Pollokshields C Glas...175 G5
Polmassick Cnwll.........4 F6
Polmont Falk..............176 C3
Polnish Highld...........200 B8
Polperro Cnwll.............5 K5
Polruan Cnwll..............5 H5
Polstead Suffk.............78 B6
Poltalloch Ag & B......182 B7
Poltimore Devon........12 C3
Polton Mdloth...........177 J5
Polwarth Border........178 F7
Polyphant Cnwll...........9 H7
Polzeath Cnwll............4 E1
Pomathorn Mdloth....177 H6
Pondersbridge
Cambs..................89 J5
Ponders End Gt Lon....45 G2

Ponsanooth Cnwll........3 K4
Ponsworthy Devon........7 G2
Pont Abraham
Services Carmth....51 H4
Pontantwn Carmth......50 F3
Pontardawe Neath......51 K5
Pontarddulais Swans...51 H5
Pont-ar-gothi Carmth...51 G2
Pontarsais Carmth......66 B8
Pontblyddyn Flints......97 L1
Pontefract Wakefd....124 C6
Pontefract
Crematorium
Wakefd...............124 C6
Ponteland Nthumb.....158 F7
Ponterwyd Cerdgn......81 G7
Pontesbury Shrops......83 H3
Pontesford Shrops......83 H3
Pontfadog Wrexhm......97 K5
Pontfaen Pembks........64 E7
Pont-faen Powys.........67 L7
Pontgarreg Cerdgn......65 K4
Ponthenry Carmth.......50 F4
Ponthir Torfn..............37 M2
Ponthirwaun Cerdgn...65 J5
Pontllanfraith Caerph...37 J2
Pontlliw Swans...........51 H5
Pontlottyn Caerph.......53 H6
Pontlyfni Gwynd..........95 G3
Pontneddfechan
Neath.....................52 D6
Pontnewydd Torfn.......37 L2
Pontrhydfendigaid
Cerdgn...................67 G2
Pont-rhyd-y-fen
Neath.....................36 C2
Pontrhydygroes
Cerdgn...................81 G8
Pontrilas Herefs.........54 B3
Pont Robert Powys......82 C2
Pontshaen Cerdgn......66 B5
Pontsticill Myr Td.......53 G5
Pontwelly Carmth.......65 L6
Pontyates Carmth.......50 F4
Pontyberem Carmth....51 G4
Pontybodkin Flints......97 L2
Pontyclun Rhondd.......37 G4
Pontycymer Brdgnd....36 D3
Pont-y-pant Conwy......96 B2
Pontypool Torfn..........53 L7
Pontypridd Rhondd.....37 G3
Pontywaun Caerph.....37 K2
Pool Cnwll....................3 H3
Pool Leeds................123 J2
Poole Poole................15 J4
Poole Crematorium
Poole.....................15 J3
Poole Keynes Gloucs...39 M2
Poolewe Highld.........219 K5
Pooley Bridge Cumb..138 C3
Poolfold Staffs............99 K1
Poolhill Gloucs............55 G3
Pool of Muckhart
Clacks..................185 L2
Pool Street Essex........77 H6
Poplar Gt Lon.............45 G4
Porchfield IoW............16 F4
Poringland Norfk........92 F3
Porkellis Cnwll.............3 J5
Porlock Somset...........24 D3
Porlock Weir Somset...24 D3
Portachoillan Ag & B..172 C6
Port-an-Eorna Highld..210 B7
Port Appin Ag & B......191 H7
Port Askaig Ag & B.....171 H5
Portavadie Ag & B......172 F4
Port Bannatyne
Ag & B...................173 J5
Portbury N Som..........38 D5
Port Carlisle Cumb.....147 M3
Port Charlotte Ag & B..170 E6
Portchester Hants.......17 H2
Portchester
Crematorium
Hants....................17 H2
Port Driseach Ag & B..173 G4
Port Ellen Ag & B......160 C1

Port Elphinstone
Abers 206 E2
Portencalzie D & G 152 B7
Portencross N Ayrs 173 K8
Port Erin IoM 237 a6
Portesham Dorset 14 B5
Portessie Moray 215 K2
Port Eynon Swans 50 F7
Portfield Gate
Pembks 48 F4
Portgate Devon 10 B7
Port Gaverne Cnwll 8 D8
Port Glasgow Inver 174 C4
Portgordon Moray 215 J2
Portgower Highld 227 H5
Porth Cnwll 4 C4
Porth Rhondd 36 F3
Porthallow Cnwll 3 K6
Porthallow Cnwll 5 K5
Porthcawl Brdgnd 36 C5
Porthcothan Cnwll 4 D2
Porthcurno Cnwll 2 C6
Port Henderson
Highld 219 H6
Porthgain Pembks 64 A7
Porthgwarra Cnwll 2 C6
Porthkerry V Glam 37 G6
Porthleven Cnwll 3 H6
Porthmadog Gwynd 95 K5
Porth Navas Cnwll 3 K5
Porthoustock Cnwll 3 K6
Porthpean Cnwll 5 G5
Porthtowan Cnwll 3 J2
Porthyrhyd Carmth 51 G3
Portincaple Ag & B 183 J8
Portington E R Yk 125 J4
Portinnisherrich
Ag & B 182 D5
Portinscale Cumb 137 H3
Port Isaac Cnwll 8 D8
Portishead N Som 38 C5
Portknockie Moray 215 K2
Portland Dorset 14 D7
Portlethen Abers 207 H6
Portling D & G 146 F4
Portloe Cnwll 4 E7
Port Logan D & G 144 D6
Portmahomack
Highld 223 H8
Portmeirion Gwynd 95 K5
Portmellon Cnwll 4 F6
Port Mor Highld 189 K1
Portnacroish Ag & B 191 H6
Portnaguran W Isls 232 g2
Portnahaven Ag & B 170 D7
Portnalong Highld 208 E7
Port nan Giuran
W Isls 232 g2
Port nan Long W Isls 232 c5
Port Nis W Isls 232 g1
Portobello C Edin 177 J4
Portobello Wolves 85 G4
Port of Menteith
Stirlg 184 D6
Port of Ness W Isls 232 g1
Porton Wilts 28 D4
Portpatrick D & G 144 B4
Port Quin Cnwll 8 C8
Port Ramsay Ag & B 191 H7
Portreath Cnwll 3 H3
Portree Highld 209 G5
Port St Mary IoM 237 b7
Portscatho Cnwll 4 D8
Portsea C Port 17 J3
Portskerra Highld 230 C3
Portskewett Mons 38 D3
Portslade Br & H 19 H4
Portslade-by-Sea
Br & H 19 H5
Portslogan D & G 144 B3
Portsmouth C Port 17 J3
Portsmouth Calder 122 D5
Port Soderick IoM 237 c6
Portsonachan Hotel
Ag & B 182 F3
Portsoy Abers 216 B2
Port Sunlight Wirral 111 K5

Portswood C Sotn 29 H8
Port Talbot Neath 36 B3
Portuairk Highld 189 K3
Portway Worcs 85 J8
Port Wemyss Ag & B 170 D7
Port William D & G 145 H6
Portwrinkle Cnwll 6 A5
Portyerrock D & G 145 K7
Poslingford Suffk 77 H5
Posso Border 166 B3
Postbridge Devon 10 F8
Postcombe Oxon 58 B7
Postling Kent 34 F6
Postwick Norfk 93 G2
Potarch Abers 206 B6
Potten End Herts 59 G6
Potter Brompton
N York 134 F4
Potterhanworth
Lincs 117 H7
Potterhanworth
Booths Lincs 117 H7
Potter Heigham
Norfk 107 J8
Potterne Wilts 39 M8
Potterne Wick Wilts 39 M8
Potters Bar Herts 59 L7
Potters Crouch Herts 59 J6
Potters Green
Covtry 86 D6
Potters Marston
Leics 87 G4
Potterspury Nhants 73 L6
Potterton Abers 207 H3
Potto N York 141 L6
Potton C Beds 75 J5
Pott Shrigley Ches E 113 L5
Poughill Cnwll 9 G4
Poughill Devon 11 K3
Poulner Hants 15 M2
Poulshot Wilts 39 L7
Poulton Gloucs 56 C7
Poulton-le-Fylde
Lancs 120 D3
Poundffald Swans 51 H6
Pound Green E Susx 20 B2
Pound Green Suffk 77 G2
Pound Hill W Susx 32 B5
Poundon Bucks 57 M3
Poundsgate Devon 7 G2
Poundstock Cnwll 9 G5
Pouton D & G 145 K5
Povey Cross Surrey 31 L3
Powburn Nthumb 168 F6
Powderham Devon 12 C5
Powerstock Dorset 13 M3
Powfoot D & G 147 K2
Powick Worcs 70 E4
Powmill P & K 185 L1
Poxwell Dorset 14 E5
Poyle Slough 43 G5
Poynings W Susx 19 H4
Poyntington Dorset 26 F7
Poynton Ches E 113 L5
Poynton Green
Wrekin 98 E8
Praa Sands Cnwll 3 G5
Pratt's Bottom Gt Lon 45 J7
Praze-an-Beeble
Cnwll 3 H4
Prees Shrops 98 D5
Preesall Lancs 120 E2
Prees Green Shrops 98 E6
Prees Heath Shrops 98 E5
Prees Higher Heath
Shrops 98 E5
Pren-gwyn Cerdgn 65 L5
Prenteg Gwynd 95 K4
Prescot Knows 112 C3
Prescott Devon 25 H8
Presnerb Angus 195 J3
Prestatyn Denbgs 110 E5
Prestbury Ches E 113 K6
Prestbury Gloucs 55 L4
Presteigne Powys 69 G2
Prestleigh Somset 26 F4
Preston Border 179 G6

Preston Br & H 19 J4
Preston Devon 7 K2
Preston Dorset 14 D5
Preston E R Yk 126 F4
Preston Gloucs 56 B7
Preston Herts 59 K3
Preston Kent 34 D3
Preston Kent 35 H3
Preston Lancs 121 H4
Preston Nthumb 169 H4
Preston Rutlnd 88 C3
Preston Somset 25 H4
Preston Suffk 77 L4
Preston Torbay 7 K4
Preston Wilts 40 B5
Preston Bagot
Warwks 71 L2
Preston Bissett Bucks 58 A3
Preston Bowyer
Somset 25 H6
Preston Brockhurst
Shrops 98 D7
Preston Brook Halton 112 E5
Preston Candover
Hants 29 L3
Preston Capes
Nhants 73 H4
Preston
Crematorium
Lancs 121 H4
Preston Green
Warwks 71 L2
Preston Gubbals
Shrops 98 C8
Preston on Stour
Warwks 72 B4
Preston on the Hill
Halton 112 E5
Preston on Wye
Herefs 69 H6
Prestonpans E Loth 177 K4
Preston Patrick
Cumb 129 L3
Preston Plucknett
Somset 26 D7
Preston-under-Scar
N York 131 K2
Preston upon the
Weald Moors
Wrekin 84 C1
Preston Wynne
Herefs 69 L5
Prestwich Bury 113 J1
Prestwick S Ayrs 163 J4
Prestwick Airport
S Ayrs 163 J4
Prestwood Bucks 58 E7
Prickwillow Cambs 90 E6
Priddy Somset 26 D2
Priest Hutton Lancs 129 L5
Priestland E Ayrs 164 B2
Priest Weston Shrops 82 F4
Primrosehill Border 179 G6
Primsidemill Border 168 B4
Princes Risborough
Bucks 58 D7
Princethorpe Warwks 72 E1
Princetown Devon 6 E2
Priors Hardwick
Warwks 72 F4
Priorslee Wrekin 84 C2
Priors Marston
Warwks 72 F3
Priors Norton Gloucs 55 K3
Priory Vale Swindn 40 C3
Priston BaNES 39 G7
Prittlewell Sthend 46 E3
Privett Hants 30 B6
Prixford Devon 23 J4
Probus Cnwll 4 E6
Prora E Loth 178 C3
Prospect Cumb 147 K6
Prospidnick Cnwll 3 H5
Protstonhill Abers 216 F2
Prudhoe Nthumb 150 D3
Publow BaNES 38 F7
Puckeridge Herts 60 C4

Puckington Somset 26 B7
Pucklechurch S Glos 39 G5
Puddington Ches W 111 K6
Puddington Devon 11 J3
Puddletown Dorset 14 E4
Pudsey Leeds 123 J4
Pulborough W Susx 18 E3
Pulford Ches W 98 A2
Pulham Dorset 14 D2
Pulham Market
Norfk 92 E6
Pulham St Mary
Norfk 92 E6
Pulloxhill C Beds 74 F7
Pumpherston W Loth 176 E4
Pumsaint Carmth 66 E6
Puncheston Pembks 49 G2
Puncknowle Dorset 14 A5
Punnett's Town
E Susx 20 C2
Purbrook Hants 17 J2
Purfleet Thurr 45 K4
Puriton Somset 25 L3
Purleigh Essex 61 K7
Purley Gt Lon 44 F7
Purley W Berk 42 A5
Purse Caundle
Dorset 27 G2
Purtington Somset 13 K2
Purton Gloucs 54 F6
Purton Gloucs 55 G7
Purton Wilts 40 C3
Purton Stoke Wilts 40 C3
Pury End Nhants 73 K5
Pusey Oxon 41 G2
Putley Herefs 70 B6
Putley Green Herefs 70 B6
Putney Gt Lon 44 E5
Putney Vale
Crematorium
Gt Lon 44 E5
Puttenham Surrey 30 F2
Puxley Nhants 73 L6
Puxton N Som 38 B7
Pwll Carmth 50 F5
Pwll-glâs Denbgs 97 H2
Pwllgloyw Powys 68 B7
Pwllheli Gwynd 94 F5
Pwllmeyric Mons 38 D2
Pwll Trap Carmth 50 C3
Pwll-y-glaw Neath 36 C2
Pye Bridge Derbys 101 H3
Pyecombe W Susx 19 J3
Pyle Brdgnd 36 C4
Pyleigh Somset 25 H5
Pylle Somset 26 E4
Pymoor Cambs 90 C6
Pymore Dorset 13 L4
Pyrford Surrey 43 H8
Pyrton Oxon 42 B2
Pytchley Nhants 88 C8
Pyworthy Devon 9 J4

Q

Quadring Lincs 103 L6
Quadring Eaudike
Lincs 103 L5
Quainton Bucks 58 C4
Quantock Hills
Somset 25 J4
Quarff Shet 235 c6
Quarley Hants 28 F3
Quarndon Derbys 101 G4
Quarrier's Village
Inver 174 C5
Quarrington Lincs 103 H4
Quarrington Hill Dur 151 H7
Quarry Bank Dudley 85 G6
Quarrywood Moray 214 E2
Quarter N Ayrs 173 L6
Quarter S Lans 175 J7
Quatford Shrops 84 D5
Quatt Shrops 84 D6
Quebec Dur 150 F6

Quedgeley Gloucs 55 J5
Queen Adelaide
  Cambs 90 E7
Queenborough
  Kent................46 E5
Queen Camel Somset 26 E6
Queen Charlton
  BaNES 38 F6
Queen Elizabeth
  Forest Park Stirlg....184 B6
Queenhill Worcs 70 F6
Queen Oak Dorset........27 H5
Queen's Bower IoW....17 H5
Queensbury C Brad......123 G4
Queensferry Flints........111 K7
Queenslie C Glas 175 H5
Queenzieburn N Lans...175 J3
Quendon Essex........60 E3
Queniborough Leics 87 J2
Quenington Gloucs......56 C7
Queslett Birm 85 J4
Quethiock Cnwll........5 L3
Quidenham Norfk 92 B6
Quidhampton Wilts......28 C5
Quinton Nhants........73 L4
Quintrell Downs
  Cnwll................4 D4
Quixwood Border 179 G5
Quoig P & K 185 H3
Quorn Leics........87 H1
Quothquan S Lans......165 J2
Quoyburray Ork........234 c6
Quoyloo Ork........234 b5

R

Raasay Highld 209 J5
Rachan Mill Border......165 L3
Rachub Gwynd........109 J7
Rackenford Devon......24 D7
Rackham W Susx......18 E3
Rackheath Norfk........93 G1
Racks D & G................155 H7
Rackwick Ork........234 a7
Radbourne Derbys......100 F5
Radcliffe Bury................113 H1
Radcliffe on Trent
  Notts................101 M5
Radclive Bucks......73 J7
Raddery Highld......213 H3
Radernie Fife........187 G5
Radford Covtry............86 D7
Radford Semele
  Warwks................72 D2
Radlett Herts 59 K7
Radley Oxon......57 K7
Radley Green Essex......60 F6
Radnage Bucks......42 C2
Radstock BaNES......27 G1
Radstone Nhants......73 H6
Radway Warwks......72 D5
Radwell Bed......74 E3
Radwell Herts......75 J7
Radwinter Essex......76 E6
Radyr Cardif........37 H4
Rafford Moray......214 C3
Ragdale Leics......102 A8
Raglan Mons......54 B6
Ragnall Notts......116 D6
Raigbeg Highld......213 J8
Rainbow Hill Worcs......70 F4
Rainford St Hel......112 C2
Rainham Gt Lon......45 K4
Rainham Medway......46 D6
Rainhill St Hel......112 C4
Rainhill Stoops St Hel..112 D4
Rainow Ches E......113 L6
Rainton N York......132 E4
Rainworth Notts......101 L2
Rait P & K......186 D3
Raithby Lincs......118 D5
Raithby Lincs......118 E7
Rake Hants......30 D5
Ralia Highld......203 H5
Ramasaig Highld......208 B5

Rame Cnwll 3 J4
Rame Cnwll 6 B6
Rampisham Dorset........14 B3
Rampside Cumb............128 F6
Rampton Cambs........76 B2
Rampton Notts 116 D5
Ramsbottom Bury......122 B6
Ramsbury Wilts........40 F6
Ramscraigs Highld........227 K3
Ramsdean Hants........30 B6
Ramsdell Hants........41 L8
Ramsden Oxon......57 G5
Ramsden Bellhouse
  Essex................46 B2
Ramsey Cambs........89 K6
Ramsey Essex 62 E2
Ramsey IoM......237 e3
Ramsey Forty Foot
  Cambs................89 K6
Ramsey Heights
  Cambs................89 J6
Ramsey Island Essex......61 M6
Ramsey Island
  Pembks................48 B3
Ramsey Mereside
  Cambs................89 K5
Ramsey St Mary's
  Cambs................89 J6
Ramsgate Kent........35 K2
Ramsgill N York......131 L5
Ramshope Nthumb......157 J2
Ramshorn Staffs......100 B4
Ramsnest Common
  Surrey................30 F5
Ranby Lincs........118 B5
Ranby Notts......116 A5
Rand Lincs......117 J5
Randalls Park
  Crematorium
  Surrey................44 D8
Randwick Gloucs......55 J6
Ranfurly Rens......174 D5
Rangemore Staffs......100 D7
Rangeworthy S Glos......39 G3
Rankinston E Ayrs......163 L6
Rannoch Station
  P & K................193 G5
Ranscombe Somset......24 E3
Ranskill Notts......116 A4
Ranton Staffs......99 J7
Ranton Green Staffs......99 J7
Ranworth Norfk......93 H1
Raploch Stirlg......185 G7
Rapness Ork......234 c4
Rascarrel D & G......146 D5
Rashfield Ag & B......173 K2
Rashwood Worcs......71 G2
Raskelf N York......133 G5
Rastrick Calder......123 H6
Ratagan Highld......200 E2
Ratby Leics......87 G3
Ratcliffe Culey Leics......86 D4
Ratcliffe on Soar
  Notts................101 J6
Ratcliffe on the
  Wreake Leics......87 J1
Rathen Abers......217 J3
Rathillet Fife......186 F3
Rathmell N York......130 F7
Ratho C Edin......176 F4
Ratho Station C Edin...176 F4
Rathven Moray......215 K2
Ratley Warwks......72 E5
Ratling Kent......35 H4
Ratlinghope Shrops......83 H4
Rattar Highld......231 J2
Rattery Devon......7 H4
Rattlesden Suffk......77 L3
Ratton Village E Susx...20 C5
Rattray P & K......195 J7
Raunds Nhants......88 E8
Ravenfield Rothm......115 J3
Ravenglass Cumb......136 F7
Raveningham Norfk......93 H4
Ravenscar N York......143 K6
Ravenscraig N Lans......175 K6
Ravensden Bed......74 F4

Ravenshead Notts......101 K2
Ravensthorpe Kirk......123 J6
Ravensthorpe Nhants....73 J1
Ravenstone Leics......86 E2
Ravenstone M Keyn......74 B4
Ravenstonedale
  Cumb................139 G6
Ravenstruther S Lans...165 H1
Ravensworth N York....140 E5
Rawcliffe C York......133 J8
Rawcliffe E R Yk......125 G6
Rawdon Leeds......123 J3
Rawdon
  Crematorium
  Leeds................123 J3
Rawling Street Kent......34 B3
Rawmarsh Rothm......115 H3
Rawreth Essex......46 C2
Rawridge Devon......12 F2
Rawtenstall Lancs......122 B6
Raydon Suffk......78 C6
Rayleigh Essex......46 D2
Rayne Essex......61 H4
Raynes Park Gt Lon......44 E6
Reach Cambs......76 E2
Read Lancs......122 B4
Reading Readg......42 B5
Reading
  Crematorium
  Readg................42 B5
Reading Services
  W Berk................42 A6
Reading Street Kent......34 B8
Reading Street Kent......35 K2
Reagill Cumb......138 E4
Realwa Cnwll......3 G4
Rearquhar Highld......223 G3
Rearsby Leics......87 J2
Reay Highld......230 D3
Reculver Kent......47 L6
Red Ball Devon......25 H7
Redberth Pembks......49 J6
Redbourn Herts......59 J5
Redbourne N Linc......116 F2
Redbrook Gloucs......54 D6
Redbrook Wrexhm......98 D4
Redbrook Street Kent....34 C7
Redburn Highld......213 L5
Redcar R & Cl......142 D3
Redcastle D & G......146 E2
Redcastle Highld......212 E4
Redding Falk......176 C3
Reddingmuirhead
  Falk................176 C3
Redditch Worcs......71 J2
Redditch
  Crematorium
  Worcs................71 J2
Rede Suffk......77 J4
Redenhall Norfk......92 F6
Redesmouth Nthumb....157 L5
Redford Abers......197 J3
Redford Angus......196 F7
Redford W Susx......30 E6
Redfordgreen Border...166 E6
Redgorton P & K......186 A2
Redgrave Suffk......92 C7
Redhill Abers......206 E4
Red Hill Bmouth......15 K4
Redhill Herts......59 M2
Redhill N Som......38 D7
Redhill Surrey......32 B3
Redisham Suffk......93 J6
Redland Bristl......38 E5
Redland Ork......234 b5
Redlingfield Suffk......78 E1
Redlingfield Green
  Suffk................78 E1
Red Lodge Suffk......77 G1
Redlynch Somset......27 G5
Redlynch Wilts......28 D7
Redmarley Worcs......70 D2
Redmarley D'Abitot
  Gloucs................55 H2
Redmarshall S on T......141 J3
Redmile Leics......102 D5
Redmire N York......131 K2

Redmyre Abers......197 J2
Rednal Shrops......98 A6
Redpath Border......167 J3
Redpoint Highld......219 H7
Red Roses Carmth......49 L5
Red Row Nthumb......159 G3
Redruth Cnwll......3 J3
Redstone P & K......186 C1
Red Wharf Bay IoA......109 G5
Redwick Newpt......38 B4
Redwick S Glos......38 D3
Redworth Darltn......141 G3
Reed Herts......75 L7
Reedham Norfk......93 J3
Reedness E R Yk......125 J6
Reeds Holme Lancs......122 B5
Reepham Lincs......117 H6
Reepham Norfk......106 D7
Reeth N York......140 C7
Reeves Green Solhll......86 C7
Regil N Som......38 D7
Reiff Highld......224 B5
Reigate Surrey......31 L2
Reighton N York......135 H4
Reisque Abers......207 G2
Reiss Highld......231 L5
Relubbus Cnwll......2 F5
Relugas Moray......214 B5
Remenham Wokham......42 C4
Remenham Hill
  Wokham................42 C4
Rempstone Notts......101 L7
Rendcomb Gloucs......56 A6
Rendham Suffk......79 H2
Rendlesham Suffk......79 H4
Renfrew Rens......174 F5
Renhold Bed......74 F4
Renishaw Derbys......115 J6
Rennington Nthumb......169 J5
Renton W Duns......174 D3
Renwick Cumb......149 G6
Repps Norfk......93 J1
Repton Derbys......100 F6
Resaurie Highld......213 H5
Resipole Highld......190 E4
Reskadinnick Cnwll......3 H3
Resolis Highld......213 G2
Resolven Neath......52 C7
Rest and be thankful
  Ag & B................183 J6
Reston Border......179 H6
Reswallie Angus......196 E6
Retford Notts......116 B5
Rettendon Essex......61 J7
Revesby Lincs......103 M1
Rewe Devon......12 B3
Rew Street IoW......16 F4
Reydon Suffk......93 K7
Reymerston Norfk......92 B3
Reynalton Pembks......49 J5
Reynoldston Swans......50 F7
Rezare Cnwll......6 A1
Rhandirmwyn
  Carmth................67 H5
Rhayader Powys......67 L2
Rheindown Highld......212 D5
Rhes-y-cae Flints......111 G7
Rhewl Denbgs......97 H1
Rhewl Denbgs......97 J4
Rhicarn Highld......224 D4
Rhiconich Highld......228 C5
Rhicullen Highld......222 F6
Rhigos Rhondd......52 E6
Rhireavach Highld......220 D3
Rhives Highld......223 H2
Rhiwbina Cardif......37 J4
Rhiwderyn Newpt......37 K3
Rhiwlas Gwynd......109 H7
Rhoden Green Kent......33 H4
Rhodes Minnis Kent......34 F6
Rhodiad-y-brenin
  Pembks................48 C3
Rhonehouse D & G......146 C3
Rhoose V Glam......37 G6
Rhos Carmth......65 L7
Rhos Neath......51 L5
Rhoscolyn IoA......108 C6

Rhoscrowther
Pembks 48 F6
Rhosesmor Flints 111 H7
Rhosgoch Powys 68 D5
Rhoshill Pembks 65 H6
Rhoshirwaun Gwynd 94 D6
Rhoslefain Gwynd 80 D3
Rhosllanerchrugog
Wrexhm 97 L3
Rhosmeirch IoA 108 F6
Rhosneigr IoA 108 D6
Rhosnesni Wrexhm 97 M3
Rhôs-on-Sea Conwy 110 B5
Rhossili Swans 50 E7
Rhostryfan Gwynd 95 H2
Rhostyllen Wrexhm 97 L3
Rhosybol IoA 108 F4
Rhos-y-gwaliau
Gwynd 96 E5
Rhosymedre Wrexhm 97 L4
RHS Garden Wisley
Surrey 43 H8
Rhu Ag & B 174 B2
Rhuallt Denbgs 110 F6
Rhubodach Ag & B 173 H4
Rhuddlan Denbgs 110 E6
Rhunahaorine Ag & B.. 172 C8
Rhyd Gwynd 95 L4
Rhydargaeau Carmth 50 F1
Rhydcymerau
Carmth 66 D6
Rhyd-Ddu Gwynd 95 K3
Rhydlewis Cerdgn 65 K5
Rhydowen Cerdgn 66 B5
Rhyd-uchaf Gwynd 96 D5
Rhyd-y-clafdy Gwynd ... 94 F5
Rhyd-y-foel Conwy 110 C6
Rhydyfro Neath 51 K4
Rhyd-y-groes Gwynd ... 109 H7
Rhyd-y pennau
Cerdgn 80 E6
Rhyl Denbgs 110 D5
Rhymney Caerph 53 H6
Rhynd P & K 186 B4
Rhynie Abers 215 L8
Rhynie Highld 223 J5
Ribbesford Worcs 84 D8
Ribbleton Lancs 121 H4
Ribchester Lancs 121 J4
Riby Lincs 126 F8
Riccall N York 124 F3
Riccarton Border 156 F3
Riccarton E Ayrs 163 K3
Richards Castle
Herefs 69 J1
Richmond Gt Lon 44 D5
Richmond N York 140 F6
Richmond Sheff 115 H4
Rickerscote Staffs 99 L7
Rickford N Som 38 C8
Rickham Devon 7 H7
Rickinghall Suffk 92 C7
Rickling Green Essex ... 60 E3
Rickmansworth Herts.... 43 H2
Riddell Border 167 H4
Riddlecombe Devon 10 F3
Riddlesden C Brad...... 123 G3
Ridge Dorset 15 H5
Ridge Herts 59 K7
Ridge Wilts 27 L5
Ridge Lane Warwks 86 C4
Ridgeway Derbys 115 H5
Ridgewell Essex 77 G6
Ridgewood E Susx 19 M2
Ridgmont C Beds 74 E7
Riding Mill Nthumb 150 C3
Ridlington Norfk 107 H6
Ridlington Rutlnd 88 B3
Ridsdale Nthumb 158 A5
Rievaulx N York 133 J3
Rievaulx Abbey
N York 133 J3
Rigg E R Yk 148 B2
Riggend N Lans 175 K4
Righoul Highld 213 K4
Rigsby Lincs 118 F6
Rigside S Lans 165 G3

Riley Green Lancs 121 J5
Rilla Mill Cnwll 5 L2
Rillington N York 134 D5
Rimington Lancs 122 B2
Rimpton Somset 26 E6
Rimswell E R Yk 127 H5
Rinaston Pembks 49 G3
Rindleford Shrops 84 D4
Ringford D & G 146 C4
Ringland Norfk 92 D2
Ringmer E Susx 19 L3
Ringmore Devon 6 F6
Ringmore Devon 7 L2
Ringorm Moray 215 G5
Ringsfield Suffk 93 J5
Ringsfield Corner
Suffk 93 J6
Ringshall Herts 59 G5
Ringshall Suffk 78 C4
Ringshall Stocks
Suffk 78 C4
Ringstead Nhants 88 E7
Ringstead Norfk 105 H4
Ringwood Hants 15 L2
Ringwould Kent 35 K5
Ripe E Susx 20 B4
Ripley Derbys 101 H3
Ripley Hants 15 M3
Ripley N York 132 D7
Ripley Surrey 31 H1
Riplington Hants 30 A6
Ripon N York 132 D5
Rippingale Lincs 103 H6
Ripple Kent 35 J5
Ripple Worcs 70 F6
Ripponden Calder 122 F6
Risabus Ag & B 160 B2
Risbury Herefs 69 K4
Risby Suffk 77 H2
Risca Caerph 37 K3
Rise E R Yk 126 E3
Risegate Lincs 103 K6
Riseley Bed 74 F3
Riseley Wokham 42 B7
Rishangles Suffk 78 E2
Rishton Lancs 121 L4
Rishworth Calder 122 F6
Risley Derbys 101 J5
Risley Warrtn 112 F3
Risplith N York 132 C5
River Kent 35 J6
River W Susx 30 F6
Riverford Highld 212 E4
Riverhead Kent 32 F3
Rivington Lancs 121 J7
Rivington Services
Lancs 121 J7
Roade Nhants 73 L4
Roadmeetings S Lans.. 176 B7
Roadside E Ayrs 164 B5
Roadside Highld 231 H4
Roadwater Somset 25 G4
Roag Highld 208 D5
Roan of Craigoch
S Ayrs 153 G2
Roath Cardif 37 J5
Roberton Border 166 F6
Roberton S Lans 165 H4
Robertsbridge E Susx ... 20 E2
Roberttown Kirk 123 J6
Robeston Wathen
Pembks 49 J4
Robgill Tower D & G... 155 M7
Robin Hood
Crematorium
Solhll 85 K7
Robin Hood
Doncaster
Sheffield Airport
Donc 116 A2
Robin Hood's Bay
N York 143 K6
Roborough Devon 6 D4
Roborough Devon 10 E2
Roby Knows 112 B4
Rocester Staffs 100 C5
Roch Pembks 48 E3

Rochdale Rochdl 122 D7
Rochdale
Crematorium
Rochdl 122 C7
Roche Cnwll 4 F4
Rochester Medway 46 C6
Rochester Nthumb 157 L3
Rochford Essex 46 E3
Rochford Worcs 70 B2
Rock Cnwll 4 E2
Rock Nthumb 169 J5
Rock Worcs 70 D1
Rockbeare Devon 12 C4
Rockbourne Hants 28 C7
Rockcliffe Cumb 148 C3
Rockcliffe D & G 146 E4
Rockend Torbay 7 L4
Rock Ferry Wirral 111 K4
Rockfield Highld 223 K5
Rockfield Mons 54 C5
Rockford Devon 24 B2
Rockhampton S Glos 38 F2
Rockhill Shrops 82 F7
Rockingham Nhants 88 C5
Rockland All Saints
Norfk 92 B4
Rockland St Mary
Norfk 93 G3
Rockland St Peter
Norfk 92 B4
Rockley Notts 116 B6
Rockwell End Bucks 42 D3
Rodborough Gloucs 55 J6
Rodbourne Swindn 40 C4
Rodbourne Wilts 39 L4
Rodden Dorset 14 B5
Rode Somset 27 J2
Rode Heath Ches E 99 J2
Rodel W Isls 232 d5
Roden Wrekin 83 L1
Rodhuish Somset 24 F4
Rodington Wrekin 83 L1
Rodington Heath
Wrekin 83 L1
Rodley Gloucs 55 H5
Rodmarton Gloucs 39 L2
Rodmell E Susx 19 L4
Rodmersham Kent 34 B3
Rodmersham Green
Kent 34 B3
Rodney Stoke Somset ... 26 C2
Rodsley Derbys 100 D4
Roecliffe N York 132 E6
Roe Green Herts 59 K6
Roe Green Herts 75 K7
Roehampton Gt Lon 44 E5
Roffey W Susx 31 K5
Rogart Highld 226 C7
Rogate W Susx 30 D6
Rogerstone Newpt 37 L3
Roghadal W Isls 232 d5
Rogiet Mons 38 C3
Roke Oxon 41 L2
Roker Sundld 151 J3
Rollesby Norfk 93 J1
Rolleston Leics 87 K4
Rolleston Notts 102 C3
Rolleston on Dove
Staffs 100 E6
Rolston E R Yk 126 F2
Rolvenden Kent 33 L6
Rolvenden Layne
Kent 33 L7
Romaldkirk Dur 140 C3
Romanby N York 132 K2
Romanno Bridge
Border 177 G3
Romansleigh Devon 24 B7
Romesdal Highld 208 F4
Romford Dorset 15 K1
Romford Gt Lon 45 K3
Romiley Stockp 113 L4
Romsey Hants 29 G6
Romsley Shrops 84 D6
Romsley Worcs 85 G7
Rona Highld 209 K3

Ronachan Ag & B 172 C7
Rookhope Dur 150 B6
Rookley IoW 17 G5
Rooks Bridge Somset ... 26 A2
Rooks Nest Somset 25 H5
Rookwith N York 132 C3
Roos E R Yk 127 G4
Roothams Green Bed.... 75 G3
Ropley Hants 29 M5
Ropley Dean Hants 29 L5
Ropsley Lincs 103 G5
Rora Abers 217 K4
Rorrington Shrops 82 F4
Rosarie Moray 215 J4
Rose Cnwll 3 K1
Rose Ash Devon 24 C6
Rosebank S Lans 175 L7
Rosebush Pembks 49 J2
Rosedale Abbey
N York 142 F7
Rose Green Essex 61 L3
Rose Green Suffk 77 L5
Rose Green Suffk 77 L6
Rose Green W Susx 18 B5
Rosehall Highld 225 K7
Rosehearty Abers 217 H2
Rose Hill Lancs 122 C4
Roseisle Moray 214 E2
Roselands E Susx 20 C5
Rosemarket Pembks 49 G5
Rosemarkie Highld 213 H3
Rosemary Lane
Devon 25 J7
Rosemount P & K 195 J7
Rosenannon Cnwll 4 E3
Rosewell Mdloth 177 J6
Roseworth S on T 141 K3
Rosgill Cumb 138 D4
Roskhill Highld 208 D5
Rosley Cumb 148 B6
Roslin Mdloth 177 H5
Rosliston Derbys 86 B1
Rosneath Ag & B 174 B2
Ross D & G 146 B6
Rossett Wrexhm 98 A2
Rossett Green N York .. 132 D8
Rossington Donc 115 L2
Rossland Rens 174 E4
Ross-on-Wye Herefs 54 E4
Roster Highld 231 J7
Rostherne Ches E 113 H5
Rosthwaite Cumb 137 H4
Roston Derbys 100 C4
Rosyth Fife 176 F2
Rothbury Nthumb 158 D2
Rotherby Leics 87 J1
Rotherfield E Susx 32 F7
Rotherfield Greys
Oxon 42 B4
Rotherfield Peppard
Oxon 42 B4
Rotherham Rothm 115 H3
Rotherham
Crematorium
Rothm 115 J3
Rotherthorpe
Nhants 73 K3
Rotherthorpe
Services Nhants 73 K3
Rotherwick Hants 30 B1
Rothes Moray 215 G4
Rothesay Ag & B 173 J5
Rothiebrisbane
Abers 216 E6
Rothiemay Moray 215 M5
Rothiemurchus
Lodge Highld 204 B4
Rothienorman Abers.... 216 D7
Rothley Leics 87 H2
Rothmaise Abers 216 D7
Rothwell Leeds 123 L5
Rothwell Lincs 117 J2
Rothwell Nhants 88 B7
Rottal Lodge Angus..... 196 B3
Rottingdean Br & H 19 K5
Rottington Cumb 136 D5
Roucan D & G 155 H6

Roucan Loch
Crematorium
D & G 155 H6
Rougham Norfk 105 K7
Rougham Green
Suffk 77 K3
Rough Common Kent 34 F3
Roughpark Abers 205 H3
Roughton Lincs 118 C8
Roughton Norfk 106 F5
Roughton Shrops 84 D5
Roundbush Green
Essex 60 F5
Round Green Luton 59 J4
Roundham Somset 13 K1
Roundhay Leeds 123 L3
Roundway Wilts 40 A7
Roundyhill Angus 196 C6
Rousay Ork 234 c4
Rousdon Devon 13 H4
Rousham Oxon 57 J3
Rous Lench Worcs 71 H4
Routenburn N Ayrs 173 L6
Routh E R Yk 126 D3
Row Cumb 129 K2
Rowanburn D & G 156 D6
Rowardennan Stirlg 183 L7
Rowarth Derbys 114 A4
Rowberrow Somset 38 C8
Rowde Wilts 39 L7
Rowen Conwy 109 L6
Rowfoot Nthumb 149 H3
Rowhedge Essex 62 B4
Rowington Warwks 72 B2
Rowland Derbys 114 E6
Rowland's Castle
Hants 17 K1
Rowland's Gill Gatesd .. 150 E4
Rowledge Surrey 30 D3
Rowley Dur 150 D5
Rowley Regis Sandw 85 H6
Rowley Regis
Crematorium
Sandw 85 G6
Rowlstone Herefs 54 A3
Rowly Surrey 31 H4
Rowner Hants 17 H3
Rowney Green Worcs 71 J1
Rownhams Hants 29 G7
Rownhams Services
Hants 29 H7
Rowrah Cumb 136 E4
Rowsham Bucks 58 D4
Rowsley Derbys 114 E7
Rowston Lincs 103 H2
Rowton Ches W 112 C8
Rowton Wrekin 98 E8
Roxburgh Border 167 L4
Roxby N Linc 125 L6
Roxton Bed 75 G4
Roxwell Essex 61 G6
Royal Botanic
Gardens, Kew
Gt Lon 44 D5
Royal Leamington
Spa Warwks 72 D2
Royal Tunbridge
Wells Kent 33 G5
Royal Wootton
Bassett Wilts 40 B4
Roy Bridge Highld 192 D1
Roydon Essex 60 C6
Roydon Norfk 92 D7
Roydon Norfk 105 H7
Roydon Hamlet Essex .. 60 C6
Royston Barns 124 B7
Royston Herts 75 L6
Royton Oldham 122 D8
Rozel Jersey 236 e6
Ruabon Wrexhm 97 L4
Ruaig Ag & B 188 D6
Ruan Lanihorne
Cnwll 4 D7
Ruan Major Cnwll 3 J7
Ruan Minor Cnwll 3 J7
Ruardean Gloucs 54 F4
Ruardean Hill Gloucs 54 F5

Ruardean Woodside
Gloucs 54 F5
Rubery Birm 85 H7
Rubha Ban W Isls 233 c9
Ruckhall Herefs 69 J6
Ruckinge Kent 34 D7
Ruckley Shrops 83 K4
Rudby N York 141 L6
Rudchester Nthumb 150 E2
Ruddington Notts 101 L6
Rudge Somset 27 J2
Rudgeway S Glos 38 F3
Rudgwick W Susx 31 H5
Rudheath Ches W 112 F6
Rudley Green Essex 61 K7
Rudloe Wilts 39 J6
Rudry Caerph 37 J3
Rudston E R Yk 135 H6
Rudyard Staffs 99 L2
Ruecastle Border 167 J5
Rufford Lancs 120 F7
Rufforth C York 124 D1
Rugby Warwks 87 G7
Rugeley Staffs 100 B8
Ruishton Somset 25 K6
Ruislip Gt Lon 43 H3
Rùm Highld 198 F5
Rumbach Moray 215 J4
Rumbling Bridge
P & K 185 L7
Rumburgh Suffk 93 H7
Rumford Cnwll 4 D2
Rumford Falk 176 C3
Rumney Cardif 37 K5
Runcorn Halton 112 D5
Runcton W Susx 18 B5
Runcton Holme Norfk .. 90 E2
Runfold Surrey 30 E3
Runhall Norfk 92 C3
Runham Norfk 93 K2
Runnington Somset 25 H6
Runswick N York 143 G4
Runtaleave Angus 195 L3
Runwell Essex 46 C2
Ruscombe Wokham 42 D5
Rushall Herefs 70 B7
Rushall Norfk 92 E6
Rushall Wilts 28 C1
Rushbrooke Suffk 77 K3
Rushbury Shrops 83 K5
Rushden Herts 60 A2
Rushden Nhants 74 D2
Rushenden Kent 46 E5
Rushford Norfk 91 K7
Rush Green Essex 62 E5
Rush Green Gt Lon 45 K3
Rush Green Warrtn 113 G4
Rushlake Green
E Susx 20 D3
Rushmere Suffk 93 K6
Rushmoor Surrey 30 E4
Rushock Worcs 70 F1
Rusholme Manch 113 J3
Rushton Nhants 88 B6
Rushton Spencer
Staffs 113 L8
Rushwick Worcs 70 E4
Rushyford Dur 141 G2
Ruskie Stirlg 184 D7
Ruskington Lincs 103 H3
Rusland Cross Cumb .. 129 H2
Rusper W Susx 31 K4
Ruspidge Gloucs 54 F5
Russell's Water Oxon .. 42 B3
Russ Hill Surrey 31 L4
Rusthall Kent 32 F5
Rustington W Susx 18 E5
Ruston N York 134 E3
Ruston Parva E R Yk .. 135 G6
Ruswarp N York 143 H5
Rutherford Border 167 K4
Rutherglen S Lans 175 H6
Ruthernbridge Cnwll 4 F3
Ruthin Denbgs 97 H2
Ruthrieston C Aber 207 H4
Ruthven Abers 215 L5
Ruthven Angus 195 L6

Ruthven Highld 203 H5
Ruthvoes Cnwll 4 E4
Ruthwell D & G 147 J2
Ruyton-XI-Towns
Shrops 98 B7
Ryal Nthumb 158 C7
Ryall Dorset 13 K4
Ryall Worcs 70 F6
Ryarsh Kent 33 H2
Rydal Cumb 137 K6
Ryde IoW 17 H4
Rye E Susx 21 H2
Rye Foreign E Susx 21 H2
Rye Street Worcs 70 D7
Ryhall Rutlnd 88 F2
Ryhill Wakefd 124 B7
Ryhope Sundld 151 K4
Ryland Lincs 117 G5
Rylands Notts 101 K5
Rylstone N York 131 H7
Ryme Intrinseca
Dorset 14 B1
Ryther N York 124 E3
Ryton Gatesd 150 E3
Ryton Shrops 84 D3
Ryton-on-Dunsmore
Warwks 86 E8

S

Sabden Lancs 122 B3
Sacombe Herts 60 B4
Sacriston Dur 151 G5
Sadberge Darltn 141 H4
Saddell Ag & B 161 K3
Saddington Leics 87 J5
Saddle Bow Norfk 90 E1
Saddlescombe
W Susx 19 H4
Saffron Walden
Essex 76 D6
Sageston Pembks 49 H6
Saham Hills Norfk 91 K3
Saham Toney Norfk 91 K3
Saighton Ches W 98 C1
St Abbs Border 179 J5
St Agnes Border 178 E5
St Agnes Cnwll 3 J2
St Agnes IoS 2 a2
St Albans Herts 59 J6
St Allen Cnwll 4 C5
St Andrew Guern 236 c3
St Andrews Fife 187 H4
St Andrews Botanic
Garden Fife 187 H4
St Andrew's Major
V Glam 37 H6
St Andrews Well
Dorset 13 L4
St Anne's Lancs 120 D5
St Ann's D & G 155 J4
St Ann's Chapel Cnwll 6 B2
St Ann's Chapel
Devon 6 F6
St Anthony Cnwll 3 K6
St Anthony's Hill
E Susx 20 D5
St Arvans Mons 38 D2
St Asaph Denbgs 110 E6
St Athan V Glam 36 F6
St Aubin Jersey 236 b7
St Austell Cnwll 4 F5
St Bees Cumb 136 D5
St Blazey Cnwll 5 G5
St Boswells Border 167 J3
St Brelade Jersey 236 b7
St Brelade's Bay
Jersey 236 b7
St Breock Cnwll 4 F2
St Breward Cnwll 5 H1
St Briavels Gloucs 54 E6
St Bride's Major
V Glam 36 D5
St Brides super-Ely
V Glam 37 H5

St Brides Wentlooge
Newpt 37 L4
St Budeaux C Plym 6 C4
Saintbury Gloucs 71 K6
St Buryan Cnwll 2 D6
St Catherines Ag & B .. 183 G6
St Chloe Gloucs 55 J7
St Clears Carmth 50 C3
St Cleer Cnwll 5 K3
St Clement Cnwll 4 D6
St Clement Jersey 236 e8
St Clether Cnwll 9 G7
St Colmac Ag & B 173 H5
St Columb Major
Cnwll 4 E3
St Columb Minor
Cnwll 4 D4
St Columb Road
Cnwll 4 E4
St Combs Abers 217 K2
St Cross South
Elmham Suffk 93 G6
St Cyrus Abers 197 J4
St David's P & K 185 K4
St David's Pembks 48 C3
St Day Cnwll 3 J3
St Dennis Cnwll 4 E4
St Dogmaels Pembks .. 65 G5
St Dominick Cnwll 6 B3
St Donats V Glam 36 E6
St Endellion Cnwll 4 F1
St Enoder Cnwll 4 D4
St Erme Cnwll 4 D6
St Erney Cnwll 6 B4
St Erth Cnwll 2 F4
St Erth Praze Cnwll 3 G4
St Ervan Cnwll 4 D2
St Eval Cnwll 4 D3
St Ewe Cnwll 4 F6
St Fagans Cardif 37 H5
St Fagans: National
History Museum
Cardif 37 H5
St Fergus Abers 217 K4
St Fillans P & K 184 F3
St Florence Pembks 49 J7
St Gennys Cnwll 8 F5
St George Conwy 110 D6
St Georges N Som 38 B7
St George's V Glam 37 H5
St Germans Cnwll 6 A4
St Giles in the Wood
Devon 23 H7
St Giles-on-the-
Heath Devon 9 K6
St Harmon Powys 81 L8
St Helen Auckland
Dur 140 F2
St Helens IoW 17 J5
St Helens St Hel 112 D5
St Helens
Crematorium
St Hel 112 C3
St Helier Gt Lon 44 E6
St Helier Jersey 236 d7
St Hilary Cnwll 2 F5
St Hilary V Glam 36 F5
St Ippollitts Herts 59 K3
St Ishmael's Pembks .. 48 E6
St Issey Cnwll 4 E2
St Ive Cnwll 5 L3
St Ives Cambs 75 K1
St Ives Cnwll 2 F3
St James's End
Nhants 73 L3
St James South
Elmham Suffk 93 G7
St Jidgey Cnwll 4 E3
St John Cnwll 6 B5
St John Jersey 236 c5
St John's IoM 237 b5
St Johns Kent 32 F3
St Johns Surrey 43 G8
St Johns Worcs 70 E4
St John's Chapel
Devon 23 H5
St John's Chapel Dur .. 149 M7

St John's Fen End
Norfk.............................90 D2
St John's Kirk S Lans.....165 J3
St John's Town of
Dalry D & G..............154 B6
St John's Wood
Gt Lon............................44 F4
St Jude's IoM.................237 d3
St Just Cnwll.......................2 C5
St Just-in-Roseland
Cnwll...............................4 D8
St Katherines Abers.......216 E7
St Keverne Cnwll..............3 K6
St Kew Cnwll.....................5 G1
St Kew Highway
Cnwll...............................5 G2
St Keyne Cnwll..................5 K4
St Lawrence Essex.........62 A6
St Lawrence IoW............17 G6
St Lawrence Jersey.......236 c6
St Lawrence Kent...........35 K2
St Leonards Bucks..........58 E6
St Leonards Dorset.........15 L2
St Leonards E Susx........20 F4
St Levan Cnwll...................2 C6
St Lythans V Glam...........37 H6
St Mabyn Cnwll.................5 G2
St Madoes P & K...........186 C3
St Margarets Herefs.......69 G7
St Margarets Herts........60 B5
St Margaret's at
Cliffe Kent.....................35 K5
St Margaret's Hope
Ork...............................234 c7
St Margaret South
Elmham Suffk..............93 G6
St Marks IoM.................237 c6
St Martin Cnwll..................3 J6
St Martin Cnwll..................5 K5
St Martin Guern.............236 d3
St Martin Jersey............236 e6
St Martin's IoS...................2 b1
St Martin's P & K..........186 B2
St Martins Shrops...........97 L5
St Mary Jersey..............236 b6
St Mary Bourne Hants...29 H2
St Marychurch Torbay.....7 L3
St Mary Church
V Glam...........................36 F6
St Mary Cray Gt Lon......45 J6
St Mary in the Marsh
Kent.............................21 L1
St Marylebone
Crematorium
Gt Lon............................44 E3
St Mary's IoS......................2 b1
St Mary's Ork.................234 c6
St Mary's Bay Kent.........21 L1
St Mary's Hoo
Medway.........................46 D5
St Maughans Green
Mons..............................54 C5
St Mawes Cnwll.................3 L5
St Mawgan Cnwll..............4 D3
St Mellion Cnwll................6 B3
St Mellons Cardif............37 K4
St Merryn Cnwll.................4 D2
St Michael Caerhays
Cnwll...............................4 F7
St Michael Church
Somset..........................25 L5
St Michael Penkevil
Cnwll...............................4 D7
St Michaels Kent.............34 B7
St Michaels Worcs..........69 L2
St Michael's on Wyre
Lancs...........................120 F3
St Minver Cnwll.................4 F1
St Monans Fife...............187 H6
St Neot Cnwll.....................5 J3
St Neots Cambs...............75 H3
St Nicholas Pembks.........64 C7
St Nicholas V Glam.........37 H5
St Nicholas at Wade
Kent.............................47 L6
St Ninians Stirlg............185 G8
St Olaves Norfk................93 J4

St Osyth Essex.................62 D5
St Ouen Jersey..............236 b6
St Owens Cross
Herefs...........................54 D3
St Pauls Cray Gt Lon......45 J6
St Paul's Walden
Herts..............................59 K4
St Peter Jersey..............236 b6
St Peter Port Guern.......236 d3
St Peter's Guern............236 b3
St Peter's Kent................35 K2
St Pinnock Cnwll...............5 J3
St Quivox S Ayrs............163 J5
St Sampson Guern.........236 d2
St Saviour Guern............236 c3
St Saviour Jersey..........236 d7
St Stephen Cnwll..............4 E5
St Stephens Cnwll............6 B4
St Stephens Cnwll............9 J7
St Teath Cnwll....................8 E8
St Tudy Cnwll....................5 G1
St Twynnells Pembks.....48 F7
St Veep Cnwll.....................5 J5
St Vigeans Angus...........197 G7
St Wenn Cnwll...................4 F3
St Weonards Herefs........54 D3
Salcombe Devon................7 H7
Salcombe Regis
Devon............................12 F5
Salcott-cum-Virley
Essex.............................61 M5
Sale Traffd.....................113 H3
Saleby Lincs..................118 F5
Sale Green Worcs...........71 G3
Salehurst E Susx............20 F2
Salem Cerdgn..................80 F6
Salen Ag & B.................190 C7
Salen Highld..................190 D4
Salford C Beds.................74 D6
Salford Oxon....................56 F3
Salford Salfd..................113 J2
Salford Priors Warwks...71 J4
Salfords Surrey...............32 B4
Salhouse Norfk...............93 G1
Saline Fife.....................185 L8
Salisbury Wilts................28 C5
Salisbury Cathedral
Wilts..............................28 C5
Salisbury
Crematorium
Wilts..............................28 D5
Salisbury Plain Wilts.......28 B3
Salkeld Dykes Cumb......148 F7
Salle Norfk.....................106 D7
Salmonby Lincs..............118 D6
Salperton Gloucs............56 B4
Salsburgh N Lans...........175 L5
Salt Staffs........................99 L6
Saltaire C Brad...............123 H3
Saltash Cnwll.....................6 B4
Saltburn Highld..............223 G7
Saltburn-by-the-Sea
R & Cl...........................142 E3
Saltby Leics...................102 D7
Saltcoats N Ayrs............163 G2
Saltdean Br & H..............19 K5
Salterbeck Cumb...........136 D3
Salterforth Lancs...........122 D2
Salterton Wilts.................28 C4
Saltfleet Lincs................118 F3
Saltfleetby All Saints
Lincs............................118 F4
Saltfleetby St
Clement Lincs.............118 F3
Saltfleetby St Peter
Lincs............................118 F4
Saltford BaNES................39 G6
Salthouse Norfk.............106 C4
Saltmarshe E R Yk.........125 J5
Saltney Flints................111 L8
Salton N York.................133 L4
Saltrens Devon................23 G6
Saltwell
Crematorium
Gatesd..........................151 G3
Saltwood Kent..................34 F7
Salvington W Susx..........18 F5

Salwarpe Worcs...............70 F3
Salway Ash Dorset...........13 L3
Sambourne Warwks........71 J3
Sambrook Wrekin............99 G7
Sampford Arundel
Somset..........................25 H7
Sampford Brett
Somset..........................25 G3
Sampford Courtenay
Devon............................10 F5
Sampford Moor
Somset..........................25 H7
Sampford Peverell
Devon............................25 G8
Sampford Spiney
Devon..............................6 D2
Samsonlane Ork............234 d5
Samuelston E Loth........178 B4
Sanaigmore Ag & B.......170 E4
Sancreed Cnwll..................2 D5
Sancton E R Yk..............125 L3
Sandaig Highld...............199 L5
Sandal Magna
Wakefd.........................123 L6
Sandavore Highld..........199 G7
Sanday Ork.....................234 d4
Sanday Airport Ork........234 d4
Sandbach Ches E.............99 H1
Sandbach Services
Ches E............................99 H1
Sandbank Ag & B..........173 K3
Sandbanks Poole.............15 K5
Sandend Abers...............216 B2
Sanderstead Gt Lon........45 G7
Sandford Cumb..............139 G4
Sandford Devon...............11 J4
Sandford Dorset..............15 H5
Sandford Hants................15 M3
Sandford IoW...................17 G6
Sandford N Som..............38 B8
Sandford S Lans.............164 E2
Sandford-on-Thames
Oxon..............................57 K7
Sandford Orcas
Dorset............................26 F7
Sandford St Martin
Oxon..............................57 H3
Sandgate Kent..................35 G7
Sandhaven Abers...........217 H2
Sandhead D & G.............144 D5
Sand Hills Leeds.............124 B3
Sandhills Oxon.................57 K6
Sandhills Surrey...............30 F4
Sandhoe Nthumb............150 B2
Sandhole Ag & B............182 E7
Sand Hole E R Yk...........125 J3
Sandholme E R Yk..........125 J4
Sandhurst Br For.............42 D7
Sandhurst Gloucs............55 J4
Sandhurst Kent.................33 K7
Sandhutton N York.........132 F3
Sand Hutton N York........133 L7
Sandiacre Derbys...........101 J5
Sandilands Lincs............119 G5
Sandleheath Hants..........28 C7
Sandleigh Oxon...............57 J7
Sandley Dorset.................27 H6
Sandness Shet...............235 b5
Sandon Essex..................61 H6
Sandon Herts...................75 K7
Sandon Staffs...................99 L6
Sandon Bank Staffs.........99 L6
Sandown IoW...................17 H5
Sandplace Cnwll................5 K4
Sandridge Herts...............59 K6
Sandringham Norfk........105 H6
Sandsend N York............143 H5
Sandtoft N Linc..............125 H8
Sandway Kent..................34 B5
Sandwich Kent.................35 J3
Sandwick Cumb...............136 D4
Sandwick W Isls.............232 g2
Sandwith Cumb..............136 D4
Sandy C Beds..................75 H5
Sandyford D & G.............155 L4
Sandygate Devon..............7 K2
Sandygate IoM...............237 d2

Sandyhills D & G.............146 F4
Sandylands Lancs..........129 J6
Sandy Lane Wilts............39 L6
Sandy Park Devon...........11 G6
Sangobeg Highld...........228 F3
Sangomore Highld.........228 F3
Sankyn's Green
Worcs.............................70 E2
Sanna Bay Highld..........189 K3
Sanndabhaig W Isls.......232 g2
Sannox N Ayrs...............162 C1
Sanquhar D & G.............164 F7
Santon Bridge Cumb......136 F6
Santon Downham
Suffk..............................91 J6
Sapcote Leics.................86 F5
Sapey Common
Herefs............................70 C2
Sapiston Suffk.................91 K7
Sapperton Gloucs............55 L7
Sapperton Lincs.............103 G5
Saracen's Head
Lincs............................104 B6
Sarclet Highld................231 L6
Sarisbury Hants...............17 G2
Sarn Gwynd....................94 D6
Sarn Powys......................81 K4
Sarn Powys......................82 E5
Sarnau Cerdgn.................65 K4
Sarnau Powys..................82 E1
Sarn Park Services
Brdgnd...........................36 D4
Saron Carmth...................51 H3
Saron Gwynd..................109 G7
Sarratt Herts....................59 H7
Sarre Kent........................47 L6
Sarsden Oxon...................56 F4
Satley Dur......................150 E6
Satterleigh Devon............23 L6
Satterthwaite Cumb.......129 H2
Sauchen Abers...............206 D3
Saucher P & K................186 C2
Sauchieburn Abers.........197 G3
Saul Gloucs......................55 H6
Saundby Notts................116 C4
Saundersfoot
Pembks...........................49 K6
Saunderton Bucks...........58 C7
Saunton Devon.................23 G4
Sausthorpe Lincs............118 E7
Savile Town Kirk.............123 K6
Sawbridge Warwks.........73 G2
Sawbridgeworth
Herts..............................60 D5
Sawdon N York...............134 E3
Sawley Lancs..................122 B2
Sawley N York.................132 C6
Sawston Cambs...............76 C5
Sawtry Cambs..................89 H6
Saxby Leics....................102 D8
Saxby Lincs....................117 G4
Saxby All Saints
N Linc...........................126 B7
Saxelbee Leics...............102 B7
Saxham Street Suffk........78 C3
Saxilby Lincs..................116 E6
Saxlingham Norfk...........106 B5
Saxlingham Green
Norfk..............................92 F4
Saxlingham
Nethergate Norfk...........92 F4
Saxlingham Thorpe
Norfk..............................92 E4
Saxmundham Suffk.........79 H2
Saxondale Notts.............102 B4
Saxon Street Cambs.........76 F3
Saxtead Suffk...................78 F2
Saxtead Green Suffk.........78 F2
Saxtead Little Green
Suffk...............................78 F2
Saxthorpe Norfk.............106 D6
Saxton N York.................124 D3
Sayers Common
W Susx............................19 H3
Scackleton N York..........133 K5
Scafell Pike Cumb...........137 H5
Scaftworth Notts.............116 A3

Scagglethorpe
  N York 134 C5
Scalasaig Ag & B 180 E8
Scalby E R Yk 125 K5
Scalby N York 134 F2
Scaldwell Nhants 73 L1
Scaleby Cumb 148 D3
Scalebyhill Cumb 148 D3
Scales Cumb 129 G5
Scales Cumb 137 K2
Scalford Leics 102 C7
Scaling N York 142 F4
Scalloway Shet 235 c6
Scalpay Highld 209 J7
Scamblesby Lincs 118 C5
Scamodale Highld 191 G2
Scampston N York 134 D4
Scampton Lincs 116 F5
Scaniport Highld 212 F6
Scapegoat Hill Kirk 123 G7
Scarba Ag & B 181 K6
Scarborough N York 135 G2
Scarcewater Cnwll 4 E5
Scarcliffe Derbys 115 J7
Scarcroft Leeds 124 B3
Scarfskerry Highld 231 J2
Scarinish Ag & B 188 D7
Scarisbrick Lancs 120 E7
Scarning Norfk 91 L2
Scarrington Notts 102 B4
Scartho NE Lin 118 C1
Scatsta Airport Shet 235 c4
Scawby N Linc 116 F1
Scawsby Donc 115 K1
Scawthorpe Donc 115 K1
Scawton N York 133 H3
Scayne's Hill W Susx 19 K2
Scethrog Powys 53 H3
Scholar Green Ches E 99 J2
Scholemoor
  Crematorium
  C Brad 123 H4
Scholes Kirk 123 H8
Scholes Leeds 124 B3
Scholes Rothm 115 H3
Scholes Wigan 112 E1
Scissett Kirk 123 K7
Scleddau Pembks 64 C7
Scofton Notts 115 L5
Scole Norfk 92 D7
Scone P & K 186 B3
Sconser Highld 209 H7
Scoonie Fife 186 F6
Scopwick Lincs 103 H2
Scoraig Highld 220 C3
Scorborough E R Yk 126 C2
Scorrier Cnwll 3 J3
Scorton Lancs 121 G2
Scorton N York 141 G7
Scotby Cumb 148 D4
Scotch Corner N York 140 F6
Scotforth Lancs 129 K7
Scothern Lincs 117 G6
Scotlandwell P & K 186 C6
Scotscalder Station
  Highld 231 G4
Scot's Gap Nthumb 158 C5
Scotsmill Abers 206 B2
Scotstoun C Glas 174 F5
Scotswood N u Ty 150 F3
Scotter Lincs 116 E2
Scotterthorpe Lincs 116 E2
Scotton Lincs 116 E2
Scotton N York 132 E7
Scotton N York 140 F7
Scoulton Norfk 92 B4
Scourie Highld 228 B6
Scourie More Highld 228 B6
Scousburgh Shet 235 c7
Scrabster Highld 231 G2
Scraesburgh Border 167 K5
Scrane End Lincs 104 C4
Scraptoft Leics 87 J3
Scratby Norfk 93 K1
Scrayingham N York 133 L7
Scredington Lincs 103 H4
Scremby Lincs 118 F7

Scremerston
  Nthumb 179 L8
Screveton Notts 102 B4
Scriven N York 132 E7
Scrooby Notts 115 M4
Scropton Derbys 100 D6
Scrub Hill Lincs 103 L2
Scruton N York 132 D2
Scullomie Highld 229 J4
Sculthorpe Norfk 105 L6
Scunthorpe N Linc 125 K7
Seaborough Dorset 13 K2
Seabrook Kent 35 G7
Seaburn Sundld 151 J3
Seacroft Leeds 124 B4
Seafield Highld 209 G5
Seafield W Loth 176 D5
Seafield
  Crematorium
  C Edin 177 J4
Seaford E Susx 20 A6
Seaforth Sefton 111 K3
Seagrave Leics 101 L8
Seaham Dur 151 K5
Seahouses Nthumb 169 J3
Seal Kent 32 F2
Seale Surrey 30 E2
Seamer N York 134 F3
Seamer N York 142 B5
Seamill N Ayrs 173 L8
Sea Palling Norfk 107 J6
Searby Lincs 117 H1
Seasalter Kent 47 H6
Seascale Cumb 136 E6
Seathwaite Cumb 137 H7
Seatoller Cumb 137 H4
Seaton Cnwll 5 L5
Seaton Cumb 136 E2
Seaton Devon 13 G4
Seaton E R Yk 126 E2
Seaton Kent 35 G3
Seaton Nthumb 159 H6
Seaton Rutlnd 88 C4
Seaton Carew Hartpl 142 B2
Seaton Delaval
  Nthumb 159 H6
Seaton Ross E R Yk 125 J3
Seaton Sluice
  Nthumb 159 H6
Seatown Dorset 13 K4
Seave Green N York 142 C7
Seaview IoW 17 J4
Seaville Cumb 147 K4
Seavington St Mary
  Somset 26 B7
Seavington St
  Michael Somset 26 B7
Sebergham Cumb 148 C6
Seckington Warwks 86 C3
Sedbergh Cumb 130 C2
Sedbury Gloucs 38 D2
Sedbusk N York 131 G2
Sedgeberrow Worcs 71 H6
Sedgebrook Lincs 102 D5
Sedgefield Dur 141 J2
Sedgeford Norfk 105 H5
Sedgehill Wilts 27 K5
Sedgemoor Services
  Somset 26 A2
Sedgley Dudley 85 G5
Sedgwick Cumb 129 L3
Sedlescombe E Susx 20 F3
Sedrup Bucks 58 D5
Seend Wilts 39 L7
Seend Cleeve Wilts 39 L7
Seer Green Bucks 42 F3
Seething Norfk 93 G4
Sefton Sefton 111 K2
Seighford Staffs 99 K7
Seion Gwynd 109 H7
Seisdon Staffs 84 E4
Selattyn Shrops 97 K5
Selborne Hants 30 C5
Selby N York 124 F4
Selham W Susx 30 F7
Selhurst Gt Lon 45 G6
Selkirk Border 167 G4

Sellack Herefs 54 E3
Sellafirth Shet 235 d2
Sellindge Kent 34 E6
Selling Kent 34 D4
Sells Green Wilts 39 L7
Selly Oak Birm 85 J6
Selmeston E Susx 20 B4
Selsdon Gt Lon 45 G7
Selsey Gloucs 55 J7
Selsey W Susx 18 B6
Selside N York 130 E4
Selsted Kent 35 G5
Selston Notts 101 J2
Selworthy Somset 24 E3
Semer Suffk 78 B5
Semington Wilts 39 K7
Semley Wilts 27 K6
Send Surrey 31 G1
Senghenydd Caerph 37 H3
Sennen Cnwll 2 C6
Sennen Cove Cnwll 2 C6
Sennybridge Powys 52 E3
Sessay N York 133 G4
Setchey Norfk 90 F2
Seton Mains E Loth 177 L4
Settle N York 130 F6
Settrington N York 134 C5
Sevenhampton
  Gloucs 56 B4
Sevenhampton
  Swindn 40 E3
Seven Hills
  Crematorium
  Suffk 78 F6
Seven Kings Gt Lon 45 J3
Sevenoaks Kent 32 F3
Sevenoaks Weald
  Kent 32 F3
Seven Sisters Neath 52 C6
Seven Star Green
  Essex 61 M3
Severn Beach S Glos 38 D4
Severn Stoke Worcs 70 F5
Severn View Services
  S Glos 38 D4
Sevington Kent 34 D6
Sewards End Essex 76 E6
Sewell C Beds 59 G4
Sewerby E R Yk 135 J5
Seworgan Cnwll 3 J5
Sewstern Leics 102 E7
Sgiogarstaigh W Isls 232 g1
Shabbington Bucks 58 A6
Shackerstone Leics 86 D3
Shackleford Surrey 30 F3
Shader W Isls 232 f1
Shadforth Dur 151 H6
Shadingfield Suffk 93 J6
Shadoxhurst Kent 34 C7
Shadwell Norfk 91 L6
Shaftenhoe End
  Herts 76 B6
Shaftesbury Dorset 27 K6
Shafton Barns 124 B7
Shakerley Wigan 113 G2
Shalbourne Wilts 40 F7
Shalden Hants 30 B3
Shaldon Devon 7 L2
Shalfleet IoW 16 E5
Shalford Essex 61 H3
Shalford Surrey 31 G3
Shalford Green Essex 61 H3
Shalmsford Street
  Kent 34 E4
Shalstone Bucks 73 J7
Shamley Green
  Surrey 31 G3
Shandford Angus 196 D4
Shandon Ag & B 174 B2
Shandwick Highld 223 J6
Shangton Leics 87 K4
Shanklin IoW 17 H6
Shap Cumb 138 E4
Shapinsay Ork 234 C5
Shapwick Dorset 15 H3
Shapwick Somset 26 B4
Shardlow Derbys 101 H6

Shareshill Staffs 85 G3
Sharlston Wakefd 124 B6
Sharnbrook Bed 74 E3
Sharnford Leics 86 F5
Sharoe Green Lancs 121 G4
Sharow N York 132 E5
Sharpenhoe C Beds 59 H2
Sharperton Nthumb 158 B2
Sharpness Gloucs 54 F7
Sharrington Norfk 106 C5
Shatterford Worcs 84 E7
Shaugh Prior Devon 6 D3
Shavington Ches E 99 G3
Shaw Oldham 122 D8
Shaw W Berk 41 J6
Shaw Wilts 39 K7
Shawbirch Wrekin 84 B2
Shawbost W Isls 232 e2
Shawbury Shrops 98 E7
Shawell Leics 87 G7
Shawford Hants 29 J6
Shawhead D & G 154 F6
Shaw Mills N York 132 C6
Shawsburn S Lans 175 K7
Shearington D & G 147 H2
Shearsby Leics 87 J5
Shearston Somset 25 L5
Shebbear Devon 10 C3
Shebdon Staffs 99 H7
Shebster Highld 230 E3
Sheddens E Rens 175 G6
Shedfield Hants 29 K8
Sheen Staffs 100 C1
Sheepridge Kirk 123 H6
Sheepscar Leeds 123 L4
Sheepscombe Gloucs 55 K6
Sheepstor Devon 6 E3
Sheepwash Devon 10 C4
Sheepy Magna Leics 86 D3
Sheepy Parva Leics 86 D3
Sheering Essex 60 E5
Sheerness Kent 46 F5
Sheerwater Surrey 43 H7
Sheet Hants 30 C6
Sheffield Sheff 115 G4
Sheffield City Road
  Crematorium
  Sheff 115 G4
Shefford C Beds 75 G6
Sheigra Highld 228 B4
Sheinton Shrops 83 L3
Shelderton Shrops 83 H7
Sheldon Birm 85 L6
Sheldon Derbys 114 D7
Sheldon Devon 12 E2
Sheldwich Kent 34 D4
Shelfanger Norfk 92 D6
Shelford Notts 102 A4
Shelley Kirk 123 J7
Shelley Suffk 78 B6
Shellingford Oxon 40 F2
Shellow Bowells
  Essex 60 F6
Shelsley Beauchamp
  Worcs 70 D2
Shelsley Walsh Worcs 70 C2
Shelton Bed 74 F2
Shelton Norfk 92 F5
Shelton Notts 102 C4
Shelton Under
  Harley Staffs 99 J5
Shelve Shrops 83 G4
Shelwick Herefs 69 K6
Shenfield Essex 45 L2
Shenington Oxon 72 D6
Shenley Herts 59 K7
Shenley Brook End
  M Keyn 74 B7
Shenley Church End
  M Keyn 74 B7
Shenmore Herefs 69 H6
Shennanton D & G 145 H3
Shenstone Staffs 85 K3
Shenstone Worcs 84 F8
Shenton Leics 86 E4
Shenval Moray 214 F7
Shephall Herts 59 L4

Shepherd's Bush
Gt Lon 44 E4
Shepherdswell Kent 35 H5
Shepley Kirk 123 J8
Shepperton Surrey 43 H6
Shepreth Cambs........... 76 B5
Shepshed Leics 101 J8
Shepton Beauchamp
Somset 26 B7
Shepton Mallet
Somset 26 F3
Shepton Montague
Somset 27 G5
Shepway Kent 33 K3
Sheraton Dur............. 151 K7
Sherborne Dorset 26 F7
Sherborne Gloucs...... 56 D5
Sherborne Somset...... 26 E1
Sherborne St John
Hants 29 L1
Sherbourne Warwks 72 C3
Sherburn Dur............. 151 H6
Sherburn N York........ 134 E4
Sherburn Hill Dur........ 151 H6
Sherburn in Elmet
N York 124 D4
Shere Surrey................ 31 H2
Shereford Norfk......... 105 L6
Sherfield English
Hants 28 F6
Sherfield on Loddon
Hants 42 B8
Sherford Devon............. 7 H6
Sheriffhales Shrops 84 D2
Sheriff Hutton N York... 133 K6
Sheringham Norfk...... 106 E4
Sherington M Keyn 74 C5
Shernborne Norfk...... 105 H6
Sherrington Wilts........ 27 L4
Sherston Wilts 39 J3
Sherwood C Nott........ 101 K4
Sherwood Forest
Notts 101 L2
Sherwood Forest
Crematorium
Notts 116 A7
Shetland Islands Shet .. 235 C5
Shettleston C Glas..... 175 H5
Shevington Wigan 121 H8
Sheviock Cnwll 6 B5
Shibden Head C Brad...123 G5
Shide IoW 16 F5
Shidlaw Nthumb 168 B2
Shiel Bridge Highld 200 E2
Shieldaig Highld 210 C4
Shieldhill D & G 155 H5
Shieldhill Falk........... 176 B3
Shieldhill House
Hotel S Lans........... 165 J2
Shields N Lans........... 175 K7
Shielfoot Highld........ 190 D3
Shielhill Angus 196 C5
Shielhill Inver 173 L4
Shifnal Shrops............ 84 D2
Shilbottle Nthumb 169 J7
Shildon Dur 141 G3
Shillford E Rens 174 E6
Shillingford Devon 24 F6
Shillingford Oxon....... 41 L2
Shillingford Abbot
Devon 11 K6
Shillingford St
George Devon.......... 11 K7
Shillingstone Dorset ... 14 F1
Shillington C Beds..... 75 G7
Shilton Oxon 56 E6
Shilton Warwks 86 E6
Shimpling Norfk......... 92 D6
Shimpling Suffk......... 77 J4
Shimpling Street
Suffk 77 K4
Shincliffe Dur........... 151 H6
Shiney Row Sundld.... 151 H4
Shinfield Wokham 42 B6
Shinness Highld 225 L5
Shipbourne Kent........ 33 G3
Shipdham Norfk......... 91 L3

Shipham Somset 38 C8
Shiphay Torbay 7 K3
Shiplake Oxon............ 42 C5
Shipley C Brad........... 123 H3
Shipley W Susx........... 31 J6
Shipley Bridge Surrey.... 32 B5
Shipmeadow Suffk...... 93 H5
Shippon Oxon............ 41 J2
Shipston on Stour
Warwks 72 B6
Shipton Gloucs........... 56 B4
Shipton N York.......... 133 H7
Shipton Shrops........... 83 L5
Shipton Bellinger
Hants 28 E3
Shipton Gorge Dorset ... 13 L4
Shipton Green W Susx ... 17 L3
Shipton Moyne
Gloucs..................... 39 K3
Shipton-on-Cherwell
Oxon 57 J5
Shiptonthorpe E R Yk...125 K2
Shipton-under-
Wychwood Oxon 56 F4
Shirburn Oxon............ 42 B2
Shirdley Hill Lancs...... 120 E7
Shirebrook Derbys...... 115 K7
Shiregreen Sheff........ 115 G3
Shirehampton Bristl.... 38 D5
Shiremoor N Tyne 159 H7
Shirenewton Mons...... 38 C2
Shireoaks Notts.......... 115 K5
Shirland Derbys 101 H2
Shirley C Sotn 29 H8
Shirley Derbys........... 100 E4
Shirley Gt Lon 45 G6
Shirley Solhll 85 K7
Shirrell Heath Hants 29 L8
Shirvan Ag & B........... 172 E2
Shirwell Devon 23 J4
Shiskine N Ayrs.......... 162 B4
Shobdon Herefs.......... 69 H3
Shobrooke Devon........ 11 K5
Shoby Leics 102 B7
Shocklach Ches W........ 98 C3
Shoeburyness Sthend... 46 F3
Sholden Kent 35 K4
Sholing C Sotn 16 F1
Shop Cnwll.................... 9 G2
Shoreditch Gt Lon....... 45 G4
Shoreditch Somset...... 25 K6
Shoreham Kent 45 K7
Shoreham Airport
W Susx 19 G5
Shoreham-by-Sea
W Susx 19 H5
Shorley Hants 29 L6
Shorne Kent 46 B6
Shortgate E Susx......... 20 A3
Shortlanesend Cnwll 4 C6
Shortlees E Ayrs........ 163 K3
Shortstown Bed.......... 74 F5
Shorwell IoW.............. 16 F5
Shoscombe BaNES...... 27 J8
Shotesham Norfk........ 92 F4
Shotgate Essex........... 46 C2
Shotley Suffk 78 F7
Shotley Bridge Dur...... 150 D4
Shotley Gate Suffk...... 78 F7
Shotley Street Suffk..... 78 F7
Shottenden Kent........ 34 D4
Shottery Warwks......... 71 L4
Shotteswell Warwks 72 E5
Shottisham Suffk........ 79 G5
Shottlegate Derbys..... 100 F3
Shotton Dur 151 K6
Shotton Flints 111 J7
Shotton Colliery Dur ... 151 J6
Shotts N Lans........... 176 B6
Shotwick Ches W 111 K6
Shougle Moray......... 214 F4
Shouldham Norfk........ 90 F2
Shouldham Thorpe
Norfk 90 F2
Shoulton Worcs.......... 70 E4
Shrawardine Shrops..... 83 H1
Shrawley Worcs.......... 70 E2

Shrewley Warwks 72 B2
Shrewsbury Shrops 83 J2
Shrewton Wilts........... 28 B3
Shripney W Susx......... 18 C5
Shrivenham Oxon........ 40 E3
Shropham Norfk......... 92 B5
Shucknall Herefs........ 69 L6
Shudy Camps Cambs.... 76 E5
Shuna Ag & B........... 181 M5
Shurdington Gloucs..... 55 L4
Shurlock Row W & M.... 42 D5
Shurrery Highld........ 230 F4
Shurrery Lodge
Highld 230 F4
Shurton Somset 25 J3
Shustoke Warwks........ 86 B5
Shute Devon 11 K5
Shute Devon 13 G3
Shutford Oxon............ 72 E6
Shut Heath Staffs........ 99 K7
Shuthonger Gloucs...... 70 F7
Shutlanger Nhants 73 K4
Shuttington Warwks..... 86 B3
Shuttlewood Derbys 115 J6
Shuttleworth Bury 122 B6
Siabost W Isls 232 e2
Siadar W Isls 232 f1
Sibbertoft Nhants....... 87 K6
Sibford Ferris Oxon..... 72 D6
Sibford Gower Oxon..... 72 D6
Sible Hedingham
Essex 77 H7
Sibley's Green Essex.... 60 F3
Sibsey Lincs 104 B3
Sibson Cambs 89 G4
Sibson Leics 86 D4
Sibster Highld........... 231 K5
Sibthorpe Notts........ 102 C4
Sibthorpe Notts........ 116 B6
Sibton Suffk.............. 79 H1
Sicklesmere Suffk....... 77 K3
Sicklinghall N York..... 124 B2
Sidbury Devon 12 E4
Sidbury Shrops........... 84 C6
Sidcot N Som 38 B8
Sidcup Gt Lon 45 J5
Siddington Ches E....... 113 J7
Siddington Gloucs....... 56 B7
Sidestrand Norfk........ 106 F4
Sidford Devon............ 12 E4
Sidlesham W Susx....... 18 B6
Sidley E Susx 20 E4
Sidmouth Devon 12 E5
Sigglesthorne E R Yk...126 E2
Sigingstone V Glam...... 36 F6
Silchester Hants 41 L7
Sileby Leics 87 H1
Silecroft Cumb 128 D3
Silfield Norfk............. 92 D4
Silkstone Barns........ 114 F1
Silkstone Common
Barns 114 F1
Silk Willoughby
Lincs 103 H4
Silloth Cumb 147 K4
Silpho N York........... 134 E2
Silsden C Brad.......... 122 F2
Silsoe C Beds 74 F7
Silton Dorset 27 H5
Silverburn Mdloth..... 177 G6
Silverdale Lancs........ 129 K4
Silverdale Staffs......... 99 J3
Silver End Essex......... 61 K4
Silverford Abers 216 E2
Silverstone Nhants 73 J5
Silverton Devon.......... 12 B2
Silvington Shrops........ 84 B7
Simonburn Nthumb ... 157 L7
Simonsbath Somset 24 B4
Simonstone Lancs...... 122 B4
Simprim Border........ 168 C1
Simpson M Keyn 74 C7
Simpson Cross
Pembks 48 F4
Sinclair's Hill Border... 179 G2
Sinclairston E Ayrs..... 163 L6
Sinderby N York........ 132 E3

Sinderland Green
Traffd 113 G4
Sindlesham Wokham..... 42 C6
Sinfin C Derb 101 G6
Singleton Kent............ 34 D6
Singleton Lancs......... 120 E3
Singleton W Susx........ 18 B3
Singlewell Kent 46 A6
Sinnarhard Abers...... 205 K3
Sinnington N York...... 134 B3
Sinton Worcs............. 70 E3
Sinton Worcs............. 70 F2
Sinton Green Worcs..... 70 E3
Sissinghurst Kent........ 33 K5
Siston S Glos............. 39 G5
Sithney Cnwll 3 H5
Sittingbourne Kent...... 34 D4
Six Ashes Shrops........ 84 E5
Sixhills Lincs 117 K4
Six Mile Bottom Cambs.. 76 E3
Sixpenny Handley
Dorset 27 M7
Sizergh Castle Cumb... 129 K3
Skaill Ork............... 234 d6
Skares E Ayrs........... 164 B6
Skateraw Abers 207 G6
Skateraw E Loth........ 178 F4
Skeabost Highld........ 208 F5
Skeeby N York.......... 140 F6
Skeffington Leics 87 L3
Skeffling E R Yk......... 127 J6
Skegby Notts............ 101 J1
Skegby Notts............ 116 C7
Skegness Lincs.......... 119 H8
Skelbo Highld........... 223 H3
Skelbo Street Highld.... 223 H3
Skelbrooke Donc....... 124 D7
Skeldyke Lincs.......... 104 B5
Skellingthorpe Lincs...116 F6
Skellow Donc........... 124 E7
Skelmanthorpe Kirk.... 123 J7
Skelmersdale Lancs.... 112 C1
Skelmorlie N Ayrs..... 173 L5
Skelpick Highld......... 229 L4
Skelston D & G 154 E5
Skelton C York........... 133 J7
Skelton Cumb........... 148 D7
Skelton E R Yk........... 125 H5
Skelton N York.......... 132 E5
Skelton R & Cl........... 142 E4
Skelwith Bridge
Cumb 137 K6
Skendleby Lincs........ 118 F7
Skene House Abers.... 206 E4
Skenfrith Mons.......... 54 C4
Skerne E R Yk........... 135 G7
Skerray Highld.......... 229 K3
Skerricha Highld........ 228 C5
Skerton Lancs........... 129 K6
Sketchley Leics.......... 86 E5
Sketty Swans............. 51 J6
Skewen Neath............ 51 K6
Skewsby N York........ 133 K5
Skiall Highld............ 230 E3
Skidby E R Yk........... 126 C4
Skigersta W Isls....... 232 g1
Skilgate Somset......... 24 F6
Skillington Lincs....... 102 E7
Skinburness Cumb..... 147 K4
Skinflats Falk........... 176 B2
Skinidin Highld........ 208 C5
Skipness Ag & B........ 172 F6
Skipper's Bridge
D & G 156 C5
Skipsea E R Yk.......... 135 J8
Skipton N York.......... 122 E1
Skipton-on-Swale
N York 132 E4
Skipwith N York........ 125 G3
Skirlaugh E R Yk........ 126 E3
Skirling Border.......... 165 L2
Skirmett Bucks 42 C3
Skirpenbeck E R Yk.... 134 B7
Skirwith Cumb.......... 149 G7
Skirza Highld........... 231 L2
Skokholm Island
Pembks 48 C6

Skomer Island
Pembks 48 C5
Skulamus Highld 199 K2
Skye Green Essex 61 L4
Skye of Curr Highld...... 204 B1
Slack Calder 122 E5
Slacks of Cairnbanno
Abers 216 F5
Slad Gloucs 55 K6
Slade Devon 23 H3
Slade Green Gt Lon 45 K5
Slade Hooton Rothm... 115 K4
Slaggyford Nthumb 149 H4
Slaidburn Lancs 130 D8
Slaithwaite Kirk 123 G7
Slaley Nthumb............. 150 B4
Slamannan Falk 176 B4
Slapton Bucks 58 F4
Slapton Devon 7 J6
Slapton Nhants............. 73 J5
Slaugham W Susx 31 L5
Slaughterford Wilts 39 J5
Slawston Leics 87 L5
Sleaford Hants............. 30 D4
Sleaford Lincs 103 H4
Sleagill Cumb............. 138 E4
Sleapford Wrekin 84 B1
Sleasdairidh Highld.... 222 E3
Sledmere E R Yk 134 E6
Sleetbeck Cumb.......... 156 E6
Sleights N York 143 H5
Slickly Highld............. 231 K3
Sliddery N Ayrs 162 B5
Sligachan Highld 209 G7
Sligrachan Ag & B 173 K1
Slimbridge Gloucs 55 H7
Slindon Staffs 99 J6
Slindon W Susx 18 C4
Slinfold W Susx 31 J5
Slingsby N York.......... 133 L4
Slip End C Beds 59 H4
Slip End Herts 75 K6
Slipton Nhants............. 88 D7
Slitting Mill Staffs 100 B8
Slockavullin Ag & B.... 182 B7
Sloncombe Devon.......... 11 H7
Sloothby Lincs 119 G7
Slough Slough............... 43 G4
Slough Crematorium
Bucks 43 G4
Slough Green Somset... 25 L7
Slumbay Highld 210 D6
Slyne Lancs 129 K6
Smailholm Border 167 K3
Smallburgh Norfk 107 G7
Small Dole W Susx 19 G3
Smalley Derbys 101 H4
Smallfield Surrey 32 B5
Small Heath Birm 85 K6
Small Hythe Kent.......... 34 B8
Smallridge Devon.......... 13 H3
Smallworth Norfk 92 B7
Smannell Hants 29 G2
Smarden Kent............... 34 B6
Smarden Bell Kent......... 34 B6
Smart's Hill Kent........... 32 F5
Smearisary Highld....... 190 D2
Smeatharpe Devon......... 12 F1
Smeeth Kent................. 34 E6
Smeeton Westerby
Leics 87 K5
Smerral Highld............ 227 L2
Smestow Staffs 84 F5
Smethwick Sandw 85 H6
Smisby Derbys............ 101 G8
Smithfield Cumb......... 148 D2
Smith's Green Essex 76 F6
Smithstown Highld...... 219 J6
Smithton Highld 213 H5
Smoo Highld................. 228 F3
Smythe's Green Essex.... 61 L4
Snade D & G 154 E5
Snailbeach Shrops 83 G3
Snailwell Cambs............ 76 F2
Snainton N York 134 E3
Snaith E R Yk............... 124 F6
Snape N York............... 132 D3

Snape Suffk 79 H3
Snape Street Suffk......... 79 H3
Snaresbrook Gt Lon 45 H3
Snarestone Leics 86 D2
Snarford Lincs 117 H5
Snargate Kent 34 D8
Snave Kent 34 D8
Sneaton N York............ 143 J5
Snelland Lincs 117 H5
Snelston Derbys 100 D4
Snetterton Norfk 92 B5
Snettisham Norfk 105 G5
Snitter Nthumb 158 C2
Snitterby Lincs............ 117 G3
Snitterfield Warwks 72 B3
Snitton Shrops.............. 83 L7
Snodland Kent............... 46 B7
Snowdon Gwynd........... 95 K2
Snowdonia
National Park
Gwynd 96 C6
Snow End Herts............. 60 C2
Snowshill Gloucs 71 K7
Soake Hants 17 J1
Soay Highld 199 G3
Soberton Hants 29 L7
Soberton Heath
Hants 29 L8
Sockburn Darltn 141 J5
Soham Cambs 90 E8
Solas W Isls 232 C5
Soldridge Hants 29 M4
Sole Street Kent 34 E5
Sole Street Kent 46 A6
Solihull Solhll 85 L7
Sollers Dilwyn
Herefs 69 H4
Sollers Hope Herefs 54 E2
Solva Pembks 48 D3
Solwaybank D & G 156 B6
Somerby Leics 87 L2
Somerby Lincs............. 117 H1
Somercotes Derbys 101 H2
Somerford Dorset.......... 15 M4
Somerford Keynes
Gloucs 40 A2
Somerley W Susx.......... 17 M3
Somerleyton Norfk......... 93 K4
Somersal Herbert
Derbys 100 C5
Somersby Lincs 118 D6
Somersham Cambs......... 89 L7
Somersham Suffk 78 C5
Somerton Oxon.............. 57 J3
Somerton Somset.......... 26 C5
Somerton Suffk.............. 77 J4
Sompting W Susx 19 G5
Sonning Wokham 42 C5
Sonning Common
Oxon 42 B4
Sopley Hants 15 M3
Sopworth Wilts............. 39 J3
Sorbie D & G 145 J5
Sordale Highld 231 G3
Sorisdale Ag & B 189 H4
Sorn E Ayrs 164 B4
Sortat Highld............... 231 K3
Sotby Lincs 117 K5
Sotterley Suffk.............. 93 J6
Soughton Flints 111 H7
Soulbury Bucks............. 58 E3
Soulby Cumb 139 H5
Souldern Oxon.............. 57 K2
Souldrop Bed................ 74 E3
Sound Ches E 98 F3
Sound Muir Moray....... 215 H4
Soundwell S Glos........... 38 F5
Sourton Devon 10 D6
Soutergate Cumb........ 128 F3
South Acre Norfk 91 J2
South Alkham Kent 35 H6
Southall Gt Lon 43 J4
South Allington
Devon 7 J7
South Alloa Falk.......... 185 J8
Southam Gloucs............. 55 L3
Southam Warwks 72 E3

South Ambersham
W Susx....................... 30 E7
Southampton C Sotn 29 H8
Southampton Airport
Hants 29 J7
Southampton
Crematorium
Hants 29 H7
South Anston Rothm ... 115 K5
South Ashford Kent....... 34 D6
South Baddesley
Hants 16 D3
South Ballachulish
Highld..................... 191 K5
South Bank C York 124 F1
South Barrow Somset.... 26 E5
South Beddington
Gt Lon 44 F7
South Benfleet Essex 46 C3
South Bersted W Susx... 18 C5
Southborough Gt Lon.... 45 H6
Southborough Kent........ 33 G5
Southbourne Bmouth.... 15 L4
Southbourne W Susx.... 17 L2
South Bramwith
Donc 124 F7
South Brent Devon 7 G4
South Brewham
Somset 27 G4
South Bristol
Crematorium
Bristl 38 E6
South Broomhill
Nthumb 159 G3
Southburgh Norfk 92 B3
South Burlingham
Norfk 93 H3
Southburn E R Yk 134 F8
South Cadbury
Somset 26 F6
South Carlton Lincs 116 F6
South Carlton Notts 115 L5
South Cave E R Yk...... 125 L4
South Cerney Gloucs 40 B2
South Chailey E Susx ... 19 K3
South Charlton
Nthumb 169 H5
South Cheriton
Somset 27 G6
South Church Dur 140 F2
Southchurch Sthend 46 E3
South Cliffe E R Yk 125 K4
South Clifton Notts 116 D7
South Cockerington
Lincs 118 D4
South Cornelly
Brdgnd 36 C4
Southcott Cnwll 9 G5
Southcott Devon........... 11 H8
Southcourt Bucks 58 D5
South Cove Suffk 93 K7
South Creake Norfk 105 K5
South Croxton Leics 87 K2
South Dalton E R Yk... 126 B2
South Darenth Kent....... 45 K6
South Downs
National Park
Br & H 19 K4
South Duffield N York .. 125 G4
Southease E Susx 19 L5
South Elkington
Lincs 118 D4
South Elmsall Wakefd.. 124 D7
Southend Ag & B.......... 161 H7
Southend Airport
Essex 46 E3
Southend
Crematorium
Sthend 46 E3
Southend-on-Sea
Sthend 46 E3
Southerndown
V Glam 36 D5
Southerness D & G...... 147 G4
South Erradale Highld.. 219 H7
Southerton Devon 12 D4
Southery Norfk 90 E5

South Essex
Crematorium
Gt Lon 45 L3
South Fambridge
Essex 46 E2
South Ferriby N Linc... 126 B6
South Field E R Yk...... 126 C5
Southfield Falk............ 175 L4
Southfleet Kent............. 45 L5
Southgate Gt Lon 44 F2
Southgate Swans 51 G7
South Gorley Hants....... 15 M1
South Gosforth
N u Ty 151 G2
South Green Essex........ 46 B2
South Green Kent 33 L2
South Green Norfk......... 92 C2
South Gyle C Edin....... 177 G4
South Hanningfield
Essex 61 H8
South Harting W Susx ... 30 E7
South Hayling Hants...... 17 K3
South Heath Bucks 58 E7
South Heighton
E Susx 19 L5
South Hetton Dur........ 151 J6
South Hiendley
Wakefd 124 B7
South Hill Cnwll 5 M2
South Hinksey Oxon..... 57 K7
South Holmwood
Surrey 31 K3
South Hornchurch
Gt Lon 45 K4
South Huish Devon 7 G7
South Hykeham Lincs .. 116 F8
South Hylton Sundld ... 151 J4
Southill C Beds............ 75 H6
Southington Hants 29 J2
South Kelsey Lincs 117 H2
South Kessock Highld .. 213 G5
South Killingholme
N Linc 126 E7
South Kilvington
N York 132 F3
South Kilworth Leics 87 H6
South Kirkby Wakefd.. 124 C7
South Kyme Lincs 103 K3
South Lanarkshire
Crematorium
S Lans 175 J7
Southleigh Devon 12 F4
South Leigh Oxon 57 H6
South Leverton Notts.. 116 C5
South Littleton Worcs... 71 J5
South London
Crematorium
Gt Lon 44 F6
South Lopham Norfk..... 92 C7
South Luffenham
Rutlnd 88 D3
South Malling E Susx ... 19 L4
South Marston
Swindn 40 D3
South Merstham
Surrey 32 B3
South Milford N York... 124 B4
South Milton Devon......... 7 G7
South Mimms Herts....... 59 L7
South Mimms
Services Herts............. 59 L7
Southminster Essex....... 62 A7
South Molton Devon...... 23 L6
South Moor Dur 150 F5
Southmoor Oxon 41 H2
South Moreton
Oxon 41 K3
Southmuir Angus........ 196 C5
South Mundham
W Susx..................... 18 B5
South Newbald
E R Yk 125 L4
South Newington
Oxon 57 H2
South Newton Wilts 28 C4
South Normanton
Derbys 101 H2

South Norwood
  Gt Lon 45 G6
South Ockendon
  Thurr 45 L4
Southoe Cambs 75 H2
Southolt Suffk 78 E2
South Ormsby Lincs...118 E6
Southorpe C Pete 88 F3
South Otterington
  N York 132 E3
Southover Dorset 14 C4
South Owersby Lincs ...117 H3
Southowram Calder 123 G5
South Park Surrey 31 L2
South Perrott Dorset 13 L2
South Petherton
  Somset 26 B7
South Petherwin
  Cnwll..............9 J8
South Pickenham
  Norfk 91 J3
South Pill Cnwll 6 B4
South Pool Devon 7 H7
South Poorton
  Dorset 13 M3
Southport Sefton 120 D6
Southport
  Crematorium
  Lancs 120 E7
South Queensferry
  C Edin 176 F3
South Raceby Lincs 103 G4
South Raynham
  Norfk 105 L7
Southrepps Norfk......106 F5
South Reston Lincs 118 E5
Southrey Lincs 117 J7
South Ronaldsay Ork 234 c7
Southrop Gloucs 56 D7
Southrope Hants 30 A3
South Runcton Norfk 90 F2
South Scarle Notts 116 D8
Southsea C Port 17 J3
South Shian Ag & B. 191 H7
South Shields S Tyne 151 J2
South Shields
  Crematorium
  S Tyne 151 J3
South Shore Bpool.......120 D4
Southside Dur 140 E2
South Stainley N York ...132 D6
South Stoke BaNES 39 H7
South Stoke Oxon 41 L4
South Stoke W Susx 18 D4
South Street Kent 34 E3
South Street Kent 47 J6
South Tarbrax S Lans 176 D7
South Tawton Devon 10 F6
South Tehidy Cnwll 3 H3
South Thoresby
  Lincs 118 E6
Southtown Norfk 93 L3
South Uist W Isls 233 c8
Southwaite Cumb 148 D6
Southwaite Services
  Cumb 148 D6
South Walsham
  Norfk 93 H2
Southwark Gt Lon 44 F4
South Warnborough
  Hants 30 B3
Southwater W Susx 31 J6
South Weald Essex 45 L2
Southwell Notts 102 B2
South West
  Middlesex
  Crematorium
  Gt Lon 43 J5
South Weston Oxon 42 B2
Southwick Hants 17 J2
Southwick Nhants 88 E5
Southwick Sundld 151 J4
Southwick W Susx 19 H5
Southwick Wilts 27 J1
South Widcombe
  BaNES 38 E8
South Wigston Leics 87 H4

South Willesborough
  Kent 34 D6
South Willingham
  Lincs 117 K5
South Wingfield
  Derbys 101 G2
South Witham Lincs ...102 F8
Southwold Suffk 93 K7
South Woodham
  Ferrers Essex 61 J7
South Wootton Norfk .105 G7
South Wraxall Wilts ...39 J7
South Zeal Devon 10 F6
Sowerby Calder 122 F6
Sowerby N York 132 F4
Sowerby Bridge
  Calder 122 F5
Sowood Calder 123 G6
Sowton Devon 6 D3
Sowton Devon 12 C4
Soyland Town Calder 142 F6
Spain's End Essex 76 F6
Spalding Lincs 103 L7
Spaldington E R Yk 125 H4
Spaldwick Cambs 89 G8
Spalford Notts 116 D7
Spanby Lincs 103 H5
Sparham Norfk 106 C8
Spark Bridge Cumb 129 G3
Sparkford Somset 26 E6
Sparkhill Birm 85 K6
Sparkwell Devon 6 E4
Sparrowpit Derbys 114 C5
Sparrows Green
  E Susx 33 H6
Sparsholt Hants 29 H5
Sparsholt Oxon 41 G3
Spaunton N York 133 L2
Spaxton Somset 25 K4
Spean Bridge Highld ..201 K8
Spearywell Hants 28 F6
Speen Bucks 58 D7
Speen W Berk 41 J6
Speeton N York 135 J5
Speke Lpool 112 C5
Speldhurst Kent 32 F5
Spellbrook Herts 60 D4
Spencers Wood
  Wokham 42 B6
Spen Green Ches E 99 J1
Spennithorne
  N York 131 L2
Spennymoor Dur 151 G7
Spetchley Worcs 70 F4
Spetisbury Dorset 15 G3
Spexhall Suffk.........93 H7
Spey Bay Moray 215 H2
Speybridge Highld ...204 C1
Speyview Moray 215 G6
Spilsby Lincs 118 E7
Spinkhill Derbys 115 J5
Spinningdale Highld ..222 F4
Spital Hill Donc 115 L3
Spittal E Loth 178 B3
Spittal Highld 231 H5
Spittal Nthumb 179 L7
Spittal Pembks 49 G3
Spittalfield P & K 195 H7
Spittal of Glenmuick
  Abers 205 G7
Spittal of Glenshee
  P & K 195 H3
Spittal-on-Rule
  Border 167 J5
Spixworth Norfk 92 F1
Splatt Devon 10 E4
Splayne's Green
  E Susx 19 L2
Splottlands Cardif 37 K5
Spofforth N York 124 B1
Spondon C Derb 101 H5
Spooner Row
  Norfk 92 D4
Sporle Norfk 91 J2
Spott E Loth 178 E4
Spottiswoode Border ...178 D7
Spratton Nhants 73 K1

Spreakley Surrey 30 D3
Spreyton Devon 11 G5
Spriddlestone Devon......6 D5
Spridlington Lincs 117 G5
Springburn C Glas 175 G5
Springfield D & G 148 B2
Springfield Essex 61 H6
Springfield Fife 186 E5
Springholm D & G 154 E7
Springside N Ayrs 163 J2
Springthorpe Lincs 116 E4
Springwell Sundld 151 H4
Springwood
  Crematorium
  Lpool 112 B4
Sproatley E R Yk 126 F4
Sproston Green
  Ches W 113 G7
Sprotbrough Donc 115 K2
Sproughton Suffk 78 D5
Sprouston Border 168 A3
Sprowston Norfk 92 F2
Sproxton Leics 102 D7
Sproxton N York 133 J3
Spurstow Ches E 98 D2
Spyway Dorset 14 A4
Stableford Shrops 84 D4
Stacey Bank Sheff 114 F4
Stackhouse N York 130 F6
Stackpole Pembks 49 G7
Staddiscombe C Plym 6 D5
Stadhampton Oxon 57 L7
Stadhlaigearraidh
  W Isls 233 b7
Staffield Cumb 148 F6
Staffin Highld 218 D7
Stafford Staffs 99 L7
Stafford
  Crematorium
  Staffs 99 L7
Stafford Services
  (northbound)
  Staffs 99 K6
Stafford Services
  (southbound)
  Staffs 99 K6
Stagsden Bed 74 E5
Stainburn Cumb 136 E2
Stainby Lincs 102 E7
Staincross Barns 123 L7
Staindrop Dur 140 E3
Staines-upon-
  Thames Surrey 43 G6
Stainfield Lincs 118 D7
Stainforth Donc 124 F7
Stainforth N York 130 F6
Staining Lancs 120 D4
Stainland Calder 123 G6
Stainsacre N York 143 J5
Stainton Cumb 129 L3
Stainton Cumb 138 C2
Stainton Donc 115 K3
Stainton Middsb 141 L4
Stainton by
  Langworth Lincs 117 H6
Staintondale N York 143 K7
Stainton le Vale Lincs ...117 K3
Stainton with
  Adgarley Cumb ...128 F5
Stair E Ayrs 163 K5
Stairhaven D & G 144 E4
Staithes N York 143 G4
Stakeford Nthumb 159 G5
Stakes Hants 17 K2
Stalbridge Dorset 27 G7
Stalbridge Weston
  Dorset 27 G7
Stalham Norfk 107 H7
Stalisfield Green Kent 34 C4
Stallen Dorset 26 E7
Stallingborough
  NE Lin 126 F7
Stalmine Lancs 120 E2
Stalybridge Tamesd 113 L2
Stambourne Essex 77 G6
Stambourne Green
  Essex 77 G6

Stamford Lincs 88 E3
Stamford Nthumb 169 J5
Stamford Bridge
  Ches W 112 C7
Stamford Bridge
  E R Yk 133 L7
Stamfordham
  Nthumb 158 D7
Stamford Hill Gt Lon 45 G3
Stanbridge C Beds 58 F3
Stanbury C Brad 122 F3
Stand N Lans 175 K5
Standburn Falk 176 C4
Standeford Staffs 85 G3
Standen Kent 33 L5
Standerwick Somset 27 J2
Standford Hants 30 D4
Standingstone Cumb ...147 J7
Standish Wigan 121 H7
Standlake Oxon 57 H7
Standon Hants 29 H6
Standon Herts 60 C4
Standon Staffs 99 J5
Stane N Lans 176 B6
Stanfield Norfk 105 M7
Stanford C Beds 75 H6
Stanford Kent 34 F6
Stanford Bishop
  Herefs 70 C4
Stanford Bridge
  Worcs 70 C2
Stanford Dingley
  W Berk 41 L6
Stanford in the Vale
  Oxon 41 G2
Stanford le Hope
  Thurr 46 B4
Stanford on Avon
  Nhants 87 H7
Stanford on Soar
  Notts 101 K7
Stanford on Teme
  Worcs 70 C2
Stanfree Derbys 115 J6
Stanghow R & Cl 142 E4
Stanground C Pete 89 H4
Stanhoe Norfk 105 J5
Stanhope Border 165 L4
Stanhope Dur 150 C6
Stanhope Kent 34 D6
Stanion Nhants 88 D6
Stanley Derbys 101 H4
Stanley Dur 150 F4
Stanley P & K 186 B2
Stanley Staffs 99 L3
Stanley Crook Dur 150 E7
Stanley Pontlarge
  Gloucs 55 M3
Stanmer Br & H 19 K4
Stanmore Gt Lon 44 D2
Stanmore Hants 29 J5
Stannersburn
  Nthumb 157 J5
Stanningfield Suffk 77 K3
Stannington Nthumb 158 F6
Stannington Sheff 114 F4
Stannington Station
  Nthumb 158 F5
Stansbatch Herefs 69 G3
Stansfield Suffk 77 H4
Stanstead Suffk 77 J3
Stanstead Abbotts
  Herts 60 C5
Stansted Kent 45 L7
Stansted Airport
  Essex 60 E4
Stansted
  Mountfitchet
  Essex 60 E3
Stanton Gloucs 71 J7
Stanton Nthumb 158 E4
Stanton Staffs 100 C4
Stanton Suffk 91 L8
Stanton by Bridge
  Derbys 101 G6
Stanton by Dale
  Derbys 101 J5

Stanton Drew BaNES......38 E7
Stanton Fitzwarren
Swindn 40 D3
Stanton Harcourt
Oxon.........................57 H6
Stanton in Peak
Derbys...................114 E8
Stanton Lacy Shrops...83 K7
Stanton Lees Derbys.....114 E8
Stanton Long Shrops......83 L5
Stanton on the
Wolds Notts...........101 M6
Stanton Prior BaNES......39 G7
Stanton St Bernard
Wilts........................40 C7
Stanton St John Oxon...57 L6
Stanton St Quintin
Wilts........................39 K4
Stanton Street Suffk...77 L2
Stanton under
Bardon Leics 86 F2
Stanton upon Hine
Heath Shrops...........98 E7
Stanton Wick BaNES...38 E7
Stanway Essex............61 M3
Stanway Gloucs...........56 B2
Stanwell Surrey 43 H5
Stanwick Nhants.........74 E1
Stanwix Cumb............148 D4
Staoinebrig W Isls 233 b8
Stape N York 143 G7
Stapeley Ches E...........99 G3
Stapenhill Staffs.........100 E7
Staple Kent..................35 H4
Staple Cross Devon......25 G7
Staple Cross E Susx......20 F2
Staplefield W Susx 32 B7
Staple Fitzpaine
Somset.......................25 K7
Stapleford Cambs.......76 C4
Stapleford Herts..........60 A5
Stapleford Leics........102 D8
Stapleford Lincs.........102 E2
Stapleford Notts........101 J5
Stapleford Wilts...........28 B4
Stapleford Abbotts
Essex........................45 K2
Staplegrove Somset......25 K6
Staplehay Somset........25 K6
Staplehurst Kent..........33 K5
Staplestreet Kent..........34 E3
Stapleton Herefs..........69 G2
Stapleton Leics............86 E4
Stapleton N York.........141 G5
Stapleton Shrops.........83 J3
Stapleton Somset........26 C7
Stapley Somset............25 J8
Staploe Bed 75 G3
Staplow Herefs............70 C6
Star Fife...................186 E6
Star Pembks...............65 H7
Star Somset.................38 C8
Starbeck N York.........132 E7
Starbotton N York......131 H5
Starcross Devon..........12 C6
Stareton Warks..........72 D1
Starlings Green Essex....60 D2
Starston Norfk.............92 F6
Startforth Dur............140 D4
Startley Wilts................39 L4
Statenborough Kent.....35 J4
Statham Warrtn..........112 F4
Stathe Somset..............26 A5
Stathern Leics...........102 C6
Staughton Green
Cambs.......................75 G2
Staunton Gloucs..........54 D5
Staunton Gloucs..........55 H3
Staunton on Arrow
Herefs........................69 G3
Staunton on Wye
Herefs........................69 G5
Staveley Cumb...........129 H3
Staveley Cumb...........138 C7
Staveley Derbys.........115 H6
Staveley N York.........132 E6
Staverton Devon...........7 J3

Staverton Gloucs..........55 K4
Staverton Nhants........73 G3
Staverton Wilts...........39 J7
Stawell Somset............26 A4
Stawley Somset............25 G6
Staxigoe Highld........231 L5
Staxton N York..........134 F4
Staynall Lancs...........120 E2
Stean N York.............131 K5
Stearsby N York.........133 J5
Steart Somset..............25 L3
Stebbing Essex............61 G3
Stedham W Susx...........30 E6
Steelend Fife.............185 L8
Steele Road Border.....156 F4
Steen's Bridge Herefs....69 K3
Steep Hants................30 C6
Steep Lane Calder......122 F5
Steeple Essex..............61 M7
Steeple Ashton Wilts....27 K1
Steeple Aston Oxon......57 J3
Steeple Bumpstead
Essex........................76 F6
Steeple Claydon
Bucks........................58 B3
Steeple Gidding
Cambs.......................89 G7
Steeple Langford
Wilts..........................28 B4
Steeple Morden
Cambs.......................75 K6
Steeton C Brad..........122 F2
Stein Highld...............208 D3
Stelling Minnis Kent......34 F5
Stembridge Somset......26 B7
Stenalees Cnwll.............4 F4
Stenhouse D & G........154 D4
Stenhousemuir Falk....176 B2
Stenscholl Highld......218 D7
Stenson Fields Derbys...101 G6
Stenton E Loth..........178 D4
Steornabhagh W Isls....232 f2
Stepaside Pembks........49 K6
Stepney Gt Lon............45 G4
Steppingley C Beds......74 E7
Stepps N Lans...........175 H5
Sternfield Suffk...........79 H3
Stert Wilts...................40 B8
Stetchworth Cambs......76 F3
Stevenage Herts..........59 L3
Stevenston N Ayrs......163 H2
Steventon Hants..........29 K2
Steventon Oxon...........41 J3
Steventon End Essex....76 E6
Stevington Bed...........74 E4
Stewartby Bed............74 E6
Stewartfield S Lans....175 H7
Stewarton E Ayrs......163 K1
Stewkley Bucks...........58 D3
Stewley Somset............25 L7
Steyning W Susx..........19 G4
Steynton Pembks.........48 F6
Stibb Cnwll...................9 G3
Stibbard Norfk...........106 B6
Stibb Cross Devon......10 C2
Stibb Green Wilts.........40 E7
Stibbington Cambs.......88 F4
Stichill Border...........167 L2
Sticker Cnwll.................4 F5
Stickford Lincs...........104 B1
Sticklepath Devon........10 F6
Stickney Lincs...........104 B2
Stiffkey Norfk...........106 A4
Stilligarry W Isls........233 b7
Stillingfleet N York.....124 F3
Stillington N York......133 J6
Stillington S on T......141 J3
Stilton Cambs.............89 H5
Stinchcombe Gloucs......55 G7
Stinsford Dorset..........14 D4
Stiperstones Shrops....83 G4
Stirchley Wrekin..........84 C3
Stirling Abers...........217 L6
Stirling Stirlg...........185 G8
Stirling Services Stirlg ...175 L2
Stirtloe Cambs.............75 H2

Stirton N York...........131 H8
Stisted Essex..............61 J3
Stithians Cnwll..............3 J4
Stivichall Covtry..........86 D7
Stixwould Lincs.........117 K7
Stoak Ches W............112 B6
Stobo Border.............166 B2
Stoborough Dorset.......15 H5
Stobs Castle Border.....167 G7
Stobswood Nthumb......158 F3
Stock Essex................61 H7
Stock N Som...............38 C7
Stockbridge Hants........29 G4
Stockbriggs S Lans......164 F3
Stockbury Kent............46 D7
Stockcross W Berk........41 H6
Stockerston Leics........88 B4
Stock Green Worcs........71 H3
Stocking Herefs............54 F2
Stockingford Warwks....86 D5
Stocking Pelham
Herts........................60 D3
Stockland Devon..........13 G2
Stockland Bristol
Somset.......................25 K3
Stockleigh English
Devon........................11 K4
Stockleigh Pomeroy
Devon........................11 K4
Stockley Wilts.............39 M6
Stocklinch Somset........26 B7
Stockport Stockp........113 K4
Stockport
Crematorium
Stockp.....................113 K4
Stocksbridge Sheff......114 E2
Stocksfield Nthumb....150 D3
Stockton Herefs...........69 K3
Stockton Norfk............93 H5
Stockton Shrops...........84 C4
Stockton Warwks........72 E2
Stockton Wilts............27 M4
Stockton Wrekin..........84 D1
Stockton Heath
Warrtn.....................112 E4
Stockton-on-Tees
S on T.....................141 K4
Stockton on Teme
Worcs........................70 C2
Stockton on the
Forest C York.........133 K7
Stockwood Bristl..........38 F6
Stockwood Dorset........14 B2
Stock Wood Worcs........71 H3
Stodmarsh Kent...........35 G3
Stody Norfk...............106 C5
Stoer Highld.............224 C3
Stoford Somset............26 E8
Stoford Wilts...............28 B4
Stogumber Somset........25 H4
Stogursey Somset........25 J3
Stoke Covtry...............86 D7
Stoke Devon................22 C6
Stoke Hants.................17 K3
Stoke Hants.................29 H2
Stoke Medway.............46 D5
Stoke Abbott Dorset.....13 L3
Stoke Albany Nhants....88 B5
Stoke Ash Suffk...........78 D1
Stoke Bardolph Notts..101 M4
Stoke Bliss Worcs.........70 B2
Stoke Bruerne
Nhants.......................73 L4
Stoke by Clare Suffk......77 G5
Stoke-by-Nayland
Suffk.........................78 B7
Stoke Canon Devon......12 B3
Stoke Charity Hants......29 J4
Stoke Climsland Cnwll....6 A2
Stoke Cross Herefs........70 B4
Stoke D'Abernon
Surrey.......................43 J8
Stoke Doyle Nhants......88 E6
Stoke Dry Rutlnd.........88 C4
Stoke Edith Herefs........69 L6
Stoke Farthing Wilts......28 B6
Stoke Ferry Norfk........91 G4

Stoke Fleming Devon......7 K6
Stokeford Dorset..........15 G5
Stoke Gabriel Devon......7 J4
Stoke Gifford S Glos......38 F4
Stoke Golding Leics......86 E4
Stoke Goldington
M Keyn.....................74 B5
Stokeham Notts.........116 C6
Stoke Hammond
Bucks........................58 E3
Stoke Holy Cross
Norfk.........................92 F3
Stokeinteignhead
Devon.........................7 L2
Stoke Lacy Herefs.........70 B5
Stoke Lyne Oxon...........57 K3
Stoke Mandeville
Bucks........................58 D6
Stokenchurch Bucks......42 C2
Stoke Newington
Gt Lon.......................45 G3
Stokenham Devon..........7 J7
Stoke-on-Trent C Stke...99 K3
Stoke Orchard Gloucs....55 K3
Stoke Poges Bucks........42 F4
Stoke Prior Herefs........69 K3
Stoke Prior Worcs.........71 G2
Stoke Rivers Devon......23 K4
Stoke Rochford Lincs...102 F6
Stoke Row Oxon...........42 B4
Stoke St Gregory
Somset.......................25 M6
Stoke St Mary Somset....25 K6
Stoke St Michael
Somset.......................26 F3
Stoke St Milborough
Shrops.......................83 L6
Stokesay Castle
Shrops.......................83 H6
Stokesby Norfk............93 J2
Stokesley N York........142 B5
Stoke sub Hamdon
Somset.......................26 B6
Stoke Talmage Oxon......58 B7
Stoke Trister Somset.....27 H5
Stoke upon Tern
Shrops.......................98 F6
Stoke-upon-Trent
C Stke.......................99 K4
Stolford Somset...........25 K3
Stondon Massey
Essex........................60 F7
Stone Bucks................58 C5
Stone Gloucs................39 G2
Stone Rothm..............115 K4
Stone Staffs.................99 K5
Stone Worcs................84 F7
Stone Allerton
Somset.......................26 B2
Ston Easton Somset.....26 F2
Stonebridge N Som......38 B7
Stonebridge Warwks....86 B6
Stonebroom Derbys....101 H2
Stone Cross Kent..........35 J4
Stonecrouch Kent........33 J6
Stoneferry C KuH......126 D4
Stonefield Castle
Hotel Ag & B...........172 E4
Stonegate E Susx.........33 H7
Stonegrave N York.....133 K4
Stonehaven Abers......207 G7
Stonehouse Gloucs.......55 J6
Stonehouse C Plym......6 C5
Stonehouse Gloucs.......55 J6
Stonehouse S Lans......175 K8
Stone in Oxney Kent.....21 J1
Stoneleigh Warwks......86 D8
Stonesby Leics...........102 D7
Stonesfield Oxon..........57 H4
Stones Green Essex.....62 E3
Stone Street Kent.........33 G3
Stone Street Suffk........93 H6
Stonewells Moray.......215 G2
Stoneybridge W Isls....233 b8
Stoneyburn W Loth.....176 D5
Stoneygate C Leic........87 H3
Stoneykirk D & G.......144 C6

Stoney Middleton
Derbys............114 E6
Stoney Stanton Leics....86 F4
Stoney Stoke Somset.....27 G5
Stoney Stratton
Somset.............26 F4
Stoneywood C Aber....207 G3
Stoneywood Falk........175 L2
Stonham Aspal Suffk....78 D3
Stonnall Staffs...........85 J3
Stonor Oxon..............42 B3
Stonton Wyville Leics....87 K4
Stony Houghton
Derbys............115 J7
Stony Stratford
M Keyn...........73 L6
Stoodleigh Devon........23 K5
Stoodleigh Devon........24 E7
Stop 24 Services Kent....34 F7
Stopham W Susx.........18 D2
Stopsley Luton..........59 J3
Stornoway W Isls........232 f2
Stornoway Airport
W Isls...............232 g2
Storrington W Susx........18 E3
Storth Cumb...........129 K4
Storwood E R Yk.......125 H2
Stotfield Moray..........214 F1
Stotfold C Beds...........75 J7
Stottesdon Shrops.......84 C6
Stoughton Leics...........87 J3
Stoughton Surrey.........31 G2
Stoughton W Susx.......17 L1
Stoulton Worcs...........70 F4
Stourbridge Dudley......84 F6
Stourbridge
Crematorium
Dudley............84 F6
Stourpaine Dorset.........15 G1
Stourport-on-Severn
Worcs..............70 E1
Stour Provost Dorset....27 H6
Stour Row Dorset.......27 J7
Stourton Staffs............84 F6
Stourton Warwks........72 C6
Stourton Wilts...........27 H5
Stourton Caundle
Dorset............27 G7
Stove Shet...............235 C7
Stoven Suffk.............93 J6
Stow Border.............167 G1
Stow Lincs..............116 E5
Stow Bardolph
Norfk 90 F3
Stow Bedon Norfk......91 L4
Stowbridge Norfk.......90 E3
Stow-cum-Quy
Cambs............76 D3
Stowe Shrops.............82 F8
Stowe by Chartley
Staffs............100 A6
Stowell Somset..........27 G6
Stowey BaNES...........38 E7
Stowford Devon...........10 C7
Stowlangtoft Suffk.......77 L2
Stow Longa Cambs......75 G1
Stow Maries Essex.......61 K7
Stowmarket Suffk........78 C3
Stow-on-the-Wold
Gloucs............56 D3
Stowting Kent..............34 F6
Stowting Common
Kent...............34 F6
Stowupland Suffk........78 C3
Straanruie Highld...........204 B3
Strachan Abers...........206 D6
Strachur Ag & B........182 F6
Stradbroke Suffk..........92 F8
Stradishall Suffk............77 H4
Stradsett Norfk............90 F3
Stragglethorpe Lincs....102 E3
Straiton Mdloth.............177 H5
Straiton S Ayrs............153 H2
Straloch Abers............207 G2
Straloch P & K..........195 G4
Stramshall Staffs..........100 B5
Strang IoM 237 c5

Strangeways Salfd........113 J2
Strangford Herefs.......54 E3
Stranraer D & G.........144 C3
Stratfield Mortimer
W Berk...........42 A7
Stratfield Saye Hants...42 B7
Stratfield Turgis
Hants............42 B7
Stratford Gt Lon........45 H3
Stratford St Andrew
Suffk.............79 H3
Stratford St Mary
Suffk.............78 C7
Stratford Tony Wilts....28 C6
Stratford-upon-Avon
Warwks...........72 B4
Strath Highld.............219 J5
Strathan Highld.........224 D4
Strathan Highld.........229 J3
Strathaven S Lans.....164 D1
Strathblane Stirlg.......175 G3
Strathcanaird Highld...220 F2
Strathcarron Highld....210 E6
Strathcoil Ag & B.......181 K2
Strathdon Abers.......205 H3
Strathkinness Fife......187 G4
Strathloanhead
W Loth...........176 C4
Strathmashie House
Highld............202 F6
Strathmiglo Fife.......186 C5
Strathpeffer Highld....212 D3
Strathtay P & K........194 E5
Strathwhillan N Ayrs...162 D3
Strathy Highld..........230 B3
Strathy Inn Highld......230 B3
Strathyre Stirlg.........184 C4
Stratton Cnwll..........9 G4
Stratton Dorset.........14 C4
Stratton Gloucs.........56 A7
Stratton Audley Oxon...57 L3
Stratton-on-the-
Fosse Somset.....26 F2
Stratton St Margaret
Swindn............40 D3
Stratton St Michael
Norfk.............92 E5
Stratton Strawless
Norfk............106 F7
Streat E Susx............19 K3
Streatham Gt Lon......44 F5
Streatley C Beds.......59 H3
Streatley W Berk.......41 L4
Street Devon............12 F5
Street Somset..........26 C4
Street Ashton Warwks...86 F6
Street Dinas Shrops....97 M5
Street End Kent.........34 F4
Street End W Susx.....18 A5
Streethay Staffs.........85 K2
Streetlam N York.......141 H7
Streetly
Crematorium
Wsall.............85 J4
Streetly End Cambs....76 E5
Street on the Fosse
Somset...........26 F4
Strelitz P & K...........186 C1
Strelley Notts..........101 K4
Strensall C York........133 K7
Strensham Services
(northbound)
Worcs............70 F6
Strensham Services
(southbound)
Worcs............70 F6
Stretcholt Somset.......25 L3
Strete Devon...........7 J6
Stretford Traffd.........113 H3
Strethall Essex.........76 C6
Stretham Cambs........90 D8
Strettington W Susx....18 B4
Stretton Derbys.........101 H1
Stretton Rutlnd.........88 D1
Stretton Staffs..........84 F2
Stretton Staffs.........100 E7
Stretton Warrtn.......112 F5

Stretton Grandison
Herefs............70 B5
Stretton-on-
Dunsmore Warwks....86 E8
Stretton on Fosse
Warwks............72 B6
Stretton Sugwas
Herefs............69 J6
Stretton under Fosse
Warwks............86 F7
Stretton Westwood
Shrops............83 L4
Strichen Abers.........217 H4
Stringston Somset......25 J3
Strixton Nhants........74 C3
Stroat Gloucs..........38 E2
Stroma Highld.........231 L1
Stromeferry Highld....210 D7
Stromness Highld......234 b6
Stronachlachar Stirlg...183 L5
Stronafian Ag & B.....173 H3
Stronchrubie Highld...224 F5
Strone Ag & B.........173 L3
Strone Highld..........192 B1
Strone Highld..........212 E8
Stronenaba Highld.....201 J8
Stronmilchan Ag & B...183 G2
Stronsay Ork...........234 d5
Stronsay Airport Ork...234 d5
Strontian Highld.......191 G4
Strood Medway........46 B6
Stroud Gloucs.........55 J6
Stroud Hants..........30 B6
Stroud Green Gloucs...55 J6
Stroxton Lincs.........102 E6
Struan Highld.........208 E6
Struan P & K..........194 C4
Strumpshaw Norfk....93 H3
Strutherhill S Lans....175 K7
Struthers Fife.........186 F5
Struy Highld..........212 B6
Stuartfield Abers.......217 H5
Stubbington Hants....17 G2
Stubbins Lancs........122 B6
Stubton Lincs.........102 E3
Stuckton Hants.......28 D8
Studham C Beds.......59 G5
Studland Dorset.......15 J6
Studley Warwks.......71 J2
Studley Wilts..........39 L6
Studley Roger N York...132 D5
Studley Royal N York...132 D5
Stuntney Cambs........90 D7
Sturmer Essex..........77 G5
Sturminster
Common Dorset.....27 H8
Sturminster Marshall
Dorset............15 H3
Sturminster Newton
Dorset............27 H8
Sturry Kent............35 G3
Sturton N Linc........116 F2
Sturton by Stow
Lincs.............116 E5
Sturton le Steeple
Notts.............116 C5
Stuston Suffk..........92 D7
Stutton N York........124 D3
Stutton Suffk..........78 D7
Styal Ches E..........113 J5
Stynie Moray.........215 H3
Styrrup Notts..........115 L4
Succoth Ag & B.......183 K6
Suckley Worcs.........70 C4
Sudborough Nhants....88 D6
Sudbourne Suffk.......79 J4
Sudbrook Lincs.......102 F4
Sudbrook Mons........38 D3
Sudbrooke Lincs......117 G6
Sudbury Derbys.......100 D6
Sudbury Gt Lon........44 D3
Sudbury Suffk..........77 K6
Suffield Norfk.........134 F2
Suffield N York........106 F6
Sugnall Staffs..........99 H6
Sugwas Pool Herefs...69 J6
Suisnish Highld........199 J3

Sulby IoM.............237 d3
Sulgrave Nhants.......73 G5
Sulgrave Manor
Nhants............73 H5
Sulham W Berk.......41 M5
Sulhamstead W Berk...41 M6
Sullom Shet...........235 C4
Sullom Voe Shet......235 C4
Sully V Glam..........37 J6
Sumburgh Airport
Shet.............235 c8
Summerbridge
N York...........132 C6
Summercourt Cnwll........4 D5
Summerfield Norfk....105 J5
Summerhill Pembks...49 K6
Summerhouse Darltn...140 F4
Summersdale W Susx...18 B4
Summerseat Bury......122 B7
Summertown Oxon.....57 K6
Sunbury Surrey........43 J6
Sundaywell D & G.....154 E5
Sunderland Ag & B......170 E5
Sunderland Cumb......147 L7
Sunderland Lancs.....129 J7
Sunderland Sundld....151 J4
Sunderland Bridge
Dur..............151 G7
Sunderland
Crematorium
Sundld............151 J4
Sundhope Border.......166 E4
Sundon Park Luton.....59 H3
Sundridge Kent.........32 E3
Sunningdale W & M....42 F6
Sunninghill W & M.....42 F6
Sunningwell Oxon......57 J7
Sunniside Dur.........150 E7
Sunniside Gatesd......150 F3
Sunnyhill C Derb.......101 G6
Sunnyhurst Bl w D....121 K6
Sunnylaw Stirlg.......185 G7
Sunnymead Oxon.......57 J6
Surbiton Gt Lon........44 D6
Surfleet Lincs..........103 L6
Surlingham Norfk......93 G3
Surrex Essex............61 L4
Surrey & Sussex
Crematorium
W Susx............32 B5
Sustead Norfk.........106 E5
Susworth Lincs........116 D2
Sutcombe Devon........9 J3
Sutcombemill Devon........9 J3
Sutterby Lincs.........118 E6
Sutterton Lincs........103 M5
Sutton C Beds..........75 J5
Sutton C Pete..........89 G4
Sutton Cambs..........90 C7
Sutton Devon...........7 G7
Sutton E Susx..........20 A5
Sutton Gt Lon..........44 E7
Sutton Kent............35 J5
Sutton N York.........124 D5
Sutton Norfk..........107 H7
Sutton Notts..........102 C5
Sutton Oxon...........57 H6
Sutton Shrops.........84 D6
Sutton Staffs..........99 H7
Sutton Suffk...........79 G5
Sutton W Susx.........18 D3
Sutton at Hone Kent....45 K6
Sutton Bassett
Nhants............87 L5
Sutton Benger Wilts.......39 L5
Sutton Bonington
Notts............101 K7
Sutton Bridge Lincs....104 D7
Sutton Cheney Leics....86 E4
Sutton Coldfield Birm...85 K4
Sutton Coldfield
Crematorium
Birm.............85 K4
Sutton Courtenay
Oxon............41 J2
Sutton cum Lound
Notts............116 B5

Sutton Green Surrey......31 G1
Sutton Howgrave
  N York..................132 D4
Sutton in Ashfield
  Notts.................101 J2
Sutton-in-Craven
  N York................122 F2
Sutton Maddock
  Shrops................84 C3
Sutton Mallet Somset...26 A4
Sutton Mandeville
  Wilts.................27 M5
Sutton Montis
  Somset................26 F6
Sutton-on-Hull C KuH...126 E4
Sutton on Sea Lincs....119 G5
Sutton-on-the-
  Forest N York........133 J6
Sutton on the Hill
  Derbys...............100 E5
Sutton on Trent
  Notts................116 D7
Sutton St Edmund
  Lincs.................89 L2
Sutton St James Lincs..104 C8
Sutton St Nicholas
  Herefs...............69 K5
Sutton Scotney
  Hants................29 J4
Sutton-under-Brailes
  Warwks...............72 C6
Sutton-under-
  Whitestonecliffe
  N York...............133 G3
Sutton upon
  Derwent E R Yk.......125 G2
Sutton Valence Kent....33 L4
Sutton Veny Wilts......27 K3
Sutton Waldron
  Dorset...............27 K7
Sutton Weaver
  Ches W...............112 D5
Sutton Wick BaNES......38 E8
Sutton Wick Oxon.......41 J2
Swaby Lincs............118 E6
Swadlincote Derbys.....100 F8
Swaffham Norfk.........91 J2
Swaffham Bulbeck
  Cambs................76 D3
Swaffham Prior
  Cambs................76 E2
Swafield Norfk.........107 G6
Swainby N York.........141 L6
Swainsthorpe Norfk.....92 F4
Swainswick BaNES.......39 H6
Swalcliffe Oxon........72 E6
Swalecliffe Kent.......47 J6
Swallow Lincs..........117 K2
Swallow Beck Lincs.....116 F7
Swallowcliffe Wilts....27 L6
Swallowfield
  Wokham...............42 B7
Swanage Dorset.........15 J6
Swanbourne Bucks.......58 D3
Swan Green Ches W......113 G6
Swanland E R Yk........126 B5
Swanley Kent...........45 K6
Swanley Village
  Kent.................45 K6
Swanmore Hants.........29 L7
Swannington Leics......86 E1
Swannington Norfk......106 D8
Swanpool Garden
  Suburb Lincs.........116 F7
Swanscombe Kent........45 L5
Swansea Swans..........51 J6
Swansea Airport
  Swans................51 H7
Swansea
  Crematorium
  Swans................51 J5
Swansea West
  Services Swans.......51 J5
Swanton Abbot
  Norfk................106 F7
Swanton Morley
  Norfk................92 B1

Swanton Novers
  Norfk................106 B6
Swanwick Derbys........101 H2
Swanwick Hants.........17 G1
Swarby Lincs...........103 H4
Swardeston Norfk.......92 E3
Swarkestone Derbys.....101 G6
Swarland Nthumb........158 F2
Swarraton Hants........29 K4
Swarthmoor Cumb........129 G4
Swaton Lincs...........103 J5
Swavesey Cambs.........75 L2
Sway Hants.............16 C3
Swayfield Lincs........103 G7
Swaythling C Sotn......29 H7
Sweetham Devon.........11 K5
Sweethaws E Susx.......32 E7
Sweets Cnwll...........8 F5
Sweetshouse Cnwll......5 H4
Swefling Suffk.........79 H2
Swepstone Leics........86 D2
Swerford Oxon..........57 G2
Swettenham Ches E......113 J7
Swilland Suffk.........78 E4
Swillington Leeds......124 B4
Swimbridge Devon.......23 K5
Swimbridge
  Newland Devon........23 J5
Swinbrook Oxon.........56 F5
Swincliffe N York......132 C7
Swinderby Lincs........116 E8
Swindon Gloucs.........55 L3
Swindon Staffs.........84 F5
Swindon Swindn.........40 D4
Swine E R Yk...........126 E4
Swinefleet E R Yk......125 H6
Swineshead Bed........74 F2
Swineshead Lincs.......103 L4
Swiney Highld..........227 M2
Swinford Leics.........87 H7
Swingfield Minnis
  Kent.................35 G6
Swingfield Street
  Kent.................35 H6
Swingleton Green
  Suffk................77 L5
Swinhoe Nthumb.........169 J4
Swinithwaite N York....131 K2
Swinside Cumb..........137 H3
Swinstead Lincs........103 G7
Swinton Border.........179 H8
Swinton N York.........132 C4
Swinton N York.........134 B5
Swinton Rothm.........115 J2
Swinton Salfd.........113 H2
Swithland Leics........87 G2
Swordale Highld........212 E2
Swordland Highld.......200 B6
Swordly Highld.........229 M3
Swynnerton Staffs......99 J5
Swyre Dorset...........13 M5
Sychtyn Powys..........81 L3
Syde Gloucs............55 L5
Sydenham Gt Lon........45 G5
Sydenham Oxon..........58 B7
Sydenham Damerel
  Devon................6 B2
Syderstone Norfk.......105 K6
Sydling St Nicholas
  Dorset...............14 C3
Sydmonton Hants........41 J8
Syerston Notts.........102 C3
Sygun Copper Mine
  Gwynd................95 K3
Sykehouse Donc.........124 F6
Symbister Shet.........235 d4
Symington S Ayrs.......163 J3
Symington S Lans.......165 J3
Symondsbury Dorset.....13 K4
Symonds Yat Herefs.....54 E5
Syre Highld............229 L6
Syreford Gloucs........56 B4
Syresham Nhants........73 J6
Syston Leics...........87 J2
Syston Lincs...........102 F4
Sytchampton Worcs......70 E2
Sywell Nhants..........74 B2

T

Tackley Oxon...........57 J4
Tacolneston Norfk......92 D4
Tadcaster N York.......124 D2
Taddington Derbys......114 C7
Tadley Hants...........41 L7
Tadlow Cambs...........75 K5
Tadmarton Oxon.........72 E6
Tadworth Surrey........44 E8
Taff's Well Rhondd.....37 H4
Taibach Neath..........36 B3
Tain Highld............223 G5
Tain Highld............231 J3
Tairbeart W Isls.......232 e4
Takeley Essex..........60 F4
Takeley Street Essex...60 E4
Talaton Devon..........12 D3
Talbenny Pembks........48 E5
Taleford Devon.........12 E3
Talerddig Powys........81 K4
Talgarreg Cerdgn.......65 L4
Talgarth Powys.........68 D7
Talisker Highld........208 E7
Talke Staffs...........99 J2
Talkin Cumb............148 F4
Talladale Highld.......219 L7
Talla Linnfoots
  Border...............165 M5
Tallaminnock S Ayrs....153 J3
Tallarn Green
  Wrexhm...............98 C4
Tallentire Cumb........147 K7
Talley Carmth..........66 E7
Tallington Lincs.......88 F2
Talmine Highld.........229 J3
Talog Carmth...........50 D1
Talsarn Cerdgn.........66 D4
Talsarnau Gwynd........95 K5
Talskiddy Cnwll........4 E3
Talwrn IoA.............109 G6
Tal-y-Bont Cerdgn......80 E5
Tal-y-Bont Conwy.......109 L7
Tal-y-bont Gwynd.......95 K7
Tal-y-bont Gwynd.......109 J7
Talybont-on-Usk
  Powys................53 H4
Tal-y-Cafn Conwy.......109 M7
Tal-y-coed Mons........54 B5
Talysarn Gwynd.........95 H2
Tamerton Foliot
  C Plym...............6 C4
Tamworth Staffs........86 B3
Tamworth Services
  Warwks...............86 B4
Tandridge Surrey.......32 C3
Tanfield Dur...........150 F4
Tanfield Lea Dur.......150 F4
Tangley Hants..........28 F2
Tangmere W Susx........18 B4
Tangusdale W Isls......233 b9
Tankerness Ork.........234 c6
Tankersley Barns.......115 G2
Tankerton Kent.........47 J6
Tannach Highld.........231 K6
Tannachie Abers........206 E8
Tannadice Angus........196 D5
Tanner's Green Worcs...85 J8
Tannington Suffk.......78 F2
Tannochside N Lans.....175 J6
Tansley Derbys.........100 F1
Tansor Nhants..........88 F5
Tantobie Dur...........150 F4
Tanworth in Arden
  Warwks...............71 K1
Tan-y-groes Cerdgn.....65 J5
Taobh Tuath W Isls.....232 d5
Taplow Bucks...........42 E4
Tarbert Ag & B.........172 B7
Tarbert Ag & B.........172 E5
Tarbert W Isls.........232 e4
Tarbet Ag & B..........183 K6
Tarbet Highld..........200 B6
Tarbet Highld..........228 B5
Tarbolton S Ayrs.......163 K4
Tarbrax S Lans.........176 D7

Tardebigge Worcs.......71 H2
Tarfside Angus.........196 D1
Tarland Abers..........205 K4
Tarleton Lancs.........120 F6
Tarlton Gloucs.........55 L7
Tarnock Somset.........26 B2
Tarporley Ches W.......112 D8
Tarrant Crawford
  Dorset...............15 H2
Tarrant Gunville
  Dorset...............27 L8
Tarrant Hinton Dorset..15 H1
Tarrant Keyneston
  Dorset...............15 H2
Tarrant Launceston
  Dorset...............15 H1
Tarrant Monkton
  Dorset...............15 H2
Tarrant Rawston
  Dorset...............15 H2
Tarrant Rushton
  Dorset...............15 H2
Tarring Neville E Susx..19 L5
Tarrington Herefs......70 B6
Tarskavaig Highld......199 J4
Tarves Abers...........217 G7
Tarvin Ches W..........112 C7
Tasburgh Norfk.........92 E4
Tatenhill Staffs.......100 D7
Tathwell Lincs.........118 D5
Tatsfield Surrey.......32 D2
Tattenhall Ches W......98 C2
Tatterford Norfk.......105 K6
Tattersett Norfk.......105 K6
Tattershall Lincs......103 K2
Tattershall Thorpe
  Lincs................103 L1
Tattingstone Suffk.....78 D6
Tattingstone White
  Horse Suffk..........78 D6
Tatworth Somset........13 J2
Tauchers Moray.........215 J4
Taunton Somset.........25 K6
Taunton Deane
  Crematorium
  Somset...............25 J6
Taunton Deane
  Services Somset......25 J7
Taverham Norfk.........92 E2
Tavernspite Pembks.....49 K5
Tavistock Devon........6 C2
Taw Green Devon........10 F5
Tawstock Devon.........23 J5
Taxal Derbys...........114 A5
Taychreggan Hotel
  Ag & B...............182 F3
Tay Forest Park P & K..194 C4
Tayinloan Ag & B.......161 H1
Taynton Gloucs.........55 G4
Taynton Oxon...........56 E5
Taynuilt Ag & B........182 E2
Tayport Fife...........187 G2
Tayvallich Ag & B......172 C2
Tealby Lincs...........117 J4
Tealing Angus..........196 C8
Team Valley Gatesd.....151 G3
Teangue Highld.........199 K4
Teanord Highld.........212 F2
Tebay Cumb.............138 E6
Tebay Services Cumb....138 E6
Tebworth C Beds........59 G3
Tedburn St Mary
  Devon................11 J6
Teddington Gloucs......55 L2
Teddington Gt Lon......44 D6
Tedstone Delamere
  Herefs...............70 C3
Tedstone Wafer
  Herefs...............70 C3
Teesside
  Crematorium
  Middsb...............141 L4
Teeton Nhants..........73 K1
Teffont Evias Wilts....27 M5
Teffont Magna Wilts....27 M5
Tegryn Pembks..........65 H7
Teigh Rutlnd...........88 C1

Teigngrace Devon 7 K2
Teignmouth Devon 12 B7
Teindside Border 166 F7
Telford Wrekin 84 C2
Telford Crematorium
Wrekin 84 D2
Telford Services
Shrops 84 D2
Tellisford Somset 27 J1
Telscombe E Susx 19 L5
Tempar P & K 193 L5
Templand D & G 155 J5
Temple Cnwll 5 J2
Temple Mdloth 177 J6
Temple Bar Cerdgn 66 C4
Temple Cloud BaNES 38 F8
Templecombe
Somset 27 G6
Temple Ewell Kent 35 H5
Temple Grafton
Warwks 71 K4
Temple Guiting
Gloucs 56 C3
Temple Hirst N York 124 F5
Temple Normanton
Derbys 115 H7
Temple of Fiddes
Abers 197 K1
Temple Sowerby
Cumb 138 E2
Templeton Devon 11 K3
Templeton Pembks 49 J5
Templetown Dur 150 E5
Tempsford C Beds 75 H4
Tenbury Wells Worcs 69 L2
Tenby Pembks 49 J7
Tendring Essex 62 D3
Tendring Green Essex 62 D3
Tendring Heath Essex 62 D3
Ten Mile Bank Norfk 90 E4
Tenterden Kent 34 B7
Terling Essex 61 J5
Ternhill Shrops 98 F6
Terregles D & G 155 G6
Terrington N York 133 K5
Terrington St
Clement Norfk 104 E7
Terrington St John
Norfk 90 D2
Teston Kent 33 J3
Testwood Hants 29 G8
Tetbury Gloucs 39 K2
Tetchill Shrops 98 B6
Tetcott Devon 9 J5
Tetford Lincs 118 D6
Tetney Lincs 118 D2
Tetsworth Oxon 58 B7
Tettenhall Wolves 84 F4
Teversal Notts 101 J1
Teversham Cambs 76 C3
Teviothead Border 156 D2
Tewin Herts 59 L5
Tewkesbury Gloucs 55 K2
Teynham Kent 34 C3
Thackley C Brad 123 H3
Thakeham W Susx 18 F3
Thame Oxon 58 B6
Thames Ditton Surrey 44 D6
Thamesmead Gt Lon 45 J4
Thanet Crematorium
Kent 35 K2
Thanington Kent 34 F4
Thankerton S Lans 165 J2
Tharston Norfk 92 E5
Thatcham W Berk 41 K6
Thaxted Essex 60 F2
Theakston N York 132 D3
Thealby N Linc 125 K6
Theale Somset 26 C3
Theale W Berk 41 M6
Thearne E R Yk 126 D3
The Beeches Gloucs 56 B7
Theberton Suffk 79 J2
The Beth Chatto
Gardens Essex 62 C3
The Braes Highld 209 H7
The Brunt E Loth 178 E4

The Bungalow IoM 237 d4
The Burf Worcs 70 E2
The Butts Gloucs 55 K5
The City Bucks 42 C2
The Common Wilts 28 E5
The Counties
Crematorium
Nhants 73 K3
Theddingworth Leics 87 J6
Theddlethorpe All
Saints Lincs 118 F4
Theddlethorpe St
Helen Lincs 119 G4
The Den N Ayrs 174 C7
The Forest of Dean
Crematorium
Gloucs 54 F5
The Forstal Kent 34 D6
The Garden of
England
Crematorium
Kent 46 E6
The Green Cumb 128 E3
The Green Essex 61 J4
The Green N York 143 G6
The Green Wilts 27 K5
The Headland Hartpl 151 M7
The Hill Cumb 128 E3
The Lee Bucks 58 E6
The Lhen IoM 237 d2
The Linn
Crematorium
E Rens 175 G6
Thelnetham Suffk 92 B7
The Lochs Moray 215 G2
Thelveton Norfk 92 E7
Thelwall Warrtn 112 F4
The Manchester
Crematorium
Manch 113 J3
Themelthorpe Norfk 106 C7
The Moor Kent 33 K7
The Mumbles Swans 51 J7
The Murray S Lans 175 H7
The Neuk Abers 206 D5
Thenford Nhants 73 G6
The Park
Crematorium
Hants 30 E2
The Reddings Gloucs 55 K4
Therfield Herts 75 L6
The Rose Hill
Crematorium
Donc 115 L2
The Ross P & K 185 G3
The Stocks Kent 21 H1
The Strand Wilts 39 L8
The Tank Museum
(Bovington)
Dorset 14 F5
Thetford Norfk 91 K6
Thetford Forest Park 91 J5
The Vale
Crematorium
Luton 59 J3
Theydon Bois Essex 60 D7
Thickwood Wilts 39 J5
Thimbleby Lincs 118 C7
Thimbleby N York 141 K7
Thingwall Wirral 111 J5
Thirkleby N York 133 G4
Thirlby N York 133 G3
Thirlestane Border 178 C8
Thirn N York 132 C3
Thirsk N York 132 F3
Thistleton Lancs 120 E3
Thistleton Rutlnd 102 E8
Thistley Green Suffk 90 F7
Thixendale N York 134 C7
Thockrington
Nthumb 158 B6
Tholomas Drove
Cambs 90 B3
Tholthorpe N York 133 G6
Thomastown Abers 216 B6
Thompson Norfk 91 K4
Thoralby N York 131 J3

Thoresway Lincs 117 K3
Thorganby Lincs 117 K3
Thorganby N York 125 G3
Thorgill N York 142 E7
Thorington Suffk 93 J8
Thorington Street
Suffk 78 B7
Thorlby N York 131 H8
Thorley Herts 60 D4
Thorley Street IoW 16 D5
Thormanby N York 133 G5
Thornaby-on-Tees
S on T 141 K4
Thornage Norfk 106 C5
Thornborough Bucks 73 L7
Thornborough N York 132 D4
Thornbury C Brad 123 J4
Thornbury Devon 9 K3
Thornbury Herefs 70 B3
Thornbury S Glos 38 F3
Thornby Nhants 87 J7
Thorncliff Staffs 100 A2
Thorncliffe
Crematorium
Cumb 128 E5
Thorncombe Dorset 13 J2
Thorndon Suffk 78 D1
Thorndon Cross
Devon 10 D6
Thorne Donc 125 G7
Thorner Leeds 124 B3
Thorne St Margaret
Somset 25 H7
Thorney C Pete 89 K3
Thorney Notts 116 E6
Thorney Somset 26 B6
Thorney Hill Hants 16 A3
Thorney Island
W Susx 17 L2
Thornfalcon Somset 25 L6
Thornford Dorset 26 E8
Thorngrafton
Nthumb 149 K2
Thorngumbald E R Yk 126 F5
Thornham Norfk 105 H4
Thornham Magna
Suffk 78 D1
Thornham Parva
Suffk 92 D8
Thornhaugh C Pete 88 F4
Thornhill C Sotn 29 J8
Thornhill Cumb 136 D5
Thornhill D & G 154 F3
Thornhill Derbys 114 D5
Thornhill Kirk 123 K6
Thornhill Stirlg 184 E7
Thornhill
Crematorium
Cardif 37 J4
Thornholme E R Yk 135 H6
Thornicombe Dorset 15 G2
Thornington Nthumb 168 D3
Thornley Dur 150 E7
Thornley Dur 151 J6
Thornliebank E Rens 174 F6
Thorns Suffk 77 G4
Thornsett Derbys 114 A4
Thornthwaite Cumb 137 H3
Thornthwaite N York 132 B7
Thornton Angus 196 C6
Thornton Bucks 73 L7
Thornton C Brad 123 G4
Thornton E R Yk 125 H2
Thornton Fife 186 E7
Thornton Lancs 120 D3
Thornton Leics 86 F3
Thornton Middsb 141 L4
Thornton Nthumb 179 K8
Thornton Curtis
N Linc 126 D6
Thornton Garden
of Rest
Crematorium
Sefton 111 K2
Thorntonhall S Lans 175 G7
Thornton Heath
Gt Lon 44 F6

Thornton Hough
Wirral 111 J5
Thornton-in-Craven
N York 122 D2
Thornton in Lonsdale
N York 130 D5
Thornton-le-Beans
N York 132 F2
Thornton-le-Clay
N York 133 L6
Thornton le Dale
N York 134 C3
Thornton le Moor
Lincs 117 H3
Thornton-le-Moor
N York 132 F2
Thornton-le-Moors
Ches W 112 C6
Thornton-le-Street
N York 132 F3
Thorntonloch E Loth 178 F4
Thornton Rust N York 131 H2
Thornton Steward
N York 132 B3
Thornton Watlass
N York 132 C3
Thornydykes Border 178 D8
Thornythwaite Cumb 137 L3
Thoroton Notts 102 C4
Thorp Arch Leeds 124 C2
Thorpe Derbys 100 D3
Thorpe E R Yk 126 B2
Thorpe N York 131 J6
Thorpe Notts 102 C3
Thorpe Surrey 43 G6
Thorpe Abbotts
Norfk 92 E7
Thorpe Arnold Leics 102 C7
Thorpe Audlin
Wakefd 124 D7
Thorpe Bassett
N York 134 D5
Thorpe Bay Sthend 46 E3
Thorpe by Water
Rutlnd 88 C4
Thorpe Constantine
Staffs 86 C2
Thorpe End Norfk 93 G2
Thorpe Green Essex 62 E4
Thorpe Green Suffk 77 L4
Thorpe Hesley Rothm 115 G3
Thorpe in Balne Donc 124 F7
Thorpe Langton Leics 87 L5
Thorpe Lea Surrey 43 G6
Thorpe-le-Soken
Essex 62 E4
Thorpe le Street
E R Yk 125 K2
Thorpe Malsor
Nhants 88 B7
Thorpe Mandeville
Nhants 73 G5
Thorpe Market Norfk 106 F5
Thorpe Marriot Norfk 92 E1
Thorpe Morieux Suffk 77 L4
Thorpeness Suffk 79 K3
Thorpe on the Hill
Lincs 116 E7
Thorpe Park Surrey 43 G6
Thorpe St Andrew
Norfk 92 F2
Thorpe St Peter Lincs 104 D1
Thorpe Salvin Rothm 115 K5
Thorpe Satchville
Leics 87 K2
Thorpe Thewles
S on T 141 J3
Thorpe Tilney Lincs 103 J2
Thorpe Underwood
N York 133 G7
Thorpe Waterville
Nhants 88 E7
Thorpe Willoughby
N York 124 E4
Thorrington Essex 62 C4
Thorverton Devon 11 L4
Thrandeston Suffk 92 D7

Thrapston Nhants 88 E7
Threapwood Ches W.......98 C4
Threapwood Staffs.......100 B4
Threave S Ayrs 163 J7
Threave Castle D & G.....146 C3
Three Bridges W Susx....32 B5
Three Chimneys Kent......33 L5
Three Cocks Powys........68 D6
Three Counties
  Crematorium
  Essex 61 J3
Three Crosses Swans 51 H6
Three Cups Corner
  E Susx 20 D2
Threekingham Lincs 103 H5
Three Leg Cross
  E Susx 33 H6
Three Legged Cross
  Dorset 15 K2
Three Mile Cross
  Wokham 42 B6
Threemilestone Cnwll 3 K3
Three Miletown
  W Loth 176 E3
Three Oaks E Susx 21 G3
Threlkeld Cumb...........137 J3
Threshers Bush Essex...... 60 D6
Threshfield N York 131 J6
Thrigby Norfk 93 K2
Thringstone Leics.........101 H8
Thrintoft N York 132 D2
Thriplow Cambs 76 B5
Throcking Herts 60 B3
Throckley N u Ty 150 E2
Throckmorton Worcs......71 H4
Throop Bmouth............15 L4
Thropton Nthumb 158 C2
Throsk Stirlg...............176 B1
Throughgate D & G......154 F5
Throwleigh Devon 11 G6
Throwley Forstal
  Kent 34 C4
Thrumpton Notts.........101 J6
Thrumster Highld.........231 L6
Thrunscoe NE Lin 127 H8
Thrupp Gloucs.............55 K7
Thrussington Leics........87 J1
Thruxton Hants 28 F3
Thruxton Herefs...........69 J7
Thrybergh Rothm 115 J3
Thulston Derbys..........101 H6
Thundersley Essex.........46 C3
Thurcaston Leics...........87 H2
Thurcroft Rothm..........115 J4
Thurgarton Norfk 106 E5
Thurgarton Notts 102 B3
Thurgoland Barns 114 F2
Thurlaston Leics...........87 G4
Thurlaston Warwks 72 F1
Thurlbear Somset 25 K7
Thurlby Lincs...............89 G1
Thurlby Lincs..............102 E1
Thurlby Lincs..............119 G6
Thurleigh Bed 74 F3
Thurlestone Devon 7 G7
Thurloxton Somset 25 L5
Thurlstone Barns 114 E2
Thurlton Norfk 93 J4
Thurmaston Leics 87 H2
Thurnby Leics 87 J3
Thurne Norfk 93 J1
Thurnham Kent 33 K2
Thurning Nhants 88 F6
Thurning Norfk 106 C6
Thurnscoe Barns 115 J1
Thurrock Services
  Thurr 45 L4
Thursby Cumb............148 B5
Thursford Norfk 106 B5
Thursley Surrey 30 E4
Thurso Highld 231 K2
Thurstaston Wirral 111 H5
Thurston Suffk.............77 L2
Thurstonfield Cumb......148 B4
Thurstonland Kirk 123 H7
Thurton Norfk 93 G4
Thurvaston Derbys......100 E5

Thuxton Norfk..............92 B3
Thwaite N York 139 K7
Thwaite Suffk 78 D2
Thwaite Head Cumb 129 H2
Thwaite St Mary
  Norfk 93 G4
Thwing E R Yk 135 G5
Tibbermore P & K........185 L3
Tibbers D & G............154 E3
Tibberton Gloucs..........55 H4
Tibberton Worcs...........70 F3
Tibberton Wrekin 99 G7
Tibbie Shiels Inn
  Border 166 C5
Tibenham Norfk...........92 D5
Tibshelf Derbys...........101 H1
Tibthorpe E R Yk........134 E7
Ticehurst E Susx 33 H7
Tichborne Hants...........29 L5
Tickencote Rutlnd.........88 E2
Tickenham N Som........38 C6
Tickhill Donc 115 L3
Ticklerton Shrops.........83 J5
Ticknall Derbys 101 G7
Tickton E R Yk 126 D3
Tidcombe Wilts............40 F8
Tiddington Oxon 57 M6
Tiddington Warwks 72 B4
Tidebrook E Susx..........33 G7
Tideford Cnwll............. 6 A4
Tidenham Gloucs..........38 E2
Tideswell Derbys 114 D6
Tidmarsh W Berk.........41 M5
Tidmington Warwks......72 C6
Tidworth Wilts.............28 E2
Tiers Cross Pembks 48 F5
Tiffield Nhants 73 K4
Tigerton Angus...........196 E4
Tigh a Ghearraidh
  W Isls 233 b6
Tigharry W Isls 233 b6
Tighnabruaich Ag & B...173 G4
Tigley Devon 7 H4
Tilbrook Cambs 74 F2
Tilbury Thurr 45 M5
Tile Hill Covtry.............86 C7
Tilehurst Readg 42 A5
Tilford Surrey 30 E3
Tilgate W Susx.............31 L4
Tilham Street Somset.....26 E4
Tillicoultry Clacks 185 J7
Tillietudlem S Lans 164 F1
Tillingham Essex..........62 B7
Tillington Herefs...........69 J5
Tillington W Susx.........30 F6
Tillington Common
  Herefs 69 J5
Tillybirloch Abers 206 D4
Tillyfourie Abers 206 C3
Tillygreig Abers 207 G2
Tillyrie P & K.............186 B6
Tilmanstone Kent 35 J4
Tilney All Saints
  Norfk 104 F8
Tilney High End Norfk..104 E8
Tilney St Lawrence
  Norfk 90 D2
Tilshead Wilts..............28 B2
Tilstock Shrops............98 D5
Tilston Ches W.............98 C3
Tilstone Fearnall
  Ches W...................98 E1
Tilsworth C Beds 59 G3
Tilton on the Hill Leics...87 L3
Tiltups End Gloucs........39 J2
Timberland Lincs.........103 J2
Timbersbrook Ches E....113 K8
Timberscombe
  Somset 24 E3
Timble N York 132 B8
Timpanheck D & G 156 B7
Timperley Traffd 113 H4
Timsbury BaNES 38 F8
Timsbury Hants 29 G6
Timsgarry W Isls 232 d2
Timsgearraidh W Isls ...232 d2
Timworth Suffk 77 J2

Timworth Green
  Suffk 77 J2
Tincleton Dorset...........14 E4
Tindale Cumb 149 G3
Tindale Crescent Dur ...140 F2
Tingewick Bucks 58 A2
Tingrith C Beds.............59 G2
Tingwall Airport Shet ...235 c6
Tinhay Devon 9 K7
Tinsley Sheff 115 H4
Tinsley Green W Susx....32 B5
Tintagel Cnwll............... 8 E7
Tintagel Castle Cnwll...... 8 D6
Tintern Abbey Mons......54 D7
Tintern Parva Mons......54 D7
Tintinhull Somset 26 D7
Tintwistle Derbys 114 A3
Tinwald D & G 155 H5
Tinwell Rutlnd..............88 E3
Tipton Sandw 85 G5
Tipton St John Devon....12 E4
Tiptree Essex................61 L5
Tiptree Heath Essex......61 L5
Tirabad Powys 67 J6
Tiree Ag & B...............188 D7
Tiree Airport Ag & B 188 C7
Tiretigan Ag & B 172 C6
Tirley Gloucs................55 J3
Tirphil Caerph 53 H7
Tirril Cumb 138 D2
Tisbury Wilts...............27 L5
Tissington Derbys 100 D3
Titchberry Devon 22 C6
Titchfield Hants 17 G2
Titchmarsh Nhants 88 E7
Titchwell Norfk...........105 J4
Tithby Notts...............102 B5
Titley Herefs................69 G3
Titsey Surrey 32 D3
Titson Cnwll................. 9 H5
Tittensor Staffs 99 K5
Tittleshall Norfk..........105 L7
Titton Worcs................70 E1
Tiverton Ches W...........98 D1
Tiverton Devon 24 E8
Tivetshall St
  Margaret Norfk.........92 E6
Tivetshall St Mary
  Norfk 92 E6
Tixall Staffs.................99 L7
Tixover Rutlnd..............88 E4
Toab Shet 235 c8
Tobermory Ag & B 189 L5
Toberonochy Ag & B ...181 L5
Tobha Mor W Isls 233 b7
Tocher Abers 216 D7
Tochineal Moray 215 L2
Tockenham Wilts..........40 B4
Tockholes Bl w D 121 K6
Tockington S Glos.........38 E3
Tockwith N York 133 G8
Todber Dorset 27 J7
Toddington C Beds........59 G3
Toddington Gloucs........56 B2
Toddington Services
  C Beds 59 G3
Todenham Gloucs.........72 B7
Todhills Angus............196 C8
Todhills Services
  Cumb 148 C3
Todmorden Calder 122 D5
Todwick Rothm 115 J3
Toft Cambs 75 L4
Toft Lincs 88 F1
Toft Shet 235 c3
Toft Hill Dur 140 E2
Toft Monks Norfk.........93 J4
Toft next Newton
  Lincs 117 H4
Toftrees Norfk 105 L6
Togston Nthumb.........159 G2
Tokavaig Highld..........199 J3
Tokers Green Oxon 42 B5
Tolastadh W Isls 232 g2
Tolland Somset 25 H5
Tollard Royal Wilts.......27 L7
Toll Bar Donc 124 E8

Toller Fratrum Dorset 14 B3
Toller Porcorum
  Dorset 14 B3
Tollerton N York 133 H6
Tollerton Notts............101 L5
Tollesbury Essex...........62 A6
Tolleshunt D'Arcy
  Essex 61 L5
Tolleshunt Knights
  Essex 61 L5
Tolleshunt Major
  Essex 61 L5
Tolpuddle Dorset...........14 E4
Tolsta W Isls...............232 g2
Tolworth Gt Lon 44 D6
Tomatin Highld 213 J8
Tomchrasky Highld......201 K3
Tomdoun Highld.........201 H5
Tomich Highld............211 L8
Tomich Highld............212 E5
Tomich Highld............222 F7
Tomich Highld............226 A7
Tomintoul Moray 204 E2
Tomnacross Highld 212 D6
Tomnavoulin Moray.....204 F1
Tonbridge Kent 33 G4
Tondu Brdgnd..............36 D4
Tonedale Somset..........25 H6
Tong C Brad 123 J4
Tong Kent 34 C4
Tong Shrops 84 E3
Tonge Leics................101 H7
Tongham Surrey...........30 E2
Tongland D & G..........146 C4
Tongue Highld 229 J4
Tong Norton Shrops 84 E3
Tongue Highld 229 J4
Tongwynlais Cardif 37 H4
Tonmawr Neath 36 C2
Tonna Neath 52 B7
Tonwell Herts 60 B5
Tonypandy Rhondd 36 F3
Tonyrefail Rhondd 36 F3
Toot Baldon Oxon 57 K7
Toot Hill Essex.............60 E7
Toothill Swindn 40 C4
Tooting Gt Lon 44 F5
Tooting Bec Gt Lon 44 F5
Topcliffe N York 132 F4
Topcroft Norfk 92 F5
Topcroft Street Norfk 92 F5
Toppesfield Essex 77 G6
Toprow Norfk 92 E4
Topsham Devon 12 C5
Torbeg N Ayrs 162 A4
Torboll Highld 223 G2
Torbreck Highld 213 G6
Torbryan Devon 7 J3
Torcastle Highld 192 B2
Torcross Devon............. 7 J7
Tore Highld 212 F4
Torinturk Ag & B........172 D5
Torksey Lincs..............116 D5
Tormarton S Glos 39 H5
Tormore N Ayrs..........161 M3
Tornagrain Highld 213 J4
Tornaveen Abers 206 C4
Torness Highld 212 E8
Toronto Dur 140 F2
Torpenhow Cumb.......147 L6
Torphichen W Loth 176 D3
Torphins Abers 206 C4
Torpoint Cnwll............. 6 C5
Torquay Torbay 7 L3
Torquay
  Crematorium
  Torbay 7 K3
Torquhan Border.........177 L8
Torran Highld 209 J5
Torrance E Duns 175 H4
Torranyard N Ayrs......163 J1
Torridon Highld 210 D3
Torridon House
  Highld 210 D3
Torrin Highld 199 J2
Torrisdale Ag & B.......161 K3
Torrisdale Highld 229 K3
Torrish Highld 227 G5

Torrisholme Lancs........129 K6
Torrobull Highld 226 A7
Torry C Aber................207 H4
Torryburn Fife.............176 D2
Torteval Guern............236 b4
Torthorwald D & G....155 H6
Tortington W Susx 18 D5
Torton Worcs 84 E8
Tortworth S Glos 39 G2
Torvaig Highld 209 H5
Torver Cumb...............137 J7
Torwood Falk..............175 L2
Torwoodlee Border 167 G2
Torworth Notts 116 A4
Toscaig Highld 209 L6
Toseland Cambs 75 J3
Tosside Lancs 130 E7
Tostock Suffk 77 L2
Totaig Highld..............208 C4
Tote Highld 208 F5
Tote Highld 209 H3
Totland IoW..................16 D5
Totley Sheff 114 F5
Totnes Devon 7 J4
Toton Notts 101 J5
Totronald Ag & B.......188 F5
Totscore Highld 208 F2
Tottenham Gt Lon 45 G3
Tottenhill Norfk..........90 F2
Totteridge Gt Lon 44 E2
Totternhoe C Beds 59 G4
Tottington Bury 122 B7
Totton Hants 29 G8
Toulton Somset 25 J5
Toulvaddie Highld 223 J5
Tovil Kent.....................33 K3
Toward Ag & B............173 K5
Toward Quay Ag & B ..173 J5
Towcester Nhants........73 K5
Towednack Cnwll...........2 E4
Towersey Oxon 58 B6
Towie Abers 205 K3
Tow Law Dur...............150 E6
Town End Cambs 90 B4
Townend W Duns 174 D3
Townhead Barns 114 D2
Townhead D & G 155 H4
Townhead of
    Greenlaw D & G...146 C3
Townhill Fife..............176 F1
Town Littleworth
    E Susx 19 L3
Towns End Hants 41 K8
Townshend Cnwll...........3 G5
Town Street Suffk 91 H6
Town Yetholm Border..168 B4
Towthorpe C York 133 K7
Towton N York 124 D3
Towyn Conwy 110 D5
Toxteth Lpool 111 K4
Toynton All Saints
    Lincs 118 E8
Toy's Hill Kent 32 E3
Trabboch E Ayrs.........163 K5
Trabbochburn E Ayrs..163 L5
Tradespark Highld.....213 K3
Trallong Powys 52 E3
Tramway Museum
    Derbys 101 G2
Tranent E Loth 177 L4
Tranmere Wirral.........111 J4
Trantelbeg Highld 230 C5
Trantlemore Highld ..230 C5
Trapp Carmth...............51 J2
Traprain E Loth 178 D4
Traquair Border 166 E3
Trawden Lancs 122 D3
Trawsfynydd Gwynd 96 A5
Trealaw Rhondd 36 F3
Treales Lancs 120 F4
Trearddur Bay IoA 108 C5
Treaslane Highld 208 F4
Trebetherick Cnwll........4 E1
Treborough Somset 24 D4
Trebullett Cnwll 5 M1
Treburley Cnwll 6 A1
Trecastle Powys 52 D3

Trecwn Pembks 64 D7
Trecynon Rhondd 52 F7
Tredegar Blae G 53 H6
Tredington Gloucs.......55 K3
Tredington Warwks......72 C5
Tredunnock Mons........38 B2
Treen Cnwll 2 D6
Treeton Rothm 115 H4
Trefasser Pembks........64 C6
Trefecca Powys 53 H2
Trefeglwys Powys........81 L5
Treffgarne Pembks......49 G3
Treffgarne Owen
    Pembks 48 E3
Trefforest Rhondd 37 G3
Trefilan Cerdgn...........66 D3
Trefin Pembks 64 B7
Trefnant Denbgs 110 E7
Trefonen Shrops 97 K6
Trefor Gwynd 94 F4
Trefriw Conwy 109 L8
Tregadillett Cnwll 9 H7
Tregare Mons 54 B6
Tregaron Cerdgn.........66 F3
Tregarth Gwynd 109 H7
Tregeare Cnwll 9 H7
Tregeiriog Wrexhm 97 J5
Tregele IoA 108 D3
Treglemais Pembks.....48 D2
Tregonetha Cnwll..........4 E3
Tregony Cnwll...............4 E6
Tregorrick Cnwll...........4 F5
Tregoyd Powys 68 E6
Tre-groes Cerdgn 65 L5
Tregynon Powys..........82 C4
Tre-gynwr Carmth 50 E2
Trehafod Rhondd 37 G3
Trehan Cnwll 6 B4
Treharris Myr Td 37 H2
Treherbert Rhondd......52 E7
Trekenner Cnwll............6 A1
Treknow Cnwll 8 D7
Trelawnyd Flints........110 F5
Trelech Carmth 65 J7
Treleddyd-fawr
    Pembks 48 C2
Trelewis Myr Td 37 H2
Trelights Cnwll 8 C8
Trelill Cnwll 5 G1
Trelissick Garden
    Cnwll 4 C7
Trelleck Mons 54 D6
Trelogan Flints..........110 F5
Tremadog Gwynd 95 K4
Tremail Cnwll 8 F7
Tremain Cerdgn...........65 H5
Tremaine Cnwll.............9 G6
Tremar Cnwll 5 K3
Trematon Cnwll.............6 B4
Tremeirchion Denbgs..110 F6
Trenance Cnwll..............4 D3
Trenance Cnwll..............4 E2
Trench Wrekin 84 C2
Trenear Cnwll 3 H5
Treneglos Cnwll 9 G7
Trent Dorset 26 E7
Trentham C Stke..........99 K4
Trentishoe Devon 23 K2
Treoes V Glam 36 E5
Treorchy Rhondd 36 E2
Trequite Cnwll 5 G1
Trerhyngyll V Glam 36 F5
Trerulefoot Cnwll 5 M4
Tresaith Cerdgn...........65 J4
Tresco IoS 2 a1
Tresco Heliport IoS 2 a1
Trescowe Cnwll 3 G5
Tresean Cnwll 4 C4
Tresham Gloucs 39 H3
Treshnish Isles Ag & B..189 G7
Tresillian Cnwll 4 D6
Treskinnick Cross
    Cnwll 9 G5
Tresmeer Cnwll 9 G7
Tresparrett Cnwll 9 G6
Tressait P & K 194 C4
Tresta Shet 235 c5

Tresta Shet 235 e3
Treswell Notts 116 C5
Treswithian Downs
    Crematorium
    Cnwll........................3 H3
Tre Taliesin Cerdgn 80 E5
Trethevey Cnwll.............8 E6
Trethewey Cnwll............2 C6
Trethurgy Cnwll.............5 G5
Tretire Herefs 54 D4
Tretower Powys 53 J4
Treuddyn Flints...........97 K2
Trevalga Cnwll...............8 E6
Trevalyn Wrexhm 98 B2
Trevarrian Cnwll............4 D3
Treveal Cnwll 4 C4
Treveighan Cnwll 8 E8
Trevellas Downs
    Cnwll 3 J2
Trevelmond Cnwll 5 K3
Treverva Cnwll 3 K5
Trevescan Cnwll 2 C6
Treviscoe Cnwll 4 E5
Trevone Cnwll 4 D2
Trevor Wrexhm 97 L4
Trewalder Cnwll 8 E7
Trewarmett Cnwll 8 E7
Trewen Cnwll 9 H7
Trewint Cnwll 9 G8
Trewithian Cnwll 4 D7
Trewoon Cnwll 4 F5
Treyford W Susx 30 D7
Trimdon Dur 151 J7
Trimdon Colliery Dur ..151 J7
Trimdon Grange Dur ..151 J7
Trimingham Norfk 107 G5
Trimley St Martin
    Suffk 78 F6
Trimley St Mary Suffk ..79 G7
Trimsaran Carmth 50 F5
Trimstone Devon 23 H3
Trinafour P & K 194 B4
Tring Herts 58 F5
Trinity Angus.............196 F4
Trinity Jersey.............236 d6
Trinity Gask P & K 185 K4
Triscombe Somset 25 J4
Trislaig Highld 191 L2
Trispen Cnwll 4 D5
Tritlington Nthumb 158 F4
Trochry P & K 194 F7
Troedyraur Cerdgn 65 K5
Troedyrhiw Myr Td 53 G7
Troon Cnwll 3 H4
Troon S Ayrs 163 H3
Tropical World
    Roundhay Park
    Leeds 123 L3
Trossachs Stirlg 184 B5
Trossachs Pier Stirlg ..184 B6
Troston Suffk 91 K8
Trotshill Worcs 70 F4
Trottiscliffe Kent 33 H2
Trotton W Susx 30 D6
Troutbeck Cumb.........137 L6
Troutbeck Bridge
    Cumb 137 L7
Troway Derbys 115 H5
Trowbridge Wilts.........39 J8
Trowell Notts 101 J4
Trowell Services
    Notts 101 J4
Trowse Newton
    Norfk 92 F3
Trudoxhill Somset 27 H3
Trull Somset 25 K6
Trumpan Highld 208 C3
Trumpet Herefs 70 B6
Trumpington Cambs ...76 C4
Trunch Norfk..............107 G5
Truro Cnwll 4 C6
Truro Cathedral
    Cnwll 4 C6
Trusham Devon 11 K7
Trusley Derbys 100 E5
Trusthorpe Lincs 119 G5
Trysull Staffs 84 F5

Tubney Oxon................57 H7
Tuckenhay Devon 7 J5
Tuckhill Shrops 84 E6
Tuckingmill Cnwll 3 H3
Tuckingmill Wilts 27 L5
Tuckton Bmouth 15 L4
Tuddenham Suffk 77 G1
Tuddenham Suffk 78 E5
Tudeley Kent................33 G4
Tudhoe Dur 151 G7
Tudweiliog Gwynd 94 D5
Tuffley Gloucs 55 J5
Tufton Hants 29 J3
Tufton Pembks 49 H2
Tugby Leics..................87 L4
Tugford Shrops............83 L6
Tughall Nthumb 169 J4
Tullibody Clacks 185 H7
Tullich Highld 212 F8
Tullich Highld 223 J6
Tulliemet P & K 194 F5
Tulloch Abers 216 F7
Tullochgorm Ag & B...182 D7
Tulloch Station
    Highld 192 F1
Tullymurdoch P & K....195 J5
Tullynessle Abers 206 B2
Tulse Hill Gt Lon 44 F5
Tumble Carmth............51 G3
Tumby Lincs 103 L1
Tumby Woodside
    Lincs 103 L2
Tummel Bridge P & K ..194 B5
Tunbridge Wells
    Kent.......................33 G5
Tundergarth D & G....155 L6
Tunley BaNES 39 G8
Tunstall C Stke............99 K3
Tunstall E R Yk 127 H4
Tunstall Kent 34 B3
Tunstall Lancs 130 B5
Tunstall N York..........140 F7
Tunstall Norfk.............93 J2
Tunstall Staffs 99 H6
Tunstall Suffk 79 H4
Tunstall Sundld 151 J4
Tunstead Derbys 114 C6
Tunstead Norfk 107 G7
Tunstead Milton
    Derbys 114 B5
Turgis Green Hants 42 B8
Turkdean Gloucs..........56 C4
Tur Langton Leics........87 K5
Turleigh Wilts 39 J7
Turnastone Herefs.......69 G7
Turnberry S Ayrs........152 E2
Turnditch Derbys.......100 F3
Turner's Hill W Susx....32 C6
Turnhouse C Edin.......177 G4
Turnworth Dorset 14 F2
Turriff Abers 216 D4
Turton Bottoms
    Bl w D 121 L7
Turves Cambs 89 L4
Turvey Bed..................74 D4
Turville Bucks 42 C3
Turweston Bucks 73 H6
Tushielaw Inn Border..166 D5
Tutbury Staffs 100 E6
Tutshill Gloucs 38 D2
Tuttington Norfk.......106 F6
Tuxford Notts 116 C7
Twatt Ork 234 b5
Twatt Shet 235 c5
Twechar E Duns 175 J3
Tweedbank Border 167 H3
Tweedmouth
    Nthumb 179 K7
Tweedsmuir Border ...165 L4
Twelveheads Cnwll 3 K3
Twemlow Green
    Ches E 113 H7
Twenty Lincs 103 J7
Twerton BaNES 39 G7
Twickenham Gt Lon 44 D5
Twigworth Gloucs.......55 J4
Twineham W Susx.......19 H2

Twinstead Essex..............77 J6
Twitchen Devon..............24 C5
Two Dales Derbys..........114 F8
Two Gates Staffs.............86 B4
Twycross Leics.................86 D3
Twycross Zoo Leics......86 C3
Twyford Bucks.................58 A3
Twyford Hants.................29 J6
Twyford Leics.................87 K2
Twyford Norfk.............106 B7
Twyford Wokham...........42 C5
Twynholm D & G.........146 B4
Twyning Green
Gloucs.....................70 F6
Twynllanan Carmth.......51 L2
Twywell Nhants.............88 D7
Tyberton Herefs.............69 H6
Tycroes Carmth.............51 H4
Tycrwyn Powys.............97 H8
Tydd Gote Lincs...........104 D8
Tydd St Giles Cambs......90 B1
Tydd St Mary Lincs......104 C8
Tye Green Essex.............76 E7
Tyldesley Wigan...........113 G2
Tyler Hill Kent...............34 F3
Tylorstown Rhondd........36 F2
Ty-nant Conwy...............96 F4
Tyndrum Stirlg.............183 K2
Ty'n-dwr Denbgs...........97 K4
Tynemouth N Tyne.......151 J2
Tynemouth
Crematorium
N Tyne.....................151 J2
Tyninghame E Loth......178 D3
Tynron D & G..............154 E4
Tyntesfield NT
N Som........................38 D6
Tynygraig Cerdgn..........66 F1
Ty'n-y-Groes Conwy....109 L7
Tyn-y-nant Rhondd........37 G4
Tyringham M Keyn.........74 C5
Tythegston Brdgnd........36 D5
Tytherington Ches E.....113 K6
Tytherington S Glos......38 F3
Tytherington Wilts.........27 K3
Tytherleigh Devon.........13 H2
Tytherton Lucas Wilts...39 L5
Tywardreath Cnwll..........5 H5
Tywyn Gwynd................80 D4

U

Ubbeston Green
Suffk........................79 G1
Ubley BaNES.................38 D8
Uckfield E Susx.............19 M2
Uckinghall Worcs...........70 F6
Uckington Gloucs...........55 K3
Uddingston S Lans.......175 J6
Uddington S Lans........165 G3
Udimore E Susx.............21 H2
Udny Abers...................207 G1
Udny Station Abers......207 G1
Uffculme Devon.............25 G8
Uffington Lincs..............88 F3
Uffington Oxon.............40 F3
Uffington Shrops...........83 K2
Ufford C Pete.................89 G3
Ufford Suffk...................79 G4
Ufton Warwks.................72 E3
Ufton Nervet W Berk.....41 M6
Ugadale Ag & B...........161 K4
Ugborough Devon............7 G5
Uggeshall Suffk.............93 J7
Ugglebarnby N York.....143 H5
Ughill Sheff.................114 E4
Ugley Essex...................60 E3
Ugley Green Essex.........60 E3
Ugthorpe N York..........143 G5
Uibhist A Deas W Isls...233 c8
Uibhist A Tuath W Isls...233 b6
Uig Ag & B..................188 F5
Uig Highld..................208 C4
Uig Highld..................208 F2
Uig W Isls...................232 d2

Uigshader Highld.........209 G5
Uisken Ag & B.............180 E4
Ulbster Highld.............231 K7
Ulceby Lincs...............118 F6
Ulceby N Linc.............126 D7
Ulceby Skitter N Linc...126 E7
Ulcombe Kent...............33 L4
Uldale Cumb...............147 M7
Uley Gloucs...................55 H7
Ulgham Nthumb...........159 G4
Ullapool Highld...........220 E3
Ulleskelf N York..........124 D3
Ullesthorpe Leics..........87 G6
Ulley Rothm................115 J4
Ullingswick Herefs........69 L4
Ullinish Lodge Hotel
Highld....................208 E6
Ullock Cumb...............136 E3
Ullswater Cumb...........138 B3
Ulpha Cumb................128 E2
Ulrome E R Yk............135 J7
Ulsta Shet...................235 d3
Ulva Ag & B................189 K7
Ulverston Cumb...........129 G4
Ulwell Dorset................15 J6
Ulzieside D & G...........164 F7
Umberleigh Devon.........23 J6
Unapool Highld...........224 F2
Underbarrow
Cumb......................129 K2
Under Burnmouth
Border....................156 E5
Undercliffe C Brad.......123 J4
Underdale Shrops..........83 K2
Under River Kent..........32 F3
Underwood Notts.........101 J3
Undy Mons....................38 C3
Union Mills IoM...........237 c5
Unst Shet....................235 d1
Unstone Derbys...........115 G6
Upavon Wilts.................28 C1
Upchurch Kent..............46 D6
Upcott Devon................24 B5
Up Exe Devon...............12 B2
Upgate Norfk...............106 D8
Uphall Dorset................14 B2
Uphall W Loth.............176 E4
Upham Devon................11 K3
Upham Hants................29 K7
Uphampton Herefs........69 H2
Uphampton Worcs.........70 E2
Uphill N Som................37 L8
Up Holland Lancs.........112 D1
Uplawmoor E Rens.......174 E7
Upleadon Gloucs...........55 H3
Upleatham R & Cl.........142 D4
Uploders Dorset............13 L4
Uplowman Devon...........24 F7
Uplyme Devon................13 H4
Up Marden W Susx........30 D8
Upminster Gt Lon..........45 K3
Up Mudford Somset.......26 E7
Up Nately Hants............30 B2
Upottery Devon..............12 F2
Upper Affcot Shrops......83 J6
Upper Ardchronie
Highld....................222 E4
Upper Arley Worcs.........84 D7
Upper Basildon
W Berk....................41 L5
Upper Beeding
W Susx....................19 G4
Upper Benefield
Nhants....................88 E5
Upper Bentley Worcs.....71 H2
Upper Bighouse
Highld....................230 C4
Upper Boddington
Nhants....................72 F4
Upper Brailes Warwks...72 C6
Upper Breakish
Highld....................199 L2
Upper Broadheath
Worcs......................70 E4
Upper Broughton
Notts.....................102 B7

Upper Bucklebury
W Berk.....................41 K6
Upper Burgate Hants....28 D7
Upperby Cumb.............148 D4
Upper Caldecote
C Beds.....................75 H5
Upper Chapel Powys.....67 L6
Upper Chicksgrove
Wilts........................27 L5
Upper Chute Wilts........28 F2
Upper Clapton Gt Lon...45 G3
Upper Clatford Hants....29 G3
Upper Cound Shrops......83 K3
Upper Cumberworth
Kirk.......................123 J8
Upper Dallachy
Moray....................215 H2
Upper Deal Kent............35 K4
Upper Dean Bed............74 F2
Upper Denby Kirk.......114 E1
Upper Dicker E Susx......20 B4
Upper Dounreay
Highld....................230 E3
Upper Dovercourt
Essex......................62 F2
Upper Drumbane
Stirlg.....................184 E6
Upper Dunsforth
N York....................133 G6
Upper Eashing Surrey...30 F3
Upper Eathie Highld....213 J2
Upper Egleton Herefs....70 B5
Upper Elkstone
Staffs....................100 B2
Upper Ellastone
Staffs....................100 C4
Upper Farringdon
Hants.......................30 B4
Upper Framilode
Gloucs......................55 H6
Upper Froyle Hants........30 C3
Upperglen Highld........208 E4
Upper Godney
Somset......................26 C3
Upper Gravenhurst
C Beds.....................75 G7
Upper Green W Berk......41 G7
Upper Grove
Common Herefs........54 E3
Upper Hale Surrey........30 D2
Upper Halliford
Surrey......................43 H6
Upper Hambleton
Rutlnd......................88 C3
Upper Harbledown
Kent........................34 F3
Upper Hartfield
E Susx......................32 E6
Upper Hatherley
Gloucs......................55 L4
Upper Heaton Kirk.......123 H6
Upper Helmsley
N York....................133 L7
Upper Hergest Herefs....68 F4
Upper Heyford
Nhants......................73 J2
Upper Heyford Oxon......57 J3
Upper Hill Herefs..........69 J4
Upper Hopton Kirk......123 J6
Upper Hulme Staffs.....100 A1
Upper Inglesham
Swindn......................40 D2
Upper Killay Swans.......51 H6
Upper Kinchrackine
Ag & B....................183 G2
Upper Lambourn
W Berk....................40 F4
Upper Landywood
Staffs......................85 H3
Upper Langford
N Som......................38 C7
Upper Langwith
Derbys....................115 K7
Upper Largo Fife.........187 G6
Upper Leigh Staffs......100 A5
Upper Lochton Abers...206 D6
Upper Longdon Staffs...85 J2

Upper & Lower
Stondon C Beds.......75 H7
Upper Lybster Highld...231 J7
Upper Lydbrook
Gloucs......................54 E5
Upper Lye Herefs..........69 H2
Uppermill Oldham.......113 M1
Upper Milton Worcs......84 E8
Upper Minety Wilts........40 A3
Upper Mulben Moray...215 H4
Upper Netchwood
Shrops......................83 L5
Upper Nobut Staffs.....100 B5
Upper Norwood
W Susx......................18 C3
Upper Poppleton
C York....................133 H8
Upper Ratley Hants......28 F6
Upper Rissington
Gloucs......................56 D4
Upper Rochford
Worcs......................70 B2
Upper Ruscoe D & G....145 L3
Upper Sapey Herefs......70 C2
Upper Seagry Wilts........39 L4
Upper Shelton C Beds...74 E5
Upper Sheringham
Norfk......................106 D4
Upper Skelmorlie
N Ayrs....................173 L5
Upper Slaughter
Gloucs......................56 D4
Upper Soudley Gloucs...54 F6
Upper Standen Kent......35 H6
Upper Stoke Norfk.........92 F3
Upper Stowe Nhants.....73 J3
Upper Street Hants........28 D7
Upper Street Norfk........93 H1
Upper Street Norfk......107 G8
Upper Street Suffk........77 H4
Upper Street Suffk........78 D4
Upper Sundon C Beds...59 H3
Upper Swell Gloucs.......56 D3
Upper Tasburgh
Norfk.......................92 E4
Upper Tean Staffs.......100 A5
Upperthong Kirk.........123 H8
Upperton W Susx..........30 F6
Upper Town Herefs........69 L5
Uppertown Highld.......231 L1
Upper Town N Som........38 D7
Upper Town Suffk..........77 K2
Upper Tumble
Carmth......................51 G3
Upper Tysoe Warwks.....72 D5
Upper Victoria Angus...187 J1
Upper Wardington
Oxon.......................72 F5
Upper Welland Worcs....70 D6
Upper Wellingham
E Susx......................19 L3
Upper Weybread
Suffk.......................92 F7
Upper Wield Hants........29 L4
Upper Winchendon
Bucks.......................58 C5
Upper Woodford
Wilts........................28 C4
Upper Wraxall Wilts......39 J5
Uppingham Rutlnd........88 C4
Uppington Shrops..........83 L2
Upsall N York...............133 G3
Upsettlington Border...168 C1
Upshire Essex................60 C7
Up Somborne Hants.......29 H5
Upstreet Kent................35 G3
Upton Bucks.................58 C5
Upton C Pete................89 G4
Upton Cambs................89 H7
Upton Ches W.............112 B7
Upton Cnwll...................5 L2
Upton Devon...................7 G7
Upton Devon.................12 E2
Upton Dorset................14 E5
Upton Dorset................15 J4
Upton Halton...............112 C4
Upton Hants..................29 G1

Upton Hants 29 G7
Upton Leics 86 D4
Upton Lincs 116 E4
Upton Norfk 93 H2
Upton Notts 102 B2
Upton Notts 116 C6
Upton Oxon 41 K3
Upton Slough 43 G5
Upton Somset 24 F5
Upton Somset 26 C6
Upton Wakefd 124 D7
Upton Wirral 111 J4
Upton Bishop Herefs 54 F3
Upton Cheyney S Glos .. 39 G6
Upton Cressett
  Shrops 84 B5
Upton Grey Hants 30 B2
Upton Hellions Devon ... 11 J4
Upton Lovell Wilts 27 L4
Upton Magna Shrops ... 83 K2
Upton Noble Somset ... 27 G4
Upton Pyne Devon 11 L5
Upton St Leonards
  Gloucs 55 K5
Upton Scudamore
  Wilts 27 K2
Upton Snodsbury
  Worcs 71 G4
Upton upon Severn
  Worcs 70 F6
Upton Warren Worcs.... 71 G2
Upwaltham W Susx 18 C3
Upwell Norfk 90 C3
Upwood Cambs 89 J6
Urchfont Wilts 40 B8
Urmston Traffd 113 H3
Urquhart Moray 215 G2
Urra N York 142 C6
Urray Highld 212 D4
Usan Angus 197 H5
Ushaw Moor Dur 151 G6
Usk Mons 54 B7
Usselby Lincs 117 H3
Usworth Sundld 151 H4
Utkinton Ches W 112 D7
Utley C Brad 122 F3
Uton Devon 11 J5
Utterby Lincs 118 D3
Uttoxeter Staffs 100 C5
Uxbridge Gt Lon 43 H4
Uyeasound Shet 235 d2
Uzmaston Pembks 49 G5

V

Vale Guern 236 d2
Vale of Glamorgan
  Crematorium
  V Glam 37 H6
Vale of Rheidol
  Railway Cerdgn 80 F7
Valley IoA 108 C5
Valtos Highld 209 H2
Valtos W Isls 232 d2
Vange Essex 46 B3
Vatsetter Shet 235 d3
Vatten Highld 208 D5
Vaynor Myr Td 53 G6
Veensgarth Shet 235 c6
Velindre Powys 68 D7
Venngreen Devon 9 K3
Venn Ottery Devon 12 D4
Ventnor IoW 17 G6
Venton Devon 6 E4
Vernham Dean Hants ... 29 G1
Vernham Street
  Hants 41 G8
Verwood Dorset 15 K2
Veryan Cnwll 4 E7
Vickerstown Cumb 128 E5
Victoria Cnwll 4 F4
Vidlin Shet 235 d4
Viewfield Moray 215 G2
Viewpark N Lans 175 J6
Vigo Kent 45 M7

Village de Putron
  Guern 236 d3
Vines Cross E Susx 20 C3
Vinters Park
  Crematorium
  Kent 33 K2
Virginia Water Surrey 43 G6
Virginstow Devon 9 K6
Vobster Somset 27 G2
Voe Shet 235 c4
Vowchurch Herefs 69 G7

W

Waberthwaite Cumb ... 128 D2
Wackerfield Dur 140 E3
Wacton Norfk 92 E5
Wadborough Worcs 70 F5
Waddesdon Bucks 58 C5
Waddeton Devon 7 K4
Waddingham Lincs 117 G3
Waddington Lancs 121 L2
Waddington Lincs 116 F8
Wadebridge Cnwll 4 F2
Wadeford Somset 13 H1
Wadenhoe Nhants 88 E6
Wadesmill Herts 60 B4
Wadhurst E Susx 33 H6
Wadshelf Derbys 114 F7
Wadworth Donc 115 K3
Wainfleet All Saints
  Lincs 104 D2
Wainfleet St Mary
  Lincs 104 D2
Wainhouse Corner
  Cnwll 9 G5
Wainscott Medway 46 C6
Wainstalls Calder 122 F5
Waitby Cumb 139 H5
Waithe Lincs 118 C2
Wakefield Wakefd 123 L6
Wakefield
  Crematorium
  Wakefd 123 L7
Wakerley Nhants 88 D4
Wakes Colne Essex 61 L3
Walberswick Suffk 93 K8
Walberton W Susx 18 C4
Walbutt D & G 146 D2
Walcombe Somset 26 D3
Walcot Lincs 103 H5
Walcot Shrops 83 L2
Walcot Swindn 40 D4
Walcote Leics 87 H6
Walcot Green Norfk 92 D7
Walcott Lincs 103 J2
Walcott Norfk 107 H6
Walden Stubbs
  N York 124 E6
Walderslade Medway .. 46 C7
Walderton W Susx 17 L1
Walditch Dorset 13 L4
Waldridge Dur 151 G5
Waldringfield Suffk 79 G5
Waldron E Susx 20 B2
Wales Rothm 115 J5
Wales Somset 26 E6
Walesby Lincs 117 J3
Walesby Notts 116 B7
Walford Herefs 54 E4
Walford Herefs 83 H8
Walford Heath
  Shrops 98 C8
Walgherton Ches E 99 G3
Walgrave Nhants 74 B1
Walkden Salfd 113 G2
Walker N u Ty 151 H1
Walkerburn Border 166 E3
Walkeringham Notts... 116 C3
Walkerith Lincs 116 C3
Walkern Herts 59 M3
Walkerton Fife 186 D6
Walkford Dorset 16 B4
Walkhampton Devon ... 6 D2
Walkington E R Yk 126 B3

Walkley Sheff 115 G4
Walk Mill Lancs 122 C5
Walkwood Worcs 71 J2
Wall Nthumb 150 A2
Wall Staffs 85 K3
Wallacetown S Ayrs ... 153 G2
Wallacetown S Ayrs ... 163 J5
Wallands Park
  E Susx 19 L4
Wallasey Wirral 111 J3
Wallingford Oxon 41 L3
Wallington Gt Lon 44 F6
Wallington Hants 17 H2
Wallington Herts 75 K7
Wallisdown Poole 15 K4
Walls Shet 235 b5
Wallsend N Tyne 151 H2
Wallyford E Loth 177 K4
Walmer Kent 35 K5
Walmer Bridge
  Lancs 121 G5
Walmley Birm 85 K5
Walpole Suffk 93 H8
Walpole Cross Keys
  Norfk 104 E8
Walpole Highway
  Norfk 90 D2
Walpole St Andrew
  Norfk 104 D8
Walpole St Peter
  Norfk 90 C1
Walsall Wsall 85 H4
Walsden Calder 122 D6
Walsgrave on Sowe
  Covtry 86 E7
Walsham le Willows
  Suffk 78 B1
Walshford N York 132 F8
Walsoken Norfk 90 C2
Walston S Lans 165 K1
Walsworth Herts 59 K3
Walter's Ash Bucks 42 D2
Waltham Kent 34 E5
Waltham NE Lin 118 C2
Waltham Abbey
  Essex 60 C7
Waltham Chase
  Hants 29 K7
Waltham Cross Herts... 60 B7
Waltham on the
  Wolds Leics 102 D7
Waltham St
  Lawrence W & M 42 D5
Walthamstow Gt Lon ... 45 G3
Walton Cumb 148 F3
Walton Derbys 115 G7
Walton Leeds 124 C2
Walton Leics 87 H6
Walton M Keyn 74 C7
Walton Powys 68 F3
Walton Somset 26 C4
Walton Suffk 79 G7
Walton W Susx 17 M2
Walton Wakefd 123 L6
Walton Wrekin 98 E8
Walton Cardiff
  Gloucs 55 K2
Walton East Pembks.... 49 H3
Walton-in-Gordano
  N Som 38 B5
Walton Lea
  Crematorium
  Warrtn 112 E4
Walton-le-Dale Lancs... 121 H5
Walton-on-Thames
  Surrey 43 J6
Walton-on-the-Hill
  Staffs 99 L7
Walton on the Hill
  Surrey 31 L1
Walton on the Naze
  Essex 62 F4
Walton on the Wolds
  Leics 101 L8
Walton-on-Trent
  Derbys 100 E8
Walton Park N Som 38 B6

Walton West Pembks 48 E5
Waltonwrays
  Crematorium
  N York 122 E1
Walworth Darltn 141 G4
Walworth Gt Lon 45 G4
Walwyn's Castle
  Pembks 48 E5
Wambrook Somset 13 H2
Wanborough Surrey 30 F2
Wanborough Swindn ... 40 E4
Wandsworth Gt Lon 44 E5
Wangford Suffk 93 K7
Wanlip Leics 87 H2
Wanlockhead D & G ... 165 G6
Wannock E Susx 20 C5
Wansford C Pete 88 F4
Wansford E R Yk 135 G7
Wanshurst Green
  Kent 33 K4
Wanstead Gt Lon 45 H3
Wanstrow Somset 27 G3
Wanswell Gloucs 55 G7
Wantage Oxon 41 H3
Wappenbury Warwks ... 72 E2
Wappenham Nhants... 73 J5
Warbleton E Susx 20 C3
Warborough Oxon 41 L2
Warboys Cambs 89 K7
Warbreck Bpool 120 D3
Warbstow Cnwll 9 G6
Warburton Traffd 113 G4
Warcop Cumb 139 H4
Warden Nthumb 150 A2
Wardington Oxon 72 F5
Wardle Ches E 98 E2
Wardle Rochdl 122 D6
Wardley Gatesd 151 H3
Wardley Rutlnd 88 B4
Wardlow Derbys 114 D6
Wardy Hill Cambs 90 C6
Ware Herts 60 B5
Wareham Dorset 15 H5
Warehorne Kent 34 D7
Warenford Nthumb 169 H4
Wareside Herts 60 C5
Waresley Cambs 75 J4
Warfield Br For 42 E6
Warfleet Devon 7 K6
Wargrave Wokham 42 C5
Warham All Saints
  Norfk 105 M4
Warham St Mary
  Norfk 105 M4
Wark Nthumb 157 L6
Wark Nthumb 168 C2
Warkleigh Devon 23 K6
Warkton Nhants 88 C7
Warkworth Nhants 72 F6
Warkworth Nthumb... 159 G2
Warlaby N York 132 E2
Warleggan Cnwll 5 J3
Warley Town Calder... 122 F5
Warlingham Surrey 32 C2
Warmfield Wakefd 124 B6
Warmingham Ches E ... 99 G1
Warmington Nhants 88 F5
Warmington Warwks... 72 E5
Warminster Wilts 27 K3
Warmley S Glos 38 F5
Warmsworth Donc 115 K2
Warmwell Dorset 14 E5
Warner Bros Studio
  Tour Herts 59 H7
Warnford Hants 29 L6
Warnham W Susx 31 J5
Warningcamp
  W Susx 18 D4
Warninglid W Susx 31 L6
Warren Ches E 113 K7
Warren Pembks 48 F7
Warrenhill S Lans 165 J2
Warren Row W & M 42 D4
Warren Street Kent 34 C4
Warrington M Keyn 74 C4
Warrington Warrtn 112 E4
Warriston C Edin 177 H4

Warriston
Crematorium
C Edin 177 H3
Warsash Hants..............16 F2
Warslow Staffs..............100 C2
Warter E R Yk...............125 K1
Warthermaske N York..132 C4
Warthill N York..............133 K7
Wartling E Susx...............20 D4
Wartnaby Leics..............102 B7
Warton Lancs.................120 E5
Warton Lancs.................129 K5
Warton Warwks................86 C3
Warwick Warwks................72 C2
Warwick Bridge
Cumb 148 E4
Warwick Castle
Warwks 72 C2
Warwick Services
Warwks 72 D3
Wasbister Ork...............234 c4
Wasdale Head Cumb......137 G5
Washaway Cnwll................5 G2
Washbourne Devon............7 J5
Washbrook Suffk...............78 D6
Washfield Devon................11 L2
Washford Somset...............25 G3
Washford Pyne
Devon 11 J3
Washingborough
Lincs 117 G7
Washington Sundld........151 H4
Washington W Susx............18 F3
Washington Services
Gatesd 151 G4
Wasperton Warwks...........72 C3
Wass N York....................133 H4
Watchet Somset................25 G3
Watchfield Oxon...............40 E3
Watchgate Cumb.............138 D7
Water Devon.....................11 H8
Waterbeach Cambs...........76 C2
Waterbeach W Susx............18 B4
Waterbeck D & G..............155 M6
Water End E R Yk..............125 J3
Waterfall Staffs................100 B3
Waterfoot E Rens...............100 B3
Waterford Herts................60 A5
Waterheads Border..........177 H7
Waterhouses Staffs...........100 B3
Wateringbury Kent.............33 H3
Waterloo Highld...............199 K2
Waterloo N Lans...............175 L7
Waterloo P & K.................195 G8
Waterloo Pembks...............49 G6
Waterloo Sefton...............111 K2
Waterlooville Hants............17 J1
Watermillock Cumb...........138 C3
Water Newton
Cambs 89 G4
Water Orton Warwks...........85 L5
Waterperry Oxon................57 L6
Waterrow Somset...............25 G6
Watersfield W Susx.............18 D3
Waterside Bl w D..............121 K5
Waterside E Ayrs..............163 K7
Waterside E Ayrs..............163 L2
Waterside E Duns..............175 J4
Waterstein Highld............208 B5
Waterstock Oxon...............57 M6
Waterston Pembks..............48 F6
Water Stratford
Bucks 73 J7
Waters Upton Wrekin..........98 F8
Watford Herts...................43 J2
Watford Nhants................73 H2
Watford Gap
Services Nhants..............73 H2
Wath N York....................132 B6
Wath N York....................132 E4
Wath upon Dearne
Rothm 115 H2
Watlington Norfk...............90 E2
Watlington Oxon................42 B2
Watten Highld.................231 J5
Wattisfield Suffk................92 B8
Wattisham Suffk................78 B4

Watton Dorset...................13 L4
Watton E R Yk.................126 C1
Watton Norfk....................91 K4
Watton-at-Stone
Herts 60 A4
Wattston N Lans..............175 K4
Wattsville Caerph...............37 J3
Waulkmill Abers...............206 C6
Waunarlwydd Swans...........51 H6
Waunfawr Cerdgn..............80 E6
Waunfawr Gwynd...............95 J2
Wavendon M Keyn...............74 C6
Waverbridge Cumb............147 L5
Waverton Ches W..............112 C8
Waverton Cumb................147 L5
Wawne E R Yk.................126 D3
Waxham Norfk..................107 J7
Wayford Somset.................13 K2
Waytown Dorset................13 L3
Way Village Devon..............11 K3
Weacombe Somset.............25 H4
Weald Oxon......................56 F7
Wealdstone Gt Lon.............44 D3
Weardley Leeds................123 K2
Weare Somset....................26 B2
Weare Giffard Devon...........23 G6
Wearhead Dur.................149 L6
Wearne Somset...................26 B5
Wear Valley
Crematorium Dur...141 G2
Weasenham All
Saints Norfk.................105 K7
Weasenham St Peter
Norfk 105 K7
Weaste Salfd...................113 J2
Weaverham Ches W............112 E6
Weaverthorpe N York ...134 E5
Webheath Worcs.................71 H2
Wedderlairs Abers.............216 F7
Weddington Warwks............86 D5
Wedhampton Wilts..............40 B8
Wedmore Somset................26 C2
Wednesbury Sandw.............85 H4
Wednesfield Wolves............85 G4
Weedon Bucks...................58 D4
Weedon Nhants..................73 J3
Weedon Lois Nhants...........73 H5
Weeford Staffs..................85 K3
Weeke Hants.....................29 J5
Weekley Nhants..................88 C7
Week St Mary Cnwll..............9 H5
Weel E R Yk....................126 D3
Weeley Essex....................62 D4
Weeley Crematorium
Essex 62 D4
Weeley Heath Essex 62 D4
Weem P & K.....................194 D6
Weethley Warwks................71 J4
Weeting Norfk....................91 H5
Weeton E R Yk.................127 H6
Weeton Lancs..................120 E4
Weeton N York.................123 K2
Weetwood Leeds...............123 K3
Weir Lancs.....................122 C5
Weir Quay Devon.................6 C3
Weisdale Shet.................235 c5
Welborne Norfk..................92 C2
Welbourn Lincs................102 F2
Welburn N York.................133 L6
Welbury N York.................141 J6
Welby Lincs....................102 F5
Welcombe Devon................22 C7
Welford Nhants..................87 J7
Welford W Berk.................41 H5
Welford-on-Avon
Warwks 71 K4
Welham Leics....................87 L5
Welham Notts..................116 B5
Welham Green Herts...........59 L6
Well Hants........................30 C3
Well Lincs.......................118 F6
Well N York....................132 D3
Welland Worcs...................70 E6
Wellbank Angus................196 D8
Wellesbourne Warwks........72 C4
Well Head Herts.................59 K3
Welling Gt Lon..................45 J5

Wellingborough
Nhants 74 C2
Wellingham Norfk.............105 L7
Wellingore Lincs..............103 G2
Wellington Cumb..............136 F6
Wellington Herefs...............69 K5
Wellington Somset..............25 H7
Wellington Wrekin..............84 B2
Wellington Heath
Herefs 70 C6
Wellow BaNES...................39 H8
Wellow IoW.......................16 E5
Wellow Notts...................116 A7
Wells Somset....................26 D3
Wells-next-the-sea
Norfk 105 L4
Wellstye Green Essex 61 G4
Welltree P & K.................185 K3
Wellwood Fife.................176 E2
Welney Norfk.....................90 D5
Welshampton Shrops...........98 C5
Welsh Frankton
Shrops 98 A6
Welsh Newton Herefs.........54 D4
Welshpool Powys...............82 E3
Welsh St Donats
V Glam 36 F5
Welton Cumb....................148 C6
Welton E R Yk.................126 B5
Welton Lincs....................117 G5
Welton Nhants...................73 H2
Welton le Marsh Lincs...119 G7
Welton le Wold Lincs......118 C4
Welwick E R Yk.................127 H6
Welwyn Herts....................59 L5
Welwyn Garden City
Herts 59 L5
Wem Shrops......................98 D6
Wembdon Somset...............25 L4
Wembley Gt Lon................44 D3
Wembury Devon..................6 D6
Wembworthy Devon............10 F3
Wemyss Bay Inver.............173 L4
Wendens Ambo Essex....76 D7
Wendlebury Oxon...............57 K4
Wendling Norfk..................91 L2
Wendover Bucks................58 E6
Wendron Cnwll....................3 H5
Wendy Cambs....................75 K5
Wenhaston Suffk................93 J7
Wennington Cambs.............89 J7
Wennington Gt Lon.............45 K4
Wennington Lancs.............130 C5
Wensley Derbys................100 E1
Wensley N York................131 K2
Wentbridge Wakefd...........124 D6
Wentnor Shrops..................83 H5
Wentworth Cambs...............90 C7
Wentworth Rothm.............115 G2
Wenvoe V Glam..................37 H6
Weobley Herefs...................69 H4
Wepham W Susx.................18 E4
Wereham Norfk...................90 F3
Werrington C Pete...............89 H3
Werrington Cnwll.................9 J7
Wervin Ches W.................112 B6
Wesham Lancs..................120 F4
Wessex Vale
Crematorium
Hants 29 J7
Wessington Derbys...........101 G2
West Acre Norfk.................91 H1
West Alvington
Devon 7 G6
West Anstey Devon.............24 D6
West Ashby Lincs..............118 C6
West Ashling W Susx...........17 M2
West Ashton Wilts..............27 K1
West Auckland Dur...........140 F3
West Ayton N York............134 F3
West Bagborough
Somset 25 J5
West Bank Halton..............112 D5
West Barkwith Lincs..........117 K5
West Barnby N York..........143 G5
West Barns E Loth.............178 E3
West Barsham Norfk.........105 L5

West Bay Dorset................13 L4
West Beckham Norfk...106 D5
West Bedfont Surrey.........43 H5
Westbere Kent...................35 G3
West Bergholt Essex.......62 A3
West Berkshire
Crematorium
W Berk 41 K6
West Bexington
Dorset 14 A5
West Bilney Norfk..............91 G1
West Blatchington
Br & H 19 J4
West Boldon S Tyne........151 J3
Westborough Lincs...........102 E4
Westbourne Bmouth..........15 K4
Westbourne W Susx...........17 L2
West Bowling C Brad...123 H4
West Bradenham
Norfk 91 K2
West Bradford Lancs........121 L2
West Bradley Somset.........26 E4
West Bretton Wakefd.....123 K7
West Bridgford Notts......101 L5
West Bromwich
Sandw 85 H5
West Bromwich
Crematorium
Sandw 85 H5
Westbrook Kent.................35 J2
Westbrook W Berk.............41 H6
West Buckland Devon.......23 K5
West Buckland
Somset 25 J7
West Burton N York.........131 J3
Westbury Bucks.................73 J7
Westbury Shrops...............83 G2
Westbury Wilts..................27 K2
Westbury Leigh Wilts.....27 K2
Westbury on Severn
Gloucs 55 G5
Westbury-on-Trym
Bristl 38 E5
Westbury-sub-
Mendip Somset 26 D2
West Butterwick
N Linc 116 D1
Westby Lancs..................120 E4
West Byfleet Surrey..........43 H7
West Cairngaan D & G..144 D8
West Caister Norfk...........93 K2
West Calder W Loth......176 D5
West Camel Somset..........26 E6
West Chaldon Dorset.......14 E5
West Challow Oxon...........41 G3
West Charleton
Devon 7 H7
West Chiltington
W Susx 18 E3
West Chinnock
Somset 26 C8
West Clandon Surrey......31 H2
West Cliffe Kent................35 J5
Westcliff-on-Sea
Sthend 46 E3
West Coker Somset..........26 D8
Westcombe Somset..........27 G4
West Compton
Somset 26 E3
West Compton
Abbas Dorset 14 B4
Westcote Gloucs................56 E4
Westcote Barton
Oxon 57 H3
Westcott Bucks.................58 B5
Westcott Devon..................12 C2
Westcott Surrey.................31 J2
West Cottingwith
N York 125 G3
Westcourt Wilts..................40 E7
West Cowick E R Yk.....124 F6
West Cross Swans............51 H7
West Curthwaite
Cumb 148 B5
West Dean E Susx............20 B5
West Dean W Susx............18 B3
West Dean Wilts................28 E6

West Deeping Lincs 89 G2
West Derby Lpool..........111 L3
West Dereham Norfk 90 F4
West Down Devon 23 H3
Westdowns Cnwll 8 E7
West Drayton Gt Lon 43 H4
West Drayton Notts 116 B6
West Dunnet Highld 231 J2
West Ella E R Yk 126 C5
West End Bed 74 E4
West End Hants 29 J8
West End N Som 38 C6
West End Norfk 93 K2
West End Surrey 42 F7
West End Wilts 27 M6
West End Green
  Hants 42 A7
Westerdale Highld 231 G5
Westerdale N York 142 E6
Westerfield Suffk 78 E5
Westergate W Susx 18 C5
Westerham Kent 32 D3
Westerhope N u Ty 150 F2
Westerland Devon 7 K4
Westerleigh S Glos 39 G4
Westerleigh
  Crematorium
  S Glos 39 G5
Western Isles W Isls 232 d5
Wester Ochiltree
  W Loth 176 D4
Wester Pitkerie Fife 187 J6
Wester Ross Highld 220 C5
Westerton of Rossie
  Angus 197 G6
Westerwick Shet 235 c6
West Farleigh Kent 33 J3
West Farndon Nhants 73 G4
West Felton Shrops 97 M7
Westfield BaNES 26 F2
Westfield Cumb 136 D2
Westfield E Susx 21 G3
Westfield Highld 230 F3
Westfield N Lans 175 J4
Westfield Norfk 92 B2
Westfield W Loth 176 C4
Westfields of Rattray
  P & K 195 J6
Westgate Dur 150 A7
Westgate N Linc 125 J8
Westgate on Sea
  Kent 35 J2
West Grafton Wilts 40 E7
West Green Hants 30 C1
West Grimstead Wilts 28 E6
West Grinstead
  W Susx 31 K6
West Haddlesey
  N York 124 E5
West Haddon Nhants 73 J1
West Hagbourne
  Oxon 41 K3
West Hagley Worcs 84 F7
Westhall Suffk 93 J7
West Hallam Derbys 101 H4
West Halton N Linc 125 L6
Westham Dorset 14 C6
Westham E Susx 20 D5
West Ham Gt Lon 45 H4
Westham Somset 26 B3
Westhampnett
  W Susx 18 B4
West Handley Derbys ...115 H6
West Hanney Oxon 41 H2
West Hanningfield
  Essex 61 H7
West Harnham Wilts 28 C5
West Harptree BaNES 38 E8
West Harting W Susx 30 C7
West Hatch Somset 25 L7
West Hatch Wilts 27 L5
West Haven Angus 187 J1
Westhay Somset 26 C3
West Heath Birm 85 J7
West Helmsdale
  Highld 227 H5
West Hendred Oxon 41 H3

West Hertfordshire
  Crematorium
  Herts..........................59 J7
West Heslerton
  N York 134 E4
West Hewish N Som 38 B7
Westhide Herefs.............69 L5
Westhill Abers..............206 F4
West Hill Devon 12 D4
West Hoathly W Susx 32 C6
West Holme Dorset.........15 G5
Westhope Herefs............69 J4
Westhope Shrops............83 J6
West Horndon Essex 45 M3
Westhorpe Lincs............103 L6
Westhorpe Suffk............78 C2
West Horrington
  Somset.......................26 E3
West Horsley Surrey 31 H2
West Hougham Kent.......35 H6
Westhoughton
  Bolton 112 F1
Westhouse N York.........130 D5
Westhouses Derbys 101 H2
West Howe Bmouth 15 K4
Westhumble Surrey 31 K2
West Huntingtower
  P & K 185 M3
West Huntspill
  Somset.......................25 L3
West Hythe Kent 34 F7
West Ilsley W Berk 41 J4
West Itchenor W Susx ...17 L3
West Kennett Wilts 40 C6
West Kilbride N Ayrs 173 L8
West Kingsdown
  Kent 45 L7
West Kington Wilts 39 J5
West Kirby Wirral 111 H4
West Knapton N York ..134 D4
West Knighton
  Dorset 14 D5
West Knoyle Wilts 27 K5
Westlake Devon 6 F5
West Lambrook
  Somset.......................26 B7
West Langdon Kent 35 J5
West Lavington
  W Susx 30 E7
West Lavington Wilts 28 A2
West Layton N York 140 E5
West Leake Notts..........101 K7
Westleigh Devon 23 G5
Westleigh Devon 25 G7
West Leigh Somset 25 H5
Westleton Suffk.............79 J2
West Lexham Norfk 91 J1
Westley Suffk.................77 J2
Westley Waterless
  Cambs 76 E3
West Lilling N York 133 K6
Westlington Bucks.........58 C6
West Linton Border......176 F7
Westlinton Cumb..........148 D3
West Littleton S Glos 39 H5
West Lockinge Oxon.......41 H3
West London
  Crematorium
  Gt Lon 44 E4
West Lulworth Dorset....14 F6
West Lutton N York.......134 E5
West Lydford Somset 26 E5
West Lyng Somset...........25 L5
West Lynn Norfk...........104 F7
West Malling Kent..........33 H2
West Malvern Worcs.......70 D5
West Marden W Susx 30 C8
West Markham Notts....116 B6
Westmarsh Kent 35 H3
West Marsh NE Lin......127 G8
West Marton N York 122 D1
West Melbury Dorset......27 K7
West Meon Hants 29 M6
West Mersea Essex 62 B5
Westmeston E Susx 19 K3
West Midland Safari
  Park Worcs................84 E7

Westmill Herts 60 B3
West Milton Dorset........13 L3
Westminster Gt Lon.......44 F4
West Minster Kent 46 E5
West Molesey Surrey......43 J6
West Monkton
  Somset 25 K5
West Moors Dorset 15 K2
West Morden Dorset 15 G4
West Morriston
  Border 167 J2
West Mudford
  Somset 26 E7
Westmuir Angus..........196 B5
West Ness N York 133 L4
Westnewton Cumb......147 K6
West Newton E R Yk....126 F3
West Newton Norfk.....105 H6
West Newton Somset.....25 L5
West Norwood
  Gt Lon 44 F5
West Norwood
  Crematorium
  Gt Lon 44 F5
Westoe S Tyne.............151 J2
West Ogwell Devon 7 J2
Weston BaNES 39 G6
Weston Ches E...............99 G3
Weston Devon 12 E3
Weston Devon 12 F5
Weston Hants 30 B6
Weston Herts 59 L3
Weston Lincs................103 M7
Weston N York 123 H2
Weston Nhants 73 H5
Weston Notts................116 C7
Weston Shrops 83 L5
Weston Shrops 97 L6
Weston Staffs.................99 L6
Weston W Berk 41 H5
Weston Beggard
  Herefs 69 L6
Westonbirt Gloucs 39 J3
Weston by Welland
  Nhants 87 L5
Weston Colville
  Cambs 76 E4
Weston Corbett
  Hants 30 B3
Weston Coyney
  C Stke 99 L4
Weston Favell Nhants ...73 L3
Weston Green Cambs.....76 F4
Weston Heath Shrops 84 D2
Westoning C Beds...........75 G2
Weston-in-Gordano
  N Som 38 C5
Weston Jones Staffs.......99 H7
Weston Longville
  Norfk 92 D1
Weston Lullingfields
  Shrops 98 B7
Weston Mill
  Crematorium
  C Plym 6 C4
Weston-on-the-
  Green Oxon 57 K4
Weston Patrick Hants ...30 B3
Weston Rhyn Shrops......97 L5
Weston-sub-Edge
  Gloucs 71 K6
Weston-super-Mare
  N Som 37 L7
Weston-super-Mare
  Crematorium
  N Som 38 A7
Weston Turville Bucks....58 D6
Weston-under-Lizard
  Staffs 84 E2
Weston under
  Penyard Herefs 54 F4
Weston-under-
  Redcastle Shrops 98 E6
Weston under
  Wetherley Warwks 72 D1
Weston Underwood
  Derbys 100 F3

Weston Underwood
  M Keyn 74 C4
Weston-upon-Trent
  Derbys 101 H6
Westonzoyland
  Somset 25 M4
West Orchard Dorset......27 J7
West Overton Wilts........40 C6
Westow N York 134 B6
West Park Abers...........206 E5
West Parley Dorset........15 K3
West Peckham Kent........33 H3
West Pelton Dur...........151 G4
West Pennard
  Somset 26 D4
West Pentire Cnwll 4 B4
West Perry Cambs 75 G2
West Porlock Somset 24 D3
Westport Somset 26 B7
West Putford Devon........9 K2
West Quantoxhead
  Somset 25 H3
Westquarter Falk 176 B3
West Rainton Dur........151 H5
West Rasen Lincs..........117 H4
Westray Ork.................234 c3
Westray Airport Ork 234 c3
West Raynham Norfk...105 L7
Westrigg W Loth..........176 B5
West Road
  Crematorium
  N u Ty 150 F2
Westrop Swindn 40 D2
West Rounton N York ..141 K6
West Row Suffk..............90 F7
West Rudham Norfk.....105 K6
West Runton Norfk......106 E4
Westruther Border 178 D7
Westry Cambs 90 B4
West Saltoun E Loth ...178 B5
West Sandford Devon....11 J4
West Sandwick Shet.....235 d3
West Scrafton N York ..131 K3
West Stafford Dorset 14 D4
West Stockwith
  Notts 116 C3
West Stoke W Susx........17 M2
West Stour Dorset..........27 H6
West Stourmouth
  Kent 35 H3
West Stow Suffk.............77 J1
West Stowell Wilts 40 C7
West Street Suffk 78 B1
West Suffolk
  Crematorium
  Suffk 77 J2
West Tanfield N York ..132 D4
West Taphouse Cnwll......5 J3
West Tarbert Ag & B ...172 E5
West Tarring W Susx 18 F5
West Thirston
  Nthumb 158 F3
West Thorney W Susx....17 L3
West Thorpe Notts.......101 L7
West Thurrock Thurr.....45 L4
West Tilbury Thurr.........46 A4
West Tisted Hants 29 M5
West Torrington Lincs...117 J5
West Town Hants 17 K3
West Town N Som.........38 C6
West Tytherley Hants 28 F5
West Walton Norfk.........90 C2
West Walton
  Highway Norfk...........90 C2
Westward Cumb...........148 B6
Westward Ho! Devon 23 G5
Westwell Kent 34 D5
Westwell Oxon 56 E6
Westwell Leacon
  Kent 34 C5
West Wellow Hants 28 F7
West Wembury
  Devon 6 D6
West Wemyss Fife 186 E7
Westwick Cambs 76 B2
West Wickham
  Cambs 76 E5

West Wickham Gt Lon.... 45 G6
West Williamston
Pembks 49 H6
West Wiltshire
Crematorium
Wilts..........................39 K7
West Winch Norfk..........90 F1
West Winterslow
Wilts..........................28 E5
West Wittering
W Susx........................17 L3
West Witton N York.....131 K2
Westwood Devon........12 C3
Westwood Kent 35 K2
Westwood Wilts..........39 J8
West Woodburn
Nthumb 157 M5
West Woodhay
W Berk......................41 H7
Westwoodside N Linc...116 C2
West Worldham
Hants.........................30 C4
West Worthing
W Susx........................18 F5
West Wratting Cambs....76 E4
Wetheral Cumb...........148 E4
Wetherby Leeds.........124 B2
Wetherby Services
N York.......................124 C1
Wetherden Suffk.........78 B3
Wetheringsett Suffk.....78 D2
Wethersfield Essex......61 H2
Wetherup Street
Suffk.........................78 D2
Wetley Rocks Staffs.....99 L3
Wettenhall Ches E.......98 F1
Wetton Staffs............100 C2
Wetwang E R Yk.........134 E7
Wetwood Staffs...........99 H5
Wexcombe Wilts..........40 F8
Weybourne Norfk.......106 D4
Weybourne Surrey.......30 D2
Weybread Suffk...........92 F7
Weybread Street
Suffk.........................92 F7
Weybridge Surrey........43 H7
Weycroft Devon...........13 H3
Weydale Highld.........231 H3
Weyhill Hants.............28 F3
Weymouth Dorset.......14 D6
Weymouth
Crematorium
Dorset.......................14 C6
Whaddon Bucks.........74 B7
Whaddon Cambs.........75 L5
Whaddon Gloucs.........55 J5
Whaddon Wilts...........28 D6
Whaddon Wilts...........39 K7
Whaley Derbys..........115 K7
Whaley Bridge
Derbys......................114 A5
Whaley Thorns
Derbys......................115 K7
Whaligoe Highld........231 K7
Whalley Lancs...........121 L4
Whalsay Shet............235 d4
Whalton Nthumb.......158 E6
Whaplode Lincs.........104 A7
Whaplode Drove
Lincs.........................89 K2
Wharf Warwks............72 E4
Wharfe N York..........130 E5
Wharles Lancs...........120 F4
Wharley End C Beds....74 D5
Wharncliffe Side
Sheff.......................114 F3
Wharram-le-Street
N York.....................134 D6
Wharton Herefs..........69 K4
Whashton N York.......140 E6
Whasset Cumb...........129 L4
Whatcote Warwks.......72 C5
Whateley Warwks.......86 B4
Whatfield Suffk...........78 B5
Whatley Somset..........13 J2
Whatley Somset..........27 G3
Whatlington E Susx.....20 F3

Whatton Notts...........102 C5
Whauphill D & G........145 J5
Wheatacre Norfk.........93 K5
Wheathampstead
Herts........................59 K5
Wheatley Hants..........30 C4
Wheatley Oxon...........57 L6
Wheatley Hill Dur.......151 J6
Wheatley Hills Donc...115 L1
Wheaton Aston Staffs....84 F2
Wheddon Cross
Somset.......................24 E4
Wheelock Ches E.........99 H2
Wheelton Lancs..........121 J6
Wheldrake C York......125 G2
Whelford Gloucs.........56 D7
Whelpley Hill Bucks.....59 G6
Whempstead Herts......60 A4
Whenby N York..........133 K5
Whepstead Suffk.........77 J3
Wherstead Suffk..........78 E6
Wherwell Hants...........29 H3
Wheston Derbys........114 C6
Whetsted Kent............33 H4
Whetstone Leics..........87 G4
Whicham Cumb..........128 D3
Whichford Warwks......72 C7
Whickham Gatesd......150 F3
Whiddon Down
Devon........................11 G6
Whigstreet Angus......196 D7
Whilton Nhants...........73 J2
Whimple Devon...........12 D3
Whimpwell Green
Norfk.......................107 H6
Whinburgh Norfk.........92 B2
Whinnie Liggate
D & G......................146 C4
Whinnyfold Abers......217 K7
Whippingham IoW........17 G4
Whipsnade C Beds.......59 G4
Whipton Devon...........12 B4
Whisby Lincs.............116 E7
Whissendine Rutlnd......88 B2
Whissonsett Norfk......105 L7
Whistlefield Ag & B.....183 J8
Whistlefield Inn
Ag & B.....................183 G8
Whistley Green
Wokham.....................42 C5
Whiston Knows.........112 C3
Whiston Nhants..........74 B3
Whiston Rothm.........115 H4
Whiston Staffs...........84 F2
Whiston Staffs..........100 B3
Whitbeck Cumb.........128 D3
Whitbourne Herefs......70 D3
Whitburn S Tyne........151 J3
Whitburn W Loth.......176 C5
Whitby N York...........143 J5
Whitchester Border.....178 F6
Whitchurch BaNES......38 F6
Whitchurch Bucks.......58 D4
Whitchurch Cardif.......37 J4
Whitchurch Devon........6 D2
Whitchurch Hants........29 J2
Whitchurch Herefs......54 D4
Whitchurch Oxon.........41 M5
Whitchurch Pembks.....48 D3
Whitchurch Shrops......98 D4
Whitchurch
Canonicorum
Dorset.......................13 K4
Whitchurch Hill
Oxon.........................41 M5
Whitcombe Dorset.......14 D5
Whitcot Shrops...........83 H5
Whitcott Keysett
Shrops.......................82 F6
Whiteacre Heath
Warwks.....................86 B5
White Ball Somset.......25 H7
Whitebridge Highld....202 D3
Whitebrook Mons.......54 D6
Whitecairns Abers......207 H2
Whitechapel Gt Lon.....45 G4
White Chapel Lancs....121 H3

Whitecliffe Gloucs........54 E6
White Colne Essex.......61 L3
Whitecraig E Loth.......177 K4
Whitecrook D & G......144 E4
White Cross Cnwll.........3 H6
Whitecross Falk.........176 C3
Whiteface Highld......222 F4
Whitefarland N Ayrs...161 L2
Whitefaulds S Ayrs....163 H7
Whitefield Bury.........113 J1
Whitefield Somset.......25 G5
Whiteford Abers........206 D1
Whitegate Ches W......112 F7
Whitehall Ork............234 d5
Whitehaven Cumb......136 D4
Whitehill and Bordon
Hants........................30 C5
Whitehills Abers........216 C2
Whitehouse Abers......206 C3
Whitehouse Ag & B....172 D6
Whitekirk E Loth........178 D3
White Lackington
Dorset........................14 D3
Whitelackington
Somset.......................26 B7
White Ladies Aston
Worcs........................71 G4
Whiteleaf Bucks..........58 D6
Whiteley Hants...........17 G1
Whiteley Bank IoW......17 G6
Whitemire Moray......214 B4
Whitemoor C Nott.....101 K4
Whitemoor Cnwll..........4 F4
Whiteness Shet.........235 c6
White Notley Essex......61 J4
Whiteparish Wilts.......28 E6
White Pit Lincs..........118 E6
Whiterashes Abers.....206 F2
White Roding Essex.....60 E5
Whiterow Highld.......231 L5
Whiterow Moray.......214 C3
Whiteshill Gloucs........55 J6
Whitesmith E Susx......20 B3
Whitestaunton
Somset.......................13 H1
Whitestone Cross
Devon........................11 K6
White Waltham
W & M......................42 D5
Whitewell Lancs.........121 K2
Whitfield C Dund.......187 G2
Whitfield Kent............35 J5
Whitfield Nhants.........73 H6
Whitfield Nthumb......149 K4
Whitfield S Glos..........38 F3
Whitford Devon..........13 G4
Whitford Flints..........111 G5
Whitgift E R Yk..........125 J6
Whitgreave Staffs.......99 K6
Whithorn D & G.........145 J6
Whiting Bay N Ayrs...162 D4
Whitkirk Leeds..........124 B4
Whitland Carmth.........49 L4
Whitlaw Border.........167 G6
Whitletts S Ayrs.........163 J5
Whitley N York..........124 E6
Whitley Readg............42 B6
Whitley Sheff............115 G3
Whitley Wilts.............39 K6
Whitley Bay N Tyne....159 J7
Whitley Bay
Crematorium
N Tyne.....................159 H7
Whitley Chapel
Nthumb.....................150 B4
Whitley Lower Kirk.....123 J6
Whitminster Gloucs.....55 H6
Whitmore Staffs..........99 J4
Whitnage Devon..........25 G7
Whitnash Warwks.......72 D2
Whitney-on-Wye
Herefs........................68 F5
Whitsbury Hants.........28 C7
Whitsome Border.......179 H7
Whitson Newpt...........38 B4
Whitstable Kent..........47 J6
Whitstone Cnwll..........9 H5

Whittingham
Nthumb 168 F6
Whittingslow Shrops....83 H5
Whittington Derbys....115 G6
Whittington Gloucs......56 A4
Whittington Lancs......130 B4
Whittington Norfk.......91 G4
Whittington Shrops......97 L6
Whittington Staffs.......84 F6
Whittington Staffs.......85 L2
Whittington Warwks....86 C4
Whittington Worcs......70 F4
Whittlebury Nhants.....73 K5
Whittle-le-Woods
Lancs.......................121 H6
Whittlesey Cambs.......89 J4
Whittlesford Cambs.....76 C5
Whitton N Linc..........125 L5
Whitton Nthumb.......158 D3
Whitton Powys...........68 F2
Whitton S on T...........141 J3
Whitton Shrops...........83 L8
Whittonstall Nthumb...150 D4
Whitway Hants...........41 J8
Whitwell Derbys........115 K6
Whitwell Herts...........59 K4
Whitwell IoW..............17 G6
Whitwell N York.........141 G7
Whitwell Rutlnd..........88 D2
Whitwell-on-the-Hill
N York.....................133 L6
Whitwell Street
Norfk.......................106 D7
Whitwick Leics...........86 E1
Whitworth Lancs.......122 D6
Whixall Shrops...........98 D5
Whixley N York.........133 G7
Whorlton Dur...........140 E4
Whyle Herefs.............69 L3
Whyteleafe Surrey......32 C2
Wibsey C Brad..........123 H4
Wibtoft Warwks..........86 F6
Wichenford Worcs......70 D3
Wichling Kent............34 B4
Wick Bmouth.............15 L4
Wick Highld..............231 L5
Wick S Glos................39 G5
Wick V Glam..............36 E6
Wick W Susx..............18 D5
Wick Worcs................71 G5
Wicken Cambs............76 E1
Wicken Nhants...........73 L6
Wicken Bonhunt
Essex........................60 D2
Wickenby Lincs.........117 H5
Wicken Green Village
Norfk.......................105 K6
Wickersley Rothm.....115 J3
Wicker Street Green
Suffk.........................77 L6
Wickford Essex..........46 C2
Wickham Hants...........17 H1
Wickham W Berk........41 H6
Wickham Bishops
Essex........................61 K5
Wickhambreaux Kent...35 G3
Wickhambrook Suffk....77 H4
Wickhamford Worcs....71 J6
Wickham Green Suffk...78 D2
Wickham Market
Suffk.........................79 G4
Wickhampton Norfk....93 J3
Wickham St Paul
Essex........................77 J7
Wickham Skeith Suffk...78 C2
Wickham Street Suffk...78 C1
Wick John o' Groats
Airport Highld.........231 L5
Wicklewood Norfk......92 C3
Wickmere Norfk........106 E5
Wick St Lawrence
N Som........................38 A7
Wickwar S Glos..........39 G3
Widdington Essex........60 E2
Widdrington Nthumb ..159 G3
Widdrington Station
Nthumb.....................159 G4

Widecombe in the
Moor Devon 7 G1
Widegates Cnwll 5 L4
Widemouth Bay
Cnwll 9 G4
Wide Open N Tyne 159 G7
Widford Essex 61 H6
Widford Herts 60 C5
Widmer End Bucks 42 E2
Widmerpool Notts 101 M6
Widmore Gt Lon 45 H6
Widnes Halton 112 D5
Widnes Crematorium
Halton 112 D4
Widworthy Devon 13 G3
Wigan Wigan 112 E1
Wigan Crematorium
Wigan 112 E1
Wigborough Somset 26 C7
Wiggaton Devon 12 E4
Wiggenhall St
Germans Norfk 90 E2
Wiggenhall St Mary
Magdalen Norfk 90 E2
Wiggenhall St Mary
the Virgin Norfk 90 E2
Wigginton C York 133 J7
Wigginton Herts 58 F6
Wigginton Oxon 57 H2
Wigginton Staffs 86 B3
Wigglesworth N York 130 F7
Wiggonby Cumb 148 B4
Wighill N York 124 D2
Wighton Norfk 105 M4
Wightwick Wolves 84 F4
Wigley Hants 29 G7
Wigmore Herefs 69 H2
Wigmore Medway 46 D6
Wigsley Notts 116 E7
Wigsthorpe Nhants 88 F6
Wigston Leics 87 H4
Wigston Parva Leics 86 F5
Wigthorpe Notts 115 L5
Wigtoft Lincs 103 L5
Wigton Cumb 148 A5
Wigtown D & G 145 J4
Wike Leeds 123 L3
Wilbarston Nhants 88 B5
Wilberfoss E R Yk 125 H1
Wilburton Cambs 90 C7
Wilby Nhants 74 C2
Wilby Norfk 92 B5
Wilby Suffk 78 F1
Wilcot Wilts 40 C7
Wilcott Shrops 98 B8
Wildboarclough
Ches E 113 M7
Wilden Bed 75 G4
Wilden Worcs 84 E8
Wildmanbridge
S Lans 175 L7
Wildmoor Worcs 85 G7
Wildsworth Lincs 116 D3
Wilford Hill
Crematorium
Notts 101 L5
Wilkesley Ches E 98 F4
Wilkhaven Highld 223 K4
Wilkieston W Loth 176 F5
Willand Devon 12 D1
Willaston Ches E 99 G3
Willaston Ches W 111 K6
Willen M Keyn 74 C6
Willenhall Covtry 86 D7
Willenhall Wsall 85 H4
Willerby E R Yk 126 C4
Willerby N York 134 F4
Willersey Gloucs 71 K6
Willersley Herefs 68 F5
Willesborough Kent 34 D6
Willesborough Lees
Kent 34 D6
Willesden Gt Lon 44 E3
Willesley Wilts 39 J3
Willett Somset 25 H5
Willey Shrops 84 C4
Willey Warwks 86 F6

Willey Green Surrey 30 F2
Williamscot Oxon 72 F5
Willian Herts 59 L2
Willingale Essex 60 F6
Willingdon E Susx 20 C5
Willingham Cambs 76 B1
Willingham by Stow
Lincs 116 E5
Willington Bed 75 G4
Willington Derbys 100 F6
Willington Dur 150 F7
Willington Kent 33 K3
Willington Warwks 72 C6
Willington Quay
N Tyne 151 H2
Willitoft E R Yk 125 H4
Williton Somset 25 H4
Willoughby Lincs 119 G6
Willoughby Warwks 73 G2
Willoughby-on-the-
Wolds Notts 101 M7
Willoughby
Waterleys Leics 87 H5
Willoughton Lincs 116 F3
Willows Green Essex 61 H4
Willtown Somset 26 B6
Wilmcote Warwks 71 L3
Wilmington Devon 13 G3
Wilmington E Susx 20 B5
Wilmington Kent 45 K5
Wilmslow Ches E 113 J5
Wilpshire Lancs 121 K4
Wilsden C Brad 123 G3
Wilsford Lincs 103 G4
Wilsford Wilts 28 C4
Wilsford Wilts 40 C8
Wilshaw Kirk 123 G8
Wilsill N York 132 B6
Wilson Leics 101 H7
Wilsontown S Lans 176 C7
Wilstead Bed 74 F5
Wilsthorpe Lincs 88 F2
Wilstone Herts 58 E5
Wilton Herefs 54 E3
Wilton N York 134 D3
Wilton R & Cl 142 C4
Wilton Wilts 28 C5
Wilton Wilts 40 E7
Wilton Dean Border 167 G6
Wimbish Green Essex 76 E7
Wimbledon Gt Lon 44 E6
Wimblington Cambs 90 B5
Wimboldsley Ches W 113 G8
Wimborne Minster
Dorset 15 J3
Wimborne St Giles
Dorset 28 B8
Wimbotsham Norfk 90 E3
Wimpole Cambs 75 L4
Wimpstone Warwks 72 B5
Wincanton Somset 27 G5
Winchburgh W Loth 176 E4
Winchcombe Gloucs 56 A3
Winchelsea E Susx 21 H3
Winchester Hants 29 J5
Winchester Services
Hants 29 K4
Winchet Hill Kent 33 J5
Winchfield Hants 30 C1
Winchmore Hill Bucks 42 F2
Winchmore Hill
Gt Lon 44 F2
Wincle Ches E 113 L7
Wincobank Sheff 115 G3
Windermere Cumb 137 L7
Winderton Warwks 72 D6
Windhill Highld 212 E5
Windlesham Surrey 42 F7
Windmill Cnwll 4 D2
Windmill Hill E Susx 20 D4
Windmill Hill Somset 25 L7
Windrush Gloucs 56 D5
Windsole Abers 216 B3
Windsor W & M 42 F5
Windsor Castle W & M 42 F5
Windsoredge Gloucs 55 J7
Windsor Green Suffk 77 K4

Windy Arbour
Warwks 72 C1
Windygates Fife 186 E7
Wineham W Susx 31 L7
Winestead E R Yk 127 G5
Winfarthing Norfk 92 D6
Winford IoW 17 G5
Winford N Som 38 D7
Winforton Herefs 68 F5
Winfrith Newburgh
Dorset 14 F5
Wing Bucks 58 E4
Wing Rutlnd 88 C3
Wingate Dur 151 J7
Wingerworth Derbys 115 G7
Wingfield C Beds 59 G3
Wingfield Suffk 92 F7
Wingfield Wilts 27 J1
Wingham Kent 35 H3
Wingrave Bucks 58 E4
Winkburn Notts 102 B2
Winkfield Br For 42 E6
Winkfield Row Br For 42 E6
Winkhill Staffs 100 B3
Winkleigh Devon 10 F4
Winksley N York 132 C5
Winlaton Gatesd 150 F3
Winless Highld 231 K5
Winmarleigh Lancs 120 F2
Winnall Hants 29 J5
Winnersh Wokham 42 C6
Winnington Ches W 112 F6
Winscombe N Som 38 B8
Winsford Ches W 112 F7
Winsford Somset 24 E4
Winsham Somset 13 J2
Winshill Staffs 100 F7
Winshwen Swans 51 K6
Winskill Cumb 149 G7
Winsley Wilts 39 J7
Winslow Bucks 58 C3
Winson Gloucs 56 C6
Winsor Hants 28 F8
Winster Cumb 129 J2
Winster Derbys 100 E1
Winston Dur 140 E4
Winston Suffk 78 E3
Winstone Gloucs 55 L6
Winswell Devon 10 D3
Winterborne Came
Dorset 14 D5
Winterborne
Clenston Dorset 14 F2
Winterborne
Houghton Dorset 14 F2
Winterborne
Kingston Dorset 15 G3
Winterborne
Monkton Dorset 14 D5
Winterborne
Stickland Dorset 14 F2
Winterborne
Whitechurch
Dorset 14 F3
Winterborne Zelston
Dorset 15 G3
Winterbourne S Glos 38 F4
Winterbourne W Berk 41 J6
Winterbourne Abbas
Dorset 14 C4
Winterbourne
Bassett Wilts 40 C5
Winterbourne
Dauntsey Wilts 28 D4
Winterbourne Earls
Wilts 28 D5
Winterbourne
Gunner Wilts 28 D4
Winterbourne
Monkton Wilts 40 C5
Winterbourne
Steepleton Dorset 14 C4
Winterbourne Stoke
Wilts 28 B3
Winteringham N Linc 131 H7
Winteringham N Linc 125 L6
Winterley Ches E 99 H2

Winterslow Wilts 28 E5
Winterton N Linc 125 L6
Winterton-on-Sea
Norfk 107 K8
Winthorpe Notts 102 D2
Winton Bmouth 15 K4
Winton Cumb 139 H5
Wintringham N York 134 D5
Winwick Cambs 89 G7
Winwick Nhants 87 J8
Winwick Warrtn 112 E3
Wirksworth Derbys 100 F2
Wirral 111 J4
Wirswall Ches E 98 D4
Wisbech Cambs 90 C2
Wisbech St Mary
Cambs 90 B2
Wisborough Green
W Susx 31 H6
Wiseman's Bridge
Pembks 49 K6
Wiseton Notts 116 B4
Wishaw N Lans 175 L7
Wishaw Warwks 85 L5
Wispington Lincs 117 K6
Wissett Suffk 93 H7
Wissington Suffk 62 A2
Wistanstow Shrops 83 H6
Wistanswick Shrops 98 F6
Wistaston Ches E 99 G2
Wiston Pembks 49 H4
Wiston S Lans 165 J3
Wiston W Susx 18 F3
Wistow Cambs 89 K7
Wistow N York 124 F4
Wiswell Lancs 121 L3
Witcham Cambs 90 C7
Witchampton
Dorset 15 J2
Witchford Cambs 90 C7
Witcombe Somset 26 C6
Witham Essex 61 K5
Witham Friary
Somset 27 H3
Witham on the Hill
Lincs 88 F1
Withcall Lincs 118 C5
Withdean Br & H 19 J4
Witherenden Hill
E Susx 33 H7
Witheridge Devon 11 J3
Witherley Leics 86 D4
Withern Lincs 118 F5
Withernsea E R Yk 127 H5
Withernwick E R Yk 126 F3
Withersdale Street
Suffk 92 F7
Withersfield Suffk 76 F5
Witherslack Cumb 129 J3
Withiel Cnwll 4 F3
Withiel Florey Somset 24 F5
Withington Gloucs 56 B5
Withington Herefs 69 L5
Withington Manch 113 J3
Withington Shrops 83 L2
Withington Staffs 100 B5
Withleigh Devon 11 K3
Withnell Lancs 121 J6
Withybed Green
Worcs 85 H8
Withybrook Warwks 86 E6
Withycombe Somset 24 F3
Withyham E Susx 32 E6
Withypool Somset 24 D4
Withywood Bristl 38 E6
Witley Surrey 30 F4
Witnesham Suffk 78 E4
Witney Oxon 57 G6
Wittering C Pete 88 F3
Wittersham Kent 21 H1
Witton Birm 85 J5
Witton Norfk 93 G2
Witton Norfk 107 H6
Witton Gilbert Dur 151 G5
Witton le Wear Dur 140 E2
Witton Park Dur 140 F2
Wiveliscombe Somset 25 G5

Wivelrod Hants.............30 A4
Wivelsfield E Susx.......19 K2
Wivelsfield Green
  E Susx....................19 K2
Wivenhoe Essex.........62 C4
Wiveton Norfk...........106 C4
Wix Essex..................62 E3
Wixford Warwks........71 K4
Wixoe Suffk................77 G6
Woburn C Beds..........58 F2
Woburn Abbey
  C Beds....................58 F2
Woburn Sands
  M Keyn...................74 D7
Woking Surrey............43 G8
Woking
  Crematorium
  Surrey....................42 F8
Wokingham Wokham...42 D6
Woldingham Surrey.....32 C3
Wold Newton E R Yk...135 G5
Wold Newton NE Lin...118 C3
Wolfclyde S Lans......165 K3
Wolferton Norfk........105 G6
Wolfhill P & K...........186 B2
Wolf's Castle Pembks...49 G3
Wolfsdale Pembks.......48 F3
Wollaston Dudley........84 F6
Wollaston Nhants........74 C2
Wollaston Shrops........83 G2
Wollaton C Nott.......101 K4
Wollerton Shrops........98 F6
Wollescote Dudley......85 G6
Wolseley Bridge
  Staffs...................100 A7
Wolsingham Dur.......150 D7
Wolstanton Staffs......99 J3
Wolston Warwks........86 E7
Wolvercote Oxon........57 J6
Wolverhampton
  Wolves...................85 G4
Wolverhampton
  Halfpenny Green
  Airport Staffs.........84 E5
Wolverley Worcs........84 E7
Wolverton Hants........41 K8
Wolverton M Keyn......74 B6
Wolverton Warwks......72 B3
Wolverton Wilts..........27 H5
Wolvesnewton Mons....54 C7
Wolvey Warwks..........86 E6
Wolvey Heath
  Warwks..................86 E5
Wolviston S on T.......141 K3
Wombleton N York....133 K3
Wombourne Staffs......84 F5
Wombwell Barns.......115 H2
Womenswold Kent......35 G5
Womersley N York.....124 E6
Wonersh Surrey..........31 G3
Wonford Devon..........12 B4
Wonston Dorset.........14 E2
Wonston Hants..........29 J4
Wooburn Bucks..........42 E3
Wooburn Green
  Bucks.....................42 E3
Woodacott Devon........9 K4
Woodall Rothm.........115 J5
Woodall Services
  Rothm..................115 J5
Woodbastwick Norfk...93 G1
Wood Bevington
  Warwks..................71 J4
Woodborough Notts...101 M3
Woodborough Wilts.....40 C7
Woodbridge Suffk.......78 F5
Woodbury Devon........12 C5
Woodbury Salterton
  Devon....................12 C5
Woodchester Gloucs...55 J7
Woodchurch Kent.......34 C7
Woodcombe Somset...24 E3
Woodcote Gt Lon........44 F7
Woodcote Oxon..........41 M4
Woodcote Wrekin.......84 D1
Woodcroft Gloucs......38 D2
Wood Dalling Norfk...106 C6

Woodditton Cambs.....76 F3
Woodeaton Oxon.......57 K5
Wood End Gt Lon........43 J4
Wood End Herts.........60 B3
Woodend Highld.......190 F4
Woodend Nhants........73 H5
Woodend W Loth......176 C4
Woodend W Susx........17 M2
Wood End Warwks......71 K1
Wood Enderby
  Lincs....................118 C8
Woodfalls Wilts..........28 D7
Woodford Cnwll...........9 G3
Woodford Gloucs........39 G2
Woodford Gt Lon........45 H2
Woodford Nhants........88 D7
Woodford Stockp......113 K5
Woodford Bridge
  Gt Lon....................45 H2
Woodford Halse
  Nhants...................73 G4
Woodford Wells
  Gt Lon....................45 H2
Woodgate Birm..........85 H6
Woodgate Devon........25 H7
Woodgate W Susx.......18 C5
Woodgate Worcs........71 H2
Wood Green Gt Lon.....44 F2
Woodgreen Hants.......28 D7
Woodhall N York.......131 J2
Woodhall Spa Lincs...117 K8
Woodham Bucks.........58 B4
Woodham Surrey........43 H7
Woodham Ferrers
  Essex.....................61 J7
Woodham Mortimer
  Essex.....................61 K6
Woodham Walter
  Essex.....................61 K6
Wood Hayes Wolves....85 G3
Woodhead Abers......216 E6
Woodhill Shrops........84 D6
Woodhill Somset........26 A6
Woodhorn Nthumb...159 H4
Woodhouse Leeds.....123 K4
Woodhouse Leics........87 G1
Woodhouse Sheff......115 H4
Woodhouse Wakefd...124 B6
Woodhouse Eaves
  Leics.....................87 G2
Woodhouselee
  Mdloth..................177 H5
Woodhouselees
  D & G....................156 D6
Woodhouses Staffs...100 D8
Woodhurst Cambs......89 K7
Woodingdean Br & H...19 K5
Woodkirk Leeds........123 K5
Woodland Abers.......207 G2
Woodland Devon..........6 F5
Woodland Devon..........7 J3
Woodland Dur..........140 D2
Woodland S Ayrs......152 E3
Woodlands Abers.....206 E6
Woodlands Donc......124 E8
Woodlands Dorset......15 K2
Woodlands Hants.......16 C1
Woodlands N York....132 E8
Woodlands (Coleshill)
  Crematorium
  Warwks..................85 L5
Woodlands Park
  W & M....................42 E5
Woodlands
  (Scarborough)
  Crematorium
  N York.................134 F3
Woodlands
  (Scunthorpe)
  Crematorium
  N Linc..................125 K7
Woodleigh Devon........7 H6
Woodley Wokham.......42 C5
Woodmancote
  Gloucs...................39 H2
Woodmancote
  Gloucs...................55 L3

Woodmancote
  Gloucs...................56 A6
Woodmancote
  W Susx..................17 L2
Woodmancote
  W Susx..................19 H3
Woodmancott Hants...29 K3
Woodmansey E R Yk...126 C3
Woodmansgreen
  W Susx..................30 E6
Woodmansterne
  Surrey...................32 B2
Woodmanton Devon...12 C5
Woodnesborough
  Kent......................35 J4
Woodnewton Nhants...88 F5
Wood Norton Norfk...106 B6
Woodplumpton
  Lancs...................121 G4
Woodrising Norfk......92 B3
Wood's Corner
  E Susx...................20 D2
Woodseaves Staffs.....99 H7
Woodsetts Rothm.....115 K5
Woodsford Dorset......14 E4
Wood's Green E Susx...33 H6
Woodside Br For........42 F6
Woodside Fife..........187 G5
Woodside Gt Lon........45 G6
Woodside P & K.......195 K8
Woodstock Oxon........57 H5
Woodston C Pete........89 H4
Wood Street Norfk....107 H7
Wood Street Village
  Surrey...................30 F2
Woodton Norfk...........93 G5
Woodtown Devon.......22 F6
Woodvale
  Crematorium
  Br & H....................19 J4
Wood Walton Cambs...89 J7
Woofferton Shrops.....69 K2
Wookey Somset.........26 D3
Wookey Hole Somset...26 D2
Wool Dorset..............14 F5
Woolacombe Devon....23 G3
Woolage Green Kent...35 H5
Woolaston Gloucs......54 E7
Woolaston Common
  Gloucs...................54 E7
Woolavington
  Somset...................25 M3
Woolbeding W Susx...30 E6
Woolbrook Devon......12 E5
Wooler Nthumb.......168 E4
Woolfardisworthy
  Devon....................11 J3
Woolfardisworthy
  Devon....................22 E7
Woolfords S Lans......176 D6
Woolhampton
  W Berk...................41 L6
Woolhope Herefs........69 L7
Woolland Dorset........14 E2
Woolley BaNES..........39 H6
Woolley Cambs..........89 G8
Woolley Wakefd.......123 L7
Woolley Edge
  Services Wakefd...123 K7
Woolmere Green
  Worcs....................71 G2
Woolmer Green Herts...59 L4
Woolminstone
  Somset...................13 K2
Woolpit Suffk............77 L3
Woolstaston Shrops....83 J4
Woolsthorpe Lincs...102 D5
Woolsthorpe-by-
  Colsterworth
  Lincs....................102 F7
Woolston C Sotn........16 E1
Woolston Shrops........97 L7
Woolston Somset.......25 H4
Woolston Somset.......26 F5
Woolston Warrtn......112 F4
Woolstone Gloucs......55 L3
Woolstone M Keyn......74 C6

Woolstone Oxon.........40 F3
Woolston Green
  Devon......................7 H3
Woolton Lpool.........112 B4
Woolton Hill Hants.....41 H7
Woolverstone Suffk....78 E6
Woolverton Somset....27 H2
Woolwich Gt Lon........45 H4
Woonton Herefs.........69 G4
Woore Shrops.............99 G4
Wootten Green Suffk...92 F8
Wootton Bed.............74 E5
Wootton Kent............35 G5
Wootton N Linc.........126 D7
Wootton Nhants.........73 L3
Wootton Oxon............57 H4
Wootton Oxon............57 J7
Wootton Staffs.........100 C4
Wootton Bassett
  Wilts.....................40 B4
Wootton Bridge IoW...17 G4
Wootton Courtenay
  Somset...................24 E3
Wootton Fitzpaine
  Dorset....................13 J4
Wootton Rivers Wilts...40 D7
Wootton St
  Lawrence Hants.....29 L2
Wootton Wawen
  Warwks..................71 L2
Worcester Worcs.......70 F4
Worcester Park
  Gt Lon....................44 E6
Wordsley Dudley.......84 F6
Worfield Shrops.........84 D4
Workington Cumb....136 D2
Worksop Notts.........115 L5
Worlaby N Linc........126 C7
Worlds End Hants.....29 M8
Worlds End W Susx....19 J2
Worle N Som.............38 A7
Worleston Ches E......98 F2
Worlingham Suffk......93 J5
Worlington Devon......11 H3
Worlington Suffk.......91 G8
Worlingworth Suffk....78 F2
Wormbridge Herefs....54 B2
Wormegay Norfk........90 F2
Wormelow Tump
  Herefs....................54 C3
Wormhill Derbys......114 C6
Wormingford Essex....61 M2
Worminghall Bucks....57 M6
Wormington Gloucs....71 J7
Wormit Fife.............186 F3
Wormleighton
  Warwks..................72 F4
Wormley Herts..........60 B6
Wormley Surrey.........30 F4
Wormshill Kent.........34 B3
Wormsley Herefs........69 H5
Worplesdon Surrey.....30 F2
Worrall Sheff...........114 F3
Worsbrough Barns...115 G2
Worsbrough Bridge
  Barns...................115 G2
Worsbrough Dale
  Barns...................115 G2
Worsley Salfd..........113 H2
Worstead Norfk.......107 G7
Worsthorne Lancs....122 C4
Worston Devon............6 E5
Worston Lancs.........122 B3
Worth Kent................35 J4
Wortham Suffk..........92 C7
Worthen Shrops.........83 G3
Worthenbury
  Wrexhm..................98 B4
Worthing Norfk.......106 B8
Worthing W Susx.......18 F5
Worthing
  Crematorium
  W Susx...................18 F4
Worthington Leics....101 H7
Worth Matravers
  Dorset....................15 H6
Wortley Barns.........114 F2

Wortley Leeds 123 K4
Worton N York 131 H2
Worton Wilts 39 L8
Wortwell Norfk 92 F6
Wotton-under-Edge
Gloucs 39 H2
Wotton Underwood
Bucks 58 B5
Woughton on the
Green M Keyn 74 C6
Wouldham Kent 46 B7
Wrabness Essex 62 E2
Wrafton Devon 23 H4
Wragby Lincs 117 J6
Wragby Wakefd 124 C6
Wrangaton Devon 7 G4
Wrangle Lincs 104 C3
Wrangway Somset 25 H7
Wrantage Somset 25 L6
Wrawby N Linc 126 C8
Wraxall N Som 38 C6
Wraxall Somset 26 E4
Wray Lancs 130 B6
Wraysbury W & M 43 G5
Wrayton Lancs 130 C5
Wrea Green Lancs 120 E4
Wreay Cumb 148 D5
Wrecclesham Surrey 30 D3
Wrekenton Gatesd 151 G3
Wrelton N York 134 B3
Wrenbury Ches E 98 E3
Wreningham Norfk 92 E4
Wrentham Suffk 93 K6
Wrentnall Shrops 83 H3
Wressle E R Yk 125 G4
Wressle N Linc 126 B8
Wrestlingworth
C Beds 75 J5
Wretton Norfk 91 G4
Wrexham Wrexhm 97 M3
Wribbenhall Worcs 84 E7
Wrinehill Staffs 99 H3
Wrington N Som 38 C7
Writhlington BaNES 27 G1
Writtle Essex 61 G6
Wrockwardine
Wrekin 84 B2
Wroot N Linc 116 B2
Wrose C Brad 123 H3
Wrotham Kent 33 G2
Wroughton Swindn 40 C4
Wroxall IoW 17 G6
Wroxall Warwks 72 B1
Wroxeter Shrops 83 L2
Wroxham Norfk 107 G8
Wroxton Oxon 72 E6
Wyaston Derbys 100 D4
Wyberton East Lincs 104 B4
Wyboston Bed 75 H3
Wybunbury Ches E 99 G3
Wychbold Worcs 71 G2
Wychnor Staffs 85 L1
Wyck Rissington
Gloucs 56 D4
Wycliffe Dur 140 E4
Wycoller Lancs 122 D3
Wycomb Leics 102 C7
Wycombe Marsh
Bucks 42 E3
Wyddial Herts 60 B2
Wye Kent 34 E5
Wyke C Brad 123 H5
Wyke Dorset 27 H6
Wyke Champflower
Somset 26 F4
Wykeham N York 134 E3
Wyken Covtry 86 D7
Wyken Shrops 84 D4
Wyke Regis Dorset 14 C6
Wykey Shrops 98 B7
Wylam Nthumb 150 E3
Wylde Green Birm 85 K5
Wylye Wilts 28 A4
Wymeswold Leics 101 L7
Wymington Bed 74 D2
Wymondham Leics 102 D8
Wymondham Norfk 92 D3

Wynford Eagle
Dorset 14 B3
Wyre Forest
Crematorium
Worcs 84 E8
Wyre Piddle Worcs 71 G5
Wysall Notts 101 L6
Wythall Worcs 85 J7
Wytham Oxon 57 J6
Wythenshawe Manch .. 113 J4
Wyton Cambs 89 K8
Wyton E R Yk 126 E4
Wyverstone Suffk 78 C2
Wyverstone Street
Suffk 78 B2

Y

Yaddlethorpe N Linc 116 E1
Yafforth N York 141 H7
Yalberton Torbay 7 K4
Yalding Kent 33 J3
Yanwath Cumb 138 D2
Yanworth Gloucs 56 B5
Yapham E R Yk 125 J1
Yapton W Susx 18 D5
Yarborough N Som 38 B8
Yarburgh Lincs 118 E3
Yarcombe Devon 13 G2
Yard Devon 24 B6
Yardley Birm 85 K6
Yardley
Crematorium
Birm 85 K6
Yardley Gobion
Nhants 73 L5
Yardley Hastings
Nhants 74 C3
Yardley Wood Birm 85 K7
Yarkhill Herefs 69 L6
Yarley Somset 26 D3
Yarlington Somset 26 F5
Yarm S on T 141 K5
Yarmouth IoW 16 D4
Yarnbrook Wilts 27 K1
Yarnfield Staffs 99 K6
Yarnscombe Devon 23 J6
Yarnton Oxon 57 J5
Yarpole Herefs 69 J2
Yarrow Border 166 E4
Yarrow Feus Border 166 E4
Yarrowford Border 166 F4
Yarwell Nhants 88 F4
Yate S Glos 39 G4
Yateley Hants 42 D7
Yatesbury Wilts 40 B6
Yattendon W Berk 41 K5
Yatton Herefs 69 H2
Yatton N Som 38 B7
Yatton Keynell Wilts 39 K5
Yaverland IoW 17 H5
Yaxham Norfk 92 B2
Yaxley Cambs 89 H5
Yaxley Suffk 92 D8
Yazor Herefs 69 H5
Yeading Gt Lon 43 J4
Yeadon Leeds 123 J3
Yealand Conyers
Lancs 129 K5
Yealand Redmayne
Lancs 129 K4
Yealmpton Devon 6 E5
Yearsley N York 133 J5
Yeaton Shrops 98 B8
Yeaveley Derbys 100 D4
Yeavering Nthumb 168 D4
Yedingham N York 134 D4
Yelford Oxon 57 G6
Yell Shet 235 d3
Yelling Cambs 75 J3
Yelvertoft Nhants 87 H7
Yelverton Devon 6 D3
Yelverton Norfk 93 G3
Yenston Somset 27 G7
Yeoford Devon 11 H5

Yeolmbridge Cnwll 9 J7
Yeovil Somset 26 D7
Yeovil Crematorium
Somset 26 D7
Yeovil Marsh Somset 26 D7
Yeovilton Somset 26 D6
Yesnaby Ork 234 b5
Yetminster Dorset 14 B1
Yettington Devon 12 D5
Yetts o'Muckhart
Clacks 185 L6
Yew Tree Sandw 85 H4
Y Felinheli Gwynd 109 G7
Y Ferwig Cerdgn 65 G5
Y Ffor Gwynd 95 G5
Y Gyffylliog Denbgs 97 G2
Yielden Bed 74 E2
Yieldshields S Lans 176 B7
Yiewsley Gt Lon 43 H4
Y Maerdy Conwy 96 F4
Ynysboeth Rhondd 37 G2
Ynysddu Caerph 37 J2
Ynyshir Rhondd 36 F3
Ynystawe Swans 51 K5
Ynysybwl Rhondd 37 G2
Yockleton Shrops 83 H2
Yokefleet E R Yk 125 J5
Yoker C Glas 174 F5
York C York 124 F1
York City
Crematorium
C York 124 F2
Yorkletts Kent 34 E3
Yorkley Gloucs 54 F6
York Minster C York ... 124 F1
Yorkshire Dales
National Park
N York 131 G4
York Town Surrey 42 E7
Youlgreave Derbys 114 E8
Youlthorpe E R Yk 134 B7
Youlton N York 133 G6
Yoxall Staffs 100 C8
Yoxford Suffk 79 H2
Y Rhiw Gwynd 94 D6
Ysbyty Ifan Conwy 96 C3
Ysbyty Ystwyth
Cerdgn 67 G1
Ysceifiog Flints 111 G7
Ystalyfera Neath 52 B6
Ystrad Rhondd 36 F2
Ystrad Aeron Cerdgn 66 C4
Ystradfellte Powys 52 E5
Ystradgynlais Powys 52 C6
Ystrad Meurig
Cerdgn 66 F2
Ystrad Mynach
Caerph 37 H2
Ystradowen V Glam 36 F5
Ythanbank Abers 217 G7
Ythanwells Abers 216 C6
Ythsie Abers 217 G7

Z

Zeal Monachorum
Devon 11 G4
Zeals Wilts 27 H5
Zelah Cnwll 4 C5
Zennor Cnwll 2 E4
Zouch Notts 101 J7
ZSL Whipsnade Zoo
C Beds 59 G4

Be alert to accident black spots even before seeing the cameras

The AA brings you a Smart Phone app that provides 'real-time' updates of safety camera locations

The AA Safety Camera app brings the latest safety camera location system to your Smart Phone. It improves road safety by alerting you to the location of fixed and mobile camera sites and accident black spots.

The AA Safety Camera app ensures that you will always have the very latest data of fixed and mobile sites on your Smart Phone without having to connect it to your computer. Updates are made available automatically.

Powered by **RoadPilot**®

Visual Countdown
To camera location

Your Speed
The speed you are travelling when approaching a camera. Dial turns red as an additional visual alert

Camera Types Located
Includes fixed cameras (Gatso, Specs etc.) and mobile cameras

Speed Limit at Camera

Smart Phone Apps

Ireland

Map pages north

Western
Isles

Steornabhagh•
(Stornoway)

232

21
Gai

•Ui

208   2
Portree•

233

198   1
Mall

188   189

180   1

170   171

160
Campb•

To help you navigate safely
and easily, see the AA's
Ireland atlases...
theAA.com/shop